OXFORD EU LAW LIBRARY

General Editors

DAVID ANDERSON, QC

Barrister at Brick Court Chambers and
Visiting Professor of Law at King's College London

PIET EECKHOUT

Professor of Law at University College London

Principles and Practice in EU Sports Law

OXFORD EUROPEAN UNION LAW LIBRARY

The aim of this series is to publish important and original studies of the various branches of EC and EU law. Each work provides a clear, concise, and critical exposition of the law in its social, economic, and political context, at a level which will interest the advanced student, the practitioner, the academic, and government and community officials. Formerly the Oxford European Community Law Library.

Principles and Practice in EU Sports Law

STEPHEN WEATHERILL

Jacques Delors Professor of European Law
University of Oxford

OXFORD
UNIVERSITY PRESS

OXFORD

UNIVERSITY PRESS

Great Clarendon Street, Oxford, OX2 6DP,
United Kingdom

Oxford University Press is a department of the University of Oxford.
It furthers the University's objective of excellence in research, scholarship,
and education by publishing worldwide. Oxford is a registered trade mark of
Oxford University Press in the UK and in certain other countries

Published in the United States of America by Oxford University Press
198 Madison Avenue, New York, NY 10016, United States of America

British Library Cataloguing in Publication Data
Data available

Library of Congress Control Number: 2017933789

ISBN 978–0–19–879365–6

Printed and bound by
CPI Group (UK) Ltd, Croydon, CR0 4YY

Series Editor's Foreword

This book on *Principles and Practice in EU Sports Law* is an outstanding contribution to the EU Law Library. Its title is deceptively unassuming. The book is not some kind of general overview of a specialized area of EU law. What it offers is a cogently constructed and sustained intellectual argument about the way in which sport and EU law interact. In developing this argument, it offers a range of fertile insights which transcend both the regulation of sports, and the particular system which constitutes EU law. Their fertility is enhanced by the uncommon encounter between sport regulation and EU law, whose natural environments are fundamentally different. Sport is regulated by sporting associations, which often operate on a global scale and try to operationalize self-contained regimes. There is moreover a significant nationalist dimension to sport. EU law, on the other hand, is supranational, averse to nationality discrimination, and indeed averse to claims to regulatory autonomy as soon as there is an economic activity with a cross-border dimension.

Stephen Weatherill's book offers a complete account of the encounter, in a way which deepens and enriches the reflection about the special nature of sport, and how its autonomy can be safeguarded without sacrificing the public good of orthodox economic regulation. He argues that EU law accepts but a *conditional* autonomy of sport, and that the route to achieving such autonomy is an interpretative or adjudicative one. Sport's autonomy needs to find its proper place within a general framework of relevant EU law principles, in particular those focused on the internal market and on competition law; and the EU institutions, guided by the Court of Justice's case law, help to implement those principles. His analysis shows that EU law is far from ideological in this respect, in that it has been willing to provide ample space for sporting autonomy. It further shows that, over a number of decades, EU law has also managed to develop sound principles governing the limits of such autonomy. It is clear, though, that this soundness is itself much enhanced by the illuminating, principled, and intellectually outstanding journey which the book undertakes.

And it bears emphasizing that this is not just a book about EU *sports* law. Even those with no interest whatsoever in the regulation of sports will find this book a joy to read, for it is embedded in the deep understanding of general EU law which characterizes Stephen Weatherill's work. Whether it is internal market law, the system of EU competences, or EU competition law: the analysis adds immense value to our general understanding of each of these fundamental areas of EU law. Written in characteristically lucid prose, and marked also by a deep love of sports, the book deserves the broadest of readerships.

Piet Eeckhout

London
March 2017

Preface

I have been writing about and teaching EU law in its application to sport for thirty years, and I am pleased to have been given the opportunity by OUP to draw together my thinking in this monograph.

The title of this book is chosen deliberately in order to convey the special challenges of sports law in general and EU sports law in particular. To refer to *principles* invites reflection on the intellectual framework of the law. I present an argument in this book that there is more to sports law than simply the application of orthodox legal rules to sporting activity: the context in which sport is organized and pursued demands that a degree of sensitivity shall inform the application and interpretation of legal rules. It is the scope of autonomy from the law typically claimed by governing bodies in sport that requires the closest attention. But there is *practice* too. Whatever one's assessment of the intellectual strength in principle of the claim to sporting autonomy one must reckon with the practical reality that sport is often rather successful in sheltering its disputes from review by ordinary courts of law. Its system of arbitration is well developed: more crudely, the length of litigation contrasted with the short span of the typical sporting career tends to deter recourse to law. The study of sports law, and of EU sports law in particular, requires an understanding of both principle and practice.

The book identifies sports law generally as being framed by sporting bodies' claims for legal autonomy from the 'ordinary law' of states and international organizations, and applies this to the particular context of EU law. Sporting bodies commonly insist on using their expertise to create a set of globally applicable rules which should not be deviated from irrespective of the territory on which they are applied. This is to appeal to the virtue of the *lex sportiva*—and to plead for its insulation from outside intervention by the courts of states or organizations such as the EU. Such pleas have foundation—a sport truly needs rules which are applied in a uniform manner wherever the game is played. But making a plea for absolute autonomy is to go too far. In many areas sporting practices have direct and significant commercial implications—for athletes, for fans, for broadcasters—which cannot be placed beyond the scope of legal review. This book demonstrates how EU law grants *conditional autonomy* to practices in sport. The vital and persisting arguments centre on just what shall be the content of those conditions. The enduring dilemma facing sports lawyers running throughout the text is whether sport should be regarded as special, and in turn how (far) its special character should be granted legal recognition.

The law is that in force on 1 January 2017.

Stephen Weatherill

Oxford
March 2017

Contents Summary

Contents

Table of Cases

Table of Cases

Table of Legislation

List of Abbreviations

GENERAL

ATP	Association of Tennis Professionals
BGH	Bundesgerichtshof (the highest civil court in the German system)
CAS	Court of Arbitration for Sport
CFCB	Club Financial Control Body (of UEFA)
CFI	Court of First Instance (known since the entry into force of the Lisbon Treaty in December 2009 as the General Court)
DRC	Dispute Resolution Chamber (of FIFA)
EC	Treaty Establishing the European Community
ECA	European Club Association
ECHR	European Convention on Human Rights (in full, European Convention for the Protection of Human Rights and Fundamental Freedoms)
EEC	Treaty Establishing the European Economic Community
EFTA	European Free Trade Association
ELPA	Elliniki Leskhi Aftokinitou kai Periigiseon (Automobile and Touring Club of Greece)
ESA	EFTA Surveillance Authority
EURO	European Football Championships
FAPL	Football Association Premier League (England)
FFP	Financial Fair Play (UEFA)
FIFA	Fédération Internationale de Football Association
FINA	Fédération internationale de natation
IOC	International Olympic Committee
ISU	International Skating Union
ITC	Independent Television Commission
MOTOE	Motosykletistiki Omospondia Ellados (Greek Motorcycling Federation)
PILA	Swiss Private International Law Act
TEU	Treaty on European Union
TFEU	Treaty on the Functioning of the European Union
UCI	Union Cycliste Internationale
UEFA	Union of European Football Associations
UNESCO	United Nations Educational, Scientific and Cultural Organization
USADA	United States Anti-Doping Agency
WADA	World Anti-Doping Agency

JOURNALS

AJCL	American Journal of Comparative Law
Arb Intl	Arbitration International
Chi J Intl L	Chicago Journal of International Law
CJICL	Camb Journal of International and Comparative Law

CLJ	Cambridge Law Journal
CML Rev	Common Market Law Review
Col J Eur L	Columbia Journal of European Law
ECLR	European Competition Law Review
EL Rev	European Law Review
ELJ	European Law Journal
ESLJ	Entertainment and Sports Law Journal
Eur J Law Econ	European Journal of Law and Economics
German LJ	German Law Journal
Intl Org	International Organization
Intl Sports L Rev	International Sports Law Review
Intl Sports LJ	International Sports Law Journal
J Intl Arb	Journal of International Arbitration
JCER	Journal of Contemporary European Research
JEPP	Journal of European Public Policy
JIDS	Journal of International Dispute Settlement
JLAS	Journal of Legal Aspects of Sport
LQR	Law Quarterly Review
MJ	Maastricht Journal of European and Comparative Law
MLR	Modern Law Review
NJW	Neue Juristische Wochenschrift
RMUE	Revue du marché unique européen
RTDE	Revue trimestrielle de droit européen
Tulane L Rev	Tulane Law Review
Yale LJ	Yale Law Journal
YEL	Yearbook of European Law

1

Sport is Special

Competitors in a sporting event need opponents. In a normal industry a supplier's sweetest dream involves the acquisition of a monopoly. That would grant freedom to behave as it chooses without fearing that its customers will switch their allegiance to a competitor. There is no competitor. By contrast, a single football or rugby or cricket club would be in a sorry state. No one would be interested in watching it play on its own. It needs competition. Moreover, the opponents that it needs must be more or less credible opponents. Spectators are likely to lose interest if the outcome of the contest is a foregone conclusion.

As part of this notion that the competition must be credible, people watching a sporting event do not expect to know the result in advance. At an opera most of the members of the audience know which character(s) will die in the end. So too in the theatre or in literature: no one watching a performance of *Romeo and Juliet* or reading *Tess of the D'Urbervilles* is expecting a happy ending. By stark contrast in sport you don't know who will win. Uncertainty of outcome is one of the principal and essential attractions of attending a game of cricket or an athletics meeting. And a match the result of which is fixed in advance is not a sporting event at all.

The key insight is that there is a mutual interdependence between sports clubs which is not found in a normal industry. It is in the nature of a sports league that some matters are pursued in common, and the implication is that the law should be more forgiving of such collaboration than it would be where pursued between rivals in a normal industry. There needs to be agreement on the rules of the game, the timing of fixtures, and the like. And the special character of sporting activity is not found solely on the supply-side. On the demand-side too, sport is special. The customer of a poorly performing supermarket will quickly choose to shop at a different supermarket. The typical sports fan enjoys no such luxury. Few fans feel able to change their team, no matter how badly it performs, no matter how poorly the fan is treated. In fact, although switching to a more successful club is in principle possible and may even seem rational, only someone who is not a fan could do it. Sport is special—the consumer of sport, the fan, is special too. You can be a true fan only if you are irrational. Supporting a club is not consumption, it is passion and it is commitment: Rudyard Kipling's famous nineteenth-century poem *If* advises that if you can meet with triumph and disaster and treat those two impostors just the same, then you'll be a man. Perhaps so. But you won't be a sports fan.

Sport is special in its patterns of governance too. Most sports are subject to regulation by a single governing body, and frequently that body claims a global reach.

It is in the typical nature of sport that the rules of the game do not differ according to the place in which the contest takes place. Offside in Bolivia is offside in Spain too. This ensures that the sport transcends national borders—it is truly a 'global game'. Normal industries may have trade associations through which matters of common concern are addressed, but they do not act as a source of agreed common production and marketing conditions that are applicable to all undertakings active in the sector. Or, at least, if they do, they can expect to be the subject of aggressive intervention by authorities responsible for the application of laws restraining anti-competitive conduct. Sport, typically regulated according to a single global regime and under the auspices of a single governing body, is special.

This provides one reason why sport is unusually resistant to control by litigation. Courts are jurisdictionally limited: sports bodies are not. In addition litigation is slow: sporting contest is fast-paced. Winning a lawsuit may take as long as a career would typically last in top-level professional sport. Bringing that lawsuit may mean that the career ends prematurely or that it never even begins. Sports bodies are not immune from litigation pursued before ordinary courts of law in either principle or practice, but they are able to resist it conspicuously more effectively than actors in most other areas of economic activity.

The claim to assert monopoly power over rule-making is also frequently combined with a claim to use that power to achieve redistribution of income and to promote solidarity within the sport. Fédération Internationale de Football Association (FIFA) is fond of asserting that it is concerned with the good of the game, which means that it wishes to sustain the sport not simply its own commercially lucrative pinnacle. Some of this rhetoric is a rather poor disguise for ruthlessly aggressive profit-maximizing practices. And it is, in any event, more audible in Europe than in North America. But some of it is true. Powerful trade associations bringing together, for example, steelmakers or pharmaceutical manufacturers do not tend to support age-group events or women's competitions. FIFA does.

Moreover sport has a cultural resonance which exceeds its purely economic impact. Publicity-hungry captains of industry may look jealously at the media coverage granted to individuals in the sports sector with access to far smaller budgets. Indeed crowding into this limelight is often a reason for choosing to become financially involved in sport. Buying a club may often not be a good way to make money, but it is often a good way to raise one's profile. Sport has a social and cultural impact which typically sets it apart from and above industries which generate similar or even much higher levels of income. And that impact is worldwide: the great European football clubs are known and followed across the globe and they structure their commercial strategies accordingly. In England, in particular, foreign ownership of the leading clubs has become the norm and, as is clear from the pattern of acquisitions by nationals of states with patchy reputations for respecting human rights, the aim is commonly not primarily profit but rather a veneer of respectability.

Sport is frequently garlanded for its ability to bring people together in a spirit of friendship, harmony, and tolerance. 'Fair play!' is an endearing appeal, which portrays sport as a model of decency and honesty. So too sport as recreation has evident benefits as a means of improving public health. No one makes virtuous claims of this type about car-making or ship-building or selling insurance.

But sport is not *that* special.

Sporting activity is not completely without analogy to normal industry and it is certainly not as special as those engaged in sports governance commonly claim. Sport is not *only* motivated by profit-making but it is without doubt a sector in which large amounts of money are made. In particular, the attachment of attractive high-profile sport to the deregulated and technologically advanced broadcasting sector has over the last twenty-five years brought wealth into professional sport to such a degree that its shape is scarcely comparable to that of the past. The fan who lives locally and pays at the turnstile was once the principal source of revenue for football clubs, but that primacy has long since shifted to the consumer of broadcasting services, and that consumer could be resident anywhere across the world. In similar vein whereas in the past the successful footballer might pay his bills by becoming a manager once he retires from playing, today the retired top-level footballer has no reason to worry about the financial need to work ever again. He is already a celebrity, and a very rich one. In 2012 Giles Clarke, then chairman of the England and Wales Cricket Board, revealed that the governing body had acted to force the closing down of 700 pirate websites providing illegal streams of matches, and he warned that they are 'the biggest danger' facing the game.[1] But the eternal beauty of cricket on the village green is not in the slightest imperilled by such trends. What he really meant was that such websites are the biggest danger facing the dependence of the *professional* game on protected revenue streams from mainstream broadcasters.

Much of the admittedly distinctive character of sport just sketched deserves careful assessment which takes due account of context. The necessary mutual interdependence between sports clubs in a professional League clearly serves as a reason to treat *some* forms of collaboration among sports clubs as legitimate where it would not be so benignly regarded in a normal industry, but it does not mean that clubs are *never* properly treated as competitors. They may compete in the market for players; they may compete for support from sponsors and from broadcasters. Different models are to be found in different countries. The intense attention paid in North American sports leagues to promoting competitive balance, through devices such as the 'draft pick' and salary caps, are largely absent from European leagues, where far less attempt is made to control the strong and support the weak. In part this is because in Europe consumers—fans, one might prefer to call them—seem more tolerant of suppliers of services—clubs, one might prefer to call them—who can never seriously compete to be the champion. In part it is also because in Europe there are many more prizes on offer to satisfy fans—avoiding relegation, qualifying to play in European competitions—than are available in the 'closed' leagues that dominate North American sport, where promotion and relegation are foreign

---

[1] <https://www.theguardian.com/sport/2012/jan/26/pirate-websites-cricket-giles-clarke> accessed 29 November 2016.

concepts and there is no interconnection between national and international competitions on the European model. So pursuit of competitive balance has much
less resonance in European than in North American professional sport. All chosen
models assume that some, but not all, forms of collaboration between clubs reflect
interdependence among competitors as a special feature of sport and that they
should therefore be not only tolerated but encouraged, but not all models adopt
precisely the same priorities.

The global pattern of governance which is characteristic of sport makes good
sense as a means to ensure that the rules of the game are not fragmented in their
geographical application, but carries with it the risk of the rise of unaccountable
and uncontrolled power. Sports bodies may have a case when they seek to insulate
the integrity of the rules of the global game from intervention by local and diverse
particularities: the matter is different when laws on transparency, taxation, corporate governance, and anti-corruption are dismissed as antithetical to the stability of
global governance in sport. Unchecked and uncheckable power is always a source
of anxiety. Sports bodies, which are not tethered to any conventional pattern of
democratic oversight or accountability, are among the more obvious sources of
such disquiet in the modern world. Typically private in form, they are nonetheless
of immense interest to the public and they wield huge power. The risk of self-
interested action untethered to any conventional chains of external accountability
is a powerful reason to plead for a system of rules governing sport that is not allowed
unconfined immunity from the parochial but democratically approved structures
of national and EU law.

The cultural resonance of sport is frequently celebrated, but it too may be
double-edged. It is plainly a splendid thing when sport provides a platform for
bringing people together in a spirit of friendship, harmony, and tolerance, but
examples abound of sport providing an opportunity for the display of base emo-
tions and regeneration of historical grievances. So, for example, in October 2014 a
football match between Serbia and Albania was abandoned after fans invaded the
pitch and attacked visiting players.[2] This is by no means the only instance in recent
years of a match being halted and left unfinished because of violence. In 2001 a
match between France and Algeria was abandoned after fans invaded the pitch.[3]
Honduras and El Salvador fought the so-called 'football war' in 1969: there was of
course much more to its causes than football, but a fiercely contested World Cup
qualifying match between the two countries did nothing to promote peace—quite
the reverse. Sport of a representative nature generates true passion. Sometimes this
goes too far. Here there is merit in distinguishing between amateur and recreational
sport, where the profit-making motive is absent and participation is of greater

---

[2] 'Serbia v Albania Abandoned after Players and Fans Brawl on Pitch' *The Guardian* (London, 14
October 2014) <https://www.theguardian.com/football/2014/oct/14/serbia-albania-euro-2016-flag-
halted> accessed 29 November 2016.

[3] 'Fans Force Abandonment of Watershed France v Alegria [sic] Match' *The Guardian* (London,
8 October 2001) <https://www.theguardian.com/football/2001/oct/08/newsstory.sport16> accessed
29 November 2016.

significance than winning or losing, and professional sport, where the partisan element is greatly heightened. Similarly, sport as a form of recreation plays a useful part of a broader strategy to promote awareness of the benefits of a healthy lifestyle, but this has negligible connection with the pay-per-view viewer who turns on his or her television to watch a Champions League match, beer(s) and burger(s) to hand, preferably (as far as the Union of European Football Associations (UEFA) is concerned) those produced by the competition's official sponsor(s). Money-making looms large in professional sport.

The challenge and delight of 'sports law' is fuelled by, first, exploration of the strength of the claim that sport is 'special' and then, second, appreciation of how such a claim, if made good, should affect the making, interpretation, and application of legal rules. This is more than simply collecting together the several areas of the law which might conceivably touch the practice of sport(s). It is a much richer enterprise—one that is built on an expectation that sport is to some extent special and that the law will sometimes, but not always, be shaped accordingly. In this sense sports lawyers must reckon with Frank Easterbrook's famous rebuke. Delivered under the title 'Cyberspace and the Law of the Horse',[4] his main target for criticism was the risk of shaping a 'cyberlaw' inadequately tethered to existing legal rules and principles, most of all associated with intellectual property. His analogy was with the imagined law of the horse: simply to gather cases concerning horses would stretch over sales law, personal injury, licensing, and so on, and would, he argued, yield shallow results and miss unifying principles. So, he counselled, 'the best way to learn the law applicable to specialized endeavors is to study general rules'.[5] Get to horses via tort and contract and property law, and so on. So should one get to sports in the same way? This sceptical inquiry is worth making—and it is not a concern that is exclusive to sport[6]—but there are satisfying answers to the accusation that 'sports law' as a category is banal and empty. Most of all the concept of 'sports law' is driven by a claim that sporting activity, because it is special, should be granted partial or total *autonomy* from the 'ordinary law' of states or of international organizations created by states. Sport, after all, is typically governed by global bodies which claim expertise in and sensitivity to their field and which insist on the vital importance of creating a single set of rules that should not be fragmented in their application or interpretation by geographical accident. If offside in Bolivia is not offside in Spain because Spanish law makes different demands or prefers a different interpretation, or even simply because Spanish judges claim authority to

[4] F Easterbrook, 'Cyberspace and the Law of the Horse' (1996) 7 University of Chicago Legal Forum <http://chicagounbound.uchicago.edu/uclf/vol1996/iss1/7> accessed 29 November 2016.
[5] ibid 207.
[6] eg on aviation law, see B Havel and G Sanchez, *The Principles and Practice of International Aviation Law* (CUP 2014) ch 1; on health care law, T Hervey and J McHale, *European Union Health Law: Themes and Implications* (CUP 2015) Pt I; on food law, N Fortin, *Food Regulation: Law, Science, Policy and Practice* (2nd edn, John Wiley 2017) Foreword; and on how to 'see something when we think about the regulation of cyberspace that other areas would not show us', see L Lessig. 'The Law of the Horse: What Cyberlaw Might Teach' (1999) <http://cyber.law.harvard.edu/publications/1999/The_Law_of_the_Horse> accessed 29 November 2016.

review decisions made on the pitch by the referee, then the very character of the sporting endeavour has been ruined. This claim to sporting autonomy is typically pitched in terms of protection of the *lex sportiva*. The *lex sportiva* is a term lacking a precise agreed definition, but it helpfully, if loosely, refers to the arrangements that define a sport's operation. The *lex sportiva* is made up of the rules and practices established by governing bodies and applied globally to ensure common treatment of a particular sport wherever it happens to be played, and increasingly it is shaped by the practice of the *lex sportiva*'s adjudicative pinnacle, the CAS, the Court of Arbitration for Sport, which is examined in Chapter 2.[7] The *lex sportiva* is not the law of a state. It may come into conflict with the law of a state or with the law of an international institution such as the EU, and it is exactly at that point that the appeal to show respect to the autonomy claimed by *lex sportiva* is heard at its loudest. Typically governing bodies in sport will seek to impress a positive view of the virtues of this sporting autonomy on those charged with the responsibility to apply 'ordinary law'. And although interference with the autonomy of the offside rule is a rather fanciful example, the matter becomes a good deal more sensitive when sports governing bodies claim that their sale of broadcasting rights or their imposition of control over the transfer of players should be immune from supervision pursuant to the 'ordinary law' of a state or a body such as the EU. Sports bodies may be suspected of pleading the autonomy of the *lex sportiva* not only as a means to protect its integrity but also in order to sustain commercial advantage. Moreover, as part of this thematically consistent strategy, sports governing bodies are remarkably skilful at portraying commercial activities in the most virtuous possible light. The flabby couch potato may be the true consumer of the Champions League and fast food and beer producers the main sponsors, but it is the value of a healthy lifestyle and tolerant generosity of spirit that will be pushed strategically into the foreground by sports governing bodies when they seek to proclaim their case for autonomy from legal supervision.

So investigation of 'sports law' promises an expedition that is more intellectually ambitious and more sharply focused than a mere desire to collect together the several types of laws—public law and private law; criminal law and competition law; national, European, and international—to which sporting activities happen to be subject. 'Sports law' has its focus on the intersection of two types of legal order: the *lex sportiva*, on the one hand, and, on the other, the law of states or of international organizations on whose territory sport is practised. Sports law therefore has two distinct, though connected, components: the claim to (some degree of) autonomy from the application of the 'ordinary' law of states and international organizations

---

[7] For a useful overview of the literature, see R Siekmann, 'What is Sports Law? Lex Sportiva and Lex Ludica: a Reassessment of Content and Terminology' (2011) 11(3–4) Intl Sports LJ 3; I Blackshaw, 'Towards a Lex Sportiva' (2011) 11(3–4) Intl Sports LJ 140; A Valero, 'In search of a working notion of lex sportiva' (2014) 14 Intl Sports LJ 3; A Duval, 'Lex Sportiva: A Playground for Transnational Law' (2013) 19 ELJ 822. See also F Latty, *La Lex Sportiva: Recherche sur le Droit Transnational* (Martinus Nijhoff 2007).

and the claim that 'internal' sports law, the *lex sportiva*, possesses sufficient coherence and procedural integrity to be treated as a legitimate system of ordering.

Sports law as a discipline explores the ability of sports bodies *in practice* to insulate their legal order from that of public regulators—the strategies they use to keep 'ordinary law' at bay. And its intellectual core explores how to make a normative assessment of the strength of the claims advanced in favour of autonomy. The detailed answers provided may plausibly vary in different jurisdictions and in different sports. And in its main part this book will focus on the law of the EU. But the core questions confronting any sports lawyer are the same: Just how special is sport really, and how, if at all, should that special character be granted legal recognition?

2

Three Strategies for Defending 'Sporting Autonomy'

2.1 Protecting Sporting Autonomy: the Contractual, Legislative, and Interpretative Routes

On occasion sports governing bodies find it strategically useful to seek the protection of the law. So, for example, the Union of European Football Associations (UEFA) has aligned itself closely with the Commission in mapping the contours of its Financial Fair Play regime for fear that it might be accused of putting together an anti-competitive scheme that unlawfully limits spending. This is examined in Chapter 10.9. And Giles Clarke, the cricket administrator met in Chapter 1, nervous about matches being shown unlawfully on 'pirate websites',[1] would doubtless be only too happy to see the coercive force of the state crack down on those damaging his commercial model by violating the property and contractual rights held by cricket's governing bodies. But it is much more common to find that the principal ambition of sports governing bodies is to isolate their practices and activities from legal supervision or at least to mould legal rules to sporting taste. So the question is normally how, and how far, may an autonomy for sporting practices be extracted.

There are three main strategies for sports federations wishing to protect their regulatory autonomy (ie the *lex sportiva*) from 'ordinary law' (ie the law of states or of international organizations established by states such as those of the EU). These three strategies are, in short, contractual, legislative, and interpretative in nature.

First, sporting bodies may require participants to contract in to the *lex sportiva*, and to agree not to solve sporting disputes before 'ordinary' courts. This is the contractual solution to achieving sporting autonomy. It is increasingly common to find this model adopted by the constitutions of major sports governing bodies, such as Fédération Internationale de Football Association (FIFA) and the International Olympic Committee (IOC), and it has lent increasing prominence to the role of the Court of Arbitration for Sport (CAS), which is the dominant adjudicative body within the system formed by the *lex sportiva*. But valuable and in practice significant though this 'contracting out' is for those espousing the virtues of sporting

---

[1] <https://www.theguardian.com/sport/2012/jan/26/pirate-websites-cricket-giles-clarke> accessed 29 November 2016.

autonomy, it does not achieve a watertight division between 'ordinary law' and the *lex sportiva*.

Second, sports federations may seek to induce states or international organizations to adopt or implement the *lex sportiva* (in whole or in part). This may be summarized as the legislative solution—although in so far as the regulator is an international organization, it is a Treaty-based solution. The lure of the rich prize of hosting a major event such as the Olympic Games or the Football World Cup has permitted sports bodies to extract remarkable concessions granting them autonomy from the normal laws of the host country and/or special protection of their commercial interests, and on other occasions narrower and more sector-specific exemptions have been secured, in particular in the shaping of tax regimes and in state subsidies. The EU, however, has been consistently resistant to pressure to grant sport an explicit exclusion from the application of EU law. And no state and no international organization goes so far as to confer on sport a *general* amnesty from legal regulation.

Third, sports federations commonly seek to persuade courts (in states and in international organizations) that the special character of sport should be taken into account in the interpretation and application of 'ordinary' law. This is the interpretative—or adjudicative—solution. It does not claim formal autonomy *from* the law of states or of international organizations, but rather it seeks to claim a functional autonomy *within* that law, by persuading judges that the application of relevant legal rules falls for modification where the peculiarities of sport are at stake. Its value to sporting bodies is plainly dependent on the level of success they enjoy in persuading judges that their special status is merited and should accordingly be translated into some form of adjusted or softened interpretation and application of the generally applicable legal rules within the particular jurisdiction at stake.

These three strategies are at heart all founded on claims that 'sport is special', but they are constructed differently, and they are here arranged in descending order of preference from the perspective of sporting federations. The contractual solution typically has most appeal, the legislative is 'next best', and the interpretative solution is likely to be the least favoured, because it involves sport making its case on 'enemy' territory, that is, according to locally applicable law. Where, under the third strategy, sports federations strive to appeal for interpretative leniency, one will commonly observe a tension whereby sporting bodies push for a more generous scope of autonomy than may be readily on offer. But it is on the third strategy that sporting bodies are frequently compelled to rely, once the contractual solution reaches its limits and where the legislative solution is unattainable, and it is here—in the practice of the institutions that interpret and apply the ordinary law of states and of international organizations—that much of the vivid excitement of 'sports law' as an intellectual concept and a practical challenge emerges as litigation erupts.

This chapter explains the possibilities but also the limits of, first, the contractual solution and, second, the legislative solution as methods to preserve sporting autonomy. It then reflects briefly on the interpretative solution, but in essence the entirety of the rest of the book addresses the interpretative solution at length in the particular context of the application of EU law to sport.

2.2 The Contractual Solution

It is quite common for sports bodies to provide in their governing statutes that disputes shall be resolved 'internally' through arbitration and that recourse to the ordinary courts shall not be pursued (sometimes on pain of sanction). The CAS has become prominent in such arrangements. This is, at one level, simply a contractual acceptance of dispute resolution outside the framework of the ordinary courts. This is not a peculiarly sports-specific concern. In sport, as elsewhere, arbitration has strong appeal as a means of providing for quick and relatively cheap resolution of disputes and also for ensuring that the matter is dealt with by parties with a higher level of sensitivity to and expertise in the matter at hand than is possessed by ordinary judges. Moreover arbitration offers the possibility of a developing uniform system of practice which is not constrained by jurisdictional boundaries. It promises common global understandings which courts operating state by state cannot provide.[2] For sport, the aspiration is to the elucidation of a *lex sportiva* which is unfragmented by jurisdictional specificity and which is informed by sports-sensitive expertise.[3]

2.2.1 Protecting arbitration

FIFA describes its Statutes as 'the constitution of FIFA and world football'.[4] This is perfectly accurate. They are not a *state* constitution, but they bring together the rules and working methods of FIFA, the organization that stands at the apex of the global governance pyramid of the sport of football. The rules *constitute* the entity—which is FIFA.

FIFA's Statutes make careful provision for the dominant role of arbitration, and they place the CAS in a presiding role. Article 59(1) of the currently applicable Statutes[5] directs that: 'The confederations, member associations and leagues shall agree to recognise CAS as an independent judicial authority and to ensure that their members, affiliated players and officials comply with the decisions passed by CAS.' The same obligation is extended to intermediaries and licensed match agents. Article 57 adds that 'FIFA recognises the independent Court of Arbitration for Sport (CAS) with headquarters in Lausanne (Switzerland) to resolve disputes between FIFA, member associations, confederations, leagues, clubs, players, officials, intermediaries and licensed match agents', and that: 'The provisions of the CAS Code of Sports-related Arbitration shall apply to the proceedings. CAS shall primarily apply the various regulations of FIFA and, additionally, Swiss law.'

---

[2] See eg W Park, 'Explaining Arbitration Law' (2015) available at SSRN <https://papers.ssrn.com/sol3/papers.cfm?abstract_id=2675268> accessed 29 November 2016.

[3] cf P Cavalieros and J Kim, 'Can the Arbitral Community Learn from Sports Arbitration?' (2015) 32 J Intl Arb 237.

[4] <http://www.fifa.com/about-fifa/fifa-congress/all-you-need-to-know/index.html> accessed 29 November 2016.

[5] The current—April 2016—version of the Statutes is at <http://resources.fifa.com/mm/document/affederation/generic/02/78/29/07/fifastatutsweben_neutral.pdf> accessed 29 November 2016.

The aim, however, is more ambitious than simply to engage CAS in dispute resolution. The FIFA Statutes seek to confer *exclusive* jurisdiction on CAS. Article 59(2) provides that 'Recourse to ordinary courts of law is prohibited unless specifically provided for in the FIFA regulations' and also that: 'Recourse to ordinary courts of law for all types of provisional measures is also prohibited.' Article 59(3) seeks to ensure the implementation of this exclusion of ordinary courts within the several lower layers of the organizational pyramid over which FIFA rules as the global body. Article 59(3) provides:

The associations shall insert a clause in their statutes or regulations, stipulating that it is prohibited to take disputes in the association or disputes affecting leagues, members of leagues, clubs, members of clubs, players, officials and other association officials to ordinary courts of law, unless the FIFA regulations or binding legal provisions specifically provide for or stipulate recourse to ordinary courts of law. Instead of recourse to ordinary courts of law, provision shall be made for arbitration. Such disputes shall be taken to an independent and duly constituted arbitration tribunal recognised under the rules of the association or confederation or to CAS. The associations shall also ensure that this stipulation is implemented in the association, if necessary by imposing a binding obligation on its members ...

Were a party to this contractual network to seek to break out of its bonds and to route a claim through the ordinary courts of a state then it would be open to FIFA to rely on these provisions as a reason why such ordinary courts should not claim jurisdiction to hear a case. An agreement to commit to arbitration and not to litigate is binding as a contract in the normal way. A national court should respect the contractually agreed exclusion of its own jurisdiction over the matter. The multi-jurisdictional excursion that would be needed to provide an exhaustive account of practice will not be pursued here: suffice to say that at national level, through judicial practice and commonly pursuant to statutory mandate, and at international level, most of all because of the Convention on the Recognition and Enforcement of Foreign Arbitral Awards of 1958, also known as the New York Convention, the promise not to litigate *is* typically enforced. Remedies vary according to circumstances and there are distinctions at the level of detail between common and civil law systems but, beyond simple refusal to consider the substance of a case which the parties have agreed to send to arbitration, they include orders to compel arbitration, antisuit injunctions, non-recognition of judgments which are obtained in breach of a valid agreement to arbitrate, and conceivably an award of damages.[6]

In the *consumer* context the EU asserts a power to check whether clauses that require that disputes be taken exclusively to arbitration are fair and, if they are not, to treat them as unenforceable.[7] This is one aspect of the EU's relative readiness to intervene in the process of arbitration in order to protect its values and it is for that

---

[6] G Born, *International Commercial Arbitration* (2nd edn, Kluwer 2014) ch 8; M Moses, *The Principles and Practice of International Commercial Litigation* (2nd edn, CUP 2012) ch 5; N Blackaby, C Partasides, A Redfern, and M Hunter (eds), *Redfern and Hunter on International Commercial Arbitration* (6th edn, OUP 2015) ch 7.
[7] Council Directive 93/13/EEC of 5 April 1993 on unfair terms in consumer contracts [1993] OJ L95/29.

reason generally treated with some hostility by arbitration specialists. The wider context of EU interventionism, and its possible application to sport, is considered more fully later.

There is, however, more to FIFA's exclusion of recourse to ordinary courts of law under its Statutes. Article 59(3)'s concluding sentence adds teeth. It provides that: 'The associations shall impose sanctions on any party that fails to respect this obligation and ensure that any appeal against such sanctions shall likewise be strictly submitted to arbitration, and not to ordinary courts of law.' Article 61 provides more broadly that 'Any violation of the foregoing provisions will be punished in compliance with the FIFA Disciplinary Code'. As shown in section 2.2.8, such sanctions are on occasion imposed, in the event that these contractual obligations are disrespected.

FIFA, then, establishes a contractual network into which other parties in the 'pyramid' of sporting governance—most prominently, the continental confederations and national associations—are locked, under which they accept and will enforce on their clubs and players the central place of the CAS and normally too, in conjunction, the exclusion of recourse to ordinary courts of law. And, moreover, sanctions are available to discipline those who would seek to break out of this system of arbitration by engaging with ordinary courts.

This amounts to a thorough and vigorous protection of the *lex sportiva*. The plan is to resolve sporting disputes internally by isolating them from the ordinary courts of law. Comparable provisions allocating to the CAS the job of arbitrating disputes may be found in the constitutions of many other sporting bodies, and usually in company with an exclusivity proviso that shuts off recourse to ordinary courts of law. For example, Article 61 of the Olympic Charter is entitled 'Dispute Resolution'. It provides that any dispute relating to the application or interpretation of decisions of the IOC 'may be resolved solely by the IOC Executive Board and, in certain cases, by arbitration before the Court of Arbitration for Sport (CAS)'; and that any dispute 'arising on the occasion of, or in connection with, the Olympic Games shall be submitted exclusively to the Court of Arbitration for Sport (CAS), in accordance with the Code of Sports-Related Arbitration'.[8]

There is in fact a high level of coordination among governing bodies. Most sports federations are based in Switzerland.[9] Reasons for this include matters of tax and transparency (in relative terms there is not much of either), but the effect is to promote shared practice. In general, sports federations have much in common with each other, though, judged according to their organizational character, functions, and strategic roles, they are not identical.[10]

---

[8] <http://www.olympic.org/Documents/olympic_charter_en.pdf> version in force from August 2015, accessed 29 November 2016. See generally AM Mestre, *The Law of the Olympic Games* (TMC Asser 2009).

[9] C Dudognon, 'The Standard International Sports Federation: An Association under Swiss Law with its Headquarters in Lausanne' [2014] Intl Sports L Rev 50.

[10] F Lefebvre-Rangeon and C Dudognon, 'Typological, Institutional and Legal Analysis of International Sports Federations' [2014] Intl Sports L Rev 79; A Geeraert, J Alm, and M Groll, 'Good Governance in International Sport Organisations: An Analysis of the 35 Olympic Sport Governing Bodies' (2014) 6 International Journal of Sport Policy and Politics 281.

2.2.2 The CAS

The CAS was founded in 1984.[11] It is based in Lausanne in Switzerland. In formal terms the CAS is a 'court' only in name. It is an arbitration tribunal that draws its authority from the agreements entered into by the parties which choose to submit to its jurisdiction. It offers the advantages offered by arbitration in general. The CAS is the sports-specific reflection of the general preference which underpins arbitration for a desirable method for streamlining access to justice through tailored procedures that are quicker and cheaper than those of the ordinary courts and possessed of more specific expertise. It is, in its own right, an intriguing example of the trend towards creating a single global adjudicative body with expertise.[12]

The CAS's profile is high and rising as the centrality of its role in the development of the *lex sportiva* is beyond dispute. The publication in 2016 of the first ever *Yearbook of International Sports Arbitration*, which is mainly though not exclusively concerned with CAS practice and decisions, emphasizes its prominence.[13] The CAS is emerging as the source of case law and of principles of an increasingly dense *lex sportiva*. The CAS does not operate according to a formal system rooted in precedent in the way that a common lawyer might recognize and expect, for it decides disputes on their facts. Writing over ten years ago, Erbsen cautioned against a complacently homogenous account of the CAS's elaboration of a *lex sportiva*.[14] In particular he pressed the need to understand where, when, and how the CAS will identify principled methods of interpretation and adjudication in circumstances where a sporting rule or code fails to provide a textually clear answer to a dispute. Foster, writing at the same time, emphasized that when faced with disciplinary cases that expose the profound asymmetry of power that prevails in the relationship between governing body and athlete, the CAS should be attentively interventionist to a degree that would not be apt in other areas where it exercises jurisdiction.[15] The caution against uncritical embrace of the label *lex sportiva* is well made. But this is not to deny that the CAS's accumulated decisions reveal themes and principles. Moreover, more recent accounts observe that it tends increasingly to cite its own previous rulings, thereby building a sense of continuity and enhancing

---

[11] It has a useful website—<http://www.tas-cas.org/en/index.html>—which includes a summary of its development over time—<http://www.tas-cas.org/en/general-information/history-of-the-cas.html> accessed 29 November 2016. On its first 20 years, see I Blackshaw, R Siekmann, and J Soek (eds), *The Court of Arbitration for Sport 1984–2004* (TMC Asser 2006).

[12] On its structure and operation, see R McLaren, 'The Court of Arbitration for Sport' in J Nafziger and S Ross (eds), *Handbook on International Sports Law* (Elgar 2011) ch 2; M Beloff, S Netzle, and U Haas, 'The Court of Arbitration for Sport' in A Lewis and J Taylor (eds), *Sport: Law and Practice* (3rd edn, Bloomsbury 2014) ch E3.

[13] A Duval and A Rigozzi (eds), *Yearbook of International Sports Arbitration 2015* (TMC Asser 2016).

[14] A Erbsen, 'The Substance and Illusion of Lex Sportiva' in I Blackshaw, R Siekmann, and J Soek (eds), *The Court of Arbitration for Sport 1984–2004* (TMC Asser 2006).

[15] K Foster, 'Lex Sportiva and Lex Ludica: The Court of Arbitration for Sport's Jurisprudence' in I Blackshaw, R Siekmann, and J Soek (eds), *The Court of Arbitration for Sport 1984–2004* (TMC Asser 2006).

predictability.[16] In particular, fairness is emerging as a guiding principle, especially well developed in its procedural (rather than its substantive) dimension.[17] It has been argued that CAS practice reveals a strain of willingness to defer to the autonomy of sporting bodies but on condition that their practice meets standards of good governance, including compliance with published rules, transparency, and ensuring a fair hearing.[18] It is propelled in this direction by the critical gaze of some national courts—this is considered later, in section 2.2.4—but the CAS's approach deserves to be understood as something more than merely instrumental. The CAS aspires to shape a procedurally respectable scheme of review of an insulated and developing *lex sportiva*, at the apex of which it sits, but beneath which is flourishing a rather dense form of governance which is largely invisible to the ordinary courts. The practice of the World Anti-Doping Agency (WADA) provides a particularly rich case study into the development of a remarkably detailed self-contained regime, which occasionally also provokes appeal decisions before the CAS.[19]

It would be a mistake to exaggerate the consistency of the CAS's practice. Its job is to resolve disputes, not to craft an intellectually pure stream of principles. Chapter 9 will explore a wild inconsistency in its approach to the calculation of compensation payable to clubs whose players have terminated their contracts without just cause. But overall there is more convergence than divergence in its accumulated decisional practice. The CAS's decisions are significant in their own right and they also set the tone for the future. Accordingly the CAS may not be a court in a formal sense, yet it is in functional terms a 'court'. It presides over a system of *private* ordering—but it *is* ordering.

The CAS has its own procedural rules, found in the *Code of Sports-Related Arbitration*.[20] They state that in ordinary arbitration: 'The Panel shall decide the dispute according to the rules of law chosen by the parties or, in the absence of such

---

[16] R van Kleef, 'Reviewing Disciplinary Sanctions in Sports' (2015) 4 CJICL 3; G Ioannidis, 'The Influence of Common Law Traditions on the Practice and Procedure before the CAS' in A Duval and A Rigozzi (eds), *Yearbook of International Sports Arbitration 2015* (TMC Asser 2016) ch 2.

[17] eg J Nafziger, 'The Principle of Fairness in the Lex Sportiva of CAS Awards and Beyond' (2010) 10(3–4) Intl Sports LJ 3; J Nafziger, 'International Sports Law' in J Nafziger and S Ross (eds), *Handbook on International Sports Law* (Edward Elgar 2011) 17–31; McLaren (n 12) 54–62; J Letnar Černič, 'Fair Trial Guarantees before the Court of Arbitration for Sport' (2012) 6 Human Rights and International Legal Discourse 259.

[18] D Mavromati, 'Autonomy and Good Governance in Sports Associations in light of the Case Law Rendered by the Court of Arbitration for Sport' [2014] Intl Sports L Rev 71.

[19] Erbsen (n 14) uses this as his main source of illustrations of CAS practice. See also R W Pound and K Clarke, 'Doping in Sport' in J Nafziger and S Ross (eds), *Handbook on International Sports Law* (Edward Elgar 2011) ch 6; V Moeller and P Dimeo, 'Anti-doping: The End of Sport' (2014) 6 International Journal of Sport Policy and Politics 259; A Duval, 'La Lex Sportiva Face au Droit de l'Union Européenne: Guerre et Paix dans l'Espace Juridique Transnational' (DPhil thesis, EUI Florence, 2015) 317–72, available via <http://cadmus.eui.eu/handle/1814/36997> accessed 29 November 2016. On anti-doping generally and the World Anti-Doping Agency (WADA) and its Code in particular, see U Haas and D Healey (eds), *Doping in Sport and the Law* (Hart 2016); J Gleaves and TM Hunt (eds), *A Global History of Doping in Sport: Drugs, Policy and Politics* (Routledge 2015).

[20] <http://www.tas-cas.org/en/index.html>. The current version has been in force since January 2016. See D Mavromati and M Reeb, *The Code of the Court of Arbitration for Sport* (Kluwer 2015).

a choice, according to Swiss law.'[21] And so in some cases the CAS will apply the law of the contract as stipulated by the parties. In arbitration before the CAS on appeal—which will be the norm where the matter has originated in a decision by FIFA or another sports governing body—it is provided that:

... the Panel shall decide the dispute according to the applicable regulations and, subsidiarily, to the rules of law chosen by the parties or, in the absence of such a choice, according to the law of the country in which the federation, association or sports-related body which has issued the challenged decision is domiciled or according to the rules of law the Panel deems appropriate.[22]

So, for example, in *Adrian Mutu v Chelsea Football Club* the relevant employment contract was governed by English law and therefore English law fell to be applied to determine the damages due to the club as a consequence of the breach of the contract by the player, whose drug use had led to a ban and his unavailability for selection.[23] A sum of compensation in excess of €17 million had been ordered through FIFA's dispute resolution procedure and this was duly approved by the CAS and an appeal to the Swiss Federal Tribunal by the player failed.[24]

There is a degree of inconsistency in the attitude of CAS Panels to the application of relevant provisions of EU law.[25] A strong statement in favour of adhesion to EU law in CAS decision-making is found in *AEK Athens and Slavia Prague*, where the parties agreed that the Panel should apply EC (as it then was) and Swiss competition law, but the Panel found that 'even if the parties had not validly agreed on its applicability to this case, it should be taken into account anyway'.[26] It added that Article 19 of the Swiss Federal Statute on Private International Law directs that an arbitration tribunal sitting in Switzerland must take into consideration foreign mandatory rules, even of a law different from the one determined through the choice-of-law process, provided that three conditions are met. These hold that, first, such rules must belong to that special category of norms which need to be applied irrespective of the law applicable to the merits of the case; second, there must be a close connection between the subject matter of the dispute and the territory where the mandatory rules are in force; and, third, the mandatory rules must aim to protect legitimate interests and crucial values and their application must allow an

---

[21] The Code, R45. See CL Haemmerle, 'Choice of Law in the Court of Arbitration for Sport: Overview, Critical Analysis and Potential Improvements' (2013) 13 Intl Sports LJ 299: the proposed improvement is to improve certainty by replacing default to Swiss law with a 'closest connection' test.

[22] The Code, R58. See U Haas, 'Applicable Law in Football-related Disputes—the Relationship between the CAS Code, the FIFA Statutes and the Agreement of the Parties on the Application of National Law' [2015] Intl Sports L Rev 9.

[23] CAS 2008/A/1644.

[24] The payment seems never to have been made. In CAS 2013/A/3365 *Juventus v Chelsea* the CAS refused to hold the club that the player joined subsequent to his ban jointly liable, citing the deterrent effect on the player pursuing his livelihood that would follow from such an award.

[25] See A Duval, 'The Court of Arbitration for Sport and EU Law: Chronicle of an Encounter' (2015) 22(2) MJ 224, 235–45; and more fully Duval (n 19) Partie II Titre 2.

[26] CAS 98/200, para 10.

appropriate decision. The three conditions were in the Panel's view met and so, pursuant to Article 19 of the Swiss Federal Statute, EU competition law has to be taken into account by the CAS.

A similar approach was taken to EU free movement law in the CAS ruling in *Celtic v UEFA*, which concerned the transfer of a player.[27] The Panel concluded that the conditions of Article 19 of the Swiss statute were satisfied and it therefore applied what is now Article 45 of the Treaty on the Functioning of the European Union (TFEU) to test the compatibility of a demand for compensation with EU law. Following the Court of Justice's reasoning in *Bosman*,[28] it decided that EU law precluded any such demand.

In *Galatasaray v UEFA* the CAS Panel expressly adopted a desire to converge with the reasoning of the Panel in *AEK Athens and Slavia Prague* and, citing Article 19 of the Swiss statute, agreed that it would take account of the Treaty rules on both free movement and on competition as mandatory provisions of EU law.[29] It then, however, resisted the claim that UEFA's Financial Fair Play regulations offended against the requirements of EU law. This point of substance is addressed in context in Chapter 10.9.

The test drawn from Article 19 of the Swiss statute and applied in the ruling is not sports-specific. It would in principle apply to any matter falling for determination by an arbitration tribunal sitting in Switzerland. However, the sporting context is relevant to the ease with which the test is met: the second in particular is readily met precisely because of the location of major football clubs. Under this reasoning the CAS is always required to take into account both EU competition law and EU free movement law in any case with a connection to the EU. Practice admittedly varies:[30] but a powerful pragmatic reason pushing the CAS to take EU law seriously lies in the likelihood that, in the absence of such respect, the finality of its rulings will in turn be disrespected by courts within the EU determined to prevent subversion of the provisions of EU internal market law which count as an expression of public policy. This is considered further later in this section.

2.2.3 How immune is the *lex sportiva* from 'ordinary' law?

Challenge to a ruling of the CAS, as to any arbitral body, is possible under Swiss law, but only to a very limited extent and very rarely with success. The clean finality of arbitration is treated as a value in its own right and it is strenuously protected.

Arbitrations are subject to the Swiss Federal Act on Private International Law. This provides for the annulment of an arbitral award on grounds set out in Article 190. But the identified grounds are limited. They cover only cases where the sole arbitrator was not properly appointed or where the arbitral tribunal was not properly constituted; where the arbitral tribunal wrongly accepted or declined jurisdiction;

---

[27] CAS 98/201 *Celtic v UEFA*, award of 7 January 2000. On the transfer system, see Ch 9.
[28] Case C-415/93 [1995] ECR I-4921. See Ch 4.
[29] CAS 2016/A/4492 *Galatasaray v UEFA*.   [30] Duval (n 25).

where the arbitral tribunal's decision went beyond the claims submitted to it, or failed to decide one of the items of the claim; where the principle of equal treatment of the parties or the right of the parties to be heard was violated; and where the award is incompatible with public policy.

Jurisdiction belongs exclusively with the Swiss Federal Tribunal and it has conscientiously adopted a narrow and restrictive approach to the possibility of intervention. This has the effect of sustaining the finality of the arbitral process. This is not a sports-specific issue, but sport has been among the contexts in which judicial reluctance to intervene in the finality of arbitration has been emphasized. The ruling in *Azerbaijan Field Hockey Federation v Fédération Internationale de Hockey* offers a vivid illustration of the reticence to intervene in decisions reached by the CAS.[31] The applicants were seeking to replace Spain in the women's field hockey competition at the Beijing Olympics of 2008. In the background were doping investigations which had been pursued against Spain but which had not led to that team's expulsion. The applicants failed before the CAS. They then brought the matter before the Swiss Federal Supreme Court. It found that the challenge was in essence an attack on the CAS Panel's interpretation of the Hockey Federation's Anti-Doping Policy. The Federal Supreme Court declared that it would not examine whether an arbitral tribunal had properly applied the law on which it rested its decision. Moreover, the claim that the CAS decision violated public policy for want of examination of the merits of the claim was also treated as unfounded.

In this case the Swiss Federal Supreme Court carefully and cautiously positioned itself far away from any pretence at serving as an appellate jurisdiction. The rulings show that normally it will not even correct errors of law perpetrated within the process of arbitration. This constitutes an aggressive protection of the process of arbitration, and in this context it entails a strongly held deference to the *lex sportiva* as shaped by the CAS.[32] This approach upholds sporting autonomy.

The Swiss Federal Supreme Court has intervened only twice in sports-related matters. The first intervention was in 2007 in *Guillermo Cañas v ATP Tour*.[33] Cañas, a professional tennis player, fell foul of anti-doping procedures and was banned for two years by the ATP, the sport's governing body. He appealed against this decision to the CAS—in fact, a large slice of the CAS's workload is taken up with challenges to such bans. Part of his claim was that the decision would contravene the law of Delaware regarding restraint of trade, but the CAS, in deciding to reduce the length of his ban, ignored this in its ruling. The Swiss Court upheld Cañas's appeal. The CAS had not met its obligation to deal with all arguments raised by parties before it. It had, in short, violated his right to be heard. This, one would suppose, is an

---

[31] 4A_424/2008 (2009) (Switz). English version at (2009) 3 Swiss International Arbitration Law Reports 57.

[32] On practice, see A Rigozzi, 'Challenging Awards of the Court of Arbitration for Sport' (2010) 1 JIDS 217; T Glienke, 'The Finality of CAS awards' (2012) 12(3–4) Intl Sports LJ 52; D Mavromati, 'Recent Jurisprudence of the Swiss Federal Tribunal on Motions to Set Aside CAS Awards: Some Lessons to be Drawn' [2014] Intl Sports L Rev 3.

[33] 4P_172/2006, 22 March 2007.

exceptional case and the flaw is easily avoided in future. The CAS has liberty to get the law wrong without fearing intervention by the Swiss Federal Supreme Court, but *Cañas* teaches that it must not refuse to engage with the law.

The second instance of intervention in a CAS award arrived in 2012, when the Swiss Federal Supreme Court decided *Matuzalem*.[34] This is of potentially wider significance than the *Cañas* case. Matuzalem was a footballer who had broken his contact with one club, Shakhtar Donetsk in Ukraine, and moved to another in Spain. He (and the acquiring club, Zaragoza) had been the subject of a decision by FIFA that compensation should be paid to the first club and, though challenged, this decision had been confirmed by the CAS.[35] Matuzalem could not afford to pay the sum. Nor could the acquiring club, Zaragoza, which was in a difficult financial position. Payment was therefore not made and a subsequent decision by FIFA imposed further sanctions pursuant to the FIFA Disciplinary Code, including both fines and a prohibition against Matuzalem playing until such time as the compensation was paid. This second adverse ruling too was challenged before, but again confirmed by, the CAS.[36]

As mentioned earlier, the Swiss Federal Act on Private International Law provides that an arbitral award may be set aside if it is incompatible with public policy. Matuzalem argued before the Swiss Federal Supreme Court that the CAS award violated his personal freedom to such an extent that it offended against public policy recognized by Swiss law within the meaning of the Act. The Swiss Court agreed. It found that a limitation of freedom is contrary to public policy if the rights of the individual concerned are clearly and severely infringed. And it took the view that an open-ended playing ban of the type that Matuzalem was facing constituted a severe infringement of the player's individual rights which was sufficient to overcome its normal reluctance to interfere with arbitral rulings.

This runs contrary to the orthodox disinclination to intervene in the finality of the CAS's rulings. It serves as a reminder that the contractual route to securing the autonomy of the *lex sportiva* which is the subject of this chapter is useful only in so far as ordinary courts of law do not take the view that a higher value, here that of public policy, shall usurp the product of contractual agreement. And if the approach taken in *Matuzalem* is broadened to a more general readiness to intervene in the CAS's rulings, the vitality of the strategy for maximizing sporting autonomy via the contractual route will be diminished. Consider, for example, attacks brought before the Swiss Federal Supreme Court against rulings by the CAS which confirm heavy penalties on, for instance, those found to have engaged in match-fixing or doping. It is at least possible that the Swiss Court will be tempted to intervene, but it is perhaps not probable. The CAS rulings upholding penalties of this type are likely to be treated as reflecting the existential need for 'clean' sport. But the transfer system, especially as applied in *Matuzalem*, is different. *Matuzalem* was a special case, and the decision is probably best understood not as a reflection of a newly

---

[34] 4A_558/2011, 27 March 2012.   [35] CAS 2008/A/1519-1520 *Matuzalem*.
[36] 29 June 2011, unreported.

interventionist mood on the part of the Swiss Federal Supreme Court but rather as a rebuke to the egregiously self-interested approach of a FIFA dispute resolution system which had sanctioned Matuzalem—twice—in circumstances where the direct beneficiary was a FIFA member, the association of the first club in Ukraine. More concretely, as the Swiss Federal Supreme Court pointed out, the second FIFA award (imposing a ban) was in any event in principle not necessary, since the first (requiring compensation) was enforceable through the ordinary courts by reliance on the New York Convention without the need for an additional second sanction imposed by FIFA. This aspect of the global system of arbitration now falls to be considered.

2.2.4 Recognition and enforcement of CAS rulings as Swiss arbitral awards

Once a ruling of the CAS has been made (and left undisturbed under Swiss law) it is to be recognized and enforced by ordinary courts of law as a Swiss arbitral award. So the CAS ruling may be enforced in whichever jurisdiction or jurisdictions is most convenient or appropriate, which will typically be the place(s) where the losing party and/or its assets are located. This is not a sports-specific matter. It is the general assumption that underpins arbitration. It applies pursuant to the New York Convention, which governs the recognition and enforcement of arbitral awards in states which have ratified the Convention. This covers some 150 states, including the United States and all of the EU's twenty-eight Member States. It is made specific by Article III: 'Each Contracting State shall recognize arbitral awards as binding and enforce them in accordance with the rules of procedure of the territory where the award is relied upon, under the conditions laid down in the following articles.' An English judge, asked to interpret and apply the Convention as incorporated into English law by the Arbitration Act 1996, has helpfully captured the intent behind this system: 'the purpose of the Convention is to ensure the effective and speedy enforcement of international arbitration awards'.[37] Were national courts inclined to ready and regular interference with awards once made, then the very purpose of arbitration as a speedier, cheaper, and expertise-driven alternative to litigation would be thwarted. Accordingly the strong emphasis is on judicial *enforcement* of arbitration awards once made.[38]

Therefore the CAS's awards, like arbitration awards generally, are final and binding on the parties, and they are enforceable internationally (as Swiss arbitral awards) by the parties by virtue of the New York Convention. So national courts outside Switzerland should and do enforce the CAS's rulings as foreign arbitration awards. In practice this is rarely necessary. The CAS's awards appear to command general respect and in any event some sports are capable of penalizing or threatening to

---

[37] *IPCO Ltd v Nigerian National Petroleum Corporation* [2008] EWCA Civ 1157 (Court of Appeal, judgment, para 14 per Tuckey LJ).
[38] See Born (n 6) ch 26.03; Moses (n 6) ch 10; Blackaby, Partasides, Redfern, and Hunter (n 6) ch 11.

penalize refusal to comply with an award of the CAS through 'internal' means without the need to seek the strong arm of the ordinary courts. FIFA's Disciplinary Code, for example, provides that failure to comply with a CAS decision exposes the party refusing to a range of penalties, both financial and sporting, including points deduction, relegation and/or a transfer ban for clubs and a ban on any football-related activity for players.[39] This happened to Matuzalem, as explained earlier, and even though he was able to go to law in Switzerland to shake off the supplementary penalties imposed as a follow-up for failure to pay the initially stipulated sum of compensation, the lesson is that it takes not only exceptional circumstances but also courage, energy, and deep pockets to resist an award of the CAS. And Matuzalem, even if freed from the ban on playing football imposed by FIFA as a result of the intervention of the Swiss Federal Tribunal, still was not released from the compensation award initially made against him.

The principle, then, holds that the ordinary courts of states that are party to the New York Convention should treat awards of the CAS as binding (foreign, ie Swiss) arbitral awards, and they should, if called upon, enforce them without further inquiry. This allows not simply for respect for the *lex sportiva* as reflected in the CAS's rulings, but in fact it serves as an active transnational promotion of that incrementally accumulated *lex sportiva*. Scope for national courts to intervene in or to decline to recognize awards made by the CAS and arbitral bodies generally is tightly limited by the Convention. But it is not wholly excluded.

Article V of the New York Convention seeks to codify the possibilities for intervention. These are exceptional. Article V(1) addresses detailed flaws in an arbitral ruling. So, for example, recognition and enforcement of the award may be refused on grounds of the incapacity of the parties, the absence of proper notice, or that the award goes beyond the term of the submission to arbitration. Article V(2) adds that recognition and enforcement of an arbitral award may also be refused if the competent authority in the country where recognition and enforcement is sought finds that (a) the subject matter of the difference is not capable of settlement by arbitration under the law of that country or (b) that the recognition or enforcement of the award would be contrary to the public policy of that country.

The principal concern animating these bases for refusal to enforce an arbitral award is *not* the merit of the legal or factual assessment visible on the face of the award but rather the (absence of) integrity of process.[40] However, the last item on this list, appeal to 'public policy' as envisaged by Article V(2), is potentially the window through which aggressive intervention by national courts might be driven to the prejudice of the autonomy of the process of arbitration. But this is not the practice.

Public policy is not defined in the Convention, but typically it is interpreted narrowly in the many jurisdictions in which the New York Convention is the governing

---

[39] Art 64 of the 2011 version <http://www.fifa.com/governance/disciplinary/> accessed 29 November 2016. See U Haas, 'The Enforcement of Football-related Arbitral Awards by the Court of Arbitration for Sport (CAS)' [2014] Intl Sports L Rev 12.

[40] Moses (n 6) 217.

text. Practice shows it is rare that it is allowed to intervene to withhold recognition and enforcement: the autonomy of arbitration awards is widely respected among the courts of the contracting states.[41]

An exhaustive survey of global judicial enforcement practice is unfeasible. Let the United States serve as an illustration. If any state is likely to have incentives to sacrifice the advantages of reciprocal enforcement of arbitral awards guaranteed by the Convention in order to assert a unilateral interventionist jurisdiction then it is likely to be the most powerful state on the planet. But it is instructive that any such temptation is not visible. A typical example of the practice of judicial deference, rooted in anxiety to make the Convention system function effectively, is provided by the US Court of Appeals Second Circuit in its ruling in *Parsons and Whittemore Overseas Co.*[42] The ruling refers to 'the general pro-enforcement bias informing the Convention' and draws from this the logically consequent trend 'toward a narrow reading of the public policy defense'. As the Court convincingly observes, 'An expansive construction of this defense would vitiate the Convention's basic effort to remove preexisting obstacles to enforcement', which led it to state that refusal to enforce foreign arbitral awards should be denied for affront to public policy 'only where enforcement would violate the forum state's most basic notions of morality and justice'. And the judgment refers explicitly to 'considerations of reciprocity' which, it advised, 'counsel courts to invoke the public policy defense with caution lest foreign courts frequently accept it as a defense to enforcement of arbitral awards rendered in the United States'. The background to the dispute which had generated the arbitral award which the American Court was asked to enforce—and was willing to enforce—was distant from sport. It was mired in the 1967 conflict involving Israel and Egypt. But, as the Court put it, 'To deny enforcement of this award largely because of the United States' falling out with Egypt in recent years would mean converting a defense intended to be of narrow scope into a major loophole in the Convention's mechanism for enforcement'. So an American court enforced a foreign arbitral award against an American corporation and in favour of an Egyptian firm. And, to underline that this attitude represents a shared understanding among judges about the virtues of the system, in 2014 the Privy Council of the United Kingdom, hearing an appeal from the Court of Appeal of the British Virgin Islands, relied explicitly on *Parsons and Whittemore* in asserting the general approach to enforcement of an award as 'pro-enforcement'.[43]

In similar vein the US Court of Appeals Fifth Circuit in *Karaha Bodas* declared: 'Erroneous legal reasoning or misapplication of law is generally not a violation of public policy within the meaning of the New York Convention.'[44]

---

[41] See Born (n 6) ch 26.05[C][9]; Blackaby, Partasides, Redfern, and Hunter (n 6) chs 10.81–87, 11.105–22.

[42] 508 F 2d 969 (1974).

[43] *Cukurova Holding AS v Sonera Holding BV* [2014] UKPC 15, [2015] 2 All ER 1061 (Lord Clarke).

[44] Co 364 F 3d 274 (2004).

This respect for the finality of the process of arbitration has been applied in the context of arbitration in sport too. Justin Gatlin was an American sprinter. He won the gold medal for the 100 metres dash at the 2004 Olympics and the 2005 World Championships. However, he was subsequently found guilty of taking prohibited performance-enhancing drugs—a doping offence. Sanctions were imposed preventing him from competing and, on appeal, they were upheld by the CAS. He brought an application before a court in the United States for an order requiring that he be treated as free to compete in the US athletics trials. He was granted a temporary injunction against the relevant agency, USADA, in June 2008, to lift his suspension by the US District Court, Northern District of Florida. The competent federal court set aside the injunction four days later because it ruled that it lacked jurisdiction to intervene in USADA's process.[45]

The court explained:

Pursuant to the United Nations Convention on the Recognition and Enforcement of Foreign Arbitral Awards, ('New York Convention'), claims that have been properly submitted to arbitration and ruled upon by entities such as CAS are barred from relitigation in this forum ... the only conceivable exception is where enforcement of the award would be contrary to public policy.... This, however, is a very slender exception reserved for decisions which violate the 'most basic notions of morality and justice' ...

The conditions of this 'slender exception' were not present in Gatlin's case. The court was therefore willing to enforce the award against him. The vigour with which the court was prepared to apply the New York Convention in such a way as to disable its own review function and to protect the ruling of the CAS in the case is strongly emphasized by the observation in the court's judgment that the actions of the authorities and of the CAS were, in its estimation, 'arbitrary and capricious'. The court, examining the basis of the investigation, found it 'troubling' that Gatlin had in the circumstances been condemned for violation. However, it explicitly concluded that a decision which is arbitrary and capricious does not qualify for re-opening in the name of public policy. This meant that the New York Convention protected the CAS ruling, which was to be recognized and enforced by the American courts. The implication is that only recourse to the Swiss courts could help Gatlin—though, as explained previously, that was and is cold comfort, even in the light of the more recent *Matuzalem* decision of the Swiss Federal Supreme Court.[46]

This is plainly important. The higher the threshold that must be crossed before a national court withholds recognition and enforcement from an award of the CAS, the sturdier the development of a genuine global *lex sportiva* which in effect ousts varying national laws that would otherwise have the potential to impose different

---

[45] *Gatlin v US Anti-Doping Agency* 2008 WL 2567657 (ND Fla 2008–24 June 2008); <http://docs.justia.com/cases/federal/district-courts/florida/flndce/3:2008cv00241/50408/36/0.pdf?1214341987> accessed 29 November 2016.

[46] The story of litigation pursued before courts in the US without success by an equally famous cheat, Lance Armstrong, is told by D McArdle, *Dispute Resolution in Sport* (Routledge 2015) 50–53.

standards of validity in different legal jurisdictions. This is immensely helpful to the aspiration of sports governing bodies to apply a consistent and even pattern of legal regulation across the world. The *lex sportiva* is their monopoly regulation, which they would wish to shelter from fragmentation consequent on the incursion of the 'ordinary law' of particular jurisdictions. The aggressive protection by national courts of rulings of the CAS as arbitral awards grants much of this wish for sporting autonomy.

It is, however, a protection which is only as valuable as national courts are prepared to make it. Any departure from this general, though not absolute, respect for the finality of decisions of the CAS would weaken the autonomy of the *lex sportiva*. Two recent cases before German courts highlight the delicacy of the relationship between the ordinary courts and the *lex sportiva*. The first was *Wilhelmshaven SV*. In December 2014 a regional court, the Oberlandesgericht of Bremen, refused to enforce a CAS ruling that imposed sanctions on the club for violation of the FIFA rules on the transfer of players, specifically those governing the payment of compensation to clubs that had committed resources to train young players. The court's objection was that the possible relevance of EU free movement law as a restraint on the transfer system had been badly misunderstood by the CAS. The second case is *Pechstein*. It was decided in early 2015. This is even more serious: it does not object to a particular rogue decision, rather it represents an assault on the very foundations of the CAS as currently constituted. The Oberlandesgericht of Munich refused to respect a clause which obliged the athlete, a speed-skater found to have committed anti-doping violations whose two-year suspension from competition had been confirmed by the CAS,[47] to pursue arbitration in the event of a dispute. The basis for the decision was that the CAS lacked the independence required of an arbitrator because its composition led to a slant in favour of governing bodies. The German court accordingly treated the clause as anti-competitive and unenforceable.[48]

Such scepticism about the virtues of the autonomy of the system of sporting arbitration would, if sustained by the German courts, be unlikely to be confined to Germany and would be capable of undermining the global integrity of the CAS-based system as a source of a uniformly applicable *lex sportiva*. But the decisions have not been sustained by the German courts: both bombs have been defused. In September 2016 the Bundesgerichtshof (BGH), the highest civil court in the German system, dealt with *Wilhelmshaven SV* by focusing only on the incompatibility with *German* law of the sanctions imposed.[49] It treated neither the FIFA rules nor EU law as relevant to its decision. As for *Pechstein*, in June 2016 the Bundesgerichtshof concluded, in contrast to the lower court, that the CAS is structured in such a way

---

[47] CAS 2009/A/1912-1913 *Pechstein v International Skating Union*, on which see D McArdle, 'Pechstein v International Skating Union' in J Anderson (ed), *Leading Cases in Sports Law* (TMC Asser 2013) ch 13.

[48] OLG München, Urteil von 15.01.2015, U 1110/14 Kart.

[49] II ZR 25/15 <http://juris.bundesgerichtshof.de/cgi-bin/rechtsprechung/document.py?Gericht=bgh&Art=pm&Datum=2016&Sort=3&anz=163&pos=0&nr=76335&linked=urt&Blank=1&file=dokument.pdf> accessed 29 November 2016.

as to guarantee due independence and that it is accordingly entitled to be treated as a genuine arbitration tribunal.[50] The BGH also noted the advantages of speed and expertise granted by the system to both governing bodies and athletes. Calm and stability was therefore restored: the decision adopts the conventional judicial stance in favour of strong, though not absolute, protection of the finality of CAS rulings. Unsurprisingly the CAS itself welcomed the ruling's confirmation of the validity of the arbitration clause and of its own status as a genuine arbitration tribunal.[51]

Wilhelmshaven SV and *Pechstein* serve as a reminder that the contractual route to preserving sporting autonomy from the application of 'ordinary' state law is not rooted in a seamlessly integrated legal order based on clear hierarchies. It is instead a system involving connections between the *lex sportiva* as a system of arbitration and national law which is mediated by the commitments made through the New York Convention. A national court that refuses to accept the finality of arbitration threatens the stability of the system, but its intransigence cannot simply be set aside, except by a higher national court. It is worth noting that one beneficial side-effect of these rough-edged arrangements is that this induces the CAS to take seriously its procedural probity: respect for the finality of its rulings is conditional on such scrupulousness. There is in fact an appealing analogy to be drawn between the conditional respect which the CAS earns from national courts and that which the Court of Justice of the EU enjoys in instructing that EU law shall be treated as supreme. In both cases national legal orders are receptive to pronouncements 'from outside' not because of any directly enforceable claim to authority made by those bodies, and still less because of any means of coercion, but rather because national law provides a basis for acceptance of those sources. National law is the door through which decisions of the CAS and the Court of Justice enter national legal practice, so national law may close that door, and it will do unless the practice of the CAS and the Court of Justice meets its standards. For the CAS this means in particular the need to attend to due standards of legal precision and procedural fairness, for the Court of Justice it has long meant in particular the need to supplement claims to the primacy of its legal order with respect for fundamental rights within it.[52] This is to point to a certain fragility in the system, but it is a creative tension.

---

[50] KZR 6/15 <http://juris.bundesgerichtshof.de/cgi-bin/rechtsprechung/document.py?Gericht=bgh&Art=pm&Datum=2016&Sort=3&anz=97&pos=0&nr=75021&linked=urt&Blank=1&file=dokument.pdf> accessed 29 November 2016. For criticism written before the BGH's reversal of the OLG decision, see U Haas, 'The Court of Arbitration for Sport in the Case Law of the German Courts' [2015] Intl Sports L Rev 71; after the fact, A Duval, 'The BGH's Pechstein Decision: A Surrealist Ruling?', Asser International Sports Law Blog, 8 June 2016 <http://www.asser.nl/SportsLaw/Blog/post/the-bgh-s-pechstein-decision-a-surrealist-ruling> accessed 29 November 2016.

[51] Media Release, 7 June 2016 <http://www.tas-cas.org/fileadmin/user_upload/Media_Release_Pechstein_07.06.16_English_.pdf> accessed 29 November 2016. CAS proudly provides an English-language translation of the BGH ruling on its website <http://www.tas-cas.org/fileadmin/user_upload/Pechstein___ISU_translation_ENG_final.pdf> accessed 29 November 2016. See also D Mavromati (Head of research and mediation at the CAS), 'The Legality of the Arbitration Agreement in favour of CAS under German Civil and Competition Law', available at SSRN <https://papers.ssrn.com/sol3/papers.cfm?abstract_id=2800044> accessed 29 November 2016.

[52] S Weatherill, *Law and Values in the European Union* (OUP 2016) ch 4.3.

For the CAS, the lesson of *Wilhelmshaven SV* should be to take proper and careful account of relevant provisions of EU law, while the lesson to draw from *Pechstein* should be to keep checking the independence of its members and its processes from the governing bodies that make such frequent use of its offices.[53] In fact the CAS welcome for the BGH's ruling in *Pechstein* includes commitment to pursue 'best practices in international arbitration law'.[54] This needs to be made real.

2.2.5 The normative case for and against the *lex sportiva* as expressed through contract/CAS

The *lex sportiva* has acquired a high level of social and commercial significance as a system of global governance. Its rise is of great practical importance but it also commands considerable intellectual interest. It is not 'law' as conventionally understood, but it is private ordering of sorts and, as explained, it is able to claim a degree of autonomy from conventional state regulation. Examination of the *lex sportiva* deserves connection to broader literature on legal pluralism, for it reveals much about how interaction between different orders, each claiming different sources of authority and legitimacy, is managed.[55] So, it has been argued, sports law should be of interest not only to sports lawyers.[56] It tells us interesting things about how legal phenomena are associated with actors other than public authorities. It is the *lex sportiva*'s global and non-governmental character that serve as the intellectual keys to appraising its distinctive place in the system of norms that regulate sport.[57] The *lex sportiva* is frequently compared to the *lex mercatoria*, the body of rules deriving from custom and practice among merchants and open to application in preference to diverse local laws.[58] This is to some extent helpful: it helps to push one's imagination away from exclusive focus on systems of rule-making that are the preserve of public authorities. Indeed the CAS itself has chosen to make precisely this analogy. In *AEK Athens and Slavia Prague* it noted that, as a result of the transnational nature of sporting competitions, international federations have to reckon not only with their own statutes and the laws of their host country where the federation is incorporated but also with a set of unwritten legal principles with which they must comply built up especially through the arbitral settlement of disputes—'a sort of *lex mercatoria* for sports'.[59]

---

[53] For suggestions see McArdle (n 46) 30–32; N De Marco, 'Compelled Consent—Pechstein and the Dichotomy and Future of Sports Arbitration' (2016) <https://www.blackstonechambers.com/news/analysis-compelled_consent_/> accessed 29 November 2016.

[54] Media Release (n 51). This concern is stressed also by Mavromati (n 51) (SSRN).

[55] A Duval, 'Lex Sportiva: A Playground for Transnational Law' (2013) 19 ELJ 822; and more fully Duval (n 19). See also A Valero, 'In Search of a Working Notion of Lex Sportiva' (2014) 14 Intl Sports LJ 3.

[56] M Mitten and H Opie, 'Sports Law: Implications for the Development of International, Comparative and National Law and Global Dispute Resolution' (2010) 85 Tulane L Rev 269.

[57] L Casini, 'The Making of a Lex Sportiva by the Court of Arbitration for Sport' (2011) 12 German LJ 1317.

[58] See eg B Kolev, 'Lex Sportiva and Lex Mercatoria' (2008) 8(1–2) Intl Sports LJ 57.

[59] CAS 98/200, para 156.

But the *lex mercatoria* has an essentially private law flavour. The *lex sportiva* more closely resembles a transnational regime of governance which, although private in form, is administrative, even quasi-legislative, in its substance. It includes significant powers to impose sanctions, most strikingly but not exclusively in connection with doping control. The emergent principles of the *lex sportiva* cover matters such as fair procedure, as discussed earlier.[60] Its flavour is much closer to that of public law. It has been astutely noted that this lends support to 'the theory that the more complex private regimes become, the more they will come to resemble public law regimes'.[61] There are intellectual connections to the debate about the development of a global administrative law, which entails 'the increasing use of administrative law-type mechanisms—in particular those related to transparency, participation, accountability, and review—within the regulatory institutions of global governance'.[62] Because sport aspires to a truly global reach in its governance regimes, it supplies an especially promising place to explore these trends.[63] Moreover, there is a good case that all this is entirely desirable: the *lex sportiva* involves an assertion of a much higher level of power to pursue the interests of the powerful, the sports governing bodies, than does the *lex mercatoria* and therefore complacent analogies with the *lex mercatoria* should be avoided for fear that they miss this reason to question the strength of the *lex sportiva*'s appeal to deserve autonomy.

There is appeal in the shaping of a system that is sensitive to the needs and expectations of the parties intimately involved and which is apt to shape a globally recognized and predictable set of applicable standards. The bright side of the *lex sportiva* is efficiency and expertise: the dark side is absence of accountability of rule-makers, dearth of transparency, and the risk that *lex sportiva* is simply an intellectually deft camouflage for entrenching private power and privilege from legal scrutiny. Even if it is accepted that the *lex sportiva*'s global and non-governmental character mark it out not only as worthy of intellectual inquiry but also serve as reasons supporting claims to its autonomy from subjection to 'ordinary' law, a question that should be asked is whether the CAS awards deserve the respect that attaches to them under the rules and practices set out in sections 2.2.3 and 2.2.4.

Pechstein, considered previously, is a vivid example of exactly this anxiety: the BGH's conclusion was that CAS awards had earned that right. The conventional judicial imposition of a narrow interpretation of the public policy exception under

---

[60] See n 17.

[61] Casini (n 57) 1340. This projects the inquiry far beyond sports law: Casini cites A Riles, 'The Anti-Network: Private Global Governance, Legal Knowledge, and the Legitimacy of the State' (2008) 56 AJCL 605; and E Meidinger, 'Competitive Supragovernmental Regulation: How Could It Be Democratic?' (2008) 8 Chi J Intl L 513.

[62] According to the website of the Global Administrative Law project <http://www.iilj.org/gal/> accessed 29 November 2016.

[63] See eg L Casini, 'The Emergence of Global Administrative Systems: The Case of Sport' (2015) 1 Glocalism: Journal of Culture, Politics and Innovation 1; K Foster, 'Global Administrative Law: The Next Step for Global Sports Law?' (2012), available at SSRN <https://papers.ssrn.com/sol3/papers.cfm?abstract_id=2014694> accessed 29 November 2016.

the New York Convention is a more generally applicable instance of the anxiety to protect the finality of arbitration. But the tension is real, the debate is necessary. Such shelter afforded to the CAS's rulings, and the shift of a large body of sports-related dispute settlement away from ordinary courts and towards a process of arbitration which has in effect become the internal world of sport, highlights the pressing need for fair procedure and competent decision-making within the CAS process.

The claim to sporting autonomy achieved through contractual provision deserves the normatively sceptical perspective that one would conventionally aim at any process whereby agreement is struck between a strong party and a party with little or no choice but to accept what is on offer. Contractual *freedom* in form may in fact in substance amount to deprivation of the freedom of the weaker party. Put another way, the assiduously respectful attitude to the process of arbitration may assume what is not present—equal standing, bargaining power, and free choice to enter into the arrangements in the first place. And if, as suggested earlier, the *lex sportiva* has a public law flavour, the question is whether it is sufficiently attentive to the need to protect the individual athlete or club from the exercise of power by strong sports federations.

Moreover, there should be no hiding from the point that appeals by sporting bodies to respect their autonomy may be driven not only by a respectable anxiety to maintain the global integrity of the rules of the game, but also by a far more strategic interest to protect their commercially advantageous position from orthodox legal regulation. That a sport needs a single global regulatory body makes perfect sense when one considers the need for a single governing set of rules, but the more that single body exercises not only regulatory but also commercial power, the more troubling its plea for autonomy becomes. Sports bodies possess monopoly power and, in the economic context, that may be pernicious. This book teems with examples drawn from the context of EU law—mandatory release of players to play in international competitions, timetabling those competitions, and so on—but the issue is not at all limited to the EU. It is an endemic question in determining the proper scope and worth of claims to sporting autonomy. Who better to decide which sports shall be admitted to the Olympic Games than the IOC? And yet, given the immense commercial as well as sporting advantages associated with admission, and the relatively cold uncommercial and invisible fate of a sport which finds itself excluded, is it really convincing to treat such a choice as properly lying beyond the reach of legal regulation as an expression of pure sporting autonomy?

These are questions best answered only after a detailed exploration of the way that sports law has developed. The discussion will be resumed in Chapter 12, the concluding chapter. It will be seen in particular that EU law's treatment of the *lex sportiva* is best understood as involving a grant of *conditional autonomy*—the practices of sporting bodies will not be disturbed by EU law on condition that they comply with key expectations of EU law, associated with both matters of substance, most obviously the demands of the internal market, and matters of procedure and good governance. It is in this inquiry that the virtues and vices of sporting autonomy are exposed and assessed.

2.2.6 The limits of the CAS's umbrella: at EU level

Whatever one's normative perspective on the virtue of sporting autonomy secured through the relative immunity from scrutiny of the rulings of the CAS, the strong, if not absolute, protection which is provided—both in Switzerland and in the many states which are parties to the New York Arbitration Convention—forms an important part of the descriptive understanding of the profile of the contractual route to securing the autonomy of the decisions and practices of sporting bodies from review by the ordinary courts.

But some sports-related disputes are not channelled through the CAS, while others cannot be, for want of material or personal jurisdiction. Cases involving parties who have not agreed to participate in the network of arrangements that confer exclusive jurisdiction on dispute settlement procedures that are internal to sport and ultimately on the CAS are routed through the ordinary courts. Those involving broadcasters are an important instance. Such cases are not contractually tied into the *lex sportiva*: they escape the limits of the largely closed internal world of sporting regulation.

In the particular case of the EU, many cases have arisen without any involvement of the CAS. The landmark rulings in *Walrave and Koch*[64] and *Bosman*[65] pre-date the establishment of the CAS. The more recent *Karen Murphy* case involved broadcasting rights and so lies beyond the jurisdiction of FIFA and the CAS.[66] Even where a ruling of the CAS is at stake, EU law tends to assume the jurisdiction of the Court of Justice and of national courts of the Member States to examine the matter. *Meca-Medina and Majcen v Commission* arose out of a ruling of the CAS which confirmed (though shortened) a period of suspension imposed on swimmers by the sport's governing body, FINA, for violation of anti-doping rules.[67] That ruling had not been appealed to the Swiss Federal Supreme Court. But the litigation that reached the Court was not a direct challenge to that ruling of the CAS. Instead it was founded on alleged violation of EU competition law and in particular it concerned the role of the Commission, which had rejected the applicant swimmers' complaint that they were the victims of a violation of those Treaty provisions.[68] The matter was considered at length and in very different ways by (what are now) the General Court and, on appeal, the Court of Justice, and it was ultimately decided that no violation of EU competition law had been demonstrated. This is explored in Chapter 5. But this conclusion was reached only after a careful (and controversial) examination of the proper interpretation of EU law in this (sporting) context. At no stage did either Court treat the matter as closed by the earlier ruling of the CAS. And no reference at all was made to the New York Convention. In similar vein the Commission's treatment of UEFA's rule forbidding multiple ownership of

---

[64] Case 36/74 [1974] ECR 1405. See Ch 4.
[65] Case C-415/93 [1995] ECR I-4921. See Ch 4.
[66] Joined Cases C-403/08 and C-429/08 [2011] ECR I-9083. See Ch 11.8.
[67] CAS 99/A/ 234, 99/A/235, unreported.
[68] Case C-519/04P [2006] ECR I-6991. See Ch 5.

clubs, which will be examined more fully in Chapter 5.2, notes that the dispute had previously been addressed by the CAS,[69] but shows not the slightest reluctance to examine the matter in the light of EU competition law and, in conducting its legal assessment, ignores the CAS's view entirely—even though in fact the CAS's assessment, favourable to the rule, draws heavily on EU competition rules and largely coincides with that reached by the Commission.[70]

On this evidence EU law has scant respect for the autonomy of the process of arbitration in general and for the *lex sportiva* in particular. EU competition law comes first. The objection to this approach insists on its tendency to fragment the consistent and even global application of the *lex sportiva*. The answer, such as it is, is that it does not so fragment it—provided that the *lex sportiva* meets the basic requirements of EU law. And if it does not meet those requirements, then it does not serve a high enough value to claim hierarchy, and must yield. That, of course, is a perspective that makes perfect sense as a means to defend the coherence of the EU's legal order. But it is much less attractive from the perspective of governing bodies in sport.

One can readily feel the force of this objection when seen from within sports governance—the global system applies in the EU only in so far as the EU permits it to. That risks fragmenting the *lex sportiva*. In one part of the world, the EU, its application is conditional on compliance with the peculiarities of local laws. And this is the heart of the inquiry into how legitimate the *lex sportiva* is: should it be allowed priority over 'ordinary' law? Is the claim to specific expertise and global reach strong enough? The counter is exactly that the *lex sportiva* is dangerous because of its devotion to sporting expertise and the exclusion of other proper social and political concerns of 'ordinary' law; and also that the aspiration to global reach is precisely what is a source of concern, for it envisages a zone of such immense power for sports bodies.

This is a tension to return to later in this book, for full assessment requires insight into how far EU law truly goes in setting aside sporting autonomy in favour of its own particular expectations. That is, it must be asked how genuine and real is the conflict between EU law and the *lex sportiva*.

2.2.7 The limits of the CAS's umbrella: before national courts in the EU

EU law's relative intolerance of the contractual strategy for asserting the autonomy of the *lex sportiva* is not only visible in proceedings advanced at EU level. *National courts of the Member States* asked to intervene in arbitration are also empowered

---

[69] CAS 98/200 *AEK Athens and Slavia Prague v UEFA*.
[70] COMP 37.806 *ENIC/UEFA*, IP/02/942, 27 June 2002. The rejection decision is available at <http://ec.europa.eu/competition/elojade/isef/case_details.cfm?proc_code=1_37806> accessed 29 November 2016.

by EU law—and again, this may be for good, it may be for ill, depending on one's standpoint.

The key ruling of the Court of Justice is *Eco Swiss China Time Ltd v Benetton International NV*.[71] A licensing agreement between Eco Swiss and Benetton provided that all disputes or differences arising between the parties were to be settled by arbitration in conformity with the rules of the Nederlands Arbitrage Instituut (Netherlands Institute of Arbitrators) and that the arbitrators appointed were to apply the law of the Netherlands. The arbitration had concluded with a finding that Benetton should pay damages for its breach of the agreement. Benetton brought proceedings for stay of enforcement of this arbitration award ordering it to pay damages, on the ground that the award in question was contrary to public policy within the meaning of the Dutch Code of Civil Procedure. The core of its claim was that the licensing agreement was incompatible with EU competition law—then Article 81 of the Treaty Establishing the European Community (EC), now Article 101 TFEU—and that accordingly it was void pursuant to that provision's second paragraph.

A preliminary reference was made to the Court of Justice seeking interpretative guidance on the meaning of EU law in such a context, where EU law is relied upon to break open an existing and apparently final arbitral award. The Court explicitly remarked on the general inadvisability of such interruption. It declared that 'it is in the interest of efficient arbitration proceedings that review of arbitration awards should be limited in scope and that annulment of or refusal to recognize an award should be possible only in exceptional circumstances'.[72] But it then found that exceptional circumstances *did* prevail.

The Court ruled that where national law requires a court to annul an arbitration award for failure to observe national rules of public policy—as Dutch law did—then it must annul the award where it fails to comply with the prohibition laid down in Article 81(1) EC, now Article 101(1) TFEU. So the Court insists that public policy which is recognized under national law must also accommodate EU competition law.

It added that 'the provisions of Article 81 EC … may be regarded as a matter of public policy within the meaning of the New York Convention'.[73] Moreover, it declared resoundingly that:

… it is manifestly in the interest of the Community [now Union] legal order that, in order to forestall differences of interpretation, every Community [Union] provision should be given a uniform interpretation … It follows that … Community [Union] law requires that questions concerning the interpretation of the prohibition laid down in Article 81(1) EC [now Article 101(1) TFEU] should be open to examination by national courts when asked to determine the validity of an arbitration award and that it should be possible for those questions to be referred, if necessary, to the Court of Justice for a preliminary ruling.[74]

---

[71] Case C-126/97 *Eco Swiss China Time Ltd v Benetton International NV* [1999] ECR I-3055.
[72] ibid para 35 of the ruling.   [73] ibid para 39.   [74] ibid para 40.

This strongly suggests that the Court's ruling is not based simply on the existing platform in Dutch law which recognized intervention in the name of public policy. Even if national law did *not* contain a public policy exception granting the power to intervene in arbitration awards, a national court should treat itself as empowered by EU law to intervene in order to check the award for compliance with EU competition law. In precisely this vein, in its subsequent ruling in *Vincenzo Manfredi*, the Court, expressly referring to *Eco Swiss*, stated that 'it should be recalled that Articles 81 EC and 82 EC [now 101 and 102 TFEU] are a matter of public policy which must be automatically applied by national courts'.[75] The same bold assertion of public policy is emblazoned in the very first Recital to Directive 2014/104 on actions for damages under national law for infringements of competition law.[76] And presumably a claim to violation of the free movement law would be treated in the same way as a claim to violation of competition law—that is, the award would be opened up on review. In *Eco Swiss* the Court described Article 81 EC, which is now Article 101 TFEU, as 'a fundamental provision which is essential for the accomplishment of the tasks entrusted to the Community and, in particular, for the functioning of the internal market'[77] and—admittedly not in the particular context of arbitration—it has in similar ambitious vein referred to the free movement of goods as 'one of the fundamental rules of the Community'[78] and as 'one of the foundations of the Community'.[79]

The merit in treating an arbitration as reliably final is therefore of inadequate weight to override the virtue in correcting misapplication of EU internal market law. This would apply to treatment of arbitration in sport in general, and to a ruling of the CAS in particular. It seems to follow from *Eco Swiss* that a national court in an EU Member State would be required to intervene in an award which disrespected EU competition law or free movement law. This follows, according to the Court of Justice's reasoning, both as a matter of EU law and pursuant to the 'public policy' exception provided for by the New York Convention. Sporting autonomy expressed through arbitration (*lex sportiva*) is not of itself set aside, but where its economic implications bring it into collision with internal market law it does not prevail. Arbitrating a sporting matter narrowly understood is one thing: arbitrating a commercial matter falling within the scope of EU law which happens to arise in a sporting context is quite different. *Eco Swiss* stands as a statement of intolerance of misapplication of EU competition law by an arbitrator in a commercial context where the achievement of the EU's internal market is jeopardized.

So in principle the arbitration is not immune from review pursuant to EU law before national courts. *Eco Swiss* shows the high significance of the Treaty

---

[75] Joined Cases C-295/04 to C-298/04 [2006] ECR I-6619, para 31.

[76] Directive 2014/104/EU of 26 November 2014 on certain rules governing actions for damages under national law for infringements of the competition law provisions of the Member States and of the European Union [2014] OJ L349/1.

[77] *Eco Swiss* (n 71) para 36.

[78] Case 120/78 *Rewe-Zentrale AG v Bundesmonopolverwaltung für Branntwein* [1979] ECR 649, para 14.

[79] Case C-194/94 *CIA Security International v Signalson & Securitel* [1996] ECR I-2201, para 40.

competition rules in this respect, and free movement law exists on the same elevated level. But the Court has also chosen to treat consumer protection as a particularly important value which under EU law constitutes a matter of public policy.[80] In *Elisa María Mostaza Claro v Centro Móvil Milenium SL* a consumer had failed to argue that an arbitration clause was unfair within the meaning of Directive 93/13 on unfair terms in consumer contracts during the course of the arbitration.[81] That Directive, which targets terms that have not been individually negotiated, includes in its Annex of terms that *may* be regarded as unfair 'excluding or hindering the consumer's right to take legal action or exercise any other legal remedy, particularly by requiring the consumer to take disputes exclusively to arbitration'. This already asserts incursion into a contractual commitment to the exclusivity of arbitration: the Court has similarly tackled terms which confer exclusive jurisdiction in respect of disputes arising under the contract on a court that is convenient to the trader but not the consumer.[82] *Mostaza Claro* goes further. The consumer had raised the matter only in subsequent proceedings contesting the (adverse) arbitral finding. As a matter of Spanish law this was too late. The Spanish court asked the Court of Justice whether the application of Directive 93/13 required that the closure under Spanish law be levered open. The Court agreed that 'it is in the interest of efficient arbitration proceedings that review of arbitration awards should be limited in scope and that annulment of or refusal to recognize an award should be possible only in exceptional circumstances'.[83] This corresponds to the judicial treatment of the New York Arbitration Convention, considered earlier. But the aim of Directive 93/13 is to strengthen consumer protection, and the Court treated it as a measure 'essential to the accomplishment of the tasks entrusted' to the Union and 'to raising the standard of living and the quality of life in its territory'. On this point the Court made an explicit analogy with *Eco Swiss*.[84] This meant that a national court seised of an action for annulment of an arbitration award must determine whether the arbitration agreement is void and annul that award where that agreement contains an unfair term, even though the consumer has not pleaded that invalidity in the course of the arbitration proceedings but rather only in the subsequent action for annulment. The Court was especially influenced by the Directive's concern to protect the consumer as the weaker party.[85] This was enough to lead it to require the adaptation of Spanish law, for otherwise the 'special protection established by the Directive would be definitively undermined'.[86] But the consequence of this was definitively to undermine the finality of arbitration.

---

[80] eg (among many examples) Case C-397/11 *Erika Joros*, judgment of 30 May 2013, para 30; Case C-488/11 *Asbeek Brusse*, judgment of 30 May 2013, para 44.

[81] Case C-168/05 *Elisa María Mostaza Claro v Centro Móvil Milenium SL* [2006] ECR I-10421.

[82] eg Case C-137/08 *VB Pénzügyi Lízing* [2010] ECR I-10847; Case C-243/08 *Pannon GSM Zrt* [2009] ECR I-4713.

[83] *Claro* (n 81) para 34.   [84] ibid para 37.

[85] ibid para 38. See also eg Case C-243/08 *Pannon GSM Zrt* [2009] ECR I-4713, para 25; Case C-415/11 *Aziz*, judgment of 14 March 2013, para 45; Case C-169/14 *Sánchez Morcillo*, judgment of 17 July 2014, para 23. On the case law, see H-W Micklitz and N Reich, 'The Court and Sleeping Beauty: The Revival of the Unfair Contract Terms Directive' (2014) 51 CML Rev 771.

[86] *Claro* (n 81) para 31.

Intrusion is, however, context-specific. EU law does not *always* mandate that the effective application of EU law shall dictate setting aside the finality of arbitration or awards that have similar conclusive effect. Elsewhere, and in the absence of the pressing concerns associated with competition law and consumer protection found in *Eco Swiss* and *Claro* respectively, the Court of Justice has been perfectly content to protect the finality of decisions that may not be re-opened under national law, even where they exhibit a flaw as a matter of EU law. It has relied on the need for legal certainty, stability, and the sound administration of justice.[87]

And even where competition law or consumer protection are involved, EU law does not wholly and inevitably destabilize national procedures simply to ram home its requirements. In *Eco Swiss* the Court of Justice accepted that a national court is *not* required to refrain from applying domestic rules of procedure according to which an interim arbitration award, which is in the nature of a final award and in respect of which no application for annulment has been made within the prescribed time limit of three months, acquires the force of *res judicata* and may no longer be called in question by a subsequent arbitration award, even if this is necessary in order to examine, in proceedings for annulment of a subsequent arbitration award, whether an agreement which the interim award held to be valid in law is nevertheless void in the light of EU competition law. Such a rule envisages that an award may remain on foot even if contrary to EU law. The Court considered that the stipulated period of three months 'does not seem excessively short compared with those prescribed in the legal systems of the other Member States, [and] does not render excessively difficult or virtually impossible the exercise of rights conferred by' EU law.[88] The concern of such a rule is to protect legal certainty and EU law is not blind to such values, even where respecting them means no correction of a misapplication of EU law. The same is sometimes true in consumer law. *Claro* ruled that the consumer who fails to plead a violation of Directive 93/13 on unfair terms in the course of the arbitration proceedings may repair that omission in a subsequent action for annulment of the arbitration award, but in *Asturcom Telecomunicaciones SL v Maria Cristina Rodriguez Noguiera* the Court held that EU law's principle of effectiveness could *not* come to the rescue where the consumer had failed even to bring a challenge to the arbitral award within the time limit stipulated by national (Spanish) law.[89]

So there are limits to EU law's recognition of public policy for these purposes and there are limits to the extent to which it insists on upsetting national procedures in the name of its conception of public policy. In fact it cannot be the case that a matter becomes public policy as a matter of EU law simply because it falls within the scope of EU competence within the meaning of Articles 2 to 6 TFEU, for otherwise everything 'from the Charter of Fundamental Rights to a directive on pressurized equipment' would count as public policy within the meaning of Article V(2)(b)

---

[87] eg Case C-234/04 *Kapferer* [2006] ECR I-2585; Case C-455/06 *Heemskerk BV* [2008] ECR I-8763; Case C-2/08 *Fallimento Olimiclub Srl* [2009] ECR I-7501.
[88] *Eco Swiss* (n 71) para 45.   [89] Case C-40/08 [2009] ECR I-9579.

of the New York Convention.[90] But, in general, EU law has an 'unusually robust notion' of public policy which leads it to an abnormally high level of intervention in international arbitration.[91] This is especially the case where application of EU free movement and competition law or the EU's law of consumer protection is at stake. Seen from the perspective of the integrity of the process of arbitration it has been complained that *Claro* is 'ill-considered and arguably contradict[s] the [New York] Convention's requirements for restraint in application of Article V(2)(b)'s public policy exception'.[92] This, however, is the Court's choice and the critic will be still more vexed by appreciation that the areas in which the Court will be prepared to expect intervention are not closed and much will depend on the Court's future approach to inquiring into clauses committing to arbitration and into arbitration proceedings which appear to be concluded and final. This is troubling in so far as it implies an unpredictable case-by-case incremental development of legal control, although it is characteristic of the ad hoc development of EU law's pursuit of the provision of effective judicial protection at national level.[93]

Possible extension in EU intervention into contractual commitments to submit a dispute to arbitration, rather than to the ordinary courts, could be motivated by a concern to protect the weaker party and, more generally, by an assumption that in a case of asymmetric power, 'freedom' of contract is an illusion. This is central to the Court's interpretation of Directive 93/13.[94] This theme is visible too in Directive 2013/11 on alternative dispute resolution in consumer disputes.[95] It reveals a similar thematic concern to preclude consumers agreeing to surrender a right to bring an action before the courts for the settlement of the dispute without having been made fully aware of that outcome.[96] Articles 38 and 47 of the Charter of Fundamental Rights of the European Union underpin these commitments to a

[90] Case C-536/13 *Gazprom OAO v Lietuvos Respublika*, para 182, Opinion of Wathelet AG delivered on 4 December 2014. His point was that the 'Brussels I' Regulation, 44/2001, should *not* be treated as a matter of public policy within the meaning of the New York Convention. In its judgment of 13 May 2015 the Court did not deal with the point, for it found the matter to fall outwith the scope of the Regulation. Within Reg 44/2001 itself the notion of 'public policy' as a basis for refusing to enforce a judgment of another Member State is to be interpreted narrowly as a matter of EU law: see eg Case C-420/07 *Apostolides* [2009] ECR I-3571; Case C-559/14 *Rūdolfs Meroni v Recoletos Ltd*, judgment of 25 May 2016.

[91] G Berman, 'Navigating EU Law and the Law of International Arbitration' (2012) 28 Arb Intl 397, 397. See also A Duval, 'The Court of Arbitration for Sport and EU Law: Chronicle of an Encounter' (2015) 22(2) MJ 224, 227–35.

[92] Born (n 6) ch 26, text at fn 1494. See similarly, if softer, M Piers, 'Consumer Arbitration in the EU: a Forced Marriage with Incompatible Expectations' (2011) 2 JIDS 209. And the Court's disrespect for national procedural autonomy has critics even within the institution: see eg Case C-169/14 *Sánchez Morcillo*, judgment of 17 July 2014, Opinion of Wahl AG (which did not sway the Court in the case).

[93] The rich, even eccentric, variety in the case law combined with the intrusive character of EU law is well captured by the title of an article by A Arnull: 'The Principle of Effective Judicial Protection in EU law: An Unruly Horse?' (2011) 36 EL Rev 51.

[94] See n 7.

[95] Directive 2013/11/EU of 21 May 2013 on alternative dispute resolution for consumer disputes [2013] OJ L165/63. On the relationship between this Directive and Directive 93/13, see N Reich, 'A Trojan Horse in the Access to Justice—Party Autonomy and Consumer Arbitration in conflict in the ADR-Directive 2013/11/EU' (2014) 10 European Review of Contract Law 258.

[96] Especially its Art 10, 'Liberty' and Art 11, 'Legality'.

high level of consumer protection and a right to an effective remedy respectively. But protecting the weaker party appears as a concern in EU employment law too. The Court has openly embraced an understanding of the employee as 'the weaker party to the employment contract' and in the context of the regulation of working time has identified the need 'to prevent the employer being in a position to disregard the intentions of the other party to the contract or to impose on that party a restriction of his rights'.[97] In the interpretation of the EU's harmonization of employment laws, the Court insists on the importance of the aim of protecting employee rights alongside the establishment and functioning of the internal market. This is readily traceable through the EU's legislative *acquis* and associated interpretative rulings of the Court stretching over several decades.[98] So there is a protective or social as well as an economic rationale for legislative harmonization.[99] This fits into a broader paradigm of EU law as a source of protection of the weaker party. Directive 93/13 does not touch employment contracts, but the case can be made that Directive 93/13 is but one manifestation of a wider concern in EU law to protect the weaker party.[100] Peering into the future, one could not leave out of account that a sports person might in this sense be treated as a weaker party able to rely on EU law to secure protection from a clause that commits a matter exclusively to arbitration or to lever open an unfavourable arbitral ruling once made even where competition law or free movement law are not at stake. The high-earning legally advised superstar might not deserve such treatment but at a lower level one could envisage a readiness to intervene to protect the weaker party to the contract. Such a push beyond *Mostaza Claro* and *Eco Swiss* would weaken further the autonomy from the ordinary courts of the contractual attachment to arbitration expressed through the *lex sportiva*.

2.2.8 The practice of sanctions

A final practical point about EU law's relatively eager tendency to disrespect the contractual sanctity of arbitral proceedings, including those conducted by the CAS, may be added. It was explained earlier that some governing bodies in sport supplement the contractual network which ties participants into the dispute resolution system foreseen by the *lex sportiva* and which excludes recourse to the ordinary courts by providing for the imposition of sanctions in the event that this channelling is disregarded. So, in principle, a national association which allows its disputes

---

[97] Joined Cases C-397/01 to C-403/01 *Pfeiffer and others v Deutsches Rotes Kreuz* [2004] ECR I-8835, para 82; Case C-429/09 *Günter Fuß v Stadt Halle* [2010] ECR I-12167, para 80.

[98] eg on transfer of undertakings Case C-164/00 *Katia Beckmann* [2002] ECR I-4893, para 29; Case C-561/07 *Commission v Italy* [2009] ECR I-4959, para 30; cf on collective redundancies, regulated by Directive 98/59, also adopted under Art 100 EEC, Case C-55/02 *Commission v Portugal* [2004] ECR I-9387, para 48; Case C-385/05 *CGT* [2007] ECR I-611, para 43.

[99] See generally ACL Davies, *EU Labour Law* (Edward Elgar 2012); C Barnard, *EU Employment Law* (4th edn, OUP 2012).

[100] N Reich, *General Principles of EU Civil Law* (Intersentia 2014) ch 2; S Weatherill, *Contract Law of the Internal Market* (Intersentia 2016) ch 4.

to leak into the domain of the ordinary courts—through its own action or by failing to assert a grip on a club within its jurisdiction which pursues such action—could find its team(s) suspended from participation in international competitions.

The threat is usually enough: there is no need for execution. Practice is in any event erratic, not to say chaotic. It was revealed in 2014, and confirmed by detailed production of documents in 2015, that the Irish FA's threat to take legal action against FIFA as a result of a refereeing error at a crucial moment in a World Cup qualifying match against France in 2009 had resulted in a payment by FIFA to the Irish FA of some £5 million.[101] It is scarcely feasible that the action would even have been heard by a court given the commitment to arbitration made by the Irish FA within the *lex sportiva*, let alone that it might enjoy the slightest chance of success (in the absence of any suggestion of fraud), and it reveals much about FIFA's puzzling system of governance under Sepp Blatter that payment was made in preference to relying on the Irish FA's contractual obligation not to pursue such litigation. In other circumstances, however, governing bodies have been more aggressive in defence of contractually agreed commitment to the autonomy of arbitration and, through that, to the preservation of a *lex sportiva* unfragmented by local jurisdictional variations. For example, in 2011 the Swiss football federation, itself under pressure from UEFA, imposed sanctions on one of its members, FC Sion, in consequence of Sion having taken an objection to its treatment by UEFA to the ordinary Swiss courts. Sion reluctantly terminated the litigation.[102] Even if a litigant were more stubborn it is easy to imagine that a national judge aware of a possible consequence, such as expulsion of the national team from UEFA and FIFA competitions, would be wary in assessing his or her jurisdiction to hear a case in which it is argued that jurisdiction lies exclusively within the *lex sportiva*.

None of this applies to the EU. It does not trouble the Court or the Commission. The EU's team cannot be excluded from the World Cup. There is no EU team.

2.2.9 Conclusion—the limits of the contractual solution as a means to protect sporting autonomy

In conclusion, there is plainly a great deal more to EU sports law than the CAS alone. Cases reach the ordinary courts notwithstanding the arrangements made to place a priority on internal dispute settlement. Some sports-related litigation simply does not fall within the scope of the CAS's jurisdiction and/or it does not involve parties that are within the contractual network which privileges and protects arbitration.

So sports bodies must move beyond their first strategy of requiring participants to contract in to the *lex sportiva* and to agree not to solve sporting disputes before

---

[101] FAI Statement 05/06/15 <http://www.fai.ie/domestic/news/fai-statement-050615> accessed 29 November 2016.
[102] See McArdle (n 46) 27. Sion had no success before the CAS: CAS 2011/O/2574 *UEFA v FC Sion*.

'ordinary' courts. The second strategy for maximizing sporting autonomy is the legislative solution.

2.3 The Legislative Solution

Where the protection provided by the contractual route to protecting sporting autonomy, which is founded on arbitration, runs out, the second available solution is to induce states to adopt or to implement the *lex sportiva* (in whole or in part) or, at least, to adopt concessions that protect the autonomy of sports governance. This is a *legislative* solution—although to the extent that the regulator might be an international organization such as the EU, it is a *Treaty-based* solution in so far as the autonomy desired is autonomy from the application of the primary rules of the system.

2.3.1 Hosting the World Cup and the Olympic Games

This strategy tends to be most conspicuously visible where large one-off events are involved. Countries which bid to host the Football World Cup or the Olympic Games are sufficiently eager to win the competition that they are commonly willing to sign contracts with the sports governing body concerned in which they offer to make concessions to the normal assumptions attached to the application and enforcement of the law. Some of these promises made to secure the right to host the major event are then typically given legal shape by legislative reform. This may typically cover enhanced protection of the intellectual property rights of the organizers of events and of other commercial interests which they hold: it may cover typically generous treatment of taxation of income.

The Olympic Games were held in London in 2012. In preparation for this event the London Olympic and Paralympic Games Act 2006 was enacted.[103] The sheer scope of some of the Act's provisions is breathtaking. So too is the extent of the protection of commercial interests and the amount of resources of the state which are placed at the service of the IOC to secure enforcement of their interests. They go far beyond what any ordinary business would expect the state to offer it in support for its normal private law rights.

The connection between the 2006 Act and the deal struck by the United Kingdom as a condition of its success in winning the right to host the 2012 Games, beating off strong competition from Paris in particular, is perfectly clear on the face of the statute. It refers explicitly to 'the Host City Contract', which is defined as the contract signed at Singapore on 6 July 2005 and entered into by the IOC, the Mayor of London (representing London), and the British Olympic Association.[104]

---

[103] <http://www.legislation.gov.uk/ukpga/2006/12/pdfs/ukpga_20060012_en.pdf> accessed 29 November 2016. The 2006 Act was subsequently supplemented by the London Olympic Games and Paralympic Games (Amendment) Act 2011.

[104] London Olympic and Paralympic Games Act 2006, s 1(3)(e).

A corporate body named the Olympic Delivery Authority is established by the Act which has a widely drawn range of functions to acquire land, conclude construction contracts, deal with planning matters and security, and address street lighting and cleaning.[105] This is not surprising. The statute also provides for the development of a dedicated Olympic transport plan for London, including powers to regulate traffic and close roads.[106] Although some controversy was created by the designation of particular routes for privileged use by IOC officials and corporate sponsors, the overall need for London's transport network to be adapted for the special pressures of two weeks of Olympic competition seems indisputable. However, it is when the statute moves to matters of a more overtly commercial impact that the true scale of the protection for the IOC granted by the United Kingdom becomes clear. This indeed is a theme that permeates this book: sporting bodies are not purely concerned with the regulation and administration that is necessary to run the sport, but rather are also intimately involved in the commercial exploitation of the events that are staged under their auspices.

The 2006 Act has a set of provisions entitled 'Advertising', sections 19 to 24, and 'Trading', sections 25 to 31. They have much in common. In both instances it is provided that the Secretary of State is empowered to make regulations about advertising and about trading 'in the vicinity of London Olympic events'.[107] This power is explicitly tied to the aim of securing compliance with the obligations imposed by the 'Host City Contract' and the Secretary of State shall have regard to 'any requests or guidance' from the IOC.[108] The envisaged content of the regulations is strikingly broad. They shall determine the places, nature, and definition of advertising and trading. Advertising 'of any kind' and 'in any form' is covered, in particular 'advertising of a non-commercial nature, and announcements or notices of any kind'.[109] Advertising is plainly and calculatedly not confined to a purely commercial context. Contravention of regulations is an offence punishable by a fine.[110] Enforcement powers include a power of entry on to land or premises where a contravention is occurring, and a power to remove, destroy, conceal, or erase any infringing article.[111]

Schedules 3 and 4 to the 2006 Act contain the provisions which set out the detailed protection of the Olympic brand. Schedule 3 protects the 'Olympics association right' and builds on and amends the Olympic Symbol Protection Act 1995. Schedule 4 protects the 'London Olympics Association Right'.

The aim is to preclude use of symbols and mottos similar to those owned and used by the IOC. This covers anything sufficiently similar as to be likely to create in the public mind an association with the Olympic Games. So, for example, Schedule 4 directs that for the purpose of considering whether a person has infringed the London Olympics association right, a court may take account of combined use of the expressions 'games', 'Two Thousand and Twelve', '2012', and 'twenty twelve':

---

[105] ibid ss 3–9.   [106] ibid ss 10–18.   [107] ibid ss 19(1), 25(1).
[108] ibid ss 19(2), 25(2).   [109] ibid ss 19(4), 19(5).   [110] ibid ss 21, 27.
[111] ibid ss 22, 28.

and gold, silver, bronze, London, medals, sponsor, and summer. Here too contravention is an offence punishable by a fine.

Regulations were duly adopted. These were the London Olympic Games and Paralympic Games (Advertising and Trading) (England) Regulations 2011.[112] Advertising and trading within the 'event zone' during 'relevant event period or periods' was forbidden: Schedules I and II respectively defined these concepts. Some aspects of the Regulations are comically detailed. An event zone covers 'the pavement on each side of an event road or, where there is no pavement, the land or water that is within two metres of each side of the road, but excluding the frontage of any building on that pavement or land';[113] displaying an advertisement includes providing for an advertisement to be displayed on an animal.[114] But the powers are real enough. Use was made of them during the Games on 896 occasions, though in the majority of cases no formal action was taken: traders simply stopped doing what they were doing (whether with an animal or not).[115]

The message is that the IOC has a direct commercial interest in suppressing activities that conflict with the interests of its official sponsors, but also a broader interest in suppressing forms of expression that might be politically controversial and therefore more broadly damaging to the value of its commercial model. And these considerations are given shape and legal protection by the UK statute.

2.3.2 Ticket 'touting'

Ticket 'touting' provides a small case study in how the normal expectations of market competition are subverted by intrusive state regulation. Section 31 of the 2006 Act is entitled 'Sale of tickets'. It creates an offence committed where a person sells an Olympic ticket in a public place or in the course of a business otherwise than in accordance with a written authorization issued by the London Organising Committee. The rest of the section spells out the ingredients of the offence: it is broadly drafted, covering, for example, offering to sell and advertising that a ticket is available for purchase, and moreover a person is to be treated as acting in the course of a business if he or she 'does anything as a result of which he makes a profit or aims to make a profit'. There were reportedly some 200 arrests during the Games for offences committed pursuant to this section of the Act.[116]

The statute does not use the legally imprecise word 'touting' but that is the conventional name for the practice at which this section is targeted. The pejorative term 'touting' hides a more mundane reality: the seller of tickets that have been purchased through so-called 'unauthorized' channels is doing no more than breaking

---

[112] SI 2011/2898, available at <http://www.legislation.gov.uk/uksi/2011/2898/contents/made> accessed 29 November 2016. A separate regime was created for the other constituent elements of the UK.

[113] ibid Sch I, para 2(b).   [114] ibid s 5(1).

[115] Department for Culture, Media, and Sport, *Post Legislative Assessment* (CM 8503, 2012) para 21 <https://www.gov.uk/government/uploads/system/uploads/attachment_data/file/235982/8503.pdf> accessed 29 November 2016.

[116] ibid para 18.

open the contractual arrangements restricting re-sale imposed by the first seller and providing a product or service that is in demand. There is a market only because the first seller's price has turned out to have been too low. If this is 'touting', then *any* market involving re-sale deserves the same intellectually silly slur. The transaction is no more than a conventional matching of demand to supply. What is really at stake in the use of the term 'touting' is an attempt to provide a cover to explain public regulation designed merely to defend a contractual position which the first seller—the organizer of the sports event—is unable through private law or through commercial strategy to defend as securely as it would wish. Justifications for legal regulation rooted in protection of public order may carry some limited purchase in the case of a particularly combustible football match, but they cannot provide a sensible justification for using legislation and public resources to suppress the re-sale of tickets for an afternoon session spent watching Olympic table tennis or an evening at the velodrome. Yet that is the meaning of the 2006 Act. It represents a surreptitious slippage of measures designed to address public disorder into wider areas of purely commercial concern.[117] There is no explanation for this pattern of public regulation of the market for tickets beyond the sheer economic power of sports bodies intent on extracting legislative protection of their commercial interests from compliant host countries. Sports governing bodies have borrowed the coercive powers of the state.

2.3.3 Ambush marketing

The driving commercial concern of sports governing bodies when they plan major events is to protect the interests of the official sponsors of the event under an assumption that, without such astute protection, the price they will pay to act as sponsors will be depressed. 'Ambush marketing' comes in as many forms as there are legal rules, specific and general, to suppress it.[118] The smiling young person outside the stadium's car parks and train station handing out a t-shirt or a cap bearing the logo of a company that is not officially associated with the event is an 'ambush marketer'. Advertising a product or service heavily during the television

---

[117] cf M James and G Osborn, 'The Olympics, Transnational Law and Legal Transplants: the International Olympic Committee, Ambush Marketing and Ticket Touting' (2016) 36 Legal Studies 93, 106–109.

[118] See eg J Hoek and P Gendall, 'Ambush Marketing: More Than Just a Commercial Irritant?' (2002) 1 Entertainment Law 72; C Watson and C Graham, 'European Regulation of Media Rights' and T Jagodic, 'Legal Aspects of International Event Sponsorship' both in J Nafziger and S Ross (eds), *Handbook on International Sports Law* (Edward Elgar 2011) chs 14 and 18, respectively; JT Marcus, 'Ambush Marketing: An Analysis of its Threat to Sports Rights Holders and the Efficacy of Past, Present and Proposed Anti-Infringement Programmes' (2011) 11(3–4) Intl Sports LJ 97; M James and G Osborn, 'London 2012 and the Impact of the UK's Olympic and Paralympic Legislation: Protecting Commerce or Preserving Culture?' (2011) 74 MLR 410, 422–26; S Stuart and T Scassa, 'Legal Guarantees for Olympic Legacy' (2011) 9(1) ESLJ 3 <http://www.entsportslawjournal.com/articles/10.16997/eslj.28/> accessed 29 November 2016; G Pearson, 'Dirty Trix at Euro 2008: Brand Protection, Ambush Marketing and Intellectual Property Theft at the European Football Championships' (2012) 10(1) ESLJ 2 <http://www.entsportslawjournal.com/articles/10.16997/eslj.21/> accessed 29 November 2016; James and Osborn (n 118) 102–106.

broadcasts of an event when the supplier is not actually a sponsor of the event is another device. The general intent is plain: the ambush marketer seeks to take a free ride on the goodwill extended towards sponsors of major sporting events by consumers without having paid the necessary fee to acquire an *official* association. The ambush is to imply such association. This is a source of alarm to those hosting events, who fear that the price they can extract from real sponsors will be reduced if those sponsors feel they are being undermined. There are obvious possible violations of private law involved—such as, in English law, passing off and/or trademark infringement. A clever ambush marketer will avoid such legal wrongs. Some jurisdictions may envisage protection pursuant to unfair competition law. The ambush marketer may violate property rights, depending on where he or she goes about his or her tactics. And contractual protection is available to combat the ambush. It is open to the official sponsor to do a deal with a television company to exclude advertisements by ambushers during the event. There are plenty of legal and commercial means to protect the interests of the official sponsors. And if the ambush is successful because the official sponsor has been outwitted, that is no more than the free market at work. Clever commercial strategies are meant to be rewarded. Perhaps a case may be made that the private law is insufficiently attentive to the phenomenon of ambush marketing and that it therefore leads to inhibited investment in major sporting events, thereby justifying public regulation. But no such case has ever been coherently made. This is a matter of economic power. Where the IOC or FIFA is concerned, the free market is aggressively suppressed by rules that the organizations are able to extract from countries as part of the price that is paid to win hosting rights. Their concern is to maximize their income.

They are very good at maximizing income—ruthlessly so. Requiring the host country to exercise a tight grip over ambush marketing is only one, albeit vivid and visible, example. The Football World Cup held in Brazil in 2014 revealed how FIFA, careful of its sponsors' interests, was able, according to one detailed account that traced the negotiation between Brazil and FIFA and the consequent adoption of the General Law of the Cup, to enjoy a 'temporary monopoly' on the economy of Brazil.[119] Broadly, FIFA was able to use the lure of staging the event as a lever to induce the Brazilian government to agree to a remarkably imbalanced business model, where FIFA was able to lay claim to much of the income while placing much of the commercial risk on Brazil. A vivid example of FIFA's power is provided by its ability to extract a (temporary) change in the law forbidding the sale of beer in Brazilian football stadiums. Jerome Valcke, FIFA Secretary General at the time, was not remotely coy in depicting the power FIFA, a sports governing body, held over Brazil, the world's fifth most populous country: 'The fact that we have the right to sell beer has to be a part of the law'.[120] And so it was.[121] Less open to view are the

---

[119] JT Wendt and PC Young, 'Protecting Spectator Rights: Reflections on the General Law of the Cup' (2014) 14 Intl Sports LJ 179.

[120] <http://www.bbc.co.uk/news/world-latin-america-16624823> accessed 29 November 2016.

[121] On other concessions, see the unofficial site Brazil 2014—<http://www.v-brazil.com/world-cup/law/> accessed 29 November 2016.

tax arrangements typically made. The IOC was able to wrest significant exemptions from the normal rules of taxation of income earned in the United Kingdom, to the point where it has been vividly noted that the taxpayer was an 'unofficial sponsor' of the 2012 London Olympic Games.[122] FIFA performs similarly. FIFA's own website declares that '[a]pproximately 90 per cent of FIFA's revenue is generated through the sale of television, marketing, hospitality and licensing rights for the FIFA World Cup™'.[123] It adds too that some 72 per cent of spending is directed at the development of the game. Its own documentation reports that its revenue in 2014 was US$2,096 million, largely as a result of the sale of broadcasting rights and other marketing deals struck in connection with the 2014 World Cup which was hosted by Brazil, and that at the end of 2014 its reserves exceeded $1,500 million.[124] A year later this had slipped to $1,340 million after 'an incredibly tough year for FIFA'.[125] Most federations, including the IOC and FIFA, are located in Switzerland and that is where they pay the tax due on the immense profits made in staging major events elsewhere in the world. And the relatively low tax rates applied in Switzerland coupled to the rules protecting commercial confidentiality are plainly a major factor for that choice of location.[126]

There are good arguments that the legal protection which has been granted is far too generous,[127] there is proper disquiet about the extent of the restrictions on freedom of expression at stake in the brand protection rules of the type just considered.[128] There is, moreover, a vast gulf between the binding commitments ruthlessly extracted from hosts in order to maximize the profits of governing bodies and the much lighter touch typically associated with securing a long-term socially useful legacy from staging a major event.[129] The extraordinary skewing of priorities is vividly illustrated by the criticism aimed by the chief executive of the (doomed) English bid to host the 2018 World Cup at the BBC as 'unpatriotic' for

---

[122] K Tetlak, 'The Taxpayer as the Unofficial Sponsor of the London 2012 Olympic Games' (2013) 13 Intl Sports LJ 97.

[123] <http://www.fifa.com/governance/finances/> accessed 29 November 2016. No one except FIFA calls the FIFA World Cup™ anything other than the World Cup.

[124] *FIFA Financial Report 2014* <http://resources.fifa.com/mm/document/affederation/administration/02/56/80/39/fr2014weben_neutral.pdf> accessed 29 November 2016.

[125] *FIFA Financial and Governance Report 2015*, p 7 <http://resources.fifa.com/mm/document/affederation/administration/02/77/08/71/gb15_fifa_web_en_neutral.pdf> accessed 29 November 2016.

[126] See eg Dudognon (n 9).

[127] eg A Louw, *Ambush Marketing and the Mega-Event Monopoly: How Laws are Abused to Protect Commercial Rights to Major Sporting Events* (TMC Asser 2012), which (as is plain from its title) argues that the legal controls over 'ambushing' have been extended too far. See also, on the London Olympics in particular, James and Osborn (n 118) 410.

[128] eg R Gauthier, 'Major Event Legislation: Lessons from London and Looking Forward' (2014) 14 Intl Sports LJ 58; K De Beer, 'Let the Games Begin … Ambush Marketing and Freedom of Speech' (2012) 6 Human Rights and International Legal Discourse 284.

[129] S Stuart and T Scassa, 'Legal Guarantees for Olympic Legacy' (2011) 9(1) ESLJ 3 <http://www.entsportslawjournal.com/articles/10.16997/eslj.28/> accessed 29 November 2016; P Bretherton, J Piggin, and G Bodet, 'Olympic Sport and Physical Activity Promotion: The Rise and Fall of the London 2012 Pre-Event Mass Participation Legacy' (2016) 8 International Journal of Sport Policy and Politics 609.

broadcasting a programme critical of FIFA shortly before the decision was taken.[130] Even the Prime Minister of the time, David Cameron, saw fit to intervene, describing the BBC's scheduling as 'frustrating'.[131] Even if the driving political attraction is association with the major event rather than with the federation responsible for selecting a host, the two come as a package and there is plenty of evidence of politicians' eagerness to work with and acquire the blessing of officials of FIFA and the IOC and Formula 1, even where the murky background is far from unknown.[132] Governing bodies in sport may sometimes appear to ask for the moon, but they have willing suppliers among national politicians. Nor is this lunacy. Given that the commonly expressed claims that hosting tournaments will be commercially lucrative for the host have been exposed as unfounded,[133] it seems plain that political gain from association with the glitter and 'soft power' of top-level sport counts as the true motivation.

Admittedly, powerful though FIFA and the IOC are, their mitigating stupidity should never be overlooked. Rules adopted by South Africa as part of the deal to host the 2010 World Cup led to a group of thirty-six women, who had been paid to attend a match wearing dresses advertising the Dutch beer Bavaria, being removed from the stadium and threatened with criminal proceedings.[134] Bavaria, an ambush marketer with no official connection to the tournament, might have hoped for a small dose of publicity but in fact, thanks to the absurdly high-handed response, gained worldwide sympathetic attention. FIFA was ridiculed. And derision can sometimes be meted out to the freeloading host politician: George Osborne, then the United Kingdom's Chancellor of the Exchequer, was roundly booed when he presented medals at the London Olympics in 2012.[135] But overall this is a sorry

---

[130] '2018 chief dubs BBC "unpatriotic"', BBC News, 17 November 2010 <http://news.bbc.co.uk/sport1/hi/football/9201248.stm> accessed 29 November 2016; 'England's Bid Chief: BBC is "Unpatriotic" and "Sensationalist"' *The Independent* (London, 18 November 2010) <http://www.independent.co.uk/sport/football/news-and-comment/englands-bid-chief-bbc-is-unpatriotic-and-sensationalist-2136835.html> accessed 29 November 2016. The fury of the tabloid press at the BBC's impertinent concern to find out the truth was still more extreme, though exceeded again by its reaction to FIFA's subsequent refusal to award England hosting rights, but such circus events do not deserve citation.

[131] 'Panorama Won't Hurt 2018 Bid—PM' BBC News, 26 November 2010 <http://news.bbc.co.uk/sport1/hi/football/9233770.stm> accessed 29 November 2016; 'Panorama Shadow Hangs Over England's 2018 World Cup Bid' *The Independent* (London, 27 November 2010) <http://www.independent.co.uk/sport/football/news-and-comment/panorama-shadow-hangs-over-englands-2018-world-cup-bid-2145005.html> accessed 29 November 2016.

[132] See eg A Jennings, *Foul! The Secret World of FIFA. Bribes, Vote Rigging and Ticket Scandals* (Harper Collins 2007); J Sugden and A Tomlinson, *Badfellas: FIFA Family at War* (Mainstream 2003); A Jennings and C Sambrook, *The Great Olympic Swindle: When the World Wanted its Games Back* (Simon and Schuster 2000).

[133] See eg A Zimbalist, *Circus Maximus: The Economic Gamble behind Hosting the Olympics and the World Cup* (2nd edn, The Brookings Institution 2016); V Matheson and R Baade, 'Mega-Sporting Events in Developing Nations: Playing the Way to Prosperity?' (2004) 72 South Africa Journal of Economics 1085; E Molloy and T Chetty, 'The Rocky Road to Legacy: Lessons from the 2010 FIFA World Cup South Africa Stadium Program' (2015) 46 Project Management Journal 88.

[134] 'How Ambush Marketing Ambushed Sport' BBC News, 17 June 2010 <http://news.bbc.co.uk/1/hi/8743881.stm> accessed 29 November 2016.

[135] 'George Osborne is Booed at Paralympic Games' BBC News, 4 September 2012 <http://www.bbc.co.uk/newsround/19473291> accessed 29 November 2016.

tale of over-intrusive public regulation designed to promote private interests and political vanity. The ability of (most of all) the IOC and FIFA and, to some extent, the organizers of Formula 1 motor racing to wring immensely lucrative concessions from large and democratic sovereign states is the main story. It is well known that the franchise system on which the North America sports model is founded allows wily owners to play cities off against each other and to extract generous concessions on, for example, financial arrangements and/or support for infrastructure under the threat of relocation.[136] To watch the race to host the Olympic Games in summer or in winter or the Football World Cup is to watch this model expanded many times over in size and projected on to the global stage.

2.3.4 *Not* hosting the World Cup or the Olympic Games

In 2013 Jerome Valcke, then Secretary General of FIFA, reflecting on the difficulties in dealing with Germany and Brazil, hosts of the 2006 and 2014 World Cups respectively, and expecting Russia, 2018 hosts, to prove easier to work with, was quoted as having said: 'I will say something which is crazy, but less democracy is sometimes better for organising a World Cup.'[137] This, from the perspective of cutting a deal and having it executed, was of course not crazy at all. But the most striking aspect of the history of hosting tournaments is how much *democratic* states are also ready to yield.

Not always. In the Autumn of 2014 Norway attracted publicity when it decided noisily to abandon its bid to stage the 2022 Winter Olympic Games. It was reported that the IOC's list of demands 'included a cocktail reception with Norway's King Harald—with drinks paid for by the royal family'; that committee members 'expected to be chauffeur-driven along lanes reserved for their use, with traffic lights adjusted to give them priority'; that 'each delegate wanted a Samsung mobile phone with a Norwegian subscription'; that 'Bars at IOC hotels were also to stay open late … while a VIP lounge at the Olympic stadium should serve them "high quality" food and a full bar during the opening and closing ceremonies'.[138] Moreover, in line with this pattern, 'Olympic organisers further demanded control over all advertising space throughout Oslo during the Games, to be used exclusively by official sponsors'.[139]

The IOC's own Olympic Charter contains within the *Fundamental Principles of Olympism* the claim that 'The practice of sport is a human right'. It is also splendidly lucrative for those at the top of its organizational structures. There is something breathtaking about the arrogance of the demands reportedly made by the IOC, but

---

[136] See eg M Mitten, *Sports Law in the United States* (Wolters Kluwer 2011) 60–64; P Anderson and W Miller, 'Sonic Bust: Trying to Retain Major League Franchises in Challenging Financial Times' (2011–12) 21 JLAS 117.

[137] BBC News, 24 April 2013 <http://www.bbc.co.uk/sport/0/football/22288688> accessed 29 November 2016.

[138] 'IOC hits out as Norway withdraws Winter Olympic bid' *Financial Times* (London, 2 October 2014).

[139] ibid.

the truly illuminating story is not that Norway chose to say 'no', but instead that so many other (mostly much poorer) states, by no means all of them M Valcke's preferred less democratic ones, have eagerly said 'yes', and continue to do so. After all, FIFA and the IOC have no power whatsoever to *oblige* states to host their events. It is powerful politicians who hold that in their gift. The lesson is of the power of sports bodies in securing a favourable legal regime which protects the *lex sportiva* or, more generally, protects and promotes the regulatory and commercial autonomy of sports governing bodies and shelters them from some of the normal assumptions of local law. It is not difficult to envisage a better bidding process applicable to hosting rights[140] but the eagerly competitive process to host major events currently grants governing bodies such leverage that incentives to promote reform are limited.

The case of Norway shows that just occasionally potential hosts baulk at the demands associated with hosting major events. Still more high-profile as confirmation that even the most dominant governing bodies are not always able to leverage that power in order to secure special treatment was the arrest in May 2015 on Swiss soil of several high-ranking FIFA officials by officials of US federal law enforcement agencies. The arrests, which also precipitated the resignation of Sepp Blatter as FIFA President later in 2015, were in connection with alleged corruption over a period of twenty-four years and were conducted pursuant to an indictment issued in a federal court in New York.[141] The final outcome will doubtless be clear only after several years. This dramatic intervention proves that the legislative solution examined in this subsection cannot buy absolute autonomy for sports bodies and their governing officials. But it can buy a high level of autonomy, whereby local rules are introduced for the special commercial interests of sports bodies. The arrests of 2015, certainly high-profile, were in association with alleged criminal conduct: and even to take these first steps in closing the net around the the individuals concerned had taken the most powerful nation on earth a remarkably long time. Meanwhile neither the EU nor its Member States had done anything useful.[142] The arrests were more a demonstration of how exceptional, rather than how routine, is the subjection of officials to legal process. Moreover, the episode does not at all bring into question the power of FIFA to raise large amounts of money by selling rights to host and to broadcast its principal events, most of all the World Cup. Whatever corrupt practices might have occurred in this instance, the most striking

---

[140] See eg R Gauthier, 'International Sporting Event Bid Processes, and How They Can Be Improved' (2011) 11 Intl Sports LJ 1. See also B Humphreys and H van Egteren, 'Mega Sporting Event Bidding, Mechanism Design and Rent Extraction' in W Maennig and A Zimbalist (eds), *International Handbook on the Economics of Mega Sporting Events* (Edward Elgar 2012) ch 3.

[141] Office of Public Affairs of the US Department of Justice, 'Nine FIFA Officials and Five Corporate Executives Indicted for Racketeering Conspiracy and Corruption', 27 May 2015 <https://www.justice.gov/opa/pr/nine-fifa-officials-and-five-corporate-executives-indicted-racketeering-conspiracy-and> accessed 29 November 2016.

[142] For cautious comment by the Commission, stressing respect for 'the autonomy of sport's governing bodies' before allegations were converted into action, see E-003340/14 [2014] OJ C341/79, Answer to WQ by Ms Vassiliou; for sanctimonious contribution after the fact, see European Parliament Resolution of 11 June 2015 on recent revelations on high-level corruption cases in FIFA [2016] OJ C407/81.

feature of FIFA's business model is that it requires absolutely no taint of corruption to be wildly commercially successful. FIFA's promises of governance reform under Gianni Infantini, who succeeded Sepp Blatter as its President in 2016, do not alter the fact that it is the monopoly supplier of a staggeringly popular spectacle nor do they change the willingness of potential hosts to grant it remarkable benefits in order to win its favour.

2.3.5 Conclusion—the limits of the legislative solution as a means to protect sporting autonomy

The *legislative* strategy for maximizing sporting autonomy works brilliantly well in the case of one-off, high-profile events. It is competition among hosts which is ideal for the elaboration and execution of this strategy. Extracting general exclusions from the law and/or special treatment for sport that is not limited in time or targeted on particular events is much harder to achieve. No state offers sport a general immunity from legal regulation. Occasional concessions or generous categorizations may be found. English law, for example, will not subject sports bodies to judicial review: they are treated as creatures of private law rather than public law.[143] Some jurisdictions in Europe offer special protection for organizers of sports events.[144] Sport is sometimes able to extract special treatment under tax law by reliance on its socially useful functions.[145] There is an echo of this in the treatment of sporting infrastructure projects under EU state aid law, where perceived social utility has promoted the Commission to draw on Article 165 TFEU to adopt a favourable view, on condition that certain key ingredients associated with the discharge of a state responsibility are present.[146] Vertical solidarity has been pressed as a basis for generous treatment of the sale of rights to broadcast sporting events under competition law: see Chapter 11.7.

But these are specific instances: this is no *general* exemption from legal supervision. Plenty of states have sports-specific legislation and even in some instances provision for sport in their constitutions,[147] but here too the issue is detailed distinctive treatment of sport, not general amnesty for sport from the law. Switzerland, admittedly, serves as a special case. It acts as host to a large number of sporting bodies, most of which choose the legal form of a not-for-profit organization. It has

---

[143] *R v Disciplinary Committee of the Jockey Club, ex parte Aga Khan* [1993] 1 WLR 919; *R (Mullins) v Appeal Board of the Jockey Club* [2005] EWHC 2197.

[144] T Margoni, 'The Protection of Sports Events in the EU: Property, Intellectual Property, Unfair Competition and Special forms of Protection' (2016) 47 International Review of Intellectual Property and Competition Law 386, especially 409–14.

[145] See R Siekmann and J Soek, 'Models of Sport Governance within the European Union' in J Nafziger and S Ross (eds), *Handbook on International Sports Law* (Elgar 2011) ch 5.

[146] eg Commission decision of 20 November 2013, *Belgium—Football stadiums in Flanders*, Case SA.37109; Commission decision of 18 December 2013, *France—EURO 2016*, Case SA.35501. See B García, A Vermeersch, and S Weatherill, 'A New Horizon in EU Sports Law: The Application of the EU State Aid Rules Meets the Specific Nature of Sport' (forthcoming).

[147] J Soek, 'Sport in National Sports Acts and Constitutions: Definitions, Ratio Legis and Objectives' (2006) 6(3–4) Intl Sports LJ 28.

been argued that the consequent generous treatment under tax law is the principal reason for the attraction of Switzerland, although others factors too are in play, such as political stability and the country's political neutrality, as well as the powerful inducement of the IOC, which has generated a clustering of governing bodies in Switzerland.[148] Immunity from anti-corruption laws is also a helpful inducement, although, as is revealed by recent events pertaining to FIFA mentioned earlier, there is no absolute immunity. Even in Switzerland, sport is far from *wholly* exempt from the application of the law.

So states do not grant sport any *general* legislative or constitutional immunity. Given the economic significance of sport, that would not be intellectually justified in principle: nor is sport strong enough politically to extract it in practice. And just as states do not grant sport general legislative or constitutional immunity, so too the EU, in the shaping of its founding documents which are the Treaties, does not permit any general immunity. Here too the economic significance of sport deprives any such request of intellectual plausibility: here too sport lacks the political muscle to seize autonomy in practice even though it lacks good arguments to extract it in principle. For all the spirited efforts made by sports bodies, the first references to sport attached to the EU's founding Treaties were not apt to grant sport the prize of autonomy from the application of EU law. They were the Amsterdam and the Nice Declarations, which are examined in Chapter 6. They reflect in ambiguous fashion the general notion that sport may have special features, but they lack operational clarity. And the long struggle over the place of sport in the Treaty of Lisbon resulted not in exclusion but in inclusion—sport was finally recognized as an EU competence. This is Article 165 TFEU, the shaping of which is traced in Chapter 6. The aspiration to sporting autonomy was moved away from the fruitless quest to carve out an exclusion of sport from the control exercised by EU law to instead seeking legal provisions that would nudge towards the softened or sensitive application of EU law to sport, taking due account of its special status as an economic activity that is more than an economic activity. And it is precisely this that—generally, and not exclusively in relation to the EU—constitutes the third strategy of sports bodies seeking to protect their autonomy. This is to persuade courts that the special character of sport should be taken into account in the interpretation and application of 'ordinary' law. This, beyond the contractual and the legislative solutions, is the adjudicative or interpretative solution.

2.4 The Adjudicative or Interpretative Solution

The adjudicative or interpretative solution is doubtless the least attractive to sports federations of the three available options. Under this approach they are forced to defend their claim to autonomy on enemy territory, as it were: to show why 'the law'—the law of states, the law of the EU—needs and deserves adaptation in their

---

[148] See Dudognon (n 9) 50.

case. Whatever degree of autonomy sport is able to extract is dependent on what the adjudicator is willing to yield in an individual case. But no court denies without nuance that 'sport is special', though available judicial receptivity to the extent that sport is truly special may vary and may, in particular, commonly not be as generous as sports bodies would assert. The real questions are *how* special is sport. And this is where the real heartland of the problematic intersection of the *lex sportiva* and 'ordinary law' arises. This is mapping the adjudicative or interpretative solution and it forms the strategic and the intellectual core of sports law as a discipline. Sport is special—but how special? Some degree of autonomy may be merited—but how much, and why? This is strategically important because this is how pleas for autonomy need to be framed. And it is intellectually significant because it is here that a normative assessment of the vigour of the claim that 'sport is special' must be delivered.

Sometimes it is clear that sport is special. For example, in a normal industry there would be neither motivation nor justification for grouping workers according to their nationality. In sport, where national representative teams are involved, that is the very nature of the activity. So EU law's normal assumptions that discrimination on the basis of nationality is sternly prohibited need to be applied with recognition of the special character of sport.[149] It is expected that the German football team is composed of Germans and that the members of the French rugby team are French, whereas no one would assume that a German car-maker should have an existential need to employ only Germans or that a French bank should have only French employees. Sport is special. Similarly the essential need to guarantee to spectators that a sporting event is not fixed in advance, that its outcome is genuinely uncertain, justifies rules that prohibit the multiple ownership of football clubs in the EU.[150] In a normal industry, attempts to prevent an owner expanding his or her portfolio of companies would amount to anti-competitive restraints with the potential to depress prices by reducing the competitive pool of potential buyers (unless exceptionally the purchase would push the buyer into an unacceptably powerful position in the relevant market). Sport is special.

But when the public authorities in Milan violated the EU rules on public contracting by failing to meet the required standards of transparency and open bidding, there was no protection available simply because the project in question involved the construction of a football stadium for the 1990 World Cup.[151] It could have been a school, it could have been a hospital: it happened to be a football stadium. There was nothing special about the sporting context. The law applied in the normal way—the law had been broken. And when a medley of suppliers were found to have fixed prices for goods, it mattered not that the goods in question happened to be replica football shirts.[152] This was a straightforward breach of UK competition law. No possible softening could be deserved simply because it was consumers of

---

[149] Case 36/74 *Walrave and Koch v Union Cycliste Internationale* [1974] ECR 1405. See Ch 4.8.
[150] COMP 37.806 *ENIC/UEFA*, IP/02/942, 27 June 2002. See Ch 5.2.
[151] Case C-103/88 *Fratelli Costanzo v Commune di Milano* [1989] ECR 1839.
[152] *Manchester United, Umbro, JJB Sports and others v Office of Fair Trading* (2005) CAT 22.

sports goods that were being cheated of price competition in the market. In similar vein the Commission found that the organizers of the 1998 Football World Cup in France had violated what is now Article 102 TFEU by abusively restricting sales of tickets 'blind'—that is, in advance of the draw for the competition, before the identity of the participating teams was even known—to nationals and residents of France.[153] The Commission quite correctly dismissed the far-fetched argument that such discrimination could be justified on the basis of public security, finding that 'such a policy was excessive because it failed to take into account the generally peaceful nature of consumers purchasing tickets at a time when the identities of participating teams are not known'; there was no 'specific security risk'.[154] Only if there were, might sport be treated as special. Since this intervention, ticket sales for major sporting events in the EU have been conducted on the basis that all nationals of EU Member States shall be treated equally.[155] One final example of sport *not* being special will suffice. When the Court of Justice was asked to rule on the burden of proof applicable under Directive 2000/78 on equal treatment in employment and occupation in cases associated with imputing to an employer discriminatory comments made by an individual, it was not of material significance that the employer happened to be the leading Romanian football club, Steaua Bucarest.[156] Determining legal responsibility for such comments as 'Not even if I had to close Steaua down would I accept a homosexual on the team.... There's no room for gays in my family, and Steaua is my family' did not depend on the sporting context. Sport is not special. In fact, the case is a helpful reminder that sport truly is *not* as special as is sometimes claimed. There is no hint here of the virtues of tolerance and respect which pious sports federations will sometimes claim to be spreading.

Sometimes sport is special. Sometimes it is not. It is the cases where sport *may* be special that are the truly interesting ones. What criteria are decisive? And who decides—how much room should sport be given to make its choices? EU law is the field of inquiry pursued in this book. And it is this third adjudicative or interpretative strategy that is the main part of the inquiry—here is where EU law's special demands are tasked to mesh with sport's. But the reader should not overlook the wider map of sports law: the first two strategies considered previously are concerned with avoiding even needing to mesh. And these are tensions and strategies that are found in the development of sports law in any jurisdiction, not only in EU law.

---

[153] Decision 2000/12 *1998 Football World Cup* [2000] OJ L5/55. See S Weatherill, '0033149875354: Fining the Organisers of the 1998 Football World Cup' [2000] ECLR 275.

[154] Decision 2000/12 (n 153) para 112.

[155] eg Euro 2000 Football European Championships, IP/00/591, 8 June 2000; 2004 Olympic Games in Athens, IP/03/738, 23 May 2003; 2006 World Cup, IP/05/519, 2 May 2005.

[156] Case C-81/12 *Asociatia ACCEPT*, judgment of 25 April 2013.

3

The Framework and the Challenges of an EU Law and Policy on Sport

3.1 Introduction

The interpretative or adjudicative approach to securing sporting autonomy was placed in context in Chapter 2. It is based on the claim that sport is 'special' and that accordingly this should condition the interpretation and application of legal rules. No doubt sport *is* to some extent special, and no court goes so far as to dismiss out of hand such pleas as a matter of principle. From the perspective of sporting bodies the complaint is typically that those adjudicating such claims tend to be inadequately sensitive in practice, rather than utterly insensitive in principle, to the extent to which sport is different from normal industries. The intellectual challenge is to assess whether this allegation has foundation or whether instead it is based on an exaggerated depiction of the merits of the appeals to autonomy commonly made by sporting bodies. It is especially where there is a commercial advantage attached to attempts to escape the normal assumptions of legal regulation that one may sense a strategic rather than an intellectually pure appeal to be permitted sporting autonomy.

Such introductory remarks fit the challenge of sports law anywhere in the world, but the preoccupation of this book is with EU law. One can make sense of the opportunities available to those involved in sports governance to secure a favourable *interpretation* of EU law only by appreciating the background structure of EU law. In particular, the EU's founding Treaties make meagre explicit provision for sport. The foundation stone of the EU's constitutional order is the principle of conferral, which according to Article 5(2) of the Treaty on European Union (TEU) provides that 'the Union shall act only within the limits of the competences conferred upon it by the Member States in the Treaties to attain the objectives set out therein'. The answer to the question 'what may the EU do?' is in principle always 'the EU may do what its Treaties permit, no more and no less'. Article 165 of the Treaty on the Functioning of the European Union (TFEU) stipulates that the Union 'shall contribute to the promotion of European sporting issues, while taking account of the specific nature of sport' and that Union action shall be aimed at 'developing the European dimension in sport, by promoting fairness and openness in sporting competitions and cooperation between bodies responsible for sports, and by protecting the physical and moral integrity of sportsmen and sportswomen, especially the youngest sportsmen and sportswomen'. To contribute to the achievement of these objectives it is provided in Article 165(4) TFEU that the EU enjoys a legislative competence to adopt incentive measures, though this explicitly excludes any harmonization of the laws. This, then, is what the EU may do in the field of sport according to the explicit terms of its Treaties.

But this is very far from the full story. Article 165 is the starting point in understanding the competence conferred on the EU to act in the field of sport. But its text is both thin and vague and it is not apt to guide the resolution of particular disputes. In particular it is of little service in framing the application of EU free movement and competition law to sporting practices which collide with the underlying assumptions of the internal market. Those Treaty provisions on free movement and competition law offer no explicit mention of sport at all, but sport, like any other sector, is subject to the rules contained in those Treaty provisions in so far as it constitutes an economic activity, for the scope of the EU Treaty system itself is driven by the subjection of economic activity to the demands of the internal market. That project is the subject of the commitment made in Article 3(3) TEU that the Union 'shall establish an internal market' and that internal market is defined as 'an area without frontiers in which the free movement of goods, persons, services and capital is ensured' by Article 26 TFEU. Much activity in sport is organized on national lines: here immediately looms the thematic tension between sport and the EU's internal market. And how to address that tension is left unaddressed by Article 165 TFEU in particular and by the EU Treaty structure more generally.

Moreover, even the slender and ill-defined competence conferred by Article 165 TFEU has been in existence *only since December 2009*. Article 165 is a creature of the reforms instituted by the amendments made to the EU Treaty system with effect from that date by the Lisbon Treaty. A great deal of evolutionary activity at the intersection of EU law and sport occurred prior to that date, at a time when the legally binding provisions of the EU Treaties had no explicit textual connection with sport at all. Sport was indeed not even mentioned in the text of the Treaties until 2009. As a result the 'interpretative strategy' for achieving sporting autonomy was deployed before EU institutions—most prominently the Court of Justice and the Commission—which had a great deal of scope and flexibility to make important interpretative choices without any direction supplied by the Treaty.

The purpose of this chapter is to map the landscape: to show how and why EU law lacks concrete rules dealing systematically with its impact on sport, and to show the background which explains the very limited success of governing bodies in sport in achieving a secure exclusion for their practices from EU law. What has instead developed is a space within which to discuss to what extent sport's special characteristics should be integrated into the application of the legal rules. This, then, is the heart of the *interpretative* strategy for maximizing sporting autonomy.

This chapter, then, sets out the scope of EU competence applied to sport. The three chapters that follow deal with the detailed articulation of that competence. This covers, first, the application of the rules that govern the building of the internal market—principally free movement, examined in Chapter 4, and competition law, examined in Chapter 5. The issue is the prohibition of sporting practices found to contradict the aims of the EU. Then attention moves to action taken by the EU in the name of regulating and legislating— that is, promulgating positive law. This is discussed in Chapter 6.

Otherwise framed, this examines, first, in Chapters 4 and 5, the decision-making of the Court and the Commission when faced with the question of whether sporting practices are compatible with EU law. Then, second, in Chapter 6, analysis moves to the shaping of Article 165 TFEU, the Lisbon Treaty's innovation, and the creation of opportunities to move beyond ad hoc adjudication in the shadow of free movement and competition law and instead to elaborate broader policy articulation by (most prominently) the Commission and, on a very limited scale, for the EU to adopt legislation setting ground rules for sporting practice in the EU. Chapter 7 then draws together the several strands and themes addressed in these chapters and presents a case for understanding EU sports law as an integrated and coherent system, giving shape to Article 165's assertion that sport has a specific nature. Chapters 8 to 11 then deal with particular substantive topics—nationality rules, the transfer system, governance, and the sale of broadcasting rights.

Running through this inquiry is the quest for 'principles'. How is EU sports law and policy framed by its shaping in the past in the shadow of the internal market and into the future by the directions mapped by Article 165 TFEU? What really is the 'specific nature of sport' to which Article 165 refers, and to what extent has this justified and does this justify sport's treatment under EU law in a way which differs from its application to other less atypical—less 'special'—areas of economic activity. This is addressed in the book's concluding chapter, Chapter 12, which summarizes the animating themes and principles of EU sports law.

3.2 'Competence' as a Constitutionally Foundational Issue in the EU

One can find in any jurisdiction the tendency of sporting bodies to be forced to deploy the interpretative or adjudicative strategy for maximizing their sporting autonomy. US law, English law, German law, Australian law, and so on all have their own particular versions of this story, and there are intriguing differences between jurisdictions in the answers given to the questions 'is sport special and, if so, how special?'. Some of these differences may be historical accident or random peculiarity, but others reflect genuine structural and cultural differences affecting the organization of sport. In the United States, for example, there is far more attention paid to the need for competitive balance in sports leagues than anything found in Europe, and this leads to interventionist features such as the 'draft pick' and long-established salary caps which are designed to go some way to evening out opportunities to succeed across all the participants.[1] So in this sense an inquiry into EU sports law is an inquiry which is readily connected to and helpfully informed

---

[1] See eg M Mitten, *Sports Law in the United States* (Wolters Kluwer 2011) Pt II, ch 4.2.

by inquiry into the sports law of any jurisdiction. Sports law scholarship deserves a comparative dimension.[2] But there are also special features of the EU's experience in the shaping of sports law and policy which are not shared by other jurisdictions.

Most of all the EU possesses only the competences and powers which are conferred on it by its Member States under the founding Treaties, as amended periodically. This is the 'principle of conferral' set out in Article 5 TEU. Article 5(1) TEU declares that 'The limits of Union competences are governed by the principle of conferral'. Article 5(2) TEU adds that pursuant to this principle, 'the Union shall act only within the limits of the competences conferred upon it by the Member States in the Treaties to attain the objectives set out therein'. As both Articles 4(1) and 5(2) TEU make explicit, this logically entails that competences not conferred upon the Union in the Treaties remain with the Member States. The principle of conferral is foundationally important to the EU's claim to exercise power in a legitimate way. When the EU acts, it does so under the authorization provided by all its Member States who, according to their own particular constitutional rules relating to the ratification of international Treaties, have approved the EU's original Treaties and its subsequent amending Treaties, most recently the Lisbon Treaty of 2009. It means too that action taken by the EU *beyond* its constitutional mandate is not legitimate: it is invalid as a matter of law.

It is not possible to attempt serious study of the EU's treatment of the sports sector without a secure grasp of this constitutional foundation. Put another way, the EU sports lawyer must start out with an education as an EU lawyer pure and simple. Most of all this is because those constitutional foundations reveal the *limits* of the EU's role—which serve as constraints that dictate the more substantive debate into what the EU *should* seek to achieve by intervening in the sports sector. So there are issues that arise in EU sports law that would be familiar to a sports lawyer from elsewhere who has no knowledge at all of the EU and its legal order, but there are also aspects that are incomprehensible without appreciation of the EU's constitutional and institutional peculiarities. EU law is, after all, the law of an international organization and has its roots in a system of international Treaties. It is not the law of a state, even if the EU functions in a manner that is readily comparable to the law of a federal state and even if the EU is a relatively, in truth uniquely, *sophisticated* international organization.

So the EU's competence is no more, no less than that conferred on it by its founding Treaties.[3] In its legislative dimension, the Lisbon Treaty was a landmark.

---

[2] See eg L Halgreen, *European Sports Law: A Comparative Analysis of the European and American Models of Sport* (Forlaget Thomson 2004); J Nafziger, 'European and North American Models of Sports Organization' in J Nafziger and S Ross (eds), *Handbook on International Sports Law* (Edward Elgar 2011) ch 4; N St Cyr Clarke, 'The Beauty and the Beast: Taming the Ugly Side of the People's Game' (2010–11) 17 Col J Eur L 601. Comparative economics has a place too: see eg W Andreff, 'Some Comparative Economics of the Organisation of Sports: Competition and Regulation in North American vs European Professional Team Sports Leagues' (2011) 8 European Journal of Comparative Economics 3.

[3] See eg S Weatherill, *Law and Values in the European Union* (OUP 2016) ch 2; R Schütze, *European Union Law* (CUP 2015) ch 7; C Barnard and S Peers (eds), *European Union Law* (OUP 2014) ch 3.

It created with effect from December 2009 a sports-specific competence: Article 165 TFEU, which, as already mentioned, directs that the EU 'shall contribute to the promotion of European sporting issues, while taking account of the specific nature of sport, its structures based on voluntary activity and its social and educational function' and that EU action shall be aimed at 'developing the European dimension in sport, by promoting fairness and openness in sporting competitions and cooperation between bodies responsible for sports, and by protecting the physical and moral integrity of sportsmen and sportswomen, especially the youngest sportsmen and sportswomen', and, to those ends, provides in Article 165(4) TFEU for a legislative competence to adopt incentive measures at EU level.

The force and intent of Article 165 TFEU is far from clear in its detail. The text is the result of tortured compromise and stop-start negotiation over several years. This is explored in detail in Chapter 6. In fact, Article 165, as a product of compromise, is in many respects designed precisely *not* to provide a tightly drawn or unambiguously clear competence for the EU. Crucially, as Chapter 6 will explore, it is the remnant of the failure of those lobbying on behalf of the sports sector to secure an express exclusion for sport from the application of EU law. That plea for complete autonomy is the specific EU version of the legislative route to securing sporting autonomy examined in Chapter 2—being, in the EU context, an attempt to write autonomy into the Treaty rather than, as at state level, into legislation. Article 165 TFEU is an expression of failure to achieve that objective. Instead it locates sport within the scope of EU law, while admitting that it is to some (ill-defined) extent 'special'. Precisely *how* special will require elucidation: this is the heart of the adjudicative or interpretative route to sporting autonomy introduced in the previous chapter.

But Article 165 TFEU is deceptive. Indeed the foundational Article 5 TEU itself, asserting the principle of conferral, is deceptive too. Both are built on the *principle* that the EU has only limited competences and powers—namely, those conferred on it by the Member States in the Treaties. But the *practice* is more slippery. And the practice is much *less* comforting to those, such as sports governing bodies, who would typically wish to understand the EU's role as reliably controlled by the principle of conferral. The limits to EU law promised by Article 5 TEU are in truth broad and, worse, they are ill-defined. There is an enduring drama in EU law, not confined to sport alone, whereby competences and powers, though limited in principle, are far-reaching in practice, often unpredictably so. There is a motor of transformation[4] or, otherwise put, of 'competence creep',[5] and this tendency was a key issue for deliberation at the Convention on the Future of Europe which ultimately shaped the Lisbon Treaty, which entered into force in 2009 and which provoked the currently applicable arrangements.[6]

---

[4] J Weiler, 'The Transformation of Europe' (1991) 100 Yale LJ 2403.

[5] M Pollack, 'Creeping Competence: The Expanding Agenda of the European Community' (1994) 14 Journal of Public Policy 95; S Weatherill, 'Competence Creep and Competence Control' (2004) 23 YEL 1.

[6] On the problems perceived during the process that led to the reforms effective from 2009, see eg A Von Bogdandy and J Bast, 'The European Union's Vertical Order of Competences: the Current

The principal anxiety is structural: it rests on the poor way in which Article 5 TEU's principle of conferral is put into operation in the Treaties. The Treaties' general *modus operandi* is not to declare particular sectors off-limits for the EU nor to reserve particular functions to the Member States. Instead the principle of conferral pronounced by Article 5 TEU is made specific in its application to particular sectoral competences by provisions granting legislative authority to the EU which are to be found in Part Three of the TFEU. In short, the Treaty system works by declaring what the EU may do, not what it may not do. It is accordingly hard to marshal operationally useful constitutional arguments *against* EU intervention. Still worse, although Articles 2 to 6 TFEU helpfully provide a brisk summary of the scope and nature of the areas in which the EU enjoys competence under its Treaties, a detailed understanding of the matter demands a laborious journey through the chaotic pattern of provisions granting legislative authority to the EU which are scattered across Part Three of the TFEU, which stretches from Article 26 to Article 197. It is no easy read. It is, in consequence, disturbingly difficult to set out clearly an account of the nature of EU competence and its effect on Member State competence which does justice to the detailed intricacy.[7] Article 5 TEU's principle of conferral is not all that it seems.

Sport was not even mentioned in the Treaties until 2009. But this did not at all mean it was reserved to the Member States. The EU's competence is not exclusively or even principally *legislative* in nature. EU law applies also even where legislative competence is lacking in so far as national practices collide with the objective of creating an internal market.

As a general structural observation, the issue at stake is that the whole EU system is driven by the functional logic of transforming the fragmented pattern of economies that have been shaped over many years, in some cases centuries, according to *national* patterns and *national* regulatory rhythms by merging 'the national markets into a single market bringing about conditions as close as possible to those of a genuine internal market'.[8] This is today inscribed in the Treaty by Article 3(3) TEU, which provides that 'The Union shall establish an internal market'. And this internal market is defined by Article 26(2) TFEU as 'an area without internal frontiers in which the free movement of goods, persons, services and capital is ensured in accordance with the provisions of the Treaties'. So any national practice which hinders the development of an internal market in the EU falls within the scope of EU law. And the free movement rules and the competition rules, which serve the achievement of the Treaty's economic objectives,

Law and Proposals for its Reform' (2002) 39 CML Rev 227; S Weatherill, 'Better Competence Monitoring' (2005) 30 EL Rev 23; G Davies, 'Subsidiarity: The Wrong Idea, in the Wrong Place, at the Wrong Time' (2006) 43 CML Rev 63; on the chosen solutions, see eg R Schütze, 'Subsidiarity after Lisbon: Reinforcing the Safeguards of Federalism' (2009) 68 CLJ 525; A Cygan, 'The Parliamentarisation of EU Decision-Making? The Impact of the Treaty of Lisbon on National Parliaments' (2011) 36 EL Rev 480. For deep critical engagement, see L Azoulai (ed), *The Question of Competence in the European Union* (OUP 2014).

[7] See especially Weatherill (n 3) ch 2. [8] Case 15/81 *Gaston Schul* [1982] ECR 1409.

therefore have startling functional breadth. Any field of national policy-making which tends to come into conflict with the quest for market integration in the EU is subject to review in the light of its impact on the Treaty rules on free movement or competition. So even though the EU may lack a *legislative* competence in a particular field does not at all mean that the matter rests in the province of national regulatory autonomy.

This accentuates the need to distrust the deceptively simple formula that is Article 5 TEU's principle of conferral. The impetus delivered by the internal market means that EU law may exert transformative effects on national practice even in areas where EU legislative competence is thin or even wholly absent. Areas such as health care,[9] social security,[10] taxation,[11] and environmental protection[12] provide good examples. Even in the rare instances where the Treaty seems explicitly to guard against disruption of national autonomy, such as Article 345 TFEU which explicitly declares that the Treaties 'shall in no way prejudice the rules in Member States governing the system of property ownership', the Court has found a way to insert internal market law. So, for example, in a case concerning Dutch rules prohibiting privatization in the gas sector, the Court agreed that Article 345 TFEU guaranteed the neutrality of EU law as far as property ownership was concerned, but it refused to read Article 345 TFEU as conferring immunity from the basic thrust of the rules of free movement and non-discrimination where property rights were being *exercised*.[13] None of this is incompatible with Article 5 TEU's principle of conferral, but it shines light on what that principle means in practice. EU law reaches only so far as its Treaties mandate—but, driven by the economic logic of market-making, in practice that is a remarkably broad reach. Areas of truly exclusive state competence are few and, were it otherwise, the achievement of the core objectives of the Treaty would be gravely imperilled.

Sport is in one sense just another illustration of these trends—it is an application of general EU law orthodoxy. But sport offers a particularly vivid illustration of this trend, not least because of the strenuous attempts of sporting bodies to preserve their autonomy from remorseless erosion in the name of the internal market. In formal terms the EU, when it checks national practices for conformity with the requirements of internal market law, is not dictating what shall be done, it is instead simply deciding whether what is currently being practised may lawfully continue. That follows logically from the limits of its role: it may not legislate, it may only check for violation of internal market law. In practice, however, EU law constricts and channels regulatory autonomy. The interpretation of the scope and impact of internal market law has a profound influence on the viability of the choices available to those subject to its supervision. In most areas this means primarily public

---

[9] eg Case C-372/04 *ex parte Watts* [2006] ECR I-4325.

[10] eg Case C-512/03 *J É J Blankaert* [2005] ECR I-7685.

[11] eg Case C-446/03 *Marks and Spencer v Halsey* [2005] ECR I-10837.

[12] eg Case 302/86 *Commission v Denmark* [1988] ECR 4607; Case C-379/98 *Preussen Elektra* [2001] ECR I-2099; Case C-573/12 *Alands Vindkraft*, judgment of 1 July 2014.

[13] Joined Cases C-105/12 to C-107/12 *Essent*, judgment of 22 October 2013.

authorities in the Member States—in sport this means primarily governing bodies and federations.

3.3 The Framework of EU Law and Policy and How it Applies to Sport

The scope of the EU's influence is best understood by beginning with the separation between negative and positive law. Negative law refers to laws that prohibit particular practices—broadly, those that conflict with the objective of creating and maintaining the EU's internal market. Most prominent among these restraints on public authorities and private actors are the rules on free movement and the competition rules. Positive law, by contrast, refers not to the role of the EU in stopping actions but rather to the EU's own—positive—capacity to put in place its own common rules—that is, centralized EU-level law-making. The negative law provisions are deregulatory in the sense that they require that the offending actions be stopped. Positive law may be deregulatory too, in the sense that a single common EU rule typically replaces in whole or in part divergent and confusing national practices, but it is also a form of re-regulation in the sense that the matter become subject to the chosen common EU standard.

3.4 Negative Law—Free Movement and Competition

The principal negative law provisions are Articles of the Treaty. The application of these provisions is predominantly the preserve of the Court and of national courts, though the Commission too plays a direct role in securing observance of the competition rules. The creation of positive law is predominantly the preserve of the EU's political institutions and the legislative process, making use of the authorizations to adopt legislation conferred by the Treaty to adopt measures of secondary legislation. For sport, this means most obviously the admittedly meagre power to adopt 'incentive measures' which is conferred by Article 165 TFEU.

The Treaty on the Functioning of the EU contains a group of provisions which prohibit practices that obstruct the achievement of the EU's objectives. Article 18 TFEU is a good starting point since its predecessor was one of the provisions at stake in the 1974 ruling in *Walrave and Koch*, which was the Court's first ever exploration of the intersection of EU law and sport.[14] Article 18 TFEU states: 'Within the scope of application of the Treaties, and without prejudice to any special provisions contained therein, any discrimination on grounds of nationality shall be prohibited.' This is repeated in Article 21 of the Charter of Fundamental Rights of the European Union, which has enjoyed binding effect since 2009. This, then,

---

[14] Case 36/74 *Walrave and Koch v Union Cycliste Internationale* [1974] ECR 1405.

is a prohibition that is central to the very purpose of the EU, but it also poses evident problems for sports which involve competition between national representative teams where selection is based squarely on the criterion of nationality. In *Walrave and Koch* the Court, respectful of the distinctive concerns of sporting interest, found a way to permit room for sporting autonomy in the matter. Sport was here 'special', as explored more fully in Chapter 4.

Beyond Article 18 TFEU's prohibition against discrimination on grounds of nationality, the driving force of the Treaty provisions relevant to sport is the project to create an 'internal market' for the EU. Article 3(3) TEU commits the Union to the establishment of an internal market. The internal market is defined in Article 26(2) TFEU as an 'area without internal frontiers in which the free movement of goods, persons, services and capital is ensured in accordance with the provisions of this Treaty'. The aim, then, is a single trading area stretching across the territory of all twenty-eight Member States, in which national political frontiers shall be of no economic relevance. The key provisions are those which govern free movement and competition. They prohibit practices that obstruct free movement across borders or operate to distort competition in the internal market, although in most instances allowing some limited scope for rule-makers to show justification for their practices.

Articles 34 to 36 TFEU deal with the free movement of goods, by subjecting to control any national practice that obstructs the free movement of goods between Member States. Articles 45 to 48, 49 to 55, and 56 to 62 TFEU perform a similar function by asserting supervision of practices which obstruct the free movement of persons, the self-employed and companies, and providers and recipients of services, respectively. These have been of particular significance in the field of sport: athletes are capable of being classified as 'workers' and both clubs and federations which organize competitions are readily treated as suppliers of services. The provisions on the free movement of workers were at stake in the first two major sports-related rulings of the Court, *Walrave and Koch v Union Cycliste Internationale* and *Bosman*, both of which will be examined more thoroughly later in this book.[15] Rules that treated workers differently on the basis of nationality and rules that required the payment of a fee as a condition of the transfer of a player's registration were treated as restrictions on the cross-border mobility of workers. The cross-border provision of services by athletes was at stake in *Deliège v Ligue de Judo*.[16] What is now Article 56 TFEU was deployed to attack selection rules which had the effect of limiting the number of participants in an international (judo) tournament, although the Court, citing *Walrave and Koch* and *Bosman*, concluded that such limiting rules were inherent in the conduct of an international event. The exact quality of this formula will be examined further in Chapter 4: it represents an important attempt to carve out a protected area for sporting autonomy even where practices exert an economic effect on the internal market. The Treaty provisions on the free movement of services are

---

[15] ibid; Case C-415/93 *Union royale belge des sociétés de football association ASBL v Jean-Marc Bosman* [1995] ECR I-4921.

[16] Cases C-51/96 and C-191/97 *Deliège v Ligue de Judo* [2000] ECR I-2549.

important too in the market for broadcasting. This sector is examined more fully in Chapter 11.

All the Treaty provisions on free movement are readily applied to national practices which discriminate on the basis of nationality, but they also apply more broadly to restrictions and impediments to cross-border trade even in the absence of overt discrimination. Measures that restrict free movement are also capable of being treated as limitations from the perspective of Articles 15 to 17 of the Charter of Fundamental Rights, which deal with the freedom to choose an occupation, the freedom to conduct a business, and the right to property, but so far the Court has taken the view that a Charter-based claim adds nothing and changes nothing when compared with the well-established structure and substance of free movement law.[17] The governing concept is to oppose the fragmentation of the EU's internal market along national lines.

The early cases decided in the growth of EU sports law were concerned with the Treaty provisions concerning free movement, but subsequently the profile of the Treaty rules on competition has become ever more prominent. The competition rules to some extent complement the free movement rules in the sense that they may apply to the same type of practice but they may also control practices that escape the reach of the free movement rules, such as price-fixing or other kinds of anti-competitive arrangements that are not tied to the particular vice at which the free movement rules are targeted, which is the partitioning of the internal market along national lines. Competition law is governed principally by Articles 101 and 102 TFEU. The former controls anti-competitive practices, the latter addresses the abuse of a dominant position. The competition rules are explicitly tied to the internal market. Article 101 targets particular practices which are 'prohibited as incompatible with the internal market'; Article 102 forbids abuse of a dominant position 'as incompatible with the internal market in so far as it may affect trade between Member States'. The two provisions share an aim, which is the 'maintenance of effective competition' within the internal market.[18]

Article 101's control of bilateral and multilateral practices that may harm the competitive structure of the market is readily applied to the network of agreements between clubs, national associations, and governing bodies at continental and global level that structure professional sport. These are potentially horizontal and vertical restraints, as the orthodox terminology of competition law would have it— that is, agreements struck between parties at the same level of the production process (such as clubs) and agreements between parties at different levels in the chain (such as clubs and governing bodies, or governing bodies and broadcasters). Since the organization of sporting competition is characterized by a much higher degree of interdependence among participants than would be normal elsewhere, one may readily expect to find practices in the organization of a sports league that are in

---

[17] eg Case C-390/12 *Pfleger*, judgment of 30 April 2014 (TFEU, Art 56); Case C-98/14 *Berlington*, judgment of 11 June 2015 (TFEU, Art 56); Case C-367/12 *Sokoll-Seebacher*, judgment of 13 February 2014 (TFEU, Art 49).

[18] Case 6/72 *Continental Can v Commission* [1973] ECR 215.

principle capable of falling within the scope of Article 101 TFEU. The question of abiding interest will be whether, and if so how, the fact that the practices do arise in the particular context of sport then conditions the nature of the legal scrutiny.

Article 102 TFEU, which loosely put deals with monopoly power, is capable of application to the rule-maker in sport, which is frequently allocated exclusive power to decide 'top down' how the activity shall be organized. In a normal run-of-the-mill industry one is required to investigate carefully whether—to choose one of the most famous examples in the Court's case law—a supplier of bananas is sufficiently free of competition from suppliers of other kinds of fruit to be correctly regarded as dominant in the market, and whether it is operating in a territory that is geographically distinct and in which it enjoys that position of economic dominance,[19] but in sport the whole point is commonly to centralize regulatory power in the hands of one governing body. It is typical of Article 102 investigations that the undertaking in question seeks to persuade that it is subject to constraint by competition in the market with the consequence that it is not dominant, and so immune from sanction pursuant to Article 102, but that line of reasoning, conducive to achieving autonomy, is not typically open to a sports federation. What is open to the sports federation is to show that its characteristic dominant regulatory power is inherent in the organization of sport. So here too the issue is the extent to which this feature of monopoly power to set rules, which is common in sport, is fed into the legal analysis of whether the dominant position frequently enjoyed by the sports regulator has in fact been abused.

Key decisions of the Commission and Court, examined more fully later in this book, have paved the way. Under an approach which has some functional and structural similarity with that adopted in the development of free movement law, the norm is to refuse to permit the *lex sportiva* any absolute immunity from the control exercised by EU law where there are economic effects at stake. Instead an intersection between sporting practices and EU law is acknowledged, within which the expression of sport's special nature is admitted and assessed. So UEFA's rules prohibiting the ownership of more than one football club were treated as restrictions on competition, because they shut out would-be buyers from the market once they had acquired one club, but were accepted as a necessary measure in ensuring that the sport was not tainted by the suspicion of collusion that would arise where clubs under the same ownership faced each other in a competitive fixture.[20] So too in the Court's pioneering decision in *Meca-Medina*, which authoritatively analysed the relationship between EU competition law and sporting practices, it was found that the imposition of sanctions for violation of anti-doping rules might in some circumstances damage the athlete's livelihood in such a way as to offend against EU law, but that provided the sanctions were neither arbitrary nor disproportionate in their restrictive effects, they should be tolerated as a necessary aspect of 'clean' sport.[21] The *lex sportiva* enjoys conditional autonomy under EU law. It is where the

---

[19] Case 27/76 *United Brands v Commission* [1978] ECR 207.
[20] COMP 37.806 *ENIC/ UEFA*, IP/02/942, 27 June 2002.
[21] Case C-519/04P *Meca-Medina and Majcen v Commission* [2006] ECR I-6991.

monopoly power to take decisions about the way the sporting events shall be organized is extended to decisions with direct commercial consequences,[22] and especially where there is a conflict of interest favouring the rule-maker's own commercial position,[23] that Article 102 TFEU is most likely to be found to have been infringed by a sporting body.

The Treaty provisions on the free movement of workers and services are interpreted as capable of application not only to measures of public authorities but also to the collectively agreed practices of private parties, which clearly embraces governing bodies in sport. This is not true of the rules governing the free movement of goods, which bind only public authorities,[24] but the provisions on goods are in any event of little significance to the major issues that arise in sports law. The competition rules are plainly designed primarily for application to private parties, and certainly engage governing bodies in sport. So sporting bodies are within the personal scope of the key Treaty provisions which supply the governing framework of the internal market. Their practices must survive scrutiny in so far as they obstruct cross-border trade or harm the competitive structure of the EU's market.

The Court has attributed high significance to these Treaty provisions. It describes freedom of movement for goods as 'one of the foundations' of the system.[25] Article 101 TFEU is 'a fundamental provision which is essential for the accomplishment of the tasks entrusted to the Community [now Union] and, in particular, for the functioning of the internal market'.[26] In *FA Premier League and others v QC Leisure and others, Karen Murphy v Media Protection Services Ltd*, the Court went so far as to state that completion of the internal market is 'the fundamental aim of the Treaty'.[27] On any literal reading of the Treaty, this is simply not true. But it clearly reveals the strong assumption that the internal market lies at the heart of the EU's ambitions to reshape the relationships between European states into a model of cooperation from which all benefit.[28]

The crucial point in understanding the impact of the rules on free movement and competition is that sport is not mentioned *at all* in any of these Treaty provisions. Sport is affected by and subject to these provisions in so far as it constitutes an economic activity, which is key to bringing sport within the scope of application of the EU Treaties. The point, in fact, is that these foundationally important Treaty provisions do not spell out their application to *any* particular sector of the economy. They cover all economic activity. They are the means to achieve functional ends—most of all, that of economic integration within the internal market. So sporting practices, as much as practices in the financial services sector or affecting car manufacture

---

[22] eg Decision 2000/12 *1998 Football World Cup* [2000] OJ L5/55.

[23] Case C-49/07 *MOTOE* [2008] ECR I-4863. See Ch 10.

[24] eg Case C-159/00 *Sapod Audic* [2002] ECR I-5031.

[25] Case C-194/94 *CIA Security International v Signalson and Securitel* [1996] ECR I-2201, para 40.

[26] Case C-126/97 *Eco Swiss China Time Ltd v Benetton International NV* [1999] ECR I-3055, para 36.

[27] Joined Cases C-403/08 and C-429/08 *FA Premier League and others v QC Leisure and others, Karen Murphy v Media Protection Services Ltd* [2011] ECR I-9083, para 115.

[28] See S Weatherill, *The Internal Market as a Legal Concept* (OUP 2017).

or regulating chemicals, fall to be checked in the light of the demands of EU law in so far as they cause impediments to cross-border trade or distort competition in the internal market. In this vein *Walrave and Koch* set an enduring tone.[29] In that pioneering ruling the Court decided that 'the practice of sport is subject to Community [Union] law only in so far as it constitutes an economic activity within the meaning of Article 2 of the Treaty': but, as has become increasingly evident, the word 'only' is deceptive, for in fact it is extremely hard to find aspects of sport which are *not* in at least some way entangled with the jurisdictional trigger of 'economic activity'. Appreciation of this was in fact not lost on perceptive commentators at the time of the ruling over forty years ago.[30]

In this sense EU law reaches sport principally as a result of its preoccupation with the construction of an internal market, and not as a consequence of its concern for sport as such. And Article 165 TFEU does not change that. But the Court, in choosing to interpret EU law in an expansive manner, is following what it sees as the logic of the Treaty itself. The Treaty does not place particular sectors of economic activity beyond the reach of its basic rules. When one is engaged in economic activity, it is very difficult to construct an argument apt to secure insulation from the application of EU free movement and competition law. In EU trade law the principal arguments tend to surround the question whether a particular practice is justified or not. There is little scope for arguing that EU law does not apply *at all*.

The question, then, is whether those challenged practices may be justified, a question which is at its most sensitive where their defence is driven by the claim that sport is 'special' and so should be treated in a way that grants it more auton-omy than would be granted to the financial services sector or car manufacture or production of chemicals. And here the Treaty provisions on free movement and competition offer no help at all, since they do not mention sport. Article 165 TFEU offers some help. But it is thin and vague. Its undeveloped reference to the 'specific nature' of sport simply opens space for debate about how special sport truly is, rather than setting out operationally useful rules and boundaries apt to resolve particular disputes at the intersection of EU internal market law and the *lex sportiva*. It was in any event added to the Treaty as late as 2009, by which time the Court and the Commission had long been forced to grapple with that intersec-tion with no guidance whatsoever provided by the EU's founding constitutional texts. So the EU's institutions have been forced to reckon with the claims to sport's special status in circumstances where they have no choice but to use their own wit to gauge their weight.

It bears repetition that this is endemic to the system of EU law. Negative law, in particular that driven by the functional concern to complete the inter-nal market across the whole sweep of economic activity pursued in the EU,

[29] *Walrave and Koch* (n 14).
[30] See G Ubertazzi, 'Le domaine du droit communautaire. A propos de l'arrêt Walrave, Union cycliste internationale' [1976] RTDE 635.

reaches further and wider than positive law underpinned by the EU's conferred legislative competence. In consequence, policy of sorts must be shaped in the application and interpretation of the Treaty's free movement and competition rules in circumstances where the Treaty offers little or no guidance as to the EU's policy-making priorities.

All this is supplemented by the constitutional character of EU law. From the very beginning, in landmark judgments delivered in the early 1960s, the Court has sought, with extraordinary success, to distance EU law from orthodox public international law governing the effects of Treaties within national legal orders, both rhetorically and in substance. It insists that EU law is *supreme*—it applies in preference to national law in the event of conflict.[31] It also stipulates that EU law is *directly effective*, which means that rules of sufficient clarity and precision fall to be applied on an everyday basis by the national courts of the Member States.[32] None of this is made explicit in the Treaty: it is the product of the Court's adventurous interpretative approach. Article 19(1) TEU dictates that Member States shall provide remedies sufficient to ensure effective legal protection in the fields covered by Union law, but even this is no more than a recent codification of the Court's long-standing interpretative approach.[33] Moreover, the Court of Justice and the national courts are organically tied together in a cooperative relationship by a procedure that is foreseen explicitly in the Treaties, the preliminary reference procedure contained in Article 267 TFEU which permits, and in some circumstances requires, awkward points of EU law raised at national level to be transmitted by national judges to the Court for authoritative resolution. Exploration of the philosophical foundations of this process and the type of legal order that has emerged are fascinating;[34] so too is investigation of the complex combination of incentives at national and EU level that have nourished and sustained it.[35] But this agenda stretches beyond the ambitions of this book. For present purposes the point is predominantly practical. The combined effect of the constitutional principles nurtured by the Court is that EU law exerts a much more powerful and immediate influence over the shaping of national law and practice than does orthodox public international law. EU law is in many respects not only international law but also national law. The legal order of the EU is much more deeply integrated into national legal practice than is the case for orthodox international treaties and the legal orders of states that are party to them. The Court has long aimed to have EU law treated as something new—as international law but as something more, something that directly controls aspects of the course of domestic legal proceedings. What this means for the practical vindication of rights conferred by EU law to challenge sporting practices is immensely

---

[31] Case 6/64 *Costa v ENEL* [1964] ECR 585.
[32] Case 26/62 *Van Gend en Loos* [1963] ECR 1.   [33] Weatherill (n 3) ch 4.5.
[34] eg M Avbelj and J Komárek, *Constitutional Pluralism in the European Union and Beyond* (Hart 2012).
[35] eg K Alter, *The European Court's Political Power* (OUP 2009); M Everson and J Eisner, *The Making of a European Constitution: Judges and Law beyond Constitutive Power* (Routledge Cavendish 2007); G Martinico and O Pollicino, *The Interaction between Europe's Legal Systems: Judicial Dialogue and the Creation of Supranational Laws* (Edward Elgar 2012).

significant. It means that litigation before the ordinary courts of the Member States designed to protect EU law rights is perfectly feasible and normal. This is quite separate from and supplementary to the role of the Commission in prosecuting violations of EU law, if necessary by bringing proceedings before the Court of Justice. The main interest of this book is EU sports law, but in the background is the distinctive constitutional flavour of EU law.

3.5 Positive Law—the Competence Conferred by Article 165 TFEU

According to the principle of conferral expressed in Article 5(1) TEU, the EU possesses only the competences and powers which are conferred on it by its Treaties. The EU has enjoyed a conferred competence to act in the field of sport since 2009, the date of entry into force of the Treaty of Lisbon. This is declared in Article 6(e) TFEU and elaborated in Article 165 TFEU.

Article 6 TFEU declares that the Union shall have competence to carry out actions to support, coordinate, or supplement the actions of the Member States in several listed areas, one of which is sport, which appears in Article 6(e) TFEU in the company of education, vocational training, and youth.

Article 165 TFEU is one of two Treaty articles (along with Article 166 TFEU) which make up Title XII of Part Three of the Treaty on the Functioning of the European Union, under the title 'Education, Vocational training, youth and sport'. Filleted of content pertaining to education in order to bring into focus what Article 165 does for sport, it reads:

1. … The Union shall contribute to the promotion of European sporting issues, while taking account of the specific nature of sport, its structures based on voluntary activity and its social and educational function.
2. Union action shall be aimed at: … developing the European dimension in sport, by promoting fairness and openness in sporting competitions and cooperation between bodies responsible for sports, and by protecting the physical and moral integrity of sportsmen and sportswomen, especially the youngest sportsmen and sportswomen.
3. The Union and the Member States shall foster cooperation with third countries and the competent international organisations in the field of education and sport, in particular the Council of Europe.
4. In order to contribute to the achievement of the objectives referred to in this Article: the European Parliament and the Council, acting in accordance with the ordinary legislative procedure, after consulting the Economic and Social Committee and the Committee of the Regions, shall adopt incentive measures, excluding any harmonisation of the laws and regulations of the Member States; the Council, on a proposal from the Commission, shall adopt recommendations.

This is and has been since December 2009 the sport-specific competence conferred on the EU. Sport is not mentioned anywhere else in the EU Treaties. Articles 6(e) and 165 TFEU are the only references to it.

The carefully limited scope of Article 165 is best understood by contrasting it with legislative competences granted elsewhere by the TFEU. The EU possesses some conferred legislative competences that are, unlike Article 165, remarkably broad in their scope. This is true in particular of two provisions. Article 114 TFEU permits harmonization of national laws as a means to improve the functioning of the internal market. It is not sector-specific: any type of national practice may in principle be harmonized at EU level provided only that it contributes to promoting market integration, typically by replacing regulatory fragmentation at national level with a common EU regime. Article 352 TFEU is similarly functionally, not sectorally, driven. It envisages action by the EU to attain the objectives set out in the Treaties, in so far as the necessary powers are not granted elsewhere in the Treaties. As a legislative competence, Article 165 TFEU on sport is emphatically *not* of this broad type.

In fact most of the sector-specific legislative competences that have been added to the EU's armoury, beginning with the first major revision of the founding Treaties in 1987 effected by the Single European Act, are typically drawn with more care and caution than Articles 114 and 352 TFEU. They betray an anxiety on the part of the Member States to equip the EU with the competence to act to address sector-specific problems which they share in common but also to rein in the exact scope and reach of that competence, in order to preserve room for state autonomy. Articles 167, 168, and 169 TFEU are good examples of this model. These provisions, addressing culture, public health, and consumer protection respectively, were added to the Treaty with effect from 1993 as a result of the amendments made by the Maastricht Treaty. Each, in slightly different and subtle ways, confines the vitality of the EU as an actor in the relevant fields, thereby preserving ample room for national action. Harmonization of culture, public health policy, and consumer protection pursuant to these Treaty provisions is excluded. Instruments available to the EU's institutions are predominantly limited to incentive and supporting measures. Social policy, under Articles 151 to 161 TFEU, is another politically highly contested field, where reservations about the extent of the role to be played by the EU have led to several types of carefully drawn constraint being locked into the Treaty. Relevant techniques include detailed limitation of the material scope of conferred competence, restricting available legal instruments of which the EU may make use, locating EU intervention at the level of setting only minimum standards, and, in some areas of particular sensitivity, providing that the applicable voting rule in Council is hard-to-achieve unanimity. The narrative tells of EU legislative competence that is carefully *controlled* by the Member States. Article 165 TFEU on sport is very much of this cautious and controlled character, except also that the autonomy that is to be to a certain degree preserved is not only that of the public authorities in the Member State but also that of the private associations that typically run sport.

In fact, the scope of Article 165, on close inspection, is both restricted and obscure. Although the *fact* of sport's addition to the list of EU competences is undeniably important as a constitutional landmark, the detailed content of this competence newly granted by the Member States to the EU is far less remarkable. In fact, the most striking aspect is not the fact that the EU has been granted an explicit role for the first time but rather that that role is drafted in terms which are both *cautiously narrow* and *calculatedly vague*.

It is in the first place important to note that there is created only a supporting competence for the EU, the weakest form of the three principal types of competence mapped in Title I of Part One of the TFEU. The basic competence descriptor found in Article 6(e) TFEU locates the Union as an entity with competence 'to carry out actions to support, coordinate or supplement the actions of the Member States'. The EU is granted a subordinate role. Moreover, Article 165 TFEU is drafted to stress that the Union shall do no more than 'contribute' to the promotion of European sporting issues. And though legislation may be adopted, it is confined to 'incentive measures, excluding any harmonisation'. This *cautiously narrow* formula is designed to reassure those who fear the rise of the EU as a sports regulator.

The *calculatedly vague* aspects of Article 165 focus on its embrace of 'the specific nature of sport' and 'the European dimension in sport'. Quite what these notions entail is not at all clear. It is an open question whether they are intended to convey anything different from the practice accumulated before 2009 in the decision-making of the Court and the Commission when applying internal market law, which is examined in depth in the next two chapters. The vocabulary chosen by the Lisbon Treaty is at least capable of being read in the light of the pre-existing practice of the Court and the Commission. It will be explained in Chapters 4 and 5 that the pre-2009 case law dealing with the internal market is readily understood with hindsight in the light of Article 165's stipulations, while so far since 2009 the Court has resisted reading internal market law any differently simply because of the rise of Article 165. In fact it has treated Article 165 TFEU as a corroboration of its case law.[36]

This openness is deliberate. Article 165 TFEU was drafted in order to reflect, but not to pin down in concrete or unambiguous form, sporting ambitions for autonomy, but precisely what is at stake—which extends only to conditional, not absolute, autonomy—requires the elaboration of institutional practice. In particular Article 165, inserted with effect from December 2009 by the amending Treaty of Lisbon, represents the failure of the strategy of securing complete insulation of sporting autonomy from the impact of EU law. Instead it is the product of adoption by the 'sports lobby' of a second best strategy, one of inclusion rather than exclusion but on terms which permit sport's special concerns to be written into the Treaty. This will be explained more fully in Chapter 6. The consequence is that sports governing bodies must pursue the interpretative or adjudicative route to protecting their interests and their autonomy.

---

[36] Case C-325/08 *Olympique Lyonnais v Olivier Bernard, Newcastle United* [2010] ECR I-2177. See Ch 7.2.

That—as previously mentioned and as elaborated in Chapters 4 and 5—is largely the position reached under internal market law long before 2009. Indeed it was exactly the failure of the strategy of exclusion under internal market law, coupled to the inability to secure a reversal at political level through Treaty revision, that finally and grudgingly brought sport to accept the strategy of conditional inclusion of which Article 165 TFEU represents the ambiguous culmination. For the future one would expect to see the vocabulary of Article 165 as a frame for the long-standing debate about how to resolve the tension between EU law's claim to exercise a supervisory jurisdiction and the desire of sporting bodies to achieve some degree of autonomy. Chapter 7 tracks the evolving narrative and argues for an integrated EU sports law built on the recognition of the specific nature of sport which is mandated by Article 165 TFEU. Chapter 12 pulls together the threads.

The arrival of Article 165 in the Treaties with effect from 2009 put to an end any claim that EU law has no connection with sport. The EU's role in the field of sport is legitimated. It leaves open the precise nature of that connection, while preparing the ground for debate about how to manage the tension between sporting autonomy and EU law. In particular, what is the 'specific nature' of sport heralded by Article 165 TFEU? What is the nature of the conditional autonomy granted by EU law to the *lex sportiva*? These are the questions that will help to illuminate just how special sport truly is, and how that is reflected in the interpretation of legal rules.

3.6 An EU Law and Policy on Sport?

Against this constitutional background, it is important to appreciate that even to discuss the prospects for an *EU law and policy on sport* is to risk skating on thin ice.

In fact the invitation to pursue an *EU law and policy on sport* immediately faces three challenges. Is it coherent to seek a role for the *EU* in developing a law and policy on sport? Is it coherent to suppose that the EU is able to deliver a *law and policy* on sport? And it is coherent to imagine that an EU law and policy is able to address *sport*?

The first issue, that pertaining to the role of the EU, is awkward because no sport is organized in such a way as to treat the EU as even relevant. Sports are in general organized under a globally applicable regime, beneath which lie continental and national federations and, lower still, clubs from the professional level down to the 'grass roots'. There is simply no place in this governance 'pyramid' for the EU. Moreover, there is no EU representative team in *any* sport. The EU flag flutters proudly at golf's Ryder Cup, but opportunistically so, since it is the continent of Europe, not the EU, which competes against the United States in that biennial extravaganza, and in most events there is no presence for the EU at all. The EU's quest to build an internal market without frontiers, which converts the territories of its twenty-eight Member States into a single economic space, has no resonance at all with the structure and ambition of sport. So the EU stands accused of clumsy engagement with an activity into which its assumptions, even its very identity and purpose, simply do not fit.

The second issue takes this scepticism about the legitimate role of the EU further. The creation of a *law and policy* requires the availability of competences and powers apt to deliver such a law and policy. As already outlined, the EU has only the competences and powers conferred on it by its founding Treaties—no more. This is Article 5 TEU's foundationally important principle of conferral. Until the entry into force of the Lisbon Treaty in 2009, sport was not even mentioned in the text of those Treaties, and even now, since the Lisbon Treaty, the provision dealing with sport, Article 165 TFEU, is pitched at a level of generality which does not promise concrete guidance. In particular, the EU's constitutional limitations dictate that it tends to be much more heavily engaged in the negative task of deciding what sport may *not* do when put to the test under EU free movement and competition law than with making positive provision for what should be done. Up until 2009 it was doing so without any help from the Treaties: since 2009 it has some help, but not much. The EU is therefore working with thin and ambiguous materials when it contemplates the construction of a law and policy on sport. It has good reason to be modest in its ambition. Its competences are tightly confined and the powers at its disposal, though apt to spill over into soft law beyond the narrow grant of binding legislative powers and embracing the 'social dialogue' foreseen by Articles 154 and 155 TFEU too, are also relatively meagre.

The third issue asks whether it is sensible for the EU (or, for that matter, any other rule-maker) to seek to construct a law and policy on *sport* rather than *sports*. Sport has many different manifestations. Amateur and recreational sport is quite distinct in its motivations and effects from professional sport. Sports may be individual, they may be team: they may be classic tests of 'higher, stronger, faster', they may be more graceful and artistic. Addressing 'sport' risks trying to make one size fit all. The particular criticism of the EU has long been that it has tended to focus on football most of all and, to a lesser extent, on Formula 1 as if they are the sports that provide a model that all others do or should follow. No doubt the economic significance of these two sports is a reason for their prominence. No doubt too that the more commercially significant sports have a particular incentive to dress themselves in the clothes of fair play, tolerance, and a healthy lifestyle as part of a strategy to strengthen their claims to deserve autonomy. But a policy agenda that lacks nuance in appreciating the diversity of 'sport' is not simply misguided, it is potentially harmful.

A helpful way to collect together these reservations is to ask whether the EU is really able to *add value* to the regulation of sport or whether instead it gets in the way of the legitimate activities of sports federations and governing bodies and applicable national and international legal rules.

These three reservations about an *EU law and policy on sport* frame the inquiry. They caution modesty. But they do not foreclose the importance of conducting that inquiry.

The central—and, notwithstanding the three aforementioned reservations, inescapable—question asks how far 'sport is special'. That then leads to an exploration into how that special character, once identified, should be reflected in the application of legal rules. That is true of inquiry into sports law in *any* jurisdiction. In the EU, however, an extra dimension is added: that the EU that has no general regulatory competence, but rather only the mandate granted by its Treaties, which is most of all Article 165 TFEU plus the commitment to creating an internal market.

In a sense, as already suggested in Chapter 1, this is an inquiry into the intersection of two forms of sports 'law'—the legal rules to which sports bodies are subjected (by states and by regional actors such as the EU) and the rules which sports bodies themselves create (the *lex sportiva*). It is, put another way, a friction between 'external' and 'internal' sports law. The quest is for an intellectually coherent framework as an essential pre-condition to detailed decision-making about just when sport has made a sufficiently compelling case to deserve some degree of autonomy from the normal assumptions of the legal rules of the jurisdiction to which it is in principle subject. And that autonomy will be delivered, if at all, through an interpretation of those legal rules which is sensitive to sport's special character—what Article 165 TFEU calls its 'specific nature'.

So, from the perspective of sports governing bodies, there are good economic and political reasons why sporting autonomy should be effectively protected. But are there good legal reasons? This is the general challenge of sports law—how far should we accept that sport is special, and how should we then allow this to affect the application of the 'ordinary' legal rules. How strong is the intellectual case? This occurs against a background in which typically and inevitably sports bodies come to court pushing for an interpretation of the law that maximizes their autonomy. The institutions of the EU, most of all the Court and the Commission, must then seek to piece together a coherent approach to the regulation of sport against a Treaty background which is not at all dedicated to elucidating the peculiarities of sport. EU law plainly erodes the self-regulatory paradigm which has for so long been dominant in sports governance. But to what effect, good or ill? Does the EU add value?

This has generated a rich literature covering the shaping of *EU law and policy on sport*, both in book-length treatment[37] and articles[38] and in more general political

---

[37] eg R Parrish, *Sports Law and Policy in the European Union* (Manchester University Press 2003); S Weatherill, *European Sports Law* (2nd edn, TMC Asser 2014); B Bogusz, A Cygan, and E Szyszczak (eds), *The Regulation of Sport in the European Union* (Edward Elgar 2007); R Parrish and S Miettinen, *The Sporting Exception in European Law* (TMC Asser 2007); J Anderson, *Modern Sports Law: A Textbook* (Hart 2010) chs 1 and 8; B Van Rompuy, 'Economic Efficiency: The Sole Concern of Modern Antitrust Policy?' (Wolters Kluwer 2012) especially ch 5; M Mataija, *Private Regulation and the Internal Market: Sports, Legal Services, and Standard Setting in EU Economic Law* (OUP 2016) especially ch V.
[38] eg S Van den Bogaert and A Vermeersch, 'Sport and the European Treaty: A Tale of Uneasy Bedfellows' (2006) 31 EL Rev 821; S Weatherill, '"Fair Play Please!": Recent Developments in the Application of EC Law to Sport' (2003) 40 CML Rev 51; R Parrish, 'Lex Sportiva and EU Sports Law' (2012) 37 EL Rev 716; A Duval, 'Lex Sportiva: A Playground for Transnational Law' (2013) 19 ELJ 822.

science literature which emphasizes the interaction of the several actors, the pattern of prevailing interests, and the strategies employed to protect and promote particular preferences.[39] Questions that are familiar within this thematic inquiry will be encountered in the detailed analysis provided chapter-by-chapter in this book, and Chapter 12, the concluding chapter, will tie the exploration together.

[39] eg L Barani, 'The Role of the European Court of Justice as a Political Actor in the Integration Process: The Case of Sport Regulation after the Bosman Ruling' (2005) 1 JCER 42; D Dimitrakopoulos, 'More than a Market? The Regulation of Sports in the EU' (2006) 41 Government and Opposition 561; B García and H Meier, 'Limits of Interest Empowerment in the European Union: The Case of Football' (2012) 34 European Integration 359; A Geeraert, J Scheerder, and H Bruyninckx, 'The Governance Network of European Football: Introducing New Governance Approaches to Steer Football at the EU Level' (2013) 5 International Journal of Sport Policy and Politics 113; A Geeraert and E Drieskens, 'The EU controls FIFA and UEFA: A Principal-agent Perspective' (2015) 22 JEPP 1448.

4

Sport in the Internal Market

Free Movement Law

4.1 Introduction

Chapter 3 set out the framework of EU law. The constitutional starting point is the principle of conferral contained in Article 5 of the Treaty on European Union (TEU), which seems to promise restraint in the subjection of sport to EU law. It declares that the EU may do no more than its Treaties mandate. However, the practice is rather different because even though the EU Treaties conferred no explicit competence to act in the field of sport until 2009, and even though since then the relevant directions in Article 165 of the Treaty on the Functioning of the European Union (TFEU) are written with caution, the EU's institutions have, since the 1970s, intervened in the field of sport in so far as practices affect the creation and functioning of the EU's internal market. Article 26 TFEU defines the internal market as an 'area without internal frontiers in which the free movement of goods, persons, services and capital is ensured in accordance with the provisions of this Treaty', and sporting practices, like practices in any other field, may collide with the aim of creating a single trading area stretching across the territory of all twenty-eight Member States, in which national political frontiers shall be of no economic relevance. The question is whether, in the interpretation and application of EU internal market law, justice has been done to sport's special features.

The story told in this chapter is of how sporting bodies have attempted to maximize their autonomy in the face of EU internal market law, and how first the Court of Justice, as the authoritative voice of the law, and then subsequently the Commission have grappled with the strength of these claims. It is free movement law which forms the focus of this chapter. Competition law is the subject of treatment in Chapter 5. The first question to address is whether, in principle, EU internal market law may apply to sport *at all*, and then, given that the EU's institutions have consistently given 'yes' as the answer to this question, the second and more complex question is how far, if at all, the special features of sport should guide the interpretation and application of EU internal market law to sporting practices. At stake is a quest to determine how EU law mediates between its own claim to exercise authority over sporting bodies active on its territory and the claimed legitimacy of the rules which sports bodies themselves create (the *lex sportiva*). A model of 'conditional autonomy' under EU law emerges: sporting bodies have room to protect and preserve their special concerns *on condition that* they demonstrate how and why EU law should be open to the accommodation of such characteristics.

The explanatory narrative traces the way in which the Court and the Commission developed an approach over the extended period lasting until 2009 in which sport was not even mentioned in the EU's governing Treaties. The more recent entry into force of the Lisbon Treaty gives a new vocabulary to the legal analysis and puts to an end any possibility of denying in principle that sport is any of the EU's business. But there is no indication that the Lisbon Treaty has changed the rules of the game. Quite the reverse: it simply provides a new form of vocabulary apt to explore how EU internal market law and the *lex sportiva* shall co-exist. Article 165 TFEU directs that the EU 'shall contribute to the promotion of European sporting issues, while taking account of the specific nature of sport' and that EU action shall be aimed at 'developing the European dimension in sport, by promoting fairness and openness in sporting competitions and cooperation between bodies responsible for sports, and by protecting the physical and moral integrity of sportsmen and sportswomen, especially the youngest sportsmen and sportswomen'. Even though this is not explicitly stated to apply beyond Article 165 TFEU, in contrast to provisions such as Articles 11 and 12 TFEU which make explicit that requirements of environmental and consumer protection (respectively) shall be woven into the definition and implementation of Union policies activities, there is no reason to doubt that it is correct to make such interconnection also in the case of sport. In fact, before 2009, exactly that connection had been frequently made by both Court and Commission and since 2009 that pattern has been maintained. And this is exactly the point. The Lisbon vocabulary may be new but the thematic questions which are arising are not new at all. The clock of EU sports law was not re-set in 2009. This is explained more fully in Chapter 7.

The concern here is not the legislative institutions (Council and Parliament) setting common EU rules that dictate the terms on which sport shall be organized, but rather the Court and the Commission establishing what may *not* be done in the field of sport, in so far as it collides with internal market law, most of all free movement and competition law. The legislative context is the subject of Chapter 6. However, there is thematic linkage between this chapter and Chapter 5, which traverse internal market law, and Chapter 6 on the legislative context. In all three chapters the story is one of how a strategy of seeking exclusion from EU law has proved ultimately inadequate to meet the aspirations of sporting bodies and how instead sporting bodies moved to a strategy of inclusion. The Treaty of Lisbon, and the insertion of Article 165 TFEU, represents the most visible manifestation of this trend, but it is already apparent in the development of EU internal market law as applied to sport. In fact, it is the failure of a strategy of exclusion before the Court and Commission that is a major reason explaining the retreat to a strategy of (conditional) inclusion within the Treaty superstructure. So, as will be explored further in Chapter 6, Article 165 TFEU is not simply a codification-of-sorts of the lesson drawn from EU internal market law that sport is to some extent special (but not as special as sports bodies commonly claim), in fact Article 165 TFEU owes its very existence to the appreciation of sports bodies that internal market law could not and would not grant them the highest level of autonomy for which they yearned. Chapter 7 then brings together the story told in this chapter (free movement law), Chapter 5 (competition law), and Chapter 6 (the conferral of a sports-specific competence on the EU) to present an integrated account of EU sports law as a programme of conditional autonomy.

4.2 The First Step: *Walrave and Koch*

Walrave and Koch, a case decided in 1974, offered the Court of Justice its first opportunity to consider how, if at all, EU law interacts with the practices of sporting associations.[1]

The sport in question was esoteric: it was paced cycling. Teams in this sport are made up of a cyclist who is supported by, and rides in the lee of, a pacemaker on a motorcycle. The applicants, Walrave and Koch, were Dutch. They were pacemakers. They were professional. But the Union Cycliste Internationale (UCI), the sport's governing body, decided that with effect from 1973 the pacemaker in the world championships must be of the same nationality as the cyclist. This damaged the professional opportunities available to the applicants and they challenged the rule change as a violation of EU law. They brought an action before a court in Utrecht, relying on the directly effective vigour of EU law. At the time, the Treaty clearly prohibited any discrimination on the basis of nationality. This prohibition was then contained in Article 7 of the Treaty Establishing the European Economic Community (EEC). Its successor today is Article 18 TFEU, and it is in all material respects identical. So surely Walrave and Koch were obvious victims of unlawful discrimination on grounds of nationality?

The twist is that the relevant Treaty provision directed then, and still directs today, that the prohibition of discrimination on grounds of nationality applies only within the scope of application of the Treaties. This is no more than an explicit and specific statement of the general rule in EU law that its bite is felt only within areas in which the EU enjoys competences and powers conferred by its Treaties. This is the principle of conferral, found today in Article 5 TEU, carefully examined in Chapter 3.2. So the question that was most enticing in *Walrave and Koch* was how the Court would deal with the confinement of EU law to the scope of application of the Treaties, which at the time did not mention sport at all. This was the question of principle which the Court was asked to address in a preliminary reference made by the court in Utrecht before which Walrave and Koch had raised their objection to the practices of the UCI. In reflecting on the practical significance of the ruling which the court was asked to give, one might be forgiven for thinking that the world championships for paced cycling are of only niche interest, but it is plain that the issue of whether a sports governing body may confine participation in championship events to teams composed of participants possessing the same nationality has

---

[1] Case 36/74 *Walrave and Koch v Union Cycliste International* [1974] ECR 1405.

immense consequences. If it may *not*, it is the end of football's World Cup, among other competitions enjoying a considerably higher profile than paced cycling.

The astute reader will immediately recognize that the Court did not reach such a cataclysmic conclusion. The football World Cup still exists, more than four decades later. The real interest in the ruling is *how* the Court negotiated a route between, on the one hand, the application of the foundational principle of EU law that condemns discrimination on grounds of nationality and, on the other, the nationality-based links that characterize the very nature of top-level international representative team sport. And, to look beyond this particular context, the *structure* of the arguments pressed on the Court in *Walrave and Koch* in 1974 still resonates today—sports governing bodies typically seek to find methods to exclude or, if not, to limit the incursion of EU law on to their territory. The extent to which they are successful dictates just how far EU law is willing to accept that sport is 'special'.

In *Walrave and Koch* the Court rejected the claim that because sport went unmentioned in the EU's founding Treaties it is simply none of the EU's business. The scope of EU law, and the practical significance of the principle of conferral, is broad because it is driven by the functional concern to achieve an economically integrated market for the EU. The objective to break down obstacles to inter-state trade 'in order to merge the national markets into a single market bringing about conditions as close as possible to those of a genuine internal market'[2] means that any economic activity, irrespective of its precise form, which is conducted in such a way as to defeat that purpose is caught by EU law. As the applicants pressed on the Court: 'By reason of the importance, in this sphere of sport, of a world title, this clause seriously limits their professional activity'.[3] The UCI's rules discriminated on the grounds of nationality in such a way as to limit opportunities and thereby to cause economic harm to providers of pacing services.

This reasoning is convincing and it persuaded the Court. In a formula which stands as the first statement of how and why sport is subjected to EU law it declared that:

Having regard to the objectives of the Community, the practice of sport is subject to Community law only in so far as it constitutes an economic activity within the meaning of Article 2 of the Treaty.[4]

What is today Union law rather than Community law applies to sport *only* in so far as it constitutes an economic activity—but sport is commonly and easily found to constitute an economic activity. The Court's formula is apt to exclude purely recreational activities from the scope of application of EU law, but according to this formula professional sport falls comfortably within the scope of EU law. It is an economic activity, just as making sausages and cars and selling financial services count as economic activities. And it is therefore subject to the rule against discrimination on grounds of nationality.

---

[2] Case 15/81 *Gaston Schul* [1982] ECR 1409, para 33; Case C-312/91 *Metalsa* [1993] ECR I-3751, para 15.
[3] *Walrave and Koch* (n 1) 1416.   [4] ibid judgment, para 4.

However, sport, though an economic activity, is not *only* an economic activity. It has a social and cultural resonance that transcends sausage- or car-making or the provision of financial services. Of more specific relevance to the governance of sport and so to its legal assessment, were producers of sausages or of cars or sellers of financial services to get together and determine the conditions that should regulate their activities on a global scale they would expect to find themselves swiftly condemned for severely anti-competitive activities. Sport is different. The very nature of sport is that it is subject to common rules which apply globally. Sport is special. And moreover sport has rules which reflect a character that is not to be found in normal industries. One such rule concerns the criteria governing the selection of national representative teams, which simply does not arise in the car or the sausage or the financial services sector. Sport is special.

In *Walrave and Koch* the Court captured this notion in enigmatic fashion. It stated that EU law's prohibition of nationality-based discrimination 'does not affect the composition of sport teams, in particular national teams, the formation of which is a question of purely sporting interest and as such has nothing to do with economic activity'.[5] The Court's formula is as fascinating as it is evasive. It is evidently a protection of sorts for certain rules, but it is ill-defined. The next paragraph in the ruling reveals the Court's anxiety lest this concession to sporting autonomy be pushed too far. It added that the 'restriction on the scope of the provisions in question must however remain limited to its proper objective'.[6]

The Court's formula is readily interpreted as a push to the national court to find that rules affecting 'the composition of sport teams, in particular national teams' do not offend against EU law. That, indeed, is how the ruling was interpreted. No one sought to relieve West Germany of the football World Cup they had lifted six months earlier on the basis that they had violated EU law by refusing to pick any Belgians or Danes. The jurisdictional point is that where economic activity is not engaged, then EU law is not engaged either. This makes perfect constitutional sense in the abstract. It is to apply the principle of conferral, today found in Article 5 TEU. The matter is outside the conferred competences to which the EU is able to lay claim where there is nothing associated with economic activity at stake. The awkward twist, however, is that it is plainly absurd to claim, as the Court in *Walrave and Koch* did claim, that the rule involves 'a question of purely sporting interest and as such has nothing to do with economic activity'.[7] International football is big business. Players enhance their profile and popularity, and therefore their earning potential, as a result of their exposure as international footballers. Restricting selection for national teams has direct and important economic consequences. A footballer able to play for, say, Spain or Germany in the World Cup will obtain clear and large advantages from the consequent worldwide exposure, of interest to employers and to sponsors, when compared with one eligible only to play for Andorra or Malta.[8] And Walrave and Koch themselves would obviously

---

[5] ibid para 8.   [6] ibid para 9.   [7] ibid para 8.
[8] cf 'Gareth Bale would have Made Millions if Real Madrid Star had Picked England over Wales, says agent Jonathan Barnett' *The Independent* (London, 8 September 2015) <http://www.independent.

have suffered financially by being restricted to pacing only Dutch cyclists in world championship events. This, in fact, was precisely why they had brought the matter before a court.[9]

The Court's ruling was important in the general sweep of EU law for it emphasized the Treaty's broad material scope, which is triggered by identification of economic activity.[10] But, as far as the particular case of sport was concerned, it was on the wrong track in groping for rules that involve 'purely sporting interest', with no association to economic activity. It is, in truth, hard to imagine such a rule, given the ubiquitous character of economic activity. Rules governing selection for national teams are sporting rules but at the same time they are *also* rules with an association to economic activity. What is really at stake is not a group of sporting rules and a separate group of economic rules, but rather a group of sporting rules which carry economic implications and which therefore fall for assessment, but not necessarily condemnation, under EU trade law. This is the core of the thesis that EU law and 'internal' sports law, the *lex sportiva*, cannot be kept separate. And it is what the Court missed, or preferred to avoid, in *Walrave and Koch*.

Unfortunately EU sports law was sent by *Walrave and Koch* in search of a red herring: a question of purely sporting interest which as such has nothing to do with economic activity. Most—almost all—sporting practices have something to do with economic activity. Few—hardly any—are *purely* sporting. *Walrave and Koch* is flawed in assuming a separation between sport and the economy which is at best fiendishly hard to make and at worst implausible. Better to treat sporting rules as economic in effect—but to find some means within EU law to protect those that truly define the nature of the activity. Eventually the Court would get to this solution, which entails a case-by-case inspection of the compatibility of sporting practices with EU law, but it would take it over thirty years: this is elucidated in Chapter 5.[11]

The Court in *Walrave and Koch* felt able to deal relatively easily with the other devices deployed which were designed to protect sporting autonomy. It held that the relevant Treaty provisions were not confined to restrictions which have their origin in acts of a public authority. Prohibition of discrimination 'extends likewise to rules of any other nature aimed at regulating in a collective manner gainful employment and the provision of services'.[12] On this point *Walrave and Koch* set the tone and is important in the general development of EU law governing the personal scope of the economic freedoms guaranteed by the Treaty, not simply in the field of

---

co.uk/sport/football/international/gareth-bale-would-have-made-millions-if-real-madrid-star-had-picked-england-over-wales-says-agent-10492331.html> accessed 29 November 2016. Bale is Welsh but, thanks to an English grandmother, could have chosen to play football for England instead.

[9] The Opinion of Warner AG in the case makes this clear.

[10] This was stressed at the time by G Ubertazzi, 'Le domaine du droit communautaire. A propos de l'arrêt Walrave, Union cycliste internationale' (1976) RTDE 635.

[11] Case C-519/04P *Meca-Medina and Majcen v Commission* [2006] ECR I-6991. Also on this trajectory, see R Parrish, 'Case 36/74 *Walrave and Koch*' in J Anderson (ed), *Leading Cases in Sports Law* (TMC Asser 2013) ch 3.

[12] *Walrave and Koch* (n 1) para 17.

sports law.[13] The Court asserted that this interpretation, apt to cover private parties, was necessary, for otherwise, were EU law confined to public bodies, 'the abolition of barriers of national origin could be neutralized by obstacles resulting from the exercise of their legal autonomy by associations or organizations which do not come under public law';[14] and it added that given that 'working conditions in the various Member States are governed sometimes by means of provisions laid down by law or regulation and sometimes by agreements and other acts concluded or adopted by private persons, to limit the prohibitions in question to acts of a public authority would risk creating inequality in their application'.[15] This reasoning has been used by the Court in cases remote from sport to subject to control the practices of bodies such as trade unions[16] and bodies that set rules for professions[17] which tend to obstruct the free movement of workers and services.

Moreover, the observation that the activities of a sporting federation are typically worldwide did not deter the Court from asserting subjection to EU law. It found that the rule on non-discrimination applies to all relationships where 'by reason either of the place where they are entered into or of the place where they take effect, [they] can be located within the territory of the Community'.[18] This is immensely important. The Court here asserts that the intersection of a regional system of law, that of the EU, with a global system, the *lex sportiva*, does not mean that the geographically less extensive regime must retreat. This is perfectly logical from the point of view of EU law. Were it otherwise, there would be a fragmentation of law within the EU: some industries would be subject to EU law, others would escape it purely because of their capacity to claim a global reach. In fact, this would be counter-intuitive, for the *more* powerful actor would be subject to reduced legal supervision when compared with the less powerful. However, seen not from the perspective of EU law but rather from that of sports governing bodies, this intrusion into the *lex sportiva* is exactly the source of pained frustration and friction. How—a sports body will ask—can we organize globally if we have to adjust locally?

This is the very heart of the intellectual case for inquiring into the worth of sporting autonomy. In *Walrave and Koch* the Court adopted a flawed analytical formula—the rule of purely sporting interest—from which, as explained later, it would eventually resile. But the wider framework within which it chose to operate has proved enduring. It refused to grant autonomy in principle from the reach of EU law, but in the interpretation and application of EU law it showed sensitivity to the special character and purpose of sport. So sporting bodies can rarely appeal to absolute autonomy from the application of EU law, but they have room to show that their subjection to EU law is on terms that reflect sport's peculiarities. This forms the core of the interpretative or adjudicative strategy for securing sporting

---

[13] See S Weatherill, *The Internal Market as a Legal Concept* (OUP 2017) ch 7.
[14] *Walrave and Koch* (n 1) para 18.   [15] ibid para 19.
[16] Case C-438/05 *Viking Line* [2007] ECR I-10779; Case C-341/05 *Laval* [2007] ECR I-11767.
[17] Case C-309/99 *JCJ Wouters, JW Savelbergh, Price Waterhouse Belastingadviseurs BV v Algemene Raad van de Nederlandse Orde van Advocaten* [2002] ECR I-1577.
[18] *Walrave and Koch* (n 1) para 28.

autonomy from the law. Nationality discrimination is for good reason outlawed across the wide sweep of economic activities within the EU, both because it operates to the detriment of creating an efficient structure for a unified EU market and because it deprives individuals of an important aspect of their right to equality. But sport is special. Nationality discrimination has a legitimate role to play. It defines the very character of international team competition.

Two years later, in 1976, the Court confirmed its approach in *Donà v Mantero*.[19] This was a preliminary reference concerning rules of the Italian Football Federation which limited eligibility to players of Italian nationality. The Court simply repeated what it had stated in *Walrave and Koch*. EU law's prohibitions may be disabled where exclusion is based on reasons which are not of an economic nature, which relate to the particular nature and context of such matches, and are of sporting interest only. This was no more satisfactory than the formula offered in *Walrave and Koch* two years earlier. But the ruling offered no amplification and the Court left the matter to be disposed of in detail by the referring Italian court.

Things then went very quiet. From the mid-1970s through to the 1990s EU sports law retreated into the background, a matter of niche interest without practical significance. Here and there a self-indulgent academic writer claimed to find intellectual intrigue in the potential collision of EU internal market law and the organization of sport.[20] But there was no practical bite.

4.3 *Bosman* Changed Everything

For almost twenty years after *Walrave and Koch* and *Donà v Mantero* in the mid-1970s the Court of Justice was not faced by any sports-related cases. This was not simply a matter of chance. That gap in time reveals the power with which sports bodies are able to resist 'ordinary law'. Challenging governing bodies in sport is no trivial task. A sporting career is short. Litigation is typically lengthy. The powers of sports bodies are immense and they are global in their reach. The cost of challenging them is likely to be high, both financially and professionally. A bad tackle can end a sportsman's career. Suing the sport's governing body carries the risk of equally devastating effects. Walrave and Koch themselves declined to pursue their complaint any further, apparently in the face of a threat by the defendant sporting body, the UCI, to withdraw their event from the world cycling championship

---

[19] Case 13/76 [1976] ECR 1333.

[20] eg S Weatherill, 'Discrimination on Grounds of Nationality in Sport' (1989) 9 YEL 55. In S Weatherill, 'The *Lex Sportiva* and EU Law: The Academic Lawyer's Path Before and After Bosman' in A Duval and B Van Rompuy (eds), *The Legacy of Bosman: Revisiting the Relationship between EU Law and Sport* (TMC Asser/Springer 2016) ch 10, I was able to find only eight academic papers and one book dealing with EU sports law published in the 20 years following *Walrave and Koch*. I do not pretend that this search is exhaustive—I subsequently also found W Schroeder, 'Sport und Europäische Integration: Die Diskriminierung von Sportlern in der EG', Band 25: Europarecht/Völkerrecht Studien und Materialen (Munich 1989), but I doubt I have missed much.

schedule.[21] Even the ban on the participation of English football clubs in highly profitable European club competition imposed in the wake of the Heysel Stadium disaster in 1985 stimulated no challenge based on EU law, even though its application to all clubs, rather than those whose fans posed actual or potential threats to public order, was surely a disproportionate interference with economic freedoms guaranteed under EU law.[22]

But along came a fading Belgian footballer, and EU sports law erupted.

Walrave and Koch involved a sport, paced cycling, that will be unfamiliar to most Europeans. Not so *Bosman*.[23] *Bosman* changed everything, in football, in sport more generally, and even more so in the suddenly and irrevocably energized discipline of EU sports law.

The Court's landmark ruling of December 1995 in *Bosman* repays the closest attention even today because it established what has become orthodoxy. It is a judgment which, in addressing the legitimate scope of sporting autonomy under EU law, is simultaneously both constraining and permissive. The Court refused to accept a string of devices that were aimed at excluding the application of EU law to sport, but then it found space for recognition of sport's particular characteristics in judging whether sporting rules were justified. *Bosman* is considerably more sophisticated in its detailed reasoning than *Walrave and Koch* but it has a close thematic correspondence to *Walrave and Koch* in that it chooses an approach that builds the argument that 'sport is special' into the *interpretation* of EU law rather than using special status as a basis for *excluding* the application of EU law. It is a shining example of the adjudicative or interpretative strategy for achieving sporting autonomy which is mapped in Chapter 2 of this book. And in this vein *Bosman* conforms to the orthodoxy of EU internal market law. Finding a practice that tends to harm the functioning of the internal market is typically readily achieved, but EU law is about more than merely economic integration. Trade-restrictive practices are put to the test, not automatically disallowed, and for sport, as for those defending interests expressed at national level in defence of matters such as consumer protection,[24] cultural diversity,[25] environmental protection,[26] and the protection of human dignity,[27] there is room for the rule-maker to choose why its choices should be treated as important enough to prevail over market-making. The Charter of Fundamental

---

[21] This is recounted, though without citation of sources, by H Van Staveren, 'The Rules of the Sports Community and the Law of the State', in *Sport and the Law* (Proceedings of the Eighteenth Colloquy on European Law, Maastricht, 12–14 October 1988), Council of Europe 1989; and G Veth, 'Uitsluiting van buitenlandse voetballers: mogelijk binnen de EEG?' (1978) 53 Nederlands Juristenblad 504.

[22] cf A Evans, 'Freedom of Trade under the Common Law and EC Law: The Case of the Football Bans' (1986) 102 LQR 510.

[23] Case C-415/93 *Union royale belge des sociétés de football association ASBL v Jean-Marc Bosman* [1995] ECR I-4921.

[24] eg Case C-441/04 *A-Punkt Schmuckhandels GmbH v Claudia Schmidt* [2006] ECR I-2093; Case C-265/12 *Citroën Belux*, judgment of 18 July 2013.

[25] eg Case C-208/09 *Ilonka Sayn-Wittgenstein v Landeshauptmann von Wien* [2010] ECR I-13693.

[26] eg Case C-379/98 *Preussen Elektra* [2001] ECR I-2099.

[27] eg Case C-36/02 *Omega Spielhallen* [2004] ECR I-9609.

Rights, endowed with binding effect since 2009, is especially significant today in providing constitutional confirmation that EU internal market law is not simply about trade liberalization: it is about regulatory values too. But this is not transformative, for the Court has long astutely embedded the possibility to justify barriers to inter-state trade into the structure of free movement law.[28] It should be appreciated that, precisely because of this room allowed to justify practices, the Court's approach is far more potentially generous to sporting autonomy than is frequently lamented by sports governing bodies aggrieved at alleged disrespect shown by EU law to the *lex sportiva*.

The factual background to *Bosman* was supplied by the transfer system. This is a long-established feature of the industry, dating back to the nineteenth century. The existence of a transfer system has long been and still is a major reason why footballers are not treated in the same way as normal employees. The basic model rests on each player being registered with a football club, in addition to having a normal contract of employment with that club. He or, given the recent rise of a professional dimension to the women's game, she cannot play for another club, even if that other club is willing to offer him or her a better deal, unless in addition the registration is transferred from the first club to the new club. And that transfer of registration occurs only if the first club agrees: which has typically involved payment of a fee to the first club. In form it is the player's registration that is transferred but in effect, and in common parlance, it is the player. Here, then, footballers are treated differently from ordinary employees in other sectors, whose status depends on contact and is not affected by collectively agreed and enforced arrangements of the type found in professional football. At its most brutal, the system provided not only that a transfer could be completed only when a fee had been paid by the new club to the first club, but also that the first club could simply refuse to agree to the transfer and could retain the player's registration—even after the contract of employment had expired, and so the player was not receiving any payment from the first club. The imbalance of power is astonishing. Footballers' freedom to choose between possible employers was far more restricted than that of other employees, which amounted to an anti-competitive restraint with a consequent depressive effect on the wages they could command.

In the United Kingdom, the original home of professional football, this extreme 'retain and transfer' system was finally brought to an end as a result of the decision of the English High Court in 1964 in *Eastham v Newcastle United*.[29] The High Court found it to be an unreasonable restraint of trade and therefore contrary to the common law. The court's principal objection was to the particularly onerous 'retain' element of the system rather than the basic underlying concept that a collectively agreed and enforced transfer system could be justified in football, whereas, in other industries, the relationship between employer and employee would be determined by contractual negotiation. This, therefore, left room for a revised system to be applied, focusing on payment of a fee in return for agreement to transfer a player's

---

[28] See Weatherill (n 13).   [29] [1964] Ch 413.

registration, while ameliorating the player's position to some extent by suppressing the ability of the first club simply to retain the registration and in practice force the footballer to abandon a career as a professional. So a revised system lived on, varying in different countries but in Europe with a layer set by UEFA on top, and it was this to which Bosman fell victim. The detail is set out at some length in the judgment,[30] but the problem is readily summarized.

Jean-Marc Bosman was a Belgian professional footballer, born in 1964. In the early part of his career Bosman had earned a reputation as a player of promise and by the time of the dispute that generated the landmark litigation he was under contract to RC Liège, a Belgian first division club. That contract expired at the end of June 1990. In April 1990 RC Liège offered him a new contract for one season, but at a much reduced salary. The brutal reality was that the best of Bosman's career was now behind him. Bosman chose to reject RC Liège's offer and instead found a club in the French second division, US Dunkerque, which was willing to make him a better offer. Were this a normal industry it would simply follow that the worker whose contract of employment had come to an end would be free to agree a contract with a new employer. But football was not and is not a normal industry. The two clubs were required to come to an agreement according to which the transfer certificate pertaining to Bosman would be released by the Belgian federation to its French counterpart. An agreement was reached, involving payment by US Dunkerque of a compensation fee of BFr1,200,000, but, apparently as a result of the French club's financial position,[31] no payment was ever made. In July 1990 Bosman found himself not only without a club but, in line with the applicable system in football, suspended from playing.

The key point deserves repetition. This was not simply a dispute between an employee and a past and future employer. Football is organized according to a hierarchical structure. Football clubs wishing to participate in official competitions must affiliate to national football associations. Each Member State of the EU has its own national association, excepting the United Kingdom alone, which has four associations, one for each home country, a pattern reflected at international level in the separate participation of England, Northern Ireland, Scotland, and Wales in international tournaments. National associations are in turn members of FIFA, the world organizing body, which is based in Switzerland. FIFA is split into confederations for each continent. The European confederation is UEFA, also based in Switzerland, and the national associations of the EU Member States are members of UEFA and as such undertake to comply with its rules. Players are contracted to clubs, but their rights and obligations as employees are not determined solely by the terms of the contract and applicable employment law. They are subject also to the collectively agreed system establishing, among other things, a transfer system which is enforced

[30] *Bosman* (n 23) paras 6–24. Also Advocate General Lenz's Opinion contains an extensive and detailed examination. For a useful collection of contemporary materials and some analysis, see R Blanpain and R Inston, *The Bosman Case: The End of the Transfer System?* (Sweet and Maxwell/Peeters 1996); see also S Van den Bogaert, *Practical Regulation of the Mobility of Sportsmen in the EU post Bosman* (Kluwer 2005) ch IV.
[31] *Bosman* (n 23) para 33 of the judgment.

through the combined power of all the involved national and international federations and clubs. Dunkerque could have concluded a contract of employment with Bosman. But they could not have picked him to play in a match without having met the overall requirements for registration. Any such attempt would have led to sanctions being imposed promptly on both player and club. Governance in the sport—the pyramid with FIFA at its apex—cuts across contractual negotiation. Footballers are less free than ordinary workers in choosing their employer.

And so began the litigation before the Belgian courts.[32]

In accordance with the rules prevailing in Belgium, RC Liège suspended Bosman so that he could not play in the 1990–91 football season. This prompted him to pursue redress before the courts. Initially, he sought an interlocutory order that the transfer rules did not apply to him. He was granted an interlocutory order in Liège in November 1990 ordering the club and the Belgian association to refrain from impeding his engagement. However, he was unable to secure employment with a leading club. As his case progressed through the courts, he was able to find only relatively small clubs in France and Belgium who were willing to offer him terms. RC Liège's readiness to cut his wage so savagely in the summer of 1990, combined with the lack of interest in acquiring Bosman's services shown by major clubs at the time, may suggest that his ability to play top-level football was in any event in doubt, but it was widely suspected that Bosman was also the victim of a boycott pursued by leading clubs after 1990, despite the interim order in his favour.

The litigation initiated by Bosman was chequered by a remarkable series of delays and aborted references to Luxembourg. Other defendants were joined. There were interventions, inter alia, by footballers' associations. During this period Bosman also attempted to challenge the Commission's approach to football before the Court, but his application was rejected as inadmissible.[33] Eventually the matter reached the Court in October 1993 by way of the preliminary reference procedure, then under Article 177 of the Treaty Establishing the European Community (EC), now Article 267 TFEU. The questions asked by the Cour d'Appel in Liège were directed at the application of Articles 48, 85, and 86 EEC—now Articles 45, 101, and 102 TFEU: that is, the provisions dealing with the free movement of workers and competition law.

The questions referred to the Court of Justice for a preliminary ruling were:

Are Articles 48, 85 and 86 of the Treaty of Rome of 25 March 1957 [now Articles 45, 101 and 102 TFEU] to be interpreted as:

(i) prohibiting a football club from requiring and receiving payment of a sum of money upon the engagement of one of its players who has come to the end of his contract by a new employing club;

---

[32] On the twists and turns, see J-L Dupont [Bosman's lawyer], 'Le droit communautaire et la situation du sportif professionale avant l'arrêt *Bosman*' [1996] RMUE 65; B García, 'He Was Not Alone: Bosman in Context' in A Duval and B Van Rompuy (eds), *The Legacy of Bosman: Revisiting the Relationship between EU Law and Sport* (TMC Asser/Springer 2016) ch 2.

[33] Case C-117/91 *Jean-Marc Bosman v Commission* [1991] ECR I-4837; an application for interim measures was rejected in Case C-117/91R *Bosman* [1991] ECR I-3353.

(ii) prohibiting the national and international sporting associations or federations from including in their respective regulations provisions restricting access of foreign players from the European Community to the competitions which they organize?

The Court was therefore asked to interpret EU law in the context of the transfer rules of which Bosman had fallen foul. It was also asked to rule on the compatibility of nationality discrimination in club football with EU law. Like the transfer system these rules too had undergone adjustment over time, but by the time of the litigation they were rules set by UEFA, the continental federation, based on a so-called '3 plus 2' requirement. It was permitted that each national association could limit to three the number of foreign players whom a club may field in any first division match in their national championships, plus two players who had played in the country of the relevant national association for an uninterrupted period of five years, including three years as a junior (so-called 'assimilated' players). The same limitation was mandatorily applicable to UEFA matches in competitions for club teams.[34] These European club competitions, today the Champions League and the Europa League, complement national tournaments. They are highly prestigious in sporting terms, but they are also extremely lucrative in the commercial context. One consequence of these rules was that clubs from countries which tolerated relatively relaxed rules at domestic level frequently found that they were unable to field the first-choice team used in their national League when they came to compete in European-level club competitions. The '3 plus 2' rule forced them to leave out some non-national players in favour of less skilled eligible national players.

This was an intriguing follow-up to the treatment of national discrimination in *international* football which the Court had supplied twenty years earlier in *Walrave and Koch*. However, the '3 plus 2' rule appeared to have nothing to do with Bosman's situation. For that reason it was far from clear that the Court even had jurisdiction to answer the questions, which seemed irrelevant to the matter before the national court. This is a technical area of EU law. There are instances in which the Court takes the view that the questions it is asked are hypothetical[35] and/or not formulated in a sufficiently helpful way to permit it to provide an answer that will assist the referring court.[36] This leads it to decline jurisdiction to answer the questions referred to it by a national court. But the Court normally takes an indulgent view, assuming in a cooperative spirit that the referring court has good reason for asking the question even if it is not immediately obvious, and that was its preference in *Bosman*.[37] It chose not to disturb the national court's assessment that application of the nationality clauses could impede Bosman's career by reducing his chances of

---

[34] *Bosman* (n 23) paras 25–27.
[35] eg Case C-83/91 *Wienand Meilicke v ADV/ORGA FA Meyer AG* [1992] ECR I-4871; C-186/07 *Club Nautico de Gran Canaria* [2008] ECR I-60.
[36] eg Cases C-320–322/90 *Telemarsicabruzzo v Circostel* [1993] ECR I-393; Case C-123/00 *Christina Bellamy* [2001] ECR I-2795; Case C-380/05 *Centro Europa 7 Srl* [2008] ECR I-349.
[37] *Bosman* (n 23) paras 55–67.

being employed or fielded in a match by a club from another Member State and that therefore challenge to them was not irrelevant to the dispute. In this respect, in setting bounds governing the inadmissibility of preliminary references, *Bosman* has become one of the judgments of the Court which it is most fond of citing in its own rulings.[38] This is remote from sports law, the current concern. But there is a sports-specific rhythm to the Court's receptivity. Sports bodies are relatively well protected from litigants for practical reasons associated with those bodies' global reach, power, and deep pockets combined too with the typical fast pace of sporting competition compared to the glacial pace of judicial process. So the Court knew that the likely consequence of a refusal to address the compatibility of the '3 plus 2' rule with EU law would have been the rule's sustained immunity in practice from judicial scrutiny. Moreover, lurking beneath the Court's generous approach to the admissibility of the reference was a further *procedural* reason. The Commission is empowered to bring infringement proceedings against states which it believes to be in violation of EU law[39] and, moreover, it has specific powers of investigation and sanction in the private sphere in so far as violation of the competition rules is concerned.[40] But it is not equipped with any power to act directly against private parties accused of violation of the Treaty rules on free movement. The use of national courts, and reliance on the preliminary reference procedure, is therefore especially significant as a means to police such infractions. This is in principle not a relevant consideration in determining the admissibility of a reference and it does not feature in the Court's explanation. But the Court was not unaware of this twist. In his Opinion, Advocate General Lenz expressly remarked upon the practical immunity that sporting associations would continue to enjoy were the Court to refuse to address the issue.[41] And, despite the tenuous connection between Bosman's plight and the rules of nationality discrimination in club football, the Court did choose to address the issue.

4.4 *Bosman*—the Structure of the Ruling: the Limits of Sporting Autonomy under EU Law

On 15 December 1995, the Court of Justice provided answers to both questions referred to it by the Cour d'Appel in Liège. However, the Court was not prepared to answer those questions in the light of all the Treaty provisions mentioned in the reference court. The Court instead carefully confined itself to analysis in the light of Article 48 EEC, today Article 45 TFEU, which concerns the free movement of

---

[38] See M Derlén and J Lindholm, 'Bosman: A Legacy beyond Sports' in A Duval and B Van Rompuy (eds), *The Legacy of Bosman: Revisiting the Relationship between EU Law and Sport* (TMC Asser/Springer 2016) ch 3.

[39] TFEU, Art 258. A fine may be imposed pursuant to TFEU, Art 260.

[40] Council Regulation (EC) 1/2003 of 16 December 2002 on the implementation of the rules on competition laid down in Arts 81 and 82 of the Treaty [2003] OJ L1/1.

[41] *Bosman* (n 23) paras 111–19, Opinion of Lenz AG.

workers. It left entirely to one side any examination of the application of the Treaty competition rules. This deliberate omission left open a number of issues of significance for the future adjustment of industry structures, and several will be discussed later in this chapter and elsewhere in this book.

The detail of the inquiry into the transfer system from which Bosman suffered will be explored in Chapter 9, the detail relating to nationality rules (from which he did not, at least not directly) will be examined in Chapter 8. The key to this chapter's preoccupation is to identify how the Court found EU free movement law applicable, but without denying that sport is special and that it therefore deserves sensitive treatment in the interpretation and application of free movement law. *Bosman* is the foundation stone of EU sports law and so it deserves forensic structural examination.

The affected sports governing bodies lined up a series of devices with the aim of excluding entirely the application of EU law. The outcome of this strategy was failure. It is worth tracking the sequence of unsuccessful arguments to understand the thematic ambition of sports bodies to secure autonomy for their practices (the *lex sportiva*) and to lay bare the way that this ambition is converted (albeit unsuccessfully) into legal arguments. However, the examination also has concrete practical significance, because the Court in *Bosman* established a set of principles to which it has adhered consistently ever since. Broadly the key to the ruling is the *conditional autonomy* afforded to sports bodies under EU law. This means that EU law does not permit sport to escape its reach—there is no absolute or unconditional autonomy. But nor does EU law expose sport to an insensitive application of the rules of the internal market. Instead it takes into account the context, and allows sport to make its case for special treatment within EU law. But sport must make that case: it is an autonomy conditional on showing that it truly has special features that justify appropriately modified interpretation and application of EU free movement law. As will be shown in Chapter 5, a similar approach has subsequently infused the application of EU competition law to sport too.

4.5 No Absolute Autonomy for Sport under EU Law …

The claims to absolute or unconditional autonomy advanced by the football authorities and methodically rejected by the Court in *Bosman* numbered eight.

Each is structurally important in understanding how broad is the reach of EU internal market law and how, accordingly, core issues tend to be settled in the substantive appraisal of their merit as a claim to protect the special features of sport, rather than by excluding EU law in principle. This is the heart of the model of 'conditional autonomy' granted to sport under EU law.

1. It was argued by the Belgian football association that only the major European football clubs may be regarded as undertakings, whereas by contrast the economic activity pursued by smaller clubs such as RC Liège is 'negligible'.[42] The German

---

[42] ibid para 70.

government pressed in similar vein that in most cases football is not an economic activity.[43] The Court did not disagree. And it repeated its finding in *Walrave and Koch* that sport is subject to EU law only in so far as it constitutes an economic activity within the meaning of the Treaty. But it found that this readily applies to the activities of professional or semi-professional footballers, where they are in gainful employment or where they provide a remunerated service. It does not matter whether the employer counts as an 'undertaking'. What matters is the existence of, or the intention to create, an employment relationship.[44] The application of EU law could not be excluded in principle.

The message here is that it is easy to find at least some economic context to sporting activity and, since that economic context is the constitutional trigger to the application of EU law, it is correspondingly easy to bring sport within the reach of EU law. This broad and deep reach is a well-established feature of EU internal market law generally.

2. It was argued by the Belgian football association that the matter 'does not concern the employment relationships between players and clubs but the business relationships between clubs and the consequences of freedom to affiliate to a sporting federation', and that as a result (what was then) Article 48 did not apply.[45] This plea is quoted here in its original form, because it is scarcely comprehensible and therefore it is incapable of helpful paraphrase. The Court politely pointed out that even if the transfer rules govern the business relationships between clubs rather than the employment relationships between clubs and players, their existence, and in particular the obligation imposed on a buying club to pay a fee, affected the players' opportunities to find employment as well as the terms under which such employment is offered.[46] The application of EU law could not be excluded in principle.

3. UEFA alerted the Court to the extreme difficulty of distinguishing between the 'economic and the sporting aspects of football' and advised that a decision of the Court concerning the situation of professional players 'might call in question the organization of football as a whole'.[47] Once again the Court saw no reason to disagree as a matter of principle. Citing *Donà*,[48] it repeated the observation that EU law does not forbid 'rules or practices justified on non-economic grounds which relate to the particular nature and context of certain matches'. As exposed earlier, this is analytically unhelpful. It continued by adding that any such restriction on the scope of the provisions must remain limited to its proper objective. There is no basis for immunizing the whole of a sporting activity from the scope of the Treaty.[49] And the Court, while accepting that 'the practical consequences of any judicial decision must be weighed carefully', would not permit possible consequences for the organization of football as a whole 'to diminish the objective character of the law and compromise its application'. Such anxieties could at most find expression in a limitation to the temporal effect of a judgment, which the Court is exceptionally prepared to sanction.[50] And, in fact, in *Bosman* the

---

[43] ibid para 72.   [44] ibid paras 73–74.   [45] ibid para 70.
[46] ibid para 75.   [47] ibid para 71.   [48] *Donà* (n 19).
[49] *Bosman* (n 23) para 76.   [50] ibid paras 76–77.

Court agreed that Article 48 EEC (now Article 45 TFEU) could not be used to attack a transfer fee which had already been paid or was due, except by those who had already lodged a claim. So, in line with its general, though infrequently exercised, power to grant its rulings only prospective effect in circumstances where they may cause serious difficulties to parties that have acted in good faith,[51] it did permit a degree of protection to the established status quo in football. The transfer system would necessarily change—but with effects for the future. By contrast, however, it saw no basis for a temporal limitation of the effects of the judgment ruling against nationality discrimination in club football.[52]

This type of reasoning would be perfectly orthodox in any legal order. Granting a specific and focused temporal limitation to the effects of a ruling that was not entirely foreseeable is one thing, but no court can be expected to adopt a general policy of setting aside the application of legal rules simply because of the disruptive effect on those subject to them. A different question, however, is determining precisely what those legal rules, properly interpreted, entail in the first place. This matter of substance is considered more closely in sections 4.7 and 4.8.

4. The German government submitted that sport has points of similarity with culture. This led it to draw the Court's attention to the direction in what was then Article 128(1) EC, now Article 167(1) TFEU, that the EU must respect the national and regional diversity of the cultures of the Member States, and it argued that by analogy the same respect should be paid to sport.[53] In response the Court did not seek to refute the alleged similarity between sport and culture. Indeed it is perfectly convincing that there is a degree of similarity: sport has its cultural dimension, even if that analogy might sometimes be exaggerated by those eager to praise sport's virtue. However, the Court observed that in the case it was not being asked to deal with the exercise of a limited competence to act conferred on the EU. Rather the matter at hand addressed the scope of one of the fundamental freedoms guaranteed by EU law.[54] Whatever respect for 'culture' is mandated by EU law cannot involve a disapplication in principle of internal market law. A cultural context is no reason to afford absolute autonomy to those engaged in and pursuing an activity with economic motivation.

This is fully in line with orthodox EU law. The creation of the internal market defined by Article 26 TFEU demands a sweeping scope to the application of the free movement and competition rules, reaching into every area of economic activity as a basis for review of public and private practices that imperil integration and, crucially, even in sectors where EU legislative competence is lacking in part or in full. This structural dimension of EU law was explained in the abstract in Chapter 3: here now is its direct and practical significance in defeating appeals for sporting autonomy from free movement law pressed on the Court in *Bosman*. Sport is slightly different from most cases involving free movement law in that it is

---

[51] eg Case 24/86 *Blaizot and others* [1988] ECR 379; Case C-402/03 *Skov and Bilka* [2006] ECR I-199; Case C-76/14 *Manea*, judgment of 14 April 2014.
[52] *Bosman* (n 23) paras 139–46.   [53] ibid para 73.   [54] ibid para 78.

in the main private actors that are concerned rather than public authorities.[55] But otherwise the basic model found in *Bosman* follows faithfully that used in other cases where free movement law is used to review national practices even in the absence of comprehensive EU legislative competence to dictate how the matter shall be regulated.[56] The point is that in such circumstances it is not for the EU to dictate how football should shape its transfer system. It *is* for the EU—specifically its Court—to rule on how football shall *not* shape its transfer system. It shall not violate EU internal market trade law.

The Court has tried to give principled expression to the limits of its role, and of EU law generally, in cases of this constitutionally sensitive type. In a case in which a patient wished to rely on free movement law to claim a right to receive medical treatment in another Member State and have it funded by her home Member State—an area where the key legislative competences plainly belong at state, not at EU, level—the Court stated that the achievement of the fundamental freedoms guaranteed by the Treaty inevitably required Member States to make adjustments to the structure and resourcing of social security systems, but it added that EU law 'does not detract from the power of the Member States to organise' such systems and that it does not 'undermine ... their sovereign powers in the field'.[57] Free movement law stops states acting, in the absence of justification for chosen practices that impede cross-border trade, but the EU does not create any legislative framework in the field. Sport follows precisely this model, albeit that it is typically private practices, rather than those of public authorities, which are put to the test. So the formula used by the Court in its cases on cross-border health aligns perfectly with the approach taken in *Bosman*: the achievement of the fundamental freedoms guaranteed by the Treaty inevitably requires adjustment to the structure of sports organization, while still leaving ultimate power to administer sport to the responsible governing bodies. It is the model of conditional autonomy under EU law. That inquiry requires the Court to proceed to make assessment of the virtues claimed for the transfer system as a method of organization and, by definition, that must occur in these cases where the reach of free movement law exceeds that of the EU's legislative competence without any useful policy framework mapped on to the affected sector by the Treaty itself.

There is perhaps something disingenuous about the Court's approach: the power of organization (of health care, of sport) is not assumed by the EU, but EU law does confine the scope of those organizational choices. State 'sovereign powers' to which the Court refers are modified in their practical exercise. The point of general structural significance is that this investigation takes place *within* the fabric of EU law: there is no immunity from free movement law simply because practices are sporting (or cultural) in intent or effect, provided they carry economic implications.

---

[55] There is jurisdictional variation in the extent to which sports organization is influenced by the State: see R Siekmann and J Soek, 'Models of Sport Governance within the European Union' in J Nafziger and S Ross (eds), *Handbook on International Sports Law* (Edward Elgar 2011) ch 5.
[56] See Ch 3.3.   [57] Case C-372/04 *Ex parte Watts* [2006] ECR I-4325, para 121.

5. The German government referred to the freedom of association and autonomy enjoyed by sporting federations under national law.[58] The Court expressly confirmed that the principle of freedom of association is one of the fundamental rights which is protected in the legal order of the EU. Today it would doubtless rely on Article 11 of the Charter of Fundamental Rights. However, it found no basis to permit freedom of association to yield sporting autonomy from EU law. The rules on which the Court had been asked to supply a preliminary ruling were not necessary to ensure enjoyment of the freedom of expression by national associations, clubs, or players, nor could they be seen as an inevitable result thereof.[59] The application of EU law could not be excluded in principle.

6. The German government, citing the principle of subsidiarity, pressed for acceptance of a general principle that intervention by public authorities, including those of the EU, must be confined to what is strictly necessary.[60] Here too the Court did not disagree, but found the claim inapt to achieve autonomy. The principle of subsidiarity cannot lead to a situation in which the freedom of private associations to adopt sporting rules restricts the exercise of rights conferred on individuals by the Treaty.[61] This is fully in line with the observations made earlier about the Court's orthodox interpretation of the structure of internal market law. It is dismissive of submissions that are designed to place restrictive practices with economic effects in a zone which excludes them in principle from scrutiny under EU law. The real test is whether or not they are justified.

7. Did Article 48 EEC, today Article 45 TFEU, apply to private parties such as the governing bodies of a sport?[62] The Court concluded that it did. The Court cited its ruling in *Walrave and Koch*, and embraced the reasoning it had provided twenty years earlier.[63] By applying Article 48 not only to the action of public authorities but also to 'rules of any other nature aimed at regulating gainful employment in a collective manner', EU law addresses obstacles to freedom of movement which would escape its grip were it concerned exclusively with state barriers and, moreover, it avoids the risk of creating inequality in application in consequence on the different patterns of private and public actors across the several Member States. UEFA's objection that such an interpretation unfairly burdens private parties who, unlike Member States, may not rely on limitations justified on grounds of public policy, public security, or public health was swiftly dismissed on the basis that individuals may rely on such justifications.[64]

This has become orthodoxy in internal market law. Adherence to this line of reasoning has admittedly taken the Court into some controversial terrain. Most of all, the logic deployed in *Walrave and Koch* and *Bosman* to subject sporting bodies to obligations rooted in EU free movement law was used subsequently in *Viking Line* to subject trade unions to obligations imposed by the Treaty rules on free movement.[65]

---

[58] *Bosman* (n 23) para 73.   [59] ibid para 80.   [60] ibid para 73.
[61] ibid para 81.   [62] ibid para 82.   [63] ibid paras 82–84.
[64] ibid paras 85–86.
[65] Case C-438/05 *Viking Line* [2007] ECR I-10779, para 55; Case C-341/05 *Laval* [2007] ECR I-11767, para 98.

So collective labour action taken to deter a company from 'reflagging' a vessel in a Member State with lower regulatory costs was treated as an obstacle to the free movement of companies and therefore required justification. The cramped approach to the scope of justification adopted by the Court in *Viking Line* has earned it severe criticism.[66] Structurally, however, the judgment conforms to *Walrave and Koch* and to *Bosman*: it confirms that the scope of free movement law is interpreted broadly with the consequence that a heavy load is carried by the often sensitive inquiry into whether practices should be treated as justified. Trade unions, like sporting bodies before them, have discovered ruefully that it is extremely difficult to persuade that Court that they should be granted an absolute autonomy from the controls exercised by EU internal market law. Conditional autonomy—autonomy that is conditional on showing practices to be justified—is the next best prize on offer. It is the heart of the adjudicative or interpretative route to securing sporting autonomy.

8. UEFA argued that the dispute concerned a situation purely internal to a single Member State, Belgium. It concerned a Belgian player detrimentally affected by the conduct of a Belgian club and a Belgian association.[67] It is indeed clear that EU free movement law bites only where there is a cross-border element to the dispute. The 'purely internal' situation escapes its reach. But, perfectly obviously, Bosman's case was not 'purely internal'. His prospective new employer was French![68]

However, there was, in truth, a bit more to this argument than meets the eye.

The situation was not purely internal to a single Member State. The basic problem was that Bosman was faced with a restriction to his movement across a border, since he wished to move from a Belgian employer to a French employer. However, in fact he would have been faced by the same problem even had he been seeking to move to another *Belgian* employer. That is to say, the obstacles created as a result of the transfer system applicable in football affected all workers in exactly the same way whether they wished to enter into a contract of employment with a new employer in the same Member State as their previous employer or whether it so happened that their preferred new employer was based in another Member State. So it was pure chance that an association with cross-border mobility was at stake. In reality the problem was the transfer system generally, which affected all workers equally in law and in fact whether or not they happened to wish to cross a border to join a new club.

Two years earlier, in its notorious ruling in *Keck and Mithouard*,[69] the Court had placed (rather imprecise) limits on the application of the rules governing the free

---

[66] cf eg L Azoulai, 'The Court of Justice and the Social Market Economy: The Emergence of an Ideal and the Conditions for its Realisation' (2008) 45 CML Rev 1335; C Barnard, 'Fifty Years of Avoiding Social Dumping? The EU's Economic and Not So Economic Constitution' in M Dougan and S Currie (eds), *Fifty Years of the European Treaties: Looking Back and Thinking Forward* (Hart 2009); ACL Davies, 'One Step Forward, Two Steps back? The Viking and Laval cases in the ECJ' (2008) 37 Industrial Law Journal 126; C Joerges and F Rödl, 'Informal Politics, Formalised Law and the "Social Deficit" of European Integration: Reflections after the Judgments of the ECJ in *Viking* and *Laval*' (2009) 15 ELJ 1.

[67] *Bosman* (n 23) para 88.   [68] ibid paras 89–90.

[69] Joined Cases C-267/91 and C-268/91 *Keck and Mithouard* [1993] ECR I-6097, cited at *Bosman* (n 23) para 102.

movement of *goods* in circumstances where challenged rules met the requirement of legal and factual equality of application. In *Bosman* it seemed open to the Court to adopt a comparable solution in the field of the free movement of *persons*. On such an understanding, the matter should not fall within the scope of application of free movement law at all (and should be tackled, if at all, by competition law). But the Court did not take this approach in *Bosman*. It found the matter to fall within the scope of free movement law. This was a practice which impeded the freedom of movement of a national of one Member State wishing to take up employment in another.[70] This, the Court stated, was not contradicted by the fact that the transfer rules applied also to transfers between clubs belonging to the same national association.[71] And it concluded that the rules were not comparable to the rules at stake in *Keck and Mithouard*.[72] That was enough, in the Court's view, to bring (what is now) Article 45 TFEU into play.

The judgment on this point is less comfortably orthodox than the reasoning provided by the Court on the other points considered earlier. In particular, it seems to assert in this vein a wider scope for the rules on the free movement of *persons* than those that apply to *goods*—but it fails to articulate just why this should be so. The Court's approach makes it difficult to piece together a coherent understanding of the scope of free movement law which bridges all the freedoms. That, however, is a puzzle for general internal market lawyers.[73] It is not of any particular specific relevance to sports law as such and it needs no further articulation here. For sports lawyers the ruling asserts the relevance of free movement law to control sporting practices that impede the free movement of workers even where that impediment is felt also within the territory of a single Member State. And in *Bosman* it meant that the legal analysis turned to whether the rules of which the player had fallen foul could be justified.

4.6 ... but a Conditional Autonomy for Sport under EU Law

The Court thus methodically refused all eight invitations to place sport in general, and the dispute involving Bosman in particular, beyond the reach of EU law. And it used reasoning which is in the main perfectly orthodox and familiar to EU lawyers. The underlying message throughout is that sport would need to make its case for special treatment *within* the interpretation of EU internal market law, not by seeking to slip beyond its reach. As the Court put it, having concluded that the transfer rules constituted an obstacle to freedom of movement for workers, EU law forbids them unless those rules pursue a legitimate aim compatible with the Treaty and are justified by pressing reasons of public interest and, moreover, they must be such

---

[70] *Bosman* (n 23) paras 96–97.   [71] ibid paras 98, 103.   [72] ibid para 103.
[73] See eg S Prechal and S De Vries, 'Seamless Web of Judicial Protection in the Internal Market' (2009) 34 EL Rev 5; Weatherill (n 13) ch 8.

as to ensure achievement of the aim in question and must not go beyond what is necessary for that purpose.[74]

Any autonomy granted to sport by EU law is *conditional* on meeting the expectations located in the tests of justification recognized by EU internal market law. And it is in the shaping of the environment of justification that sport needs to aspire to embed its claims to be 'special'.

In *Bosman*, when the Court turned to justification, it immediately accepted that sport *is* special. This is the ruling's famous paragraph 106:

In view of the considerable social importance of sporting activities and in particular football in the Community, the aims of maintaining a balance between clubs by preserving a certain degree of equality and uncertainty as to results and of encouraging the recruitment and training of young players must be accepted as legitimate.[75]

This statement is foundationally important in the development of EU sports law. Article 165, which entered into force in 2009, embraces 'the specific nature of sport': here, in the 1995 ruling in *Bosman*, are its fertile roots.

The structural point is that the Court, having spent much time explaining why it was refusing to accept the claims of sports bodies to absolute autonomy from the application of EU law, turned to address the possibility of justifying practices that fall within the scope of EU law, and immediately it embraces a recognition that sport has distinct characteristics. Sport is special—in at least two respects. The Court accepts as legitimate the aims of maintaining a balance between clubs by preserving a certain degree of equality and uncertainty as to results and of encouraging the recruitment and training of young players. The Court had no basis whatsoever in the Treaty for recognizing any such concessions. The Treaty made no mention of sport. In fact, the Court, which notes in its ruling that it had had these virtues pressed on it by the Belgian football association, UEFA, and the French and Italian governments,[76] was making its own choices about the nature and purpose of sport and its claim to a degree of special treatment in the interpretation and application of EU internal market law. This is one of the direct consequences of the point that EU legislative competence is narrower than the reach of internal market law. It demands a creative Court.

In fact, UEFA had in some respects done an astonishingly poor job in defending the special character of sport. The game's governing bodies plainly held a complacent expectation that Bosman would be induced or intimidated to settle the matter without his day in court. In April 1995, just eight months before the ruling was delivered, UEFA was reported as 'reluctant to believe that Bosman might win, because there is a feeling generally that the player will be approached by one of the interested parties to settle the matter out of court and drop the case'.[77] As late as 16 November 1995, a month before the ruling, UEFA requested the Court to order a measure of inquiry under Article 60 of the Rules of Procedure of the Court with

---

[74] *Bosman* (n 23) para 106.   [75] ibid para 106.   [76] ibid para 105.
[77] 'Bosman case could end transfers' *The Guardian* (London, 4 April 1995) 18.

a view to obtaining fuller information on the role played by transfer fees in the financing of small or medium-sized football clubs, the machinery governing the distribution of income within the existing football structures, and the presence or absence of alternative machinery if the system of transfer fees were to disappear.[78] But the Court dismissed this application. It was made at a time when, in accordance with the Rules of Procedure, the oral procedure was closed. Such an application can be admitted only if it relates to facts which may have a decisive influence and which the party concerned could not put forward before the close of the oral procedure. But here the Court held that UEFA could have submitted its request before the close of the oral procedure: such questions had in any event been raised, in particular by Bosman in his written observations.

In *Bosman* the Court proceeded to take a negative view of the possibility to justify the particular transfer system of which Bosman himself had fallen foul. But it was plainly receptive to the maintenance of a less restrictive system, even though no such system would be tolerated in a normal industry. It accepted that sport is special.

4.7 Failing to Justify the Transfer System

The Court decided that the transfer system was not an adequate means of maintaining financial and competitive balance in the world of football. It did not do this in any remotely systematic way. The rules did not preclude the richest clubs from acquiring the best players nor did they 'prevent the availability of financial resources from being a decisive factor in competitive sport, thus considerably altering the balance between clubs'.[79] The Court agreed that the prospect of receiving a transfer fee is 'likely to encourage football clubs to seek new talent and train young players'.[80] But it could not see that that prospect could serve as a decisive factor in encouraging recruitment and training or as an adequate means of financing such activities, given that it is not possible to predict the sporting future of young players with any certainty.[81] Some will make it as professional players, most will not. Transfer fees are uncertain and in any event unrelated to the actual cost borne by clubs of training both future professional players and those who will never play professionally.[82] The Court added that 'the same aims can be achieved at least as efficiently by other means which do not impede freedom of movement for workers', and on this point it made reference to the fuller discussion of possible models provided in the rich and thoughtful Opinion of Advocate General Lenz.[83]

---

[78] Noted at *Bosman* (n 23) paras 52–54.   [79] ibid para 107.   [80] ibid para 108.
[81] ibid para 109.   [82] ibid.
[83] ibid para 110. Mr Lenz reminisces—including recall of 'phone calls from the German political world' during the preparation of his Opinion—in C-O Lenz, 'Foreword' in A Duval and B Van Rompuy (eds), *The Legacy of Bosman: Revisiting the Relationship between EU Law and Sport* (TMC Asser/Springer 2016).

So the system of which Bosman had fallen foul was damned. But the Court had clearly left open the possibility of renovation of a system that might meet the demands imposed by EU law, especially (and perhaps only) where a connection between fees paid and expenses incurred could be established, thereby reflecting the legitimate concern to induce training of young players. Moreover, the ruling's condemnation was aimed explicitly at a system requiring a payment on the expiry of the player's contract with a club, leaving open the possibility to justify collectively imposed restraints on players wishing to change clubs while still under contract. It is, however, not for the Court to spell out exactly what is permitted, still less to direct what should be done by the governing bodies in football. The Court's job is strictly to decide whether challenged practices comply with EU internal market law or not. But *Bosman* plainly provided clues as to possible avenues of reform, and the transfer system, adjusted and refined, lives on today. The interest in whether it complies with the demands of EU law is, however, certainly not exhausted: this is pursued in Chapter 9.

4.8 Failing to Justify Nationality Discrimination in Club Football

The Court was far less generous in its treatment of the nationality discrimination practised under the '3 plus 2' rule in European club football. This was quickly and easily identified as an instance of discrimination within the scope of EU law. Clubs were not limited in the players they could add to their squad, but they were limited in the players they could select to play in official matches. This influenced their economic decisions by pushing them to prefer players whose nationality met the rules. The effect was to induce favouritism for particular nationals at the expense of nationals of other Member States.

The matter therefore rested on whether the Court could be persuaded that the nationality-based rules were justified. It could not.

The structure of the argument is once again richly instructive. There was no realistic prospect of arguing that the transfer rules were without economic character or effect, but in relation to the nationality rules the Court was invited to re-visit its finding in *Walrave and Koch* that EU law 'does not affect the composition of sport teams, in particular national teams, the formation of which is a question of purely sporting interest and as such has nothing to do with economic activity'.[84] At the level of detail, the question in *Bosman* was whether this reasoning could be extended to grant autonomy to nationality discrimination practised in *club* football. More broadly the question arose whether the Court would stick to its claim in *Walrave and Koch* that such practices have nothing to do with economic activity—which, as exposed earlier, is simply not correct.

---

[84] *Walrave and Koch* (n 1) para 8.

Drawing on *Walrave and Koch*, the Belgian football association, UEFA, and the German, French, and Italian governments argued that the nationality clauses were 'justified on non-economic grounds, concerning only the sport as such'.[85] What was at stake, they argued, was preservation of 'the traditional link between each club and its country, a factor of great importance in enabling the public to identify with its favourite team and ensuring that clubs taking part in international competitions effectively represent their countries'.[86] So *Walrave and Koch* accepted that there is a natural obligatory tie between the nationality of a player and the *international* team he represents; in *Bosman* governing bodies in sport attempted to persuade the Court to extend this logic to authorize also that same natural obligatory tie between the nationality of a player and the *club* team he represents. So French clubs should be mainly made up of French players, Germans clubs of Germans, and so on.

The Court refused to accept this. In *Walrave* the Court had cautioned that any restriction on the scope of EU law must 'remain limited to its proper objective'[87] and it repeated precisely this point in *Bosman*.[88] The Court's thematic concern is not to open up an unjustifiably large space for the expression of sporting autonomy in contradiction of the orthodox norms of EU law. And in *Bosman* the Court decided that sport was asking for too much. The Court refused to accept that the permissive approach under EU law taken to the composition of international teams should be extended to the composition of club sides. It pointed out that the application of the nationality clauses was so broad as to apply to 'the essence of the activity of professional players', and that accordingly their acceptance would be to deprive Article 48 of its practical effect and to eliminate the fundamental right of free access to employment conferred by the Treaty.[89] The Court's view was, in short, that sport is not special *enough* to make such an exorbitant claim to autonomy.

At bottom, the Court refused to accept that a link based on nationality was in any sense inherent to the structure of club football. No rule restricts clubs to a choice of players from their own region, town, or locality. And, the Court concluded, a club's links with the Member State in which it is established are no more inherent in its sporting activity than its links with its region, town, or locality.[90] The Court added that clubs qualify to participate in international competitions on the basis of success achieved in national competitions, without any particular significance being attached to the nationality of their players.[91]

The Court is probably right, although more detailed assessment of the extent to which sport's special character might justify origin-based rules governing the selection of players is reserved for Chapter 8. The broader thematic point which is of direct relevance to this chapter is that in interpreting and applying EU free movement and anti-discrimination laws, the Court was required to fashion its own view of the character of football, in particular club football, against an entirely barren Treaty background. The Court, exploring the scope and limits of justified trade barriers, is

---

[85] *Bosman* (n 23) para 122.   [86] ibid para 123.   [87] *Walrave and Koch* (n 1) para 9.
[88] *Bosman* (n 23) paras 76 and 127: although in fact the Court cites Case 13/76 *Donà* (n 19) rather than Case 36/74 *Walrave and Koch* (n 1) in making this point.
[89] *Bosman* (n 23) paras 128–29.   [90] ibid para 131.   [91] ibid para 132.

forced to behave in a creative manner. In his Opinion in *Bosman*, Advocate General Lenz had been more flowery. He reached the conclusion that supporters are primarily attached to their club rather than the background of individual players by remembering players who had been especially popular when playing in a country that was not their own: Petar Radenkovic, a charismatic Yugoslavian goalkeeper who played for TSV 1860 München in the 1960s, English international Kevin Keegan at Hamburger SV in the late 1970s and, more recently, Eric Cantona, a Frenchman at Manchester United, and Jürgen Klinsmann, a German at Tottenham Hotspur. There was a hint here of the robust and very personal approach taken by Advocate General Warner in *Walrave and Koch*, when he simply noted that the permissibility of national sporting teams was no more than a simple matter of common sense. Some Advocates General are *very* creative.

Three other arguments in support of the rules requiring nationality discrimination in club football were advanced. Each was crisply rejected.

First, it was argued that the clauses were necessary to create a sufficient pool of national players to supply adequate resources for the international representative teams.[92] The Court responded that international representative teams are composed of players having the relevant nationality, but that they are not confined to players registered to play for clubs in that country. This means that a wider pool of players available for selection for the international side already exists. Moreover, rules set and enforced by governing bodies require the release of such players to appear for their country's international representative team in certain matches.[93] The Court added that even if free movement of workers within the EU has the consequence that the chances of workers, including footballers, to find employment within their own Member State are reduced as a result of competition from migrants, the other side of that same coin is that they are able to enjoy the increased opportunity to travel across borders and to find work in every other Member State.[94]

Second, the rules were defended as a means to help maintain a competitive balance between clubs by preventing the richest clubs from acquiring the services of the best players.[95] To which the response could simply but plausibly have been: 'No they do not, they ensure precisely that happens!' The Court was slightly less curt, though still dismissive of the claim, adding that the rules in any event were not sufficient to achieve the aim of maintaining a competitive balance, since even if they limited the access of the richest clubs to the best *foreign* players, they did not limit the possibility for such clubs to recruit the best *national* players.[96]

Finally, UEFA pointed out that the '3 plus 2' rule had been drawn up in collaboration with the Commission.[97] This was perfectly true. The rule was widely known as the 'Bangemann compromise', after Martin Bangemann, the Commissioner responsible for internal market affairs at the time it was agreed, in 1991, to offer

---

[92] ibid para 124.   [93] ibid para 133. Ch 10.7 covers player release rules.
[94] *Bosman* (n 23) para 134. Ch 8.6 explains why this misses the point, though it is not there argued that the outcome of the case should be different.
[95] *Bosman* (n 23) para 125.   [96] ibid para 135.   [97] ibid para 126.

UEFA an informal green light.[98] It was, in an unappealing anachronism, described as a 'gentlemen's agreement'.[99] Protests, led in particular by a Dutch MEP, James Janssen van Raay, who had a strong track record in criticizing the stringencies of the *lex sportiva* in Europe in general[100] and who now turned his fire on this legally dubious concession,[101] had been loud and, the Court now confirmed, they had been entirely justified. The Commission has no authority to validate a violation of EU free movement law.[102] So this background was of no assistance to football's governing bodies. Put another way, they had been *politically* astute enough to extract a concession to their autonomy which protected the *lex sportiva* from the Commission, but they could not make that stick *legally* before the Court. This emphasizes still further the scale of Bosman's victory: he was cracking open a cartel that included not only governing bodies and football clubs, but also the Commission itself.

4.9 *Bosman*—the Aftermath

Assessment of the detail of the Court's analysis deserves treatment in separate chapters dealing with the transfer system (Chapter 9) and nationality rules (Chapter 8). As will be elaborated, there are holes in the Court's reasoning in *Bosman* on both points: in particular, the Court's treatment of the transfer system is too generous, its treatment of the nationality rules not generous enough. However, for present purposes, the most important point is structural. The Court was implacably opposed to permitting sporting practices any autonomy in principle from the scope of application of EU law. But it was not opposed to taking account of the claim that 'sport is special' in considering how to interpret and apply EU internal market law. Quite the reverse! Article 165 TFEU today asserts that sport possesses a 'specific nature', and that theme is plainly visible in *Bosman*. The Court was open in its embrace of the legitimate aims of sport in principle—its point was that it did not consider them properly advanced by the particular transfer system of which Bosman was the victim. And the Court did not refuse in principle to consider whether nationality discrimination might be permitted in club football—but, after examining the absence of attachment of club football to the nationality of individual players, it decided it should not be.

---

[98] The Commission's position is examined in P Karpenstein, 'Der Zugang von Ausländern zum Berufsfussball innerhalb der EG'; and G Renz, 'Freizügigkeit von Berufsfussballspielern innerhalb der EG' in M Will (ed), *Sportrecht in Europa* (CF Müller Juristischer Verlag 1993).

[99] eg Commission Press Release IP/95/411, para XII <http://europa.eu/rapid/press-release_IP-95-1411_en.htm> accessed 29 November 2016.

[100] He was Rapporteur for a critical report on restrictions on the freedom of movement of professional footballers—'a modern form of serfdom', para 9—drawn up and published in 1989 on behalf of the Parliament's Committee on Legal Affairs and Citizens' Rights, Document A 2-415/88, 1988/89 [1989] OJ C120/25.

[101] B3-1695/91, European Parliament, *The Week*, 18–22 November 1991.

[102] *Bosman* (n 23) para 136.

Bosman was, however, greeted with dismay by governing bodies in sport. Newspaper reports on the day after the publication of Mr Lenz's Opinion in September 1995 were apocalyptic. 'This is sending lesser clubs to the wall', the owner of Wimbledon was quoted as saying in literally front page news.[103] Elsewhere it was reported that 'A Football League spokesman claimed that "75 per cent" of its players could lose their jobs'.[104] By December, the mood was no less dismayed. The day after the Court gave judgment the President of UEFA, Lennart Johansson, described it as 'an attack on football, the implications of which we do not know'.[105] 'Football was plunged into chaos ...'[106]

At best such remarks are disingenuous. At worst they are outright misleading. In its ruling in *Bosman* the Court recorded that:

UEFA argued, *inter alia*, that the Community authorities have always respected the autonomy of sport, that it is extremely difficult to distinguish between the economic and the sporting aspects of football and that a decision of the Court concerning the situation of professional players might call in question the organization of football as a whole. For that reason, even if Article 48 of the Treaty were to apply to professional players, a degree of flexibility would be essential because of the particular nature of the sport.[107]

The reality is that UEFA were rewarded with exactly this 'flexibility' in the Court's ruling! Sporting rules fall readily within the scope of application of the Treaty and are therefore put to the test. But EU internal market law dictates only what may not be done, not what shall be done. So there is space for sporting bodies to find other ways to protect and promote their interests—provided always that they comply with EU law. EU free movement law, then, is an agent for change, but it does not impose a particular system on those subject to its requirements. And the Court showed generous flexibility to the claim that 'sport is special'. The transfer system and the nationality rules attacked in the case itself did not pass muster, but the Court was clearly receptive to adapted rules that would survive review pursuant to EU law because of the sporting context, when they would not be tolerated in a 'normal' industry. As Chapter 9 shows, the transfer system lives on, but shorn of its objectionable application to out-of-contract players.

It is striking how the protests of football's governing bodies in *Bosman* closely resemble the pleas for sporting autonomy made before, in, and after the *Eastham* case before the English courts over thirty years earlier.[108] The claim made in that case in favour of a transfer system was that 'If a player could do just as he liked at the end of the football season, the wealthier clubs would at once snap up the best players':[109] this may be summarized as an argument for the transfer system to serve as a means to achieve *balance* in sport. It was, moreover, argued that 'All professional football leagues elsewhere in the world have the combined retention and transfer

---

[103] 'Ruling Brings Soccer Chaos' *The Guardian* (London, 21 September 1995) 1.
[104] 'Smaller Clubs Threatened by Transfer Ruling' *The Independent* (London, 21 September 1995) 28.
[105] 'UEFA Vows to Fight after Illegal Transfers Ruling' *The Times* (London, 16 December 1995) 44.
[106] 'Chaos after Bosman Ruling' *The Guardian* (London, 16 December 1995) 20.
[107] *Bosman* (n 23) para 71.   [108] *Eastham* (n 29).   [109] ibid 424.

system or one that amounts to it, which shows that it has the unqualified approval of those best fitted to judge':[110] this is an argument rooted in relative expertise. The submission that 'In considering the system as a whole, it should be borne in mind that the present system, based on a stable league, does secure benefits to players which a smaller organisation might not be able to secure'[111] is simply a dogged refusal to imagine that the sporting world could ever be different. The thematic core of the defence of the transfer system advanced in *Eastham* is concern to allow sport autonomy from legal regulation: not only that theme but indeed even similar detailed arguments are recycled in *Bosman*. The outcomes of the two cases in detail are not precisely the same, because restraint of trade under the English common law does not exactly match EU internal market law, but overall both rulings exhibit a refusal to treat football as so special that it can claim to maintain a system as restrictive and burdensome as that at stake in the cases.

This is in a sense merely ancient history. But it helps to emphasize how significant is the shift caused by Article 165 TFEU, the innovation of the Lisbon Treaty with effect from 2009. It represents an abandonment of a refusal by sporting bodies even to entertain the legitimacy of the EU's role, and instead shows that sporting bodies have been induced to accept a strategy of inclusion as far as engagement with the EU is concerned. This story, and the more general shift of (some) sporting bodies to seek a more cooperative relationship with the Commission (in particular) is addressed directly in Chapter 6.

Meanwhile Jean-Marc Bosman had won his case. At the time of the judgment he was playing low-level football at the relatively advanced age (for a football player) of 31, having endured a series of problems caused by his plight.[112] In 1998 he received a payment from the Belgian Football Union,[113] but in 2015, on the twentieth anniversary of the ruling which will bear his name forever, he reflected ruefully that 'I earn nothing now … in the past I got a lot of promises but never received anything'.[114] For him it was largely a hollow victory. His 'success' alerted potential litigants to the costs of challenging the game's structure. To this extent *Bosman* confirmed that sports governing bodies, while not immune from legal challenge, are unusually powerful entities wielding global influence. They are in practice frequently able to operate on the assumption that they enjoy immunity from challenge. Sport is extraordinarily resilient to change.

But that obstinacy is much less sturdy than it was before *Bosman*. *Bosman* is one of the causes of the 'juridification' of EU sports law. It is certainly not the only one. Beginning in the 1980s and continuing apace today, technological change and governmental deregulation has transformed the broadcasting sector. Increasing demand for rights to show high-profile events has caused money to cascade into

---

[110] ibid 424.   [111] ibid 425.
[112] 'A Revolutionary Rebuilds His Life' *The Independent on Sunday* (London, 18 February 1996) 24.
[113] 'Bosman Action Settled at £312,000' *The Independent* (London, 23 December 1998) 20.
[114] 'Jean-Marc Bosman: I think I Did Something Good—I Gave Players Rights' *The Guardian* (London, 12 December 2015) <https://www.theguardian.com/football/2015/dec/12/jean-marc-bosman-players-rights-20-years> accessed 29 November 2016.

professional sport in Europe as never before. The creation of the English Premier League and the conversion of the European Cup into the Champions League, which both occurred in 1992, both pre-date *Bosman*. Football and Formula 1 are the most sought-after sports but, as a glance at today's television schedules shows, these are by no means the only ones. Law is part of the changing landscape. The increasing commercial significance—and often astonishing profitability—of sporting events brought with it a rising inability to present sport as something pure and noble that lies beyond legal control. Sports bodies could be challenged. They did not enjoy autonomy in principle from the application of EU law. They had to seek their protection within the interpretation of EU law. *Bosman* provided the vocabulary. If we looked at this today in the light of the Lisbon Treaty we might readily argue that the Court in *Bosman* was determining what falls within the notion of 'the specific nature of sport', as provided for in Article 165(1) TFEU. But this would be presentational, and would cause no change in substance. The Lisbon Treaty offers a particular twist in the detailed legal formula but all it does is (re-)frame long-standing questions rather than provide concrete answers to the questions 'Is sport special?' and 'If so, *how* special?' *Bosman*, most of all, showed clearly that the Court would not simply take the claims of sporting bodies at face value. EU sports law was taking shape, and it would not simply be a rubber-stamping of the *lex sportiva*.

4.10 Beyond *Bosman*

Bosman generated pioneering game-changing energy. In sharp contrast to *Walrave and Koch*, it did not sit in a glass case, intriguing in principle but unused in practice. Its value in litigation made it truly the 'birth' of European sports law.[115] And yet at an intellectual level *Bosman* remained at heart unsatisfying in its reasoning.

The Court in *Bosman* did not abandon its misguided and misleading understanding of exactly how and why it was open to football's governing bodies to escape condemnation under EU law. Citing and repeating *Donà* and therefore by implication also the parallel reasoning in *Walrave and Koch*, the Court stated:

... the Treaty provisions concerning freedom of movement for persons do not prevent the adoption of rules or practices excluding foreign players from certain matches for reasons which are not of an economic nature, which relate to the particular nature and context of such matches and are thus of sporting interest only, such as, for example, matches between national teams from different countries.[116]

---

[115] S Van den Bogaert, 'From Bosman to Bernard' in J Anderson (ed), *Leading Cases in Sports Law* (TMC Asser 2013) 97. See also S Weatherill, 'Bosman Changed Everything: The Rise of EC Sports Law' and S Van den Bogaert, 'Bosman: The Genesis of European Sports Law' both in MP Maduro and L Azoulai (eds), *The Past and Future of EU Law: The Classics of EU Law Revisited on the 50th Anniversary of the Rome Treaty* (Hart 2010) ch XII.2 and ch XII.3, respectively.
[116] *Bosman* (n 23) para 127.

It supplemented this with the proviso that that restriction on the scope of the provisions must remain limited to its proper objective, which provided the cue for its finding that no such concession should be admitted in the case of nationality discrimination in *club* football. But the Court's formula remains intellectually fragile. The reasons may not be 'of an economic nature', but they plainly exert economic effects: and in consequence they cannot convincingly be described as 'of sporting interest only'. *Bosman* shares with *Walrave and Koch* a readiness to integrate the notion that sport is special into the interpretation and application of EU internal market law but it also shares with it a fractured intellectual basis for articulating just why that is so.

After *Bosman* the Court was faced with a rising tide of litigation, but also with the need to craft a more intellectually satisfying pivot on which to rest the interaction between EU law and sporting autonomy, the *lex sportiva*.

The Court's ruling in *Deliège v Ligue de Judo* was not associated with a sport that attracts high levels of income;[117] it concerns judo. But it is significant for its analytical change of direction, and in that vein it represents an improvement. The case concerned the selection of individual judokas for international competition. An athlete could not simply enter. He or she had to be chosen by the national federation. A similar pattern operates in the Olympic Games and in many other events where individuals compete on their own behalf, but as a qualifying member of a national team. Plainly *failure* to secure selection would damage the athlete's sporting profile. It would be economically damaging too, to the extent that a would-be participant could have expected commercial advantage from involvement. The system was attacked by a disgruntled judoka who had not been selected. Litigation alleging a violation of EU internal market law was commenced before the Belgian courts and was the subject of a preliminary reference to the Court of Justice in Luxembourg. The questions referred invited the Court to address both free movement and competition law, but, as in *Bosman*, the Court chose not to examine competition law at all. The Court confined its analysis to the Treaty provision dealing with the free movement of services, at the time Article 49 EC and today Article 56 TFEU, treating the matter as a potential restriction on the cross-border provision of services by the athlete.

The Court cited both *Walrave and Koch* and *Bosman* in repeating that 'sport is subject to Community law only in so far as it constitutes an economic activity'.[118] It then accepted that the applicable selection rules had the effect of limiting the number of participants in a tournament. It then added the crucial remark that 'such a limitation is inherent in the conduct of an international high-level sports event, which necessarily involves certain selection rules or criteria being adopted'.[119] This was enough for it to conclude that the rules did not in themselves constitute a restriction on the freedom to provide services prohibited by the Treaty.[120]

---

[117] Cases C-51/96 and C-191/97 *Deliège v Ligue de Judo* [2000] ECR I-2549.
[118] ibid para 41.   [119] ibid para 64.   [120] ibid para 64.

The Court therefore ignored the unreliable notion of the rule of purely sporting interest. It was wise to do so. Properly understood, the rule of which *Deliège* had fallen foul was of sporting interest but it was not of *purely* sporting interest. The Court in *Deliège* found a functionally similar but intellectually more satisfying route to protecting sporting autonomy from the incursion of EU law than that which it had pursued previously. What is 'inherent' in the conduct of a sports event escapes condemnation under EU law—not because it does not restrict the cross-border provision of services, still less because it is devoid of economic effects, but instead because the very nature of the event is based on it. It is a conditional autonomy—sports must demonstrate that the choices define the competition.

It is clearly of central importance for these purposes what truly is 'inherent', and who decides. But this is the route to protecting sporting autonomy within the framework of EU internal market law. Finding such rules to be inherent in the organization of the event (as in *Deliège*) is a more rational basis than claiming that such rules are purely sporting in character (as in *Walrave and Koch*). There is no virtue in denying the economic effects of (most) sporting rules, but the key point is that the presence of restrictive economic effects does not, without more, disable sporting bodies from demonstrating why their rules are necessary and therefore compatible with the demands of EU law. This is to express the centrally important notion that sport enjoys a conditional autonomy under EU law.

In this vein the Court added in *Deliège* that the delegation of the task of making selections to the national federations is the norm in sport and that such federations 'normally have the necessary knowledge and experience'.[121] As a general observation, assessment of relevant expertise dictates a preference for deferring to sports bodies, and this is here, in *Deliège*, judicially acknowledged. The Court added that 'the selection rules at issue in the main proceedings apply both to competitions organised within the Community and to those taking place outside it and involve both nationals of Member States and those of non-member countries'.[122] Sensitivity to the global reach of the *lex sportiva* was therefore part of the Court's assessment, designed to avoid the interference that would have been caused by the inevitably fragmenting effect of EU law, had the selection rules been condemned in their application to EU nationals.

In sum, a detrimental effect felt by an individual athlete did not mean that sporting rules were *incompatible* with the Treaty. The *Deliège* judgment is respectful of sporting autonomy, but according to reasoning which treats EU law and 'internal' sports law (the *lex sportiva*) as potentially overlapping. Sport enjoys a *conditional* autonomy from EU free movement law. The condition is that it must show why its practices are necessary for the organization of the sport, even where they exert restrictive effects on cross-border economic activity. This also requires engagement with procedural aspects: selection procedures for judokas would not have been treated as compatible with EU law if arbitrary or intransparent.[123] In this sense

---

[121] ibid para 68.   [122] ibid para 68.
[123] cf eg Case C-219/07 *Nationale Raad van Dierenkwekers en Liefhebbers* [2008] ECR I-4475, especially paras 33–37.

EU law pushes for good governance and fair administration in sporting practice, a matter addressed more fully in Chapter 10. This approach fits Article 165 TFEU's embrace of 'the specific nature of sport', which is readily understood as an encapsulation of the Court's attitude in free movement law that sport does not enjoy any general autonomy from EU law, but that it is entitled to express its special characteristics as a basis for contextual application of EU law to sport. This is the heart of the interpretative or adjudicative strategy. Since *Bosman* and *Deliège*, most of the activity at the intersection between EU law and sport has concerned competition law rather than free movement law, but here too the focus is on the interpretative strategy as the route for sporting bodies to press for their—conditional—autonomy. And in the development of competition law, to which attention turns in Chapter 5, the Court has developed further an approach which leaves behind the misplaced reliance on 'purely sporting' rules that tainted the first steps taken in *Walrave and Koch* and in *Bosman*, and which instead takes a more realistic approach to practices which are typically both sporting and economic in their effects and intent. The Court has never gone so far as to embrace openly a convergence of the interpretative approach connecting both free movement and competition law, but it will be suggested in the next chapter that this is possible and in Chapter 7.3 it will be argued that, especially in the light of Article 165 TFEU, this is the proper way to develop an integrated approach to the specific nature of sport recognized pursuant to EU law's grant of conditional autonomy to sport.

5

Sport in the Internal Market

Competition Law

5.1 Competition Law

The previous chapter focused on the significance of the *Bosman* ruling in the shaping of EU free movement law in cases involving sport.[1] The preliminary reference made to it by the Belgian court in *Bosman* invited the Court of Justice to consider the application to sport of not only the free movement rules but also the Treaty competition rules. Having found violations of the free movement rules, the Court simply declined to discuss the relevance of competition law.[2] The same was true in *Deliège*, the case concerning judo, also met in Chapter 4.[3] The Court's ruling focused on examination of free movement law, but, despite the referring court's invitation, no discussion of competition law was forthcoming. In *Deliège* the Court considered it had not been provided with sufficient information, most of all about the structure of the market, to be able to supply an informed ruling.[4]

Most of the sports-related cases since *Bosman* and *Deliège* have dealt with the application of EU competition law rather than the free movement rules. Competition law, as explained in Chapter 3, is founded on the twin pillars of Articles 101 and 102 of the Treaty on the Functioning of the European Union (TFEU), which deal respectively with bilateral and multilateral restrictive practices and with the abuse of a position of economic dominance by a single undertaking. The regulation of sport, typically conducted according to networks of agreements between governing bodies and participants, and underpinned by the typically global reach of a single rule-maker, is plainly vulnerable to supervision according to the dictates of EU competition law. That is the concern of this chapter.

EU competition law does not run on precisely the same lines as free movement law. So, to skate over the principal points of detailed distinction, Article 101 rests heavily on finding concerted practices whereas free movement law focuses on the adoption of measures; market analysis is much more prominent in competition

---

[1] Case C-415/93 *Union royale belge des sociétés de football association ASBL v Jean-Marc Bosman* [1995] ECR I-4921.
[2] ibid para 138.
[3] Cases C-51/96 and C-191/97 *Deliège v Ligue de Judo* [2000] ECR I-2549.
[4] ibid paras 36–38.

law than in free movement law (so, for example, an explicit *de minimis* threshold for the invocation of EU law applies to the former but not the latter); and there are differences in the personal scope of the provisions. The proper relationship between competition law and free movement law needs careful description and it is normatively contested too.[5] The separation of competition law and free movement law is on occasion a friction in the shaping of EU sports law, but the bigger picture is their practical alignment for most purposes. In short, what they have in common far exceeds what separates them. This is largely because both are part of the broader scheme designed to build and maintain the EU's internal market. Articles 101 and 102 TFEU share an aim, which is the 'maintenance of effective competition' within the internal market.[6] The free movement provisions too are dedicated to the achievement of the internal market, which is defined in Article 26 TFEU as 'an area without internal frontiers in which the free movement of goods, persons, services and capital is ensured in accordance with the provisions of the Treaties'.

Bosman was a free movement case, but it set the scene and it set the tone. The Commission, interpreting and applying competition law to sport, quickly came to adopt a functionally comparable approach to that employed by the Court in the interpretation and application of the free movement provisions. It refused to exclude sport from supervision pursuant to the relevant Treaty provisions, but equally it did not rule out that sport might present some peculiar characteristics that should be taken into account in the legal analysis. This is to confirm the adjudicative or interpretative approach to securing sporting autonomy which was mapped in Chapter 2.

5.2 *ENIC/UEFA*

The Commission's *ENIC/UEFA* decision offers an early illustration of the emergence of the model of 'conditional autonomy' granted to sport in the Commission's treatment of practices in the light of EU competition law.[7]

ENIC was an investment company with a stake in six football clubs in four different EU Member States plus Switzerland. They were Glasgow Rangers, Basel, Vicenza, Slavia Prague, AEK Athens, and Tottenham Hotspur. Its difficulties arose as a result of the adoption of a UEFA rule in 1998, which under the title 'Integrity of the UEFA Club competitions: Independence of clubs' stipulated that no two (or more) clubs participating in a UEFA club competition may be directly or indirectly

---

[5] eg J Baquero Cruz, *Between Competition and Free Movement: The Economic Constitutional Law of the European Community* (OUP 2002); K Mortelmans, 'Towards Convergence in the Application of the Rules on Free Movement and Competition?' (2001) 38 CML Rev 613; V Hatzopoulos, 'The Economic Constitution of the EU Treaty and the Limits between Economic and Non-Economic Activities' [2012] European Business Law Review 973.

[6] Case 6/72 *Continental Can v Commission* [1973] ECR 215.

[7] COMP 37.806 *ENIC/UEFA*, IP/02/942, 27 June 2002. The rejection decision is available at <http://ec.europa.eu/competition/elojade/isef/case_details.cfm?proc_code=1_37806> accessed 29 November 2016.

controlled by the same entity or managed by the same person. The aim, in short, was to eliminate any whisper of suspicion of a fixed match. ENIC considered that the rule distorted competition by preventing and restricting investment in football clubs. Their point was that the rule restricted the freedom of action of club owners and would-be owners: once they had bought one club they could not buy another, to the detriment of demand-side competition in the market to buy clubs. As mentioned in Chapter 2, a challenge pursued within the *lex sportiva* did not help ENIC, for the CAS ruled that the ban was necessary to protect the authenticity of sporting competition.[8] So ENIC lodged a complaint with the Commission. Citing the familiar proviso, pioneered by the Court, that pursuit of economic activity brings the practice of sport within the scope of EU law, the Commission agreed in principle that the UEFA rule was capable of amounting to an arrangement that fell within the scope of what was then Article 81(1) of the Treaty Establishing the European Community (EC), now Article 101(1) TFEU, but, referring to the need to guarantee the integrity of the affected competitions, it decided not to pursue the matter further and it rejected ENIC's complaint. ENIC did not pursue the matter either, although it would have been possible in principle to challenge the Commission's decision before the Court in Luxembourg pursuant to Article 263 TFEU. That was the end of that particular matter.

Broadly, then, the Commission had adopted a model of 'conditional autonomy': the practice fell within the scope of EU law because of its effect on the market for clubs (ie no absolute autonomy), but autonomy was permitted provided it met the conditions set by EU law which here were attuned to the special sensitivity in sport to achieve a rigorous separation of ownership between clubs that are supposed to be rivals on the pitch. However, the precise language employed by the Commission in its rejection decision deserves attention. Its starting point was 'to assess whether the effect of the rule is restrictive and if so, whether this effect is inherent in the pursuit of the objective of the rule which is to ensure the very existence of credible pan European football competitions'.[9] Plainly this has close association with the reasoning adopted in *Deliège*, in connection with free movement law.[10] And the Commission had had pressed on it by UEFA the central relevance of that ruling,[11] but, in examining the matter, the Commission preferred to rely on the Court's ruling in *Wouters*, delivered in February 2002.[12] This, unlike *Deliège*, is a competition law case. On the other hand, its factual context has nothing at all to do with sport. *Wouters* has nonetheless established itself as centrally important in the evolution of EU sports law. *ENIC* was the start.

In *Wouters* the Court was asked to consider the compatibility with what is now Article 101 TFEU of a Dutch rule forbidding the creation of multi-disciplinary partnerships involving barristers and accountants. The Court took the view that

---

[8] CAS 98/200 *AEK Athens and Slavia Prague v UEFA*.
[9] *ENIC/UEFA* (n 7) rejection decision, para 30; see also para 3.
[10] *Deliège* (n 3); see Ch 4.10.   [11] *ENIC/UEFA* (n 7) rejection decision, para 21.
[12] Case C-309/99 *JCJ Wouters, JW Savelbergh, Price Waterhouse Belastingadviseurs BV v Algemene Raad van de Nederlandse Orde van Advocaten* [2002] ECR I-1577.

the national rule 'has an adverse effect on competition and may affect trade between Member States'.[13] A multi-disciplinary partnership could offer a wider range of services, as well as benefiting from economies of scale generating cost reductions. The prohibition was therefore liable to limit production and technical development.

Having found unambiguously that the 'rules restrict competition',[14] the Court proceeded in *Wouters* to state that the application of what is now Article 101 TFEU is conditioned by the overall context in which the bilateral or multilateral decision that restricts commercial freedom has been taken, specifically that account must be taken of its objectives. The core question is then 'whether the consequential effects restrictive of competition are inherent in the pursuit of those objectives'.[15]

In *Wouters* this drew the Court into reflection on the claimed virtues of the Dutch rules prohibiting partnerships between barristers and accountants. The stated aim was to guarantee the independence and loyalty to the client of members of the Bar as part of a broader concern to secure the sound administration of justice. Though there were—the Court repeated—'effects restrictive of competition',[16] they did not go beyond what was necessary in order to ensure the proper functioning of the legal profession in the Netherlands. There was no breach of EU competition law. In short, the question addressed: Was the practice of the legal profession 'special'? And the answer: it was. And in *ENIC* the Commission applied the same model to sport. Asking the same question, it arrived at the same answer.

Adopting the language of *Wouters*, the Commission in *ENIC* asked whether the consequential effects of UEFA's rule were inherent in the pursuit of the very existence of credible pan-European football competitions. And, embedding in its analysis the particular context in which the rule is applied, it took the view that the limitation placed on freedom to act was justified. This was not a restriction of competition, for without such a rule, and the consequent emergence of public scepticism about the fair and honest character of the event, 'the proper functioning of the market where the clubs develop their economic activities would be under threat', and damage would be done to 'interest and marketability'.[17]

The Commission reached the conclusion that rules forbidding multiple ownership of football clubs suppressed demand, but that they were indispensable to the maintenance of a credible competition marked by uncertainty as to the outcome of all matches. A competition's basic character would be shattered were consumers to suspect that the clubs were not true rivals. The aim was 'clean competition', without which there could be no credible competition at all.[18] Moreover the rule went no further than was necessary to achieve its aim: no less restrictive means could be devised. The key insight informing the decision is that sport may be culturally special, but it is economically special too: there is a need to restrain the power of buyers of companies in sports leagues that simply would not arise in a normal market until

---

[13] ibid para 86 of the judgment.   [14] ibid para 94.   [15] ibid para 97.
[16] ibid para 110.   [17] *ENIC/UEFA* (n 7) rejection decision, para 32.
[18] ibid paras 29, 38.

such time as the threshold of dominant power addressed in EU law by the Merger Regulation is approached.[19] The principal message here is that sporting practices typically have an economic effect and that accordingly they cannot be sealed off from the expectations of the Treaty. However, within the area of overlap between EU law and 'internal' sports law (the *lex sportiva*) there is room for recognition of the features of sport which may differ from 'normal' industries.

In its reasoning, *ENIC* is not presented in *exactly* the same way as *Wouters*. In the latter the Court found the rules were restrictive of competition but, having assessed the context and objectives, it concluded that they did not go beyond what was necessary in order to ensure the proper practice of the legal profession, and so they did not fall to be condemned as violations of Article 101(1) TFEU.[20] By contrast, in *ENIC* the Commission, having cited the key part of the *Wouters* ruling, then declared that there was not a restriction of competition.[21] However, the difference is more apparent than real. The Commission reached that conclusion after stating the need to examine the context in which the rule was applied and its objectives. And it agreed with UEFA that the rule protected the proper functioning of the market by ensuring maintenance of the public's perception that the sporting competition was fair and honest. In applying the *Wouters* formula the key issue, as the Commission correctly identified,[22] was whether the consequential effects of the rule were inherent in the pursuit of the very existence of credible pan-European football competitions. They were, and what the Commission intended in introducing its analysis by commenting that there was not a restriction of competition was that there was not a restriction of competition *within the meaning of the conduct that is subject to the prohibition contained in Article 101(1)*—as indeed later parts of the decision seem to make plain.[23]

ENIC follows *Wouters*: the key point is that Article 101(1) TFEU is not violated where the rules, though admittedly restrictive of competition, serve interests that are necessary for or inherent in the organization of the relevant activity. Within the interpretation and application of EU competition law and subject to the controlling requirement that measures must be limited to what is necessary to ensure the implementation of legitimate objectives, any regulated sector is given space to demonstrate what its particular special features and needs entail. *Wouters*, remote from sport, shows how EU competition law generally is porous to concern for particular sector-specific sensitivities.[24] *ENIC* is simply a sports-specific application.

This is in close alignment with the earlier ruling in *Deliège*.[25] There too the Court crafted an interpretation of EU law which concedes conditional autonomy to sport,

---

[19] The current version of the Merger Regulation is Regulation (EC) 139/2004 [2004] OJ L24/1.
[20] *Wouters* (n 12) paras 94, 109.   [21] *ENIC/UEFA* (n 7) para 32.   [22] ibid para 32.
[23] ibid especially paras 40, 42.
[24] The approach reappears in subsequent judgments remote from sport: eg Case C-1/12 *OTOC (Ordem dos Técnicos Oficiais de Contas)*, judgment of 28 February 2013; Case C-136/12 *Consiglio Nazionale dei Geologi*, judgment of 18 July 2013; Joined Cases C-184/13 to C-187/13, C-194/13, C-195/13, and C-208/13 *API*, judgment of 4 September 2014.
[25] *Deliège* (n 3).

albeit in the context of free movement law. The inquiry asks just why particular practices with economic effects are pursued—are they inherent in the organization of sport? The Court in *Deliège* treated the questions about competition law it had been asked by the referring Belgian court as inadmissible for want of adequate detailed information, but Advocate General Cosmas, though advising the Court to treat the questions as inadmissible, added brief comment. Drawing on general EU competition law, beyond its sport-specific application, he cited the Court's ruling in *DLG*, on which the Court would also rely three years later in *Wouters*,[26] and stated that what is now Article 101(1) TFEU 'does not apply to restrictions on competition which are essential in order to attain the legitimate aims which they pursue'.[27] Here the rules prevented judokas from taking part in international competitions for which they were not selected, but they were indispensable to the proper functioning of the sport. He added that were the matter assessed from the perspective of Article 102, the particular organizational demands involved would preclude any finding of abuse.

As *Wouters* would confirm soon afterwards in the context of competition law, the point is not to deny that there is a restrictive effect felt by individuals, still less to pretend that an economic context is missing, but rather to allow for an interpretation of the Treaty rules that is contextually sensitive—to allow room within EU law for sport's special characteristics to be weighed and to inquire into what really is 'inherent' in the sport's organizational model. Free movement law and competition law clearly have detailed elements that do not run in common, but, of much greater significance, they share this broader structural openness to contextual appreciation of the reasons for choosing particular organizational patterns. Both Court and Commission are receptive to sector-specific special features in the interpretation and application of EU internal market law. Article 165 TFEU's embrace of 'the specific nature of sport' post-dates these developments, but in fact reflects and is provoked by them.

5.3 *Meca-Medina and Majcen v Commission*

It is competition law rather than free movement law that has come to provide the main basis for addressing the intersection of the law of the EU's internal market with sporting autonomy, the *lex sportiva*. The Commission's reliance on *Wouters* in its *ENIC* decision was plainly significant in charting the way forward, but the authoritative voice of the Court was required to confirm the direction of travel. In the summer of 2006 the Court brought a welcome degree of analytical clarity to the matter. *Meca-Medina* is a landmark in the development of EU sports law which deserves to stand in bold prominence alongside *Bosman*.[28]

---

[26] Case C-250/92 *DLG* [1994] ECR I-5641, cited at *Wouters* (n 12) para 109.
[27] *Deliège* (n 3) para 110, Opinion of Cosmas AG.
[28] Case C-519/04 P *Meca-Medina and Majcen v Commission* [2006] ECR I-6991.

5.3.1 The importance of *Meca-Medina*

In *Meca-Medina* the Court took the opportunity to confirm that the approach it had used in *Wouters* in connection with the regulation of the bar and the administration of justice was suitable for the application and interpretation of EU competition law in the context of sport. And this allowed it to shape an intellectually convincing understanding of how and why—and how far—sport is treated as special under EU law. In particular the Court in *Meca-Medina* was presented with the opportunity to develop more firmly the notion that the 'sporting exception' does not mean that a practice falls outwith the scope of the Treaty altogether but rather that the rules have an economic effect and so fall within the scope of the Treaty—but that they are not condemned by it in so far as they are shown also to exert virtuous effects in order to secure the sport's effective organization.[29] This is why the ruling matters so much. Autonomy is permitted to sport under EU law on condition that adequate reason for the prevailing pattern of sports governance is shown to the Court's satisfaction.

5.3.2 The path to litigation

David Meca-Medina and Igor Majcen were professional swimmers. They had failed a drug test administered as part of the control exercised by swimming's governing body, FINA. As a result they had been banned from competition for a period which, after an appeal pursued before the CAS, was fixed at two years.[30] This deprived the athletes of their means of making a living and so the consequential economic detriment was obvious and unarguable. But it was equally obvious and unarguable that this was not *only* a matter of an economic impact. Sport is structured by rules which define the essence of the endeavour. Keeping out drug cheats has an economic motivation not least by securing the attraction of the event to sponsors and broadcasters: 'clean' sport sells, and only clean sport is readily connected to the wider claims associated with a healthy lifestyle commonly made on behalf of sport. At the same time it is an existential choice: sport is only sport if there is a level, drug-free playing field for competitors. The champion should have the most talent and commitment, not the best pharmacist. To use the language considered earlier, anti-doping seems convincingly understood as an inherent element in the organization of sport.

The swimmers complained to the European Commission that their exclusion from the sport constituted a violation of the EU's competition rules. The Commission rejected their complaint. Meca-Medina and Majcen then applied to the Court of First Instance (CFI: known since the entry into force of the Lisbon

---

[29] For extended analysis, see R Parrish and S Miettinen, *The Sporting Exception in European Law* (TMC Asser 2007); also S Weatherill, 'On Overlapping Legal Orders: What is the "Purely Sporting Rule"?' in B Bogusz, A Cygan, and E Szyszczak (eds), *The Regulation of Sport in the European Union* (Edward Elgar 2007) ch 3; G Auneau, 'Jurisprudence' (2007) 43 RTDE 361.

[30] *Meca-Medina* (n 28) para 3 of the judgment, which also notes that the swimmers had not appealed the CAS ruling before the Swiss Federal Court. On the CAS, see Ch 2.

Treaty in December 2009 as the General Court) for annulment of the Commission's decision to reject their complaint. The CFI rejected their application.[31] The swimmers then appealed to the Court of Justice. It subsequently set aside the CFI's judgment, though it still ultimately concluded that the swimmers' application for annulment of the Commission decision had to fail.[32] But it is worth dwelling briefly on the CFI ruling. In *Meca-Medina and Majcen v Commission* the CFI did sterling, if entirely unintended, service to the development of EU sports law by adopting an approach that was so absurd that it illuminated just what had been missed in previous judicial practice, beginning with *Walrave and Koch* and continuing in *Bosman*. And it provoked the Court, dealing with the appeal, to think much more carefully about the underlying basis for subjecting sport to EU law and to yielding it a degree of conditional autonomy. Most of all the Court's ruling on the appeal in the case is significant for taking a much less generous approach to the scope of sporting autonomy than had been admitted by the CFI. The litigation in general, and the two judgments in particular, capture the choice to be made about the extent to which the law should respect sporting autonomy.

5.3.3 The ruling of the CFI

The CFI began its analysis with faithful adherence to the line of case law reaching back to *Walrave and Koch*. Sport, it repeated, is subject to EU law only in so far as it constitutes an economic activity. But from that starting point, which indeed reflects the EU's very constitutional foundation, it then ran off in quite the wrong direction. It insisted that anti-doping rules concern exclusively non-economic aspects of sport, designed to preserve 'noble competition'[33] and that therefore they lie outwith the scope of the Treaty. Such an approach is plainly immensely favourable to sports federations' conventional appeals for sporting autonomy. It upholds a plea to absolute autonomy from the application of EU law.

The gist of the CFI's judgment is well captured by the summary that 'Purely sporting rules—like anti-doping rules—fall outside Article ... [101(1)] because they do not relate to an economic activity'.[34] And that is exactly why the judgment is flawed. This is intellectually unsupportable.

Anti-doping rules do relate to an economic activity—that of the athlete and that of the organizer of the competition. They are perfect examples of rules that are sporting in nature, but not *purely* sporting: they also have economic effects.

Put another way, the CFI's ruling is driven by the entirely correct perception that the EU's competence is limited by its founding Treaties: this is what we know today as the principle of conferral located in Article 5(1) TEU, which was examined in Chapter 3. Sport was not an explicit EU competence at the time of *Meca-Medina*, and it did not become one until the arrival in the Treaty, with effect from 2009, of

---

[31] Case T-313/02 *Meca-Medina and Majcen v Commission* [2004] ECR II-3291.
[32] *Meca-Medina* (n 28).   [33] ibid para 49.
[34] E Loozen, 'Professional Ethics and Restraints of Competition' (2006) 31 EL Rev 28, 46.

Article 165 TFEU. So the CFI referred to 'purely sporting rules, that is to say rules concerning questions of purely sporting interest and, as such, having nothing to do with economic activity' and juxtaposed this to a description of regulations which relate to the particular nature and context of sporting events which 'are inherent in the organisation and proper conduct of sporting competition and cannot be regarded as constituting a restriction on the Community rules on the freedom of movement of workers and the freedom to provide services'.[35] Such observations are sensitive to the constitutional limits of EU competence. This, however, is to conflate two different points. Plausibly there exists a (small) category of 'purely sporting' rules which are truly unassociated with economic activity, but regulations inherent in the organization and proper conduct of sporting competition form a much larger category in which economic effect is commonly present. Similarly the CFI observes that 'the campaign against doping does not pursue any economic objective'.[36] That is probably not true, and in fact the CFI itself recognizes the economic value of a 'clean' sport to its organizers,[37] but even if it *is* true, this is not of itself a reason for locating the campaign outside the EU Treaty scheme. EU internal market law is driven by assessment of a practice's effect, not merely its objective. It is the broad reach of the internal market that provides the constitutional basis for the EU's claim to assert competence in matters of sport. This is the true context within which to understand the operation of the principle of conferral found in Article 5(1) TEU. Anti-doping rules certainly have economic effects on those found to have contravened them. The CFI's attempts to present such rules as 'sporting' and not 'economic' are as unhelpful as they are unconvincing. They are both.

5.3.4 On appeal, the Court of Justice

The CFI ruling was the subject of an appeal to the Court of Justice.[38] The Court's judgment was largely directed at exposing the intellectual inadequacy of the attempt to establish a separation between sporting rules (which escape the scope of application of EU law) and rules of an economic nature (which do not). In this respect it was successful. This, however, was ultimately of no practical value to the applicant swimmers: Meca-Medina and Majcen joined Bosman and Walrave and Koch before them in doing far more service to EU law than EU law ever did for them.[39]

The Court of Justice in *Meca-Medina* was on familiar ground when it began by asserting that sport is subject to EU law 'in so far as it constitutes an economic activity'.[40] It added that the Treaty prohibitions against restrictions on free movement 'do not affect rules concerning questions which are of purely sporting interest and, as such, have nothing to do with economic activity', citing *Walrave and Koch*, its very first ruling applying EU law to sport.[41] It then referred to 'the difficulty of severing the economic aspects from the sporting aspects of a sport', a deft phrase

---

[35] *Meca-Medina* (n 31) para 41.   [36] ibid para 44.   [37] ibid para 57.
[38] *Meca-Medina* (n 28).   [39] Ch 11.8 will tell a similar story about Karen Murphy.
[40] *Meca-Medina* (n 28) para 22.   [41] ibid para 25.

deriving from *Bosman*,[42] confirming its view that the free movement provisions in the Treaty 'do not preclude rules or practices justified on non-economic grounds which relate to the particular nature and context of certain sporting events'. It then added, in line with its conventional practice, that such a restriction on the scope of the provisions in question must remain limited to its proper objective.

Up to this point this is largely familiar reasoning, although it is of note that the Court draws freely on its free movement case law to inform its treatment of a competition law case. This points to the functional connections between the two as instruments of internal market law.[43] The Court's retention of the notion of matters that are 'purely sporting' in nature, though understandable given its pedigree in the Court's case law and its use by the CFI in *Meca-Medina*, is nevertheless apt to mislead. The *effect* of a practice is what drives EU internal market law and, as explained, rules that are 'purely sporting' in effect are extremely rare. However, in *Meca-Medina* the Court moved beyond the limiting formula of the rule that is purely sporting in nature. It was far more thorough in its examination. It added that even where one finds such a rule, this 'does not have the effect of removing from the scope of the Treaty the person engaging in the activity governed by that rule or the body which has laid it down'.[44] It is, the Court explained, necessary to examine the applicable conditions set by the Treaty, in particular those concerning free movement and competition. The CFI had made an error of law in holding that rules could be excluded from the scope of the Treaty provisions on competition on the sole ground that they were regarded as purely sporting with regard to the application of the free movement provisions. A more detailed appraisal of the demands of what were then Articles 81 and 82 of the Treaty Establishing the European Community (EC), now Articles 101 and 102 TFEU, was required.[45]

The contested CFI judgment which dismissed the swimmers' application was therefore set aside. This, however, was the limit of the athletes' joy. The Court, after reviewing the matter, concluded that, despite the error of law made by the CFI, nonetheless it was appropriate to dismiss the application for annulment of the Commission decision rejecting their complaint. There was, in the Court's view, no substance to the criticism made of the Commission. The CFI had taken the wrong route in its legal analysis, but it had reached the right conclusion.

Meca-Medina and Majcen were therefore not able to use EU law to disturb their two-year suspension from swimming. But what is of enduring importance to the evolution of EU sports law is the Court's view in its ruling of how the analysis *should* have been conducted. The Court stated that the compatibility of rules with EU competition law cannot be assessed in the abstract. This is because not every agreement between undertakings which restricts the freedom of action of one or more of the parties necessarily falls within the prohibition laid down in (what is now) Article 101(1) TFEU. In applying Article 101(1), 'account must first of all be

---

[42] ibid para 26. *Deliège* too is cited in para 26.   [43] On this convergence, see further Ch 7.3.
[44] *Meca-Medina* (n 28) para 27.   [45] ibid para 33.

taken of the overall context in which the decision of the association of undertakings was taken or produces its effects and, more specifically, of its objectives'; and it 'has then to be considered whether the consequential effects restrictive of competition are inherent in the pursuit of those objectives ... and are proportionate to them'.[46] In support of these propositions the Court cited paragraph 97 of its ruling in *Wouters*.[47] As explained previously, *Wouters* was the Commission's interpretative rock in its decision in favour of UEFA's ban on multiple club ownership in *ENIC*:[48] the Court's reliance in *Wouters* on interpreting (what is today) Article 101 TFEU in *Meca-Medina* is of much higher and more authoritative significance.

Relying on the model shaped in *Wouters*, the Court envisages that a practice may generate effects that are restrictive of competition, yet may be saved from condemnation pursuant to Article 101(1) TFEU in the light of the objectives pursued. This inquiry shall also involve assessment of the necessity to tolerate the restrictive effects in pursuit of those objectives. This is to open up the legal assessment of sporting practices that have the *effect* of restricting competition also to include appraisal of their sporting *objective*. And the use of the word 'inherent' in the Court's formula[49] echoes the ruling in *Deliège*, which similarly insisted on the application of free movement law in a manner that is sensitive to context and, in particular, does not cut across sporting practices that are inherent in the sport's organization.

This then brought the Court to an examination of the anti-doping rules at stake in *Meca-Medina*. It decided that even if they were treated as a decision of an association of undertakings which limited the swimmers' freedom of action, they did not necessarily constitute a forbidden restriction of competition within the meaning of (what is now) Article 101 TFEU, since they were 'justified by a legitimate objective'.[50] This is consistent with the ruling in *Wouters* on which the Court placed explicit reliance. It is also comfortably in line with the Court's view in *Bosman* that the transfer system pursued 'legitimate' objectives, albeit in that case it was examined in the context of free movement law. It was every bit as true in *Meca-Medina* as it was in *Bosman* that the Court's view of what was 'legitimate' was not based and could not be based on the explicit terms of the Treaty, which at the time was barren of any mention of sport. Instead the Court had to think creatively and devise its own view. It stated that the Commission could rightly take the view that the general objective of the rules was to combat doping in order for competitive sport to be conducted fairly; and that it included the need to safeguard equal chances for athletes' health, the integrity and objectivity of competitive sport, and ethical values in sport.[51] Moreover, the effect of penalties for breach restricted the athletes' freedom of action but was 'inherent' in the rules, given that penalties were necessary to ensure enforcement of the ban on doping.[52]

The limitation placed on the swimmers' freedom of action was found to be 'inherent in the organisation and proper conduct of competitive sport and its very

---

[46] ibid para 42.   [47] *Wouters* (n 12).   [48] *ENIC/UEFA* (n 7).
[49] *Meca-Medina* (n 28) para 42.   [50] ibid para 45.   [51] ibid para 43.
[52] ibid para 44.

purpose is to ensure healthy rivalry between athletes'.[53] One might today choose to frame this analysis with reference to Article 165 TFEU, and treat the imposition of sanctions in a way that curtailed the swimmers' freedom of action as a reflection of 'the specific nature of sport'. But this would be to do more than repackage the willingness of the Court to interpret EU competition law in a manner sensitive to the particular context of sport well in advance of the arrival of Article 165 in the Treaty with effect from 2009.

That the restriction must be 'inherent' in organizational rules which are in turn justified by a legitimate objective ensures that the Court is able to apply Article 101 to forbid rules that are found to be excessive. Restrictions must be limited to what is necessary to ensure the proper conduct of competitive sport. This is the competition law version of the Court's careful refusal in *Bosman* to accept in the context of free movement law that nationality discrimination, inherent in *international* sport, could lawfully be extended to player selection policies in *club* football. In *Meca-Medina* the Court suggested the line might be crossed where the conditions laid down for defining the circumstances which amount to doping in respect of which penalties may be imposed lack any scientific credibility and are too readily met, or where penalties imposed are disproportionately severe. This would go beyond what is needed to ensure that sporting events take place and function properly and would therefore generate unlawful adverse effects on competition.[54] So this is the route for athletes and other interested parties to use EU competition law in future to attack sporting practices. *Meca-Medina* is not a concession of an absolute autonomy to sport. It grants a conditional autonomy under EU law. The judgment displays a proper wariness of questioning the expertise practised by sports federations, *in casu* in doping control, but the Court refuses to place such practices beyond the scope of review as a matter of principle. So, in similar vein, in *Motosykletistiki Omospondia Ellados NPID (MOTOE) v Elliniko Dimosio* the Court did not call into question the conferral on a sports governing body of an exclusive right to decide whether or not to sanction the staging of new events on its territory, but it did envisage that a violation of Article 102 TFEU could arise where such a governing body itself also organized and commercially exploited events.[55] Article 102 comes into play only where an undertaking holds a position of economic dominance, but this threshold requirement, the crossing of which normally entails careful examination of the structure of the market in order to decide whether the required level of economic power unrestrained by competitive pressure is present,[56] is typically satisfied with ease in application to a sports governing body, precisely because such bodies typically claim an existential sporting need to establish globally common applicable rules. So the question in *MOTOE* was whether there was an abuse of dominant

---

[53] ibid para 45.   [54] ibid para 47.

[55] Case C-49/07 [2008] ECR I-4863. On governance, see further Ch 10.

[56] eg Case 27/76 *United Brands and United Brands Continental v Commission* [1978] ECR 207; Case 85/76 *Hoffmann-La Roche v Commission* [1979] ECR 461; Case 322/81 *Nederlandsche Banden-Industrie-Michelin v Commission* [1983] ECR 3461, all cited at para 37 of *MOTOE*. See also Commission Notice on the definition of relevant market [1997] OJ C372/5.

power. The Court found there was. There would be, in short, a conflict of interest: the governing body would be in a position to use its regulatory power to further its own economic interests by favouring its own events over those of rival operators, a 'situation of unequal conditions of competition'.[57] But in *Meca-Medina* the Court found no such flaws.[58] EU law concedes conditional autonomy to sporting practices and, in the absence of any compelling evidence that the doping procedures were flawed or the sanctions disproportionate, the conditions set by EU law were met. FINA could ban the swimmers without infringing EU law.

5.4 The Significance of *Meca-Medina*

It is of central significance that the Court of Justice's analysis in *Meca-Medina* does *not* claim that the anti-doping rules are 'purely sporting' in their nature or effect. In fact it could not be more plain that they are *not* of this type. From the perspective of the swimmers, the rules have a very severe economic effect. They are unable to earn a living. And organizers of sports events too are doubtless motivated not only by the aim of protecting the sporting integrity of their event but also by the damage done to sponsorship and broadcasting opportunities by an association with doping.[59] Instead of pursuing the fictional or at least extremely rare creature that is the 'purely sporting' rule, the Court in *Meca-Medina* finds a different and more intellectually credible means to express the special character of sport within the interpretation and application of EU law. *Meca-Medina* constitutes a rejection of the notion that a 'purely sporting' rule is of itself apt to escape the scope of application of the Treaty. Instead the Court appreciates that a practice may be of a sporting nature—and perhaps even 'purely sporting' in *intent*—but that it must be tested against the demands of EU law where it exerts economic *effects*. EU law operates on the basis of a limited mandate—this is Article 5(1) TEU's principle of conferral—but that mandate is broad in consequence on the empowering project to complete the internal market.

Then the Court in *Meca-Medina* put sporting practices to the test, but it invested that test with recognition of the particular context in which sport is organized. So EU law overlaps with 'internal' sports law (the *lex sportiva*)—but it absorbs, albeit not uncritically, the special expectations of sports governance. It grants it a conditional autonomy.

This assertion of a sensitivity to the special character of sport in the interpretation of EU law is not a concession that is unique to sport. This, in fact, is generally

---

[57] *MOTOE* (n 55) para 51.   [58] *Meca-Medina* (n 28) paras 49–56.
[59] ibid para 46 of the judgment touches on this without placing any emphasis on it. Waning interest among sponsors and broadcasters was a factor in promoting reform of anti-doping procedures in professional cycling: see eg W Lagae and D Van Reeth, 'Paradoxes in Professional Road Cycling: A Plea for a New Cycling Industry' in Y Vanden Auweele, E Cook, and J Parry (eds), *Ethics and Governance in Sport: The Future of Sport Imagined* (Routledge 2016) ch 13. Part of the story is also a fear that *until* commercial pressure provides sufficient inducement, governing bodies are slow to adopt a rigorous approach to doping control for fear that this will harm the commercial attraction of their competitions.

applicable EU law: it is not EU sports law as an exotic rare breed. In *Wouters*, which was nothing to do with sport, there were 'effects restrictive of competition'[60] but, on examination of the objectives of the relevant restrictions (on multi-disciplinary partnerships), they did not go beyond what was necessary in order to ensure the proper functioning of the legal profession in the Netherlands. There was no breach of EU competition law. So too in *Meca-Medina*. Anti-doping rules cannot simply be excluded from the scope of review by reference to their role in ensuring 'fair play' or 'clean sport'. They must be examined in their proper context, which cannot ignore their economic effect. However, placing the rules within the ambit of the Treaty does not mean they will be forbidden by it. The general objective of the rules was to combat doping in order for competitive sport to be conducted on a fair basis; and the effect of penalties on athletes' freedom of action was treated as inherent in the anti-doping rules. This *contextual* examination of the rules was crucial in the Court's conclusion that rules affected the athletes' freedom of action but that they did not constitute a restriction of competition incompatible with EU competition law.

The CFI's ruling in *Meca-Medina* was exposed as badly flawed on appeal, but its errors remain illuminating. The CFI had suppressed the significance of *Wouters* for reasons that were logical once it had chosen to misdiagnose the anti-doping rules as 'purely sporting'. The CFI considered that *Wouters* concerned 'market conduct', an 'essentially economic activity, that of lawyers'. Anti-doping cannot be likened to market conduct without distorting the nature of sport, which 'in its very essence … has nothing to do with any economic consideration'.[61] This was doubtless sweet music to the ears of sports governing bodies intent on securing their most coveted prize, which is absolute autonomy from legal regulation. But it is profoundly unpersuasive. Although this approach, walling off sport from economic activity, reeled in the CFI, it was deservedly set aside on appeal. The Court instead preferred to accept an overlap between EU law and 'internal' sports law (*lex sportiva*), while also accepting that the peculiar demands of the latter may be used to nourish a submission that an apparent restriction is nevertheless an essential element in sports governance. This, following *Wouters*, is the heart of *Meca-Medina*.

In *Meca-Medina* the Court took a broad view of the scope of the Treaty, but emphasized its receptivity to the importance of matters not explicitly described as 'justifications' in the Treaty as a route to permit the continued application of challenged practices which are shown to be necessary to achieve legitimate sporting objectives and/or are inherent in the organization of sport. What is really at stake is not a group of sporting rules and a separate group of economic rules, but rather a group of sporting rules which carry economic implications and which therefore fall for assessment, but not necessarily condemnation, under EU competition law. This is the heart of the model according to which EU law grants sporting bodies a *conditional* autonomy. Free movement law follows a structurally comparable model: although at a detailed level free movement law and competition law differ,

---

[60] *Wouters* (n 12) para 110.   [61] *Meca-Medina* (n 31) para 65.

the inquiry into whether a sporting rule is properly treated as inherent in and neces-sary for a sport's organization runs in common. The Court in *Meca-Medina* warned that restrictions imposed by rules adopted by sports federations 'must be limited to what is necessary to ensure the proper conduct of competitive sport':[62] in simi-lar vein in *Bosman* it insisted that the transfer system must 'not go beyond what is necessary' to achieve its aims.[63] The key to EU sports law is: are the economic effects of the rule which seem to offend against core EU provisions dealing with the internal market a necessary consequence of their contribution to the structure of legitimate sports governance? If so, the *lex sportiva* prevails: the conditions for autonomy under EU law are satisfied.

Meca-Medina establishes that few rules are sporting but not also economic in nature and/or effect. The majority of rules are both. The intersection of EU law and 'internal' sports law (the *lex sportiva*) is therefore recognized, and sporting bodies have room to show how and why the rules are necessary to accommodate their particular concerns—fair play, credible competition, national representative sides, and so on.

The consequence of this approach is a need for a case-by-case examination of the compatibility of sporting practices with the Treaty. There is no blanket immu-nity: there is no zone of 'sporting autonomy' that can be treated as naturally and inevitably beyond the reach of EU law. Most positive accounts of the Court's rul-ing in *Meca-Medina* have tended to emphasize the scope allowed by the Court for debate about what is truly 'special' in the governance of sport, while also appreci-ating the improved intellectual quality of the analysis, in particular its rejection of the ill-shaped concept of the 'purely sporting' rule—which was and is rarely 'purely' sporting at all, but rather both sporting and economic in its implications.[64] On the other hand, *Meca-Medina* is, admittedly, troubling for sports bodies, not only because it represents a setback for those who would in principle champion the virtues of sporting autonomy but also for more urgently practical reasons. The need for a case-by-case examination of the compatibility of sporting practices with EU law is vulnerable to the criticism that it breeds uncertainty and unpredictabil-ity. Such anxieties had been audible for many years, but *Meca-Medina* certainly sharpened the intensity of the critical debate. The ruling attracted pained criticism about EU law's disregard for the special features of sport from those close to sports governing bodies.[65] A typical complaint was that of the EU Office of the European

---

[62] *Meca-Medina* (n 28) para 47.   [63] *Bosman* (n 1) para 104.

[64] See, at the time and in largely approving vein, S Weatherill, 'Anti-doping Revisited—the Demise of the Rule of "Purely Sporting Interest"?' [2006] ECLR 645; E Szyszczak, 'Competition and Sport' (2007) 32 EL Rev 95; M Wathelet, 'L'arrêt Meca-Medina et Majcen: plus qu'un coup dans l'eau' [2006/41] Revue de Jurisprudence de Liège, Mons et Bruxelles 1799; M Wathelet, 'Sport Governance and EU Legal Order' (The 'Wathelet Report') (2007) 7(3–4) Intl Sports LJ 3; A Rincon, 'EC Competition and Internal Market Law: on the Existence of a Sporting Exemption and its Withdrawal' (2007) 3 JCER 224.

[65] See eg G Infantino [at the time Director of Legal Affairs at UEFA, now President of FIFA], '*Meca-Medina*: A Step Backwards for the European Sports Model and the Specificity of Sport?' UEFA paper 02/10/06 <http://www.uefa.com/MultimediaFiles/Download/uefa/KeyTopics/480391_DOWNLOAD.pdf> accessed 29 November 2016; J Zylberstein, 'Collision entre idéaux sportifs et continges économiques dans l'arrêt *Meca-Medina*' (2007) 48 Cahiers de Droit Européen 218.

Olympic Committees, which considers that the notion of the specificity of sport 'suffers from the lack of a complete and precise definition' and criticizes *Meca-Medina* as 'unsuitable because it produces legal uncertainty and incomprehension', adding that the Court 'has failed ... to draw clear boundaries between EU law and sport related matters'.[66] Other sources too have expressed anxieties about, inter alia, the expertise of the Court in Luxembourg to investigate such matters.[67] The vibrant *contestability* of the practice of EU intervention in sport is plain.

This is the wider context within which *Meca-Medina* has been attacked for stripping away some of the autonomy to which sports governing bodies regularly lay claim as necessary and appropriate. And it is pertinent to appreciate that sporting bodies have unrivalled expertise in persuading the media to take their side when they are faced by legal constraint. In October 2007 the *Financial Times* ran the following story under the title 'Olympics Chief Fears EU Grip on Doping Rules':

The Olympic movement faces the frightening prospect of anti-doping rules coming under the responsibility of the European Union unless the Lisbon summit agrees to exempt sport from EU free market rules, the president of the International Olympic Committee has warned.... Mr Rogge highlighted the so-called Meca-Medina doping case in which the European Court of Justice ruled last year that anti-doping laws contravened EU competition law by taking away freedom to compete from two banned swimmers ...[68]

This is towering nonsense. The Court did no such thing! That even the *Financial Times*, by far the most reliable British newspaper, should publish the very opposite of the truth reveals the remarkable ability of sport to use the media to advance its tendentious claims for autonomy. But, stripped of its inaccuracy, this quote is helpful in capturing the abiding ambition of sports federations to keep the law in general and EU law in particular at arm's length. It illuminates too the way they approached the negotiation of what finally emerged as the Lisbon Treaty in 2009, in which sport was for the first time included in the EU Treaties: this story is told in Chapter 6. The proper retort to M Rogge and to the Court's other critics is that via the *Wouters* formula, absorbed by the Court in *Meca-Medina*, EU law accommodates the special concerns of sports governance in the interpretation and application of the law—just as it is open to any sector to seek to persuade the Court that it has particular requirements that are inherent in its operation which are apt for recognition despite their restrictive effect on competition. It is true that the case-by-case examination required by *Meca-Medina* deprives the Commission of the ability to produce a binding formula which gives sport its desired sanctuary by capturing the unsurpassable limits of the scope of EU law. The Commission's

[66] *Guide to EU Sport Policy* (2011), 11, 12, and 18 <http://www.euoffice.eurolympic.org/files/guide_to_eu_sport_policy_final_versionwithlinks.pdf> accessed 29 November 2016.

[67] See eg R Subiotto, 'The Adoption and Enforcement of Anti-Doping Rules Should Not Be Subject to European Competition Law' [2010] ECLR 323; also D Dixon, 'The Long Life of Bosman—a Triumph of Law over Experience' (2008) 6(2) ESLJ 3 <http://www.entsportslawjournal.com/articles/10.16997/eslj.60/> accessed 29 November 2016.

[68] 'Olympics Chief Fears EU Grip on Doping Rules' *Financial Times* (London, 18 October 2007) 11.

document 'Mapping and Analysis of the Specificity of Sport', published in June 2016, is a perfectly well-written overview of practice but falls far short of the type of concrete guidance that would satisfy sports governing bodies eager for certainty.[69] But although EU law operates on a case-by-case basis, its pattern of examination is sensitive to the peculiarities of sport. Article 165 TFEU, the provision inserted with effect from 2009 by the Lisbon Treaty, recognizes and confirms exactly that by endorsing 'the specific nature of sport'. Moreover, although sporting bodies have a legitimate antipathy to any judicial aspiration to micromanagement of the conduct of sporting competition, in *Meca-Medina* the Court does not make any heavy-handed claim to greater expertise than sporting bodies in the matter of doping control. It expects only that restrictions imposed shall be limited to what is necessary to ensure the proper conduct of competitive sport, specifically that procedures shall not be founded on poor science nor that sanctions shall be disproportionately severe.[70] EU law places conditions on the autonomy of sports bodies, but that autonomy, even if not absolute, is still generously sensitive to the special features of sport.

5.5 How *Meca-Medina* Has Come to Frame the Debate about EU Sports Law

The significance of the approach chosen by the Court in *Meca-Medina* is readily appreciated when one examines the contrasting tone of the 'Arnaut Report'—the so-called *Independent European Sport Review* published in October 2006.[71] The Arnaut Report is among the most revealing of all documents ever produced in the field of EU sports law—though certainly not for the reasons and aspirations of those interests that were behind its production. Like the CFI ruling in *Meca-Medina*, the Arnaut Report pines for maximum sporting autonomy but it fails utterly to present an intellectually sturdy case in favour. It is illuminating because it is wrong.

The review process that led to the Arnaut Report was initiated by the United Kingdom's Presidency of the EU in 2005, but it was dominated by the interests of those who exercised control of patterns of sports governance in Europe. Despite its name, there was little that was 'independent' about the Arnaut Report. It is, in short, heavily supportive of the status quo in sport. The Arnaut Report almost entirely ignores the Court's judgment in *Meca-Medina*.[72] It prefers instead to load its analysis on the back of the CFI's judgment, which had been set aside on appeal

---

[69] <http://ec.europa.eu/assets/eac/sport/library/studies/mapping-analysis-specificity-sport_en.pdf> accessed 29 November 2016.

[70] *Meca-Medina* (n 28) especially paras 47–56.

[71] The launch of the Arnaut Report was announced in a UEFA Press Release of 20 October 2006 <http://www.uefa.org/mediaservices/mediareleases/newsid=943432.html> accessed 29 November 2016, but its dismal quality is accentuated by the fact that its host website no longer functions: it was at <http://www.independentfootballreview.com>. A copy is held at <http://eose.org/wp-content/uploads/2014/03/independant_european_sports_review1.pdf> accessed 29 November 2016.

[72] The Arnaut Report (2016), the only exception is at p 14.

to the Court some months in advance of the publication of the Arnaut Report. So the Report claims that EU law does not affect 'rules concerning questions of purely sporting interest and, as such, having nothing to do with economic activity' and adds that it 'follows that, provided the rules in question remain limited to their proper objective ... they must be considered as pure sports rules and not subject to the prohibitions of European Community law'.[73]

As sporting bodies jealous of their autonomy and their earning potential would wish! But it is exactly this vision that was decisively rejected by the Court of Justice in the appeal in *Meca-Medina*. The Arnaut Report's account of EU law is *legally* unsound, contaminated throughout by its improperly inflated assessment of EU law's readiness to accept the notion of the 'purely sporting rule'.[74] In truth the Arnaut Report lacks any serious *legal* weight, and it amounts to little more than *politically* motivated propaganda designed to promote the ambition of sports federations to relax the intensity of their subjection to EU law. Even here the Arnaut Report is compromised by its uncritical acceptance of exaggerated claims that European football at the time was marked by vigorous vertical redistribution of wealth.[75] Nevertheless, the flawed selectivity of which the Arnaut Report stands both accused and convicted helps to reveal the full implications of the choice that was on offer in *Meca-Medina*. The CFI's approach would have maximized sporting autonomy. The Court instead insisted on a more cautious case-by-case examination of whether sporting practices with economic effects apt to bring the matter within the Treaty are compatible with EU law. Sporting autonomy is conditional on demonstrating compliance with EU law.

The European Commission's White Paper on Sport, issued in July 2007,[76] is a great deal more reliable. It largely ignores the Arnaut Report.[77] It places heavy reliance for its legal analysis on the Court's ruling on appeal in *Meca-Medina*. It presents it—entirely correctly—as a landmark ruling. In fact it is the only decision of the Court of Justice explicitly referred to in the body of the White Paper, which comprises twenty pages. It is stated that:

... in respect of the regulatory aspects of sport, the assessment whether a certain sporting rule is compatible with EU competition law can only be made on a case-by-case basis, as recently confirmed by the European Court of Justice in its *Meca-Medina* ruling. The Court provided a clarification regarding the impact of EU law on sporting rules. It dismissed the notion of 'purely sporting rules' as irrelevant for the question of the applicability of EU competition law to the sport sector.[78]

---

[73] ibid paras 3.50–3.51.

[74] eg ibid paras 3.19, 3.26, 3.40–3.41, 3.89, 5.55, 6.28, 6.60, 6.70. The Arnaut Report is stated to have been prepared with the advice of José Luis da Cruz Vilaca. It seems implausible that such a distinguished jurist could have approved the final text of the Report.

[75] cf H Moorhouse, 'Financial Expertise, Authority and Power in the European Football "Industry"' (2007) 3 JCER 290.

[76] White Paper on Sport, COM (2007) 391, 11 July 2007, available via <http://ec.europa.eu/sport/index_en.htm> accessed 29 November 2016.

[77] There is no more than a (probably calculatedly) bland reference, ibid 13, in fn 7.

[78] ibid 15.

This is correct! The Staff Working Document entitled 'The EU and Sport: Background and Context', a much fuller document which accompanied the Commission's White Paper, supplies more detailed legal analysis.[79] Its Annex I, entitled 'Sport and EU Competition Rules', explains that in so far as concessions are made to sporting 'specificity' they are made on terms dictated by EU law; and, moreover, a case-by-case analysis of sporting practices is required. This means that, in the Commission's estimation, a general exemption is 'neither possible nor warranted'.[80] Here too the legal analysis is carefully and correctly built on the foundation stone of *Meca-Medina*. It concludes that the Court's ruling reveals an interpretation of EU competition law which:

> ... provides sufficient flexibility to take account of the specificity of sport and does not impede sporting rules that pursue a legitimate objective (such as the organisation and proper conduct of sport), are indispensable (inherent) to achieve the objective and proportionate in light of the objective pursued.[81]

The Annex to the Staff Working Document proceeds to a survey of existing decision-making practice in order to provide guidance on what is permitted by EU law and what is not. This is largely intended to be descriptive although, in more ambitious vein, it seeks to explain some pre-existing EU case law on the basis of *Meca-Medina*. It suggests that the *ENIC* decision, concerning rules forbidding multiple ownership of football clubs,[82] is now capable of being understood as a finding that the measure involved no breach of Article 101(1) TFEU 'on the basis of the *Wouters* criteria applied in *Meca Medina*'.[83] This is convincing: it is fully in line with the discussion presented earlier in this chapter. As explained, such a rule suppresses demand and it therefore serves to restrict competition in the market for clubs, but it is necessary in order to eliminate suspicions of collusion that would arise were clubs under the same ownership to face each other in matches. *Lehtonen*, a case dealing with transfer windows,[84] is similarly considered with the advantage of hindsight as in line with *Meca-Medina*.[85] One should be cautious in interpreting the past in the light of what has become known in the future, for it may conceal the true pattern of reasoning adopted at the time. However, the landmark significance of *Meca-Medina* justifies an attempt to pursue such repackaging, and the Commission's analysis in the 2007 White Paper on Sport and its supporting Staff Working Document is properly cautious and astute.

It is possible to be still more ambitious than the Commission in its 2007 White Paper in reframing the early landmarks of EU sports law in the light of the method of reasoning adopted by the Court in *Meca-Medina*. The shape of EU sports law developed in the interpretation of provisions of the Treaty dealing with competition

---

[79] Staff Working Document, 'The EU and Sport: Background and Context', also available via <http://ec.europa.eu/sport/index_en.htm> accessed 29 November 2016.

[80] ibid 69, 78.   [81] ibid 69.

[82] COMP 37.806 *ENIC/ UEFA*, IP/02/942, 27 June 2002. See sect 5.2.

[83] 'The EU and Sport: Background and Context' (n 79) 71.

[84] Case C-176/96 *Lehtonen and others v FRSB* [2000] ECR I-2681.

[85] 'The EU and Sport: Background and Context' (n 79) 72.

law in *Meca-Medina* is capable of being exported also to inform the interpretation of free movement law. *Meca-Medina*'s distaste for the notion of the 'purely sporting' rule and preference instead for case-by-case examination of sporting practices deserves to be applied also to free movement law.

Free movement law, like competition law, should be treated as based on an overlap between EU law and 'internal' sports law, with minimal scope for the total exclusion of EU law, combined with a sensitive willingness to assess claims that the *lex sportiva* contains particular unusual features that are essential in sports governance. Embrace of this approach would not change the *outcome* of key free movement cases such as *Walrave and Koch* or *Bosman*, but it would make the analysis more intellectually credible. This argument is, however, better reserved for Chapter 7. Delay is helpful because it leaves space in Chapter 6 for examination of the path that led to Article 165 TFEU, and it is Article 165, and in particular its explicit embrace of the 'specific nature' of sport, that provides the constitutional impetus to argue in favour of a convergence in the treatment of sport under the model of conditional autonomy developed under both competition and free movement law as an integrated EU internal market law.

5.6 Conclusion

The Court, abandoning in practice the notion of the rule of 'purely sporting' interest, has taken a broad view of the scope of EU law—but having brought sporting rules within the scope of the Treaty it shows itself readily prepared to draw on the importance of matters not explicitly described as 'justifications' in the Treaty in order to permit the continued application of challenged practices which are shown to be necessary to achieve legitimate sporting objectives and/or inherent in the organization of sport. That, then, becomes the core of the argument when EU law overlaps with sports governance, the *lex sportiva*: can a sport show why prejudicial economic effects (for some athletes) must be tolerated? This is a statement of the *conditional autonomy* of sports federations under EU law which has been the thematic core of this chapter and the two that preceded it. This is 'the specific nature of sport' asserted but not elaborated by Article 165 TFEU, which is examined more fully in the next two chapters. An overlap between EU law and 'internal' sports law is recognized, but within that area of overlap sporting bodies have room to show how and why the rules are necessary to accommodate their particular concerns. This line of reasoning does not make it simple in contested cases to discover which rules are necessary for the effective organization of sport. And attention must be paid to how much room should be allowed to sports bodies in defining what is truly necessary for or inherent in their sport. But as a minimum this line of analysis ensures the right questions are asked. It prevents intellectually wasteful arguments about what is 'sporting' and what is 'commercial', and instead embraces the overlap of the two spheres. Then, within that zone of overlap, there is room for serious discussion of what is necessary for and/or inherent in the structure of sports governance. This then conditions the interpretation and application of EU law.

This forms the core of EU sports law in its negative dimension—it expresses the conditional autonomy that is thematically central to understanding the operation of EU sports law. And a strategy of inclusion, not exclusion, should inform sporting bodies' dealings with the EU's institutions: they must engage with the EU on its terms, but they can expect that those terms include sensitivity to the sports-specific context within which practices are reviewed. Exactly this theme is now engaged with once again in Chapter 6, in examination of the legislative—positive—dimension of EU sports law and policy.

6

The EU's Legislative Competence in the Field of Sport

6.1 Introduction

The EU possesses only the competences and powers which are conferred on it by its Treaties. This, as explained in Chapter 3, follows from the foundationally important Article 5 of the Treaty on European Union (TEU). The EU has enjoyed a conferred competence to act in the field of sport since 2009, the date of entry into force of the Treaty of Lisbon. This is declared in Article 6(e) of the Treaty on the Functioning of the European Union (TFEU) and elaborated in Article 165 TFEU. That provision, already encountered in Chapter 3, provides that the Union 'shall contribute to the promotion of European sporting issues, while taking account of the specific nature of sport, its structures based on voluntary activity and its social and educational function'; and that Union action shall be aimed at 'developing the European dimension in sport, by promoting fairness and openness in sporting competitions and cooperation between bodies responsible for sports, and by protecting the physical and moral integrity of sportsmen and sportswomen, especially the youngest sportsmen and sportswomen'.

Chapter 3 has already explained that the key provisions appear to carry rather more constitutional significance than is their effect in practice. In part this is because the grant of legislative competence which has been made is carefully and narrowly drawn. Article 165 TFEU provides that the aspirations quoted in the previous paragraph may be advanced by the adoption of EU legislation, but the legal instruments available are confined to incentive measures adopted by the Parliament and Council and recommendations adopted by the Council. Regulations, Directives, and Decisions, the triple pillars of EU law-making foreseen by Article 288 TFEU, may not be adopted pursuant to Article 165 TFEU. And the harmonization of laws and regulations is explicitly excluded. But the primary reason why Article 165 is less significant in stepping up the EU's role in the field of sport than might be initially supposed is that the text of the Treaty prior to the amendments made with effect from 2009, though barren of *explicit* reference to sport, was nonetheless long interpreted in such a way as to exercise a significant influence over the autonomy enjoyed by sports federations. This is because of the functionally broad project to create an internal market and, in particular, because of the application and interpretation of the EU rules on free movement and competition.

Chapter 4 explored the development of the intersection between the law of the EU's internal market and sport with reference to the free movement provisions. Chapter 5 performed the same function with reference to the competition rules of the Treaty. Chapters 4 and 5 explained how the case law reaching back to *Walrave and Koch*[1] and embracing *Bosman*[2] and *Meca-Medina*[3] is readily understood in the light of Article 165 TFEU's stipulation that the EU shall take into account 'the specific nature of sport'. The entry into force of the Lisbon Treaty in 2009 offered a new vocabulary with which to express old challenges—how, if at all, the special characteristics of sport shall form part of the interpretation and application of EU internal market law, in particular free movement and competition law. Sports governing bodies will doubtless argue that Article 165 serves to *strengthen* the value that should be attached to sporting autonomy, but in relation to internal market law it is much more probably mere confirmation of existing practice, and this is so far the Court's approach.[4] Article 165 has no transformative effect on the interpretation and application of free movement and competition law.

The long road leading to entry into force of the Treaty of Lisbon in 2009 and the grant of the competence found in Article 165 TFEU, which is the journey traversed in this chapter, have strong thematic similarities with the road travelled in connection with the shaping of internal market law examined in the previous two chapters. In particular, just as sports bodies have, with determination but without success, sought to exclude their activities from review in the light of EU internal market law, so too have sports bodies long sought to achieve a much broader exclusion of their activities from the Treaty superstructure itself. And just as sports bodies have been forced to fight their battles within EU internal market law—by persuading the Court and Commission that EU law be *interpreted* in a manner that is sensitive to sport's special concerns—so too sports bodies have been required to surrender their ambition to secure exemption from the scope of the Treaties and instead to accept, as second best, that sport be included in the Treaties but under an understanding that it is not simply an economic activity like any other. Article 165 is the culmination of the failed strategy of *exclusion* from EU law and represents instead grudgingly accepted and carefully designed *inclusion* within EU law.

This chapter is an exploration of the *political* dimension of how the quest for sporting autonomy in the EU shifted from a strategy of exclusion to one of (conditional) inclusion, whereas Chapters 4 and 5 looked at that same pattern of development in relation to *judicial* interpretation and application of the law.

So the purpose of this chapter is to explain how and why Article 165 TFEU came to be inserted in the Treaty. The fact that Article 165 exists at all, and the more detailed questions associated with exactly how it is written, are direct consequences of that long fruitless struggle for absolute sporting autonomy. This chapter tells a

---

[1] Case 36/74 *Walrave and Koch v Union Cycliste International* [1974] ECR 1405.
[2] Case C-415/93 *Union royale belge des sociétés de football association ASBL v Jean-Marc Bosman* [1995] ECR I-4921.
[3] Case C-519/04 P *Meca-Medina and Majcen v Commission* [2006] ECR I-6991.
[4] Case C-325/08 *Olympique Lyonnais v Olivier Bernard, Newcastle United* [2010] I-2177.

story of inclusion as a second-best option for sports governing bodies unable to extract a political promise of exclusion from the grip of EU law. It then explores just how the competence newly conferred on the EU to act in the field of sport has been exercised so far and reflects on how it *should* be exercised. The relevant provisions were envisaged by sporting bodies principally as devices designed to restrain the EU's interventionist tendencies. And they have been drafted with some care in order to locate the EU in a role that is subordinate to that of the Member States and sporting organizations in the regulation of sport. That too has been a theme of the Commission's own general policy articulation, found in the 2007 White Paper[5] and the 2011 Communication on sport.[6] However, given the endemic tendency of the exercise of the EU's competence to 'creep' outwards, the question is how sustainable is this promise of subordination. The worst fear of sporting bodies is that the EU, having been granted a carefully limited competence in sport, may extend and absorb new ambitions and interrupt the practice in a sport in a clumsy and insensitive manner. Article 165 is an attempt to engage with the EU on sport's terms. But the terms belong within the EU Treaty system now, and it is the EU's institutions that will play a central role in their practical elaboration.

The arrival of Article 165 TFEU in the Treaties with effect from 2009 put to an end any claim that EU law has no connection with sport. But it leaves open the precise nature of that connection, while preparing the ground for debate about how to manage the tension between sporting autonomy and EU law in the elaboration of the 'specific nature of sport'. The question is just what is and should be the shape of EU law and policy's contribution to sport in a more active sense than may be achieved through the control exercised by free movement and competition law. Even to ask such a question invites expressions of anxiety from sports governing bodies, who will immediately appeal to the need to grant them autonomy from an EU system that lacks any obvious institutional expertise in sports governance and which, moreover, in so far as it chooses to set norms that are specific to the EU, risks forcing fragmentation on the typically global pattern of sports governance. The EU must show that it adds value to the governance of sport for its intervention to be regarded as legitimate.

6.2 The Amsterdam Declaration

The Amsterdam Treaty entered into force in 1999. It is an amending Treaty: it amends the founding Treaties of the EU. Its primary preoccupations were rather technical and addressed detailed matters of institutional design. Sport was certainly on the distant outer margins of the political negotiation on the text and

---

[5] White Paper on Sport, COM (2007) 391, 11 July 2007, available via <http://ec.europa.eu/sport/index_en.htm> accessed 29 November 2016.

[6] COM (2011) 12, available via <http://ec.europa.eu/sport/policy/index_en.htm> accessed 29 November 2016.

garnered little attention or visibility. However, homing in on the particular matter of sport, the negotiation of the Amsterdam Treaty was informed by the delivery of the *Bosman* ruling in 1995. Any hint that the Treaty might be revised to allow sport to escape the consequences of *Bosman* lacked political momentum.[7] What instead emerged from the political negotiation was the so-called Amsterdam Declaration on Sport—to be more precise, a Declaration on Sport annexed to the Treaty of Amsterdam. It was short:

The Conference emphasises the social significance of sport, in particular its role in forging identity and bringing people together. The Conference therefore calls on the bodies of the European Union to listen to sports associations when important questions affecting sport are at issue. In this connection, special consideration should be given to the particular characteristics of amateur sport.

In legal terms, a Declaration is *not* binding. Its significance is predominantly political. Weighing in at just fifty-eight words, the Declaration displays the virtue of brevity, but it scores less well on clarity. Sport has 'social significance', but precisely what this entails is left unspecified, save for embrace of the vague but cheerfully expressed notions of 'forging identity and bringing people together'. The Declaration calls for the bodies of the EU to 'listen' to sports associations—but it is what they *do* that really counts. And the Declaration helpfully suggests that amateur sport is different from other forms, but offers no fuller articulation of what might be at stake in such differences nor what are or should be their implications.

The Amsterdam Declaration is not helpful at the level of detail. However, it vividly reveals the surrounding political sensitivity. It in no way subverts *Bosman*. It falls spectacularly far short of the absolute exclusion from EU law for which governing bodies in sport would earnestly wish, and which would have been the very pinnacle of strategic success in protecting their autonomy. There was not the political will to support such a plea. Nor is the Declaration in even the faintest sense a grant of legislative competence to the EU. The Declaration is soft in effect, intent, and tone. It is scarcely any more than a *recognition* of the tension between the reach of EU law and the sporting thirst for autonomy. It does not even begin to provide any resolution of that tension.

The Declaration, though not legally binding, is capable of providing guidance in judicial decision-making and in broader policy articulation. The Court acted accordingly. In both *Deliège*[8] and in *Lehtonen*[9] it referred to the Amsterdam Declaration. However, it simply treated the Declaration as a confirmation of its own case law, not as a basis to call it into question. Given the anodyne terms of the Declaration, the Court's approach was entirely understandable. From the perspective of the quest for sporting autonomy, this served only to highlight that the Amsterdam Declaration

---

[7] cf M Fernández Salas, 'De la possibilité de renverser l'arrêt *Bosman* par une modification du Traité. Perspectives juridiques' [1996] RMUE 155.

[8] Cases C-51/96 and C-191/97 *Deliège v Ligue de Judo* [2000] ECR I-2549, paras 41–42.

[9] Case C-176/96 *Jyri Lehtonen and Castors Canada Dry Namur-Braine ASBL v Fédération royale belge des sociétés de basket-ball ASBL (FRBSB)* [2000] ECR I-2681, paras 32–33.

had done nothing to nudge EU law into a more generous place. The Declaration was attributed no transformative effect. But the Declaration's embrace of the 'social significance of sport' also reflected the notion that sport is *to some extent* special, though this too was not transformative. In *Bosman* itself the Court had, after all, already acknowledged 'the considerable social importance of sporting activities'.[10]

6.3 The Nice Declaration

The Treaty of Nice entered into force in 2003. It was, like the Treaty of Amsterdam before it, a rather technical amending Treaty. It was largely aimed at adapting the EU's working system to permit absorption of new Member States in central and Eastern Europe: the EU's membership jumped from fifteen to twenty-five in 2004. Like the Treaty of Amsterdam, the negotiation of the Treaty of Nice attracted attention from the point of view of sport, although again it must be appreciated that sport was very far from the main priorities that were addressed in the political negotiation that ultimately generated the agreement of the Treaty of Nice.

On this occasion, the Declaration was attached not to the Treaty itself, but rather to the Conclusions of the European Council meeting held in Nice in December 2000. This difference carries no legal or political significance. As with the Amsterdam Declaration, the Nice Declaration lacks binding legal force and it reveals only the lack of political consensus with regard to taking any hard steps towards agreeing a clearly defined role for the EU—or to agreeing that there should *not* be any such role. The Nice Declaration is, however, a good deal longer than the Amsterdam Declaration, stretching to seventeen paragraphs, and its helpfully full title declares that it is a 'Declaration on the specific characteristics of sport and its social function in Europe, of which account should be taken in implementing common policies'. There are six sections to the Nice Declaration, entitled 'Amateur sport and sport for all', 'Role of sports federations', 'Preservation of sports training policies', 'Protection of young sportsmen and -women', 'Economic context of sport and solidarity', and 'Transfers'.

This is a mix. Support for amateur sport is rather uncontroversial and, in any event, remote from the formal influence of EU law. This is true too of the protection of younger people. By contrast, addressing the role of federations and the economic context of sport comes much closer to the most awkward of tensions that arise when EU law comes into contact with professional sport.

The Nice Declaration is suitably and illuminatingly cautious on these matters. It 'solves' nothing. But it does vividly capture the challenge of finding a role for the EU when it comes into contact with the increasingly prominent commercial dimension of sport. The Nice Declaration does not serve to be set out in full here, both because it is too long and because it is too dull.[11] However, it is book-ended by

[10] *Bosman* (n 2) para 106.
[11] The full text of the Nice Declaration is at <http://eur-lex.europa.eu/legal-content/EN/TXT/?uri=URISERV:l35007> accessed 29 November 2016.

anodyne comments with which it is impossible to disagree but which offer no concrete guidance, and which convey accurately the general flavour of the document:

1. The European Council has noted the report on sport submitted to it by the European Commission in Helsinki in December 1999 with a view to safeguarding current sports structures and maintaining the social function of sport within the European Union. Sporting organisations and the Member States have a primary responsibility in the conduct of sporting affairs. Even though not having any direct powers in this area, the Community must, in its action under the various Treaty provisions, take account of the social, educational and cultural functions inherent in sport and making it special, in order that the code of ethics and the solidarity essential to the preservation of its social role may be respected and nurtured.

2. The European Council hopes in particular that the cohesion and ties of solidarity binding the practice of sports at every level, fair competition and both the moral and material interests and the physical integrity of those involved in the practice of sport, especially minors, may be preserved.
   …

17. The Community institutions and the Member States are requested to continue examining their policies, in compliance with the Treaty and in accordance with their respective powers, in the light of these general principles.

One can hardly disagree. But equally one can hardly rate these comments as operationally useful in any concrete sense.

The adoption of both the Amsterdam and the Nice Declarations is important in the sense that it demonstrates that the tension between the EU's absence of explicit competence in the field of sport and the activity of its Court and Commission in applying the rules on free movement and competition had squeezed out a political response. But the legal form and the chosen content is telling: these are non-binding Declarations which do little more than sketch broad aspiration and generalities. This was the best that sport was able to extract from the political process. These Declarations emphatically do not subvert the core of the *Bosman* ruling's firm application of the fundamental Treaty rules governing free movement law to sport.

Underlying this narrative is the appreciation that for sport to secure protection from the EU and its legal order it must in some way engage with it, not dismiss it as irrelevant. After all, as the practice of the Court and the Commission accumulated it became increasingly plain that the EU's institutions did not merely show rhetorical acceptance of the claim that 'sport is (sometimes) special'. Chapters 4 and 5 track this strategy of inclusion in the context of free movement and competition law respectively, as a second-best choice after the strategy of exclusion had proved unfeasible. They show how internal market law had been used to supervise but not to condemn rules governing selection for international representative teams,[12] anti-doping sanctions,[13] a modified transfer system,[14] and rules against multiple club ownership.[15] The Union of European Football Associations

---

[12] *Walrave and Koch* (n 1).   [13] *Meca-Medina and Majcen* (n 3).
[14] *Bosman* (n 2); *Bernard* (n 4).   [15] COMP 37.806 *ENIC/UEFA*, IP/02/942, 27 June 2002.

(UEFA), in particular, was notable for adapting its strategy towards a more cooperative model.[16]

The Amsterdam and Nice Declarations have much in common with this strategy, whereby recognition of sport's special character is inscribed into EU law, but in an ambiguous manner that places heavy emphasis on subsequent detailed elaboration of policy. Chapters 4 and 5 showed the Court's involvement. In the wake of the rising political salience of the EU's intersection with sport, made manifest at the level of Treaty negotiation in the Amsterdam and Nice Declarations, it fell to the Commission to try to provide policy framing that was more *concrete* than that on offer from the Amsterdam and Nice Declarations and more *systematic* than could be extracted from the ad hoc decision-making undertaken by the Court and (less authoritatively) by the Commission in the application of the free movement and competition rules.

6.4 The Helsinki Report

The rise of a political willingness at the time of Treaty revision to address, however ambiguously, the interaction of EU law and sport first at Amsterdam and then at Nice was mainly fuelled by the Court's transformative ruling in *Bosman* in 1995. This ruling sharpened awareness of the practical significance of EU law as a means to challenge sporting autonomy after its twenty-year slumber following *Walrave and Koch* and *Donà v Mantero*.[17] The Commission too was awakened. It sought to provide some sort of guidance on policy.

Paragraph 1 of the Nice Declaration, quoted earlier, mentions the Helsinki Report. The Commission was constrained in its ambition by want of legislative competence conferred at the time by Treaties, but it was pushed in the direction of seeking to provide a framework for sports law by the rising tide of individual decisions of the Court and of the Commission. The constitutional landscape today is dominated by Article 165 TFEU and the practice of EU sports law and policy has grown much deeper over time, but these developments did not occur on a blank canvas and they need to be understood in the wider context of the Commission's policy documents in order to grasp the mapping of EU sports law and policy.

In 1999 the Commission published its so-called Helsinki Report on Sport.[18] In December 1998 the European Council meeting in Vienna had—expressing recognition of the social role of sport and acknowledging the Declaration attached to the Amsterdam Treaty—invited the Commission to submit a report to the European Council twelve months later. The Commission pursued consultation with actors such as the Olympic movement, sporting federations, media, governments, and

---

[16] See especially B García, 'UEFA and the European Union: From Confrontation to Co-Operation' (2007) 3 JCER 202.

[17] *Walrave and Koch* (n 1); Case 13/76 *Donà v Mantero* [1976] ECR 1333. See Ch 4.2.

[18] COM (1999) 644 and 644/2.

EU institutions, in particular at a 'European Union Conference on Sport', organized in May 1999, and it presented its report to the European Council meeting of December 1999. This was held in Helsinki—hence the Helsinki Report.

The brief handed to the Commission by the European Council in Vienna in 1998 was riddled with preconceptions. The invitation was to submit a report 'with a view to safeguarding current sports structures and maintaining the social function of sport within the Community framework'.[19] The Commission was no less uncritical in the report which it produced. The Helsinki Report adopted precisely this language as its formal title—it was a report from the Commission to the European Council 'with a view to safeguarding current sports structures and maintaining the social function of sport within the Community framework'. The Helsinki Report began with the ambitious assertion that it 'gives pointers for reconciling the economic dimension of sport with its popular, educational, social and cultural dimensions'. Its Introduction stated:

This social function of sport, which is in the general interest, has for some years been affected by the emergence of new phenomena which sometimes call into question the ethics of sport and the principles on which it is organised, be they violence in the stadiums, the increase in doping practices or the search for quick profits to the detriment of a more balanced development of sport.

The first section following the Introduction is entitled 'The Development of Sport in Europe risks weakening its educational and Social Function'. This has the feel of assertion rather than scientific inquiry. All of this is frankly tendentious.

There are two principal anxieties about this self-set agenda. The first is that it offers an inaccurate or, at least, narrowly selective and uncritically benign depiction of the role of sport in society. The second is that it raises expectations about the role of the Commission in particular and the EU more generally in nurturing these claimed virtues which cannot constitutionally be met and, arguably, given the EU's limited expertise and its restricted geographical scope, *should* not be met.

To refer to sport's 'social function' invites questions about whether one can plausibly identify such a coherent phenomenon, given that 'sport' embraces such a wide range of activities, from a recreational jog in the park to the glittering and commercially lucrative showcase of competing at the Olympic Games. This calls for caution when invited to construct a single 'policy' on sport. This was noted in Chapter 3.6. But the Helsinki Report falls headlong into this trap. The Helsinki Report expressed concern that commercial forces in sport are increasingly endangering the social function of sport, but this supposed conflict needs a more careful and context-sensitive explanation than that provided by the Commission. In truth, professional sport has much less to do with the social function of sport mentioned in the Helsinki Report than is there admitted. Conversely, recreational sport normally has no economic motivation. The 'search for quick profits to the detriment of a more balanced development of sport', which the Commission chooses to lament,

---

[19] Presidency Conclusions, para 95 <http://www.europarl.europa.eu/summits/wie1_en.htm> accessed 29 November 2016.

is not a problem in a context which treats sport as a means to improve public health. It is not at all clear that what is at stake here is a tension within 'sport'; it may more plausibly simply involve two quite distinct types of activity that happen to fall under the very loose and wide notion of 'sport'. In short, the Helsinki Report does not do justice to the complex influence of sports in modern society.[20]

The second group of anxieties about the tone of the Helsinki Report are associated with competence as a matter of law. The Treaty at the time was barren of any reference to sport, and even today Article 165 TFEU is certainly not sturdy enough to support the type of broad-based intervention hinted at by the Helsinki Report. In addition, the Commission in particular and the EU in general lack the material resources and the necessary sports-specific expertise to address these issues with a high degree of persuasiveness. The risk is that the EU strains its own legitimacy by taking on tasks that it is ill-suited to discharge. It is certainly true that in the Helsinki Report the Commission astutely insists on consultation between interested levels of governance, encompassing most of all sports governing bodies, Member States, and European institutions. It claims to wish to progress in partnership. But there is a taint of over-ambition in sketching the EU's ability to add value to the regulatory landscape in sport.

The most prominent instance of this—constitutional and substantive—overambition lies in the 'European Sports Model' sketched by the Commission in the Helsinki Report. This possesses a number of features, most prominently grouped around the contrasts drawn with North American sports practice. In important respects, professional sport in Europe is structured according to different expectations as compared with North American professional sport.[21] In Europe, leagues are connected, top to bottom, by promotion and relegation on a season-by-season basis, whereas in North America, leagues are typically 'closed'. There is no way in for a new club in North America—except by buying up a franchise, and moving the club from one city to another. This is anathema to the European sports fan—to call a club a 'franchise' is to insult it. North American sport is characterized by much heavier centralized control than the European model. The 'draft pick' and the salary cap reveal an intensely aggressive attachment to competitive balance and an assumption in North American sport that every team must be able to win (now and again). There can be no perennial also-ran.[22] The majority of clubs in the major football Leagues of Europe—those of Spain, England, Germany, and Italy—have

---

[20] See S Weatherill, 'The Helsinki Report on Sport' (2000) 25 EL Rev 282; S Weatherill, 'Sport as Culture in European Community Law' in R Craufurd Smith (ed), *Culture in European Union Law* (OUP 2004) ch 4.

[21] cf S Weatherill, 'Resisting the Pressures of Americanization: the Influence of European Community Law on the European Sport Model' in S Greenfield and G Osborn (eds), *Law and Sport in Contemporary Society* (Frank Cass 2000) ch 9; L Halgreen, *European Sports Law: a Comparative Analysis of the European and American Models of Sport* (Forlaget Thomson 2004); J Nafziger, 'European and North American Models of Sports Organization' in J Nafziger and S Ross (eds), *Handbook on International Sports Law* (Edward Elgar 2011) ch 4; N St Cyr Clarke, 'The Beauty and the Beast: Taming the Ugly Side of the People's Game' (2010–11) 17 Col J Eur L 601.

[22] Not even the Chicago Cubs.

not the slightest expectation of competing to win the championship. They are fated to remain perennial also-rans—though it is enough to compete occasionally for qualification into European club competition, to win a Cup competition, or even simply to escape relegation to a lower Division. As a general observation the model found in North American professional sport involves a far higher degree of central coordination than is found in Europe, where by contrast one finds concern that the elite level should support the grass roots, rather than that competing clubs should be managed to ensure a high degree of equality of opportunity. North American closed Leagues offer 'a regulated "quasi-socialist" economy' in contrast to open Leagues in Europe, which are 'almost completely deregulated'.[23] It is right to be a little cautious about how profound this dichotomy really is, for European commitment to 'vertical solidarity' may be only skin-deep in modern, highly commercialized professional sport.[24] However, it remains a plausible starting point that engagement with vertical solidarity but negligible concern for promoting competitive equality through horizontal coordination between clubs serves to distinguish European sport from the model found in North America.

There is a fascinating field of inquiry in pursuing these comparisons and contrasts. The problem, however, is that although the European Model of Sport is a suggestive basis for *describing* the governance patterns found in Europe, the Commission in its Helsinki Report injects also a normative preference for the supposed virtues of the Model. And that is perilous, because it neglects the very real limits of the EU's ability to permit the protection or promotion of the Model. The Helsinki Report's assertion that it 'gives pointers for reconciling the economic dimension of sport with its popular, educational, social and cultural dimensions' should sound warning bells. The risk is that the Commission skates over the EU's want of constitutional legitimacy, resources, and expertise.

The same unsettling sense of inflated self-perception is visible in individual decisions adopted by the Commission around the time of the Helsinki Report. In 2001 the Commission adopted a Decision concerning UEFA's rules permitting national football associations to prohibit the broadcasting of football matches within their territory during a two-and-a-half-hour period corresponding to the normal time at which fixtures are scheduled in the relevant country. This restricts the commercial freedom of broadcasters to conclude deals to show matches at designated 'blocked' times, but it is typically presented as a means to sustain a lively atmosphere in stadia by encouraging spectators to attend matches 'live' rather than merely watch

---

[23] W Andreff, 'Some Comparative Economics of the Organisation of Sports: Competition and Regulation in North American vs European Professional Team Sports Leagues' (2011) 8 European Journal of Comparative Economics 3. See also D McArdle, *Dispute Resolution In Sport* (Routledge 2015) ch 5, 'Antitrust and Competitive balance'; J Borland, 'The Production of Professional Team Sports' in W Andreff and S Szymanski, *Handbook on the Economics of Sport* (Edward Elgar 2006) ch 2.

[24] Judged in absolute terms, the English Premier League shares more income with the rest of the game than was the case prior to its creation in 1992, but the percentage shared is much smaller. Increasing the commercial vitality of the 'product' while reducing commitments to those outside the charmed circle of the Premier League was a major motivation in the establishment of the Premier League. A comparable story attaches to UEFA's Champions League.

television coverage. The Commission, examining the matter as a potential anti-competitive practice, concluded that the rules fell beyond the scope of application of what was then Article 81 of the Treaty Establishing the European Community (EC), now Article 101 TFEU.[25] The Decision is based on conventional market analysis of the type that would be regarded as routine by a competition lawyer: the Commission found in a straightforward manner that the UEFA rules did not appreciably restrict competition.[26] There is nothing sports-specific about this: and in fact the Commission explicitly stated that, given this conclusion, it had no need to assess the extent to which the televising of football might exert a negative impact on attendance at matches.[27] However, by unfortunate contrast, in the Press Release concerning this matter Mr Monti, at the time the Commissioner responsible for competition policy, was quoted as observing that the decision 'reflects the Commission's respect of the specific characteristics of sport and of its cultural and social function'.[28] This is correct in the limited sense that the Decision shows how orthodox competition law analysis is capable of leaving undisturbed unusual practices preferred in sport, but it is misleading in so far as it suggests that sport's special features played any role in the substantive analysis of the 'blocking rules' with EU law. Mr Monti's exaggeration may be rooted in a strategy to claim credit for the Commission in the face of accusations that its application of EU internal market law is liable to upset the foundations of sport. But the Commission is storing up trouble for itself in making extravagant claims about its competence to cater for cultural and social matters which do not correspond to the reality of the EU Treaty's much more limited mandate.

The Helsinki Report and the Commission's decisional practice of the time is vulnerable to the accusation that they over-estimate the constitutional reach of EU law and that, in addition, they suggest that the EU has an expertise in making choices about preferred models of sports governance. The Helsinki Report was in its detail a mis-step, but the very fact of its publication in 1999 demonstrated a rising tide of sports-related material that pressed the EU in general and the Commission in particular to try to offer a clearer and more coherent account of the proper role of the EU. This was the momentum that eventually generated Article 165 TFEU. But the next milestone was the Commission White Paper on Sport published in 2007.

6.5 The 2007 White Paper

The Commission's White Paper on Sport, released in the summer of 2007, is an immensely more reliable document than the Helsinki Report.[29] It is the product of wide-ranging consultation conducted by the Commission, and it is a thoroughly

---

[25] Comm Dec 2001/478 [2001] OJ L171/12.

[26] ibid paras 49–61. The Commission declared an intention to monitor change in market structure, particularly in the wake of what it called the 'Internet revolution', para 56.

[27] ibid para 59.   [28] IP/01/583, 20 April 2001.   [29] White Paper on Sport (n 5).

impressive piece of work. Even if it lags behind Article 165 TFEU in constitutional weight, it outstrips it in concrete analysis and intellectual ambition. It is of enduring value in the development of EU sports law.

Its Introduction claims that:

This initiative marks the first time that the Commission is addressing sport-related issues in a comprehensive manner. Its overall objective is to give strategic orientation on the role of sport in Europe, to encourage debate on specific problems, to enhance the visibility of sport in EU policy-making and to raise public awareness of the needs and specificities of the sector. The initiative aims to illustrate important issues such as the application of EU law to sport. It also seeks to set out further sports-related action at EU level.

These claims are bold, but the White Paper does not fall short. The White Paper ranges across sport as a means to improve public health, education, and the promotion of 'active citizenship' and goes so far as to encourage the use of sport in the EU's external assistance and development policies, but it also dedicates close attention to the commercial implications of sport. It cites evidence to suggest that sport accounts for 3.7 per cent of EU GDP, and employment for 15 million people. It adds, however, that 'notwithstanding the overall economic importance of sport, the vast majority of sporting activities takes place in non-profit structures, many of which depend on public support to provide access to sporting activities to all citizens'.[30] This offers an appropriately nuanced depiction of the place of sport in society: in fact, it shows a proper recognition that a discourse of *sports* is superior to one of *sport*. The White Paper generally deserves praise for its contextual sensitivity and its determination not to impose one-size-fits-all solutions as well as for its readiness to situate the EU alongside, not above, other relevant actors with responsibility for governance in sport.[31]

The White Paper itself is twenty pages long and separated into 'The Societal Role of Sport', 'The Economic Dimension of Sport', and 'The Organisation of Sport', accompanied by an Action Plan, a Staff Working Document and an Impact Assessment which is designed to provide a basis for assessing the costs and benefits of EU regulatory choices. It 'considers that certain values and traditions of European sport should be promoted'. But it accepts that there are 'diversities and complexities' in European sport, and that 'it is unrealistic to try to define a unified model of organisation of sport in Europe'.[32] It considers that 'governance is mainly the responsibility of sports governing bodies and, to some extent, the Member States and social partners'; and that 'self-regulation respectful of good governance principles' will address most challenges.[33]

---

[30] ibid 11.

[31] See S Weatherill, 'The White Paper on Sport as an Exercise in Better Regulation' (2008) 8(1–2) Intl Sports LJ 3; B García, 'Sports Governance after the White Paper: The Demise of the European Model?' (2009) 1 International Journal of Sport Policy and Politics 267. For agreement that the White Paper retreats from the Helsinki Report, but critical of that trend, see J Hill, 'The European Commission's White Paper on Sport: A Step Backwards for Specificity' (2009) 1 International Journal of Sport Policy and Politics 253.

[32] White Paper on Sport (n 5) 12.   [33] ibid 13.

The White Paper is also laced with careful respect for sites of governance beyond the EU in general and the Commission in particular, such as the World Anti-Doping Agency (WADA) and the United Nations Educational, Scientific and Cultural Organization (UNESCO). This follows the lead set by the Nice Declaration. It expresses a mood of deference which is today reflected in Article 165 TFEU, according to which the EU's role, though formally recognized, is left imprecise and is plainly designed to be limited. Article 6 TFEU reinforces the impression that the EU's role in sport is strictly subsidiary to that of the Member States and governing bodies in sport. The 2007 White Paper's suggestion that 'The Commission can play a role in encouraging the sharing of best practice in sport governance' astutely locates the EU as facilitator rather than top-down rule-maker.[34] Relative levels of expertise strongly support such an understanding of the EU's proper place. There is here an appealing flavour of regulatory modesty, even humility. The underlying theme is a desire to discover how and where the EU is able to add value, and to act according to that focus.

The notion of a European Model of Sport may have the type of explanatory value considered previously, especially as a contrast with an American Model of Sport, but in its 2007 White Paper the Commission decided to retreat quietly from the notion of using it in a prescriptively forceful manner. The relatively aggressive search for common organizing concepts or principles which marked the Commission's Helsinki Report is noticeably subdued. This makes the White Paper less adventurous, but this is a well-judged adjustment. It notes that 'the political debate on sport in Europe often attributes considerable importance to the so-called European Sport Model'; and adds that 'certain values and traditions of European sport should be promoted'. However, referring to 'the diversity and complexities of European sport' it concedes that 'it is unrealistic to try to define a unified model of organisation of sport in Europe'.[35] This is balanced and it is cautious—and it is wise. In similar vein the Commission astutely draws attention to the limits of the EU as an appropriate agent for change: 'European sport is generally organised according to continental structures, and not at EU level'.[36] Sport is (organizationally) special!

The White Paper's examination of 'The Societal Role of Sport' covers seven pages of the twenty. It begins with treatment of the public health advantages of physical exercise. There is not much the EU can contribute here. Its legal competence is thin, its material resources few, and its expertise in the field questionable. The Commission merely encourages the exchange of good practice, addressing both Member States and sports organizations. The matter of doping is treated in a similar fashion. The Commission confines itself to encouraging action against doping by Member State law enforcement agencies and sports organizations. It also urges better coordination at international level, referring explicitly to the contributions to be expected from the Council of Europe, WADA, and UNESCO.[37] Sport's role in education and training should be promoted, but here too competence to act is limited and the Commission avoids advancing any grand claims. The same is true

---

[34] ibid 12.   [35] ibid 12.   [36] ibid 18.   [37] ibid 4–5, para 2.2.

in the matter of promoting volunteering and active citizenship and using sport to improve social inclusion, integration, and equal opportunities. In the latter case the Commission refers to use of sport as a tool and indicator in the pursuit of the 'Open Method of Co-ordination' on social protection and social inclusion. The White Paper conspicuously avoids making any commitment to proposing more ambitious binding forms of top-down EU law-making. The Commission also expresses support for strengthening the prevention of and fight against racism and violence, but stresses the need for dialogue between Member States, international organizations, law enforcement services, and other stakeholders such as supporters' organizations and local authorities. The concern that animates the White Paper is to avoid any impression of top-down direction imposed by the EU. Instead, the Commission urges exchange of best practice among the several responsible actors and institutions.

The section in the White Paper entitled 'The Economic Dimension of Sport' is much shorter. It occupies just two of the total of twenty pages. It promises to seek to develop a European statistical method for measuring the economic impact of sport. This is presented as central to 'moving towards evidence-based policies'. This is self-evidently sensible, though such promises are often hard to maintain in circumstances where a matter attains a high level of political salience.

Section 4.1 of the White Paper, within the section on 'The Organisation of Sport', is entitled 'The specificity of sport'. The detailed examination of the application of EU internal market law to sport is reserved to the Staff Working Document and its annexes.[38] Here, in the body of the White Paper itself, the Commission states that 'sport has certain specific characteristics, which are often referred to as the "specificity of sport"'.[39] It sets out the specificity of European sport as apt to be 'approached through two prisms':

The specificity of sporting activities and of sporting rules, such as separate competitions for men and women, limitations on the number of participants in competitions, or the need to ensure uncertainty concerning outcomes and to preserve a competitive balance between clubs taking part in the same competitions;

The specificity of the sport structure, including notably the autonomy and diversity of sport organisations, a pyramid structure of competitions from grassroots to elite level and organised solidarity mechanisms between the different levels and operators, the organisation of sport on a national basis, and the principle of a single federation per sport.[40]

This is a helpful framework for analysis, but it is not designed to be innovative in its substance. This account is the Commission's own attempt to capture the development of the intersection of EU internal market law and sport which was covered in Chapters 4 and 5. The 'specificity of sport' is linguistically a rather clumsy phrase,[41] but it is intended to capture the failure of the strategy of absolute exclusion (of EU

---

[38] Available via <http://ec.europa.eu/sport/index_en.htm> accessed 29 November 2016.
[39] ibid 13.   [40] ibid.
[41] On its francophone origins, see A Duval, 'La Lex Sportiva Face au Droit de l'Union Européenne: Guerre et Paix dans l'Espace Juridique Transnational' (DPhil thesis, EUI Florence 2015) 198–99, available via <http://cadmus.eui.eu/handle/1814/36997> accessed 29 November 2016.

law) as a means to protect sporting autonomy and instead the embrace of what is, from the perspective of sporting bodies, the second-best strategy, that of inclusion (within EU law) but on terms which are sensitive to assessment of the special features of sport. Reference to the 'specificity of sport' nods to the content of the adjudicative or interpretative method for securing sporting autonomy which was introduced in Chapter 2. It is the model whereby sport enjoys conditional autonomy from EU law. And, as will be elaborated further later, the 'specificity of sport' has a close association with Article 165 TFEU's assertion of the 'specific nature of sport'.

In this vein, the Commission observes that it is in line with established case law that the specificity of sport falls to be considered in the interpretation and application of EU law, but it rejects any possibility of the grant of a general exemption from the application of EU law.[42] The assessment of 'whether a certain sporting rule is compatible with EU competition law can only be made on a case-by-case basis, as recently confirmed by the European Court of Justice in its *Meca-Medina* ruling'.[43] This entails that 'the formulation of general guidelines on the application of competition law to the sport sector' is not feasible, and it is explicitly excluded by the Commission.[44]

Meca-Medina is the only judgment of the Court which is explicitly mentioned in the Commission's 2007 White Paper. This emphasizes the ruling's landmark status in EU sports law and, as explained in full in Chapter 5, this prominence is fully justified. The Commission Staff Working Document, which accompanies and elaborates the narrative presented over just twenty pages in the White Paper, includes substantial Annexes dealing with 'Sport and EU Competition Rules' and 'Sport and Internal Market Freedoms'.[45] It repeats that *Meca-Medina* is to be interpreted to mean that the qualification of a rule as 'purely sporting' is not sufficient to remove the athlete or the sports association adopting the rule from the scope of the Treaty competition rules and that a case-by-case analysis is therefore required. A general exemption is 'neither possible nor warranted'.[46] Consequently sport's specificity becomes part of the assessment of the conformity of the rule with EU law, not a basis for immunizing it from review. The Staff Working Document offers detailed legal analysis against a background assumption that EU law is appropriately respectful of necessary sporting values. The Staff Working Document also places great emphasis on the role of the many other public and private, national and international bodies and actors with a stake in the governance of sport. Like the White Paper, it shows scrupulous care not to promote the EU as a top-down rule-maker in sport.

Having adopted *Meca-Medina* as the focal point of the legal analysis, the White Paper proceeds to mention the application of EU law to nationality-based discrimination, transfers, players' agents, the protection of minors, corruption, licensing

---

[42] White Paper on Sport (n 5) 13.　　[43] ibid 14.　　[44] ibid.　　[45] See n 29.
[46] White Paper on Sport (n 5); Staff Working Document, 'The EU and Sport: Background and Context', 69; see also 78.

systems for clubs, and the media (where the Commission recommends that sports organizations should pay attention to the creation and maintenance of solidarity mechanisms). However, the Commission's discussion of these matters, most of which are the subject of detailed treatment in later chapters of this book, is relatively brief. In the White Paper the Commission does not pretend that it has all the answers, nor does it suggest that the EU more generally entertains an ambition to become intensively involved in directing the shape of governance in sport.

The 2007 White Paper on Sport deserves respect and attention. It has set the tone for much of the EU's subsequent practice in the field of sport and, carefully written and appropriately modest about the EU's capacity, it is a stable foundation stone. Most of all, the 2007 White Paper represented a vast improvement on the 1999 Helsinki Report. It avoids inflated claims about the EU's actual and potential role in matters of sports governance. It avoids any suggestion that the EU has adequate legal competence, material resources, and basic knowledge and expertise to act as a primary site for addressing challenges that confront sport—or rather, sports—in Europe. It places the possible value of a role for the EU in the matter of sports governance within a context that pays due respect to the legitimate role to be played in sport by other public and private, national and international actors, including sports governing bodies themselves. Sports bodies intent on securing absolute autonomy from EU law will not be satisfied: they will scorn the claim that the EU is respectful of self-regulation in sport while simultaneously insisting on the priority of its unpredictable and intrusive legal rules.[47] However, the White Paper's sober depiction of the state of EU law shows how sport, a sector of considerable economic significance, cannot enjoy immunity from EU law, but it also carefully and convincingly sustains the argument that the 'special' features of sport—its 'specificity', in the terms preferred by the White Paper—can be and are accommodated within the interpretation and application of EU internal market law. In line with the Court's case law explored in Chapter 5, this shows that EU internal market law is *not* impervious to the legitimate demands of sporting federations. This is the conditional autonomy of the *lex sportiva* under EU law. It is an EU 'policy' of sorts which is sensitive to the needs of sporting bodies while not at all purporting to intervene by establishing binding legislative standards.

The White Paper's Conclusion noted that:

A mandate has been given by the European Council of June 2007 for the Intergovernmental Conference, which foresees a Treaty provision on sport. If necessary, the Commission may return to this issue and indicate further steps in the context of a new Treaty provision.[48]

This invites that attention shall turn to the formal addition of sport to the EU's list of legislative competences. This occurred in 2009, when the Treaty of Lisbon came into force, but the negotiation of what eventually became Article 165 TFEU was under way during the preparation of the 2007 White Paper, and so to some extent

---

[47] cf eg S Cuendet, 'The EU Commission's White Paper on Sport: An Official Coherent, Yet Debated Entrance of the Commission in the Sports Arena', Special Addendum to (2007) 7(3–4) Intl Sports LJ.
[48] White Paper on Sport (n 5) 20.

informs its background. That is, Article 165 TFEU and the 2007 White Paper did not emerge from entirely separate processes.

6.6 The Road to Article 165 TFEU: Abandoning the Dream of Absolute Exclusion for Sport

There is a common theme to the Court's case law dealing with the application of internal market law to sport examined in Chapters 4 and 5 and the material covered in this chapter, stretching from the Amsterdam Declaration on Sport and its follow-up at Nice, through the 1999 Helsinki Report, and culminating in the superior account provided in the 2007 Commission White Paper on Sport. All are marked by a refusal to locate sport beyond the reach of EU law, despite the absence of any explicit treatment of sport in the Treaty texts. However, in their approach to sport they leave room for recognition of the possibility that sporting practices may be shown to deserve sensitive examination rather than a brutal assumption that sport is simply an economic sector like any other. So the Court, the Member States, and the Commission are all broadly committed to a model whereby sporting autonomy under EU law is conditional on a demonstration of precisely why EU law should adapt its core assumptions when confronted by the 'specificity' of sport. It is the adjudicative or interpretative means to respect sporting autonomy, which was introduced in Chapter 2. Sport enjoys no absolute autonomy.

Article 165 TFEU bears the same stamp. EU law enjoys a formal competence in the field of sport based on this provision, which was added to the Treaty on the Functioning of the European Union with effect from 2009 as a result of the amendments made by the Treaty of Lisbon. No longer is there any room to deny that sport is any proper part of the EU's activities. But the terms of Article 165 are written with conspicuous care and caution. They attribute to the EU a legislative competence that is confined to the adoption of incentive measures. Moreover, Article 165 openly embraces the notion that sport is special in its reference to 'the specific nature of sport'.

Article 165 reflects in far more concrete form than the Amsterdam and Nice Declarations a political view that EU law and sport interact—that there is no *exclusion*—and the stated terms of *inclusion* are crafted to admit sensitivity to sport's concerns.

Quite how and why Article 165 TFEU is drafted in the way it is requires a look back over a period of almost ten years within which the long process of negotiation that ultimately led to the Lisbon Treaty's entry into force in 2009 was conducted. Sport, of course, was a long way distant from the top of that reform agenda pursued erratically during a turbulent decade. But it was part of the reforming rhythm, albeit at a level of relatively low political salience. An exhaustive account of the negotiation of what is today Article 165 is not called for.[49] The narrative is

---

[49] This section is an abbreviated account of the story, based on B García and S Weatherill, 'Engaging with the EU in order to minimize its impact: sport and the negotiation of the Treaty of

nonetheless worth brief attention because it reveals how the most coveted status sought by sports governing bodies, exclusion or absolute autonomy from EU law, was sought but proved politically unfeasible and how instead a strategy of inclusion combined with constitutionally entrenched respect for sport's special character was ultimately arrived at. As Article 165 now makes clear, it is this 'conditional autonomy' which forms the basis for the future elaboration of EU sports law and policy.

The basic story is simply told. Sporting bodies sought to accept sport's explicit admission to the EU Treaty structure in order to extract the maximum protection for their autonomy from the influence of the EU. This might seem a paradox, but in fact it is a reflection of a widespread though doubtless reluctant sense felt by sporting bodies that ignoring the EU and hoping it would go away had been exposed as a failed strategy, and that instead fighting for a favourable adjudicative and interpretative solution within the framework of EU law was the next best, and certainly most realistic, strategy.

6.7 From the Convention on the Future of Europe via the Failure of the Treaty Establishing a Constitution to the Lisbon Treaty

Periodic revision of the EU Treaties occurs as a result of the agreement and ratification of an amending Treaty by the Member States, acting unanimously.[50] The internal operation of the EU system has a momentum and sophistication that transcends that found in an orthodox international organization, but the process of Treaty revision, achieved externally by the choices made by the Member States, is the moment at which the EU's roots as a Treaty-based system of which the Member States are the masters is most vividly recalled and asserted. Typically the process of negotiation occurs at an intergovernmental conference, which eventually yields a text that is open to ratification by all the Member States according to their particular domestic constitutional arrangements. This was the pattern that led to the amending Single European Act (which entered into force in 1987), the Maastricht Treaty (1993), the Amsterdam Treaty (1999), and the Nice Treaty (which after some delay entered into force in 2003).

It was increasingly felt that this process was conspicuously elite-driven, and the behind-closed-doors nature of Treaty revision began to be condemned as one element in mounting popular dissatisfaction with and alienation from the EU's endeavours. In December 2001, when the European Council met in Laeken in Belgium, it decided to convene a Convention on the 'Future of Europe'. This was

---

Lisbon' (2012) 19 JEPP 238. I take the chance here to repeat my thanks to my co-author Borja García for his detailed understanding of the pattern of the negotiation and also his brilliant insight into the lessons to be learned.

[50] See now TEU, Art 48.

designed to prepare the ground for the next intergovernmental conference in a way that would be calculatedly more transparent and inclusive than had applied under previous practice. It was hoped that this would make the process a good deal more appealing and, under an optimistic diagnosis that held that the more people knew about the EU's operation the more they would feel positively engaged with it, ultimately more legitimate. The Convention held its inaugural session under the chairmanship of Valery Giscard d'Estaing in February 2002. Representatives of heads of state and government, the core of a conventional intergovernmental conference, were joined by representatives of the Parliament, the Commission, national Parliaments, and candidate accession countries. This was the planned wider participatory model.

The Convention's working method was initially founded on eleven working groups.[51] They concluded their reports by early 2003, allowing a complete draft Treaty to be knitted together in the spring and then submitted to the European Council in Rome in July 2003. Laborious negotiation followed and some detailed amendments were made to the text, but in June 2004 a Treaty establishing a Constitution for Europe was agreed by the Member States and then signed in Rome in October 2004. Much of what was at stake concerned improving the comprehensibility and presentation of what had already been done in the name of the EU, not in effecting radical change. The name was misleading too—called a Constitution, it was in form and in law simply a Treaty. It was hoped and, by some, it was expected that use of the language of a Constitution would cut through the rising popular resistance to the elite-driven nature of the project. The opposite reaction proved to be the reality. In France and the Netherlands 'no' votes were recorded in popular referenda in 2005 and so those states, founder members of the EU, could not ratify the Treaty establishing a Constitution. It was placed on ice pending a so-called 'period of reflection', and then abandoned.

In 2007 there emerged what would become the Treaty of Lisbon. In substance it had a lot in common with the Treaty establishing a Constitution, so the Convention's work was not wasted. The basic intent remained the improved operation of the existing system, not a radical overhaul. But the new text was presented with aggressive modesty as just another incremental revision of the Treaties. It abandoned the label 'constitution' and dropped some other more ambitious trappings embraced by the Convention on the Future of Europe, such as a motto and an anthem for the EU.[52] The main purpose of the calculatedly low-key emergence of the Lisbon Treaty was precisely to avoid the awkward need to secure popular approval by referendum. In fact only in Ireland was the Treaty put to this test. It failed it in 2008 but passed in a second run in 2009. The Treaty of Lisbon also had to survive inquiry by several constitutional courts in Member States anxious lest ratification should

---

[51] Documentation is available at <http://european-convention.europa.eu/EN/bienvenue/bienvenue2352. html?lang=EN> accessed 29 November 2016.

[52] European Council Presidency Conclusions, '... the constitutional concept which consisted in repealing all existing treaties and replacing them by a single text called *Constitution* is abandoned' (June 2007).

violate domestic constitutional standards,[53] but it eventually passed these tests too. The amending Treaty of Lisbon entered into force at the beginning of December 2009. Since then the EU has been founded on two treaties of equal value, the Treaty on European Union and the (longer and intricately detailed) Treaty on the Functioning of the European Union.

Article 165 TFEU was one of the Lisbon Treaty's innovations. But where did sport fit into the process of negotiation that ran through most of the decade, from the Convention on the Future of Europe, which opened in early 2002, to the entry into force of the Lisbon Treaty in late 2009?

6.8 Sport at the Convention on the Future of Europe and Beyond

At the Convention on the Future of Europe sport was not at any stage a high-profile issue in the debates. Most of the relatively few documents that referred to sport were confined to no more than brief comment or reference.[54] Contributions which engaged more actively and directly with sport tended to display an anxiety in common that the special character of sport has been undermined by the intervention of EU law.[55] Such a perspective, which would be favourably inclined to adopting more legally durable protection for sporting autonomy than had been provided by the Amsterdam and Nice Declarations, is plainly in line with that typically promoted by sporting federations. But that perspective was never carried forward with the backing of any intellectual momentum, nor did it ever gain political traction at the Convention.

It is pertinent to appreciate how very difficult it is to construct a suitable exclusion, even if one is favourably disposed towards such a model. Just as Chapters 4 and 5 tracked the case law to reveal largely fruitless attempts to attach an absolute immunity from EU law to sporting practices, so too here a symmetrical inability to draft an effective exclusionary Treaty provision infuses the more intensely political context discussed in this chapter.

One of the few contributions to the Convention to deal explicitly with sport, although sport was only one of its preoccupations, was the so-called 'Freiburg draft'.[56] Article 24 of this proposal was entitled 'Respect for the Sovereignty of the Member States'. It provided that when exercising the competences assigned by the Treaty, the Union shall respect the sovereignty of the Member States especially

---

[53] Most notably in Germany: see the *Lisbon* ruling of the BVerfG, <http://www.bundesverfassungsgericht. de/entscheidungen/es20090630_2bve000208en.html> accessed 29 November 2016.

[54] See eg CONV 189/02, 12 July 2002 (Hänsch et al), CONV 234/02, 3 September 2002 (Duff), CONV 335/02, 19 November 2002 (Ornella Paciotti), CONV 325/1/02/REV1, 6 December 2002 (Brok), CONV 541/03, 6 February 2003 (Brok), CONV 325/2/02/REV2, 7 March 2003 (Brok), CONV 495/03, 20 January 2003 (Teufel).

[55] CONV 33/02, 17 April 2002 (Duhamel), CONV 337/02, 10 October 2002 (Tajani), CONV 478/03, 10 January 2003 (Haenel et al).

[56] CONV 495/03, 20 January 2003.

in listed areas which 'are characteristic for their national identity and their fundamental constitutional legal order'. Among the several items on the list was 'sports
policy'. Union measures, it was stated, shall not 'encroach upon the core area of
these sovereign rights'.

There was no political appetite among the majority of delegates to introduce
such a brake. In general the Convention's chosen means to correct the alleged harm
done by the EU to 'sovereignty' were pitched at the modest end of the spectrum.[57]
However, it should also be noted how awkward is this formulation in its detail. In
the first instance it is not clear to which institutions of the Union this direction is
addressed. If it is a control over the exercise of *legislative* competence then it is of
little consequence as far as sport is concerned, because there is scarcely any such
legislative activity. If it is apt to serve as a restraint on the application of the law
of the internal market to sport then, given the overlap between these two spheres
traced in the previous two chapters, it is capable of exerting a much more significant
impact, but equally it is in that vein remarkably imprecise. How wide an exclusion
is intended? It is inconceivable that *all* of the commercial activities undertaken in
the field of sport, such as sales of merchandise and payment of wages, would be
immune to EU law. So the Freiburg draft's formula simply throws up awkward
boundary disputes of the type already visible in the Court's case law and in the cautious terms of the Amsterdam and Nice Declarations. In short, it does not really
help. As a general observation, any attempt to carve out sectoral protection from
the reach of EU law, especially internal market law, faces the structural difficulty
(introduced in Chapter 3) that the logic of the Treaty is rooted in a broadly based,
functionally driven regime.

The provision in the Treaty post-Lisbon which comes closest to Article 24 of the
Freiburg draft is Article 4(2) TEU, but its direction that the Union shall respect the
national identities and essential functions of the Member States does not mention
sport and is unlikely to be apt to cover it, or at least *all* of it. Moreover, in any event
it envisages a process of assessing the worth of particular state features in the context
of the achievement of the EU's objectives, whereas by contrast the Freiburg draft
sought to seal off core areas of 'sovereignty' from EU intervention.[58]

The connection to Chapters 4 and 5 is marked. It is fiendishly difficult to find
intellectually credible methods for securing a durable protection of sporting autonomy. Part of the problem is the functional breadth of the EU legal order: part of
the problem is that sport is special, but not as special as is sometimes claimed.
Ultimately sport is special but determining exactly how far it is special, and with
what consequences for the interpretation and application of the law, requires a case-
by-case examination. The Court's ruling in *Meca-Medina* is a more viable platform

---

[57] For a survey see S Weatherill, 'Competence Creep and Competence Control' (2004) 23 YEL 1.
[58] One might understand the concern to protect national constitutional identity in the BVerfG's
Lisbon judgment (n 53) as a version of the Freiburg draft wrapped up in national, rather than EU,
constitutional dress, but here too it would be a surprise if (all aspects of) sport were found to form part
of that identity.

on which to stand this inquiry than the Freiburg draft or any similarly elusive abstract model.

However, the strategic concern of the Freiburg draft to include reference to sport in the Treaty precisely in order to protect its particular special features was thematically significant, and the debate (and eventually Article 165 TFEU) followed this track. The only question was how exactly to frame this.

A 'Digest of contributions to the Forum', prepared in the summer of 2002 in advance of a plenary session of the Convention on civil society, advised of a 'call for a specific legal basis for support for sport'.[59] However, Working Group V within the Convention on 'Complementary Competencies', chaired by Henning Christophersen, a Danish politician and former member of the Commission, had considered the case for bringing in explicit mention of sport as an area in which the EU might be empowered to adopt supporting measures and, though there was some support for the idea, had rejected it.[60] Moreover, a 'preliminary draft Constitutional Treaty' prepared by the Praesidium for a plenary session of the Convention on 28 October 2002, had no place for sport.

The crucial shift was achieved in late 2002 and early 2003. The draft text proposed by the Praesidium and released on 6 February 2003 listed sport as an area where the EU would be competent to take 'supporting action'. The breakthrough had been achieved predominantly as a result of skilful lobbying by sports organizations 'off the record'.[61] The President of the International Olympic Committee (IOC), Jacques Rogge, was involved: he was able to gain access directly to Giscard d'Estaing, Chair of the Convention. Ministers of sport in some, but not all, of the Member States were also engaged in pressing the political case for sport's inclusion in the Treaty. So too was the European Commission Sports Unit. The political intervention of Commissioner Viviane Reding, who at the time held responsibility for sport as part of her Education and Culture portfolio, was also influential in pushing the Praesidium.

The lobbying process succeeded. Once sport was 'in', with effect from February 2003, it was never in danger of being pushed out. Ultimately the Praesidium's decision to incorporate sport, once taken, went largely unopposed. In fact, to put sport in its due context, its emergence was probably unnoticed by most members of the Convention. Energetic work behind the scenes was necessary to get sport across the threshold, but it was more a question of finding enough supporters than having to face down opponents. In relative terms sport was not a hot topic at the Convention nor in the subsequent intergovernmental conference that agreed the (ill-fated) Treaty establishing a Constitution.

The text agreed at the Convention placed sport alongside education, vocational training, and youth as an area of 'supporting, coordinating or complementary action' and added detailed provisions in a brand new Article, under the title 'Education,

---

[59] CONV 112/02, 17 June 2002.
[60] CONV 375/1/02 <http://european-convention.europa.eu/pdf/reg/en/02/cv00/cv00375-re01.en02.pdf> accessed 29 November 2016.
[61] On the detail see García and Weatherill (n 49).

Vocational Training, Youth and Sport'. This provided (inter alia) that 'The Union shall contribute to the promotion of European sporting issues, given the social and educational function of sport'. Union action was to be aimed at 'developing the European dimension in sport, by promoting fairness in competitions and cooperation between sporting bodies and by protecting the physical and moral integrity of sportsmen and sportswomen, especially young sportsmen and sportswomen'.

This, then, does *not* mention 'the specific nature of sport', which has become the lynchpin of the case that 'sport is special', made explicit in Article 165 TFEU. That phrase was added between the middle of 2003, when the Convention concluded, and late 2004, when the Treaty establishing a Constitution was finally agreed by the Member States. It included sport alongside education, youth, and vocational training as an 'area of supporting, coordinating or complementary action' while the substantive elaboration stated that: 'The Union shall contribute to the promotion of European sporting issues, while taking account of the specific nature of sport, its structures based on voluntary activity and its social and educational function.'

Once again the explanation was that the progress of negotiation had been influenced by astute behind-the-scenes lobbying which achieved textual adjustment that was designed to accentuate sport's coveted special status.[62] There was clearly no magic intended in the phrase 'the specific nature of sport'. Some contributions at the Convention preferred recognition of 'the specificity of the sport',[63] the phrase that, as explained earlier, in section 6.5, would come to feature heavily in the Commission's 2007 White Paper. The point was to capture, in an admittedly imprecise way, the general notion that sport deserves some degree of sensitive treatment in the application of legal rules. Excluding sport from the grip of the EU is politically unfeasible. Including *within* EU law explicit respect for its distinctive character was, however, attainable, and it is exactly in this direction that lobbying in favour of the stipulation to take account of the 'specific nature of sport' tended. It represents an acceptance of a strategy of conditional, not absolute, autonomy. Otherwise put, it is to press for an interpretative softening—to put faith in the adjudicative or interpretative approach to achieving sporting autonomy.

6.9 The Treaty of Lisbon

The story is told elsewhere of how the Treaty of Lisbon was prepared so as to be sufficiently different from the Treaty establishing a Constitution to justify withdrawal of the promise of a referendum (except in Ireland) but not so different that the substance of the planned institutional reforms would be lost.[64] But in the case of sport, that story is of no direct relevance. For sport, what was agreed at the end of 2004

---

[62] On the detail see García and Weatherill (n 49).

[63] eg CONV 398/02, 12 November 2002 (Duhamel and Beres) 4; CONV 337/02 10 October 2002 (Tajani) ('specificita'). On the francophone background, cf Duval (n 41).

[64] See eg M Dougan, 'The Treaty of Lisbon 2007: Winning Minds, Not Hearts' (2008) 45 CML Rev 617.

in the Treaty establishing a Constitution was left untouched in 2007, as the Lisbon Treaty was negotiated and agreed. So when sport was added to the armoury of the EU's legislative competences with effect from December 2009, when the Treaty of Lisbon entered into force, the terms were those mapped and planned much earlier at the Convention on the Future of Europe.

Article 6(e) TFEU states that 'The Union shall have competence to carry out actions to support, coordinate or supplement the actions of the Member States. The areas of such action shall, at European level, be: ... education, vocational training, youth and sport ...'. This grants the EU a competence in the field of sport that is the most slender of the three basic types of competence mapped out in Articles 2 to 6 TFEU. It is neither an exclusive nor a shared competence, but instead merely a supporting competence. The EU's involvement in sport is declared to be subordinate to the actions of the Member States. Moreover, although this is not made explicit, the legitimate claims to organizational autonomy of sports governing bodies are also apt to confine the EU's pretensions.

For sport, as for all EU activities, the details of the legislative competence conferred on the Union are located in the ramblingly huge Part Three of the TFEU, which is entitled 'Union Policies and Internal Actions', specifically in Title XII of Part Three 'Education, Vocational Training, Youth and Sport'. The relevant Treaty Articles are Articles 165 and 166 TFEU, though only Article 165 TFEU applies directly to sport.

Stripped down to its sports-related content, Article 165 TFEU provides:

1. ... The Union shall contribute to the promotion of European sporting issues, while taking account of the specific nature of sport, its structures based on voluntary activity and its social and educational function.
2. Union action shall be aimed at: ... developing the European dimension in sport, by promoting fairness and openness in sporting competitions and cooperation between bodies responsible for sports, and by protecting the physical and moral integrity of sportsmen and sportswomen, especially the youngest sportsmen and sportswomen.
3. The Union and the Member States shall foster cooperation with third countries and the competent international organisations in the field of education and sport, in particular the Council of Europe.
4. In order to contribute to the achievement of the objectives referred to in this Article: the European Parliament and the Council, acting in accordance with the ordinary legislative procedure, after consulting the Economic and Social Committee and the Committee of the Regions, shall adopt incentive measures, excluding any harmonisation of the laws and regulations of the Member States; the Council, on a proposal from the Commission, shall adopt recommendations.

6.10 Lisbon—How Much Changed?

Article 165 TFEU places beyond question the EU's legitimate claim to act in the field of sport. It is a statement of inclusion. Since 2009 the 'keep out!' reflex of sporting bodies insistent on absolute autonomy has been unsustainable because, on the entry into force of the Lisbon Treaty, sport became an explicit competence conferred on the EU.

For the first time, Article 165 equips the EU with a legislative competence that is explicit to sport. The EU has on occasion adopted legislation that has touched sport, but until 2009 the route was necessarily through a conferred competence that was not explicitly tied to sport. A sectoral committee covering employment in professional football was established in 2008, but this is a product of the 'social dialogue' foreseen by Articles 154 and 155 TFEU: it reaches sport via EU social policy.[65] A further good example is provided by the designation of 2004 as the European Year of Sport. This was presented in the governing EU legal measure as the European Year of Education through Sport, based on what was then Article 149 EC on education.[66] Its Preamble mentions the Amsterdam and Nice Declarations, and a small budget was allocated to the co-financing of projects developed at national level, but the strict constitutional basis is rooted in education, not sport. The absence of any legislative competence explicitly devoted to sport closely cir-cumscribed the EU's role until 2009. The reforms made by the Treaty of Lisbon change this. But they do not change it much.

The key to Article 165's legislative potential lies in its tightly confined terms. The Parliament and Council, acting in accordance with the ordinary legislative proced-ure, may adopt 'incentive measures'—although harmonization of national laws is excluded—and the Council too may adopt recommendations. This is a power that goes beyond the EU's previous remit. Anything that goes beyond nothing is something. For the first time sport is subject to explicit reference within the Treaties establishing and governing the EU. Given the fundamental principle that the EU possesses only the competences conferred upon it by its Member States, the nov-elty achieved by this express attribution in the field of sport counts as immensely constitutionally significant. But the legislative competence is written with caution in order to preclude the EU adopting a dominant role which would infringe the privileges of the Member States, and by implication also those of governing bodies in sport. So the EU's newly acquired competence in fact represents a modest, even meagre, grant made by the Member States.

In this sense, the principle—that the EU is granted an explicit legislative competence—is far less compelling than the practice—which is that there is not much of substance or potential to that competence. Moreover, the apparently trans-formative character of Article 165 is undermined by appreciation of the story told in Chapters 4 and 5, according to which (as a consequence of the internal market project) the EU has long exercised significant influence over the autonomy enjoyed by sports federations operating on its territory.

Exactly what *should* be the purpose of the legislative competence conferred by Article 165 is presented with a flourish, albeit one that is—again, calculatedly—an

---

[65] <http://ec.europa.eu/social/main.jsp?catId=480&intPageId=1848&langId=en> accessed 29 November 2016.
[66] Dec 291/2003/EC [2003] OJ L43/1.

ambiguous mix. Union action is to be aimed at 'developing the European dimension in sport', which immediately raises the question just what this 'European dimension' might comprise. It is questionable whether there is anything distinctively 'European' about sport, still less anything specifically EU in character. The identified concerns to promote cooperation between bodies responsible for sports, protect the physical and moral integrity of sportsmen and sportswomen, and to foster cooperation with third countries and competent international organizations are relatively concrete and readily understood. The promotion of fairness and openness in sporting competitions is strikingly less tangible. And the direction in the first paragraph of Article 165 that the Union shall contribute to the promotion of European sporting issues, while taking account of the specific nature of sport, its structures based on voluntary activity, and its social and educational function is in similar vein aspirationally uncontentious but in detail puzzling. What are these 'European sporting issues'? How should we understand the 'specific nature of sport'? And while the 'social and educational function' of sport has resonance in some areas, it has little to do with *professional* sport as a generator of income, even if those engaged in that lucrative activity delight in dressing themselves in such virtuously tailored clothes.

The arrival of Article 165 in the Treaties with effect from 2009 put to an end any claim that EU law has no connection with sport. But it leaves open the precise nature of that connection. It turns the focus on to precisely how far, and in what way, those special features—that 'specific nature'—will and should affect the interpretation and application of EU law. In short, the vocabulary introduced by the Lisbon Treaty provides the material with which to frame the discussion about the nature of EU sports law and policy, but it makes no concrete commitments. Therefore what matters most is the elaboration of EU sports law and policy in the shadow of Article 165. Plainly sports bodies will seek to press the virtue of permitting them autonomy though the lens of Article 165's 'specific nature of sport', but the institutions they must impress are the EU's own, most of all the Commission and the Court. For sports governing bodies, the main anxiety attached to the embrace of conditional autonomy—the strategy of inclusion within the Treaty but accompanied by explicit reference to sport's special features—is that any choices will be made on the EU's terms.

6.11 Article 165 in Legislative and Policy-making Practice

In January 2011 the Commission published a fourteen-page Communication, 'Developing the European Dimension in Sport'.[67] The changes wrought by the Lisbon Treaty are of course mentioned. However, it is thematically significant

---

[67] Commission Communication, January 2011, 'Developing the European Dimension in Sport' COM (2011) 12 <http://ec.europa.eu/sport/news/doc/communication/communication_en.pdf> accessed 29 November 2016.

that the Communication does not treat Article 165 as transformative. The 2011 Communication's principal source of inspiration is the 2007 White Paper, to which reference is made in the Communication's very first sentence. Three main themes are sustained: the societal role of sport, the economic dimension of sport, and the organization of sport. The Communication 'does not replace the White Paper but builds on its achievements'.[68] It is asserted that 'implementation of the White Paper has confirmed that, in a number of areas, action at EU level can provide significant added value',[69] and in its strongest portrayal of consistency in policy practice, unbroken but confirmed by the arrival of Article 165, the Commission in the 2011 Communication holds that:

The specific nature of sport, a legal concept established by the Court of Justice of the European Union which has already been taken into account by the EU institutions in various circumstances and which was addressed in detail in the White Paper on Sport and the accompanying Staff Working Document, is now recognised by Article 165 TFEU. It encompasses all the characteristics that make sport special, such as for instance the interdependence between competing adversaries or the pyramid structure of open competitions.[70]

The 2007 White Paper, Article 165 TFEU, and the 2011 Communication share common themes. In fact the 2007 White Paper was *already* influenced by what would become the Lisbon Treaty reforms, which, as the account above makes clear, were already visible as the 2007 White Paper was under preparation, even if they were not yet in force. All three texts are directed at the key thematic question—sport is special, but how special? So the Commission, in releasing its 2011 Communication, shows a confidence that the Lisbon Treaty was not in substance a change of direction for EU sports law and policy.

However, Article 165 TFEU certainly does provide a constitutionally undisputable starting point in developing EU sports law and policy.

That the EU possesses an explicit competence in the field of sport has permitted the dedication of a budget to sport. This is handled by the Directorate General for Education and Culture within the Commission.[71] As with Article 165 TFEU itself, the importance is more symbolic than substantive. The budget is relatively small. In the 2013 call for proposals 135 applications were received and the Commission decided to finance fifteen projects with a total amount of €2.8 million.[72] These covered the strengthening of good governance and dual careers in sport through support for the mobility of volunteers, coaches, managers and staff of non-profit sport organizations; protecting athletes, especially the youngest, from health and safety hazards by improving training and competition conditions; and promoting traditional European sports and games. Since 2014 a number of these activities have been the subject of development under the auspices of the ERASMUS+ programme for education, training, youth and sport.[73] This is based on Regulation

---

[68] ibid 2.   [69] ibid para 1.2.   [70] ibid 10.

[71] Its website is at <http://ec.europa.eu/sport/index_en.htm> accessed 29 November 2016.

[72] <http://ec.europa.eu/sport/policy/preparatory-actions/preparatory-actions-2013_en.htm> accessed 29 November 2016.

[73] <https://ec.europa.eu/programmes/erasmus-plus/node_en> accessed 29 November 2016.

1288/2013.[74] So, for example, support has been given to projects on strengthening Europe's traditional sports[75] and safeguarding youth sport.[76] The 2017 Work Programme promises a focus on grassroots sport, as well as on social inclusion, promotion of good governance principles, and the fight against violence and intolerance in sport.[77] It is supported by a budget for the year of some €38 million, which is less than 2 per cent of the total budget for ERASMUS+, the lion's share of which is spent on education and training. Support is targeted in particular at cross-border collaborative partnerships and setting up not-for-profit sports events.

At a more general level, Article 165 TFEU means that it is open to the EU's institutions to shape a policy and even, in the form of incentive measures, to adopt legislative initiatives which are openly tied to sport, rather than routed through another area where competence exists, such as education. There have, however, been no such incentive measures adopted, and so the principal interest in the elaboration of Article 165 lies in the chosen policy priorities.

In November 2010 the Council adopted a Resolution on structured dialogue in sport, which referred to Article 165 TFEU as heralding 'a new era in EU priorities in the field of sport'.[78] This was hyperbole and the Resolution itself is anodyne. But it demonstrated a new political confidence in connecting the EU to sport.[79] In 2011 a Council Resolution adopted a European Union Work Plan for Sport to cover 2011–14. It begins by embracing 'the competence assigned to the European Union, in particular by Article 6 and Article 165 of the Treaty on the Functioning of the European Union, according to which sport is an area where action at EU level should support, coordinate and supplement the actions of Member States'.[80] This did not purport to write on a blank slate: it recognized and took into account 'the achievements of the work in the informal structures established prior to the Lisbon Treaty'. Moreover, it built expressly on the themes identified in the 2007 White Paper and the 2011 Communication to address the societal role of sport, the economic dimension of sport, and the organization of sport. The constitutional point was that at this stage in the development of EU sports law the accusation that sport is none of the EU's business has been silenced. The Resolution fixed on three priority themes: the integrity of sport, in particular the fight against doping, match-fixing, and the promotion of good governance; the social values of sport, in particular health, social inclusion, education, and volunteering; and the economic aspects of sport, in particular sustainable financing of grassroots sport and evidence-based policy making. It avoids any hint that the EU should take the lead: it insists on the

---

[74] Regulation (EU) 1288/2013 of 11 December 2013 establishing 'Erasmus+': the Union programme for education, training, youth and sport [2013] OJ L347/50.

[75] <http://www.europeantraditionalsportsforum.eu/> accessed 29 November 2016.

[76] <http://www.safeguardingyouthsport.eu/> accessed 29 November 2016.

[77] C(2016) 5571, 5 September 2016, para 2.2.4. The document is available at <http://ec.europa.eu/dgs/education_culture/more_info/awp/docs/c-2016-5571_en.pdf> accessed 29 November 2016.

[78] [2010] OJ C322/1, point 3(i).

[79] See similarly Council Resolution on the role of sport as a source of and driver for active social inclusion [2010] OJ C326/5.

[80] [2011] OJ C162/1.

place of the Member States and also on the need for the EU 'to work closely with the sport movement and relevant competent organisations at national, European and international levels such as the Council of Europe'. In addition, Member States are instructed to respect 'the principle of subsidiarity and the autonomy of sport's governing structures' when developing policy at national level.

In 2014 the Commission issued a report on the implementation of this, the EU's first Work Plan for Sport, which covered 2011–14.[81] It describes a strengthened cooperation between the EU and the Member States in line with Article 165 TFEU in an effort to develop further the European dimension in sport. Following the Council's Resolution, work focused on priority themes—the integrity of sport, social values of sport, and economic aspects of sport. The point was to orient the EU's supporting competence to provide 'a valuable framework for all actors to cooperate in a coordinated way and in mutual respect of national and EU competences'.[82]

The Report notes that many of the competences in the area of sport lie with the Member States, and draws from this that it is 'important that priorities for a new EU Work Plan focus on actions delivering unambiguous value-added at EU level'.[83]

The follow-up Work Plan covers 2014–17. It was founded on a further Council Resolution on a European Work Plan for Sport to cover 2014 to 2017.[84] This follows the model of its predecessor by beginning with reference to 'the competence assigned to the European Union, in particular by Article 6 and Article 165 of the Treaty on the Functioning of the European Union'. Its content is familiar too. The three main themes to be pursued are the integrity of sport, the economic dimension of sport, and sport and society. Anxiety to work with the sports movement and relevant competent organizations at national, European, and international levels—such as the Council of Europe and WADA—remains prominent.

6.12 Article 165 as a Means to Frame the Debate

The principal significance of Article 165 does not lie at the level of detail. Instead its primary significance is that the EU's role in the field of sport is legitimated. Sporting bodies can no longer claim that sport is none of the EU's business. Instead one would expect them to claim that it is the EU's business but only to a very limited extent, and only in so far as respect is shown for its 'specific nature'. This is an important change, constitutionally and strategically, even if it may not lead to any substantial differences in the control exercised by EU law over particular sporting practices. The theme here is consistent: sports bodies must engage with the EU as part of a strategy to minimize its perceived detrimental effect on their practice. They cannot simply ignore the EU but nor are they strong enough to extract a promise of immunity. So what is left is the ambiguous middle ground of conditional

---

[81] 'Work Plan for Sport' COM (2014) 22.   [82] ibid 2.   [83] ibid 9.
[84] [2014] OJ C183/12.

autonomy, which is framed by the Lisbon Treaty's inclusion of sport in the text of the Treaty but on terms which are far from clear.

This is in many ways the position that the more astute sports governing bodies had already reached before 2009, as a strategy of exclusion had been so consistently exposed as unsuccessful before the Court and the Commission. This had been incrementally and grudgingly replaced with the recognition of a need to get closer to and to try and influence the key EU institutions by adapting a strategy moving towards a more cooperative model with the EU, especially with the Commission. UEFA was a pioneer.[85] This might be wise as a means to secure peaceful negotiation of potential flashpoints. The post-*Bosman* renegotiation of the transfer system, explained in Chapter 9, reveals a high level of cooperative engagement between UEFA, Fédération Internationale de Football Association (FIFA), and the Commission. The story of 'Financial Fair Play' (FFP), met in Chapter 10.9, also fits this description. Adopting a more active approach, it may be that sports governing bodies will sometimes find themselves able to rely on EU law, and the Commission's coercive powers, when they are themselves confronted by powerful antagonists. The potential application of EU law to restrain breakaway leagues is addressed in Chapter 10.11. The Lisbon Treaty's ambiguities are capable of serving to push the EU and sporting organizations closer together as all those involved seek to make sense of the 'principles' contained in Article 165 TFEU. In this vein it is striking that UEFA went so far as to publish its own 'Position paper'.[86] This states that Article 165 is 'not intended to prejudice the legitimate autonomy and discretionary decision making power of sports federations', and that it 'requires that the specific nature of sport must be recognised'. This, in summary, means that:

… sport is not 'above the law', there is now a provision in the Treaty itself recognising that sport cannot simply be treated as another 'business', without reference to its specific characteristics (*the 'specificity of sport'*).

This seems absolutely correct. It embraces conditional autonomy: a strategy of inclusion, not exclusion. Doubtless what is at stake in detail will require attention and debate over time. But UEFA concludes optimistically and constructively that:

Provided it is applied in a way that harmoniously reconciles the pursuit of these objectives and principles with the requirements of EU law, Article 165 of the TFEU could be beneficial for European sport.

In 2014 the Commission made a Decision adopting an arrangement for cooperation between itself and UEFA.[87] This asserts 'a common goal to promote and

---

[85] See in particular B García's pathbreaking article, 'UEFA and the European Union: From Confrontation to Co-operation' (2007) 3 JCER 202; also B García, 'The New Governance of Football: What Role for the EU?' in S Gardiner, R Parrish, and R Siekmann (eds), *EU, Sport, Law and Policy* (TMC Asser 2009) ch 7.

[86] 'UEFA's Position on Article 165 of the Lisbon Treaty' (sic) <http://www.uefa.com/MultimediaFiles/Download/uefaorg/EuropeanUnion/01/57/91/67/1579167_DOWNLOAD.pdf> accessed 29 November 2016.

[87] C(2014) 7378, 14 October 2014.

safeguard the values of fairness and openness in sport'. A commitment is made to respect all relevant rules, including competition law. The agreement makes much play of the virtuous aspects of sport: it refers to 'contributions to education, social integration and public health'. It also mentions financial solidarity, and recommends redistribution mechanisms concerning audiovisual media revenues and training compensation fees. It also commits to promoting social dialogue in sport. Regular bilateral meetings are planned. There is nothing particularly surprising about the content of this agreement, which traverses in rather bland fashion most of the matters discussed in this book. The interest lies principally in its very existence. It demonstrates that dialogue is the envisaged way forward to manage the intersection of EU law and the *lex sportiva*.

In similar vein, the Olympic and Sports Movement adopted a 'Common Position' in January 2010.[88] Greeting the specific nature of sport as 'a cornerstone of a new EU policy in the field of sport', it urges the EU to 'reaffirm its support for the independence and autonomy of sports federations and their right to determine autonomously their organisation and the promotion of their respective sport'. This was followed by the publication in 2011 of a *Guide to EU Sport Policy* by the EU Office of the European Olympic Committees, which considers that the notion of the specificity of sport 'suffers from the lack of a complete and precise definition' and urges that the Olympic movement 'be a key player in defining which sporting rules shall be recognised as specific'.[89] It makes the case for the autonomy of sports governing bodies but it does not deny the legitimate involvement in principle of the EU. Practical elaboration awaits. It is to some extent forthcoming in the recent Council Resolutions and Commission practice discussed earlier. But the difference in tone from the obstinacy surrounding *Bosman* and *Meca-Medina* is marked, and gratifyingly so.

6.13 Conclusion

Article 165 TFEU is both revolutionary and trivial. At the constitutional level it seems to carry great weight as the EU's first ever explicit conferred competence in the field of sport and, indeed, it (along with Article 6 TFEU) carries the first ever mention made of sport in the Treaties. However, in practice its effect is palpably less significant because of its narrowly drawn boundaries. Moreover, much of the content of Article 165 TFEU, especially the direction to take into account the specific nature of sport, is already familiar as a result of the Court's creative interpretation

---

[88] 'Common Position of the Olympic and Sports Movement on the implementation of the new Treaty on the Functioning of the European Union on sport' (January 2010) <https://www.idrettsforbundet. no/globalassets/idrett/idrettsforbundet/english/common_position_of_the_olympic_and_sports_ movement.pdf> accessed 29 November 2016.
[89] *Guide to EU Sport Policy* (2011) 11 <http://www.euoffice.eurolympic.org/files/guide_to_eu_ sport_policy_final_versionwithlinks.pdf> accessed 29 November 2016.

and application of internal market law when it collides with sporting practices (the *lex sportiva*).

So in this sense Article 165 TFEU serves as a continuation of the story of EU sports law. It is a re-statement and acceptance of conditional autonomy. Sport is not able to extract a grant of absolute autonomy from the reach of EU law: politically it was not strong enough and in any event intellectually the case is without merit. Many sporting practices have clear and immediate economic consequences and to wall them off from the EU, in particular from internal market law, would damage the integrity of the EU system and grant a concession that no other sector is allowed. But sport is allowed an autonomy *on condition that* it is able to show just why its practices are necessary, despite the attentive scrutiny of EU law.

Chapters 4 and 5 examined the development of this model of conditional autonomy in the decisions of the EU institution which was first into the field to engage with the question of whether sport is special—the Court of Justice. This required it to shape the law in the face of the determined attempts of sports governing bodies to exclude EU law's application to their practices or, at least, to secure an interpretation of EU law that was most favourable to their desire for autonomy. The more recent entry into force of the Lisbon Treaty gives a fresh vocabulary to the legal analysis and puts to an end any possibility of denying that sport is any of the EU's business. But so far there is no indication that the Lisbon Treaty has changed the rules of the game. Article 165 TFEU recognizes and, as the Court put it in *Olympique Lyonnais v Olivier Bernard*, 'corroborates' the specific nature of sport as an element in the law of the internal market.[90] This chapter has accordingly explored the theme of conditional autonomy in the political and legislative context.

The next chapter attempts to draw together the common themes of this chapter and the two that precede it. The aim is to use the 'specific nature' of sport to which Article 165 TFEU refers as a means to present an integrated account of the law of conditional autonomy which EU law applies in its dealings with the *lex sportiva*.

---

[90] *Bernard* (n 4).

7

The Specific Nature of Sport

An Integrated Account of the Law
of Conditional Autonomy

7.1 Introduction

The three previous chapters are linked by a common thread: EU law grants conditional autonomy to sport. Sporting bodies have room to protect and preserve their special concerns *on condition that* they demonstrate how and why EU law should be open to accommodation of such characteristics.

Chapter 4 explains how EU free movement law has been shaped by the Court of Justice, the first EU institution which was forced to grapple with the question of whether sport is special, to accommodate demonstrated organizational necessities in sporting competition. Chapter 5 tells a similar story in connection with competition law, where the demand for a case-by-case analysis, rather than blanket immunity, forms the essence of the legal control. Chapter 6 approaches the issue from the perspective of law and policy-making at EU level rather than the control of sporting practices pursuant to free movement and competition law, but it reveals a similar recognition of the specific nature of sport, albeit in a context which also assumes that the EU may play some role in shaping governance through the development of the European dimension in sporting and the promotion of fairness and openness. EU law does not intervene in sport unless, in short, it adds value: seen from the perspective of governing bodies, sporting autonomy is preserved provided it is exercised in a way that respects the conditions laid down by EU law.

The key structural point, then, is that there is negligible scope for arguing that sporting practices fall outside the scope of EU law, but rather ample scope for arguing that, once they are accepted as falling within that scope, sport may advance arguments associated with its specific nature in order to provoke a context-sensitive application of EU law. This is the adjudicative or interpretative strategy to securing sporting autonomy which was introduced in Chapter 2. It is the intellectual heart of EU sports law. The Amsterdam and Nice Declarations capture perfectly the political readiness of the Member States to embrace and express the distinctive qualities and particular virtues of sport, but not to go so far as to immunize sport from the reach of EU law. Article 165 of the Treaty on the Functioning of the European Union (TFEU) is no departure from this overall structural framework;

it is in fact a more elaborate version of that balanced approach. And the political negotiation that shaped it has conferred a legislative competence on the EU which is itself redolent of the notion of conditional autonomy. It does not at all elevate the EU to a position of top-down rule-maker. The EU's role is supplementary only. To this extent sporting autonomy is respected. But not in absolute terms.

Therefore the negotiation and entry into force of Article 165 was important as a firm recognition by sporting bodies that a strategy of securing absolute autonomy was simply not obtainable, and it placed the fact of the EU's engagement with sport on a secure constitutional footing. Henceforth it is inclusion not exclusion that dictates the *lex sportiva*'s engagement with EU law. Indeed it is the failure of a strategy of exclusion before the Court and Commission that counts as a major reason explaining the retreat to a strategy of (conditional) inclusion within the Treaty superstructure.

However, the significance of Article 165 TFEU in practice should not be exaggerated. It is in substance continuation, not reformation. The purpose of this chapter is to show how the several strands of EU sports law which emerged before 2009 are readily understood as having informed the drafting of Article 165. It then adopts a more forward-looking perspective to show how Article 165 provides a basis for an integrated, albeit modest, programme of EU sports law into the future. The aim is to show that Article 165's insistence on respect for the specific nature of sport aligns with the model of conditional autonomy developed by the Court and the Commission and provides a basis for coexistence between EU law and the *lex sportiva*. It is a theme that will be re-addressed in Chapter 12, the book's concluding chapter, after subsequent chapters which deal with concrete collisions between EU law and the *lex sportiva* in four distinct areas, namely nationality discrimination, the transfer system, governance, and the sale of broadcasting rights. The concern now is to draw together the themes of the previous three chapters to show the actual and potential pattern of an integrated sports law in the EU. In short, what are the *conditions* that attach to conditional autonomy?

7.2 Article 165 TFEU and Internal Market Law

The Treaty provisions on free movement and competition were not revised by the Treaty of Lisbon to add any reference to sport. They remain barren of any reference to sport. The sports-specific competence introduced with effect from 2009, Article 165 TFEU, is found elsewhere in the Treaty and it lacks any explicit organic link with the Treaty rules governing the internal market.

Article 165 TFEU is different from provisions such as Articles 11 and 12 TFEU which make explicit that requirements of environmental and consumer protection (respectively) shall be integrated into the definition and implementation of Union policies and activities, including the building of an internal market, but there is no room to doubt that Article 165 deserves to be read in this 'horizontal' manner. The Court treated free movement and competition law as open to interpretation in the light of the special features of sport in its case law decided before the entry into force of the Lisbon Treaty. The Court's rulings in landmark cases, such as *Walrave and Koch*,[1] *Bosman*,[2] *Deliège*,[3] and *Meca-Medina*[4] all demonstrate receptivity in principle to the claim that sport is special, albeit the Court has not always been persuaded that sport is special enough to justify the particular practices with which it is asked to deal. Moreover, the Court was explicitly willing to absorb the non-binding Amsterdam Declaration in applying the rules of internal market law in both *Deliège*[5] and in *Lehtonen*.[6] Therefore, given the grant of explicit and binding status to the 'specific nature' of sport under Article 165, it would be perverse to insist on attributing a less muscular role to the new Treaty provision. And the Court has not been perverse. *Olympique Lyonnais v Olivier Bernard* concerned the application of football's transfer system to young players.[7] The Court cited its familiar acceptance, first found in *Bosman*, that the considerable social importance of sporting activities, and in particular football in the EU, leads to the finding that the objective of encouraging the recruitment and training of young players must be accepted as legitimate.[8] This, it added, meant that assessment of the transfer system, as a restriction on free movement, shall embrace 'the specific characteristics of sport in general, and football in particular, and of their social and educational function'.[9] The Court then added that: 'The relevance of those factors is also corroborated by their being mentioned in the second subparagraph of Article 165(1) TFEU.'[10] So the Court chose to treat the apparent constitutional innovation of the Lisbon Treaty as no more than a confirmation of its own pre-existing practice. The ruling in *Bernard* is significant for its confirmation that although Article 165 is not explicitly tied to the Treaty provisions governing the internal market, it will nevertheless be read by the Court as if integrated into the interpretation and application of the provisions on free movement and competition law. But, in substance, Article 165 has no transformative effect on internal market law. The same emerges from the ruling in *Karen Murphy*, in which the Court, finding that sporting events have a unique and original character which can transform them into subject matter that is worthy of protection at law, briefly referred to Article 165, but in a way that merely confirmed rather than adjusted its orthodox approach.[11] The Court is perfectly justified in adopting this consistent approach: Article 165 could have been, but plainly is not, written to change the state of the law. Article 165 expresses what the Court has always conceded—that in the application of internal market law sport is special.

---

[1] Case 36/74 *Walrave and Koch v Union Cycliste Internationale* [1974] ECR 1405. Ch 4.2.
[2] Case C-415/93 *Union royale belge des sociétés de football association ASBL v Jean-Marc Bosman* [1995] ECR I-4921. Ch 4.3.
[3] Cases C-51/96 and C-191/97 *Deliège v Ligue de Judo* [2000] ECR I-2549. Ch 4.10.
[4] Case C-519/04 P *Meca-Medina and Majcen v Commission* [2006] ECR I-6991. Ch 5.3.
[5] *Deliège* (n 3) paras 41–42.
[6] Case C-176/96 *Jyri Lehtonen and Castors Canada Dry Namur-Braine ASBL v Fédération royale belge des sociétés de basket-ball ASBL (FRBSB)* [2000] ECR I-2681, paras 32–33.
[7] Case C-325/08 *Olympique Lyonnais v Olivier Bernard, Newcastle United* [2010] I-2177.
[8] ibid para 39, citing *Bosman* (n 2) para 106.   [9] ibid para 40.   [10] ibid.
[11] Joined Cases C-403/08 and C-429/08 *FA Premier League and others v QC Leisure and others, Karen Murphy v Media Protection Services Ltd* [2011] ECR I-9083 (Grand Chamber), para 101. See more fully Ch 11.8.

It would not be difficult today to treat the Court's rulings in landmark cases such as *Walrave and Koch*,[12] *Bosman*,[13] *Deliège*,[14] and *Meca-Medina*[15] as expressions of Article 165 TFEU's direction that the EU 'shall contribute to the promotion of European sporting issues, while taking account of the specific nature of sport'. This 'Lisbon vocabulary' captures and confirms the pre-existing model of 'conditional autonomy' enjoyed by the *lex sportiva* under EU law, which was developed by the Court and the Commission over the extended period lasting until 2009 during which sport was not even mentioned in the EU's governing Treaties. The ambivalent relationship between EU law and the *lex sportiva* crafted through the case law is now to be found at the heart of the provisions in the Treaty itself. Relying on Article 165's language would be a reframing of the analysis, nothing more: the outcome of the investigation would not change at all.

In fact the Commission's 2007 White Paper on Sport, and its accompanying Staff Working Document, are considerably more helpful than the spare terms of Article 165 in elucidating in detail what is at stake in the application of EU internal market law to sport.[16] The 'specificity of sport' is used as an organizing concept in the White Paper and the Staff Working Document.[17] But, as is true of Article 165, the point is not at all to propose a shift to something new in mediating the tension between EU law and the *lex sportiva*.

Exactly the same narrative of confirmation rather than reformation attaches to another innovation of the Lisbon Treaty, the grant of binding force to the Charter of Fundamental Rights of the European Union.[18] It too has been treated by the Court as exerting no transformative effect on internal market law. The key provisions are Articles 15 to 17 of the Charter, dealing with the freedom to choose an occupation, the freedom to conduct a business, and the right to property. In *Pfleger*, a post-Lisbon ruling, the Court treated controls on gambling as a restriction of the freedom to provide services within the meaning of Article 56 TFEU, and it added that the challenged national measures were restrictive not only from the point of view of Article 56 TFEU but were also limitations from the perspective of Articles 15 to 17 of the Charter.[19] But then it simply declared that there was no need for separate examination of the Charter-based claims. Consideration of whether the rules were restrictions and, if so, whether they were justified as a means to address concerns such as consumer protection and the prevention of both fraud and incitement to squander money on gambling, was pursued in the same orthodox way as it had been in pre-Lisbon case law.[20] The Court has similarly accepted

---

[12] *Walrave and Koch* (n 1).   [13] *Bosman* (n 2).   [14] *Deliège* (n 3).
[15] *Meca-Medina* (n 4).
[16] See Ch 5. The White Paper on Sport, COM (2007) 391, 11 July 2007, and the accompanying Staff Working Document, 'The EU and Sport: Background and Context', are both available via <http://ec.europa.eu/sport/index_en.htm> accessed 29 November 2016.
[17] White Paper on Sport (n 16) section 4.1; Staff Working Document, 'The EU and Sport: Background and Context' (n 16) see especially, but not only, 35–41.
[18] TEU, Art 6.   [19] Case C-390/12 *Pfleger*, judgment of 30 April 2014.
[20] See also Case C-98/14 *Berlington*, judgment of 11 June 2015 (TFEU, Art 56); Case C-367/12 *Sokoll-Seebacher*, judgment of 13 February 2014 (TFEU, Art 49).

that *legislative* intervention in the internal market inspired by public interest concerns, such as consumer protection and public health, may be permitted provided a fair balance is struck between the several fundamental rights at stake.[21] This is no different from its pre-existing approach in balancing competing interests. The Charter has acquired presentational prominence but it has not changed the structure or substance of internal market law generally nor in its particular application to sport. It has this in common with Article 165 TFEU.

In summary, Article 165 TFEU in particular and the reforms made with effect from 2009 by the Lisbon Treaty in general should not be regarded as transformative. They confirm the pre-existing trajectory of EU sports law, which holds that sport is special, but not always quite as special as governing bodies claim. The most useful contribution that may be drawn from Article 165 is to use it to propel with more confidence an argument that was already latent in *Meca-Medina*: that EU internal market law, embracing not only competition law but also free movement law, demands a case-by-case assessment of the compatibility of sporting practices with EU law. Only exceptionally does it immunize them from review, but, within its rather broad scope, it is open to, but not uncritically ready to accept, the claim that sport is special. Article 165's embrace of 'the specific nature of sport' is readily understood as an encapsulation of the Court's attitude in free movement law that sport does not enjoy any general autonomy from EU law, but that it is entitled to express its special characteristics as a basis for contextual application of EU law to sport. This is the heart of the interpretative or adjudicative strategy set out in Chapter 2.

Since *Bosman* and *Deliège*, most of the activity at the intersection between EU law and sport has concerned competition law rather than free movement law, but here too the focus is on the interpretative strategy as the route for sporting bodies to press for their—conditional—autonomy. *Meca-Medina* stands as an invitation by the Court to sporting bodies to show exactly what they do and why—what is 'specific'—in order to secure a contextually sensitive interpretation and application of EU law to their practices. This matches Article 165 TFEU's proviso that EU action shall be aimed at 'developing the European dimension in sport, by promoting fairness and openness in sporting competitions and cooperation between bodies responsible for sports, and by protecting the physical and moral integrity of sportsmen and sportswomen, especially the youngest sportsmen and sportswomen'. This fits a model of approval of anti-doping as an essential ingredient of modern sporting competition.

Within this explanation lies an important component in the case for an integrated EU sports law—that free movement law and competition law deserve to be read in a convergent manner. This is addressed in the next section.

---

[21] eg Case C-544/10 *Deutsches Weintor eG v Land Rheinland-Pfalz*, judgment of 6 September 2012; Case C-12/11 *Denise McDonough v Ryanair Ltd*, judgment of 31 January 2013. The case of this type which is closest to sport is Case C-283/11 *Sky Österreich GmbH*, judgment of 22 January 2013: this is considered at Ch 11.9.7.

7.3 The Convergence of Free Movement and Competition Law in Application to Sport: the Integrated Law of the Internal Market

Walrave and Koch and *Bosman* are usefully read in the light of *Meca-Medina*, in order to correct the analytical mis-steps there taken. And this is to proceed on the basis that the shape of EU sports law developed in the interpretation of provisions of the Treaty dealing with competition law in *Meca-Medina* should be exported also to inform the interpretation of free movement law.

True, the Court makes no such explicit insistence on convergence between competition law and free movement law in *Meca-Medina*. And in fact the Court rebuked the CFI for failing to separate out the different detailed elements at stake in an analysis under free movement law, on the one hand, and competition law, on the other. This, however, is not a rejection of broad convergence in purpose between the relevant Treaty provisions. Instead, the Court is best understood as simply drawing attention to the CFI's neglect of possible *detailed* differences between the provisions, such as personal scope, the need for and nature of market analysis, the role of 'internal situations', and the burden of proof.[22] The Commission's 2007 White Paper on Sport is cautious, indeed equivocal, on the point of convergence. The Staff Working Document seems in places readily to assume that *Meca-Medina* is equally relevant to free movement as to competition law,[23] yet in others it takes pains to accept that there is no convergence brought about by *Meca-Medina*.[24]

However, the most significant aspect of *Meca-Medina* is its distaste for the notion of the 'purely sporting' rule and preference instead for case-by-case examination of sporting practices, and it is this insight which deserves to be applied also to free movement law. In *Walrave and Koch* the Court treated the composition of national sports teams as unaffected by the prohibition against nationality-based discrimination now found in Article 18 TFEU, where their formation is 'a question of purely sporting interest and as such has nothing to do with economic activity'.[25] That unfortunate formula was recycled in *Bosman* in connection with (what is now) Article 45 TFEU on the free movement of workers.[26] Perhaps there are some such rules which are beyond the reach of the Treaty—the detail of the offside rule perhaps, the height of the goalposts, or the length of a match—but most rules of sporting interest are not *purely* of sporting interest, they also impinge on economic activity. In practice, the Court's consistent insistence that any restriction on the scope of the Treaty provisions in question must remain limited to its proper objective has helped to contain inflated claims to sporting autonomy via this unhappy 'purely sporting

---

[22] So the Court of Justice, in *Meca-Medina* (n 4) paras 32–33 of the appeal, is merely drawing attention to the inadequacy of para 42 in the CFI's judgment, Case T-313/02 *Meca-Medina and Majcen v Commission* [2004] ECR II-3291.

[23] 'The EU and Sport: Background and Context' (n 16) 101 and 104.

[24] ibid especially 70.   [25] *Walrave and Koch* (n 1). See Ch 4.2.

[26] *Bosman* (n 2). See Ch 4.3.

interest' formula. That is how and why the Court in *Bosman* refused to sanction discrimination in *club* football. But, in its treatment of the substance of the application in *Meca-Medina*, the Court chose not to mention the 'purely sporting' rule, and this is a change of real substance. Rather than seeking in vain for an intellectually credible basis for immunizing sports rules which have an economic effect from review under EU law, *Meca-Medina* prefers instead to find that there is an overlap between EU law and 'internal' sports law, but that the peculiar demands of the *lex sportiva* may be used to nourish a submission that an apparent restriction is nevertheless an essential element in sports governance. *Meca-Medina* was concerned with competition law, and on some points of detail competition law is different from free movement law, but the overall shape of the approach used in *Meca-Medina* is easily transplanted to free movement law. So free movement law, like competition law, should be treated as based on an overlap between EU law and 'internal' sports law, with minimal scope for the total exclusion of EU law, combined with a sensitive willingness to assess claims that the *lex sportiva* contains particular unusual features that are essential in sports governance.

Embracing this approach would not change the *outcome* of *Walrave and Koch* or *Bosman*, but it would make the analysis more intellectually credible. Using this approach, nationality-based discrimination is treated as necessary to sustain the very existence of international representative football competitions. The economic effects of the rule—confining the opportunities enjoyed by players to choose which country to play for and making international football appealing to spectators, sponsors, and broadcasters—are best understood as a necessary consequence of their contribution to the structure of sports governance. So they are not beyond the reach of EU law—rather, they are within the scope of EU law but, because of the special features of sport, not forbidden by it. By contrast, as decided in *Bosman*, nationality-based discrimination in club football has economic effects, but the Court will *not* treat it as inherent in the organization of the game and therefore it is fatally exposed to the prohibitions contained in EU law. *Meca-Medina* rinses the analysis of the unhelpful search for rules of *purely* sporting interest. This may make little, if any, difference to the *result* of litigation involving the subjection of sports governance to EU law but it provides a more realistic and intellectually sound legal basis for assessing the legitimate nature of the *lex sportiva*, the web of rules that frames modern sport while also generating profound financial implications.

The background concern is to place the economic objectives of EU internal market law in their wider Treaty-directed social and economic context for the purposes of the interpretation of the basic prohibitions. The Court in and since its landmark ruling in *Cassis de Dijon*, has interpreted Articles 34 and 56 TFEU to the effect that national rules which serve a sufficiently important interest may be treated as justified trade barriers without explicit recourse to the derogations foreseen by the Treaty in Articles 36, 52, and 62 TFEU.[27] In the same vein, *Wouters* provides a supple and context-sensitive interpretation of Article 101(1) TFEU, rather than

---

[27] Case 120/78 *Rewe-Zentrale AG v Bundesmonopolverwaltung für Branntwein* [1979] ECR 649.

an inflated interpretation of Article 101(3) TFEU.[28] Exactly this common model spills over into sport. *Meca-Medina*'s acceptance that the anti-doping rules did not constitute a restriction of competition incompatible with Article 101 TFEU, since they pursued a legitimate objective, is functionally aligned with the Court's Article 45 TFEU judgment in *Bosman*. That judgment accepts as 'legitimate' the perceived sports-specific anxiety to maintain a balance between clubs by preserving a certain degree of equality and uncertainty as to results and to encourage the recruitment and training of young players.[29] So too, in *Deliège*, an Article 56 TFEU case, the Court found that selection rules limited the number of participants in a tournament, but were 'inherent' in the event's organization.[30] Such rules are not beyond the reach of the Treaty, but they are not incompatible with its requirements.

Article 165 TFEU is a helpful basis on which to rest this argument for convergence. Its direction that the Union shall take account of 'the specific nature of sport' is not tied to either free movement law or to competition law. It should be understood as applying to both. It is an insistence that all aspects of EU law should be infused by an appreciation of the special features of sport. Such respect is not switched on or off dependent on which particular provisions of the Treaty are engaged.

So where concrete assessment of the extent to which sport is 'special' is at stake, EU free movement law and EU competition law should be taken to run in alignment.[31] The possibility that action taken by sports governing bodies may fall under both free movement and competition law reveals their unusual, if not quite *sui generis*, quasi-regulatory nature. The rules of sporting federations need to be assessed in the same contextually sensitive way irrespective of the Treaty provision against which they happen to be reviewed. Were it otherwise, there would be instability caused by strategic selection by litigants between either free movement or competition.

Steve Ross has concluded that 'the common law and the statutory competition regimes applicable in major Western countries converge, all finding that dominant sports league rules are lawful if reasonably tailored to achieve a legitimate goal'.[32] The analysis provided in this chapter and those that precede it fully endorses this finding, and adds that, in the EU context, this convergence spans not only competition but also free movement law. The scope of conditional autonomy properly allowed to sporting bodies under EU law depends on identifying what is truly necessary for the proper organization of sport, and this should not differ depending on whether the search is conducted in the name of free movement or competition. This is to assert

---

[28] Case C-309/99 *JCJ Wouters, JW Savelbergh, Price Waterhouse Belastingadviseurs BV v Algemene Raad van de Nederlandse Orde van Advocaten* [2002] ECR I-1577.
[29] *Bosman* (n 2) para 106.   [30] *Deliège* (n 3). See Ch 4.10.
[31] The same should apply to the state aid rules too, TFEU, Arts 107–109.
[32] S Ross, 'Competition Law and Labor Markets' in J Nafziger and S Ross (eds), *Handbook on International Sports Law* (Edward Elgar 2011) ch 12, at 313.

the virtue of a convergence in outcome between free movement law and the competition rules.[33] Article 165 TFEU points in exactly this direction, for it mandates a respect for the specific nature of sport which cuts across all areas of EU law.

7.4 A Sporting Margin of Appreciation

The Court's approach narrows the circumstances in which a sporting practice is likely to fall outwith the scope of EU law, and instead loads a heavy emphasis on the question whether those practices may be treated as justified in view of their place within the *lex sportiva*. This, as explained in this chapter and those that precede it, is firmly in line with the Court's approach to internal market law generally, which has within it an embedded functionally broad dynamic. It is also, as argued earlier, intellectually credible: rare will be the sporting practice that does not have the economic effect or intent that acts as the crucial jurisdictional trigger for the application of EU law. This approach does, however, make heavy demands of the Court and the Commission, as the bodies charged with deciding *how far* sport should be treated as 'special' within the scope of EU law. And there is a legitimate concern that the Treaty provides no clear mandate or useful guidance.

Article 165 TFEU directs that 'the specific nature of sport' shall be taken into account by the EU. The Court in *Bernard* accepted that this influences the interpretation of internal market law even if no explicit tie is made between Article 165 and the free movement or competition rules in the Treaty.[34] But in *Bernard* the Court also simply treated Article 165 in this context as nothing new: it corroborates the case law. And in fact Article 165 does nothing concrete to address the key questions about *how* special sport is. Nor does the Treaty more widely. The structural peculiarity of the EU system, which is particularly acutely felt in internal market law, is that the provisions on free movement and competition law stretch more widely than the legislative competences conferred on the EU. This has provoked vivid inquiry into the risk that EU law tends to promote a deregulatory dynamic which is inadequately compensated for by re-regulatory potential: to be more institutionally specific, the fear is that the Court undermines national choices, while the EU legislative process is (constitutionally and politically) unable to re-impose solutions at the EU level.[35] Most of the critical literature addresses matters of social welfare

---

[33] See eg M Mataija, *Private Regulation and the Internal Market: Sports, Legal Services, and Standard Setting in EU Economic Law* (OUP 2016) chs IV and V; K Mortelmans, 'Towards Convergence in the Application of the Rules on Free Movement and on Competition' (2001) 38 CML Rev 613. cf S Weatherill, ' "Fair Play Please!": Recent Developments in the Application of EC Law to Sport' (2003) 40 CML Rev 51, 80–86; R O'Loughlin, 'EC Competition Rules and Free Movement Rules: An Examination of the Parallels and their Furtherance by the ECJ *Wouters* Decision' [2003] ECLR 62; S Weatherill, 'On Overlapping Legal Orders: What is the "Purely Sporting Rule"?' in B Bogusz, A Cygan, and E Szyszczak (eds), *The Regulation of Sport in the European Union* (Edward Elgar 2007) ch 3.

[34] *Bernard* (n 7).

[35] See eg F Scharpf, 'The Asymmetry of European Integration, or Why the EU Cannot be a Social Market Economy' (2010) 8 Socio-Economic Review 211; M Höpner and A Schäfer, 'Embeddedness and Regional Integration: Waiting for Polanyi in a Hayekian Setting' (2012) 66 Intl Org 429; D Schiek,

and labour market regulation: the present concern is the way this tension operates in application to sport. In the gap between the relatively broad and functionally driven provisions on free movement and competition, on the one hand, and, on the other, the cramped scope for EU legislative action, yawns the most awkward task of adjudication: how to judge whether a practice that impedes the creation of the internal market should be treated as justified in circumstances where, by definition, the Treaty is deficient in providing useful guidance on EU policy goals. On this model it was necessary to judge the compatibility of sporting practices with EU law where they cut across the creation of the internal market without any explicit help from the Treaty: since 2009 there has been explicit help, in Article 165 TFEU, but this is not of any concrete assistance to the task of case-by-case adjudication.

There is a good *normative* argument that appreciation of this structure should induce the Court to be especially cautious when it applies internal market law to areas where the EU's *legislative* competence is slim or non-existent and where the Treaty offers it little or no guidance on policy and priorities. There is also a good *descriptive* argument that this caution characterizes the Court's treatment of sport under EU free movement and competition law. The Court has never refused to address the argument that sport is 'special'. Quite the reverse. In *Walrave and Koch* it took seriously the legitimate place of nationality discrimination in representative sport;[36] in *Bosman* it famously embraced 'the considerable social importance of sporting activities' and the legitimacy of 'maintaining a balance between clubs by preserving a certain degree of equality and uncertainty as to results and … encouraging the recruitment and training of young players';[37] in *Deliège* it found selection rules that excluded some athletes to be 'inherent' in sporting competition;[38] and in *Meca-Medina* it endorsed the place of anti-doping rules and the imposition of sanctions in the event of breach.[39] The Commission too has openly treated sport as an economic sector with distinctive characteristics that must inform the interpretation and application of EU law: so in *ENIC* it approved a restriction on competition in the market for acquisition of clubs as necessary to sustain uncertainty of outcome and the integrity of sporting competition.[40] None of this comes explicitly from the Treaty. It comes instead from the creative approach to mediating the intersection of internal market law and context-specific practices shaped over time by the Court and the Commission. Article 165 TFEU's assertion that sport has a 'specific nature' reflects and confirms this. In summary, EU law accommodates the special concerns of sports governance in the interpretation and application of its rules.

'The EU Constitution of Social Governance in an Economic Crisis: In Defence of a Transnational Dimension to Social Europe' (2013) 20(2) MJ 185; F De Witte, 'The Architecture of a Social Market Economy' LSE Law, Society and Economy Working Paper 13/2015; A Veldman and S De Vries, 'Regulation and Enforcement of Economic Freedoms and Social Rights: A Thorny Distribution of Sovereignty' in T Van den Brink, M Luchtman, and M Scholten (eds), *Sovereignty in the Shared Legal Order of the EU* (Intersentia 2015) ch 4.

[36] *Walrave and Koch* (n 1).   [37] *Bosman* (n 2) para 106.   [38] *Deliège* (n 3).
[39] *Meca-Medina* (n 4).
[40] COMP 37.806 *ENIC/UEFA*, IP/02/942, 27 June 2002. See Ch 5.2.

This is an application of EU internal market law more generally. The Court is noticeably careful to allow public authorities in the Member States a discretion or a margin of appreciation in circumstances where particularly sensitive social and cultural choices made at national level come into collision with trade integration, *a fortiori* where the matter generating tension escapes in whole or in part the EU's legislative competence.[41] Sport engages the practices of private parties, but the thematic openness of EU law to its special concerns is plain. In fact, albeit the language used differs, there are parallels between the interpretative or adjudicative approach to sporting autonomy under internal market law and the Court's treatment of acts of the EU's own institutions. The Court enjoys a jurisdiction conferred by the Treaty to review the legality of not merely administrative acts but also legislative acts adopted at EU level.[42] It is, however, sensitive to the limits of the judicial role and, in particular, its relationship to the political process. So it has crafted a consistently used formula which expresses its reticence to intervene aggressively in chosen legislative solutions. The Court insists that the legislature must be allowed a broad discretion in an area which entails political, economic, and social choices on its part, and in which it is called upon to undertake complex assessments.[43] In consequence, a measure must be manifestly inappropriate having regard to its objective before the legislative choice made at EU level will be regarded as invalid: 'the criterion to be applied is not whether a measure adopted in such an area was the only or the best possible measure'.[44] This means that there is a margin of appreciation granted to the EU's legislative institutions in deciding which of several options to choose. This does not discharge the Court from its proper constitutional function of ensuring that the scheme of the Treaty is respected. On occasion legislative choices have been upset, for example for want of competence,[45] misuse of institutional powers,[46] or violation of fundamental rights.[47] But where political, economic, and social choices are at stake, a discretion is allowed: only legislative choices that verge on the absurd are likely to be condemned as manifestly inappropriate. The impression is that the Court is anxious to respect the expertise and legitimacy of the political process.

The review of the *lex sportiva* practised by the Court has something in common with this relatively deferential approach. The comparison is between the relatively

---

[41] eg Case C-112/00 *Schmidberger v Austria* [2003] ECR I-5659; Case C-36/02 *Omega Spielhallen* [2004] ECR I-9609; Case C-391/09 *Runevic-Vardyn* [2011] ECR I-3787; Case C-156/13 *Digibet*, judgment of 12 June 2014; *Wouters* (n 28). Admittedly there are exceptions where the Court lacks caution and sensitivity to the full breadth of the values at stake, most of all Case C-438/05 *Viking Line* [2007] ECR I-10779; Case C-341/05 *Laval* [2007] ECR I-11767.

[42] TFEU, Art 263 provides for a direct action before the Court, but there are also other routes to bringing a challenge on validity before the Court, including the Article 267 preliminary reference procedure.

[43] eg Case C-84/94 *United Kingdom v Council* [1996] ECR I-5755, para 58; Case C-491/01 *Ex parte BAT* [2002] ECR I-11453, para 123; Case C-58/08 *Vodafone* [2010] ECR I-4999, para 52.

[44] *Vodafone* (n 43) para 52.

[45] eg Case C-376/98 *Germany v Council and Parliament* [2000] ECR I-8419.

[46] eg Case C-28/12 *Commission v Council*, judgment of 28 April 2015.

[47] eg Joined Cases C-293/12 and C-594/12 *Digital Rights Ireland Ltd*, judgment of 8 April 2014; Case C-236/09 *Association belge des Consommateurs Test-Achats and others v Council* [2011] ECR I-773.

large measure of discretion allowed to the EU institutions in making complex assessments about matters of socio-economic importance and the room allowed to private actors such as sports bodies to govern their own affairs in circumstances where the Court lacks the expertise and the Treaties lack the relevant guiding principles required to make detailed assessments of choices made. A broad discretion should be admitted. A measure within the *lex sportiva* must be manifestly inappropriate having regard to its objective before the choice will be regarded as invalid; the criterion to be applied is not whether a measure adopted in such an area was the only or the best possible measure. Decisions such as *Walrave and Koch*, *Deliège*, and *Meca-Medina*, as well as the Commission's Decision in *ENIC* fit this model. *Bosman* too did not outlaw the very idea of a transfer system, but rather the excessively restrictive version in force at the time, which held even out-of-contract players within its grip. The Court's refusal in *Bosman* to accept nationality discrimination in club football is a reminder that there are limits to the Court's readiness to review and approve the *lex sportiva*, but a red light is not the norm in the case law.

Insertion of a genuine social dialogue should enhance the width of the margin of appreciation allowed to sports governing bodies. Commitment to social dialogue is written into the Treaty. Article 152 TFEU directs that the EU 'recognises and promotes the role of the social partners at its level, taking into account the diversity of national systems' and that it 'shall facilitate dialogue between the social partners, respecting their autonomy'. Article 154(1) TFEU adds that the Commission 'shall have the task of promoting the consultation of management and labour at Union level and shall take any relevant measure to facilitate their dialogue by ensuring balanced support for the parties'. Article 155 envisages that dialogue between management and labour may lead to agreements apt for conversion into EU legislation.

'Social dialogue' has been promoted within the EU in recent years and it has exerted some influence in sport.[48] A committee was created in 2008: it is chaired by the Union of European Football Associations (UEFA) and in 2012 it agreed minimum requirements for standard player contracts.[49] Its impact on the application of internal market law deserves to be taken seriously. Sporting practices would and should be more likely to survive review pursuant to EU law if structured around a more inclusive participatory framework of dialogue and rule-making—to distance them from a horizontal restrictive practice struck between and favouring employers

---

[48] See R Branco Martins, 'Agenda for a Social Dialogue in the European Professional Football Sector' in S Gardiner, R Parrish, and R Siekmann (eds), *EU, Sport, Law and Policy* (TMC Asser 2009) ch 21; D McArdle, *Dispute Resolution in Sport* (Routledge 2015) ch 10; R Parrish, 'Social Dialogue in European Professional Football' (2011) 17 ELJ 213; R Parrish, 'The European Social Dialogue: A New Mode of Governance for European Football?' in A Duval and B Van Rompuy (eds), *The Legacy of Bosman: Revisiting the Relationship between EU Law and Sport* (TMC Asser/Springer 2016) ch 8; M Colucci and A Geerraert, 'Social Dialogue in European Professional Football' (2011) 11(3–4) Intl Sports LJ 56.

[49] <http://ec.europa.eu/social/main.jsp?catId=480&intPageId=1848&langId=en> accessed 29 November 2016. See Parrish (2016) (n 48) 197–201; Colucci and Geerraert (n 48) 64–67.

and instead to structure the arrangements more coherently as a genuine framework to govern the industry in a way that ensures representation of all affected interests.[50] In a sense this is to push for respect for the *lex sportiva* on condition that it becomes more closely comparable with 'ordinary' law that is the product of some kind of open democratic and transparent process. The *lex sportiva* should not be treated as illegitimate just because it is the product of private ordering, but the legitimacy of its claim to a deferential margin of appreciation when reviewed under EU law is much stronger if the power wielded in its name is accompanied by a demonstrated concern to reflect and represent all affected interests, not just those of the powerful top-down rule-makers.

In summary, the *conditional autonomy* of sports federations under EU law, which has been the thematic core of these chapters dealing with internal market law, reflects 'the specific nature of sport' asserted but not elaborated by Article 165 TFEU. An overlap between EU law and 'internal' sports law is recognized, but, within that area of overlap, sporting bodies have room to show how and why the rules are necessary to accommodate their particular concerns. This line of reasoning does not make it simple in contested cases to discover which rules are necessary for the effective organization of sport. And attention must be paid to how much margin should be allowed to sports bodies in defining what is truly necessary for or inherent in their sport. But as a minimum this line of analysis ensures the right questions are asked. It prevents intellectually wasteful arguments about what is 'sporting' and what is 'commercial', and instead embraces the overlap of the two spheres. Then, within that zone of overlap, there is room for serious discussion of what is necessary for and/or inherent in the structure of sports governance. Accordingly, a strategy of inclusion, not exclusion, should inform sporting bodies' dealings with the EU's institutions: they must engage with the EU on its terms, but they can expect that those terms include sensitivity to the sports-specific context within which practices are reviewed.

7.5 Using Article 165 to Frame the EU's Contribution

The examination of Article 165 TFEU presented in Chapter 6 shows a clear association with the treatment of sport under free movement and competition law which is discussed in Chapters 4 and 5. Article 165, like Articles 45, 56, 101, and 102, leaves decision-making competence primarily in the hands of sporting bodies but creates space for an EU contribution. Articles 6 and 165 TFEU place the EU in a subordinate role. What should be the shape of its contribution?

---

[50] This book does not aspire to a comparative treatment of sports law, but it is notable that in the US relatively generous treatment of sporting autonomy under antitrust law is premised on precisely this type of wider engagement in the shaping of the *lex sportiva*. See eg McArdle (n 48) ch 4 'Collective Bargaining in US Professional Sports' and ch 5 'Antitrust and Competitive Balance'; M Mitten, *Sports Law in the United States* (Wolters Kluwer 2011) Pt I ch 5.3, Pt II ch 4.2.

It was explained in Chapter 6 that in January 2011 the Commission published a fourteen-page Communication, 'Developing the European Dimension in Sport'.[51] Its principal feature was a thread of continuity with the Commission's 2007 White Paper. Article 165 TFEU was of course integrated into the examination, but it was not at all suggested that it changed the existing assumptions of the intersection between EU law and the *lex sportiva*. It treats the specific nature of sport as a concept established by the Court and taken into account by the Commission in the White Paper on Sport, and so now recognized by Article 165. The Communication asserts that 'implementation of the White Paper has confirmed that, in a number of areas, action at EU level can provide significant added value'.[52]

This notion that the EU should be shown to add value is a helpful basis for assessing its proper role. This focus is also plain from the Council Resolution on a European Union Work Plan for Sport to cover 2011 to 2014[53] and from the Commission's Report on that programme.[54] There are two distinct dimensions to the notion that the EU should add value: first in connection with what the EU does and second in connection with the space it leaves for other actors.

The Council's Resolution insists on the place of the Member States and also on the need for the EU 'to work closely with the sport movement and relevant competent organisations at national, European and international levels such as the Council of Europe'. Moreover, Member States are instructed to respect 'the principle of subsidiarity and the autonomy of sport's governing structures' when developing policy at national level.

In its Report the Commission treats the Work Plan as having provided 'a valuable framework for all actors to cooperate in a coordinated way and in mutual respect of national and EU competences'.[55] The Report notes that many of the competences in the area of sport lie with the Member States, and draws from this that it is 'important that priorities for a new EU Work Plan focus on actions delivering unambiguous value-added at EU level'.[56]

The notion that the EU should be engaged in adding value is a helpful way to understand the notion that it should supplement rather than replace existing structures of governance in sport.

In similar vein, the follow-up Work Plan, founded on a further Council Resolution on a European Work Plan for Sport to cover 2014 to 2017,[57] shows that anxiety to work with the sports movement and relevant competent organizations at national, European, and international levels, such as the Council of Europe and the World Anti-Doping Agency (WADA) remains prominent.

There is evidence that the mandate provided by Article 165 TFEU has provided a framework within which the EU has been able to contribute to the process of reform

---

[51] Commission Communication, of January 2011, 'Developing the European Dimension in Sport' COM (2011) 12 <http://ec.europa.eu/sport/news/doc/communication/communication_en.pdf> accessed 29 November 2016.
[52] ibid para 1.2.   [53] [2011] OJ C162/1.   [54] COM (2014) 22.   [55] ibid 2.
[56] ibid 9.   [57] [2014] OJ C183/12.

of WADA's World Anti-Doping Code.[58] Answers provided by the Commission to questions from MEPs have on occasion provided more concrete detail on how Article 165 might help to structure EU action. So, for example, the Commission announced a focus on tackling transnational threats that are specific to sport, such as doping, violence, racism, and intolerance, or issues relating to the integrity of competitions and sportspersons; developing European cooperation in sport through, for example, guidelines for dual careers of athletes or benchmarks for good governance of sporting organizations; and supporting grassroots sports organizations which can play a role in addressing wider socio-economic challenges, such as social inclusion.[59] Here too it was explicitly stated that this would 'bring EU added value to issues arising from the specific nature of sport'. This is a helpful means to focus on where the EU should and should not devote its attention, although it plainly does not supply concrete guidance on which priorities to choose. A glance at the website of the Directorate General for Education and Culture within the Commission reveals the principal areas of activity.[60] They cover the three main themes tracked earlier: the *societal role*, which covers education and training, health and participation, social inclusion and dual careers; the *economic dimension*, which covers matters that have long been subjected to EU internal market law and which makes up the majority of this book; and matters of *integrity*, covering anti-doping, good governance, match-fixing, and sports agents. The list headed 'Integrity' also covers free movement of sportspersons and transfers, which could as easily count as matters within the economic dimension: these categories are not watertight.

Since the entry into force of the Lisbon Treaty in December 2009, it has been open to the Commission to propose legislative initiatives based on Article 165(4) TFEU 'to contribute to the achievement of the objectives referred to' in Article 165. So far the Commission has been reticent. In part this is simply a consequence of the tightly confined grant of legislative competence made by Article 165. More generally it reflects a shrewd unwillingness to propel the EU into areas where its ability to add value is contested.

For example, in the light of disorder in Poland during the Euro 2012 football competition, the Commission was asked whether it would introduce measures concerning safety inspections and standard-setting. Ms Vassilou was not tempted.[61] The EU has a role in promoting cross-border cooperation in policing, she noted, but safety and security arrangements are the preserve of Member States and UEFA. The Council of Europe too has a role: after all, there are no sporting events where only countries that are members of the EU may participate, so EU action would tend to fragment treatment of a pan-European matter of concern between the 'EU' and the 'non-EU'. The Euro 2012 competition was a case in point: it was

---

[58] J Kornbeck, 'The Stamina of the *Bosman* Legacy: The European Union and the Revision of the World Anti-Doping Code (2011–13)' (2015) 22(2) MJ 283.

[59] E-006293/2011, Answer given by Ms Vassiliou on behalf of the Commission, 12 August 2011 [2012] OJ C128E.

[60] Its website is at <http://ec.europa.eu/sport/index_en.htm> accessed 29 November 2016.

[61] P-006468/12 [2013] OJ C203E/65.

co-hosted by Poland, which is an EU Member State, and Ukraine, which is not. In similar vein, when invited to comment on plans to demolish the Heysel stadium in Brussels, scene of ghastly loss of life before the European Cup Final in 1985, Ms Vassilou observed that the matter rested solely with the Belgian authorities; and, asked to comment on EU rules placing obligations on sports clubs to monitor the safety of facilities, she simply remarked that Article 165 TFEU 'expressly excludes any harmonisation of laws' and that the Commission therefore 'has no competence to regulate this matter at EU level'.[62] She was equally cautious, and eager to assert the autonomy of sporting organizations, when invited to comment on the selection of Israel as host country for the 2013 European Under-21 football championships.[63] It is implausible that an EU intervention into such a delicate matter would add value. High Representative Catherine Ashton was similarly circumspect when invited to address the likelihood of depriving Qatar of the right to host the 2022 World Cup as a result of the conditions applicable in that country to migrant workers: she insisted that 'human rights should be respected at all times' but that she was required 'to respect the autonomy of sport organisations'.[64] In a thematically similar vein of restraint exercised by the Commission, Ms Vassilou, asked about the EU's role in combating match-fixing, stated that a small budget would be available to support transnational projects aimed at preventing match-fixing, but emphasized the need for exchange of good practice and dialogue with sports federations and public authorities.[65] In similar vein she has excluded the regulation of betting services, but plans to address betting-related match-fixing through the preparation of recommendations on best practice in cooperation with Member States, industry, and sports.[66] Once again, there is here no hint of temptation to adopt a top-down approach. In fact, it is illuminating that in 2014 it was decided to address match-fixing through a Convention on the Manipulation of Sports Competitions, which was produced through the Council of Europe, not the EU.[67]

Subsidiarity as a legal principle is defined in unhelpfully formal terms by Article 5(3) of the Treaty on European Union (TEU), but this is subsidiarity in a more general sense. It shows a restraint on the exercise of a conferred competence which reflects a general concern to use the EU to solve problems only where it is demonstrably well equipped so to do. Article 165 TFEU has been used primarily as a framing device, not as a springboard to legislative ambition.

The virtue of the Commission's restraint is best appreciated by contrasting it to the Council's occasional frankly silly exaggeration of the role of sport. A particularly vivid example is presented by the Council conclusions on the contribution of sport to the EU economy, and in particular to addressing youth unemployment

[62] P-007040/13 [2014] OJ C81E/64.   [63] P-004857/13 [2014] OJ C35E/607.
[64] E-013138/13 [2014] OJ C237/44.   [65] E-007011/12 [2013] OJ C219E/220.
[66] E-013033/13 [2014] OJ C86E/596. On national and transnational practice, see Asser Institute, 'Study on Risk Assessment and Mangement and Prevention of Conflicts of Interest in the Prevention and Fight against Betting-related Match Fixing in the EU 28' (July 2014) <http://www.asser.nl/media/2625/betting-related-match-fixing_final-report-2014.pdf> accessed 29 November 2016.
[67] CETS No 215 <https://www.coe.int/en/web/conventions/full-list/-/conventions/treaty/215> accessed 29 November 2016. It is not yet in force.

and social exclusion.[68] These offer unobjectionable comments on the economic impact of sport and its potentially valuable role in playing a part in addressing youth unemployment. However additional claims about the virtue of sport in combating social exclusion are at best supported by flaky logic and minimal reasoning. 'Sporting activities are ... an excellent means for integrating minority and marginalized groups'; sport 'can contribute significantly to a sense of togetherness, helping to bring stability, cohesion and peace to commmunities'.[69] Such praise doubtless delights sports governing bodies, eager to show their most virtuous face as they press for autonomy from regulation, but such bland comments lack any precision. Most of all this rhetoric misleadingly conflates professional sport, built on winning and losing and often inflamed by antagonism, with recreational sport and sport pursued for health benefits.

Any hint that the Commission in particular and the EU in general might be tempted to take an inflated approach to their involvement in sport would meet resistance.[70] As shown in Chapter 6, however, Article 165 TFEU legitimates the EU's role in the field of sport. Sporting bodies can no longer claim that sport is none of the EU's business. Instead one would expect them to claim that it is the EU's business but only to a limited extent, and only in so far as respect is shown for its 'specific nature'. The theme here is consistent: sports bodies are better advised to engage with the EU as part of a strategy to minimize its perceived detrimental effect on their practice. They cannot simply ignore it but nor are they strong enough to extract a promise of immunity. So what is left is the ambiguous middle ground of conditional autonomy.

This is largely the position that the more politically aware sports governing bodies had already reached before 2009, aware that a strategy of exclusion had been so consistently exposed as unsuccessful before the Court and the Commission. UEFA was prominent among those bodies seeking constructive engagement.[71] Its 'Position paper', mentioned in Chapter 6, states that Article 165 TFEU is 'not intended to prejudice the legitimate autonomy and discretionary decision making power of sports federations', and that it 'requires that the specific nature of sport must be recognised'.[72] The 2014 arrangement for cooperation between the Commission

---

[68] [2014] OJ C32/2.   [69] ibid Recital 8.

[70] The House of Lords Select Committee on the European Union, while noting the increased profile of sport in the Treaty post-Lisbon, urged the government 'to ensure that the European institutions adhere to this provision' (Tenth Report 2007–08) para 8.49 <http://www.publications.parliament. uk/pa/ld200708/ldselect/ldeucom/62/6202.htm> accessed 29 November 2016. There are intriguing strains in the literature which make the case for moving beyond competition law to embrace sector-specific public regulation of sporting autonomy—eg N Grow, 'Regulating Professional Sports Leagues' (2015) 72 Wash and Lee L Rev 573—but materially and constitutionally the EU is poorly resourced to lay claim to carry out such a supervisory function.

[71] See in particular B García, 'UEFA and the European Union: From Confrontation to Cooperation' (2007) 3 JCER 202; on subsequent practice, see A Geeraert and E Drieskens, 'The EU Controls FIFA and UEFA: A Principal–Agent Perspective' (2015) 22 JEPP 1448.

[72] UEFA's Position on Article 165 of the Lisbon Treaty (sic) <http://www.uefa.com/MultimediaFiles/ Download/uefaorg/EuropeanUnion/01/57/91/67/1579167_DOWNLOAD.pdf> accessed 29 November 2016.

and UEFA shares this intent.[73] It is an embrace of conditional autonomy: a strategy of (wary) inclusion, not exclusion.

In similar vein, also met in Chapter 6, the Olympic and Sports Movement adopted a 'Common Position' in January 2010.[74] Greeting the specific nature of sport as 'a cornerstone of a new EU policy in the field of sport', it urges the EU to 'reaffirm its support for the independence and autonomy of sports federations and their right to determine autonomously their organisation and the promotion of their respective sport'. This was followed by the publication in 2011 of a *Guide to EU Sport Policy* by the EU Office of the European Olympic Committees, which is heavy-handed enough to dwell on the Greek roots of the word 'autonomy' in stressing its role 'in the pyramidal structure of sport' and presses that 'The autonomy of sports organisations can be considered an essential component of the specificity of sport'.[75] The document makes the case for the autonomy of sports governing bodies but it does not deny the legitimate involvement in principle of the EU, and in fact its contents show careful appreciation of the nuances of the EU's role and operation. Practical elaboration awaits. It is to some extent forthcoming in the recent Council Resolutions and Commission practice considered previously, and in particular the evident concern to confine EU intervention to cases where it adds value should provide a modestly reassuring basis for planning by sports governing bodies. It is their different and more conciliatory tone when contrasted with the obstinacy surrounding *Bosman* and *Meca-Medina* which is particularly marked. This is as gratifying as it is well judged.

7.6 Conclusion

Article 165 TFEU is both revolutionary and trivial. At the constitutional level it seems to carry great weight as the EU's first ever explicit conferred competence in the field of sport and, indeed, it, with Article 6 TEU, carries the first ever mention made of sport in the Treaties. However, in practice its effect is palpably less significant because of its narrowly drawn boundaries. Moreover, much of the content of Article 165 TFEU, especially the direction to take into account the specific nature of sport, is already familiar as a result of the Court's creative interpretation and application of internal market law when it collides with sporting practices (the *lex sportiva*).

So in this sense Article 165 TFEU serves as a continuation of the story of EU sports law. It is a re-statement and acceptance of conditional autonomy. Sport is not

---

[73] C(2014) 7378, 14 October 2014.

[74] Common Position of the Olympic and Sports Movement on the implementation of the new Treaty on the Functioning of the European Union on sport (January 2010) <https://www.idrettsforbundet.no/globalassets/idrett/idrettsforbundet/english/common_position_of_the_olympic_and_sports_movement.pdf> accessed 29 November 2016.

[75] *Guide to EU Sport Policy* (September 2011) 13 <http://www.euoffice.eurolympic.org/files/guide_to_eu_sport_policy_final_versionwithlinks.pdf> accessed 29 November 2016.

able to extract a grant of absolute autonomy from the reach of EU law: politically it was not strong enough and intellectually the case is without merit. Many sporting practices have clear and immediate economic consequences and to wall them off from the EU, in particular from internal market law, would damage the integrity of the EU system and grant a concession that no other sector is allowed. But sport is allowed an autonomy *on condition that* it is able to show just why its practices are necessary despite the attentive scrutiny of EU law.

Chapters 4 and 5 examined the development of this model of conditional autonomy in the decisions of the first EU institution which was forced to grapple with the question of whether sport is special—the Court of Justice. The more recent entry into force of the Lisbon Treaty gives a fresh vocabulary to the legal analysis and puts to an end any possibility of denying that sport is any of the EU's business. But so far there is no indication that the Lisbon Treaty has changed the rules of the game. Article 165 recognizes and, as the Court put it in *Bernard*, 'corroborates' the specific nature of sport as an element in the law of the internal market.[76]

Chapter 6 explored the theme of conditional autonomy in the political and legislative context. The Amsterdam and Nice Declarations capture perfectly the political readiness of the Member States to embrace and express the distinctive qualities and particular virtues of sport, but not to go so far as to immunize sport from the reach of EU law. Article 165 TFEU is simply a more elaborate version of that balanced approach. And the political negotiation that shaped it has conferred a legislative competence on the EU which is itself redolent of the notion of conditional autonomy. It does not at all elevate the EU to a position of top-down rule-maker. The EU's role is supplementary only. To this extent sporting autonomy is respected. But not in absolute terms. There is space, admittedly slender, for the EU to act. And the Commission's quest to focus on action that adds value is a particularly appealing method of making more concrete the conditions that should attach to the autonomy the EU allows sports bodies. The EU should add value—if it does not, its intervention deserves a sceptical reception. This provides a framework for critical analysis in the four chapters that follow, each of which deals with a particular area of intersection between EU law and the *lex sportiva*. Chapter 8 deals with nationality discrimination, Chapter 9 with the transfer system, Chapter 10 with governance, and the broadcasting sector is addressed in Chapter 11. Chapter 12 concludes.

---

[76] *Bernard* (n 7).

8

Rules Based on Nationality

8.1 Introduction

Discrimination based on nationality is at the very heart of some sporting competitions. National anthems are sung before international football matches. The anthem of the winner is played at the medal ceremony following events at the Olympic Games. Athletes in these circumstances are representing their country, and accordingly they are selected on the basis of nationality. An Estonian, however talented, may not apply to join the Italian national football team, nor may the Italians seek to recruit him or her. EU law, however, places a prohibition on discrimination on the grounds of nationality within the scope of application of the Treaties. This is stipulated by both Article 18 of the Treaty on the Functioning of the European Union (TFEU) and Article 21(2) of the Charter of Fundamental Rights. This chapter therefore examines an inescapable tension between the foundations of the *lex sportiva* and the values of the EU. How, if at all, may the discrimination founded on nationality which lies at the heart of international representative sport avoid condemnation when practised within the reach of EU law?

8.2 International Sport

The Court of Justice's earliest case law touching sport, decisions dating from the 1970s, addressed questions of discrimination based on nationality in sporting competition. It ruled in favour of the permissibility of such practices in the selection of national representative teams, even though such discrimination would appear to offend against foundational values of EU law and would certainly not be tolerated in other 'normal' industries. Chapter 3 introduced and Chapter 4 examined the pioneering decision in *Walrave and Koch v Union Cycliste Internationale*.[1] The Court, asked for the first time to inquire into EU law's application to sport, ruled that the prohibition against nationality-based discrimination 'does not affect the composition of sport teams, in particular national teams, the formation of which is a question of purely sporting interest and as such has nothing to do with economic activity'.[2] It has already been explained in Chapters 3 and 4 that this

---

[1] Case 36/74 *Walrave and Koch v Union Cycliste Internationale* [1974] ECR 1405.
[2] ibid para 8.

formula is tainted by its unconvincing assumption that selection for a national team is convincingly classified as a matter of 'purely sporting interest', because clearly such rules *also* have significant commercial implications associated with the value of exposure as an international footballer. Today, in the light of both the Court's seminal ruling in *Meca-Medina* examined in Chapter 5[3] and the framing power of Article 165 TFEU examined in Chapter 7, one would sensibly withdraw from the claim that such rules are purely sporting in character and instead treat them as a necessary element in the structure of international representative competition, and therefore as a reflection of the specific nature of sport. That is, this should be treated as 'sporting discrimination' which defines the very nature of the activity and which, notwithstanding its economic effects, therefore escapes prohibition under EU law. But this is simply to structure the examination conducted in the name of EU law in a different way from that preferred in 1974: it would not affect the *outcome* of the subjection of such rules to EU law. Such rules are not unlawful. In *Walrave and Koch* the Court decided that nationality discrimination in international representative football is not called into question by EU law and two years later in 1976 the Court confirmed its approach with no elaboration in *Donà v Mantero*.[4] Nothing that has happened since has changed that finding. Germany's victory in the 2014 football World Cup was not achieved in violation of EU law.

8.3 Club Sport

It has already been explained in Chapter 4 that twenty years after *Walrave and Koch* the Court in *Bosman* refused to extend similarly generous treatment under EU law to nationality discrimination in *club* football.[5] This, the Court concluded, would go too far: it would deprive the Treaty provision governing the free movement of workers, today Article 45 TFEU, 'of its practical effect and the fundamental right of free access to employment which the Treaty confers individually on each worker in the Community [would be] rendered nugatory'.[6] The Court refused to accept the submission made in defence of the rules (the *lex sportiva*) that in club football there was a particular significance attached to the nationality of players. It added that freedom of movement for workers, by opening up the employment market in one Member State to nationals of the other Member States, has the effect of reducing workers' chances of finding employment within the Member State of which they are nationals, but equally it offers them prospects of employment in other Member States.[7] This is true of all workers in the EU. Club footballers, in the analysis of the Court, are not special. In the past, practice governing nationality requirements

---

[3] Case C-519/04 P *Meca-Medina and Majcen v Commission* [2006] ECR I-6991.
[4] Case 13/76 *Donà v Mantero* [1976] ECR 1333.
[5] Case C-415/93 *Union royale belge des sociétés de football association ASBL v Jean-Marc Bosman* [1995] ECR I-4921.
[6] ibid para 129.   [7] ibid para 134.

in national Leagues varied:[8] within the EU *Bosman* changed this at a stroke. The Court also dismissed the submission that nationality clauses prevent the richest clubs from employing the cream among foreign players and thereby maintaining a competitive balance between clubs, because, as it tersely noted, no rules limit the possibility for such clubs to recruit the best national players, 'thus undermining that balance to just the same extent'.[9]

The Court in *Bosman* maintained the misplaced reliance on the notion that there are rules motivated by 'reasons which are not of an economic nature ... and are thus of sporting interest only'.[10] Any damage that this may do to the integrity of EU law by excluding from review practices with an economic effect was mitigated by the Court's supplementary observation that restriction on the scope of application of EU law 'must remain limited to its proper objective'.[11] And so it refused to sanction nationality-based discrimination in club football. This, as mentioned earlier and as fully articulated in Chapter 7, would be better *presented* today with recognition of the ruling in *Meca-Medina* and the embrace of 'the specific nature of sport' in Article 165 TFEU as a discriminatory practice with economic effects that offends against EU law and is not a necessary element in the organization of club football. Reliance on the notion of rules that are of purely sporting interest is thoroughly unhelpful. But, to reinforce the point made previously, this would be merely a matter of superior presentation. It would not alter the outcome.

Advocate General Trabucchi, in *Donà v Mantero*, had suggested a rather generous approach to the ability of clubs to exercise discrimination in player selection without infringing EU law.[12] He considered that it would be a matter of purely sporting interest, and therefore permissible, were a national association to limit the participation of foreign players in championship matches 'so as to ensure that the winning team will be representative of the State of which it is the champion team'. He added that this view was strengthened in the light of the fact that the champion club proceeds to represent the state at international level. These observations were not examined by the Court at all in its brief judgment in the case. They were not regarded as persuasive in the limited amount of academic writing that addressed the issue in the years before *Bosman* opened the floodgates.[13] And they seem still less persuasive today, especially because it is no longer the case that participation in European club football's primary competition, then the European Cup and now the (mis-named) Champions' League, is confined to clubs that are champion of their country. But nevertheless Mr Trabucchi's views deserve to be remembered, because they show that there was and is room to argue about just how 'special' sport truly is.

---

[8] See P Lanfranchi and M Taylor, *Moving with the Ball: The Migration of Professional Footballers* (Bloomsbury 2001). See also R Elliott and J Harris (eds), *Football and Migration: Perspectives, Places and Players* (Routledge 2015).

[9] *Bosman* (n 5) para 135.　　　[10] ibid para 127.　　　[11] ibid.　　　[12] *Donà* (n 4).

[13] S Weatherill, 'Discrimination on Grounds of Nationality in Sport' (1989) 9 YEL 55, 60–63; G Renz, 'Freizügigkeit von Berufsfussballspielern innerhalb der EG' in M Will (ed), *Sportrecht in Europa* (CF Müller Juristischer Verlag 1993); M Hilf, Die Freizügigkeit des Berufsfussballspielers innerhalb der Europäischen Gemeinschaft 1984/10 *Neue Juristische Wochenschrift* 517.

After all, at the time nothing at all provided any direction in the Treaty about how to resolve such questions, because the Treaty did not even mention sport, and even today the framing provided by Article 165 TFEU offers no concrete guidance on exactly what the admitted 'specific nature of sport' entails. It is submitted that Mr Trabucchi mistakenly conflated the separate issues of whether a club may be taken to represent a country and whether that club's players possess any such representative function. The Court's approach in *Bosman* is to be preferred: it is motivated by rejection of the claim that the identity of the players has any connection with a club's representative function. It refused to accept that a link based on nationality was in any sense inherent to the structure of *club* football, so a violation of EU free movement law was declared. But this was in no sense the inevitable consequence of a diligent reading of the Treaty. It required an infusion of sports-specific knowhow. Exactly this—almost intuitive—basis for interpreting EU law is visible too in the Opinion of Advocate General Lenz in *Bosman*. He, unlike Mr Trabucchi in *Donà v Mantero*, was not prepared to accept that nationality discrimination played any necessary part in club football and his Opinion set the Court on a course to reach the same conclusion. Mr Lenz was a good deal more vivid in his explanation of his reasoning in *Bosman* than the Court. He agreed with the submissions made on behalf of the Commission and Bosman that 'the great majority of a club's supporters are much more interested in the success of their club than in the composition of the team', and added too that the participation of foreign players does not 'prevent a team's supporters from identifying with the team'.[14] And, adding colourful detail, he noted that 'One of the most popular players ever to play for TSV 1860 München was undoubtedly Petar Radenkovic from what was then Yugoslavia', and referred too to Kevin Keegan at Hamburger SV, Eric Cantona at Manchester United, and Jürgen Klinsmann at Tottenham Hotspur.[15] So—his final point in this vein—only a few of the players at Bayern Munich come from Bavaria (let alone Munich), yet this does not destroy their identity as Bayern Munich.[16]

None of this is found in the EU's legal texts. But the quest to understand the intersection of EU internal market law and the *lex sportiva* demands that the former engage with and critically assess the key ingredients of the latter's claim that sport is 'special'.

8.4 The Immediate Aftermath of *Bosman*

The essence of the ruling in *Bosman* is that the Court did not deny that sport is special, but it refused to accept that sport was quite as special as had been pressed on it by sporting bodies, and as had long been the practice.

The Court's ruling in *Bosman* was delivered in December 1995. This meant that the 1995–96 football season was cut in half. There were at the time three major club competitions in European football—the European Cup, which had become

---

[14] *Bosman* (n 5) Opinion of Lenz AG, para 143.   [15] ibid.   [16] ibid.

the Champions League in 1992, the European Cup Winners Cup, which was discontinued in 1999, and the UEFA Cup, which would become the Europa League in 2009. Before *Bosman*, clubs were limited by the applicable nationality-based rules. After *Bosman* had exposed the incompatibility of the rules with EU law, the second half of the season proceeded with no restrictions permitted in principle on the availability of EU nationals. As is common when law meets sport, the practice was different from the principle. The initial response of the Union of European Football Associations (UEFA) to *Bosman* was to declare that the '3 plus 2' nationality restrictions should continue to be observed in the European club competitions for that season. This was surely unlawful, and the Commission made clear this was so.[17] UEFA reluctantly agreed in late February 1996 that it would comply with the ruling.[18] However, no formal challenge was initiated and the '3 plus 2' rules were in practice maintained. Juventus beat Ajax in the 1996 European Cup Final: the Italian team comprised nine Italian players and, in midfield, a Frenchman (Didier Deschamps) and a Portuguese (Paulo Sousa), while Ajax fielded eight Dutchman, a Finn (Jari Litmanen), and two non-EU nationals, the Nigerian forwards Finidi George and Kanu. But that was the last glimpse of the old world. In 1997 the Juventus team that lost the Final 3–1 to Borussia Dortmund contained only six Italians. When Manchester United beat Chelsea in the all-English 2008 Final in Moscow, only ten out of the twenty-eight players who appeared across the 120 minutes were English, although Ryan Giggs, a Welshman, swelled the number of British nationals to eleven. It is common today to find that the leading clubs in Europe have only a minority of players holding the nationality of the state in which the club is based.

In the immediate aftermath of *Bosman* in December 1995 some domestic leagues, including that in England, promptly abandoned existing restrictions on EU nationals.[19] Elsewhere, including in Germany, there were rumours that informal agreements had been struck under which clubs agreed to complete the competitions in season 1995–96 in accordance with the pre-existing rules, notwithstanding the immediate effect in law of the *Bosman* ruling. Here too there was no legal challenge. And in time practice fell into line with EU law. This means that all EU nationals must be treated equally for the purposes of eligibility for selection for club matches. Clubs were therefore enabled to pursue much more flexible recruiting strategies. An English club is consequently as free to pick a Dutch or Italian player as it is an English player. A number of clubs, particularly but not only the richer English clubs, have fielded an entire eleven comprising 'footballing foreigners'.

---

[17] eg 'EU Orders UEFA to Act on Bosman' *The Independent* (London, 20 January 1996) 27; 'Bosman Rebels Face Huge Fine' *The Guardian* (London, 1 February 1996) 20. Any such fine could have been imposed only under competition law: the Commission has no power to take action against a private party for violation of the free movement rules on which the judgment was based.

[18] 'UEFA Yields on Bosman Ruling' *Financial Times* (London, 20 February 1996) 2.

[19] 'Premiership Scraps Foreigner Rule' *The Independent* (London, 23 December 1995) 24.

8.5 *How* Has This Assessment of the Limits of Respect for the *Lex Sportiva* View Been Reached in EU Law?

In 2005 Sepp Blatter, President of Fédération Internationale de Football Association (FIFA) at the time, wrote an article entitled 'Greed threatens the Beautiful Game', and in it he asked 'is it really still "their" team when one club in England has a squad with 19 nationalities?'[20] EU law's answer is—*yes*. And EU law gets that answer not from the explicit terms of the Treaty, but from the view taken by its Court of the nature of the relationship between clubs, players, and fans. And that view is different from the view asserted by football's governing bodies. The *lex sportiva*, which mandated a tie between the nationality of a club's footballers and its team selection policies, had to be relaxed in application to nationals of EU Member States.

Who is right? It is, after all, a plausible starting-point that UEFA and FIFA have superior expertise in the matter of football governance than the constitutionally constrained Court in Luxembourg. However, I believe the Court is right. A club's attachment to its locality is a distinctive feature of European sport. Whereas in North America it is well understood that a club is a franchise and can be and will be moved from one city to another and re-named should it prove commercially expedient so to do, in Europe this is culturally unacceptable. The Brooklyn Dodgers became the LA Dodgers in 1957. The Winnipeg Jets left Canada for the United States and became the Phoenix Coyotes in 1996 when the City of Winnipeg refused to provide funding that was demanded.[21] But it would be unimaginable for Borussia Dortmund to become Borussia Berlin or for Real Sociedad to leave San Sebastian for, say, Alicante, still less for Doha. In fact, on one of the very few occasions on which a club in Europe was allowed to change its home because of the associated claimed commercial advantages—when Wimbledon, English FA Cup winners in 1988, were allowed to become Milton Keynes Dons as a result of a decision taken by the English FA in 2002—the new club, relocated 60 miles north of its traditional home, was rejected by fans of Wimbledon, who formed a new entity to sustain their club's tradition, and the cuckoo club in Milton Keynes remains widely reviled among fans of other clubs—indeed it is commonly derided as 'Franchise FC'.[22] Even attempts to change a club's name tend to be ferociously controversial, as illustrated by a concerted and successful campaign conducted by fans in 2014 and 2015 to prevent the English club Hull City's owners restyling the club 'Hull Tigers'.

But *players* are not part of this identified necessary connection. On this the Court in *Bosman* and, in even more fully reasoned terms, Advocate General Lenz

---

[20] *Financial Times* (London, 12 October 2005) 19.

[21] The Phoenix Coyotes are now the Arizona Coyotes; the Jets came home to Winnipeg in 2011 when the franchise was bought from the Atlanta Thrashers.

[22] Happily the successor Wimbledon club achieved promotion back to the Football League in 2011; less happily MK Dons remain members of the Football League.

seem convincing. Fans may typically identify with and particularly admire players who are local, but in general what really matters is not whether a player is from the locality, the region, the same country as the club or beyond. What really matters is whether the player contributes to the success of the team. And this is not a new phenomenon. The first great club side of English football was Preston North End, first ever Champions in 1889, and they were well known for importing talent from Scotland, where in the early days of the sport far more skilful footballers were bred.[23]

So I contend that the Court understood the sporting context perfectly well when it refused to agree that nationality discrimination has any necessary place in club football. The key insight is that the very fact that such an inquiry falls to be conducted reveals much about the ambitious construction of European sports law in the absence of directly relevant material in the Treaties. In *Bosman* the Court refused to allow the *lex sportiva* to dictate the scope of nationality discrimination in football and required its elimination in club football practised within the EU. Sport enjoys conditional autonomy from EU law: here the conditions were not met. Today we would frame *Bosman* in the light of *Meca-Medina* and Article 165 TFEU, and, in line with the explanation provided in Chapter 7, we would find that nationality discrimination practised in club football is simply neither necessary for nor inherent in its organization—that it is not part of 'the specific nature of sport'.[24] But the key insight is that the Court simply refused to accept that sports governing bodies could rely on their supposedly superior expertise and their status as the game's global regulator to exclude review in the name of EU law, and, in the conduct of that review, the Court was not persuaded by the case made in defence of nationality discrimination in club football. Perhaps the Court perceived this assertion of the virtue of the *lex sportiva* as a means to protect the existing commercial model; perhaps it reckoned this as no more than an unthinkingly stubborn defence of an anachronistic status quo. In any event, overall—and exceptionally in EU law—the case made to defend sporting autonomy was treated by the Court as simply not powerful enough.

8.6 The Court in Error

A point that has widely been overlooked is that in *Bosman* part of the Court's analysis is wrong. As explained previously, the Court's conclusion that, contrary to the case pressed on its by football's governing bodies, there is no necessary connection between the identity of a club and the origin of its players is persuasive, even

---

[23] In short, Scots were the first to build the game round passing the ball instead of kick-and-rush. Some might think the English have still not absorbed this lesson (and that the Scots have forgotten it).

[24] And today we could rely on some empirical evidence that changes to the composition of club squads wrought by *Bosman* have not significantly altered fans' sense of identification with their club: D Ranc, *Foreign Players and Football Supporters: The Old Firm, Arsenal and Paris-St Germain* (Manchester University Press 2012).

if nothing in EU law explicitly supports it. However, that positive assessment does not attach to all of the Court's reasoning.

It was pressed on the Court in *Bosman* that the removal of quotas restricting the number of non-national players selected by a club would damage the international game. An influx of footballing migrants would diminish the places available in clubs for local players, with the result that the national representative eleven of the country experiencing a net inflow of players would find it increasingly difficult to pick from a large enough pool. So—the argument runs—club football needs to be made to 'buy national' in order to sustain the vitality of the international game.[25]

In *Bosman* the Court swept this argument aside. As mentioned earlier, it based its rejection on an assumption about the release of cross-border trade that follows the application of EU free movement law to restrictive practices within a Member State. So opening up the employment market in one Member State to nationals of other Member States increases competition in that market, which makes life less comfortable for nationals of that Member State who were previously protected by the discriminatory practices. But the same is true in every other Member State. So the workers concerned are able to look to opportunities for employment in the markets of other Member States, which are equally cleansed of their discriminatory obstacles.[26]

In 2003 the same brand of argument was advanced before the Court in *Deutscher Handballbund eV v Maros Kolpak*.[27] The affected sport in *Kolpak* was handball. The complainant was a Slovak national: the case concerned the Association Agreement with Slovakia, which was not then a Member State. It was submitted that Germany needed to maintain nationality-based discrimination at club level in order to sustain and promote the strength of the German national handball side.[28] The Court had no need to address the meat of this submission because the rules in question discriminated against the applicant, a Slovak, but otherwise treated all EEA nationals alike. So the claimed concern to protect *German* handball players was simply not reflected in the rule. But the Court showed no sympathy for such a rule in any event, and repeated its refusal in *Bosman* to treat nationality discrimination at *club* level as permissible under EU law. It did not deal separately with the argument that the opportunities that a national loses in his or her home market as a result of the abolition of discrimination are compensated by those that become available in other states' markets and that this addresses anxiety that the pool of players available for selection in the national side will be drained, but Advocate General Stix-Hackl did. She noted the earlier treatment of the matter by the Court in *Bosman*[29] and, following the Court's approach, she pointed out that 'up-and-coming young German players are not restricted to playing for a German club' and may instead play with foreign clubs.[30]

---

[25] It is unlikely that the major clubs would wish to support this argument, for it limits their access to the best talent. On the rules requiring the release of players for international matches, see Ch 10.7.

[26] *Bosman* (n 5) para 134.

[27] Case C-438/00 *Deutscher Handballbund eV v Maros Kolpak* [2003] ECR I-4135.

[28] ibid para 52.   [29] ibid Opinion of Stix-Hackl AG, para 68.

[30] ibid Opinion of Stix-Hackl AG, para 69.

So the Court's understanding of the effect of the application of the Treaty rules on the freedom of movement for workers is that the employment markets of all the Member States will be opened up to competition on the basis of ability, not nationality. It assumes that the pool of players eligible for the national team and playing locally may diminish, but that this will be compensated by the ability of players to move abroad and find work elsewhere, while still retaining eligibility for the national side of their 'home' state.[31] However, this is to neglect an important element in sport's special character.

The Court makes assumptions about the virtues of economic integration in the EU that fail to take account of the specific nature of sport. Orthodoxy would admittedly dictate that an integrated market is a more efficient market, but in football there are clear limits on the degree of market restructuring that will follow the elimination of national borders. Integration of the labour market will not create more jobs. The number of clubs will remain stable. And it is improbable that, in the absence of quotas, the same distribution of players by nationality will prevail. States that supply a lot of skilled labour will be able to take advantage of access to newly opened markets, while less productive states with clubs that can afford to import players will find they lose the share of local players they were previously able to protect and this will be far from made up by export opportunities. Some states will be net importers of players, some will be net exporters.[32] So the pool of players available to the national team will in some states dwindle in size, which will normally tend to weaken the strength of that state's national team. It is entirely plausible to argue that that is simply a price that international teams must pay in order to improve labour mobility in the internal market and to protect the rights of individual workers in accordance with Article 45 TFEU. So the legal analysis would hold that a rule which discriminates on the basis of nationality in club football as a means to protect the size of the pool of players available for selection for the national side goes beyond what is necessary to sustain the existence of the national side and so goes beyond what will be tolerated by EU law. But that is not how the Court dealt with the matter in *Bosman*. In *Bosman* it denied that eliminating nationality discrimination in club football would have any detrimental effect on the strength of national representative teams. But in states which are net importers of footballers it probably will.

So preservation of nationality discrimination in the club game could be defended with reference to the *sport-specific* concern to preserve the continued vitality of national representative teams. Restricting the number of 'footballing foreigners' that a club may use protects the national team, a concern that simply does not arise in connection with the regulation of labour markets in car-making or the provision

---

[31] The role of the 'player release' rules in this context are made explicit at *Bosman* (n 5) para 133: on their compatibility with EU law, see Ch 10.7.

[32] European Commission, 'The Economic and Legal Aspects of Transfers of Players' (January 2013) ch 3 provides evidence of such variation <http://ec.europa.eu/assets/eac/sport/library/documents/cons-study-transfers-final-rpt.pdf> accessed 29 November 2016.

of financial services, where the very idea of a national representative team would be preposterous.

As an intellectual challenge, it would be intriguing to see the issue re-tested in litigation. My own view is that the argument should *not* succeed. The benefits are not certain: the claim is simply that more players will be available for selection for the national team in countries which are net importers of players, and it does not necessarily follow that quality levels among the very best players who make up the national side will be affected. Indeed one consequence of mandating preference in labour markets for a particular nationality is to increase demand for qualifying players, which will typically lead to an increase in price—that is, in the wages that the qualifying player can command. So the result of nationality-based preference may not be better quality footballers but rather better paid (and perhaps lazier) players. In any event, it is highly improbable that the Court will choose to re-open a matter it plainly feels it dealt with successfully in *Bosman*. My point, to sum up, is that the Court did not fully address the worth of arguments in favour of nationality-based discrimination in club football. It missed an appreciation that sport's embrace of national representative teams is special. But I think that ultimately the Court's conclusion against the compatibility of such rules with EU law is nevertheless correct.

However, the argument may have traction in other sports, in part because they are not the sport that was at stake in *Bosman* in respect of which the Court has set a course on which it seems dependent and in part because the case may carry still more force in a context other than football.

8.7 Sport is Not Just Football! The Case of Cricket, and of Rugby

Is cricket different? This is a tempting line of inquiry because it provides a concrete illustration of the inquiry into whether this is a law of sport or a law of *sports*. The league structure of English professional cricket is based on eighteen counties who play each other in four-day championship cricket (which is currently split into two Divisions) and in two principal one-day competitions. The best players are selected to play for the English national representative side, which competes in Test match and one-day competition against other countries round the world. In the past, the best English cricketers would play both for their county and, when selected, for the national side. More recently the expansion of the international programme, driven heavily by its much greater attraction to fans, sponsors, and broadcasters when compared with the county game, has meant that the best players appear only rarely at county level and have become almost exclusively full-time international cricketers.

The question is to what extent would it be lawful to introduce nationality-based discrimination into the criteria governing selection for county cricket as a means to establish a priority in favour of English players, and thereby to protect and deepen the pool of players available to play at international level for England. There *are* such rules. They have been adjusted over time. Rules on 'overseas players' in county cricket pre-date the United Kingdom's accession to the EU. Subsequent changes have in part been driven by perceptions of the effect of EU law: *Bosman* had little effect, because cross-border movement in the EU is rare since in Europe there is no Test cricket played outside the United Kingdom, but *Kolpak* had a greater impact as nationals of states outside Europe with association agreements similar to that with Slovakia, which was at stake in *Kolpak*, sought equal treatment with domestic players. The phrase 'Kolpak player' has resonance in cricket: South Africans have been the most notable beneficiaries. These EU-influenced rules too have changed over time. There are, moreover, instances of cricketers who are not qualified to play for England because they have already represented another (non-European) country acquiring the nationality of another Member State and then claiming entitlement to play county cricket in England as a matter of EU law, with the result that an England-qualified player is ousted. The concern in this analysis is not the detail nor the currently applicable arrangements.[33] The concern here is principle and in particular whether the antipathy shown by the Court in *Bosman* to nationality discrimination outside the context of international representative football has the same force when applied to cricket.

It does not have the same force.[34] The example of cricket sharpens awareness of the argument which the Court chose to miss in *Bosman*. Imagine a rule introduced by cricket administrators concerned about the future health of the England team that requires counties, in assembling their squads, to select only players qualified to play international cricket for England, or, at least, to reserve a certain percentage of the places on the squad to players who are so qualified. This would involve discrimination against EU nationals who do not carry the required sporting connection with England. Another variant would be to distribute income raised from the international game on terms that favour those counties who prioritize the selection of England-qualified players: again, the result would be to discriminate against EU nationals who are *not* England-qualified. It was argued earlier that the Court's logic that national football teams will not suffer from the abolition of nationality discrimination because players unable to find a place locally will be able to cross borders in search of work misses the point that the patterns of migration will not be consistent: some states will be net losers. But the logic *clearly* does not work in the context of cricket. An England-qualified cricketer whose place is lost to an EU national who is not English-qualified cannot work as a cricketer anywhere else in the EU. So the presence of the migrant unarguably restricts the size of the available pool of English-qualified players and risks damaging the strength of the national representative side. So the rejection in *Bosman* of the need for nationality-based restrictions in club competition as a device to sustain the national side is based

---

[33] The currently applicable ECB Regulations are at <https://www.ecb.co.uk/news/105903> accessed 29 November 2016.

[34] cf S Boyes, 'Caught Behind or Following-On? Cricket, the European Union and the Bosman Effect' (2005) 3(1) ESLJ 2 <http://www.entsportslawjournal.com/article/10.16997/eslj.120> accessed 29 November 2016.

on the economic pattern of football, which is played professionally in almost all European states, and even if I have previously argued that it is not fully convincing in the context of football, it simply does not apply at all to cricket, which is played professionally in only one European state, the United Kingdom. So this means that cricket should be able to exclude or at least limit opportunities for EU nationals who lack the necessary qualification to play international cricket for England, for otherwise the production of an England international team that is good enough to compete with the other Test-playing nations will be imperilled.

So EU nationals do *not* have to be treated alike but can be separated out on the basis of qualification to play cricket for England.[35] There are other reasons for treating cricket differently from football. Football supporters watch both club and international football in large numbers, live, on television, and increasingly through other audiovisual media. Both club and international football are commercially highly significant. But in cricket attendance at county games is dwarfed by the numbers that pay to see international cricket, live or on television or through other media. Broadcasting of county cricket games is of trivial significance. County cricket would be unsustainable in anything remotely comparable to its present shape were it not for the substantial income transferred to the counties from the pot filled by income from ticket sales, sponsors, and broadcasters of international cricket. Nothing of this sort occurs in football, where the relationship between club and country is strikingly less hierarchical. The richer football clubs might plausibly consider the international game a drain on their resources, not a supplement, in part because there is competition between club and international competitions to attract sponsors and broadcasters and in part because clubs must release their best players to play—and get weary or even injured—at international level.[36] In cricket it is well understood that the best players will rarely appear for their county. In football many supporters have an ambivalent attitude to the national side—they typically want it to succeed, but feel a stronger tie to the club they follow week in, week out—whereas by contrast in cricket it is more readily accepted that the primary function of the county game is to produce players capable of representing the national side. Country stands unarguably above club in cricket; not so in football.

In *Walrave and Koch* the Court insisted that any restriction on the scope of EU law must 'remain limited to its proper objective',[37] and although the precise understanding of just how and why sport intersects with EU law has been adjusted by the Court over time, as explored in the previous chapters, this basic controlling formula has not been abandoned. So the Court's insistence in *Meca-Medina* that EU competition law is not infringed on condition that restrictions 'must be limited to what is necessary to ensure the proper conduct of competitive sport' and that they do not 'go beyond what is necessary in order to ensure that sporting events take place and function properly' is a functional equivalent.[38] To insist on *no* players lacking

---

[35] Is this even direct discrimination at all, since it is based on sporting nationality rather than passport-based nationality? See sect 8.9.
[36] On the compatibility of this system with EU law, see Ch 10.8.
[37] *Walrave and Koch* (n 1) para 9. [38] *Meca-Medina* (n 3) paras 47, 54.

English qualification in the county cricket game might be the subject of challenge by an EU national on the basis that such a stringent approach goes beyond what is needed to sustain the national game. In this vein, it might be possible and sensible to differentiate players not qualified to play for England and who never will be qualified, on the one hand, and, on the other, those not currently qualified to play for England but who might become so as a result of meeting residence requirements.[39] The latter appear to have a stronger claim to being allowed admission. But it is improbable that these refinements would be the subject of intense or sceptical review by the Court, provided the basic point—that all EU nationals do *not* have to be treated alike but can be separated out on the basis of qualification to play cricket for England—is accepted.

Cricket, then, is different from football. In so far as one seeks to argue that nationality-based discrimination is permissible because of its contribution to sustaining the health of the national side, one is making a much stronger case in relation to cricket as contrasted with football because in cricket, but not in football, there is clear acceptance that the national representative team stands culturally and commercially at the summit of the sport.

Rugby would provide another intriguing case study into the possible adaptation in the interpretation and application of EU law in the face of sporting discrimination and the scope to understand that a law of sports, not sport, is at stake. Rugby, like cricket, has 'Kolpak players', and so similar questions arise about the extent to which eligibility for a national team may be used as a basis for distinguishing between players in the selection rules laid down by the *lex sportiva*. However, practice in rugby has a particular twist. The English Rugby Union has agreed with the clubs in its main competition, the Premiership, that players who choose to play professionally for a club outside England will be considered for selection for the English national side only in exceptional circumstances.[40] Strong preference is therefore given to a player who works for an English club. In practice the deterrent effect largely applies to players tempted to play professionally in France, the only other country in Europe apart from England which has a significant number of professional rugby clubs. This plainly brings EU law into play.

As in the case of cricket, the argument would be to defend an apparent restriction on rights granted by EU law in the light of the contribution to sustaining the health of the national side, on the basis that the relationship between club and country is not the same as that found in football and addressed in *Bosman*. But in rugby the argument is not convincing. There is a cross-border market for

---

[39] Some of the best England cricketers of recent years have qualified in this way.

[40] The policy dates from 2011: 'England to Only Pick Home-based Players from 2011' BBC Sport, 2 December 2010 <http://news.bbc.co.uk/sport1/hi/rugby_union/english/9250944.stm> accessed 29 November 2016. It continues: 'Eddie Jones [England's coach, an Australian] insists he is happy not to pick overseas players for England' *The Guardian* (London, 20 November 2015) <https://www.theguardian.com/sport/2015/nov/20/eddie-jones-happy-not-to-pick-overseas-players-for-england-new-head-coach> accessed 29 November 2016.

players in club rugby, in contrast to cricket, and the rules governing eligibility for the English national side distort that market by deterring cross-border movement, to the advantage of commercial operators in the state where the rule is made and enforced. The most obvious consequence, and arguably the motivation, of such rules is that they encourage English-qualified players to play in England rather than France. This tends to reduce the competition on wages in the (cross-border) market to the commercial advantage of owners of English clubs and helps to improve the appeal of the English Premiership at the expense of competing events. Observations by those engaged in agreeing and enforcing the rules readily bring to mind the dismissive attitudes of governing bodies in the run-up to *Bosman*. Mark McCafferty, chief executive of the English Premiership, was reported to have described it as a 'joint policy' and stated that 'Nobody is doing it against anybody's will in terms of the partnership between England, the RFU and ourselves'.[41] This complete blindness to the effect of the rules on players helpfully underlines that this is a horizontal restraint agreed by and for the advantage of employers. Moreover, the rule, in so far as it leads to some players choosing to forgo international recognition in favour of a lucrative deal in France, weakens the strength of the English national team.[42] The only sporting reason that might be advanced to defend the rule would relate to difficulties that might arise in securing the release of a player based in France for an England match— but this cannot justify a general unwillingness even to consider the selection of such players, which therefore constitutes a disproportionate interference with free movement rights granted by EU law.

The footballing equivalent would be to withhold selection for the English national side to a player who chose to play for Juventus or Real Madrid, rather than for Chelsea or Liverpool. There could be no good reason for this—only the bad reason of protecting Chelsea and Liverpool's chances of contracting with the player. And the national side would be weakened by such obstinacy. The rule would not be allowed in football and its equivalent in rugby should not be allowed either.

A broader observation, introduced earlier, asks whether it is sound policy to restrict access to the labour market on the basis of nationality or proxies such as qualification to play for the local international representative side. The result is to create a cosy advantage for those players that meet the stipulated criteria which is not the result of their talent and which will grant them artificially enhanced power in the market for wages. If X gets the job ahead of equally able Y simply because X has the 'right' nationality, the result *may* be that the national team will be improved (if X improves as a result of his or her privileged position) but the result *will* be that

---

[41] 'England to Continue Overseas Ban' PlanetRugby, 17 September 2015 <http://www.planetrugby.com/news/england-to-continue-overseas-ban/> accessed 29 November 2016.

[42] There was much grumbling about its damaging effects in the wake of England's failure to reach even the quarter-finals of the World Cup, which it hosted in 2015: eg 'England Overseas Selection Policy Criticised by Nick Abendanon' Sky Sports, 5 October 2015 <http://www.skysports.com/rugby-union/news/12504/10019044/abendanon-slams-selection-policy> accessed 29 November 2016.

X is paid more than Y in that market—unless there is a vast supply of Xs, which defeats the argument in favour of granting X any advantage in the first place. It also may be the result that X will become lazy because he or she does not need to be better than or even as good as Y to get the job they are both chasing.

The rules in rugby confer an automatic advantage on a player simply because he has chosen to stay at home. One might wonder whether the rules are in fact counter-intuitive. Surely the player who broadens his horizons by playing elsewhere would be more likely to improve, unless it were clear that the French game is much weaker than that in England, which is demonstrably not the case. This might add a suspicion that the real aim of the rule is to give English clubs a competitive advantage in the (cross-border) market for (English) players.

But the point of this discussion has been to make the case that *if* governing bodies in sport want to introduce such rules they should not treat *Bosman* as an inevitable bar. It will, however, depend on the particular circumstances prevailing—this is in its practical application a law of sports, not a homogenous law of sport. Cricket is special. If it is believed that cricketing counties are tempted by short-term success to hire EU nationals who are not English-qualified and that such tactics will lead to a weakening of the national team and that a rule imposed by the authorities of the sport is needed to sustain that core activity, then EU law would not preclude this. It would be necessary to sustain the very existence of genuinely competitive, international representative cricket. This argument should have been treated with more care by the Court in *Bosman*, where the judgment mistakenly assumes that the reciprocal nature of worker migration cures any problem of diminished talent available for national representative sides. It does not, in states with net inflows of workers. Even so, there were strong enough other reasons in *Bosman* to conclude that, overall, nationality discrimination in club football should not be permitted as a matter of EU law. As explained, in rugby the deterrent effect on free movement of English rules that favour players who work in England is also not justified as a matter of EU law. However, the case for nationality discrimination in cricket below international level is a good deal more powerful.

8.8 The Incentives to Seek a Reformed System That Would be Tied to the Origins of Players

Governing bodies in sport were and remain thoroughly grumpy about the intrusion of EU law into practices which engage discrimination on the basis of nationality. Sepp Blatter's disdain for a club in England with a squad containing nineteen nationalities is entirely typical.[43]

The Court yielded to the *lex sportiva* in the matter of nationality discrimination in international representative football. It refused to do the same in relation

---

[43] See n 20.

to *club* football. It is here that EU law in general and the Court in particular is most vulnerable to the accusation that it claims to know the needs of sport better than its governing bodies, and in circumstances where there is no explicit constitutional mandate on which to base the EU's chosen direction. This, the criticism holds, is the arrogance of EU law. And yet the point is that the model of conditional autonomy under EU law, shaped by the Court, leaves space for governing bodies to explain just why their practices are necessary elements in the structure of the sport. The real problem is not that the Court brushes aside the legitimate claims of sports bodies: the real problem is the thin arguments advanced in favour of the status quo by those sports bodies. This is a recurrent theme of this book. As explained, the Court's reasoning in *Bosman* was unpersuasive on one dimension alone, that associated with the incorrect claim that what a state loses by accepting incoming workers it gains as a result of its own workers migrating to other Member States, but otherwise it was full and careful. The Court's rejection of the claim that the origin of players is relevant to the identity of clubs places EU law's assumptions about the vice of nationality discrimination ahead of the claims to autonomy and expertise expressed through the *lex sportiva*, but, as explained previously, the Court's analysis seems more persuasive and in tune with the attitudes and expectations of fans than that pressed on it by UEFA and other sports bodies.

Governing bodies in football have not given up.

In principle, as previous chapters have shown, EU internal market law dictates only what may not be done, not what shall be done. In reality the Court seems to have left very little scope for doing anything at club level that smacks of discrimination on grounds of nationality. However, governing bodies have continued to search for an adapted system. The two principal motivations typically advanced in support of rules that restrict the freedom of clubs to select players irrespective of their background are the encouragement of youth training and sustaining the vitality of the national representative teams without falling foul of EU law. The main argument would be that the financial implications of failure (most obviously, relegation) felt by such clubs are so severe that they tend to acquire fully trained players rather than developing younger players, and that rules limiting the hiring of foreign players would be a justified response to this peril.[44] The point is to find a justification for rules that will satisfy the Court, in accordance with the model of conditional autonomy enjoyed by sporting bodies under EU law.

There are two principal models: a renovated system based on nationality, which is highly unlikely to survive examination conducted pursuant to EU law, and one based on the location in which a player is trained, the so-called 'home-grown' system, which has more chance of meeting the demands placed on sporting autonomy by EU law. These are considered in turn.

---

[44] See J-P Dubey, *La libre circulation des sportifs en Europe* (Staempfli Editions/Bruylant 2000) 506–11.

8.9 Rules Based (Directly or Indirectly) on Nationality: 'Quotas' in Club Football

FIFA has periodically aired the idea of requiring that a certain number of players in a club side must be eligible for the international representative team in that country. A so-called '6 plus 5' rule was suggested by FIFA in 2008, according to which six players in a team had to be eligible for the national team of the association in which the club was located. It has not been adopted by FIFA, even though as late as 2015 its then-President, Sepp Blatter, repeated his support for the idea.[45]

A major obstacle was and remains EU law. Direct discrimination on grounds of nationality in club football seems unsustainable under EU law unless the Court reconsiders its approach in *Bosman*. There is at least one flaw in the reasoning used in *Bosman*. As explained earlier, the Court was wrong to brush aside the argument that unlimited labour migration would not diminish the pool of players available to the national team. But even were the Court to change its mind and accept that the defence of national teams has a stronger foundation than it allowed in *Bosman*, it still seems probable that other factors weigh heavily against accepting nationality discrimination in club football. A club has historic connections with its locality, and this endures to some extent even in the case of high-profile clubs which have acquired the status of global brands. However, this does not apply to the players. The identity and origin of players does not matter in club football in the way that it matters in international representative football.

In consequence, since rules that tie clubs to select at least some players according to their nationality are not necessary for the organization of the sport, they fall foul of EU law as instances of direct discrimination on grounds of nationality. And it is orthodox that there is no scope to justify such direct discrimination, except in closely defined circumstances envisaged by the Treaty, which do not apply here.[46] In exactly this vein, the Commission's 2007 White Paper on Sport warns firmly against the reintroduction of nationality-based rules.[47] It issues a reminder that 'Discrimination on grounds of nationality is prohibited in the Treaties ... The Treaties also aim to abolish any discrimination based on nationality between workers of the Member States as regards employment, remuneration and other conditions of work and employment' and, in a nod to *Kolpak*,[48] adds that 'Equal treatment also concerns citizens of States which have signed agreements with the EU that contain non-discrimination clauses, and who are legally

---

[45] 'Sepp Blatter Urges Europe to Back His 6 plus 5 Local Talent Rule' Associated Press (New York, 13 August 2015) <http://www.espnfc.co.uk/fifa-world-cup/story/2561968/sepp-blatter-urges-europe-to-revive-his-6-plus-5-rule> accessed 29 November 2016.

[46] eg TFEU, Art 45(4) a narrowly interpreted provision concerning employment in the public service.

[47] White Paper on Sport, COM (2007) 391, 11 July 2007, available via <http://ec.europa.eu/sport/index_en.htm> accessed 29 November 2016. See Ch 6.5.

[48] *Kolpak* (n 27).

employed in the territory of the Member States'.[49] The 2011 Communication on Sport is equally stern on this point.[50] It states that 'the Treaty prohibits discrimination based on nationality and enshrines the principle of free movement of workers' and that 'rules entailing direct discrimination (such as quotas of players on the basis of nationality) are not compatible with EU law'.[51] The 2011 Commission Staff Working Document, 'Sport and Free Movement' is cut from the same cloth:

Rules leading to direct discrimination on grounds of nationality are not compatible with EU law. The same is true for rules based on criteria directly linked to nationality. For example, rules establishing quotas of players in clubs based on eligibility to play for the national team of the country where the club is located, when the main criterion for such eligibility is nationality, are not compatible with EU law.[52]

The Commission has also taken this uncompromising view in answers to questions posed by MEPs.[53] It will not accept quotas of the type proposed by FIFA. They violate EU law.

Heroic attempts have been made to find a way round the restrictions imposed by EU law on the '6 plus 5' model. They are, however, typically an analytically mushy attempt to revive the concept of the 'purely sporting' rule and to claim defence of national identity, laced too by the frankly absurd claim that such a rule would not restrict access to the labour market because it applies only to the selection of players for individual games.[54] This is utterly unpersuasive: it is in fact simply an attempt to re-fight *Bosman*. If there is any life left in the argument in defence of FIFA's mooted '6 plus 5' rule it might lie in the point that 'sporting nationality' is not necessarily congruent with passport-carrying nationality. The '6 plus 5' rule would insist that six players be eligible for the national representative side of the country in which the club is based: this could feasibly discriminate against a player holding the passport of that country as much as a player who does not, where that first player happens to be ineligible to play football for the representative side in question, typically because he is qualified through birth or blood to play for and has played for another country. This is, to be precise, not direct discrimination based on nationality but rather direct discrimination based on, in short, 'sporting nationality', which is a distinct concept.[55] There certainly are instances, some high-profile, of players holding a nationality which is not the same as that held for the purposes

---

[49] White Paper on Sport (n 47) 14–15, section 4.2.

[50] Commission Communication of January 2011, 'Developing the European Dimension in Sport' COM (2011) 12, available via <http://ec.europa.eu/sport/policy/index_en.htm> accessed 29 November 2016. See Ch 6.11.

[51] ibid para 4.3.

[52] Staff Working Document, 'Sport and Free Movement', SEC (2011) 6, p 5. The document is available via <http://ec.europa.eu/sport/index_en.htm> accessed 29 November 2016.

[53] eg E-4038/08 Parliamentary Question, WQ by De Rossa [2009] OJ C40; P-5529/09 Parliamentary Question, WG by Papastamkos [2011] OJ C10E.

[54] Institute of European Affairs, 'Expert Opinion on the Compatibility of the 6+5 rule with European Community Law' (2009).

[55] cf J Guillaumé, 'L'autonomie de la nationalité sportive' (2011) 138 Journal du droit international 313.

of international representative football.[56] Most players would plainly hold parallel sporting and political nationality, but a minority would not. So, the argument would run, a requirement that a certain number of players in a club side are eligible for the international representative team in that country would be direct discrimination on the basis of footballing nationality and only indirectly discriminatory on the basis of nationality in the political sense. The crucial legal point in EU law is that indirect discrimination on grounds of nationality is capable of objective justification, whereas direct discrimination is much less generously treated. This opens up scope to press the virtue of the '6 plus 5' rule as an expression of the discretionary power of sports governing bodies to promote youth training and to sustain national teams.[57]

This possibility cannot be conclusively ruled out. Nothing quite like it has ever reached the Court. But footballing nationality is tantamount to 'ordinary' nationality and the gap between the two concepts, though admittedly observable on occasion, is so slender that probably no distinction should be made. And in *Bosman* the Court saw no difficulty in treating the '3 plus 2' rule as a case of direct discrimination based on nationality. Early in the judgment it noted that the rules defined nationality in relation to whether the player can be qualified to play in a country's national representative team[58] but thereafter it simply treated the matter as discrimination based on nationality, ignoring any issue of footballing nationality. Even if the argument that this is indirect discrimination were accepted, and room were thereby created to argue that the rules are objectively justified, it is far from clear that the argument would succeed. This is considered more fully later, in connection with a more orthodox type of indirect discrimination, that arising where restrictions are imposed with reference to the place where the player has been trained. Even there, as will be shown, the argument is not easily made. The fact, however, that the case supporting a certain degree of action in favour of local players may be made in relation to home-grown rules is probably fatal to the claim that discrimination in favour of 'sporting nationals' of the relevant country should be permitted, because it offers a less restrictive means to achieve the end in view.

FIFA has abandoned interest in the '6 plus 5' rule, at least for the time being. The major clubs would certainly not welcome its resurrection. As a matter of EU law the correct view seems to be that such a system of discrimination would be unlawful.[59] It goes beyond the zone of conditional autonomy granted to sport by EU law.

---

[56] The UK provides a particularly odd example; there are four football nationalities in a single Member State. But other examples with the necessary cross-border element exist: UK nationals have played for Ireland, for example.

[57] See U Battis, A Ingold, and K Kuhnert, 'Zur Vereinbarkeit der 6+5 Spielregel der FIFA mit dem Unionsrecht' (2010) 45 Europarecht 3, which also draws on TFEU, Art 165 to argue for EU law to show greater respect for the cultural character of sport.

[58] *Bosman* (n 5) para 25.

[59] See also S Gardiner and R Welch, 'Bosman—There and Back Again' (2011) 17 ELJ 828; S Gardiner and R Welch, 'Nationality Based Playing Quotas and the International Transfer System Post-Bosman' in A Duval and B Van Rompuy (eds), *The Legacy of Bosman: Revisiting the Relationship between EU Law and Sport* (TMC Asser/Springer 2016) ch 4.

8.10 Home-grown Rules

A more promising approach is the adoption of rules that require that a certain minimum number of players in a team or in a squad who are registered as eligible to play in a particular competition shall have been produced through the training system that exists within the country in which the club is located. Such players are *likely* to have the nationality of the state in which a club is based, but this need not be so. There is no mandatory connection fixed on nationality. The point is to eliminate the direct discrimination based on nationality which taints FIFA's '6 plus 5' rule and instead to establish a system which, by distinguishing on the basis of training location, amounts only to indirect discrimination based on nationality. This opens up greater scope for justifying such rules as an expression of the specific character of sport.

There *are* such rules in football. They are commonly known as 'home-grown' rules. UEFA's current system deems a player 'home grown' where registered with a club for three seasons between the ages of 15 and 21, so in fact a player can count as home-grown in State A having played all his football and received all his training up to the age of 18 in State B.[60] However, the purpose of the current analysis is not to consider the arrangements in detail: their precise shape regularly changes in any event. The current concern is how to treat such rules as a matter of EU law: do they respect the terms of the conditional autonomy which EU grants to sport?

The aim of such rules is plainly to encourage investment in young talent with a view to sustaining the long-term supply of good quality players. So the scheme favours the 'home-grown', and it stops a club simply filling its team-sheet and its squad with fully developed mature players. This opens up room to argue that the rules are necessary to support the interest of encouraging investment in youth training, the matter of competitive balance between clubs, and the wider health of the national representative side.

No ruling of the Court of Justice deals directly with the compatibility of such rules with EU law. However, the Commission has accepted that 'home-grown' rules are potentially compatible with the Treaty. The Staff Working Document accompanying the 2007 White Paper merely mentions this as one of several important outstanding issues,[61] but in May 2008 the Commission, publishing an independent study on the compatibility of the scheme with EU law, announced a firmer view. It considered the home-grown rule compatible with EU law in the light of its contribution to promoting balance in sporting competition and encouraging the training of young players.[62]

---

[60] For UEFA's own explanation, see <http://www.uefa.com/news/newsid=943393.html> accessed 29 November 2016.

[61] Staff Working Document, 'The EU and Sport: Background and Context', 76, available via <http://ec.europa.eu/sport/index_en.htm> accessed 29 November 2016.

[62] IP/08/807, 28 May 2008: the report (by INEUM Consulting) is available at <http://ec.europa.eu/sport/library/studies/study-on-the-training-executive-summary_en.pdf> accessed 29 November 2016.

The 2008 study is disappointingly thin and descriptive. It does not deserve to command a high level of respect, for it is uncritically generous to the claims made on behalf of the *lex sportiva*. Nevertheless the Commission has stuck to its point of view. Its 2011 Communication on Sport is openly receptive to the 'home-grown' model.[63] It notes that the Court's case law is receptive to 'the need to preserve certain specific characteristics of sport', and adds that:

... rules which are indirectly discriminatory (such as quotas for locally trained players), or which hinder free movement of workers (compensation for recruitment and training of young players), may be considered compatible if they pursue a legitimate objective and insofar as they are necessary and proportionate to the achievement of such an objective.[64]

The accompanying 2011 Commission Staff Working Document, 'Sport and Free Movement' is even more precise in its guidance. It declares that:

... rules such as UEFA's 'home-grown players' which aim to encourage the recruitment and training of young players and ensure the balance of competitions, can be compatible with EU free movement provisions (i) in so far as they are able to achieve efficiently those legitimate objectives, (ii) if there are no other measures available which can be less discriminating and (iii) if the rules in question do not go beyond what is necessary to the attainment of their objectives.[65]

It adds that the Commission 'will nevertheless monitor the application of these rules closely on a case by case basis in order to verify that the criteria are met'.[66] The insistence on case-by-case examination, rather than the adoption of any generalized exemption, is in line with the Court's landmark ruling in *Meca-Medina*.[67]

It is of course the Court's view, rather than the Commission's, which is authoritative. But at least in principle, in accepting the virtues pursued, the Commission appears to be on solid ground. The 'home-grown' rules would be defended as means to promote balance in sporting competition (because richer clubs could not simply fill their squads with expensively purchased finished products) and as a device to encourage the training of young players. Both concerns have been recognized by the Court as legitimate in sport. Both *Bosman*[68] and *Bernard*[69] openly accept the legitimate concern of sport to promote youth training, albeit there in the context of the transfer system, rather than in the context of shaping quotas favouring locally trained players. Article 165 TFEU's direction that the Union shall take 'account of the specific nature of sport, its structures based on voluntary activity and its social and educational function' frames the analysis advanced in support of the need for such rules, although, as explained in Chapter 7, it is not argued that this is any way a change of substance.

However, the case that the home-grown rule is compatible with EU law in the light of its contribution to promoting balance in sporting competition and

---

[63] Commission Communication of January 2011 (n 50).   [64] ibid 11.
[65] 'Sport and Free Movement' (n 52) 4.   [66] ibid 4.
[67] *Meca-Medina* (n 3). See Ch 5.   [68] *Bosman* (n 5).
[69] Case C-325/08 *Olympique Lyonnais v Olivier Bernard, Newcastle United* [2010] I-2177.

encouraging the training of young players deserves a sceptical examination. The argument rooted in competitive balance is thin: rich clubs will plainly still acquire the best players while poorer clubs will find that the available pool of talent in which they can fish has been artificially diminished by the requirement to hire a defined number of 'home-grown' players. And it is far from clear that creating a protected class of 'home-grown' players, who will certainly enjoy higher wages than equally skilled non-qualifying players simply because clubs need to hit their quotas, is sensible as a means to improve the quality of training. Better, one might think, to open up the market so that young players have to sink or swim rather than enjoy artificial buoyancy because of where they happen to have been 'grown'. Given these objections and given that there are other and plausibly more appropriate ways to achieve the objectives pursued by the home-grown rules, it is at least arguable that they are incompatible with EU law.

In 2013 the Commission published an independent study into the effects of the home-grown rule applied by UEFA. It was prepared by a team from the University of Liverpool and Edge Hill University and appeared under the names of Murray Dalziel, Paul Downward, Richard Parrish, Geoff Pearson, and Anna Semens.[70] This is a thoroughly impressive piece of work: detailed, thoughtful, and fully referenced. It is an important contribution because it seeks to initiate an examination of the rules in the light of an empirical investigation into their effects. This, then, is to push EU sports law and policy towards an evidence-based foundation rather than one based on loose references to common sense[71] and Kevin Keegan.[72]

The rules which provide the background to the examination are those introduced by UEFA to govern European club football competitions with effect from the 2006–07 season. Under that scheme all qualifying teams must operate a quota of at least eight home-grown players in their squad of twenty-five. Four of the eight players must have been registered with the club for a period, continuous or non-continuous, of three entire seasons or of thirty-six months whilst between the ages of 15 and 21. The others may qualify under the same criteria where they have been trained by another club in the same association. It is explicitly provided that nationality is not relevant. And, as the Report notes, this model has been adopted in some other sports too.

The study found that the rules had exerted negligible effect—positive or negative. It argues that although the aims—to improve competitive balance and to induce the training and development of young players—are in themselves compatible with EU law, in the light of the Court's case law and now with reference to Article 165 TFEU, the absence of any adequately compelling evidence that these

---

[70] European Commission, Study on the Assessment of UEFA's 'Home Grown Player Rule' Negotiated Procedure EAC/07/2012 (2013) <http://ec.europa.eu/assets/eac/sport/library/studies/final-rpt-april2013-homegrownplayer.pdf> accessed 29 November 2016. For a summary and an explanation, see P Downward, R Parrish, G Pearson, and A Semens, 'An Assessment of the Compatibility of UEFA's Home Grown Player Rule with Article 45 TFEU' (2014) 39 EL Rev 493.

[71] AG Warner in *Walrave and Koch* (n 1), see Ch 4.

[72] AG Lenz in *Bosman* (n 5), see Ch 4.

ends are in fact advanced other than to a very modest degree should lead to a healthy preliminary scepticism that the scheme is compatible with EU law. Nearly all clubs interviewed suggested that the scheme had either 'no impact' or 'little impact' upon their strategies for the training and development of players.[73] Only four clubs interviewed, a small minority, identified any real impact.[74] The claimed capacity of the rule to sustain the quality of the national representative side is particularly hard to substantiate. And there are identified negative aspects of the rule, such as the inducement to poach qualifying young players from other clubs in order to hit the quota.[75]

Even if small benefits can be identified, the Report advances good arguments that there are other equally effective ways to attain these objectives which impose a less restrictive effect on the mobility of players. In this area the point is always to justify just why obligations should be placed on players as employees where 'normal' employees would not be so burdened. So one could envisage club licensing schemes as a means to require the maintenance of youth training, financial inducements so to do, revenue sharing, and so on. If these are equally apt to achieve the stated aims, the condemnation of the home-grown rules as incompatible with EU law seems inevitable. The Report makes the argument that where faced with a choice to intervene in football between measures affecting clubs and measures affecting players, then, all other things being equal, the presumption should be in favour of the use of the former over the latter. The latter are more likely to affect the rights of workers, including free movement rights, and so should be viewed more sceptically. Nothing in the Court's case law explicitly supports this view, but it is an elegant and convincing way to understand the protection and priorities embedded in EU law. And it acts as a valuable corrective to the often unexplained tendency to assume that footballers are inevitably vulnerable to treatment that would not be meted out to ordinary employees. The Report is spot on when it notes that it is common, but simply not acceptable, for such treatment to be defended as historically rooted in sport, nor should the relatively high level of remuneration of some professional athletes count as a reason to load burdens on them when the aims in view can be achieved at least as well by addressing the clubs or federations. So, the Report declares with persuasive vigour, 'labour market restrictions should be considered the *last* resort and it is recommended that the institutions of the EU adopt this approach as their foundation principle when assessing measures that may conflict with the freedoms of athletes'.[76]

The Report concludes that the rules cannot be described as compatible with EU free movement law until the viability of less restrictive alternatives has been examined, particularly those that do not carry discriminatory effects and are not located within the labour market. This seems thoroughly persuasive. The Report recommends that a further analysis should be conducted in three years' time by UEFA in

---

[73] European Commission, 2013 Study (n 70) 68.
[74] ibid 71: the clubs are not named, for reasons of confidentiality.   [75] ibid 100–101.
[76] ibid 7; see also 106–107, 111.

order to assess whether effects pertinent to the pursuit of competitive balance have been maintained, improved further, or have declined; whether a closer connection between the rule and improvements in youth development can be identified; and whether less restrictive alternatives can deliver more substantial improvements to competitive balance and the quality of youth development. The bottom line assumption is that 'if less restrictive alternatives are able to achieve more substantial improvements in competitive balance and the quality of youth development, the proportionality of the Rule will not have been made out and the Rule should be removed from the UEFA Regulations'.[77] The ends may be lawful, but the means used are not.

The findings of the Report have provoked neither litigation nor Commission intervention. Doubtless this is in part a reflection of the relatively closed world in which sporting autonomy is practised. Were the home-grown rules to be attacked as restrictions on free movement and distortions of competition within the EU, the best chance to defend them would probably lie in a claim that they fall within the sporting margin of appreciation considered in Chapter 7.4. In line with the aforementioned Report, it seems much easier to show that the home-grown rule is exerting an effect on buying policies than it is to show that it is encouraging a higher level of investment in youth training. The richer clubs have an obvious incentive to acquire players who meet the home-grown requirements to ensure they meet their quota.[78] The causal link to encouraging training of home-grown players in the first place is harder to establish: this is exactly the finding of the Report. And the effect of such a rule is certainly to increase the wages commanded by the home-grown player, because the system makes it harder to replace him as it restricts the supply of players who qualify. Defence of the system as a contribution to the specific nature of sport, in particular the concern to encourage an emphasis on youth training, would require production of empirical evidence of such benefits that is currently lacking. Were the scheme challenged, it is doubtless the case that sporting bodies would seek such evidence, while also pleading for a zone of autonomy within which their choices would be subjected to EU law in principle but within which in practice they would be granted a large measure of discretion in determining the 'specific nature of sport' mandated by Article 165 TFEU. This sporting margin of appreciation, considered in Chapter 7.4, draws on two strands of the Court's case law: that which yields public authorities in the Member States a discretion in resolving cases pitting trade integration against sensitive social and cultural choices made under national law, especially where an EU legislative solution is constitutionally or politically

---

[77] ibid 8, 112. For similar scepticism concerning the compatibility of the system with EU law, see Gardiner and Welch (2016) (n 59); L Freeburn, 'European Football's Home-Grown Players Rules and Nationality Discrimination under the European Community Treaty' (2009–10) 20 Marquette Sports Law Review 177.

[78] eg 'Cresswell on City's Radar as Hierarchy Bows to Demands of Home Rule' *The Times* (London, 15 April 2015) 64: 'Manchester City have identified Aaron Cresswell, the West Ham United left back, as a potential transfer target in their attempt to bolster the number of home-grown players in their squad as part of a planned reshape this summer.'

improbable,[79] and also that permitting the EU's own institutions a broad discretion in matters that entail complex assessment and a readiness to intervene only where action is manifestly inappropriate.[80] Sporting autonomy would try to take shelter under this formula. Its chances are increased where the percentage of players that must be home-grown is kept relatively small: in 2014 the Commission took the view that rules in Spanish basketball were unduly restrictive because they reserved between 40 and 88 per cent of jobs available in basketball teams to players meeting criteria associated with local training.[81]

The strength of the claim to autonomy would be improved where the social dialogue is well developed and infuses the choices made, so that the scheme is representative of all affected interests, not just the 'top-down' rule-makers. Article 165 TFEU's reference to the promotion of 'openness' could be given concrete shape through the adoption of a more lenient review of the necessity of sporting practices which appear to interfere with the internal market in circumstances where the procedures through which such practices are made are genuinely open to all affected parties, including players. This is, admittedly, an issue that could strain the governance arrangements within football. There is evidence that some larger clubs are not at all in agreement with the worth of home-grown rules. Their commitment to the health of the national team is ambiguous at best: and home-grown rules simply reduce the pool of talent within which they are able to fish and cause an artificial inflation in the costs of labour that complies with the home-grown rules.[82]

8.11 Eligibility for a National Team—Changing Country

Is it compatible with EU law to prevent someone from changing 'sporting nationality'? If not, could a time restriction be imposed before such a change is effective?

This inquiry has in common with the previous discussion the plain fact that footballers and some other athletes who represent national teams are not treated in the same way as 'ordinary' employees. A player can change club: the transfer system is examined in Chapter 9. But, at international representative level, a player cannot simply switch to another employer. Different sports have different rules.[83] In football flexibility prevailed in the past: over fifty years ago two of the finest players in history won international caps for two different countries: Ferenc Puskás for Hungary and then Spain, Alfredo di Stéfano for Argentina, then Spain. Today the rules are tighter. FIFA permits a player to appear for one country at youth level

---

[79] eg Case C-112/00 *Schmidberger v Austria* [2003] ECR I-5659; Case C-36/02 *Omega Spielhallen* [2004] ECR I-9609; Case C-391/09 *Runevic-Vardyn* [2011] ECR I-3787.
[80] eg Case C-491/01 *Ex parte BAT* [2002] ECR I-11453; Case C-58/08 *Vodafone* [2010] ECR I-4999.
[81] MEMO/14/293, 16 April 2014.
[82] This has been apparent lately in England: eg 'Premier League Fights Dyke's Homegrown Plan' *The Guardian* (London, 28 March 2015) 6.
[83] See A Wollmann, O Vonk, and G-R De Groot, 'Towards a Sporting Nationality?' (2015) 22(2) MJ 305.

and in friendly internationals and then subsequently to choose to change sporting nationality and play for another country, but once he or she has played a competitive full international then the freedom to pick and choose is at an end.[84] Other sports have different rules, but no sport allows an athlete an unrestricted freedom to play for a series of different countries.

There is evidence that a market exists for high-profile athletes: recruiting foreign athletes is a means to achieve prestige by boosting Olympic medal counts.[85] In some sports the ease with which nationality may be changed by players who have not already represented the country with which they have their closest link—usually by residence, sometimes by distant blood ties through, for example, a grandparent—has created a degree of disquiet that the very heart of international representative sport is being undermined. Rugby and cricket have tended to attract particular anxieties,[86] but football too has its tensions. Smaller countries with a long history of emigration, such as Scotland and Ireland, might be forgiven or even praised for looking hard into the sporting wealth of their diaspora. Smaller countries trawling anxiously simply to find better players abroad than they have produced at home deserve to be viewed with less indulgence.

In so far as a sports governing body chooses to introduce impediments to an athlete's ability to select his or her sporting nationality, whether this is applicable to athletes who have already competed for another country and wish to switch or more generally, where no adequate link between athlete and flag exists to the satisfaction of the governing body, then a claim might arise if the usual requirements of EU law are met. Free movement law and the competition rules would in principle be applicable where the blockage affects inter-state mobility within the EU.

This immediately invites questions about how special sport is. In a normal industry, of course, the possibility to represent a national team would not even arise. In sport the core defence of such rules would rest on the need to maintain the integrity of international competition by sustaining the connection between the origin of the player and the team that he or she represents, which the Court accepted as legitimate as long ago as 1974 in *Walrave and Koch*.[87] There is no other practice of the Court or the Commission on which to draw. However, there is room for intriguing debate. In football one might argue that the prohibition against representing more than one country in competitive international matches goes too far. A five-year waiting period would be a less restrictive rule and there is room to argue that current rules are disproportionate. The retort is that it is embedded in the very nature

---

[84] FIFA's Statutes govern the matter, they are available at <http://www.fifa.com/about-fifa/who-we-are/the-statutes.html> 29 November 2016.

[85] J Horowitz and S McDaniel, 'Investigating the Global Productivity Effects of Highly Skilled Labour Migration: How Immigrant Athletes Impact Olympic Medal Counts' (2015) 7 International Journal of Sport Policy and Politics 19. See also D Reiche, 'Investing in Sporting Success as a Domestic and Foreign Policy Tool: The Case of Qatar' (2015) 7 International Journal of Sport Policy and Politics 489.

[86] eg 'March of the Foreign Legion: It's Time for World Rugby to Stop Exodus of Talent to Play under Flags of Convenience' *Sunday Times* (London, 10 May 2015) Sports section, 11.

[87] *Walrave and Koch* (n 1).

of international representative sport, unlike the club game, that there is a one-shot opportunity only. Here too, as stated earlier, much depends on identification of the specific nature of sport and on how much deference is accorded to the *lex sportiva* as source of expertise in line with the sporting margin of appreciation considered in Chapter 7.4.

A normatively appealing case has been made that changing nationality in sport should be approached in a more fluid, less exclusive way in order to promote a healthier culture of openness and egalitarianism in preference to a discourse of 'traitors and token patriots' that attaches in particular to the Olympics.[88] There is no sign of federations being minded to take this view. In so far as part of the reluctance is attributable to the commercial lure of an event that can inflame passion by 'othering' rather than promote reconciliation, then this is the very reason why legal control is justified and in the EU's case constitutionally legitimate. But it is probably a stretch too far to move beyond normative disapproval of rules that place some restriction on athletes changing sporting nationality and to condemn them as violations of EU law.

8.12 Equal Treatment of Non-nationals in National Championship

In 2011 the Commission published a funded study into the extent to which a non-national may be excluded from a competition which is designed to identify the national champion.[89] This had been mentioned as an issue deserving attention in the Staff Working Document accompanying the White Paper,[90] and in 2008, the Commission, answering a question by MEP Ivo Belet, contented itself with a cautious reply setting out its basic approach to the application of EU law to sport and promising the very study which subsequently emerged in 2011.[91]

The Report of the study funded by the Commission makes clear that access restrictions vary state by state, sport by sport. It steers an intelligent route between the expectations of non-discriminatory treatment on the basis of nationality which is required by EU law and the legitimate concerns associated with the organization of sporting competition. A non-national plainly could not demand to be crowned as national champion, for that would destroy the very nature of the contest: but a less rigid approach could plausibly be adopted with regard to participation by non-nationals in the event. In line with the thematic investigation provided in this

---

[88] D Kostakopoulou and A Schrauwen, 'Olympic Citizenship and the (Un)Specialness of the National Vest: Rethinking the Links between Sport and Citizenship Law' Warwick Law School Legal Studies Research Paper No 2015/05.

[89] 'Study on the Equal Treatment of Non-Nationals in Individual Sports Competitions', <http://ec.europa.eu/assets/eac/sport/library/studies/study_equal_treatment_non_nationals_final_rpt_dec_2010_en.pdf> accessed 29 November 2016.

[90] 'The EU and Sport: Background and Context' (n 61) 45.

[91] WQ P-4798/08 [2009] OJ C40.

chapter, proportionality and the necessity of the restriction are the principles that are of most operational significance in EU law.

Take a chess (or squash, or snooker, or darts) tournament with generous prize money, attractive to all players irrespective of nationality, but which is also designed to identify the chess champion of a country. One could easily imagine a model according to which the best six players of that country compete along with six non-nationals in an all-play-all format. The winner of the competition would not be declared the national champion if he or she was not a national of that country, but whichever player finishes highest among the six nationals would wear the crown. That would seem to maintain the integrity of the competition to find the national champion: there is no reason to exclude non-nationals, whose interest in participation is purely economic, from participation, there is reason only to exclude them from the possibility of being national champion. So limiting entry to nationals would be unnecessary as a means to reveal the champion player of that state and would therefore be incompatible with EU law.

Imagine by contrast one were to hold such a competition, but on a knock-out basis. The problem is that although the best player will normally win, there is a bias built in depending on the pairings. It is the luck of the draw: the player who is a national of the country concerned that survives longest could be declared national champion but that may not be because he or she has proved his or her worth in competition against all the other participants but rather because he or she has been drawn to play relatively weak players in early rounds. Here there may be a good reason to confine the competition to nationals alone, for only in this way will the best player be reliably identified.

It is at least possible that the recognition in Article 165(2) TFEU of the promotion of 'openness' as a feature of the European dimension of sport would strengthen the force of a legal challenge by an excluded participant. However, the sporting margin of appreciation met in Chapter 7.4 deserves respect. It would go too far to demand that as a matter of EU law it is not permitted to use a knock-out format to determine a national champion because of its exclusionary effect on non-nationals.

A related question would ask whether EU law could be used as a lever by a club in one Member State to gain access to the league championship of another Member State. Here too Article 165 TFEU's embrace of 'openness' would assist. The matter would not concern natural persons but legal persons, but the same issue, the tension between national-based competition under the *lex sportiva* and the EU's integrated internal market, would arise. Analysis is best left for wider discussion of governance in sport in Chapter 10: this chapter is limited to the consequences of nationality for individual athletes.

8.13 Conclusion

Nationality discrimination is part of sport—it defines the activity. The organization of a competition between sausage-makers or bankers from different countries might be a bit of fun but no one would ever suppose that the labour market for makers of sausages or bankers would be constructed on the basis of political nationality. By contrast, the World Cup would lose its point if it were to be robbed of nationality as a basis for the selection of representative teams. An Olympic Games without flags and anthems would be viable, perhaps even healthier thanks to suppression of aggressive nationalism, but it would be an existentially different event.

Sport is special. Article 165 TFEU consolidates that perception within EU law. The question is only how far to allow concession to practices that would normally be offensive under EU law in the name of sporting specificity. The Court has drawn a sharp line between international representative sport and club competition. Its work reveals much about the need for creativity forced upon it by the functionally broad project of the internal market which collides with interests that are not expressed or only thinly articulated in the Treaty yet which must be taken into account in determining the transformative potential of internal market law on the sectors that it reaches. The Court does accept that sport is special but not always as special as governing bodies insist. There remains room for intriguing litigation, especially where the home-grown rules are at stake, and there is also scope for exploring the procedural dimension. It remains open to question what level of intensity of review should apply to determining the scope of the conditional autonomy afforded to sports governing bodies, and how this is affected by the presence or absence of social dialogue.

9

The Transfer System

9.1 The Transfer System—Collective Plus Individual

A transfer system exists in several sports, but football's version is by far the most high-profile, longest-established, and the one which involves the largest amount of money. Different versions have existed at different times, but the basic idea holds that an athlete in a sport that operates a transfer system does not have a choice between employers which is determined exclusively by the law of contract. A transfer system provides that where an athlete wishes to change employer it will be necessary to comply with the collectively agreed and enforced rules of the sport, which typically involves payment of a fee by the buying club to the selling club in return for the transfer of the athlete's registration as an eligible player by the sport's governing body. The normal employee—of a bank, of a supermarket, of a University—may bring a contract of employment to an end in accordance with its terms or, if it is limited in time, simply let it expire and then conclude a contract with a new employer, or may choose to break the contract with the first employer and sign a new one with a preferred replacement and face whatever consequences are dictated by the employment law of the jurisdiction applicable to the contract. Not so the athlete in a sport with a transfer system. He or she faces *extra* collectively imposed restraints on his or her freedom. Whatever may be the position as a matter of contract law and employment law, he or she will be required to meet the stipulations imposed by the transfer system on pain of sanction, which may even result in a suspension from playing if the transfer system is disregarded. Sportsmen and sportswomen are not treated as normal employees. They are more tightly restrained. Sport is special.

In both *Bosman* and *Olympique Lyonnais v Olivier Bernard*, decided in 1995 and 2010 respectively,[1] the Court of Justice ruled that aspects of the transfer system in football were not compatible with EU law. They were condemned as unlawful restrictions on the free movement of workers within the internal market. But in both rulings the Court openly embraced sport's special and legitimate concerns, and it clearly indicated that some sort of transfer system, though not the one at

---

[1] Case C-415/93 *Union royale belge des sociétés de football association ASBL v Jean-Marc Bosman* [1995] ECR I-4921; Case C-325/08 *Olympique Lyonnais v Olivier Bernard, Newcastle United* [2010] I-2177.

stake in the litigation, could survive scrutiny pursuant to EU law. So the Court accepts that sport is special, and the key question is only *how* special: which, for athletes as workers, means that the key question arising under EU law asks how much less favourably they may be treated than ordinary employees. That is the inquiry pursued in this chapter.

9.2 The Rationales for and the History of the Transfer System

Why is there a transfer system? There are at least three rationales that have been conventionally advanced in its defence. First, clubs invest in the training of their players, especially young players. The transfer system offers them compensation for such investment and therefore induces them to commit resources to training the stars (and the flops) of the future. Second, transfer fees help to circulate money within the game, to promote competitive balance. In the absence of a transfer system more powerful clubs would simply poach talent from smaller clubs without having to provide compensation. Third, the transfer system promotes stability. Players are not individuals: they are identified and selected as part of a team. The loss of one player may disrupt the playing system which forms the long-term plan for the entire team, because an exactly comparable replacement will simply not exist. So, it is argued, the transfer system offers some degree of protection to a club that does not want to lose the key to its carefully planned collective system. This protects the integrity of the competition more generally.

All three explanations are delivered from the perspective of the club, the employer, and, arguably, from the perspective of the sport more generally. The immediate interests of players as employees are here set aside. Athletes in a sport which operates a transfer system are plainly allowed less freedom to choose their employer than are employees in a normal industry. And the transfer system is based on the transfer of money between clubs, as employers, which otherwise would have been available to swell the players' salaries. The transfer system depresses wages, and an athlete's career is short.

As Johan Cruyff is reported to have said, reflecting on the footballer's need to maximize income while pursuing a career as a player that is typically unlikely to last much beyond his 30th birthday: 'When my career ends, I cannot go to the baker and say I'm Johan Cruyff, give me some bread.'[2] In fact this is not true. Certainly in the Netherlands and probably in many other countries too, Johan Cruyff would, until his death in March 2016, have been showered with bread—and cake too—in most, if not all, bakeries, at least if the baker is old enough to remember the brilliant Dutch team at the 1974 World Cup and the imperious Ajax Amsterdam side that won the European Cup in 1971, 1972, and 1973. But most players, who do not share Cruyff's glittering genius, would not be so honoured. They would have to pay

---

[2] Quoted in D Winner, *Brilliant Orange: The Neurotic Genius of Dutch Football* (Bloomsbury 2001) 19.

for their bread. For them a career as a footballer is short, and money that they do not earn because of the existence of a transfer system is money they are denied as they plan for life after their short spell working as a professional sportsman.

Money that in normal circumstances would be received by an employee in wages instead goes to clubs as a transfer fee. On the account presented by clubs and governing bodies the money is designed to support the training of future talent and to achieve a degree of redistribution among clubs, to address financial and sporting inequality. On a more sceptical reading, what is happening is the privileging of employer interests over those of employees. And this occurs in a way that certainly would not even be contemplated among bakers, bankers, supermarket workers, and University teachers.

In truth, the explanations that have been advanced to justify the transfer system are largely post hoc rationalizations. The system has its roots in the early years of the development of the sport when the relationship between employers and employees generally was far removed from that of today. The football authorities enforced a transfer system which protected the interest of owners at the expense of players, largely because they could: it was simply a reflection of the gross asymmetry of power between employers and employees.

As briefly introduced in Chapter 4, the transfer system dates back to the nineteenth century and the first wave of imposing order and organization on sport which, in the wake of the industrial revolution, occurred in the United Kingdom. Its emergence was connected to the rise of professional status and an associated concern to standardize regulation of the game.[3] The basic model of the transfer system rests on each player being registered with a football club, in addition to having a normal contract of employment with that club. He or, of more recent significance, she cannot play for another football club, even if that other club is willing to offer a better deal, unless in addition the registration is transferred from the first club to the new club. And the typical incentive provided to the first club to agree to transfer of the registration (and in effect if not in form the player) is payment of a fee to the first club. The point is that footballers are treated differently from ordinary employees in other sectors, whose status depends on contract negotiation and is not affected by collectively agreed and enforced arrangements of the type found in professional football. This has the perfectly straightforward consequence that players are in a relatively poor bargaining position when compared with employees in other sectors. They cannot pick and choose their employer by bringing a contract to an end in accordance with its terms and concluding a new one: they cannot even break a contract, suffer the consequences stipulated by applicable employment law, and conclude a new one. They must attend also to the demands and constraints of the transfer system. The organizational structure of the sport limits their freedom while ensuring a generous advantage, compared to normal industries, to the economic

---

[3] See eg D McArdle, *From Boot Money to Bosman: Football, Society and the Law* (Cavendish 2000); J Magee, 'When is a Contract More than a Contract? Professional Football Contracts and the Pendulum of Power' (2006) 4 ESLJ <http://www.entsportslawjournal.com/articles/10.16997/eslj.89/> accessed 29 November 2016.

position of the first club as employer. Footballers are treated profoundly differently from ordinary employees.[4]

Even today, although the rigidity of the transfer system has been relaxed over time, one hears an echo of these Victorian-era assumptions as players are commonly referred to as 'servants' of a club, a label that would never be attached to sausage-makers or car-makers or providers of financial services. In 2008, at a time when he was widely suspected to be eager to leave Manchester United and play for Real Madrid (a move which was eventually completed a year later) the star Portuguese player, Cristiano Ronaldo, attracted indignation and ridicule for comparing his position to that of a slave.[5] This was doubtless a tasteless exaggeration: but the relationship between the player and the club is, as a consequence of the industry-wide grip exercised through the transfer system, an echo of hierarchical labour practices of the distant past which, in normal industries, have long been discarded, albeit sometimes only after a struggle. In similar vein it is common to hear footballer's wages decried as excessive, even obscene, or, a slightly more subtle but still scornful variant, to suggest that restrictions such as the transfer system should be of no concern to individuals who are so well paid. At least until the economic crisis of 2008 it was rare to hear any such concern directed at highly-paid bankers or hedge fund managers and even today criticism is muted. There is a mean-spirited and elitist sense that working-class men should think themselves lucky to be able to afford to buy good bread.

9.3 Challenging the Transfer System: George Eastham

In the United Kingdom, the original home of professional football, the decision of the English High Court in 1963 in *Eastham v Newcastle United* found unlawful a system which had in barely modified form existed since the nineteenth century.[6] This had allowed a club not simply to demand a transfer fee but also to 'retain' the player if an acceptable fee were not offered by another club and, in certain circumstances, not to pay him at all. This demonstrated an immense imbalance and could and did force players out of the game to seek employment elsewhere even where another football club wanted to offer employment: Eastham brought his case because Newcastle United's intransigence had had precisely this effect on him.

Eastham may seem like very ancient history, but it is not, because, as will be explored, it set the scene for *Bosman* in Luxembourg over thirty years later, and it still has resonance today, given that a form of the transfer system endures in football

---

[4] The matter does not concern football alone: see eg S Greenfield, 'The Ties that Bind: Charting Contemporary Sporting Contractual Relations' in S Greenfield and G Osborn (eds), *Law and Sport in Contemporary Society* (Frank Cass 2000) ch 8.

[5] 'I Am a Slave, Says Ronaldo as He Pushes for Madrid Move' *The Guardian* (London, 11 July 2008) <http://www.theguardian.com/football/2008/jul/11/manchesterunited.premierleague1> accessed 29 November 2016.

[6] [1964] Ch 413. See S Boyes, 'Eastham v Newcastle United FC' in J Anderson (ed), *Leading Cases in Sports Law* (TMC Asser 2013) ch 5.

which remains of legally questionable status. The judgment of Wilberforce J in the case tells a story with a strong flavour of a nineteenth-century master and servant relationship. He notes a maximum wage, applicable at the time of the dispute although abandoned by the time *Eastham* was decided, which was fixed within the industry at £20 per week during the football season. It is commonplace nowadays to read of top footballers being paid £200,000 a week. Wilberforce J in the High Court found that the 'retain' element of the system amounted to an unreasonable restraint of trade and that it was therefore contrary to the English common law. The objection was that it went too far in prioritizing employer interests over those of the employee.

The court did not rule against the possible application of *any* form of collectively agreed and enforced transfer system. Wilberforce J was prepared to take the view that the system 'provides a means by which the poorer clubs can on occasions, obtain money, enabling them to stay in existence and improve their facilities' and more generally 'it provides a means by which clubs can part with a good player in a manner which will enable them to secure a replacement'.[7] He did not declare explicitly how a revised system should be shaped: this would go beyond the judicial function in a restraint of trade case. But he clearly left room in his explanation of the role of the restraint of trade doctrine for football's governing bodies to devise a system that was less rigid and more balanced. A revised system focusing on the payment of a fee in return for an agreement to transfer a player's registration, while ameliorating the player's position to some extent by suppressing the ability of the first club simply to retain the registration and in practice drive the footballer out of his chosen profession, was accordingly crafted in the wake of the ruling.

In this way a revised system lived on after the *Eastham* decision in the summer of 1963. This was the road that led eventually to *Bosman* over thirty years later in the Court of Justice in Luxembourg.[8] The rulings deserve to be considered as a pair, even if they arise in different legal orders and concern transfer regimes that are not identical, because of the striking similarity between the arguments advanced and largely rejected in *Eastham* and those deployed later in *Bosman*. In *Eastham* the club and the Football League sought to defend the transfer system on the basis that 'If a player could do just as he liked at the end of the football season, the wealthier clubs would at once snap up the best players'.[9] This is best summarized as an argument for the transfer system to serve as a means to achieve *balance* in sport. The claim that 'All professional football leagues elsewhere in the world have the combined retention and transfer system or one that amounts to it, which shows that it has the unqualified approval of those best fitted to judge'[10] is an argument rooted in expertise: sport knows best, and judges should keep out. The supplementary submission that 'In considering the system as a whole, it should be borne in mind that the present system, based on a stable league, does secure benefits to players which a smaller organisation might not be able to secure'[11] is nothing more than an

---

[7] *Eastham* (n 6) 437.   [8] *Bosman* (n 1).   [9] *Eastham* (n 6) 424.
[10] ibid 424.   [11] ibid 425.

obstinate refusal to imagine that the sporting world could ever be different. In fact this final claim carries a deeply unpleasant sense that players should do as they are told and stop complaining, and it was rightly treated as inapt to defend the practices challenged in the case.

In short, these interventions taken in combination put forward one central claim—that sport should be granted autonomy from legal regulation. That was the core of the case made in defence of the transfer system in *Bosman* too. In fact, much of what was argued in *Eastham* was recycled in *Bosman*. It was dismissed in both cases in a way that was not precisely in line, because restraint of trade under the English common law does not exactly match EU free movement law. However, the rejection was thematically consistent. Both tribunals concluded that, however special football might be, it is not so special that it can claim a justification to maintain a system as restrictive and burdensome as that at stake in the cases. It is to *Bosman* that attention now turns.

9.4 Challenging the Transfer System: Jean-Marc Bosman

In the EU it was the litigation in *Bosman* that finally brought the matter before the gaze of the Court of Justice in Luxembourg.[12] *Eastham* focused on the English game. *Bosman* had a more international dimension. The background was provided by the network of governance populated by clubs, national associations and, continental associations—in Europe, the Union of European Football Associations (UEFA)—and, at the apex of the organizational pyramid, Fédération Internationale de Football Association (FIFA), the world organizing body, which is based in Switzerland. Footballers, contracted to their club as employees, are subject to the rules decided within this system of governance: the rule-makers are at the top of the organizational pyramid, the players at the base.

Chapter 4 told the story of how Jean-Marc Bosman, a Belgian national employed in his home country as a footballer, came to rely on EU law when prevented from joining a new employer, a French football club, Dunkerque. As there explained, even though his contract of employment with RC Liège had come to an end, he was not free to enter into a new contract of employment with a new employer until such time as approval for the transfer of his registration had been given. Typically this would entail payment of a transfer fee by the new club to the old—the size of the fee would vary in rough association with the quality and age of the player. Plainly no such obstruction would affect an employee in a normal industry. But sport is special; football is different. Since the relevant transfer of registration from the Belgian to the French club did not occur, Bosman was unable to join his prospective new club. Indeed, in the absence of compliance with the transfer regulations imposed collectively within the sport, Dunkerque would not have been able to select him to play without being subject to prompt, collectively enforced sanctions. It is exactly

---

[12] *Bosman* (n 1).

here that football operates in a way that cannot be traced elsewhere. The process of contractual negotiation between employer and employee occurs in the shadow of the wider network of horizontal and vertical arrangements governing the player's status, enforced through the *lex sportiva*. Rules made and applied through the collective network of governance—the pyramid with FIFA at its apex—cut across contractual negotiation. Footballers are less free than ordinary workers in choosing their employer.

The Court found that Bosman had been victim of a violation of what was then Article 48 of the Treaty Establishing the European Economic Community (EEC), today Article 45 of the Treaty on the Functioning of the European Union (TFEU), the Treaty provision dealing with the free movement of workers. The Court did not deny that sport is special. Quite the contrary. But sport was not special enough to protect such an extremely restrictive system from the condemnation of EU law. The operative part of the ruling finds that it is incompatible with EU law to provide that a professional footballer who is a national of one Member State may not, on the expiry of his contract with a club, be employed by a club of another Member State unless the latter club has paid to the former club a transfer, training, or development fee. In this sense *Bosman* has close structural similarities with the ruling in *Eastham*. There is an acceptance that sport is special—but not as special as was assumed by the governing bodies. So a transfer system could feasibly survive—but not the transfer system attacked in the case, which was too restrictive. So in *Bosman*, just as over thirty years earlier in *Eastham*, the judges left it to the governing bodies in sport to respond to the demands of the law by reducing and reshaping the *lex sportiva*.

The centrally important paragraph in *Bosman* is paragraph 106, in which the Court declared:

In view of the considerable social importance of sporting activities and in particular football in the Community, the aims of maintaining a balance between clubs by preserving a certain degree of equality and uncertainty as to results and of encouraging the recruitment and training of young players must be accepted as legitimate.

Chapter 4 explores the importance of this declaration at a general level: it set the tone for extracting from a barren Treaty background an acceptance that the interpretation of EU law shall be sensitive to the sporting context and, as articulated in particular in Chapter 7, it is a source of the commitment to 'the specific nature of sport' now found in Article 165 TFEU. The concern in this chapter is more concrete. What precisely does this concession to the social importance of sporting activities entail in the shaping of a transfer system that can withstand scrutiny conducted in the name of EU law?

That examination now follows. However, a final observation on the *Bosman* ruling itself is deserved. It is the starting point of modern EU sports law. *Walrave and Koch* in 1974 was the first decision of the Court dealing with the intersection of EU law and sport, but its ripples were intellectual rather than practical in significance.[13]

---

[13] Case 36/74 *Walrave and Koch v Union Cycliste Internationale* [1974] ECR 1405. See Ch 4.2.

Sport resisted any litigious torrent. *Bosman*, by contrast, was the springboard to a far more juridicalized landscape in European sport, in association with a far more commercialized landscape (most of all in the sphere of broadcasting: Chapter 11). Given the transformative practical effect of *Bosman*, it is remarkable to note with hindsight how the governing bodies in football seemed to sleepwalk into *Bosman*. The arguments presented were thin. As mentioned in Chapter 4.6 the impression is that the governing bodies assumed Bosman would be induced or intimidated to settle the matter out of court. Moreover, in November 1995, a month before the Court ruled, UEFA had requested the Court to order a measure of inquiry under its Rules of Procedure with a view to obtaining fuller information on the role played by transfer fees in the financing of small or medium-sized football clubs.[14] But the Court dismissed this application. It was made at a time when, in accordance with the Rules of Procedure, the oral procedure was closed. UEFA was foolishly late. One would do well to improve on the following as a pointedly critical summary of the complacent and self-regarding attitude of the governing bodies in the sport:

> … it was said that this system, the combined system of registration, retention and transfer fees, or something like it, is operated in all professional leagues and has been so operated for a long time. This is claimed as evidence that those who know best consider it to be in the general interest of the game. I do not accept this line of argument. The system is an employers' system, set up in an industry where the employers have succeeded in establishing a united monolithic front all over the world, and where it is clear that for the purpose of negotiation the employers are vastly more strongly organised than the employees. No doubt the employers all over the world consider the system a good system, but this does not prevent the court from considering whether it goes further than is reasonably necessary to protect their legitimate interests …

Perfectly judged—and yet this rebuke was not aimed at the arguments advanced in *Bosman* at all. It is in fact an extract from the judgment of Wilberforce J in *Eastham v Newcastle United* in 1964, over thirty years before *Bosman*.[15] The feature to note is continuity. The same dogged and shabbily reasoned arguments advanced without success in *Eastham* were recycled in *Bosman*—without success. In *Bosman*, as in *Eastham*, the background assumption of the governing bodies was that one way or another the *lex sportiva* would prevail. But it did not.

9.5 The Legal and Economic Implications of the *Bosman* Ruling: Contract Negotiation and 'Player Power'

Bosman required the abolition of a system that required payment of a transfer fee by the new club not only where the player remained in contract with the former club but also even where the player's contract with his previous club had expired. The sole concession made by the Court to the alarm expressed by the

---

[14] *Bosman* (n 1) paras 52–54.   [15] *Eastham* (n 6) 439.

governing bodies about the effects of such an intervention was to concede that for reasons of legal certainty a claim could not be brought relating to a fee which had already been paid or was already payable unless the claim had already been lodged at the time of the *Bosman* ruling.[16] But clearly for the future the system had to change: the transfer system could no longer be used to affect the freedom of choice and earning capacity of a player whose contract of employment had come to an end. The footballer whose contract had ended was placed by *Bosman* in the same position as any other worker whose contract has come to an end. He or she can negotiate new terms with a new employer. And so it quickly became common to refer to an out-of-contract player being 'on a Bosman': which means only that, like a car-maker or a banker, the footballer is free to choose a new employer without any regard for the concerns of the employer with whom his or her contractual agreement has reached an end.

The diminution in scope of the transfer system which followed the *Bosman* ruling led immediately to significant commercial consequences within the industry. Money that would previously have been paid by one club to another when an out-of-contract player was transferred was now available for other purposes, most of all to increase the wages offered to the player to entice him or her to enter into a new contract. The player would now be able to negotiate to seek to gain a share of the sum that would previously have gone to the previous club.

It happened quickly. Precisely this pattern could be identified over the summer of 1996. 'Out-of-contract' players were able to secure better deals by joining clubs in other Member States and obtaining part of the pot that would otherwise have been grabbed by the previous club as a transfer fee. The player's previous club had now lost the entitlement guaranteed it under the transfer system condemned by the Court in *Bosman*. John Collins, the Scottish midfield player whose most famous moment arrived in 1998 when he scored for his country against Brazil in the opening match of the World Cup Finals in France, changed club in the summer of 1996. He left Glasgow Celtic for Monaco, despite interest from English sides. He commented: 'I was going to cost an English team £3 million whereas Monaco could get me for nothing'.[17] The crucial factor was that moving from Scotland to England is cross-border in football terms, but it is not cross-border in the context of the EU. But moving from Scotland to France triggers the necessary cross-border element which brings EU free movement law into play and allowed John Collins, as a player out-of-contract, to take immediate advantage of the path broken by Jean-Marc Bosman. Celtic took its claim for compensation to the CAS, but lost: the CAS ruling is based on the application of EU free movement law and it explicitly relies on the effect of *Bosman*.[18] The amount of wages the player could command would be favourably affected by the £3 million that thanks to EU law Monaco had *not* had to pay Celtic, though of course exactly how much of that sum he could trouser

---

[16] *Bosman* (n 1) paras 139–46.
[17] 'Collins Primed to Lead by Example' *The Independent* (London, 9 October 1996) 30.
[18] CAS 98/201 *Celtic v UEFA*, award of 7 January 2000. On the CAS, see Ch 2.

would depend on the skill of those representing him in contract negotiations with his new club.

Out-of-contract players were placed in a stronger negotiating position by *Bosman*. This, it should immediately be noted, did no more than bring the position of the footballer as an employee closer to that of *any* employee who chooses to change employer in conformity with his or her contractual rights and obligations. In principle, one would expect player wages to rise simply because the pot is swelled by money that would otherwise have been paid to another club as a transfer fee. The precise effect post-*Bosman* could not possibly be measured. In part this is because clubs would doubtless do their best not simply to recycle *all* the money saved from abolition of transfer fees as wages: exactly how much would be so used would depend on the relative skills of contract negotiation between player representatives and clubs. Moreover, at the time, the mid- to late 1990s, one would anyway have expected player wages to rise, because sport's, and especially football's, money-making capacity was higher than it had ever been and increasing, principally as a result of the intensification of competition in broadcasting markets. This is addressed in Chapter 11 which, without denying the transformative significance of *Bosman*, shows that deregulation and technological advance in the broadcasting sector has been the principal source of enhanced commodification and juridification in sport.

Wages did rise quickly post-*Bosman*. For example, the wage bill at Tottenham Hotspur was reported to have risen by 20 per cent to £10 million a year as a result of renegotiation of contracts after the ruling.[19] An increase of £5 million was reported at Manchester United as a result of a restructuring of existing deals.[20] These adjustments to the nature of the relationship between players and clubs led in turn to alteration in the treatment of players as club assets for accountancy purposes.[21] Moreover, footballers were able to command fees for more than simply playing the game. Image rights and commercial sponsorship became an increasingly important part of the financial pattern of the game.[22] Football clubs are a brand: so are footballers.

But footballers had not been placed in *exactly* the same position as a typical employee. The transfer system applicable to players who were still under contract had not been addressed in *Bosman*. It lived on. A footballer under contract wishing to change employer would have to reckon with contract and employment law,

[19] 'Bosman Ruling Costs Spurs £7.3m' *The Independent* (London, 11 October 1996) 22 (£7.3m refers to adjustment of balance sheet value).

[20] 'United Wages Soar after Bosman' *The Independent* (London, 9 October 1996) 22.

[21] cf at the time P Morris, S Morrow, and P Spink, 'EC Law and Professional Football: *Bosman* and Its Implications' (1996) 59 MLR 893.

[22] See eg I Blackshaw, *Sports Marketing Agreements: Legal, Fiscal and Practical Aspects* (TMC Asser 2012); K Gordon, *Guide to the Tax Treatment of Specialist Occupations* (Bloomsbury 2012) ch 15; J Davis, 'Fame and Its Exploitation: The Legal Protection of Celebrity in the United Kingdom' in B Bogusz, A Cygan, and E Szyszczak (eds), *The Regulation of Sport in the European Union* (Edward Elgar 2007) ch 9; L Colantuoni and C Novazio, 'Intellectual Property Rights in Sports: A Comparative Overview of the USA, UK and Italy' and S Cornelius, 'Image Rights' in J Nafziger and S Ross (eds), *Handbook on International Sports Law* (Edward Elgar 2011) ch 15 and ch 17, respectively.

as would any employee, but the transfer system and the typical demand for a fee added an extra restraint on the player's freedom of action. So the player 'in contract' was more valuable to the club than the player out of contract. Clubs accordingly changed their own strategies. If a player could simply walk away once the contract expired—as a car-maker or a banker can walk away—then clubs had an incentive to keep players *in* contract so that, if it emerged that a player was determined to leave, the club could at least still, as before, enjoy the protection of the transfer system. So clubs shaped their strategies with the aim of tying players to longer contracts or to 'rolling' contracts (which automatically continue until a break-clause is activated).[23] The reported increase at Manchester United, mentioned earlier,[24] was explicitly tied to contracting on a longer-term basis. To induce players to sign such a deal the club would typically need to provide an incentive. Higher wages offer the most obvious method, although there are other supplementary strategies too, such as offering loyalty bonuses that become more lucrative the longer the player stays at a club. This is not so very different from the normal labour market, but football remained different because of the transfer system's application to players 'in contract'. In fact refining incentives for sportsmen and sportswomen, especially in team sports, is something of an art in its own right.[25] Loyalty bonuses and contracts that are automatically renewed have a role, but so too performance-related pay has appeal as a means of allowing owners to call poorly performing players to account for losses incurred and also, if well balanced, as a means to induce players to exceed their norm. On the other hand, offering individual-focused rewards in a team sport may be unwise. For example, paying a striker by goals may discourage him from passing; paying a defender by clean sheets may discourage him from coming forward to the extent required by the team.[26]

9.6 Olivier Bernard: Confirming the Favourable Approach in Principle of EU Law to the Transfer System

The first opportunity since *Bosman* to review aspects of the transfer system reached the Court in 2010. It was *Olympique Lyonnais v Olivier Bernard, Newcastle United*.[27] Once again, as in *Bosman*, the Court chose to show a receptivity to the claim that sport is special and that, in particular, this may be reflected in the existence of a

---

[23] See eg B Frick and R Simmons, 'The Footballers' Labour Market after the Bosman Ruling' in J Goddard and P Sloane (eds), *Handbook on the Economics of Professional Football* (Edward Elgar 2014) ch 13; B Buraimo, B Frick, M Hickfang, and R Simmons, 'The Economics of Long-term Contracts in the Footballers' Labour Market' (2015) 62 Scottish Journal of Political Economy 8.

[24] See n 20.

[25] See eg F Carmichael and D Thomas, 'Team Performance: Production and Efficiency in Football' in J Goddard and P Sloane (eds), *Handbook on the Economics of Professional Football* (Edward Elgar 2014) ch 10.

[26] Ian Lynam, 'In the Financial Fair Play Era Clubs Must Pay Smart, Not Pay More' *Financial Times* (London, 11 June 2013) 47. On 'Financial Fair Play' (FFP), see Ch 10.9.

[27] *Bernard* (n 1).

transfer system which imposes collectively agreed and enforced restraints on the contractual freedom of individual workers; but, following *Bosman*, it refused to accept that the particular system under attack could be maintained.

Olivier Bernard was a young French footballer under contract to Olympique Lyonnais, one of the most prominent clubs in French professional football. He was a 'joueur espoir', which means a player between the ages of 16 and 22 who is employed as a trainee under a fixed-term contract. The term of the contract in Bernard's case was three years. Before the expiry of that contract Olympique Lyonnais offered him a professional contract which would have lasted one year. Bernard rejected that offer. Instead he accepted an offer of a contract to play for Newcastle United in England.

Controversy and ultimately litigation arose because what Bernard had chosen to do was in contravention of the French 'Charter', *charte du football professionnel*, which governed the employment of footballers in France at the time. The Charter required a 'joueur espoir' to sign his first professional contract with the club that had trained him, provided the club wished to offer him a contract. The club had, in effect, an option to buy, designed to reflect and reward the investment already made in training the young player. The Charter did not provide for the payment of compensation in the event that the player refused to agree to sign a contract, but it did envisage that in such circumstances the club which had provided the training could bring an action for damages against the 'joueur espoir' under the French *code du travail* for breach of the contractual obligations set out in the Charter. Olympique Lyonnais, deprived of the player as a result of his decision to move to England, followed this route. A tribunal in Lyon found that Bernard had committed a unilateral breach of contract contrary to the Charter. It therefore ordered Bernard and Newcastle United jointly to pay damages of €22,867,35.

The *Cour d'appel* in Lyon set that judgment aside. It relied on EU law. It ruled that the French system under the Charter restricted the player's freedom to choose his contracting partner once his training was complete, in violation of what was then Article 39 of the Treaty Establishing the European Community (EC), now Article 45 TFEU, governing the free movement of workers. Olympique Lyonnais appealed against that decision. The French *Cour de Cassation* then made a preliminary reference to Luxembourg in July 2008. It asked whether the Treaty, in particular the provision governing free movement of workers, covered the situation. This was the easy part. It obviously did. The award of damages in the circumstances that had arisen, as foreseen by the Charter, served to discourage and was intended to discourage a player from exercising a right of free movement. But the court, referring to the *Bosman* ruling,[28] also asked a more difficult question. It asked the Court of Justice whether the need to encourage the recruitment and training of young professional players constituted a legitimate objective or an overriding reason in the general interest which was capable of justifying the French scheme.

---

[28] *Bosman* (n 1).

This provided the Court with its first opportunity to address the application of EU law to sport since the entry into force of the Lisbon Treaty in 2009 and the arrival of the sports-specific competence which is Article 165 TFEU. However, as explained in Chapter 7.2, the Court in *Bernard* showed no inclination to allow any deflection from the pattern of the case law which had steadily accumulated over the previous years. The Court cited both *Bosman* and *Meca-Medina and Majcen v Commission* and, embracing 'the specific characteristics of sport in general, and football in particular, and of their social and educational function',[29] treated the relevance of those factors as 'corroborated' by their mention in the second sub-paragraph of Article 165(1) TFEU.[30] This is a statement of continuity. The Court reached its conclusion in *Bernard* with reference to its own case law, most of all *Bosman*, and only then does it mention the Lisbon Treaty.

The Court, finding that Bernard's situation fell for examination in the light of Article 45 TFEU on the free movement of workers, proceeded to an analysis that was conventional and familiar. As explained in Chapter 4, Article 45 is interpreted to control not only the actions of public authorities but also rules of any other nature aimed at regulating employment in a collective manner, and accordingly the French Charter on which the claim against Bernard was founded was subject to review. As the *Cour de Cassation* had correctly recognized, the Charter tended to discourage the exercise of a player's right of free movement by granting an option over the player to the club which had provided training. The Court agreed with Olympique Lyonnais that 'such rules do not formally prevent the player from signing a professional contract with a club in another Member State' and in fact that is exactly what had happened, but the rules make 'the exercise of that right less attractive'.[31]

The Court then turned to the matter of justification. Could the French scheme governing 'joueurs espoir' be justified, despite its restrictive effect on labour mobility within the EU and despite the absence of any such scheme in normal labour markets. The Court asserted continuity in its case law by once again citing *Bosman* in explaining that:

> A measure which constitutes an obstacle to freedom of movement for workers can be accepted only if it pursues a legitimate aim compatible with the Treaty and is justified by overriding reasons in the public interest. Even if that were so, application of that measure would still have to be such as to ensure achievement of the objective in question and not go beyond what is necessary for that purpose ...[32]

This is not a sports-specific concession. As explained in Chapter 7, it is an orthodox statement of EU internal market trade law generally. In this vein Advocate General Sharpston, writing a particularly thoughtful and helpful opinion in *Bernard*,

---

[29] *Bernard* (n 1) para 40.
[30] ibid para 40 of the judgment. French: corroborée; the German version is differently structured: Für die Relevanz dieser Faktoren spricht außerdem ihre Erwähnung in Art. 165 Abs. 1 Unterabs. 2 AEUV.
[31] ibid para 36.   [32] ibid para 38 of the judgment.

explained that the specific characteristics of sport must 'be considered carefully when examining possible justifications for any such restriction—just as the specific characteristics of any other sector would need to be borne in mind when examining the justification of restrictions applicable in that sector'.[33] The Court's judgment, in assessing the justification of the French practice, then turned to the particular context of professional sport. It confirmed what it had articulated almost fifteen years earlier in the famous and centrally important paragraph 106 of *Bosman*, that:

> … in view of the considerable social importance of sporting activities and in particular football in the European Union, the objective of encouraging the recruitment and training of young players must be accepted as legitimate.[34]

So the *end* is permitted; what matters is whether the *means* used are suitable to attain that end and do not go beyond what is necessary to attain it.

The Court accepted that 'the prospect of receiving training fees is likely to encourage football clubs to seek new talent and train young players' and once again it explicitly cited *Bosman*.[35] So in principle there is room for a system that encourages the training of young players. But—in line with *Bosman*—it proceeded to find that the scheme under examination could not meet the demands of EU law. The Court acknowledged that a club's returns on investments in training are necessarily uncertain. Some you win, most you lose—only a minority of players proceeds to a professional career at the end of the training period. In any event there is no precise co-relation between costs incurred in training and benefits accruing to the club providing the training. The Court was persuaded that clubs might be discouraged from investing in the training of young players if they could not obtain reimbursement of the amounts spent for that purpose where a player moves on to another club at the end of the period of training. It expressed a particular concern in this light for *small* clubs 'whose investments at local level in the recruitment and training of young players are of considerable importance for the social and educational function of sport'.[36] So a scheme providing for the payment of compensation for training where a young player changes club at the end of his training 'can, in principle, be justified by the objective of encouraging the recruitment and training of young players'.[37]

But the Court objected to the system of which Bernard had fallen foul. At stake was *not* compensation for training, but instead damages for breach of contract. It focused on the point that the amount was unrelated to the training costs actually incurred by the club.[38] Instead the amount was calculated in relation to the total loss suffered by the club; moreover, the amount was established on the basis of criteria which were not determined in advance. This prompted the Court to treat the system as going 'beyond what was necessary to encourage recruitment and training of young players and to fund those activities'.[39] It was in breach of Article 45 TFEU.

---

[33] ibid para 30, Opinion of Sharpston AG.   [34] ibid para 39.
[35] ibid 41, citing *Bosman* (n 1) para 108.   [36] ibid para 44.
[37] ibid para 45.   [38] ibid para 46.   [39] ibid para 48.

Bernard, like *Bosman* before it, reveals a generous receptivity to professional sport's claim that it needs a scheme whereby training costs can be recouped as a means to promote incentives to invest in training, even if the result is that a player's exercise of contractual freedom and right to move between Member States is affected in a way that would not be tolerated in a normal industry. Sport is special. *Bernard,* like *Bosman* before it, finds the particular system under review to be too restrictive and poorly designed. The 'specific nature of sport' announced by Article 165 TFEU is capable of framing this analysis but it does not change anything. Sport is not special *enough* to justify treating the French system of 'joueur espoir' as compatible with EU law.

The Court having in *Bernard* accepted that a compensation scheme (re-)designed to reward clubs that invest in training may be accepted under EU law, it rested with the football authorities (in France) to decide what to do. But the Court, though in formal terms confined to ruling on whether the chosen and challenged practices comply with EU law and not competent to provide a quasi-legislative blueprint for a revised transfer system, offered clues (as it frequently does).[40] A compensation scheme must be capable of attaining the objective of encouraging the recruitment and training of young players and be proportionate to it, 'taking due account of the costs borne by the clubs in training both future professional players and those who will never play professionally'.[41] This is slightly evasive on the question how far compensation may cover costs incurred beyond the case of the trained player alone. The more one chooses to read *Bernard* as requiring that compensation be closely tied to, or even limited to, the costs incurred in training a particular player, the less 'special' football is permitted to be—and the less comfortable the governing authorities in sport will doubtless feel. Probably, however, the ruling is best interpreted to mean that the compensation payable by those who succeed as professionals should be inflated beyond the costs incurred in their particular case to allow also some coverage of training costs incurred but wasted on those players who fall by the wayside. The calculation is any event complicated by the practical reality that players are trained in groups, not individually: the cost of training twenty players is lower than the cost of training one multiplied by twenty thanks to the realization of economies of scale.

Bernard provides an authoritative judicial statement that *some* kind of system which compensates clubs which invest in youth training may be devised in compliance with EU law. This, it should be noted, is in line with earlier political and policy statements.

The Nice Declaration on Sport lauds training policies for young sportsmen and sportswomen as 'the life blood of sport' and adds that sports federations 'are justified in taking the action needed to preserve the training capacity of clubs affiliated

---

[40] For comment, see J Lindholm, 'Annotation' (2010) 47 CML Rev 1187; K Pijetlovic, 'Another Classic of EU Sports Jurisprudence' (2010) 35 EL Rev 857; S Weatherill, 'The Olivier Bernard Case: How, If At All, to Fix Compensation for Training Young Players?' (2010) 10(1–2) Intl Sports LJ 3; B Eichel, 'Anmerkung' (2010) 45 Europarecht 685.

[41] *Bernard* (n 1) para 45, citing *Bosman* (n 1) para 109.

to them and to ensure the quality of such training'.[42] It also has a special section dedicated to the transfer system, although it does not offer concrete approval but rather expresses the European Council's keen support for 'dialogue on the transfer system between the sports movement, in particular the football authorities, organisations representing professional sportsmen and -women, the Community and the Member States, with due regard for the specific requirements of sport, subject to compliance with Community law'.[43]

The 2007 Commission White Paper on Sport mentions discussions in 2001 between the Commission and the football authorities in connection with the revision of the FIFA Regulations on international football transfers.[44] It declares that the Commission 'considers such a system to constitute an example of good practice that ensures a competitive equilibrium between sport clubs while taking into account the requirements of EU law'.[45]

The 2011 Commission Staff Working Document, 'Sport and Free Movement' offers specific comment on *Bernard*.[46] It notes that the Court confirmed what had already been decided in *Bosman*, that the recruitment and training of young players is to be considered a legitimate objective of general interest. It added that the Court had ruled that such schemes must be related to the actual cost of training players. The Commission went rather further than the Court in setting out an explicit view on whether the costs of training should cover those borne by the clubs in training both future professional players and those who will never play professionally, although it claimed to be simply following the Court. It is claimed that:

The Court affirmed hereby the principle that training costs may be calculated on the basis of the so-called 'player factor', i.e. the number of players that need to be trained in order to produce a professional player.[47]

As mentioned earlier, this is probably the correct understanding of *Bernard*. Were compensation confined exclusively to the costs of training players who succeed in developing a professional career, the inducement to clubs to invest in training would be small and uncertain. But the Court did not spell that out as clearly as the Commission claims in its 2011 Communication.

In similar but slightly more cautious vein the Commission has, in an answer to a question put by an MEP, commented that 'training compensation schemes may be considered compatible with EU free movement rules insofar as compensation is related to the actual cost of training'.[48]

---

[42] Nice Declaration on Sport, para 11. The full text is at <http://eur-lex.europa.eu/legal-content/EN/TXT/?uri=URISERV:l35007> accessed 29 November 2016. See Ch 6.3.

[43] ibid paras 16–17.

[44] White Paper on Sport, COM (2007) 391, 11 July 2007, available via <http://ec.europa.eu/sport/index_en.htm> accessed 29 November 2016. See Ch 6.5.

[45] ibid section 4.3, p 15.

[46] Staff Working Document, 'Sport and Free Movement' SEC (2011) 66 <http://ec.europa.eu/sport/news/doc/communication/communication_en.pdf> accessed 29 November 2016.

[47] ibid 6.

[48] Question for written answer E-007477/12, Peter Simon: answer given by Ms Vassilou on behalf of the Commission, 4 September 2012 [2013] OJ C270E/68.

In 2014 the European Club Association published its own a 'Study on the Transfer System in Europe'.[49] Given the source of this study, it is not a surprise that it takes a favourable view of the transfer system. It treats it as part of a system that ensures the redistribution of income from top to bottom and so it acts as a counter-weight to competitive imbalance. This approval is rather uncritical, but much the same can be said of the Court's general positive view of the concept of a transfer system in both *Bosman* and *Bernard*.

9.7 Beyond *Bosman*

Bosman concerned only the application of the transfer system to the out-of-contract player who is an EU national wishing to move from a club in one Member State to another. *Bernard* too involved a player whose (fixed-term, three-year) contract had come to an end. And in both cases the Court addressed free movement law alone. However, after *Bosman* attention had quickly turned to just how much of the rest of the transfer system might be endangered at law, were *Bosman* to be exploited beyond its particular context. It was quickly predicted that on at least three points one could anticipate attempts by eager litigants to stretch *Bosman* beyond its relatively narrow factual and legal matrix and to exploit EU law to achieve an even greater relaxation of the transfer system to the benefit of players.[50]

First, in formal terms, the ruling did not touch circumstances that were internal to a Member State—a French player moving from one French club to another French club or, in the peculiar case of the United Kingdom, a single state for EU purposes but home to four separate members of UEFA and FIFA, a transfer between England and Wales or Scotland and Northern Ireland. For the purposes of free movement law this would be a situation purely internal to a single Member State and so the necessary jurisdictional trigger of EU law, the cross-border dimension, would be missing. It was, however, not difficult to summon the dog that didn't bark in the Court's ruling in *Bosman*, EU competition law, in order to imagine a way for EU law to exercise control over circumstances of this type. Even before *Bosman* there were decisions subjecting football to EU competition law,[51] and in his Opinion

---

[49] European Club Association, 'Study on the Transfer System in Europe', available via <http://www.ecaeurope.com/news/european-club-association-publishes-study-on-the-transfer-system-in-europe/> accessed 29 November 2016.

[50] eg S Weatherill, 'Annotation of the European Court's ruling in *Bosman*' (1996) 33 CML Rev 991; D O'Keeffe and P Osborn, 'The European Court Scores a Goal' (1996) 12 International Journal of Comparative Labour Law and Industrial Relations 111; M Uilhoorn, 'The Bosman Case: Freedom of Movement for Sports Players and Its Implications' [1998] European Current Law (October) xi; G Campogrande, 'Les règles de concurrence et les entreprises sportives professionnelles après l'arrêt *Bosman*' [1996] RMUE 45; M Thill, 'L'arrêt *Bosman* et ses implications pour la libre circulation des sportifs à l'intérieur de l'Union européenne dans des contexts factuels différents de ceux de l'affaire *Bosman*' [1996] RMUE 89; L Nyssen and X Denoël, 'La situation des ressortissants de pays tiers à la suite de l'arrêt *Bosman*' [1996] RMUE 119; M Hilf and E Pache, 'Das Bosman-Urteil des EuGH: Zur Geltung der EG-Grundfreiheiten für den Berufsfussball' (1996) 18 NJW 1169.

[51] eg [1992] OJ L326/31, distribution of package tours for the 1990 World Cup incompatible with Article 85 [now TFEU, Art 101].

in *Bosman* Advocate General Lenz examined that aspect too. The Court did not, but the competition rules in this instance reach where the free movement rules do not. Put simply, if a club is forced to pay a transfer fee to a club in its own Member State in circumstances where it would not have to pay a fee to a club situated in another Member State, then there will be inevitable repercussions for the patterns of cross-border trade. A matter apparently purely internal to a state is in fact not of such limited effect on the EU's internal market. The distortive effect on the wider market of the transfer system as a horizontal agreement between clubs strengthened by the involvement of football's governing bodies brings it within the scope of application of Article 101(1) TFEU. This does not inevitably mean it will be unlawful but, translating the refusal in *Bosman* to endorse under free movement law the claimed need for a system that catches even out-of-contract players to the field of competition law, it probably would be treated as unlawful. In the determination of how 'special' sport truly is there seems no reason to adopt separate treatment of practices depending on whether they fall under Article 45 TFEU or Article 101 TFEU. This case is made in Chapter 7 with particular emphasis on the value of Article 165 TFEU's acceptance that sport has a 'specific nature' as a means to frame an integrated law of the internal market in application to sport.

Second, in formal terms, the ruling in *Bosman* dealt only with nationals of an EU Member State. It did not address the position of non-nationals, and most pertinently it did not inquire into the status of nationals of states, including other European states, with which the EU has association agreements and which were and are the source of plenty of good professional footballers. It therefore seemed highly plausible that the type of claim made by Bosman could not be limited to nationals of EU Member States alone. The general validity of this line of reasoning was subsequently confirmed by the Court in 2003 in its ruling in *Deutscher Handballbund eV v Maros Kolpak*.[52] A Slovak handball player sought to rely on the Association Agreement between the EU and Slovakia, which was not then a Member State, to defeat rules in Germany that discriminated against him on the basis of his nationality. The Court agreed with him, and repeated its refusal in *Bosman* to treat nationality discrimination at *club* level as permissible. The ruling is on its terms confined to claimants *already* lawfully employed by a club established in a Member State, so it does not fully align the position of the non-EU migrant to that privileged status of the national of a Member State. This approach was confirmed in *Igor Simutenkov*, which concerned a Russian national playing football in Spain.[53] Both cases are, however, a firm demonstration that *Bosman* has implications beyond the borders of the twenty-eight Member States. They would be pertinent too to athletes working in the United Kingdom were it to leave the EU and strike some type of association agreement to regulate its future trade relations with the EU twenty-seven.

---

[52] Case C-438/00 *Deutscher Handballbund eV v Maros Kolpak* [2003] ECR I-4135. See J-P Dubey, 'Annotation' (2005) 42 CML Rev 499.
[53] Case C-265/03 [2005] ECR I-2579.

Third, in formal terms the ruling in *Bosman* attacked only the transfer system in application to players whose contracts had expired. It did not address the application of the transfer system to players whose contracts were still on foot. This causes the sharp division noted previously which creates commercial incentives for clubs to avoid contracts for high-performing players coming to an end. However, it cannot be excluded that EU law can be used to attack the transfer system even in its narrowed down application to players who remain in contract. After all, the system exerts a restrictive effect on such players which is at its heart the same as that from which Bosman himself suffered—that is, the player must contend not only with the orthodox effects of contract and employment law but also with the collectively agreed and vigorously enforced transfer rules dictated by the *lex sportiva*. This is an obstacle with which no normal employee outside sport would have to contend. A transfer system applicable to players who are in contract is a system that is capable of restricting the free movement of workers and causing distortion of competition in the internal market, and for that reason it does not escape the application of EU law.

Football's governing bodies, having been forced by *Bosman* to scrap the transfer system as applied to out-of-contract players, were not inclined to go further and abandon it for all players. A renovated system lives on. But it may be legally vulnerable.

The renovated system now deserves consideration. Section 9.8 examines the transfer system as it has been rearranged in the light of *Bosman*. This is to some extent a moving target, both because it has been periodically amended by FIFA and UEFA and also because of the increasing prominence of the CAS in giving concrete shape to its meaning, but nonetheless its overall shape is readily identified and explained. The following analysis then places the system more fully in its legal context. Footballers' liberty is restricted by the transfer system in a way that does not apply generally to employees, but—so it seems in general discourse under EU law—football is special enough to justify such practices. That assumption is challenged. It is argued that both the justifications for the transfer system embraced by the Court in *Bosman* and in *Bernard* are in fact—in different ways—flawed. The argument is made that a different basis should be relied on to justify a transfer system, albeit that only a less restrictive version than the current model should be accepted within which other means are found to meet its professed objectives, particularly the redistribution of income. Put another way, sport is special, and so is the position of footballers as employees with unusually restricted capacity to change employer, but sport is not special enough to justify all aspects of the current regime to which footballers are uniquely subject.

9.8 The Renovated System

The Court in *Bosman* accepted that the transfer system pursued legitimate objectives,[54] but that the transfer system of which Bosman had fallen foul went too far,

---

[54] *Bosman* (n 1) especially para 106 of the judgment.

most obviously in its restraining effect even on players whose contracts had expired. The system was the subject of a thorough renovation. The process was naturally complex as the competing interests of freedom of choice for players, retention of contractual stability as an element in team-building and planning, and the concern to use fees for sold players as inducements to invest in youth training were played out in negotiation involving several actors.[55] The characteristic obstinacy of sports governing bodies remained evident and familiar shrieks of doom and dismay about the very idea of change were expressed from within the game.[56] Disagreement between UEFA and FIFA caused further wobbles in the process.[57] Moreover, the remarkable skill of sport in enlisting the support of prominent politicians was evident: Chancellor Schröder of Germany and Tony Blair, the UK Prime Minister, issued a Press Release in September 2000 expressing concern about the effects of reform and urging that the 'special situation that exists in professional soccer' be taken into account.[58]

The institutional arrangements established under the EU's founding Treaties mean that the Commission should, as an institution charged to ensure the application of the Treaties, stand above thinly reasoned political grandstanding of this type.[59] But this was the febrile environment within which the Commission became involved in the process. Troubled by the sluggish pace of reform post-*Bosman*, it sent a statement of objections to FIFA in December 1998. Plainly it had no power to direct the adoption of a particular model, rather, as a matter of form, it could only warn against the consequences of adopting a model which in its view would offend against EU law. In practice, this allowed it significant influence.

9.8.1 Eventual agreement

The negotiation of an adjusted transfer system acceptable to the governing bodies and to the Commission was successfully concluded in March 2001, when the Commission declared it had formalized the matter in an exchange of letters between Mr Monti, the Commissioner for Competition, and Sepp Blatter, President of FIFA.[60] In fact it was only later in 2001 that FIFPro, the players' union, was finally persuaded to add its support to the deal. Pending litigation was

---

[55] On the interplay of actors and ideas in crafting a new system, see D Dimitrakopoulos, 'More Than a market? The Regulation of Sport in the EU' (2006) 41 Government and Opposition 561. See also G Pearson, 'Sporting Justifications under EU Free Movement and Competition Law: The Case of the Football Transfer System' (2015) 21 ELJ 220, 223–26.

[56] eg 'Chaos Ahead in a World Without Transfers: The Chairman of Leeds Utd Says Whole Communities Could Suffer if an EU Proposal were to Succeed' *The Independent on Sunday* (London, 20 August 2000) Sports section, 5.

[57] eg 'Uefa Widens Rift with Fifa Over Transfers' *The Independent* (London, 16 January 2001) 26. See J Irving, 'Red Card: The Battle over European Football's Transfer System' (2001–02) 56 University of Miami Law Review 667, 693–709.

[58] Press Release No 425/00 of the German Government, 10 September 2000.

[59] TEU, Art 17. The same independence from direct political accountability is guaranteed to the Court by TEU, Art 19.

[60] IP/01/314, 5 March 2001. On this legally imprecise notion, see sect 9.10.

then settled and brought to an end, both in the context of proceedings initiated at national level[61] and in actions challenging the Commission's failure to investigate complaints about the transfer system.[62] The Commission announced closure of its own investigation in June 2002, on the basis that all interested parties had expressed satisfaction with it, and presenting it as striking a balance between players' free movement rights and contractual stability.[63]

Part of the background was certainly that the Commission had wearied of its attritional battle with politically savvy governing bodies. It was reluctant to invest further resources in probing the compatibility of the renovated system with EU law. It had, however, plainly extracted some movement towards change within the *lex sportiva*. The story is accurately understood as revealing a more horizontal process of cooperation than would be captured by a conventional depiction of the Commission standing above governing bodies and demanding their conformity with EU law. The process has more nuance.[64] It is only a slight exaggeration, justified to emphasize the significance of the shift, to describe the Commission as able to act with sports bodies as a 'co-producer' of norms in the shadow of EU competition law.[65] The renovation of the transfer system was one of the most notable early instances in the development of EU sports law whereby governing bodies were induced ultimately to work with the Commission, rather than seeking to keep it at arm's length.[66]

Moreover, given the need for a globally applicable *lex sportiva* apt to secure the integrity of the sport there could be no question of an adapted system applicable only within Europe, still less within the EU. The transfer system required worldwide alteration, and this is what occurred. The EU exports its norms. A rich literature explores how the EU's rule-making energy is globally influential;[67] the story

---

[61] Most strikingly Case C-264/98 *Tibor Balog v Royal Charleroi Sporting Club*, in which the reference was withdrawn by the referring (Belgian) court the day before AG Stix-Hackl was due to deliver her Opinion: its hearing was 'cancelled', according to Court Press Release No 11/2001, 29 March 2001. It is widely assumed that A Egger and C Stix-Hackl, 'Sports and Competition Law: A Never-Ending Story?' [2002] ECLR 81 is that lost opinion.

[62] Case T-42/01 *SETCA-FGTB v Commission*, removed from the Register by Order of 24 January 2002 [2001] OJ C118.

[63] IP/02/824, 5 June 2002. See M Bennett, 'They Think It's All Over ... It is Now!—How Extra Time was Required to Finally Settle Football's Transfer Saga' (2001) 9 Sport and the Law Journal 180; S Van den Bogaert, *Practical Regulation of the Mobility of Sportsmen in the EU post Bosman* (Kluwer 2005) ch V; B Dabscheck, 'International Unionism's Competitive Edge: FIFPro and the European Treaty' (2003) 58 Relations Industrielles/Industrial Relations 85; Irving (n 57).

[64] See especially A Duval, 'The FIFA Regulations on the Status and Transfer of Players: Transnational Law-Making in the Shadow of Bosman' in A Duval and B Van Rompuy (eds), *The Legacy of Bosman: Revisiting the Relationship between EU Law and Sport* (TMC Asser/Springer 2016) ch 5.

[65] A Duval, 'La Lex Sportiva Face au Droit de l'Union Européenne: Guerre et Paix dans l'Espace Juridique Transnational' (DPhil thesis, EUI Florence 2015), available via <http://cadmus.eui.eu/handle/1814/36997> accessed 29 November 2016, especially at 245–56.

[66] B García, 'UEFA and the European Union: From Confrontation to Co-Operation' (2007) 3 JCER 202; 208–13 deal in particular with the matter of transfers. See also Duval (n 64); Pearson (n 55) 223–26.

[67] eg A Young, 'The European Union as a Global Regulator? Context and Comparison' (2015) 22 JEPP 1233.

of football's transfer system shows how this occurs also in the shadow of the EU's negative agenda-setting capacity, exercised by application of the prohibitions of internal market law.

The system finally agreed in 2002 has been gently adapted since. The key source today is the FIFA Regulations on the Status and Transfer of Players.[68]

The Regulations provide for the registration of players. This is a requirement for a player to appear in an official match. A player may be registered with only one club at a time[69] and limits are placed on the number of clubs a player may play for in a single season, in order to protect 'the sporting integrity of the competition'.[70] Registration periods—otherwise known as 'transfer windows'—are dealt with explicitly in Article 6 of the Regulations.

The registration system is the starting point in grasping how footballers are different from normal employees. Applying sanctions to clubs that play unregistered players is the means to ensure that the Regulations' special rules channelling the way players may change their employer are respected.

9.8.2 International transfers

The Regulations govern international transfers—transfers between players of clubs belonging to different associations. As far as the EU is concerned, this will normally mean an inter-state transfer and the consequent application of EU law, but, because of the particular case of the United Kingdom—which contains one member of the EU but four members of UEFA—this will not always be the case. Domestic transfers—those between clubs belonging to the same association—are governed by the regulations of the local governing body, subject to the inclusion of certain mandatory provisions which ensure a degree of convergence between the FIFA rules on international transfers and domestic rules.[71] However, as already explained, even rules governing transfers within a single EU Member State are likely to fall for examination in the light of EU competition law in so far as they affect inter-state trade patterns. In fact in most material respects domestic transfer systems follow the model of the FIFA rules. This is perfectly understandable. It promotes coherence and avoids points of friction that might create perverse incentives to prefer a domestic transfer over an international one or vice versa.

9.8.3 Minors

International transfers involving minors—which means players under the age of 18—are not permitted, subject to limited exceptions set out in Article 19 of the

---

[68] The governing texts of the FIFA Regulations are at <http://www.fifa.com/aboutfifa/officialdocuments/doclists/laws.html> accessed 29 November 2016. The current version, in force since April 2015, is at <http://resources.fifa.com/mm/document/affederation/administration/02/55/56/41/regulationsonthestatusandtransferofplayersapril2015e_neutral.pdf> accessed 29 November 2016.
[69] ibid Art 5(2).   [70] ibid Art 5(4).   [71] ibid Art 1(3).

Regulations.[72] Breach of these rules led to a high-profile prohibition on transfer activity by FC Barcelona during 2015, a sanction upheld on appeal to the CAS.[73]

This concern to protect minors readily fits with statements made periodically at EU level. The Nice Declaration includes 'concern about commercial transactions targeting minors in sport, including those from third countries, inasmuch as they do not comply with existing labour legislation or endanger the health and welfare of young sportsmen and -women'.[74] The Commission's White Paper on Sport of 2007 also expresses anxiety about the exploitation of young players, in particular sexual abuse and harassment.[75] Its principal concern is recruitment of children from third countries where it detects exploitation falling short of trafficking in human beings, but nevertheless 'unacceptable given the fundamental values recognised by the EU and its Member States [and] … also contrary to the values of sport'.[76]

9.8.4 Contractual stability and its limits

Article 13 of the Regulations governs 'Respect of contract'. It provides that 'A contract between a professional and a club may only be terminated upon expiry of the term of the contract or by mutual agreement'.

There is, of course, no provision for a transfer fee in the case of the transfer of a registration of a player whose contract has come to an end. This is precisely what was outlawed in *Bosman*. So the out-of-contract player may simply negotiate a contract with a new employer. It is also stipulated by Article 18(3) of the Regulations that a player may enter into contract negotiations with a new employer within the final six months of the term of the existing contract. The generosity of this concession is entirely relative. A normal employee outside football could enter into such negotiations at any time, subject only to the restraints imposed by local contract and employment law: he or she would not face any collectively imposed industry-wide restrictions. By contrast contractual stability in football is aggressively protected.[77]

Termination of contract where there is just cause is recognized by Article 14 of the Regulations, and Article 15 creates a special case of 'sporting just cause', which allows for case-by-case examination of the possibility of early release from a contract where a player has played in fewer than 10 per cent of a club's official matches over the course of a season.

Article 16 of the Regulations provides that a contract cannot be unilaterally terminated during the course of a season.

Article 17 of the Regulations deals with the consequences of a terminating a contract *without just cause*. This, then, is the player who refuses to continue to play

---

[72] See D McArdle, *Dispute Resolution in Sport* (Routledge 2015) ch 8.
[73] CAS 2014/A/3793 *Barcelona v FIFA*.
[74] The Nice Declaration (n 42) para 13. On the Nice Declaration, see Ch 6.3.
[75] White Paper on Sport (n 44). See Ch 6.5.   [76] ibid 16.
[77] And in some other sports too: see L Kurlantzick, 'The Tampering Prohibition, Antitrust, and Agreements between American and Foreign Sports Leagues' in J Nafziger and S Ross (eds), *Handbook on International Sports Law* (Elgar 2011) ch 13.

for a club with which he has a contract, because he wishes instead to join another club. This is the critically and centrally important test of just how special a footballer really is. A 'normal' employee who chose to break his or her contract would be subject to the remedies for breach of contract available under the law of the contract and, in addition, to whatever provisions of local employment law might govern the matter. There is a huge variety in approaches taken across Europe, often sensitive to the particular context—affected by, for example, the level of confidential knowledge or know-how held by the employee. Applicable laws range from rather strict rules that might prevent the contract-breaker joining a new employer for a considerable length of time to much less interventionist rules that tend to prioritize the return of the contract-breaker into the labour market as quickly as possible.[78] The control exercised over footballers as employees is much stronger. By virtue of these FIFA Regulations the concern to protect contractual stability and sporting integrity is translated into a system of sanctions imposed by the *lex sportiva* on the contract-breaker, quite independently of any consequences that apply under national law.

According to Article 17, compensation is payable by the party in breach. This shall be calculated 'with due consideration for the law of the country concerned, the specificity of sport and any other objective criteria'—though it is also specified that this applies 'unless otherwise provided for in the contract'. It is well known that some deals include a specific contractual provision for the sum to be paid where a player does leave early. For example, Lionel Messi is reported to have such a 'buy-out' clause set at €250 million.[79] This has much the same function as a transfer fee. At least where the player is prized and well-advised one can see good reason to treat such provisions as enforceable as an expression of private autonomy, though this will depend on national law.

An additional provision is made for 'training compensation' by Article 20 of the Regulations. This applies when the player signs a first contract as a professional and each time a professional is transferred until the end of the season in which the player's 23rd birthday falls. An Annex to the Regulations sets out a method of calculation, but each case will need to be assessed according to its own facts. For young players, as defined, transfers out of contract are not free: to be 'on a Bosman', with the consequence that money that would be payable as a fee is available for negotiation as enhanced salary, is the preserve of older players.

Article 21 covers a *solidarity mechanism*: this is payable where a player is transferred before the expiry of a contract by the club he is leaving to any club that has contributed to his education and training. Annex 5 to the Regulations amplifies how the detailed calculation shall be made.

---

[78] See European Commission, 'The Economic and Legal Aspects of Transfers of Players' (January 2013) ch 2 <http://ec.europa.eu/assets/eac/sport/library/documents/cons-study-transfers-final-rpt.pdf> accessed 29 November 2016. The Study is examined further in sect 9.11; see also Van den Bogaert (n 63) 282–91.

[79] <https://www.theguardian.com/football/2015/jan/12/lionel-messi-manchester-united-move-barcelona> accessed 29 November 2016.

Under the Regulations the consequences of contract-breaking are not limited to compensation alone. 'Sporting sanctions' may also be imposed on the contract-breaking player. These may involve suspension from eligibility for official matches, up to a maximum period of six months. But the possibility of such extra sanctions being imposed depends on the player's age and the precise time at which the contract has been broken. Sporting sanctions may be imposed only where the breach without just cause occurs within the 'protected period'. This is a period of three seasons or three years (whichever comes first) following the entry into force of a contract where that contract is concluded before the player's 28th birthday, or two seasons/two years where the contract is concluded after the 28th birthday. It is also envisaged that sporting sanctions may be imposed on a club in breach of contract or inducing a breach of contract within the protected period. A ban from registering new players may be imposed on the offending club.

This 'protected period', which lasts for three years for players who were under 28 when they signed their contract and two years for older players, is plainly designed to promote contractual stability with still more vigour than is achieved through the compensation system. Its corollary is to deter contract-breaking by players with more venom than would apply under normal contract and employment law. The free movement of the player enjoyed within the terms allowed by local contract and employment law is weakened by the interests of the club in 'contractual stability', reflected through the sanctions regime created by FIFA's Regulations. The legal assessment of this restrictive system, which is unique to sport, will be addressed later, in section 9.10.

9.9 CAS: the Operation of the Transfer System

The transfer system is plainly designed to deter players from breaking their contracts and it thereby intends to promote contractual stability in the interest of clubs. It does so by envisaging the possible imposition of an obligation to compensate in the event of termination of contract without just cause plus, in defined cases arising within the contractual 'protected period', supplementary sporting sanctions. It bears repetition that these restraints would not be tolerated in 'normal' industries, where the position of the employee wishing to change employer is dictated by contract law and employment law. The transfer system adds an extra level of constraint. The question to be addressed is always not whether the transfer system is justified but rather whether the transfer system is justified *in sport but not elsewhere*. Is sport's special character justification enough? Those defending the system tend to emphasize the virtues of contractual stability in team-building; those attacking it prefer the importance of the autonomy of the individual employee and the prevalence of contractual negotiation as a means to retain valued workers.[80] The practical

---

[80] See eg S Gardiner and R Welch, 'The Contractual Dynamics of Team Stability versus Player Mobility: Who Rules the Beautiful Game?' (2007) 5(1): 3 ESLJ, available via <http://www.entsportslawjournal.com/articles/10.16997/eslj.74> accessed 29 November 2016.

operation of the system depends heavily on how compensation is calculated and how severe and frequent is the imposition of sporting sanctions. The higher the compensation, the more severe and frequent the sanctions, the more the interest of the clubs prevails over the interest of players. The lower the compensation, the milder and the more uncommon the sporting sanctions, the more that the freedom of the player to choose an employer is enhanced. Moreover, as will be examined more fully later, the place at which this balance is set is also highly significant in determining the extent to which the FIFA Regulations are likely to withstand scrutiny when reviewed under EU law.

Inspection of FIFA's Annual Reports[81] shows that a very large number of disputes between players and clubs are settled before the Dispute Resolution Chamber (DRC), which is established under the governing Regulations.[82] Transfers of players who are in contract happen, compensation is paid, they do not go to national courts. The system works!

The CAS, the Court of Arbitration for Sport, was met in Chapter 2. It has become especially influential in shaping the transfer system.[83] Its treatment of cases involving termination of contract without just cause, as defined in the Regulations, is especially revealing. Such cases reach the CAS as appeals against decisions taken by the DRC and they typically involve sanctions imposed on players of a type that certainly would not be known outside sport. This is where the FIFA Regulations have teeth. The CAS has begun to piece together a—so far rather inconsistent—set of guiding principles.

The first ruling of the CAS which grabbed attention was *Webster*.[84] Andy Webster was a Scottish international defender who played in Scotland for Hearts. He refused offers of a new extended contract and, relying on Article 17 of the Transfer Regulations, he elected to leave before the existing contract had expired and he signed a contract with Wigan Athletic in England. Hearts brought a claim for compensation before the DRC, the decision of which was duly appealed to the CAS.

The CAS decided that compensation should not be calculated according to the player's value on the transfer market, for that would have the effect of reinstating the situation existing before the Regulations were introduced. Nor is compensation to be calculated with reference to the wages payable under the new contract, that is, the one offered by the new club, Wigan. Instead, the CAS ruled, the club which the player has quit should receive only what would have been due to the player

---

[81] <https://www.fifatms.com/> accessed 29 November 2016.

[82] FIFA Regulations (n 68) Art 24. See F De Weger, *The Jurisprudence of the FIFA Dispute Resolution Chamber* (2nd edn, TMC Asser 2016).

[83] The website of the Court of Arbitration for Sport is at <http://www.tas-cas.org/>. The case law is at <http://jurisprudence.tas-cas.org/sites/caselaw/help/home.aspx>. For discussion of the case law, see McArdle (n 72) ch 8; A Wild (ed), *CAS and Football: Landmark Cases* (TMC Asser 2012) ch 4; 'The Economic and Legal Aspects of Transfers of Players' (n 78) ch 2 (this Study is examined further at sect 9.11).

[84] CAS 2007/A/1298-1300.

under the residual length of the contract which he had broken. Hearts had sought in excess of £4 million. The DRC had decided they should receive £625,000. But by the CAS, Hearts were awarded just £150,000.

Webster generated instant and acute anxiety. The ruling was criticized as vastly unbalanced in favour of the short-term interests of players and against the need to promote stability in the game. The DRC decision was reported as clearing a 'path for hordes to follow'.[85] The subsequent CAS ruling, which reduced the size of the payment due, was greeted with still greater dismay by clubs and federations since it seemed to encourage contract-breakers by confining monetary compensation to (usually) a relatively low amount and, moreover, one readily calculated in advance by the player who is able to make a shrewd calculation of what suits his or her interests best.[86]

The CAS quickly changed its tune. *Webster* had been decided by the CAS in January 2008. A differently constituted panel decided *Matuzalem* in May 2009. And a quite different approach was taken.[87] Much heavier emphasis was placed on the promotion of contractual stability and, contrary to *Webster*, it was accepted that value *is* related to the transfer fee foregone by the 'losing' club.

Matuzalem was a Brazilian player. He played for Shakhtar Donetsk in Ukraine. He terminated his contract pursuant to Article 17 of the Regulations—that is, without just cause—and he joined Real Zaragoza in Spain. Later he was loaned to Lazio in Italy. Shakhtar claimed compensation.

Having found there was no agreed contractual provision, the CAS then took the view, contrary to that which reigned in *Webster*, that calculation should be assessed with reference to the transfer fee foregone. The player, having left Shakhtar, had subsequently been the subject of a valuation agreed between Zaragoza and Lazio, so there was helpfully concrete evidence of the value placed by the market on his services. This was duly relied on as the principal means of calculation. However, the CAS also chose 'to take into due consideration the specific nature and needs of sport', which directed that not only the interests of player and club but also 'those of the whole football community' should be taken into account.[88] It was in this vein considered relevant that the breach had occurred with fully two years remaining on a five-year contract, rather than just a few months; and that the player left the club just a few weeks before the start of the qualifying rounds of the lucrative UEFA Champions League. The CAS therefore set an additional indemnity amount equal to six months of salary payable under the contract by Shakhtar Donetsk, which amounted to €600,000.

---

[85] 'Pioneer Webster's Contract Buy-Out Clears Path for Hordes to Follow' *The Guardian* (London, 9 May 2007) 4.

[86] eg D Castles, 'Wenger Sees the End of Transfer Fees: Arsenal Manager Says the Power has Shifted from Clubs to Players' *The Observer* (London, 29 June 2008) Sports section; D Hytner, 'FIFA Transfer Rule Undermines My Youth-Team Policy, Says Wenger' *The Guardian* (London, 22 April 2008) Sports section, 5.

[87] CAS 2008/A/1519-1520.   [88] *Matuzalem* (n 87) para 153.

In total an award in favour of Shakhtar of almost €12 million was made to cover the two years of the contract 'lost' to Shakhtar, whereas, had the 'Webster methodology' been followed, only €2.4 million would have been payable.

The inquiry will be harder where there is no subsequent evidence of market value of the type that was helpfully available in *Matuzalem*. The process of arbitration tends typically to generate smudgier lines in its accumulated practice than the case law of 'ordinary' courts, but even so there is something troublingly ad hoc about this process of calculation. *Matuzalem* has attracted astute criticism for its thin reasoning and the uncertainty it creates.[89] However, the approach adopted in *Matuzalem* plainly enhances the deterrent effect of Article 17 of the Transfer Regulations, and is much more conducive to contractual stability. As far as clubs and governing bodies are concerned, it was a welcome re-orientation in favour of deterring contract-breaking.

A key message for those alarmed by the unpredictability of the likely calculation of compensation, especially given the insistence in Article 17 and the CAS's rulings that the specificity of sport shall inform the assessment, is that it remains possible to address the matter in the contract itself. This allows all involved, including poacher clubs, to know where they stand. The CAS has made it clear that it will normally treat a contractual clause setting out an agreed sum payable in the event of unilateral breach of contract as enforceable. This allows players seeking to terminate their relationship with their current club to 'buy out' the contract. The CAS has also emphasized that it is important for the parties to make clear that that is what they have in fact done.[90] It seems right to be cautious about deferring to the contractual autonomy of players, especially where younger players or at least players without access to good legal advice are concerned.[91] If the CAS did not take that point, a national court asked to deal with the matter probably would.[92]

In 2010 in its *De Sanctis* decision, the CAS stressed the wide range of potentially relevant factors in the assessment of due compensation, none of which on its own would be decisive, save only that it would give effect to a liquidated damages clause.[93] In the absence of such a clause, it would consider costs incurred, lost transfer fee(s), the player's level of remuneration, the time remaining under the old contract, whether or not the breach has occurred within the protected period, the law of the country concerned, and the 'specificity of sport'. This, the ruling stresses, is not an additional head of compensation but rather a 'correcting factor', allowing consideration of other objective elements not explicitly covered by Article 17 of the Regulations.[94] In the case itself De Sanctis had broken his contract with Udinese in Italy and moved to Sevilla in Spain. The DRC made an award of some

---

[89] eg B Dabscheck, 'Being Punitive: The Court of Arbitration for Sport Overturns *Webster*' (2009) 9(3–4) Intl Sports LJ 20.

[90] eg *Matuzalem* (n 87) para 74.

[91] See M Giancaspro, 'Buy-Out Clauses in Professional Football Player Contracts: Questions of Legality and Integrity' (2016) 16 Intl Sports LJ 22.

[92] On EU law's insistence on the protection of the weaker party, see Ch 2.2.

[93] CAS 2010/A/2145-2147.   [94] ibid para 96.

€4 million, but the CAS, criticizing the lack of detailed reasoning in the DRC decision, awarded a lower sum, €2,250,055. It did, however, take the view that the loss suffered when a 'hero' leaves a club may not be readily provable in euros and it is here that an increased award inspired by the specificity of sport may be appropriate. Explicitly following the reasoning on this point advanced in *Matuzalem*, it was decided that the award should include a sum of €690,789, being six months' pay under the new contract.

Admittedly the CAS rulings are internally not fully consistent. *Juventus v Chelsea* involved an attempt by Chelsea to make Juventus jointly liable for the sum of some €17 million due under a CAS award in favour of Chelsea and payable by Adrian Mutu, a Romanian player who had been dismissed by Chelsea after being suspended for doping.[95] He had not paid, but had joined Juventus on the expiry of his ban. The CAS treated the question of how far to protect 'contractual stability [as] … at the centre of the debate' about Article 14(3) of the Regulations.[96] The CAS was particularly concerned that were Chelsea's claim to succeed, then players in Mutu's position would find it hard to find a new employer. This, the ruling noted, would reach back to 'pre-Bosman times', offer 'disproportionate' protection to Chelsea, and upset the balance between 'players' rights and an efficient transfer system'.[97] So Chelsea could have decided not to sack the player or they could, having sacked him, pursued him for compensation—but they could not also pin liability on the club that had offered the player a chance to resume his career. This approach shows how the reasoning in *Matuzalem* is open to criticism as excessively detrimental to the contract-breaking player, even seen from within the CAS's own case law. But *Matuzalem* shows that the CAS is capable of interpreting the power to make a compensation award in a way that leads to a very high amount.

There is much less relevant practice dealing with sporting sanctions as distinct from compensation. However, Matuzalem has played his part in developing the *lex sportiva* and its limits here too. In 2012 the Swiss Federal Supreme Court decided *Matuzalem*.[98] This was a follow-up to the original finding that he should pay compensation to Shakhtar. He had not paid it. He was then banned from playing for a specified period by FIFA: this was a sporting sanction of the type envisaged by the FIFA Regulations. A subsequent CAS ruling affirmed the imposition on Matuzalem of this sanction.[99] Article 190(2)(e) of the Swiss Private International Law Act (PILA) provides that an arbitral award may be set aside if it is incompatible with public policy. Matuzalem argued before the Swiss Court that the CAS award violated his personal freedom to such an extent that it offended against this notion. The Swiss Court agreed. It found that an excessive limitation of freedom is contrary to public policy if the rights of the individual concerned are clearly and severely infringed. The Swiss Supreme Court found that an open-ended playing ban, such as the one Matuzalem was facing, which could be triggered at the sole discretion of a former employer, constituted a severe infringement of the player's individual rights.

---

[95] CAS 2013/3365.   [96] ibid para 158.   [97] ibid paras 174–75.
[98] 4A_558/2011, 27 March 2012. See also Ch 2.2.   [99] 29 June 2011, unreported.

Moreover, the Court noted, the ban was intended to secure enforcement of the monetary claim against the player to the advantage of a member of FIFA and indirectly to FIFA itself: in short, the sanction was applied in circumstances of a conflict of interest.[100] Moreover, the sporting sanction was not necessary for the purpose of enforcing the monetary award of compensation, since the claim by the previous club against Matuzalem, which has been upheld by the CAS, could anyway be enforced in a national court against him by reliance on the New York Convention on the Recognition and Enforcement of Foreign Arbitral Awards without the need for an additional private sanction. All this was examined in Chapter 2—this is the contractual protection afforded by the *lex sportiva*'s embrace of arbitration which in the Swiss Court's estimation had plainly been pursued with exorbitant aggression. But none of this changed the original finding that Matuzalem was liable to pay compensation to Shakhtar under the FIFA Regulations for having terminated his contract without just cause.

9.10 The Compatibility of the Renovated System with EU Law

The renovated transfer system has not been tested for its compatibility with EU law. As explained earlier, in section 9.8, in 2002 the Commission closed its investigation into the system, observing that interested parties, including FIFPro, the players' union, had expressed satisfaction with it, and hailing it as striking a balance between players' free movement rights and contractual stability.[101] The examination of the transfer system that has been conducted since *Bosman* makes clear that the EU's institutions are inclined to accept that sport is special, in particular in the matter of encouraging youth training, and that the revised transfer system is lawful. This was covered earlier.

But even at the time of the successful renegotiation of the system there were reasons to criticize it as *too* generous to the claimed virtues of contractual stability.[102] The Commission's 'exchange of letters' in March 2001, mentioned in subsection 9.8.1, expressed satisfaction with FIFA and UEFA's plans and ended the Commission's pursuit of the matter, but the legal foundation of the deal was calculatedly obscure. The exchange of letters was declared to have 'formalised' the situation,[103] but, just as the 'Bangemann compromise' on UEFA's '3 plus 2' rule was exploded by the Court's ruling in *Bosman*,[104] so too the 2002 compromise could yet be dislodged by judicial intervention. A sceptical inquiry into its compatibility with EU law remains merited. Two justifications for the transfer system were accepted in

---

[100] More generally on legal supervision of conflicts of interest in sporting governance, see Ch 10.

[101] IP/02/824, 5 June 2002.

[102] See eg Van den Bogaert (n 63) ch V; R Blanpain, *The Legal Status of Sportsmen and Sportswomen under International, European Belgian National and Regional Law* (Kluwer 2003) Pt I.

[103] IP/01/314 (n 60). In French, 'formalisées', in German, 'formell besiegelt', which are as legally imprecise as the English version.

[104] See Ch 4.8.

principle by the Court in *Bosman*.[105] The first was the need to preserve a degree of competitive balance and equality between clubs. The second, which was confirmed in *Bernard*,[106] was to encourage the search for and training of young players, the stars of the future. In the circumstances at stake in both cases, the justifications were not met, but the Court had left room for a reshaped system and, as explained, this has duly emerged and, in 2002, the Commission declared itself satisfied.

But both justifications, even in principle, are highly questionable. It is far from clear that the transfer system is the most effective or the least restrictive way to preserve a degree of competitive balance and equality between clubs. A method for more direct redistribution of income between clubs would be superior. Sport may well be special because of the interdependence of participant clubs, but the means used to promote that special feature are disproportionately burdensome on players. And although it is doubtless true that the transfer system serves to encourage the search for and training of young players, it has never been explained why this should be permitted in sport when it is not permitted in other industries. That is, even if one accepts that the transfer system encourages the training of future talent, the question is why that logic should not apply beyond sport, to supermarkets, to car-makers, to sellers of financial services and so on. The Court treats sport as special on this point but it has never explained why, and so the counter is that sport is simply not special. This is not to argue in favour of the complete abandonment of the transfer system, but rather to argue that a better justification for it needs to be found. That must lie in protecting the integrity of the game from relatively short-term changes in playing personnel, consequent on the—varied—patterns of national contract and employment law. The Court mentioned this point in *Bosman* but did not elaborate upon it at all.[107] But it is a strong point. The *lex sportiva*, as a global system, requires some degree of control over player mobility which is not dependent on local legal variation, but there are aspects of the current system which go too far. The sections that follow expand in detail on this critique. The story of EU law's capacity to curtail the *lex sportiva* governing transfers is not yet complete.

9.11 Competitive Balance and Equality between Clubs

The Court in *Bosman*, examining the transfer system then in force, stated that 'the same aims can be achieved at least as efficiently by other means which do not impede freedom of movement of workers'.[108] In making that point, it expressly cited its Advocate General, Mr Lenz. He accepted that a system stopping rich clubs becoming ever richer and poor ever poorer could be justified. This is a reason in the general interest which may justify the imposition of restrictions on free

---

[105] *Bosman* (n 1) paras 105–14.   [106] *Bernard* (n 1) paras 38–50.

[107] *Bosman* (n 1) 'It has also been argued that the transfer rules are necessary to safeguard the worldwide organization of football', para 111.

[108] ibid para 110.

competition. Mr Lenz mentioned two particular alternative methods for preserving financial and sporting balance between clubs. First, a collective wage agreement which specified limits on salaries to be paid to players—commonly known as a salary cap; second, a system of distribution of income from the sale of tickets and broadcasting rights among all the clubs. Mr Lenz seemed little interested in the salary cap—with good reason, for there are several variants of this device in several sports around the world[109] and all are hard to police as well as being of questionable validity at law, given their restrictive effect on competition and, in particular, their emphasis on players as the focus of cost-cutting.[110] Given the much greater attention he paid to it, it is the second approach, income distribution, which was plainly Mr Lenz's preference. This, he noted, would reflect the interdependence of clubs in a sports league.

One can draw from this a claim that the transfer system cannot be justified on the basis that it is required to promote financial and competitive balance between clubs. Instead that stated aim should be achieved, if at all, through arrangements *between clubs* organized through the governing associations of the sport, and not by a system that involves employers imposing restrictions on employees, the players.[111]

In 2013 the Commission published a study entitled 'The Economic and Legal Aspects of Transfers of Players'.[112] The study, the body of which covers more than 250 pages, aims to document the different layers of rules applicable to transfers and to consider their interactions.

It explains that transfer rules in sport are a derogation from normal employment practices in the following ways:

i) They limit the freedom of players to move from one employer to another and set restrictive conditions for such moves. Contracts may be terminated by either party without consequences (such as sporting sanctions) only if justified by 'just cause';
ii) They establish a system of transfer fees between clubs in order to prevent a total ban on players' mobility.

The study explains that free movement of players is restricted under transfer rules with a view to maintaining fair and balanced competition. The question is whether

---

[109] See eg S Késenne, *The Economic Theory of Professional Team Sports: An Analytical Treatment* (2nd edn, Edward Elgar 2014) ch 7; N St Cyr Clarke, 'The Beauty and the Beast: Taming the Ugly Side of the People's Game' (2010–11) 17 Col J Eur L 601; McArdle (n 72) especially 120–23; C Davies, 'The Financial Crisis in the English Premier League: Is a Salary Cap the Answer?' [2010] ECLR 442; G Basnier, 'Sports and Competition Law: The Case of the Salary Cap in New Zealand Rugby Union' (2014) 14 Intl Sports LJ 155; R Parrish and S Miettinen, *The Sporting Exception in European Law* (TMC Asser 2007) 219–22.

[110] However, for an argument based on Case C-309/99 *Wouters* (Ch 5) in favour of the lawfulness of a cap, see S Hornsby, 'The Harder the Cap, the Softer the Law?' (2002) 10 Sport and the Law Journal 142.

[111] See also S Késenne (n 109) chs 2 and 5. One may be sceptical whether, if the load could not be placed on players, the clubs would share revenue (much). On the pursuit of competitive balance in the organization of team sports, which varies between Europe and North America, see S Szymanski, 'The Economic Design of Sporting Contests' (2003) 41 Journal of Economic Literature 1137.

[112] 'The Economic and Legal Aspects of Transfers of Players', January 2013 <http://ec.europa.eu/assets/eac/sport/library/documents/cons-study-transfers-final-rpt.pdf> accessed 29 November 2016.

this remains justified. It correctly identifies the transfer system as atypical and there-fore, if it is justified, it represents a special concession to the autonomy of sports institutions. The study relies on *Meca-Medina* as its legal platform.[113] The rules must pursue a legitimate aim compatible with the Treaty; they must be applied in a non-discriminatory manner; they must be justified by overriding reasons in the public interest; they must be suitable for securing the attainment of the objective they pursue; and they must not go beyond what is necessary for that purpose.

The study finds that the transfer rules make no effective contribution to a fight against competitive imbalance. There is a demonstrated strong link between trans-fer expenditure and sporting results, in particular since 2001. The identity of the clubs that dominate the later stages of the annual Champions League competi-tion changes little; supremacy is consolidated. Payments directly linked to trans-fers made for training compensation and as part of the solidarity mechanism only account for 1.84 per cent of the total agreed transfer fees within Europe. This can-not have a sufficient impact to affect competitive balance in a positive way and it seems implausible that it serves as a well-targeted inducement to invest in training either. The study argues that solidarity mechanisms and youth development pro-grammes should play a more important role. The study explicitly does 'not argue for the end of transfer rules as implemented by sports governing bodies'.[114] But it suggests firmer commitment to improving fair and balanced competition through better and increased redistribution between clubs. It proposes, inter alia, a 'fair play levy' on transfer fees beyond a certain amount in order to fund a redistribution mechanism from rich to less wealthy clubs. It also suggests a limit on transfer fees, involving particular attention to contract extension and to potentially abusive 'buy-out' clauses. The strengthening of solidarity payments is also suggested.

The Commission has not initiated any concrete follow-up to this mildly sceptical report, though it is still freely available on its website.[115]

This criticism seems convincing. It follows the route mapped out in the pre-vious chapter in discussion of the compatibility of the home-grown rules with EU law, and would insist that a choice between addressing sporting concerns by measures affecting clubs or measures affecting players should be resolved in favour of the former unless compelling reasons justify the need to prefer the latter. As with the home-grown rules, so with the transfer system: the sceptical view taken of their compatibility with EU law reflects a broader scepticism that it is justified to treat footballers in a way that differs from the treatment of ordinary employees. One might in this vein supplement the argument by reliance to Article 15 of the Charter of Fundamental Rights of the European Union, which declares that every-one, including footballers, has the right to engage in work and to pursue a freely chosen or accepted occupation, although so far the Court has treated economic

---

[113] Case C-519/04 P *Meca-Medina and Majcen v Commission* [2006] ECR I-6991.
[114] 'The Economic and Legal Aspects of Transfers of Players' (n 112) 8, 252.
[115] <http://ec.europa.eu/sport/policy/organisation_of_sport/transfers_en.htm> accessed 29 November 2016.

rights recognized by the Charter as running in parallel to the free movement rights contained in the TFEU, so the Charter probably adds only presentational force to the case.[116]

So in *Eastham v Newcastle United* in 1964 Wilberforce J, in the English High Court, took the view that the transfer system 'provides a means by which the poorer clubs can on occasions, obtain money, enabling them to stay in existence and improve their facilities'.[117] *Bosman's* famous paragraph 106, delivered in 1995 in Luxembourg, is carried by a similar sense. But there are other ways to achieve this which do not impinge on the position of the player as employee. So, in short, labour market restrictions have not been but *should* always be regarded as the *last* resort available in defence of the *lex sportiva*.[118]

9.12 Sport as a Special Case in Youth Training

The Court in *Bosman* adopted an approach that it subsequently repeated entirely uncritically in *Bernard*: encouraging the recruitment and training of young players must be accepted as legitimate in sport.[119]

The Court in *Bosman* commented that a transfer fee paid had no relation to the costs of training that player and the pool of other players who were trained but did not succeed in making the grade, and for whom no transfer fee would ever be recovered. So it refused to accept that the prospect of receipt of the fee could be 'a decisive factor in encouraging recruitment and training of young players or an adequate means of financing such activities'.[120] The strong implication was that a system tied in some way to costs incurred in training players would be much more likely to receive a green light. This is confirmed by the discussion in *Bernard*, albeit the system examined in that case also did not satisfy the Court. *Bernard* in particular approves a system that is motivated to encourage clubs, especially small clubs, to invest in training young players. However, it insists on a calculation which is based on compensation for the costs actually incurred. The further a system is distanced from this model and, in particular, the higher the deterrent effect on the player's right to exercise contractual freedom by moving to a club in another Member State, the more likely it is that the system will be found to violate EU law.

---

[116] See Case C-390/12 *Pfleger*, judgment of 30 April 2014 (TFEU, Art 56); Case C-98/14 *Berlington*, judgment of 11 June 2015 (TFEU, Art 56); Case C-367/12 *Sokoll-Seebacher*, judgment of 13 February 2014 (TFEU, Art 49).

[117] See n 6.

[118] cf M Dalziel, P Downward, R Parrish, G Pearson and A Semens, 'Study on the Assessment of UEFA's Home Grown Player Rules' (2013) 7; 106–107, 111 <http://ec.europa.eu/assets/eac/sport/library/studies/final-rpt-april2013-homegrownplayer.pdf> accessed 29 November 2016, and discussed in Ch 8.10.

[119] *Bosman* (n 1) para 108; *Bernard* (n 1) para 41. This was accepted too by the Oberlandesgericht in *Wilhelmshaven SV*, considered in Ch 2.2.4: its objection was only to the CAS's neglect of EU law, not to the assumptions within EU law.

[120] *Bosman* (n 1) para 109.

That the prospect of receiving training fees is likely to encourage football clubs to seek new talent and train young players is perfectly plausible. But this has never been accompanied by any explanation of why football clubs *uniquely* need such incentives to invest in youth training. The prospect of receiving training fees might be likely to encourage car-makers, banks, or supermarkets to seek new talent and train young workers, but no one has ever suggested that therefore it should be permitted that car-makers, banks, and supermarkets shall set up collectively enforced arrangements that inhibit the exercise of contractual freedom by their employees once they have been trained. It is conventionally assumed that employers train young talent and try to keep the workers they particularly value by offering them attractive contractual terms and conditions. This is how a market for labour functions. But in stark contrast football superimposes an industry-wide compensation system to benefit the training club and to the disadvantage of the employee. Why is professional football different? The Court has never explained this. It has accepted in both *Bosman* and *Bernard* that the transfer system encourages youth training but it has not explained why football deserves and needs this where other sectors do not. And it is fiendishly difficult to imagine any justification.

The closest the Court has got to addressing this issue is in *Bernard*, where it commented that the disincentive to invest in training would in particular 'be the case with small clubs providing training, whose investments at local level in the recruitment and training of young players are of considerable importance for the social and educational function of sport'.[121] This chimes with the famous paragraph 106 of *Bosman*, which recognizes legitimate concerns of sport, and it also echoes both the Amsterdam and the Nice Declarations' embrace of the virtues of sport's social function. However, the Court's explanation is remarkably thin. Some small clubs likely do a fine job in this vein: some likely do not. There is no evidence base for the Court's warm remarks. Perhaps one might argue that the market for players is so very open, because barriers such as linguistic competence play an insignificant role in recruiting employees in professional sport compared with most other sectors of the economy, that clubs in countries with high costs attached to training young talent prefer instead to shop elsewhere and buy mature players. Perhaps sport is special because the capacity of a player to improve is unknown in advance, yet quickly and atypically becomes known to all as a result of on-field performance, with the consequence that because an investing club would rapidly lose the advantage it enjoys in having more information than predator employers about an employee's developing skills, it suffers an unusually strong sport-specific unwillingness to invest in training.[122] But no claims of this type have ever been advanced before the Court of Justice. Even if they were, it would be hard to treat the transfer system as

---

[121] *Bernard* (n 1) para 44.

[122] E Fees and G Mühlheuber, 'Economic Consequences of Transfer Fee Regulations in European Football' (2002) 13 Eur J Law Econ 221; H Dietl, E Franck, and M Lang, 'Why Football Players may Benefit from the "Shadow of the Transfer System"' (2008) 26 Eur J Law Econ 129. It is questionable whether the claim, even if in itself valid, is truly sports-specific: eg the logic seems applicable also to musicians and actors.

a proportionate response: the home-grown rule, considered in Chapter 8, seems more apt. In truth *Bernard*, like *Bosman* before it, is remarkably *generous* to sport. It accepts that sport is special in its need to provide incentives to invest in training, inter alia, for social and educational benefit in circumstances where little, if any, evidence has been presented to demonstrate that sport—especially in its professional guise—is different from normal industries in this particular matter.

So, in the absence of evidence, the transfer system should be regarded as unnecessary to achieve the sports-specific concern to promote youth training, because there is no such sports-specific concern. Therefore even a system rearranged to achieve a closer tie between costs incurred in providing training and compensation payable should not be accepted as lawful. It has not been demonstrated that in the matter of the need to encourage youth training sport is special—even if the Court depicted it as such in *Bosman* and *Bernard*.

9.13 So What is Left ...?

In summary, I am highly sceptical that either of the reasons provided by the Court in *Bosman*—the need to preserve a degree of competitive balance and equality between clubs and encouragement to train young players—are sufficient to justify a transfer system. This, however, is to not to say that footballers are *always* to be treated in the same way as car-makers and bankers.

Governing bodies may preclude the movement of players between clubs at the sharp end of the season as part of their legitimate concern to maintain fair competition: a so-called 'transfer window' is not condemned by EU law, provided it is not contaminated by arbitrary or discriminatory features.[123] Such a restriction would not be found in the market for car-makers or bankers, because there is no comparable period of intensified competition across the calendar year. Sport is special. The restriction confines the opportunities for mobility of athletes, but, as the 2007 Commission White Paper accurately put it, in the absence of such rules, 'the integrity of sport competitions could be challenged by clubs recruiting players during a given season to prevail upon their competitors'.[124] Moreover, as Chapter 8 has shown, footballers are different from car-makers and bankers in the matter of selection for international representative sport. But these are exceptional instances. It takes a very good argument to justify the treatment of footballers as employees which differs from that of employees in other sectors of the economy. The two reasons given by the Court in *Bosman*—the need to preserve a degree of competitive balance and equality between clubs and the encouragement to train young players—are not good enough reasons to accept a transfer system.

---

[123] Case C-176/96 *Jyri Lehtonen and Castors Canada Dry Namur-Braine ASBL v Fédération royale belge des sociétés de basket-ball ASBL (FRBSB)* [2000] ECR I-2681. The system dealt with in that case was so contaminated, and thus did not comply with EU law.

[124] White Paper on Sport (n 44) section 4.3, p 15.

But there is a good reason for a transfer system. The matter of 'transfer windows' is one aspect of the genuine need to structure the mobility of players in such a way as to ensure the integrity of the competition in the context of a global game.

Abandoning the transfer system entirely would mean that clubs could no longer rely on the transfer system to retain players or to extract a fee for them if they leave. They would instead have to turn to the private law to protect their commercial interests, by drafting appropriately attractive contracts. The consequences of a player changing club during the term of the contract would be assessed exclusively in the light of relevant rules of private law, accompanied by the relevant provisions of local employment law. Footballers would be like car-makers and bankers. The best argument for a continuation of a *lex sportiva* which governs a transfer system would hold that this model would lead to instability in the international market for playing talent, because the enforceability of contracts would vary according to local contract and employment laws. There would be an obvious problem if a player in State X is able under local law to bring a contract to an end by payment of a small sum to the employer, while in State Y a player is required to complete the contractual term in all circumstances: a club in State Z would be more likely to look for new players in X than in Y. This suggests a need for some common rules on the amount of flexibility allowed to players wishing to change clubs while still under contract. This, in short, would be to argue for a *lex sportiva* for a global game that is not fragmented along national lines. There is validity to this claim.

The current FIFA Regulations were examined earlier. They take special account of the position of young players, though they also envisage that transfer fees shall be payable for older players who remain in contract but wish to change clubs. It follows from the discussion in section 9.12 that I am sceptical that distinct treatment of young players is justified in the absence of better reasons why football clubs are uniquely unlikely to invest in youth training without the help of such inducements. That apart, the Regulations, seen more generally, probably represent a legitimate method for attending to the need for common rules which shape the composition of club squads and therefore the integrity of the competition by regulating the mobility of players between clubs. A sporting 'margin of appreciation', addressed in Chapter 7.4, would also argue in favour of their compatibility with EU law: this would be reinforced by a genuinely participatory framework, embracing all affected interests, including players, within which the rules are produced.[125]

But detail matters. Much must depend on the level at which compensation for termination without just cause is fixed, as well as the frequency with which sporting sanctions are imposed. The more burdensome the intervention from the perspective of the player, the more probable that it will be treated as a disproportionate

---

[125] On 'social dialogue', see Chs 7.4 and 6.10. On assessing the legal status of the transfer system in the light of social dialogue, see S Gardiner and R Welch, 'Nationality Based Playing Quotas and the International Transfer System post-Bosman' and R Parrish, 'The European Social Dialogue: A New Mode of Governance for European Football?' both in A Duval and B Van Rompuy (eds), *The Legacy of Bosman: Revisiting the Relationship between EU Law and Sport* (TMC Asser/Springer 2016) ch 4 and ch 8, respectively.

restriction under EU law, were an appropriate case to arise and to provoke litigation. It is likely to be the new system *as interpreted by the CAS* that is eventually the subject of challenge before the Court of Justice. It was, after all, a CAS ruling imposing sanctions that generated the highly important ruling of the Court of Justice in *Meca-Medina*[126] and it cannot be excluded that a CAS ruling imposing an obligation on a player to pay compensation and/or to submit to a suspension from playing could similarly come to be tested pursuant to EU law. Expression of doubt that the revised transfer system will survive is especially pertinent in the light of the model of compensation used by the CAS in *Matuzalem*.[127]

As explained earlier, in section 9.9, Matuzalem himself could not rely on EU law, because he was Brazilian. But a player who falls within the personal scope of EU law would doubtless argue that an award calculated in the way that the CAS preferred in *Matuzalem* should be treated as a restriction on free movement and/or a distortion of competition which exceeds that necessary to achieve the stated sporting objectives. Bernard was a 'joueur espoir', whereas Matuzalem was an established high-level player, but the Court's anxiety in *Bernard* was to exclude that disproportionately onerous transfer fees might be dressed up as 'compensation payments' and so the analysis in *Bernard* should not be confined to the case of restrictions faced by young players. An 'EU Matuzalem' might plausibly argue that an award of approaching €12 million payable by the player to the club goes beyond what is permitted under Article 45 TFEU. The award is very high: the method of calculation relatively intransparent. In fact one of the Court's objections to the French system under review in *Bernard* was that the club's loss 'was established on the basis of criteria which were not determined in advance'.[128] Uncertainty associated with the size of the compensation that will be deemed payable, plus the fear that it may turn out to be high, acts as a stern deterrent to the player considering a unilateral breach of his contract. This tips the balance firmly towards contractual stability as the main winner—which means a priority for the interests of the clubs. The strong dissuasive effect on the player's readiness to change clubs is arguably to claim too much protection for clubs under the cover of the specificity of sport. There therefore is a solid argument that the way that Article 17 of the FIFA Regulations has been interpreted and applied by the CAS places a much heavier emphasis on the virtues of contractual stability than the players' rights under EU law and that, as an unbalanced and disproportionately restrictive system, it is for that reason incompatible with EU law.[129] Put another way, the choices made by the CAS mean that the transfer system which the Commission approved in 2002[130] is no longer the system as currently operational.

The more modest 'Webster calculation', initially preferred by the CAS in determining the compensation due, would probably comply with EU law as interpreted

---

[126] *Meca-Medina* (n 113). See Ch 5.   [127] *Matuzalem* (n 87).

[128] *Bernard* (n 1) para 47.

[129] On the lawfulness of the system, see eg Pearson (n 55); P Czarnota, 'FIFA Transfer Rules and Unilateral Termination without Just Cause' (2013) 2 Berkeley Journal of Entertainment and Sports Law 1; R Parrish, 'Article 17 of the FIFA Regulations on the Status and Transfer of Players: Compatibility with EU Law' (2015) 22(2) MJ 256; J-C Drolet, 'Extra Time: Are the New FIFA Transfer Rules Doomed?' in S Gardiner, R Parrish, and R Siekmann (eds), *EU, Sport, Law and Policy* (TMC Asser 2009) ch 10.

[130] IP/02/824, 5 June 2002.

by the Court.[131] Something a little more onerous might too, if based on a clearly articulated and objective set of criteria apt to reflect the specificity of sport and, in particular, the virtues of encouraging training, contractual stability, and team-building. *Matuzalem* looks to go too far, both in the size of the award and in the level of uncertainty. It is, after all, a requirement of EU law that individuals are able to understand their legal position in order to adapt their conduct accordingly. This is a manifestation of the principle of legal certainty[132] and it also appears in the context of free movement law, where the Court has consistently taken the view that transparency and openness are necessary elements in the justification of any system that inhibits free movement.[133] Indeed it is a principle elsewhere embraced by the CAS itself.[134]

Reliance on EU law to challenge sporting sanctions under the FIFA Regulations seems equally plausible, should the necessary connecting factors to EU law feature in a particular case. It was explained previously that Matuzalem was successful in persuading the Swiss Federal Supreme Court to find that the extra sanctions, including a suspension from playing, imposed on him under a CAS ruling as a result of failure to pay the compensation award made against him were unlawful.[135] The extra sanctions infringed public policy, given the restriction on his rights as an individual, and in any event they were unnecessary, given that the compensation claim by the previous club against Matuzalem which had been upheld by the CAS could anyway be enforced before the ordinary courts by reliance on the New York Convention on the Recognition and Enforcement of Foreign Arbitral Awards. There was no need for an additional private sanction imposed under the *lex sportiva*.

One would expect no different outcome under EU internal market law, provided of course that the player possessed the right nationality to rely on EU law, which Matuzalem did not. It would go too far to say that sporting sanctions could never conceivably be justified under EU law, but the case would be arduous, for it must be shown why conduct is treated as so egregious that it leads to a denial of the player's right to do his or her job. And—to repeat—it should be borne in mind that such repressive measures would never be meted out to an ordinary employee outside the world of sport, whose legal concerns would arise only as matters of contract and employment law.

There are therefore aspects of the current FIFA Regulations which are vulnerable to challenge under EU law, in particular when one looks at the associated, but inconsistent, practice of the CAS. This sharpens the importance of the story told in Chapter 2 of how EU law does not grant rulings of the CAS, and the *lex sportiva* more generally, autonomy from its application. Sport has a specific nature, according to Article 165 TFEU, but it seems highly unlikely that the transfer system as developed, especially

---

[131] See n 84.
[132] eg Case C-110/03 *Belgium v Commission* [2005] ECR I-2801, para 30; Case C-386/06 *R (International Association of Independent Tanker Owners (Intertanko)) v Secretary of State for Transport* [2008] ECR I-4057, para 69.
[133] eg Case C-219/07 *Nationale Raad van Dierenkwekers en Liefhebbers* [2008] ECR I-4475.
[134] Czarnota (n 129) 42.   [135] 4A_558/2011, 27 March 2012.

by the CAS and especially in *Matuzalem*, can be justified, given the way in which it prioritizes the interests of the clubs and the governing bodies over those of the players. These are disproportionate restrictions, achieved through the strong grip exercised by the powerful over the regulatory structure in sports governance. A suitable case would give the Court of Justice a chance to rule in this vein: a superior outcome would be for the CAS to absorb the controlling influence of EU law into its practice with greater fidelity and consistency.[136]

9.14 Concluding Comments

The transfer system was amended in the light of *Bosman*, but even today aspects of its operation remain vulnerable to attack driven by EU law. It is a truly intriguing case study into the extent to which sport is special, and how this should be reflected in law.

It has been argued that both justifications for a transfer system accepted by the Court in *Bosman* are unpersuasive. The transfer system is a poorer way to preserve a degree of competitive balance and equality between clubs than a horizontal revenue-sharing scheme. Sport is special because of the interdependence of participant clubs, but the transfer system is not a necessary or even well-targeted means to promote that special feature. And youth training is not a demonstrated sports-specific concern at all, at least not on the evidence addressed by the Court of Justice in *Bosman* and *Bernard*. This is not to argue in favour of the complete abandonment of the transfer system, but rather to argue that a better justification for it needs to be found. That must lie in protecting the integrity of the game from relatively short-term changes in playing personnel, consequent on the—varied—patterns of national contract and employment law. This is a legitimate concern of the *lex sportiva*. But although that is a good reason for establishing a uniformly applicable transfer system under the *lex sportiva* which transcends the diverse patterns of national contract and employment law, it is far from clear that anything so restrictive as the current system can be justified under EU law. Advocate General Lenz took this view over twenty years ago in *Bosman*: the full implications of his scepticism about the compatibility of the transfer system with EU law have not yet been fully worked out. Motivated by exactly this perception, the players' union, FIFPro, announced in September 2015 an intention to challenge the current system by submitting a complaint to the Commission.[137] It is likely that the trail of litigation pitting the transfer system against the demands of EU law which was initiated by *Bosman* is not yet at an end.

---

[136] See Ch 2.2.

[137] It is backed by a critical paper written by a leading sports economist: S Szymanski, 'The Economic Arguments Supporting a Competition Law Challenge to the Transfer System', published on FIFPro's website <https://fifpro.org/news/economic-report-makes-uncomfortable-reading/en/> accessed 29 November 2016.

10

The Influence of EU Law on Sports Governance

10.1 Introduction

The notion of 'governance' covers the whole range of practices conducted by sporting bodies in the name of the proper regulation of their sport. It is here that foundational claims to sporting autonomy are commonly made. Who, sports bodies typically argue, can know what is best for a particular sport other than those with the expertise and accumulated experience—that is, the governing bodies themselves? And that argument rooted in expertise is typically accompanied by one rooted in the need for geographical integrity. So it is claimed that decisions taken about the structure of sporting governance should not be questioned by local rules, for that would fragment the global scheme of organization to which most sports are wedded and which, they argue, is essential to ensure that the sport means the same thing whether it is played in Bolivia, Bulgaria, or Borneo.

As has been consistently observed in this book, EU law's developed approach is to permit conditional, not absolute, autonomy to sports bodies. This applies also to matters of governance. Respect is paid to claims of this type made by sports bodies in favour of autonomy in choices about governance, but it is not absolute. Sport must demonstrate a sufficiently compelling reason for its choices when they collide with the expectations of EU law. The theme of this chapter will resemble that found in other chapters: EU law accepts that sport is entitled to claim it has special features, but sometimes it makes inflated claims.

Two questions put to the Commission by Members of the European Parliament and answered in March 2013 helpfully capture the tension and the subtlety. Pressed to respond to reports of on-field violence in a Spanish football match, Ms Vassiliou calmly drew attention to the EU's limited competence in the field of sport and expressed the view that disciplinary measures should be applied, if at all, by the Spanish Football Federation and/or by other competent authorities in Spain.[1] The autonomy of sports governance was plainly and sensibly respected. But when asked to reflect on a decision of the International Amateur Boxing association to require that materials used in events shall be approved by that body,

---

[1] E-000828/12 [2013] OJ C82E/27 (20 March 2012).

Mr Almunia was far less deferential to what one might have initially thought was a matter of internal governance.[2] The appointment of suppliers, especially where this is on an exclusive basis, may have economic benefits that outweigh the restrictive effects, but the Commission's orthodox approach in applying EU competition law has been to expect an open tender with selection on a transparent, open, and non-discriminatory basis, and with limited duration. Only in this way is anticompetitive market closure prevented. Mr Almunia advised that assessment of such stipulations by a governing body should proceed 'on a case-by-case basis' and 'in the context of the concrete legal and economic circumstances'. This is fully in line with the Court's landmark ruling in *Meca-Medina and Majcen v Commission*,[3] and it reveals once again a central theme of EU sports law—the inability to place large areas of activity *automatically* outside the reach of EU law. The autonomy of sports governance in the shadow of EU law depends on a case-by-case examination. It is an autonomy that is conditional on demonstration that there is an adequate reason for the choice of particular governance patterns in sport.

10.2 The Political and Policy Background

The EU has no authority under its Treaty to adopt legislation dictating how governing bodies in sport should act. Article 165 of the Treaty on the Functioning of the European Union (TFEU) limits the EU to the adoption of incentive measures and recommendations. This was examined in Chapter 6. The EU's role in matters of governance is shaped by the broad functional reach of the relevant rules of EU internal market law—free movement and competition law, supplemented by the basic prohibition against nationality-based discrimination. These were examined in Chapters 4 and 5. So sports governance becomes a matter for examination in the light of EU law because its practices may collide with the basic economic project mapped by the Treaty. The key questions therefore focus on the consequences of that intersection.

By no means for the first time in this book it proves helpful to refer to the Nice Declaration of 2000.[4] In it the European Council 'stresses its support for the independence of sports organizations and their right to organise themselves through appropriate associative structures' and adds that 'it is the task of sporting organisations to organise and promote their particular sports, particularly as regards the specifically sporting rules applicable and the make-up of national teams, in the way which they think best reflects their objectives'.[5] Sports federations 'have a central role in ensuring the essential solidarity between the various levels of sporting practice, from recreational to top-level sport, which co-exist there', and, moreover, they

---

[2] E-000578/12 [2012] OJ C75E/278 (6 March 2012).

[3] Case C-519/04P *Meca-Medina and Majcen v Commission* [2006] ECR I-6991. See Ch 5.

[4] See Ch 6.3. The full text of the Nice Declaration on Sport is at <http://eur-lex.europa.eu/legal-content/EN/TXT/?uri=URISERV:l35007> accessed 29 November 2016.

[5] ibid para 7.

pursue social functions such as ensuring access to sports for the public at large, promotion of equal access for men and women alike, youth training, health protection, and measures to combat doping, acts of violence, and racist or xenophobic occurrences which 'entail special responsibilities for federations and provide the basis for the recognition of their competence in organising competitions'.[6] Federations provide a guarantee of sporting cohesion.[7]

The Nice Declaration is widely and correctly regarded as a document weak in bite but strong in vague aspiration, but its treatment of the role of federations contains within it the seeds of an intriguing challenge to the central role claimed by sports bodies in the governance of their sport. The autonomy envisaged by the Nice Declaration is *conditional*. So recognition that 'it is the task of sporting organisations to organise and promote their particular sports' is conditional on 'due regard for national and Community legislation and on the basis of a democratic and transparent method of operation'.[8] Federations must continue to be the key feature of a form of organization providing a guarantee of sporting cohesion but also 'participatory democracy'.[9]

The Nice Declaration makes certain assumptions about the standards of governance expected in sport as a matter of EU law. Those standards are not far removed from those that would be expected of public bodies.[10] It is easy to take this as a reflection of the power enjoyed by sporting federations, projected on a global level, but it does not fully coincide with governing bodies' own self-perception and formal legal status as private bodies.

Clearly the Nice Declaration has no binding force. But its thematic reluctance to accede to an absolute notion of sporting autonomy in matters of governance is capable of being transplanted to the interpretation and application of EU internal market law.

The Commission's 2007 White Paper on Sport tackles the matter with care and subtlety.[11] Its Section 4 is entitled 'The Organisation of Sport'. This acknowledges the 'diversity and complexities of European sport structures' and so treats it as 'unrealistic to try to define a unified model of organisation of sport in Europe'. This, as discussed in Chapter 6.5, amounts to a welcome retreat from the insensitive ambition of the 1999 Helsinki Report to promote a 'European Sport Model'. In the 2007 White Paper the Commission 'acknowledges the autonomy of sporting organisations and representative structures (such as leagues)' and it 'recognises that governance is mainly the responsibility of sports governing bodies and, to some extent, the Member States and social partners'.[12] However, in line with the Nice Declaration, the explanation does not stop here. An EU gloss is added to the discourse of autonomy. Self-regulation shall be 'respectful of good governance principles' and must respect EU law. The Commission puts itself forward as able to 'play a

---

[6] ibid paras 8 and 9.   [7] ibid para 10.   [8] ibid para 7.   [9] ibid para 10.
[10] See Ch 2.2.5.
[11] White Paper on Sport, COM (2007) 391, 11 July 2007, available via <http://ec.europa.eu/sport/index_en.htm> accessed 29 November 2016. See Ch 6.5.
[12] ibid 13.

role in encouraging the sharing of best practice in sport governance' and to 'help to develop a common set of principles for good governance in sport, such as transparency, democracy, accountability and representation of stakeholders (associations, federations, players, clubs, leagues, supporters, etc.)'. It adds: 'Attention should also be paid to the representation of women in management and leadership positions.'[13]

The Commission Communication of January 2011, 'Developing the European Dimension in Sport', is initially less assertive.[14] It begins by declaring that the Commission 'respects the autonomy of sport governing structures as a fundamental principle relating to the organisation of sport'.[15] But in its later stages it joins the thematic insistence that the EU shall pay attention to the quality of governance. It offers an explicit embrace of the notion that EU law grants conditional autonomy to sport: 'Good governance in sport is a condition for the autonomy and self-regulation of sport organisations.'[16] The Commission agrees there is no single model of governance in European sport, but it proclaims 'inter-linked principles that underpin sport governance at European level, such as autonomy within the limits of the law, democracy, transparency and accountability in decision-making, and inclusiveness in the representation of interested stakeholders'.[17] And so, to repeat, 'Good governance in sport is a condition for addressing challenges regarding sport and the EU legal framework'.[18]

Article 165 TFEU, as a binding Treaty provision, is constitutionally more sturdy than the Nice Declaration, the White Paper, and the 2011 Communication but it is also less concrete. The 'specific nature of sport' embraced by Article 165 is a concept that is apt to capture the peculiar governance arrangements that one commonly finds in sport. But it offers no operationally useful direction on just when the claim to autonomy is durable and should be respected. In line with the findings made elsewhere in this book, the point is that Article 165 provides a basis for exploration of the proper scope of the claim that 'sport is special', but it does not itself offer any answers. However, Article 165's direction that Union action be aimed at 'promoting fairness and openness in sporting competitions' might be taken as a basis for supervising the autonomy of sports bodies, in particular by challenging the arbitrary or self-serving exercise of power. This, as is examined in this chapter, is in fact the most striking feature of the cases involving reliance on EU law to intervene in the governance of sports.

10.3 The Court of Justice: *Meca-Medina*

Meca-Medina, which was introduced in Chapter 3 and examined in Chapter 5, is itself a case about governance.[19] The Court of Justice in *Meca-Medina* insisted on a

---

[13] ibid 12 and 13.
[14] 'Developing the European Dimension in Sport' COM (2011) 12, 18 January 2011, available via <http://ec.europa.eu/sport/policy/index_en.htm> accessed 29 November 2016. See Ch 6.11.
[15] ibid para 1.2.   [16] ibid 10.   [17] ibid 10.   [18] ibid 10.
[19] *Meca-Medina* (n 3).

jurisdiction to inspect procedures governing doping control to ensure they did not interfere with competition in the internal market to an extent that went beyond what was necessary. That inspection was, in line with the ruling in *Wouters*, on which *Meca-Medina* is founded,[20] receptive to the context and particular objectives at stake. This implies a need for proper administration and procedural fairness in anti-doping controls in particular and in sports governance in general, albeit such matters are left unexplored at the level of detail by the Court in *Meca-Medina*.[21]

In practice one may readily suppose that it will normally be found that chosen procedures do *not* fall foul of EU law, and this was indeed the outcome of the Court's examination conducted in *Meca-Medina* itself. The superior expertise of sports federations, as well as the anxiety to avoid fragmenting the *lex sportiva* along geographical lines, plead for a restrained application of EU law. The Court is accordingly attentive to the need to allow room to respect the detailed intricacies of decision-making within sport. This is given concrete shape in the *Meca-Medina* ruling by the Court's acceptance that the general objective of the rules was 'to combat doping in order for competitive sport to be conducted fairly'[22] and its refusal to find that the controls were excessive either in defining precisely when doping had occurred or the severity of penalties imposed. So *Meca-Medina* does not immunize sports governance from review conducted in the name of EU law, but it shows an appreciation of the sporting context within which the review takes place.

It has been explained at length in Chapters 5 and 7 that the ruling in *Meca-Medina* is of great significance in the shaping of EU sports law because of the break it makes with methodologically more ambiguous decisions of the Court in the past. *Meca-Medina* accepts that few rules are sporting but not *also* economic in their nature and/or their effect. The majority of sporting practices are not *purely* sporting, and their compatibility with EU law falls to be assessed on a case-by-case basis. This is a grant of conditional autonomy, not absolute autonomy: EU law puts sporting practices *to the test* where they conflict with its purposes, most conspicuously the creation and maintenance of the internal market.

The claim of governing bodies in sport to exercise monopoly power to set the rules of the game has a rational basis. It is necessary to define the very nature of the game in a way that is beyond contestation. And this will normally require a common approach globally. As is commonly the case, the problems arise, and the invocation of EU law is common, where that core regulatory role spills over to generate decisions that have commercial consequences.

This is particularly sensitive where the governing body in question has a direct stake in the outcome. There was a hint of this risk of a conflict of interest

---

[20] Case C-309/99 *JCJ Wouters, JW Savelbergh, Price Waterhouse Belastingadviseurs BV v Algemene Raad van de Nederlandse Orde van Advocaten* [2002] ECR I-1577. See Ch 5.

[21] See *Meca-Medina* (n 3) paras 46–55 of the judgment. cf discussion in this vein of global administrative law in Ch 2.2.5. On anti-doping, and the World Anti-Doping Agency (WADA) and its Code in particular, see U Haas and D Healey (eds), *Doping in Sport and the Law* (Hart 2016); M Viret, *Evidence in Anti-Doping at the Intersection of Science and Law* (TMC Asser 2016); J Gleaves and TM Hunt (eds), *A Global History of Doping in Sport: Drugs, Policy and Politics* (Routledge 2015).

[22] *Meca-Medina* (n 3) para 43.

in *Meca-Medina*. The swimmers complained that the anti-doping rules were not merely a choice associated with the governance of the sport, but that they were 'also intended to protect the IOC's own economic interests' and so they should not be treated as 'inherent in the proper conduct of competitive sport'.[23] The Court did not disagree that there might be a commercial motivation behind the suppression of doping. A 'clean' sport is likely to be readily associated with claimed public health benefits and it will be of greater appeal to sponsors and broadcasters. But in *Meca-Medina* the Court believed anti-doping control was also a legitimate element in protecting the integrity of the sport and so EU law did not forbid it, provided it was not arbitrary or excessive in its application.

10.4 The Court of Justice: *MOTOE*

The ruling in which the Court was enabled to engage more closely with choices about governance in sport which carried with them direct commercial conse-quences for the organizing body involved is *Motosykletistiki Omospondia Ellados NPID (MOTOE) v Elliniko Dimosio*.[24] The ruling, conveniently abbreviated to *MOTOE*, is a decision of the Grand Chamber of the Court of Justice and so it car-ries a high level of authority.

The sport is motorcycling; the territory is that of Greece. MOTOE was the Greek Motorcycling Federation. It was a non-profit-making association governed by pri-vate law. Under Greek law state authorization was required to organize motorcy-cling competitions. MOTOE had asked for authorization. But it had been refused.

The Greek State had not acted unilaterally in refusing MOTOE. Greek law pro-vided that authorization would be granted only after consent had been secured from the official representative in Greece of the Fédération Internationale de Motocyclisme (the International Motorcycling Federation). That official repre-sentative was ELPA (Elliniki Leskhi Aftokinitou kai Periigiseon, Automobile and Touring Club of Greece). It too organized sporting competitions in Greece. ELPA had entered into negotiation with MOTOE. It had supplied MOTOE with infor-mation about regulations which had to be observed in the planning of competitions and had asked MOTOE for information about the events which MOTOE planned to organize. But ELPA did not give its consent. The Greek State therefore did not authorize MOTOE to proceed to organize motorcycle competitions.

MOTOE claimed it was the victim of unlawful treatment by the Greek State. It sought compensation before the Greek courts. As a matter of EU law its claim was that a violation of what were then Articles 82 and 86(1) of the Treaty Establishing the European Community (EC), which are now Articles 102 and 106(2) TFEU, had occurred. MOTOE argued, in short, that the Greek law in question conferred

---

[23] ibid para 46.
[24] Case C-49/07 *Motosykletistiki Omospondia Ellados NPID (MOTOE) v Elliniko Dimosio* [2008] ECR I-4863.

on ELPA a position of dominance over the organization of motorcycle events in Greece which, MOTOE claimed, ELPA had abused by refusing to grant consent to MOTOE. So both the state and ELPA were accused of action in violation of EU law.

MOTOE reached the Court of Justice in Luxembourg as a preliminary reference made by the Diikitiko Efetio Athinon.

The Court found it relatively easy to decide that ELPA occupied a dominant position for the purposes of (what is now) Article 102 TFEU. Cases involving occupation of an alleged dominant position frequently involve complicated and contested analysis of market structure and market power in order to ascertain whether a commercial undertaking which is economically powerful has crossed a threshold which confers on it a 'power to behave to an appreciable extent independently of its competitors, customers and ultimately of its consumers'.[25] Acquisition of such power is not *of itself* a basis for legal intervention. But at that point the threat to competition in the market causes the undertaking to be loaded with a 'special responsibility not to allow its conduct to impair genuine undistorted competition'.[26] In the precise terms of Article 102 it must not abuse its dominant position. The identification of a dominant position will commonly be relatively straightforward in application to governing bodies in sport. The *whole point* of the governing body's existence is to claim monopoly power: one of the features that makes sport special is the presence of a single body that is responsible for setting common rules that ensure the sport maintains a global integrity. This is then typically enforced by a continent-wide association, below which lie national associations. All hold monopoly power under the 'pyramid' structure of governance according to which most sports with aspirations to global relevance operate.[27] It is conceivable that on occasion a sports governing body may hold monopoly power because it supplies a product or service which consumers regard as 'standing alone', incapable of being replaced by an alternative.[28] It is, however, entirely normal that such a body is not in competition with other suppliers of *rules*. This was ELPA's role in Greek motorcycling. The relevant market identified by the Court was the 'functionally complementary'[29] organization of motorcycling events allied to their commercial exploitation by means of sponsorship, advertising, and insurance contracts on Greek territory.[30]

---

[25] eg Case 27/76 *United Brands and United Brands Continentaal v Commission* [1978] ECR 207; Case 85/76 *Hoffmann-La Roche v Commission* [1979] ECR 461; Case 322/81 *Nederlandsche Banden-Industrie-Michelin v Commission* [1983] ECR 3461, all cited at *MOTOE* (n 24) para 37. See also Commission Notice on the definition of relevant market [1997] OJ C372/5.

[26] Case 322/81 *Michelin v Commission* [1983] ECR 3461, para 57.

[27] Boxing is an exception: some major North American sports are also different.

[28] The narrowest market definition of all is found in the Commission's Decision on the 1998 Football World Cup in which the market for match tickets for the tournament stood alone from the perspective of the consumer: Comm Dec 2000/12 *1998 Football World Cup* [2000] OJ L5/55, according to which the organizers were fined for discriminatory practices in violation of EC, Art 82 now TFEU, Art 102. See also Ch 11 for narrow market definition in broadcasting.

[29] *MOTOE* (n 24) para 33 of the judgment.

[30] At ibid para 60, Opinion of Kokott AG, she raises the (perfectly logical) possibility that the market may extend beyond motorcycling, but the Court does not pursue this.

ELPA dominated that market as a sports regulator equipped with the statutory protection conferred on it by Greek law.[31]

A clutch of other attempts to resist the application of Article 102 TFEU to the *lex sportiva* and, in particular, to the Greek system for authorizing motorcycling met a fate that should be familiar to the reader of this book. Chapter 4 showed how the Court in *Bosman* systematically dismantled a series of pleas designed to shelter sporting autonomy from EU law, and a similar pattern is found in *MOTOE*, albeit in connection with competition law, not free movement. The Treaty rules on competition apply to an 'undertaking'. The concept of 'undertaking' goes undefined in the Treaty, but it has been consistently interpreted by the Court to involve engagement in economic activity, and neither legal form nor the method of financing is of significance. It is a functional test.[32] Accordingly attempts to place ELPA beyond the reach of the EU's competition rules failed. A body performing public functions and fulfilling (more or less well) defined social tasks which also carry economic implications may not count as an 'undertaking' where the activity is not pursued in the market in actual or potential competition with other economic operators. An example drawn from the Court's case law is institutions dealing with air traffic control.[33] But providing facilities for which airlines pay constitutes an economic activity.[34] And in *MOTOE* the reference made by the Diikitiko Efetio Athinon stated that ELPA's activities were not limited to purely sporting matters—it was not a 'pure regulator'. It also engaged in economic activities such as entering into sponsorship, advertising, and insurance contracts. These activities generated income for ELPA. Moroever it organized its own sporting events. ELPA was engaged in 'the organisation and commercial exploitation of motorcycling events'.[35] Even if its stated objectives were non-profit making, its activities potentially coexisted with those of other operators seeking to make a profit. It was an 'undertaking' and accordingly it could not operate autonomously of EU competition law.

The final seawall swept away by the Court's broad jurisdictional interpretation of Article 102 TFEU was an appeal that the Treaty competition rules apply only on condition that trade between Member States is affected. This is correct, but the Court pointed out that even where the undertaking's conduct appears to relate only to a single Member State it is perfectly possible that it may 'have the effect of reinforcing the partitioning of markets on a national basis, thereby holding up the economic interpenetration which the Treaty is designed to bring about'.[36] In her

---

[31] TFEU, Art 106(2) allows Member States to confer exclusive rights which may be damaging to the competitive process in so far as they promote the operation of services of general economic interest, but the conditions for reliance on this provision were clearly not satisfied in the case.

[32] eg Case C-41/90 *Höfner and Elser* [1991] ECR I-1979; Joined Cases C-264/01, C-306/01, C-354/01, and C-355/01 *AOK Bundesverband and others* [2004] ECR I-2493, all cited in *MOTOE* (n 24) para 21 of the judgment.

[33] eg Case C-364/92 *SAT Fluggesellschaft* [1994] ECR I-43; Case C-82/01 P *Aéroports de Paris v Commission* [2002] ECR I-9297, both cited at *MOTOE* (n 24) para 24.

[34] Case C-82/01 P *Aéroports de Paris v Commission* [2002] ECR I-9297, paras 68–83, cited at *MOTOE* (n 24) para 24.

[35] ibid para 26 of the judgment.   [36] ibid para 42 of the judgment.

Opinion Advocate General Kokott followed the Commission: 'the business of sport is becoming international'.[37] The Greek rules hindered that evolution by deterring non-Greek undertakings from operating on Greek territory and, since their actual or potential effect was, as a result, not felt solely on Greek territory, the Court held that they fell within the scope of EU law.

ELPA held a dominant position in the market for supply and the commercial exploitation of motorcycling events on Greek territory. But had it *abused* that position of power?

In short, it had. The key to the Court's condemnation of ELPA's practices as a sports regulator is felicitously captured by a phrase which the Court does not explicitly adopt, but which is used by Advocate General Kokott in her Opinion: there is a *conflict of interest*.[38] ELPA organizes and markets motorcycling events; it is granted a power under Greek law to decide whether other suppliers shall be allowed to enter the Greek market in circumstances where its own economic interests are directly engaged by the decision. These are the germs of abuse within the meaning of Article 102 TFEU.

The Court insisted that a 'system of undistorted competition, such as that provided for by the Treaty, can be guaranteed only if equality of opportunity is secured as between the various economic operators'.[39] This was missing in the circumstances before it, given ELPA's privileged position. It has 'an obvious advantage over its competitors'; its right may lead it 'to deny other operators access to the relevant market'.[40] It could 'distort competition by favouring events which it organises or those in whose organisation it participates'.[41]

The Court noted that a violation of Article 102 TFEU occurs where rights of the type conferred on ELPA are liable to create a situation in which that undertaking is led to commit such abuses; or where they give rise to a risk of an abuse of a dominant position.[42] The judgment comes very close to an approach that can be termed 'inevitable abuse'. The identification of a dominant position is in principle distinct from a determination whether that dominant position has been abused, but where it has been found that in practice the conditions that lead to the creation of a dominant position carry with them an inevitable slide into abusive conduct, then the formal separation between the identification of a dominant position and the finding of its abuse loses practical bite. The one leads to the other. This lies at the heart of the Court's approach in *MOTOE*. This is not unique to sport. The Court in *MOTOE* carefully cited other rulings in EU competition law, remote from sport, which tack close to the notion of 'inevitable abuse'.[43] Decisions subsequent

---

[37] ibid para 66, Opinion of Kokott AG. In similar vein, aid to relatively small football clubs has been treated as having an effect on inter-state trade within the meaning of TFEU, Art 107: see eg SA.40168 *Willem II*, especially paras 15, 39–40; SA.41614 *Den Bosch*, paras 7, 62–63.

[38] *MOTOE* (n 24) para 98, Opinion of Kokott AG.   [39] ibid para 51 of the judgment.

[40] ibid. The Court cites, as analogies, Case C-202/88 *France v Commission* [1991] ECR I-1223; and Case C-18/88 *GB Inno BM* [1991] ECR I-5941.

[41] *MOTOE* (n 24) para 52 of the judgment.   [42] ibid para 50 of the judgment.

[43] eg Case C-41/90 *Höfner and Elser* [1991] ECR I-1979; Case C-260/89 *ERT* [1991] ECR I-2925; Case C-179/90 *Merci convenzionali porto di Genova* [1991] ECR I-5889; Case C-323/93 *Centre d'insémination de la Crespelle* [1994] ECR I-5077; Case C-380/05 *Centro Europa 7* [2008] ECR I-0000,

to *MOTOE* too show that this is a reflection of general EU competition law. So, for example, in *OTOC* the Court drew on *MOTOE* in insisting on the importance of preserving an equality of opportunity among economic operators in a context where a chartered accountants' body which provided professional training was able to decide on whether to issue a licence to would-be competitors.[44] It is, however, a model likely to be found in sport relatively readily, given the orthodox pattern whereby the regulator is attributed monopoly power to set rules. The problem, however, is not the creation of centralized regulatory power: the problem is its exploitation to serve the commercial interests of the regulator. Put another way, EU law is suspicious of the operation in practice of the *lex sportiva*, not its attachment in principle to a top-down rule-making governance model.

A few years before *MOTOE* the Commission had hinted at similar concerns in its decision in *FIA (Formula One)*.[45] Part of the Commission's objections in *FIA* targeted rules that provided a financial disincentive for contracted broadcasters to show motor sports events that competed with Formula One. The Commission announced itself satisfied with a solution according to which the FIA relaxed its grip by releasing broadcasters to make their own commercial choices about which events to show. *MOTOE* takes the matter on to a more authoritative plane. Moreover, it is a ruling of the Grand Chamber.

10.5 *MOTOE* and Review of Sports Governance

MOTOE asserts a power of review over governance arrangements in sport pursuant to EU law. In particular, it focuses on the potentially abusive mix of functions pursued by a sports regulator. The core problem—the conflict of interest—is the leverage of *regulatory* power to achieve *commercial* advantage. ELPA had, as Advocate General Kokott notes on several occasions in her Opinion, a dual role.

It is, however, thematically important to reinforce the model of conditional autonomy under EU law. EU law does not wipe out the possibility to sustain the model of governance favoured by sport, which is focused on a single federation for a single territory and, ultimately, at the apex of the 'pyramid' of governance, a single global authority. Instead EU law requires that it be shown why such a model is necessary for governance in sport, and in particular it refuses to accept that more objectionable—abusive—aspects of the system's detailed operation which are *not* necessary in sport governance may be maintained. So, in line with the thematic investigation contained in this book, EU internal market law is a force for reform in sports governance, but it is not implacably insensitive to the legitimate and

---

all cited in *MOTOE* (n 24) paras 49 and 50 of the judgment. See R Whish and D Bailey, *Competition Law* (8th edn, OUP 2015) ch 6.48, dealing in particular with cases on 'conflict of interest'.

[44] Case C-1/12 *OTOC (Ordem dos Técnicos Oficiais de Contas)*, judgment of 28 February 2013, especially para 88.

[45] COMP 35.163, Notice published at [2001] OJ C169/5.

distinctive concerns of sport. As Article 165 TFEU declares, sport has a 'specific nature' and the question here is to fit that into the concept of abuse within Article 102 TFEU.

MOTOE does not demand that the supply of competitive sporting events shall become a wholly unregulated market. Sports governing bodies remain able in principle to arrange the calendar, to decide how many events should be permitted, and to perform a gate-keeping function as far as would-be organizers are concerned. Prior approval is a potentially proper and lawful feature of a governance regime applicable to the staging of sports events. The objection in *MOTOE* is not to regulation of sport but rather to *this* system of which MOTOE fell foul, most of all the conflict of interest under which ELPA, equipped with a dual role, laboured.

The Court is properly focused on finding just why the arrangements which it is asked to inspect constitute a violation of EU law, rather than on elaborating in any detail an appropriate model for the future which would conform with EU law. However, there are crumbs within the ruling that suggest the sort of features that would be favourably regarded under a reshaped model of governance. In *MOTOE* the Court has a clear concern for 'equality of opportunity ... between the various economic operators',[46] which was missing in the case of Greek motorcycling because of the advantages enjoyed by ELPA.

The Court noted in particular ELPA's power to give consent to applications for authorization to organize motorcycling events 'without that power being made subject by that rule to restrictions, obligations and review'.[47] The problem, then, is primarily the absence of constraint over a decision-making power conferred on ELPA which is contaminated by its conflict of interest.

The Opinion of Advocate General Kokott in *MOTOE* is characteristically fuller in reflecting on what is allowed rather than simply what is condemned as abusive. She explicitly embraced the virtue of relying on the expertise of governing bodies. She believed there could be 'no objection if the national legislature provides in certain cases that the relevant authorities should obtain expert advice before granting authorisation for an activity'; this would permit the involvement of sports associations in a way apt to ensure the taking into account of the 'particular characteristics of sport and of the sport in question'.[48] Refusal of consent to authorize an event could be justified by objective reasons associated with the need to take precautions to address the safety of the racers and spectators. However, the Advocate General expressly accepted that objective reason for refusing consent need not be restricted exclusively to technical safety requirements.[49] She referred to the need for each sport to operate according to rules that are as uniform as possible; for individual competitions in a particular sport to be incorporated into an overarching framework run under a timetable that prevents clashes; and, more generally and citing the Commission's 2007 White Paper on Sport,[50] she approved the *pyramid structure*

---

[46] *MOTOE* (n 24) para 51.   [47] ibid paras 52, 53 and the operative part of the ruling.
[48] ibid para 101, Opinion of Kokott AG.   [49] ibid para 91, Opinion of Kokott AG.
[50] See n 11.

of governance found in most sports which is apt to deliver uniform rules and a uniform timetable.[51] Sport can certainly be regulated. The objection arises where the structure tips over into one that confers a power to promote the organization's own economic interest, to the detriment of other potential service providers. That strips away objective justification in the interests of sport and converts the governance arrangements into an abuse. Precisely when this tipping-point is reached requires a close examination of each aspect of the system, not a generalized assessment. This is exactly in line with the Court's insistence in *Meca-Medina* on a case-by-case examination.[52] There are and can be no bright lines that limit the reach of EU law, beyond which sporting autonomy reigns supreme: the law of the internal market is by nature a broad, functionally driven system. This is the message of the Commission's 2007 White Paper on Sport, into which the reasoning in *MOTOE* could comfortably be integrated. Most of all, for Advocate General Kokott 'the maintenance of effective competition and the ensuring of transparency require a clear separation between the entity that participates in the authorisation ... of ... events and, where appropriate, monitors them, on the one hand, and the undertakings that organise and market such events, on the other'.[53]

So what is needed is a separation of function, with the regulatory function focused on what is objectively justified as necessary in the governance of the sport, coupled to decision-making according to objective, non-discriminatory criteria, which are moreover open to review. These are the 'restrictions, obligations and review' to which the preliminary reference made by the Greek court refers and on which the Court insists in its ruling.[54] Sports federations are *not* required to give prior approval to new events. They may protect and preserve the structure of the calendar over which they preside and which they have typically created. The key issue is the conduct of the prior approval system. A sports regulator can clearly be centrally involved, indeed exclusively responsible, but the procedure must be shaped in such a way as to reflect and restrain any commercial self-interest on the part of the decision-maker. In addition the procedures and criteria for selection must be transparent, objectively justified, and non-discriminatory on paper and in their practical application and there should moreover be a right to a hearing, a duty to give reasons for decisions taken, and the possibility of review by an independent body; otherwise—abuse. This approach is visible elsewhere in case law dealing with Article 101 TFEU[55] and, in fact, it is consistent too with the Court's approach to the law of free movement, where systems requiring prior approval before a product or service may be marketed can be justified only if the restriction on trade is proportionate to the objective pursued and provided applicable criteria are objective,

---

[51] *MOTOE* (n 24) paras 91–96, Opinion of Kokott AG. See S Weatherill, 'Is the Pyramid Compatible with EC Law?' (2005) 5(3–4) Intl Sports LJ 3.
[52] See Chs 5.3, 7.3.   [53] *MOTOE* (n 24) para 102, Opinion of Kokott AG.
[54] See ibid paras 18, 48, 52, 53 and the operative part of the judgment.
[55] Case C-67/96 *Albany International BV* [1999] ECR I-5751 paras 88–122, especially para 120 on respect for the expertise of a decision-making body and para 121 on safeguards attached to its decision-making process.

non-discriminatory, and known in advance.[56] The point is that there is a procedural dimension to internal market law generally.[57] The concern is to define as tightly as possible the basis of the decision-making process in order to prevent arbitrary or self-motivated choices.

MOTOE, as a ruling requiring adaptation in but not abandonment of established patterns of sports governance, stands with other landmark judgments of the Court concerning sport. In *Bosman* the very idea of a transfer system was not ruled incompatible with EU law: the particular system of which Bosman was victim was condemned.[58] In *Lehtonen* a discriminatory transfer window was found to be incompatible with EU law, but the Court did not at all deny that sport may have a particular need for restrictions on the mobility of employees at the sharp end of a season.[59] So too *Meca-Medina*: doping controls were not treated as incompatible with EU law, though rules that were excessive judged with reference to the method of finding an offence or with regard to the severity of penalties would be.[60] So in *MOTOE* the whole notion of regulated access to the market for staging sports events was not ruled unlawful, but rather the particular challenged Greek system, which generated a profound conflict of interest, was condemned as abusive.

Practice will doubtless develop over time.[61] In October 2015 the Commission announced the opening of an investigation into the eligibility rules of the International Skating Union (ISU)[62] and in September 2016 it took the matter on to a more formal level by issuing a statement of objections.[63] The problem lies in the ISU's treatment of skaters who take part in events that are not approved by the ISU. It reserves the power, conferred on it because it is the sole governing body in the sport recognized by the International Olympic Committee (IOC), to ban such skaters from the Olympic Games and the World Championship. This throws up an obvious conflict of interest: the ISU is able to act in a way that protects and promotes the events which it organizes at the expense of competing suppliers. The ISU has a proper role as regulator of the sport, but the Commission's view is that it reserves to itself powers that exceed what is necessary for the organization of the sport and maintenance of its integrity.

A sports regulator might choose to surrender completely its commercial activities. This might in fact be the best route to achieving autonomy: it might not even

---

[56] eg Case C-390/99 *Canal Satellite Digital SL* [2002] ECR I-607, especially para 35; Case C-432/03 *Commission v Portugal* [2005] ECR I-9665, especially para 50; Case C-219/07 *Nationale Raad van Dierenkwekers en Liefhebbers* [2008] ECR I-4475, especially paras 33–37; Joined Cases C-458/14 and C-67/15 *Promoimpresa srl*, judgment of 14 July 2016, especially paras 64–74.

[57] cf C Barnard, *The Substantive Law of the EU: The Four Freedoms* (5th edn, OUP 2016) 193–94.

[58] Case C-415/93 *Union royale belge des sociétés de football association ASBL v Jean-Marc Bosman* [1995] ECR I-4921. See Ch 9.

[59] Case C-176/96 *Jyri Lehtonen and Castors Canada Dry Namur-Braine ASBL v Fédération royale belge des sociétés de basket-ball ASBL (FRBSB)* [2000] ECR I-2681.

[60] *Meca-Medina* (n 3) para 48 of the judgment.

[61] There is a growing body of case law, not only at EU but also at national level: see B Van Rompuy, 'The Role of EU Competition Law in Tackling Abuse of Regulatory Power by Sports Associations' (2015) 22(2) MJ 179, 198–206.

[62] IP/15/5771, 5 October 2015.   [63] AT.40208 *ISU*, IP/16/3201, 27 September 2016.

constitute an 'undertaking' within the meaning of EU law in such circumstances[64] and, even if it does, the risk of abuse would be minimized by the elimination of any conflict of interest between regulatory and commercial functions. But EU law, as interpreted in *MOTOE*, does not go so far as to *require* that commercial activities be stripped from a sports regulator. It is a conflict of interest of the type of which ELPA was egregiously guilty which raises concerns. They may feasibly be met by structural separation of regulatory and commercial activities within a sports regulator combined with effective procedural safeguards to ensure fairness in the decision-making process.

It is the commercial consequences of governance choices made in sport which bring EU law into play. The more the system is shaped by and responsive to the interests of governing bodies and the less the voice of would-be organizers, participant clubs, and athletes is taken into account in the drafting and application of the rules, the more likely it is that an *abuse* condemned by Article 102 TFEU will be found. This provides the basis for exploration of other aspects of sports governance to discover whether they may be contaminated by an endemic conflict of interest to the extent that they fall foul of EU law.

10.6 Multiple Ownership of Clubs

The Commission's *ENIC/UEFA* decision concerns rules forbidding the multiple ownership of clubs.[65] It has already been examined in Chapter 5.2, as part of the survey of the development of competition law in application to practices in sport. It deserves brief re-appraisal in this chapter, because it is directly concerned with EU law's supervision of sports governance and, in particular, because it confirms that EU law is receptive to sincere arguments that sport may legitimately be characterized by patterns of intervention that are more intrusive than would be found in other sectors of economic activity.

The Nice Declaration of 2000 already signalled a receptivity to rules forbidding multiple ownership.[66] Under the heading 'Economic Context of Sport and Solidarity' it declared the view of the European Council that 'single ownership or financial control of more than one sports club entering the same competition in the same sport may jeopardise fair competition'.[67] In *ENIC* the Commission had the opportunity to apply this perception to legal assessment of a Union of European Football Associations (UEFA) rule adopted in 1998 which provided that no two (or more) clubs participating in a UEFA club competition could be directly or indirectly controlled by the same entity or managed by the same person. ENIC, which controlled several clubs across Europe, attacked the rule as a distortion of competition prohibited by EU law. It complained to the Commission. But the Commission did not share ENIC's view. The Commission agreed in principle

---

[64] *SAT Fluggesellschaft* (n 33).   [65] COMP 37.806 *ENIC/UEFA*, IP/02/942, 27 June 2002.
[66] See Ch 6.3. Nice Declaration on Sport (n 4).   [67] ibid para 14.

that the UEFA rule was capable of amounting to a practice that fell within the scope of what was then Article 81(1) EC, now Article 101(1) TFEU. After all, it suppressed demand: the owner of one club could not compete in the market to buy another one. However, the Commission relied on the need to guarantee the integrity of sporting competitions, which was the motivating factor behind the rule, as a reason to reject ENIC's complaint. ENIC did not pursue the matter further.

This, as explained in full in Chapter 5, reflects the model of 'conditional autonomy' granted to sport under EU law. The Commission refused to grant absolute autonomy to UEFA. It treated the rule as falling within the scope of EU law because of its restrictive effect on competition in the market for clubs. But it permitted autonomy provided UEFA met the conditions set by EU law, which here were interpreted in the context of the sporting need to eliminate any suspicion of collaboration off the pitch that would taint the rivalry of clubs on the pitch. As also explained in Chapter 5, the Commission relied heavily on the Court's ruling in *Wouters*:[68] *ENIC* is a milestone in the shaping of EU competition law's intersection with sport. In the language of Article 165 TFEU, the Commission in *ENIC* acknowledged 'the specific nature of sport' and fed it into its interpretation and application of Article 101 TFEU.

The consequence is that a choice about governance which was driven by the peculiar character of sport, specifically the need for uncertainty of outcome, was reviewed with sensitivity to that objective and so was not condemned by EU law.

10.7 Rules on Player Release

10.7.1 The rules

The rules governing release of players by clubs to allow their selection for international representative teams are vivid examples of the truth that sport is special. Their most high-profile version is found in football.

The currently applicable rules are contained in the FIFA Regulations on the Status and Transfer of Players,[69] Annex I of which is entitled 'Release of Players to Association Teams'.

Its first paragraph is uncompromising:

Clubs are obliged to release their registered players to the representative teams of the country for which the player is eligible to play on the basis of his nationality if they are called up by the association concerned to play in an international match between two representative teams belonging to different associations. Any agreement between a player and a club to the contrary is prohibited.

---

[68] *Wouters* (n 20).
[69] The text of the FIFA Regulations on the Status and Transfer of Players is available at <http://www.fifa.com/governance/dispute-resolution-system/index.html> accessed 29 November 2016.

The Annex applies the same regime to the women's game.

The Annex provides in detail for the length of the period of release: it is longer for competitive than for friendly matches. But the basic point, made explicit in the second paragraph, is that release of players under the conditions specified is *mandatory*. This applies not only to clubs, but also to players, who are 'obliged to respond affirmatively when called up by the association', subject only to a carefully written exception in the case of an existing injury or illness. Sanctions may be imposed on club and/or player in the event of non-compliance. It is, moreover, stipulated in section 2 of the Annex that clubs releasing a player are not entitled to financial compensation; and that the club with which the player is registered shall be responsible for insurance cover against illness and accident during the entire period of release, including in respect of injuries sustained by the player during the match(es) played during the period of release.

Disputes are typically routed through the Dispute Resolution Chamber of Fédération Internationale de Football Association (FIFA) and then, if necessary, through the Court of Arbitration for Sport (CAS), as explained in Chapter 2. So, for example, a disagreement about whether clubs were required to release players for the 2008 Olympic Games' football tournament was resolved, in principle, by the CAS in favour of the clubs—although, not least because of the eagerness of the players to travel to Beijing in search of a coveted Olympic medal, in practice release did occur.[70]

This is a governance choice that, on first inspection, seems to be a necessary element in the organization of football. There are no permanent international representative teams. Instead international fixtures are placed in agreed slots through the calendar: friendly matches and qualifying matches lead to summer tournaments such as the World Cup (which takes place once every four years) which are the most high-profile events. It is club football which dominates the calendar. And players are contracted to clubs, which pay their wages as employees. If selected, players are released for a short period of time to play for international representative teams. FIFA's rules, as just summarized, guarantee this. No 'normal' industry would require that employees be (in effect) loaned out to support another related activity, but no 'normal' industry is based on a mix of club and international representative football in the way that football and some other team sports are.

A second glance is needed to appreciate the scale of the oddity. Club football and international football are *to an extent* engaged in competition in the same markets. Resources devoted by sponsors, advertisers, and broadcasters to football are finite, and their allocation to support, say, FIFA's World Cup will reduce the sums available to support club competitions at European or at national level—and vice versa. The player release rules make international representative football more commercially attractive than it would be were clubs entitled to choose whether to allow their players to perform also at international level. This creates a problem associated with the distortion of the competitive structure of the market. And FIFA is no

[70] CAS 2008/A/1622-1623-1624 *Schalke 04, Werder Bremen, Barcelona v FIFA*.

neutral regulator. FIFA has a direct commercial interest in the matter. The World Cup is an immensely lucrative resource for FIFA. It ensures its commercial attraction by requiring that clubs (in effect) loan it their best players for the duration of the tournament. There is something perfectly breathtaking about the requirement that an employer release its often very highly paid and carefully trained employee to work briefly for another entity that has made no investment in that labour resource and which does not even pay for that privilege and yet which benefits directly as a result. What is in fact at stake is one commercial undertaking, FIFA (plus the national associations), using its regulatory power within sports governance to force other competing commercial undertakings, clubs, to strengthen the vitality of its, FIFA's, business model at the expense of that of the clubs. This is the problem, visible in *MOTOE*, of the sports federation labouring under a conflict of interest because its choices about governance and regulation are entangled with and directly serve its commercial objectives.

The question is whether sport is *so* special that it can withstand the allegation that player release rules, which are imposed top-down by federations and national associations on clubs and players through the governance structure of the sport, amount to an abuse of a dominant position of the type forbidden by Article 102 TFEU.

10.7.2 The litigation

The matter has not been tested before the Court. But it *nearly* was, and the litigation that was discontinued before the Court had a chance to rule is in many respects as illuminating as some of the Court's actual rulings in exploring the EU law's intersection with and impact on governance in sport.

The story begins in November 2004. Its location is Belgium. Charleroi's promising young footballer, Abdelmajid Oulmers, had been released to play at international level for his country, Morocco. He was seriously injured and consequently he was unavailable for selection by Charleroi for several months. Such events are, to the dismay of clubs, far from uncommon in football.[71] Charleroi's results suffered a downturn. However, under FIFA's Regulations, set out earlier, the club continued to have to pay his wages while being unable to claim any compensation for his unavailability for selection. Charleroi initiated litigation before the Belgian courts. It claimed damages from FIFA, alleging that it was the victim of abusive practices in violation of what was then Article 82 of the Treaty Establishing the European Community (EC), now Article 102 TFEU. In May 2006 the Tribunal de Commerce in Charleroi rejected a number of arguments advanced by football's governing bodies which were designed to maximize sporting autonomy under the

---

[71] eg 'Wenger Blames French FA for Henry's Injury' *The Independent* (London, 14 March 2007) 56; 'Fifa Offers Newcastle £1m for Owen Injury' *The Guardian* (London, 1 March 2007) Sports section, 5; 'Bayern Blame Irresponsible Dutch for Robben Injury' *The Guardian* (London, 4 August 2010) Sports section, 4; 'Fractures impayées: suite à la blessure d'Eric Abidal, l'OL menace de poursuivre la FFF …' *Les Cahiers du Football* 18 November 2005 <http://www.cahiersdufootball.net/article-fractures-impayees-2015> accessed 29 November 2016.

lex sportiva. Some involved technical points of procedure, others were of a more fundamental nature. Some were rooted in Belgian law, others stemmed from EU law. The Tribunal concluded that, as a matter of Belgian public policy, it would not defer to the jurisdictional exclusivity claimed by FIFA for the Court of Arbitration in Sport: this is fully in line with the account provided in Chapter 2 of this book, which emphasizes EU law's predilection to crack open claims to the contractually enforced autonomy of the *lex sportiva*. Moreover, the Tribunal was not deterred by pleas to treat the rules as purely sporting in nature. It took the view that the complexity of the case law, combined with the transnational importance of the issue under examination, made it an appropriate case for referral to the Court of Justice in search of an authoritative uniform interpretation of EU law. And so the reference was made in May 2006 as *SA Sporting du Pays de Charleroi, G-14 Groupment des clubs de football européens v Fédération internationale de football association (FIFA)*.[72]

The question referred asked:

Do the obligations on clubs and football players having employment contracts with those clubs imposed by the provisions of FIFA's statutes and regulations providing for the obligatory release of players to national federations without compensation and the unilateral and binding determination of the coordinated international match calendar constitute unlawful restrictions of competition or abuses of a dominant position or obstacles to the exercise of the fundamental freedoms conferred by the EC Treaty and are they therefore contrary to Articles 81 and 82 of the Treaty [*now Articles 101 and 102 TFEU*] or to any other provision of Community law, particularly Articles 39 and 49 of the Treaty [*now Articles 45 and 56 TFEU*]?

But the Court of Justice did not answer this question.

The reference was the subject of an appeal before the Belgian courts. That appeal was set for hearing in the summer of 2008. The Court of Justice decided to wait, pending resolution of the Belgian appeal. But the litigation was settled out of court in early 2008. And in 2009 the case was recorded as having been removed from the Court's register.[73]

Two distinct lines of inquiry deserve pursuit. First, why and with what consequence was the litigation discontinued? Second, how should the question asked, but never answered, about the compatibility of the mandatory player release rules with EU law be properly answered? Both lines of inquiry reveal much about EU law's influence on governance in sport.

10.7.3 The settlement of the litigation

In the proceedings before the Tribunal de Commerce in Charleroi the might of football's governance structure was ranged against Charleroi, a small Belgian football

---

[72] Case C-243/06, referred to the Court of Justice by Tribunal de Commerce de Charleroi in May 2006. For further background, see Weatherill (n 51) 3.
[73] [2009] OJ C69/30.

club. FIFA enjoyed the support of interventions from over fifty continental and national associations. But Charleroi was not on its own. The club was supported by the so-called 'G-14' group of eighteen (sic) major football clubs. Charleroi had a particular grievance over the loss of their injured player Oulmers, but the clubs of the G-14 had a much greater long-term interest in attacking the rules governing player release. These are the clubs with the highest number of employees who are also regulars in international representative squads and these are the clubs that pay the highest wages. Consequently they had, and still today retain, a strong incentive to seek adjustment of rules which favour FIFA's commercial interests over their own. They backed Charleroi in the litigation on player release for very sound commercial reasons. And it was this background context that led to the abandonment of the litigation.

In short, a deal was done in early 2008. The threat to the established system of governance was clear and well advertised[74] and, in stark contrast to *Bosman*, the Court of Justice was prevented from taking a stance. The litigation in the case was terminated and the G-14 group of major clubs was wound up.[75] In return for this outbreak of peace the governing bodies in football agreed, first, to allocate a portion of the funds raised from the marketing of major international championships to establish a scheme to compensate clubs which release players and, second, to allow the clubs a louder voice in governance matters at transnational level. This was to be directed through a newly instituted European Club Association (ECA).[76]

The ECA was a successor to the G-14, but its membership is much broader. It currently has 220 member clubs from fifty-three national associations in Europe. Its place in football's governance structure is formally recognized. In short, the G-14 group was on the outside, lobbying to promote its members' interests, whereas by contrast the ECA is on the inside. A Memorandum of Association struck between UEFA and the ECA in 2012 provided a basis for cooperation until 2018.[77] In 2015 it was agreed to extend this until 2022.[78] The Memorandum of Association is stated to be a binding agreement, governed by Swiss law. Disputes arising out of the agreement are to be exclusively decided by the CAS. It declares a shared recognition of the benefits of both national team and club football, and commits the parties to promote cooperation in the interests of European football and to

---

[74] eg 'Oulmers Test Case has FIFA Under-Siege' *The Irish Times* (Dublin, 28 March 2006) <http://www.irishtimes.com/sport/oulmers-test-case-has-fifa-under-siege-1.1289561> accessed 29 November 2016.

[75] This was reported on G-14's website <http://www.g14.com/main.php>, but it is no longer available. On G-14's lifecycle, see W Grant, 'The Representation of Football in the European Union: UEFA versus G-14' in S Gardiner, R Parrish, and R Siekmann (eds), *EU, Sport, Law and Policy* (TMC Asser 2009) ch 22.

[76] <http://www.ecaeurope.com/> accessed 29 November 2016. For media comment at the time, see eg 'G14 Disbands but Wins Wider Role' *The Guardian* (London, 4 December 2007) Sports section, 4.

[77] Available via <http://www.ecaeurope.com/Documents/20120321_UEFA-ECA%20MoU%20 2012.pdf> accessed 29 November 2016.

[78] <http://www.ecaeurope.com/news/eca-and-uefa-renew-memorandum-of-understanding-until-2022/> accessed 29 November 2016.

ensure that the views of the clubs are 'properly' represented in the decision-making process in European football structures. Annex 1 deals with questions of insurance, and provides that UEFA will conclude an insurance policy to cover the risk of 'Temporary Total Disablement' of players registered for European clubs when released for defined international fixtures. The required scope and scale of the insurance cover is defined in some detail.

The clubs have been able to extract a share of the profits made from major events (in part) thanks to reliance on their players. Within Europe, the 2020 UEFA EURO will generate 8 per cent of income from broadcast, commercial, and ticketing/hospitality for clubs, with the minimum set at €200 million, which represents a €50 million increase on the clubs' share of UEFA EURO 2016 revenues.[79] In the particular matter of release of players it was announced in early 2015 that all clubs which had released players to appear at the 2014 FIFA World Cup staged in Brazil would receive compensation.[80] A total pot of US$70 million was shared according to the number of appearances made. So Real Madrid received $1,297,800, Chelsea $1,253,233, Benfica $501,900, Hull City $91,933, and Mysterious Cape Coast Ebusua Dwarfs $7,000. It was, moreover, made known in 2015 that the sums payable would be elevated for the Russia World Cup of 2018 and the 2022 event in Qatar.[81]

Other matters of governance which have been addressed with the involvement of the ECA include the scheduling of the international match calendar. It is plain that FIFA and its continental associations including UEFA, as sports regulators, need to play a role in overseeing the international calendar in order to prevent unnecessary clashes between attractive competitions. But here, once again, there is a risk of a conflict of interest. Clubs have incentives to push for a reduction in the number of international matches or, at least, to press for the programme to be streamlined.[82] The success of their input is reflected in the deletion, with effect from 2014, of the August date for friendly international matches and the rise of 'double-headers' in the international calendar, so that players' absence from their clubs is reduced. Similarly clubs are eager to persuade the African Football Confederation to schedule its bi-annual Cup of Nations as early as possible in January, to maximize its overlap with the winter breaks found in many European leagues, when the clubs do not need access to their players. However, FIFA, in deciding the pattern of the

---

[79] <http://www.ecaeurope.com/news/eca-and-uefa-renew-memorandum-of-understanding-until-2022/> accessed 29 November 2016.

[80] '396 Clubs to Receive Share of 2014 World Cup Benefits' <http://www.ecaeurope.com/news/396-clubs-to-receive-share-of-2014-world-cup-benefits> accessed 29 November 2016.

[81] 'World Cup: Clubs to Receive £142 Million for Releasing Players' <http://www.bbc.co.uk/sport/football/31984954> accessed 29 November 2016.

[82] eg 'Fifa Risks War with Clubs over International Friendlies' *The Guardian* (London, 15 June 2011) Sports section, 1; 'Scudamore [chief executive of the English Premier League] Warns Fifa over Fixture List' *The Daily Telegraph* (London, 3 August 2011) Sports section, 10; 'UEFA Plays Hardball with European Football's Elite Clubs over Demand for International Fixtures Reduction', February 2012 <http://www.telegraph.co.uk/sport/football/international/9052780/Uefa-plays-hardball-with-European-footballs-elite-clubs-over-demand-for-international-fixtures-reduction.html> accessed 29 November 2016.

calendar, has its own incentives which are not only regulatory but also commercial. Its income streams are heavily dependent on the success and on the size of its own tournaments. In recent years FIFA has created a Confederations Cup, which occurs every four years, and it has greatly enlarged the world club competition. It has lengthened the list of events on the calendar in a way that directly benefits its own commercial interests. The IOC too is involved in this congestion: it is not at all exclusively sporting considerations that have led to the much higher profile lately attached to football at the Olympic Games, to the detriment of clubs that must release their players.[83]

There is scope here for future friction and litigation. The continental championships—in Africa, in Europe, in South America, in Asia—are scattered across the year, which maximizes disruption for clubs forced to release players. There are naturally some reasons of climate for the selected dates, but this is not a total explanation. Part of the story is a desire to avoid competition between continental championships in order to maximize revenues from the sale of broadcasting rights and luring of sponsors. So, as with the player release system, the planning of the match calendar has embedded within it an identifiable commercial dimension, which reveals once again the endemic problem of a conflict of interest.[84] The current pattern could readily be adjusted—in particular by aligning as many international tournaments as the weather will allow in the European summer—in order to rebalance a governance system currently loaded heavily against the clubs. The designation by FIFA of the 2022 World Cup in Qatar as a *winter* event shows where predominant power lies. The ECA allows the clubs a louder voice in governance design than they previously had, but litigation provoked that change and resort to litigation, inter alia, to challenge the design of the calendar, remains a potential strategy. Most of all, decisions about the calendar by a governing body which favour the competitions from which it stands to gain most are legally vulnerable.

The overall story behind the *Charleroi* case is that the clubs won concessions associated with governance by using litigation as a method to put pressure on governing bodies otherwise obstinately opposed to ceding clubs a stronger role. So, even without the need for a final formal ruling of the Court of Justice, the saga shows how EU law provides a lever with which to achieve change in the governance of sport—*not* to demolish the pyramid according to which football is regulated *but instead* to secure adaption in the application of the rules and to claim a right of participation in rule-making. In short, EU law's notion of conditional autonomy provokes governance design to be sensitive to the crossover between the regulatory and commercial purposes of governing bodies.

---

[83] *Schalke 04* (n 70). cf also Cases C-51/96 and C-191/97 *Deliège v Ligue de Judo* [2000] ECR I-2549, para 55, Opinion of Cosmas AG.

[84] Football tends to dominate the debate but there are other examples of such conflict: see eg A Cygan, 'Competition and Free Movement Issues in the Regulation of Formula One Motor Racing' in B Bogusz, A Cygan, and E Szyszczak, *The Regulation of Sport in the European Union* (Edward Elgar 2007) ch 4.

10.7.4 How would the litigation have been resolved, had the Court been allowed the opportunity to rule on it?

The issues raised by the 'lost ruling' in *Charleroi* are worth attention. They provide a convenient context in which to explore how and why choices about models of governance in sport may be affected by EU law. It will be argued here that the player release model challenged in *Charleroi* had much in common with the transfer system at issue in *Bosman* and the prior authorization system attacked in *MOTOE*: that is, sport is special enough to justify in principle a system that would not be visible in a 'normal' industry, but the particular system addressed in the case went beyond the limits of what could be considered legitimate. The player release rules exhibit the conflict of interest which is the classic problem found in governance systems that seek to insulate the autonomy of rule-makers from legal control even where the choices involved are of direct commercial interest to that rule-maker. The arrangements are based on an unbalanced representation of affected interests.

It is obvious that the player release rules, which have immediate consequences for clubs (in a prejudicial way) and for national associations and governing bodies (in a positive way), have economic effects within the internal market.[85] They fall for examination in the light of EU law and, in particular, its framework, which grants conditional autonomy to sports governance. So, following *Meca-Medina* as a platform for reviewing the player release rules, account must be taken of:

> ... the overall context in which the decision of the association of undertakings was taken or produces its effects. More particularly, account must be taken of its objectives ... It has then to be considered whether the consequential effects restrictive of competition are inherent in the pursuit of those objectives.[86]

The essence of the inquiry asks whether the objectives pursued by the sporting practice can be achieved by measures which exert a less prejudicial impact on affected parties. If so, the practice is unlawful. In the terms used in association with Article 102 TFEU, it would not be proportionate, nor could it be held to be objectively justified. It would be an abuse of a dominant position.

The best way to show that a rule requiring player release is a necessary element in sports governance is, first, to show that nothing in EU law calls into question the legitimacy of international representative football, which exists alongside and connected to club football. This was made clear in the Court's first ever excursion into EU sports law, *Walrave and Koch*, examined in Chapter 3.[87] Were clubs free to *choose* whether to release players, international football would be reduced to a competition dependent for its quality and intensity on the diverse attitudes of clubs. It would be uneven and unpredictable. *Mandatory* player release seems indispensable if international football is to survive as a credible activity. But despite this insight

---

[85] The Arnaut Report, examined critically in Ch 5.5, argues at paras 3.42–3.48 that they are motivated by purely sporting considerations: this offers a perfect example of an intellectually baseless plea for absolute sporting autonomy from EU law.

[86] *Meca-Medina* (n 3) para 42. See Ch 5.

[87] Case 36/74 *Walrave and Koch v Union Cycliste Internationale* [1974] ECR 1405.

the system that operated at the time of *Charleroi* is highly unlikely to have survived legal scrutiny, had the Court not had the chance whisked away by the out-of-court settlement of the dispute.

As explained previously, it is a fair summary of the prevailing system of player release that it requires clubs to subsidize competing undertakings. Clubs were obliged on pain of sanction to continue to pay wages to their players while those players adorned international tournaments from which other entities—FIFA, UEFA, national associations—made lucrative profits. Any advantage to clubs was received only indirectly, via proceeds transferred to the national association of which they are a member, and as a hard-to-quantify potential increase in the value of the player to the club as a consequence of exposure to a wider audience watching international representative football. In any event, with those often intangible benefits to clubs came countervailing costs: after international games and especially after major summer tournaments clubs often found that they had to nurse injured and tired players back to health. A player release system is needed to underpin the international game's viability, but the argument runs that *this* player release system goes too far in protecting one set of commercial interests—those of the regulator—at the expense of another.

The system in place at the time of *Charleroi* offered no compensation to the clubs. This seems unjustifiably unbalanced in favour of governing bodies and national associations. Admittedly a player release scheme that forced national associations to cover the wages of players in full while they are on international duty would mean that some poorer national associations would simply be unable to call up their very best players: consider the financial impossibility faced by some African associations were they expected to pay wages of English- or Spanish-based players for even a short period. But this argues against a system according to which released players' wages are paid *in full*: it does not defeat the argument that an uncompensated system of release could and should be replaced by one in which clubs are compensated *in part* by national associations or, probably even better as a device to sustain the competitive vitality of international football, that part of the income from international football should be diverted into a pool from which clubs shall be compensated on a fair basis tied to the contribution made by a player equally and without reference to the depth of the pockets of a particular national association. Rich associations would subsidize poorer associations, whereas under the system as it applied at the time of *Charleroi* it was clubs that subsidized all associations (and FIFA).

Moreover, the rules in force at the time of *Charleroi* had been shaped with no formal input provided by directly affected parties, the clubs. Football's 'pyramid' structure of governance ruled out any direct formal contact between clubs and international governing bodies, instead routing the representation of club interests through national associations.

It is therefore submitted that the system of which Charleroi and Oulmers fell foul would have been condemned by the Court of Justice as an abuse of a dominant position had the litigation not been cut short. The system of governance was indefensibly unbalanced in favour of the commercial interests of the bodies which set the applicable rules. It follows from this analysis that the current version of the system is much more likely to survive attack rooted in Article 102 TFEU. The provision of some compensation to clubs that release players, combined with the louder voice permitted to clubs through the formal integration of the ECA as representative of the clubs into the 'pyramid', alters the governance structure towards a model that is less aggressively concerned to leverage the long-established power of the governing bodies to commercial advantage.[88] A mandatory player release system is necessary to sustain international football and it is therefore justifiable, but it needs to be and has been remodelled since that attacked in *Charleroi* went too far. The current system probably complies with EU law—it meets the demands of conditional autonomy and falls within the sporting margin of appreciation explained in Chapter 7.4—but it should be borne in mind that it exists in its current form only because of the indirect transformative influence of EU law.

10.8 Club Relocation

Leagues are typically organized along national lines. Clubs typically belong to leagues in the territory in which they are located. The winner is the national champion. Football is the most obvious example: the League is normally organized by the national association of the relevant territory which in Europe is in turn a member of UEFA and of FIFA. There are a tiny number of anomalies, which are driven by historical twists. Berwick Rangers are based in England but play in the Scottish League. Berwick is a town close to the Scottish border and it is a great deal closer to the major population centres of Scotland than those of England: and the town itself has a disputed past from the days when contests between England and Scotland were not confined to the sports field. Cardiff City and Swansea City are Welsh clubs which play in the English League: here too the story is of the distant past and the particular nature of the relationship between England and Wales, a separate nation but, unlike Scotland, deprived of its distinct political (but not cultural) identity by English invasion in the fourteenth century. There are oddities elsewhere in Europe too, such as Monaco and Derry City.

The norm, however, is clear: German clubs play in the German League, Italian clubs play in the Italian League, and so on. But what if a club wanted to move from one League to another? An obvious incentive would arise if a club from a relatively small League wanted to move to a larger and more lucrative League. This has been mooted periodically in connection with the two dominant clubs in Scottish football, Rangers and Celtic, who would gain financially by a move to England. Another slightly different issue might arise if a club wanted not to move from one League to another, but rather to move to another territory while remaining a member of the League based in the territory it has left. The attraction would be the opportunity to exploit a bigger fanbase in the new location. This was aired as an option in connection with Wimbledon, which some twenty years ago raised

---

[88] For this proposal advanced without the advantage of hindsight, see Weatherill (n 51) 67–72.

the possibility to move from London to Dublin while remaining members of the English League, although the plan never took real shape after it was made clear that (as a minimum) the consent of both national associations would be required. This was not forthcoming.[89] A move of this type has obvious echoes of the 'franchise' system common in North American sport.[90]

For an intricate set of largely sporting reasons no such cross-frontier move has ever taken place. Nor has the matter been the subject of litigation. But would there be a right under EU law to move between leagues or between territories? At the level of detail there are obvious problems. A Scottish club prevented from moving to England—either because the English League refuses admission or because the Scottish League refuses permission, or both—is not impeded from moving *between* Member States, although, in the same way as *Bosman* impacted more deeply on the transfer rules than first appreciated,[91] there might be a basis under EU competition law to attack even a practice apparently internal to a single Member State because of its implications for the wider competitive structure of the EU market.

The deeper question asks whether sport is special. A sausage-maker or a supplier of financial services could certainly rely on EU law to combat rules that deterred it from extending its commercial activities across borders within the EU or from changing the location of its corporate base. Sport, however, has a different governance structure: one based on the vitality of the national market—the national League.

It seems probable that protection of this governance model would survive review under EU law. It is in the nature of the organization of sport that Leagues are *national*, and it is therefore compatible with EU law to confine the choice of clubs as to which League they might wish to join. The 'specific nature of sport', heralded by Article 165 TFEU, captures this. It was reported in the Scottish press in 2013 that:

Rangers could sue the [English] Football Association and any other opposing football authorities in competition law for orders forcing their entry to the English football leagues ... It would be Bosman for the clubs.[92]

This is not convincing. In fact it is wildly optimistic. The report claims that 'the English football authorities are cartels which abuse their dominant position on those markets in the UK by having rules which exclude professional clubs that do not play their home games in England or Wales' which 'is a hard core competition abuse, worse than price fixing ...'. It might very well be a hard core violation of EU internal market law were it to involve collective action by private parties dedicated

---

[89] 'Dons' Dublin Move Blocked' *The Independent* (London, 9 June 1998) 31.

[90] And in fact Wimbledon ultimately were allowed to move within England, to Milton Keynes, in a manner that attracted opprobrium precisely because of the sense that the club had been allowed to act as a franchise rather than a club with local roots.

[91] Ch 9.7.

[92] 'Rangers have Route into English Football by Suing FA' *The Scotsman* (Edinburgh, 26 January 2013) <http://www.scotsman.com/sport/football/english/rangers-have-route-into-english-football-by-suing-fa-1-2760303> accessed 29 November 2016.

to territorial exclusion of new entrants into a market for, say, sausages, cars, or financial services. But sport is special. The most attractive Treaty-based argument in favour of a claim made by a club in the position of Rangers would be to supplement reliance on free movement and competition law with resort to the principle of 'openness in sporting competitions' recognized by Article 165(2) TFEU, but it seems highly unlikely that this carries sufficient force to prevail. National Leagues, composed of clubs located within the territory of the organizing association, are part of the game and may accordingly be maintained.[93]

In its *Lille/Mouscron* decision the Commission refused to proceed with a complaint about UEFA's refusal to allow a Belgian club to play a home match in a stadium just across the border in France.[94] The report is only brief, but declares that this 'is a sports rule that does not fall within the scope of the Treaty's competition rules'; and that 'UEFA has exercised its legitimate right of self-regulation as a sports organisation in a manner which cannot be challenged by the Treaty's competition rules'. The Commission noted that EU law does not 'call into question the geographic organization of football in Europe along national lines'. One would today repackage this analysis in the light of *Meca-Medina* and Article 165 TFEU and, as articulated in Chapter 7, the scope of conditional autonomy properly allowed to sporting bodies under EU law depends on identifying what is truly necessary for the proper organization of sport according to its specific nature. In this vein, the protection of national league structures from attempts to promote the cross-border access of non-national clubs is a justified exercise of sporting autonomy within the *lex sportiva*.

10.9 Financial Fair Play

Financial Fair Play (FFP) is a relatively recent addition to the pattern of governance applicable to football in Europe. UEFA's Executive Committee committed itself to the idea in 2009, and the system has been shaped and put into practice beginning in 2011. It is contained in UEFA's Financial Fair Play Regulations.[95] UEFA describes it as 'about improving the overall financial health of European club football'.[96] The overall intent of FFP is to impose a break-even requirement. Clubs must not spend more than they earn over a defined period. Beginning in season 2013–14 the acquisition of the licence which a football club requires to play in UEFA's European

---

[93] See also R Parrish and S Miettinen, *The Sporting Exception in European Law* (TMC Asser 2007) 209–11.

[94] IP/99/965, 9 December 1989; COMP/ IV/36.851 (unpublished).

[95] Available via <http://www.uefa.org/protecting-the-game/club-licensing-and-financial-fair-play/> accessed 29 November 2016. The Procedural Rules governing the CFCB, including the list of sanctions, are available at <http://www.uefa.org/MultimediaFiles/Download/Tech/uefaorg/General/02/28/72/46/2287246_DOWNLOAD.pdf> accessed 29 November 2016. Some national leagues have their own variants—see eg <http://www.financialfairplay.co.uk/financial-fair-play-explained.php> accessed 29 November 2016.

[96] <http://www.uefa.com/community/news/newsid=2064391.html> accessed 29 November 2016.

club competitions involves account being taken of the club's compliance with the demands of FFP.

There is not the slightest doubt that these rules will keep accountants and law-yers as engaged as ordinary fans. Their *detailed* application is forbiddingly difficult. It is in the hands of the UEFA Club Financial Control Body. Annex X of the Regulations deals directly with 'Calculation of the Break-Even Result'. It seeks to exercise control over transactions above or below 'fair value', but there are obvious objections to such quantification. Consider, for example, the case of an owner who pays what is criticized as an inflated sum for sponsorship rights at his or her club. Is this a way artificially to increase revenue to disguise over-spending? Such ruses are not unknown elsewhere in EU law[97] and they have counterparts elsewhere in sports law and practice too[98] but nowhere are they easy to define and police. Disputes are certain: disputes have already emerged. However, the overall aim of FFP is helpfully captured as an attack on *financial doping*, as part of an attempt to align sporting success more closely with skill and judgment rather than access to vast sums of investors' ready cash.

Clubs that have qualified for UEFA competitions are assessed by the Club Financial Control Body (CFCB) to ensure compliance with the requirements of the scheme. The CFCB, which is divided into an investigative and an adjudica-tive chamber, is empowered to take measures and impose sanctions. Decisions are published.[99] Available sanctions range from a mere warning through more formal interventions including a fine or a restriction on the number of players that a club may register for participation in UEFA competitions, all the way to exclusion from future competitions or even withdrawal of a title or award. But the system also embraces rehabilitation, and the CFCB commonly comes to an agreement with a club whereby it will commit to a path that targets compliance with the break-even requirement. Such settlements, which typically involve a financial contribution made by the club and an agreed monitoring process, negate the need to proceed to the adjudicative stage of the process. So, for example, leading English club Hull City agreed in 2015 to a programme designed to bring it into line with FFP, including also a payment of €200,000 to UEFA.[100] In early 2016 it was announced that the terms of the settlement had been met and the process brought to a conclusion.[101]

Sanctions for violation of the FFP Regulations, though not automatic, are poten-tially severe, especially where the possibility of limited access to or even exclusion

---

[97] Public authorities commonly try to evade the Treaty's state aid rules by arguing that they are behaving no differently from a normal private market investor: such claims need to be checked, see eg Commission Notice on the definition of a State Aid [2016] OJ C262/1, section 4.2, and for success in deploying this argument in a sporting context, see Case COMP/ SA.41613 *Aid to Dutch football club PSV* Dec 2016/1849 [2016] OJ L282/75.

[98] See eg the salary cap in rugby <http://www.premiershiprugby.com/salary-cap/> accessed 29 November 2016.

[99] <http://www.uefa.org/disciplinary/club-financial-controlling-body/cases/index.html> accessed 29 November 2016.

[100] <http://www.uefa.org/ MultimediaFiles/ Download/ OfficialDocument/ uefaorg/ ClubFinancialControl/02/21/63/14/2216314_DOWNLOAD.pdf> accessed 29 November 2016.

[101] <http://www.uefa.org/disciplinary/news/newsid=2325368.html> accessed 29 November 2016.

from the immensely lucrative competitions run by UEFA arises. So, for example, for the season 2014–15 Manchester City's past violations of FFP led to it being subject to a spending cap and a reduction in the size of the squad it was allowed to select for Champions League matches. The club chose not to contest the penalty.[102] The Spanish club Málaga, quarter finalist in the 2012–13 Champions League, was banned from European football altogether for season 2013–14 because of violation of the FFP rules. It had overspent. Málaga appealed against the sanction, but it was upheld by the CAS.[103] A fine of €300,000 was also imposed and upheld, all of which doubtless hinders the ability of Málaga to restructure its finances. In its ruling, the CAS refused to allow the consequences of the overdue sums under *Spanish* tax law to have any relevance. Instead it insisted on the need to adopt a uniform approach applicable in international club competitions which is not affected by the club's domicile. This is a strong assertion of the independence of the *lex sportiva* and the need for its even transnational application. A similar fate befell the Turkish club Galatasaray: in 2014 it had agreed a route back to financial stability with the CFCB[104] but in 2016 it was decided that the club had failed to fulfil its promises and so the Adjudicatory Chamber excluded it from European club competition for one season.[105] Galatasaray brought the matter before the CAS, but, like Málaga, it had no joy. Its appeal, which included a challenge to the compatibility of FFP with EU law, was dismissed.[106]

CAS rulings are arbitrations and they are subject to the Swiss Federal Act on Private International Law. As explained in Chapter 2, the only recourse for appeal is to the Swiss Federal Tribunal. It is strongly protective of the finality of arbitration and therefore it rarely intervenes in the CAS's affairs. Chapter 2 explains that it did so exceptionally in *Matuzalem*, which concerned an order for compensation backed by a suspension from playing as a result of a player's termination of contract in breach of FIFA's Transfer Regulations.[107] The Swiss court in *Matuzalem* took the view that an open-ended ban of the type that the player was facing constituted a severe infringement of the player's individual rights which was sufficient to overcome its normal reluctance to interfere with arbitral rulings. It is not inconceivable that the Swiss court could intervene similarly where a club's position is prejudiced as a result of sanctions inspired by breach of FFP. However, it is not likely. A sanctioned club is after all still eligible to play in its *national* league, which provides the majority of fixtures during a season.

It is likely that challenge to findings associated with FFP, both concerning breach and consequent sanctions, will in the first instance be contained within the FFP's

---

[102] <http://www.uefa.org/MultimediaFiles/Download/OfficialDocument/uefaorg/ClubFinancialControl/02/10/69/00/2106900_DOWNLOAD.pdf> accessed 29 November 2016.

[103] CAS 2013/A/3067 *Málaga v UEFA*, 8 October 2013.

[104] <http://www.uefa.org/MultimediaFiles/Download/OfficialDocument/uefaorg/ClubFinancialControl/02/10/69/01/2106901_DOWNLOAD.pdf> accessed 29 November 2016.

[105] <http://www.uefa.org/MultimediaFiles/Download/OfficialDocument/uefaorg/ClubFinancialControl/02/34/35/81/2343581_DOWNLOAD.pdf> accessed 29 November 2016.

[106] CAS 2016/A/4492 *Galatasaray v UEFA*, 3 October 2016.

[107] 4A_558/2011, 27 March 2012.

own decision-making structures and then channelled to the CAS. But challenge to measures taken pursuant to FFP is not capable of being contained unconditionally within the *lex sportiva*. Chapter 2 has explained how the contractual exclusivity claimed by sports-related arbitration has its limits, and how EU law in particular is relatively quick to crack it open because of its designation of internal market law as public policy.[108] A challenge to FFP rooted in EU law would be readily advanced before a national court, triggering a reference to the Court of Justice.

The legal status of FFP under EU law is intriguingly uncertain.[109] In fact, it is arguable that FFP is another instance where sport's concern to act is legitimate, because there are problems to be addressed which do not arise to the same degree or at all in other sectors, but where the means used are not justifiable. Most of all the objection is that FFP loads burdens on employees. FFP is a horizontal restraint on competition struck between football clubs backed by the framework and sanctioning power of UEFA. It is vulnerable to challenge as a violation of EU law.

The motivations behind FFP are listed in Article 2(2) of the Regulations and they are helpfully summarized on UEFA's own website.[110] The version on the website declares they aim to introduce more discipline and rationality in club football finances; to decrease pressure on salaries and transfer fees and limit inflationary effect; to encourage clubs to compete with(in) their revenues; to encourage long-term investments in the youth sector and infrastructure; to protect the long-term viability of European club football; to ensure clubs settle their liabilities on a timely basis.

The suspicion is that FFP's noble discourse of rationality in financing is a camouflage for an anti-competitive agreement which is designed to limit spending by all employers in the sector in order to maximize profits. Remarkably and surprisingly that suspicion is converted into an explicit confession by UEFA's own website. Most of all the stated aim 'to decrease pressure on salaries' simply screams illegality: employers clubbing together to fix prices (paid to labour) is as pernicious

---

[108] Especially Case C-126/97 *Eco Swiss China Time Ltd v Benetton International NV* [1999] ECR I-3055; see Ch 2.2.7.

[109] See, taking the view the arrangements are lawful, C Davies, 'Labour Market Controls and Sport in the Light of UEFA's Financial Fair Play Regulations' [2012] ECLR 435; A Mestre, 'The Striani Case: UEFA's Break-Even Rule and EU Law' July 2013 World Sports Law Report 3; that they are probably lawful, C Flanagan, 'A Tricky European Fixture: An Assessment of UEFA's Financial Fair Play Regulations and their Compatibility with EU Law' (2013) 13 Intl Sports LJ 148; that they may be unlawful, S Bastianon, 'The Striani Challenge to UEFA Financial Fair Play. A New Era after Bosman or Just a Washout?' (2015) 11 Competition Law Review 7; that they are unlawful, T Peeters and S Szymanski, 'Vertical Restraints in Soccer: Financial Fair Play in the English Premier League', Department of Economics, University of Antwerp (2012) <http://ideas.repec.org/p/ant/wpaper/2012028.html> accessed 29 November 2016; N Petit, 'Fair Play Financier ou Oligopoleague de clubs rentiers?: Eléments d'analyse en droit européen de la concurrence' (2014) <http://papers.ssrn.com/sol3/papers.cfm?abstract_id=2438399> accessed 29 November 2016; V Kaplan, 'UEFA Financial Fairplay Regulations and European Union Antitrust Complications' (2015) 29 Emory International Law Review 799.

[110] <http://www.uefa.org/protecting-the-game/financial-fair-play/index.html> accessed 29 November 2016.

an anti-competitive arrangement as can be imagined. This aim is missing from Article 2(2) of the Regulations themselves.

FFP is a horizontal agreement between suppliers (of sports services: clubs) which includes commitments to restrain spending (inter alia, on players' wages).[111] It is also strengthened by vertical restraints (in the form of licensing requirements) enforced by UEFA, the governing body. It is a restriction on competition (to acquire players' services) which has the *effect* of depressing the levels of remuneration payable to players; and, judged by the website if not by the terms of the Regulations themselves, it has that *object* too.[112] That sets alarm bells ringing. It is the province of Article 101 TFEU.

Moreover, the effect of the rules is to protect already well-established clubs from potential new market entrants capable of providing fresh competition. Under FFP clubs that are already 'financially doped' are walling off their territory from those who would wish to improve by resorting to financial doping in future. Put less tendentiously, FFP consolidates the advantages in the market of current incumbents.

Can FFP be saved as a matter of EU law?

In *Albany International* the Court accepted that restriction of competition is inherent in collective agreements between organizations representing employers and workers, but that the social policy objectives pursued by such agreements would be seriously undermined if management and labour were subject to Article 101 TFEU when seeking jointly to adopt measures to improve conditions of work and employment.[113] This contextual approach is dictated by a concern to prevent the Treaty competition rules damaging other objectives set by the Treaties.[114] It serves to grant autonomy to the process of negotiation of collective agreements unaffected by EU competition law. It is, however, limited in scope. Both key elements—collective action and improvement of conditions of work—are missing from FFP. FFP is a horizontal agreement and is designed to address the club owners' financial interests. So the '*Albany* exception' cannot help UEFA if it is asked to defend FFP.

More generally, EU competition law accepts that effects that are restrictive of competition may not lead to condemnation pursuant to Article 101 TFEU where those effects are inherent in the pursuit of recognized and justified objectives. This admittedly rough-edged 'exception' was developed by the Court most conspicuously in *Wouters*[115] and it was relied on in the sporting context by the Court in

---

[111] The significance of this is underestimated in *Galatasaray* (n 106) see especially para 76.

[112] So it is reported that in the English Premier League, which introduced its own FFP rules in 2013, players' pay increased in season 2013–14 by 5.5% while overall income rose by 22%: 'Premier League Clubs Turn Loss into Profit as Fair Play Rules Kick In' *The Guardian* (London, 29 April 2015). More rigorous analysis would be required to support a legal inquiry, but it is striking to a competition lawyer how open those involved are about the aims of FFP: the same article quotes the owner of Stoke City as saying: 'In previous years, every time the money came in, before you could blink it had all gone in players' wages ... I didn't believe we could continue being the world's richest league while all losing money.'

[113] Case C-67/96 *Albany International* [1999] ECR I-5751, paras 59–64.

[114] See Whish and Bailey (n 43) ch 1.36. For criticism at the time, see R van den Bergh and P Camesasca, 'Irreconcilable Principles? The Court of Justice Exempts Collective Labour Agreements from the Wrath of Antitrust' (2000) 25 EL Rev 492.

[115] *Wouters* (n 20).

its treatment of anti-doping in *Meca-Medina and Majcen v Commission*, in which *Wouters* is explicitly cited.[116] This ruling was examined in depth in Chapter 5 and it has re-emerged several times since in this book: as explained in Chapter 7, it is central to understanding how review in the light of EU internal market law is sensitive to the particular context in which the impugned practices occur. Anti-doping was treated as a restriction of competition, but not one incompatible with EU law, because it was justified by a legitimate objective, and it is inherent in the organization and proper conduct of competitive sport.

FFP is not a rule that is *necessary* for the conduct of sporting activity or of itself an inherent ingredient of sport. Football has survived without it for a long time. But there is in principle room to justify it on the basis that its effects, which are restrictive of competition, are inherent in the pursuit of legitimate objectives—not simply to decrease pressure on salaries but also to improve the economic and financial capability of the clubs, to introduce more discipline and rationality in club football finances, to encourage clubs to operate on the basis of their own revenues, to encourage responsible spending for the long-term benefit of football, and so on.

The best argument in favour of FFP is that it is a response to the over-spending and consequent chronic indebtedness of clubs.

In a 'normal' industry this would be disciplined by bankruptcy. A company that over-stretches vanishes, leaving the field clear for more prudent operators. In football, by contrast, it is inconceivable that famous clubs with a huge fanbase and immense cultural resonance should be consigned to oblivion in this way. Sport is special—and this, arguably, justifies stronger *ex ante* controls to prevent financial irresponsibility than would be tolerated in 'normal' industries, given that the *ex post* sanction of bankruptcy is unacceptable in football. UEFA and the clubs would therefore present FFP's effects, which are restrictive of competition (in the market for players), as inherent in the pursuit of legitimate objectives associated with the long-term stabilization of an industry that is notoriously prey to competitive over-spending.

But the argument needs nuance. In truth FFP cannot be defended as a means to prevent historic but financially reckless football clubs vanishing, because the sport already has other less restrictive means in place to address the problem of financial irrationality.

Traditional clubs with a century and more of history do *not* vanish because of the crash of bankruptcy. Football copes with such problems thanks to the separation between the corporate entity—which is extinguished by bankruptcy—and the club registered with the relevant national association—which lives on and typically retains a place in the League and, though typically acquired by and controlled by a new *company*, retains too the affection of a fanbase that is attached to club not company. Some Leagues in Europe attach penalties to a club that has undergone such a background change of corporate identity consequent on financial irresponsibility, by, for example, deducting points or even imposing relegation on the club. This

---

[116] *Meca-Medina* (n 3) para 42.

happened in the case of Glasgow Rangers, which—after well-publicized financial problems leading the company in 2012 to enter administration and subsequently to undergo liquidation—was forced to restart season 2012–13 at the lowest tier of professional football in Scotland, three Divisions below its previous home in the top Division, which it had inhabited since the League's formation as long ago as 1890. A new company acquired assets from the administrators of the liquidated company and proceeded to steer Rangers back to the top tier in 2016, but the identity of the *club*, including its fanbase, history, and honours, lived on.[117] Several English clubs have in recent years been placed into administration pursuant to the corporate rescue procedures established by the Insolvency Act 1986,[118] and since 2004 this has normally led to a deduction of points—though strictly it is the *company* that is placed into administration and the *club* that is docked points. The key point is that there may be a change in corporate form but the club does not vanish. True, bankruptcy may have a severe detrimental effect on players at the club concerned, but FFP is at best an indirect method of addressing that problem, which UEFA could address more directly and appropriately by a salary guarantee fund. So football already has in place a viable system for preventing its grand and traditional names disappearing, and FFP cannot be justified by the perceived need to bring clubs back from the brink of corporate bankruptcy. That is, sport can deal and has dealt with matters addressed by FFP because of the well-understood separation of club and company.

The properly focused argument in favour of FFP therefore lies in its role in preventing financially doped clubs from winning championships that they would not win were they constrained to match their spending to income. In this sense FFP aims at the prevention of distortion of competition.[119] In the absence of FFP, reckless over-spending distorts the nature of the sporting competition itself as well as inducing other clubs to join the 'arms race' of profligacy. The *ex post* sanction of bankruptcy for the *company* and sporting sanctions such as relegation for the *club* does not take away, nor in an effective way deter, the attraction of over-spending that will put silverware in the club's trophy room and honours on its historical record at the expense of more prudent competitors. Portsmouth FC was a member of the English Premier League in 2010 but, after financial collapse consequent on long-term over-spending and entry into administration, it was by 2013 playing in the lowest of the four tiers of the English professional game. But this did not deprive it of the FA Cup it had won in 2008 nor of its UEFA Cup participation in season 2008–09. Even though the FFP scheme envisages the exceptional possibility

---

[117] Some Glasgow Celtic fans disagree. Nowhere is sport more 'special' than in the West of Scotland and nowhere are the associated virtues and the vices more visible.

[118] See S Szymanski, 'Long-term and Short-term Causes of Insolvency and English Football' in P Rodriguez, S Késenne, and R Koning (eds), *The Economics of Competitive Sports* (Edward Elgar 2015) ch 5.

[119] This—strong—argument plays an important part in the CAS Panel finding in *Galatasaray* (n 106) that FFP complies with EU law; see paras 76–79, which include explicit reliance on *Wouters* (n 20).

of withdrawing a title from an offending club[120] this in no way adequately compensates the runner-up club that was denied the chance to lift silverware in front of its celebrating fans, just as being awarded an Olympic gold medal years after the event as a result of doping sanctions imposed on a disgraced rival is small consolation. So FFP, as an *ex ante* control based on expenditure control and licensing, is aimed at securing the integrity of club football competitions.

The Commission appears inclined to take this favourable attitude towards the compatibility of FFP with EU law. In answer to a Parliamentary Question in August 2010, Commissioner Barnier declared that the rationale of FFP 'seems to be in accordance with one of the objectives of the EU's action in the field of sport, namely with the promotion of fairness in sporting competitions (Article 165 TFEU)', although he added that 'any measure taken in this framework has to respect the EU's Internal Market and competition rules'.[121] It is significant in the developing of EU sports law to see Article 165's embrace of sport as an EU competence used to frame the explanation. It is, however, thin. Presumably 'fairness' is an allusion to FFP's suggested aim to rein in clubs that are dependent on 'financial dopers' and instead to protect competition based on the break-even requirement. But one should question whose 'fairness' is being protected. It seems to be that of the clubs with access to most income accrued through their football activities at the expense of those clubs seeking new routes to prominence, for FFP enshrines the advantages of those clubs that have climbed the ladder one way or another in the past, potentially thanks to financial doping, while refusing access to the ladder to new entrants. Put another way, from this perspective, FFP does not contribute to competitive balance—it enshrines competitive imbalance. After all, Article 165 lauds not only 'fairness' but also 'openness' in sporting competitions: FFP discourages openness. It seems, however, that the Commission is eager to find reasons not to interfere with FFP. This was confirmed in 2012 when a 'Joint Statement' by Commissioner Almunia and Michel Platini, then the President of UEFA, declared that FFP's 'break even' rule is based on sound economic principle and added that its objectives are consistent with EU state aid policy.[122] The Statement claims that both FFP and the Treaty state aid rules, found in Articles 107 to 109 TFEU, aim for a 'level playing field' on which is preserved 'fair competition'. This comparison is something of a stretch: the state aid rules control public authorities intervening in the market to grant a selective advantage to particular operators, whereas FFP, by contrast, concerns internal and formally private arrangements struck by the clubs and UEFA to cover the whole sector in the same way. The 'Joint Statement' is not legally binding, but

---

[120] The Procedural Rules, Art 29 <http://www.uefa.org/MultimediaFiles/Download/Tech/uefaorg/General/02/28/72/46/2287246_DOWNLOAD.pdf> accessed 29 November 2016.

[121] E-4628/10. <http://www.europarl.europa.eu/sides/getAllAnswers.do?reference=E-2010-4628&language=MT> accessed 29 November 2016. Similarly, Financial Fair Play in Football: Answer given by Ms Vassilou on behalf of the Commission, E-004268/13 [2014] OJ C33E/131.

[122] IP/12/264, 21 March 2012. The statement is at <http://ec.europa.eu/competition/sectors/sports/joint_statement_en.pdf> accessed 29 November 2016.

the fact of its generation and the (not entirely convincing) reasoning which it contains reveals that UEFA and the big football clubs have done a very successful job in getting close to the Commission and persuading it to work harmoniously with them.

In summary, the compatibility of FFP with EU law is on a knife-edge. It restricts competition on wages to the detriment of players; it consolidates the advantages of the existing powerful clubs at the expense of new entrants into the higher echelons of the sport. But it serves to protect the integrity of the competition by stopping wildly irresponsible spending from achieving short-term success on the field to the detriment of those clubs which have taken a longer-term and more realistic view of their spending potential.

Expertise in matters of sports governance belongs firmly with governing bodies and not with the Court or the Commission, and FFP is probably best defended as falling within the margin of appreciation properly claimed by sports governing bodies. This was examined in Chapter 7.4. Sports governing bodies should argue that the large measure of discretion allowed to both the Member States and to the EU's political institutions in making complex assessments about matters of socio-economic importance should be extended to private actors, such as sports bodies, in circumstances where the Court lacks the expertise and the Treaties lack the relevant guiding principles required to make a detailed assessment of choices made. In particular, the argument would be that FFP deserves to be tested to determine the extent to which it improves financial rationality. It has correctly been observed that much would depend on the empirical evidence that could be presented in support of FFP, and that the evidence is mixed.[123] And one might add that the insertion of a genuine social dialogue should enhance the width of the margin of appreciation allowed to sports governing bodies. FFP would and should be more likely to survive if structured around a more inclusive participatory framework of dialogue and rule-making, in order to distance it from the whiff of a horizontal restrictive practice struck between and for the advantage of employers (clubs). UEFA is sensitive to this dimension: its own FFP website claims that 'The concept has also been supported by the entire football family'.[124]

Whether any party has a sufficient incentive to challenge FFP raises another set of questions again. The already dominant clubs in Europe are content with the arrangements—indeed they provoked their adoption. Other less fortunate clubs are likely to be deterred from taking legal action by UEFA's sanctioning power, enforced through their national associations. The Commission is therefore the most appropriate actor, but, as explained, the clubs and UEFA have shrewdly stayed close to the Commission in the negotiation of FFP. Daniel Striani, a players' agent, complained to the Commission that FFP violates EU competition law, but in late 2014 it declared that it would not take the matter any further,[125] which led UEFA

---

[123] Especially C Flanagan (n 109).　　　[124] See n 110.
[125] AT.40105 <http://ec.europa.eu/competition/antitrust/cases/dec_docs/40105/40105_220_6.pdf> accessed 29 November 2016. See Bastianon (n 109).

to comment that it was 'very pleased'.[126] This reaction was entirely unsurprising yet serves as a helpful reminder that relations between UEFA and the Commission are far more convivial than in the past. Private challenge to the compatibility of FFP with EU law always remains possible despite inaction on the part of the Commission, as *Bosman* (the case) reminds us, even if the eventual outcome may not be happy, as Bosman (the man) reminds us.[127] In fact the Commission's stated reason for declining to help Striani was that it was open to him to pursue the matter at national level. He did so, and in early 2015 provoked a preliminary reference to Luxembourg by a court in Brussels, but in *Striani v UEFA, URBSFA* the Court of Justice treated the reference as inadmissible for want of clarity and detail.[128] The Court's ruling is brutally critical of the national court's inadequately presented questions, but further and better framed litigation by Striani or other interested parties in future cannot be ruled out.

10.10 Third Party Ownership

Third party ownership of players refers, in short, to a situation where the economic value of a player's registration belongs not only (or even not at all) to the club but to one or more third parties. Questions associated with third party ownership of players were initially raised in connection with the transfer system, which was examined in Chapter 9, and in fact the currently applicable rules which govern third party ownership are to be found in the FIFA Regulations on the Status and Transfer of Players.[129] However, the evolution of the phenomenon of third party ownership and the associated mutation of the rules that apply to it means that the matter is more sensibly addressed as part of a general inquiry into the pattern of governance in the game which is the preserve of this chapter.

Simply put, third party ownership allows clubs to acquire players who are better than they could otherwise afford. It is a means to attract investment in labour. The consequence is that if a player is transferred to another club, then the fee that is received is shared between the parties that own the economic rights attached to the player's registration—which, in formal terms, is what is the subject of the transfer. So the third party invests in talent in the hope that the player in question will improve and add value by becoming an attractive commodity in the market for labour. The club wins, by acquiring better players; the player wins, by getting the opportunity to play for a higher profile club than would apply in the absence of this source of investment; the third party investor wins provided it is smart enough to identify players whose ability can be improved and clubs which are able to assist

---

[126] 'Uefa defeats legal challenge to financial fair play rules', *The Guardian* (London, 20 May 2014) <https://www.theguardian.com/football/2014/may/20/uefa-defeats-financial-fair-play-challenge> accessed 29 November 2016.

[127] Ch 4.   [128] Case C-299/15 Order of 16 July 2015. See Bastianon (n 109).

[129] <http://www.fifa.com/about-fifa/official-documents/law-regulations/> accessed 29 November 2016.

in such development. This model has been used widely in Europe, although rules differed among national associations. Clubs in Portugal in particular are noted for use of such arrangements, though by contrast they have been banned in England since 2008.[130]

So what is the problem? The problem lies in the risk that the third party owner may seek to influence the club's decision-making on sporting matters. The third party owner has an interest in its player being picked for the first team as often as possible; it may have an interest in pushing for the sale of the player, in order to realize profits on its investment.

Third party ownership is a problem because the transfer system itself exists and therefore creates incentives which are awkward from the point of view of the integrity of the game, contractual stability, and team building. So the problem with third party ownership is that it may lead to economic incentives subverting the integrity of the sporting competition.

Until April 2015 the FIFA Regulations asserted supervision of what is termed 'Third-party influence on clubs'. It was provided that:

1. No club shall enter into a contract which enables any other party to that contract or any third party to acquire the ability to influence in employment and transfer-related matters its independence, its policies or the performance of its teams.
2. The FIFA Disciplinary Committee may impose disciplinary measures on clubs that do not observe the obligations set out in this article.

This does not forbid third party ownership, but it, in short, seeks to relegate the third party investor to a purely passive role. Sporting decisions must be strictly walled off from economic motivations. But this is hardly realistic. It is, moreover, plainly very hard to police a rule of this type.

A clutch of instances of alleged interference in sporting decisions by third party investors eager to provoke the transfer of 'their' player to another club prompted UEFA to change the rules.[131] With effect from May 2015 a much more restrictive regime has been imposed. The current rules in full are as follows:

18*bis* Third-party influence on clubs

1. No club shall enter into a contract which enables the counter club/counter clubs, and vice versa, or any third party to acquire the ability to influence in employment and transfer-related matters its independence, its policies or the performance of its teams.
2. The FIFA Disciplinary Committee may impose disciplinary measures on clubs that do not observe the obligations set out in this article.

18*ter* Third-party ownership of players' economic rights

---

[130] This was in consequence of a dispute concerning Carlos Tevez, then a player registered to West Ham: *FAPL v West Ham*, unreported, see A Lewis and J Taylor, *Sport: Law and Practice* (3rd edn, Bloomsbury 2014) ch H4.39. See also D Geey, 'Third Party Investment from a UK Perspective' (2016) 16 Intl Sports LJ 245.

[131] eg 'Rojo Deal Prompts Third-party Revolt: Sporting Lisbon's President Calls for Action over Offshore Funds with Stakes in Players' *The Guardian* (London, 11 September 2014).

No club or player shall enter into an agreement with a third party whereby a third party is being entitled to participate, either in full or in part, in compensation payable in relation to the future transfer of a player from one club to another, or is being assigned any rights in relation to a future transfer or transfer compensation.

...

[plus transitional arrangements governing agreements entered into before May 2015]

...

6. The FIFA Disciplinary Committee may impose disciplinary measures on clubs or players that do not observe the obligations set out in this article.

So this removes the commercial incentives underpinning third party ownership which are conducive to harming the sporting integrity of the game.

There are obvious practical questions about whether this regime can be effectively policed. But there are questions of law too. There are transitional questions about whether existing agreements between clubs and third parties are even valid in the light of their arguably anti-competitive effect and in particular their impact on the individual player, as well as questions whether the restrictions on third party ownership which applied prior to May 2015 are lawful. But the main question for the future is whether the restrictive regime that has been in force since May 2015 is itself compatible with EU law. After all, it amounts to a restriction on the demand-side of the market for players, and has the consequence of reducing competition. It risks being condemned as an unlawful restriction on free movement and/or as anti-competitive. The question would arise whether sport is so special as to require such a rule: does it, in the terms of Article 165 TFEU, fall within 'the specific nature of sport' as a rule necessary for its organization.

In determining whether the rules are compatible with EU law, the most significant question appears to be whether they are really necessary to achieve their ends or whether instead a less restrictive version would be adequate.[132] This is another instance where governing bodies would doubtless appeal to the sporting margin of appreciation presented in Chapter 7.4. The argument would be that room should be permitted to shape the *lex sportiva* according to the special concerns of preserving the integrity of sport from the corrupting influence of short-term economic pressures. EU law is, as has been consistently shown, capable of accommodating such motivations, and therefore the rules which govern third party ownership, though restrictive of competition in the market for players, are open to defence as representing a genuine need in the governance of the sport. As devices designed to protect sporting integrity, they are probably compatible with EU law.

---

[132] cf C Duve and F Loibl, 'Why FIFA's TPO Ban is Justified' (2016) 15 Intl Sports LJ 248. For a contrary view, see J Lindholm, 'Can I Please Have a Slice of Ronaldo? The Legality of Fifa's Ban on Third-party Ownership under EU Law' (2016) 15 Intl Sports LJ 137; and (arguing for a less restrictive rule) La Liga, 'FIFA must Regulate TPO, not Ban It' (2016) 15 Intl Sports LJ 235. Also on law and practice, see A Duval, 'Unpacking Doyen's TPO Deals: The Final Whistle' Asser International Sports Law Blog, 20 April 2016 <http://www.asser.nl/SportsLaw/Blog/post/unpacking-doyen-s-tpo-deals-the-final-whistle> accessed 29 November 2016.

10.11 Breakaway Leagues

From time to time noises emerge about an interest on the part of some of the leading clubs in European football to abandon the existing pyramid of governance in favour of a new and separate 'closed' European league on the American model. In 1998 the so-called 'Project Gandalf' was notified to the Commission.[133] It was a plan for a European Football League prepared by Media Partners International. It did not go any further, but periodic press reports suggest a persisting readiness to dabble in the idea.[134] The aim, in short, is to maximize revenue, both by creating a competition that is more lucrative than the existing UEFA-organized arrangements and by removing any obligation to participate in wealth distribution through the solidarity schemes that currently exist. It is unclear how serious these plans are. A plausible motivation is that they are aimed principally at provoking UEFA to pay full attention to the aspirations of the richest clubs, rather than at in fact breaking away. It is no coincidence that UEFA increased the number of clubs admitted to the lucrative knockout stages of the Champions League from twenty-four to thirty-two in 1999, in the shadow of 'Project Gandalf'.[135]

The 2006 Independent European Sport Review—the Arnaut Report—was one of the earliest attempts by UEFA to shape a strategic reliance on EU law to defend its interests.[136] It considers there is no legal means to prevent clubs going their own way, but it adds that they could not then 'cherry pick' by choosing to continue to play in UEFA competitions as it suited them.[137] It has already been noted in section 10.4 that governing bodies that use their regulatory power to suppress the emergence of competing competitions are likely to violate EU law. The problem is the conflict of interest that is involved, which in terms of EU law is translated into suspicion of an abuse prohibited by Article 102 TFEU. However, once a viable competing competition has emerged and established itself, it seems improbable that the clubs that have chosen to break away could claim that a refusal of access to competitions organized by the entity which they have chosen to leave could violate EU law.[138]

However, there is weight to the argument that it would be incompatible with EU law to establish a breakaway League in the first place. Much would depend on the precise structure envisaged: it is a new league operating on the basis of a closed structure that would be most vulnerable.[139] Promotion and relegation are properly

---

[133] Case IV/37.400 [1999] OJ C70/5. See K Pijetlovic, *EU Sports Law and Breakaway Leagues in Football* (TMC Asser 2015) ch 3.

[134] eg 'Europe's Top Football Teams in Plot to Go It Alone' *The Guardian* (London, 18 March 2006).

[135] 'The threat of a breakaway football super league in Europe was averted yesterday when 14 of the continent's biggest clubs agreed to accept a revamp of the elite Champions League competition by UEFA …', 'Clubs Reject Breakaway League Plan' *Financial Times* (London, 18 November 1998) 2.

[136] Its failings in this regard are explained in Ch 5.5. A copy is held at <http://eose.org/wp-content/uploads/2014/03/independant_european_sports_review1.pdf> accessed 29 November 2016.

[137] Arnaut Report, paras 3.30–3.32.   [138] cf Pijetlovic (n 133) ch 7.

[139] See Parrish and Miettinen (n 93) 211–15; C Hellenthal, *Zulässigkeit einer supranationalen Fussball-Europaliga nach den Bestimmungen des europäischen Wettbewerbrechts* (Peter Lang 2000).

treated as devices that improve the competitive structure of the market[140] and to abandon them in favour of a structure that walls off existing participants from challenge and sunders completely any ties of vertical solidarity within the sport is open to attack as a violation of EU competition law. The objection in law would be strengthened by reliance on Article 165 TFEU, which asserts a need for openness in European sport.

The intrigue is that it would be UEFA that would mount such an argument in order to secure protection of its existing model of governance and, most of all, its premier club competition, the Champions League. So, in contrast to the majority of the issues examined in this book, sport governing bodies would be relying on EU law to defend themselves from attack, rather than acting as the parties subject to an attack sourced in EU law. UEFA's increasing readiness to cooperate with the Commission has been noted on several occasions in this book, including in relation to the transfer system (Chapter 9), and FFP is the most obvious current example (section 10.9). There is no doubt that UEFA would be delighted were the Commission to express itself hostile to the pretensions of the would-be breakaway clubs.

10.12 Good Governance

The Commission's White Paper on Sport, released in the summer of 2007, was met in Chapter 6.5.[141] Its section 4 is entitled 'The Organisation of Sport', and it notes that the Commission 'can play a role in encouraging the sharing of best practice in sport governance' and that it 'can also help to develop a common set of principles for good governance in sport, such as transparency, democracy, accountability and representation of stakeholders (associations, federations, players, clubs, leagues, supporters, etc.)'. The Commission accepted that 'most challenges can be addressed through self-regulation respectful of good governance principles, provided that EU law is respected', and expressed itself 'ready to play a facilitating role or take action if necessary'.

In the Communication of January 2011, 'Developing the European Dimension in Sport', which was met in Chapter 6.11, the Commission returned to this theme.[142] Its section 4, also entitled 'The Organisation of Sport', declares that 'Good governance in sport is a condition for the autonomy and self-regulation of sport organisations' and asserts that there are 'inter-linked principles that underpin sport governance at European level, such as autonomy within the limits of the law,

---

[140] eg S Ross and S Szymanski, 'Open Competition in League Sports' (2002) Wisconsin Law Review 625.

[141] COM (2007) 391, 11 July 2007, available via <http://ec.europa.eu/sport/white-paper/index_en.htm> accessed 29 November 2016.

[142] COM (2011) 12, 18 January 2011 <http://ec.europa.eu/sport/news/doc/communication/communication_en.pdf> accessed 29 November 2016.

democracy, transparency and accountability in decision-making, and inclusiveness in the representation of interested stakeholders'.

An EU Expert Group on 'Good Governance' held its first meeting in December 2011. In October 2013 the Group adopted 'Recommendations on the Principles for Good Governance of Sport in the EU'.[143]

The Recommendations portray good governance as 'a set of standards and operational practices leading to the effective regulation of sport'; good governance is a concern that stands above the adoption of specific sports regulations, but 'the application of good governance principles should facilitate the development and implementation of more effective sports regulation'.[144]

The Recommendations are a rather impressive piece of work. There is no attempt to dictate what should be done nor to seek to elevate the EU to a position of prime responsibility in arranging governance in sport. The aim, in short, is to prepare a framework of best practice. The EU seeks to offer a model or models.

The Introduction to the 'Role of the EU' deserves to be set out in full:[145]

Whilst sport is by definition a global phenomenon and good governance principles are not intrinsically linked to any particular territory, the European Union, for its particular role and mission, can provide guidance for the good governance of sport at national, European and international level. For instance, the EU is an organisation based on values and on the rule of law which it has the task to promote. This includes the following:
— Decision making systems based on separation of powers between the legislative, executive and judiciary bodies;
— Public procurement based on the principles of impartiality, transparency and equal opportunities;
— Recognition of social dialogue and of the role of social partners in the fields of labour law and employment.
In addition, the EU is uniquely positioned to facilitate the exchanges of good practices, transfers of knowledge and the networking of stakeholders active at national and international level. In this respect, the EU institutions have a role to play in ensuring that good governance principles adopted at EU level are recognised and implemented in all the Member States. The EU can also facilitate the promotion of principles of good governance in sport beyond its borders with both sporting bodies and public authorities of third countries.

In this way the EU is framed as a means to add value to governance in sport. It is a facilitator. Annex I contains a list of best practices identified by the projects in the field of good governance supported by the Commission's 2011 Preparatory Action in the field of Sport. Two are explained relatively fully—these cover democracy and minimum standards (Rugby League) and sport for good governance (Dutch Olympic Committee)—and there is further detail on matters of practice.

One might be forgiven for thinking the Commission was over-optimistic when it referred to the value of the work on good governance principles in sport

---

[143] Recommendations on the Principles for Good Governance of Sport in the EU <http://ec.europa.eu/sport/policy/organisation_of_sport/good_governance_en.htm> accessed 29 November 2016.
[144] ibid 5.   [145] ibid 5–6.

undertaken by the Expert Group in the context of an appeal 'to put pressure on FIFA and other relevant bodies to genuinely combat corruption in the sport'.[146] And, as explained in Chapter 2.3.4, the EU's responses to the recent revelations of criminal conduct at FIFA which led to the resignation of its President, Sepp Blatter, occurred after the fact and, in their high-minded tone, were unappealingly opportunistic.[147] However, the EU admittedly lacks the resources for intensive investigation of crime, and there are doubtless less intractable problems than FIFA where the EU can generate an interest in improving the quality of sporting governance by advocating greater transparency and accountability. The Resolution of the Council and of the Representatives of the Governments of the Member States of 21 May 2014 on the European Union Work Plan for Sport 2014–17 promises continuing attention to the promotion of good governance.[148] That Resolution is cited at the beginning of a set of conclusions adopted by the Council at its meeting of 30 and 31 May 2016 on enhancing integrity, transparency, and good governance in major sport events.[149] The conclusions carry an unmissable flavour of 'too little, too late', but it would be churlish to deny that the EU has at least the potential to become one of the several actors that are needed to push for improved governance in international sports federations.

10.13 Conclusion

Sports governance has changed under the influence, though not the detailed direction, of EU law. Collecting together the fragments allowed by the ad hoc accumulation of decisions and near-misses considered in this chapter allows reflection on the themes which animate EU law's influence over choices made in the governance of sport. In short, what are the *conditions* according to which EU law grants conditional autonomy to sporting bodies in setting rules to govern their game?

MOTOE pushes towards the elimination of a conflict of interest held by the decision-maker and also, more broadly, to a need for a transparent system of decision-making and openness to review. Similar trends may be observed in consequence of the *Charleroi* litigation, albeit this is visible in practical reshaping of the system of player release in the shadow of EU law rather than in consequence of a specific decision of the Court or the Commission. FFP reveals a thematically similar concern that regulatory choices and their commercial implications tend to become fused within the governance of sport, which immediately raises legal

---

[146] Question for written answer E-003340/14 to the Commission Diane Dodds, answer given by Ms Vasiliou, 30 May 2014 [2014] OJ C341/79: Subject: Corruption in sport.

[147] European Parliament Resolution of 11 June 2015 on recent revelations on high-level corruption cases in FIFA [2016] OJ C407/81.

[148] [2014] OJ C183/12. See Ch 6.11.

[149] <http://data.consilium.europa.eu/doc/document/ST-9644-2016-INIT/en/pdf> accessed 29 November 2016.

anxieties. The best argument in favour of the compatibility of FFP with EU law rests in its contribution to the integrity of sporting competition, notwithstanding its clear anti-competitive effects. The story of the regulation of third party ownership shares a concern about the need for some attention to be paid to the separation of the integrity of sporting competition from the influence of economic motivation.

There is in general an argument that EU-proof governance in sport depends on something more procedurally open and, in short, more democratic than the orthodox 'pyramid'. That is, the conditions attached to autonomy under EU law include requirements of good governance. This is to absorb and convert soft law commitments into a basis for interpretation of internal market law. As explained earlier, in section 10.2, it is easy to extract from the Amsterdam and Nice Declarations exactly this respect for the autonomy of sports governance which is laced by conditions—that, as the Nice Declaration puts it, sports federations are centrally important in the organization of sport, but that in addition they shall operate 'on the basis of a democratic and transparent method of operation' and shall provide 'participatory democracy'.

The Commission has embedded such concern into its documentation. Its 2007 White Paper makes no grandiose claims to elevate the EU to a position of primary responsibility for sport.[150] Indeed it 'acknowledges the autonomy of sporting organisations and representative structures (such as leagues)'.[151] But this is not unconditional. It identifies challenges in the future governance of sport in Europe and it declares an aim to develop a common set of principles of good governance, 'such as transparency, democracy, accountability and representation of stakeholders (associations, federations, players, clubs, leagues, supporters, etc.)'.[152] One aspect of this is promotion of the social dialogue. In fact Article 165 TFEU itself points in this direction, for it refers to the promotion of 'cooperation between bodies responsible for sports'. The Commission's Communication of January 2011, 'Developing the European Dimension in Sport', is a little more pointed.[153] It states that 'Good governance in sport is a condition for the autonomy and self-regulation of sport organisations'; and that 'Good governance in sport is a condition for addressing challenges regarding sport and the EU legal framework'.[154] This has legal bite in so far as failure to pay due respect to standards of good governance, including transparency and participation, results in withdrawal of conditional autonomy when sporting practices are examined for their effect on the internal market. In this way EU law has a more powerful influence than might be appreciated from inspection of Article 165 TFEU and the relatively soft policy documents, especially those concerning 'good governance' (section 10.12) that have been published by the Commission. EU law cracks open the high level of autonomy that previously prevailed in the production of the *lex sportiva*, but it does not replace it with top-down

---

[150] See n 11.   [151] White Paper on Sport (n 11) 13.   [152] ibid 12.
[153] COM (2011) 12, <date?><http://ec.europa.eu/sport/news/doc/communication/communication_en.pdf> accessed 29 November 2016.
[154] ibid para 4.1.

decision-making. Instead it expands the range of actors involved in the process of 'co-production' of norms.[155]

One consequence of this trend is to provide incentives for sports federations to work more closely and cooperatively with the EU, most of all the Commission. In this sense the account provided in this chapter amounts to a more broadly applicable version of the story told in Chapter 6 about how Article 165 TFEU represents the culmination of a process whereby sports governing bodies, having concluded that acquiring absolute autonomy from EU law was simply not politically feasible (nor, as argued in Chapter 6, is it intellectually credible), chose instead to accept inclusion within EU law but on terms which they hoped could be used and applied to grant them a wide zone of autonomy in practice. The discussion in this chapter shows how governance in sport is not immune from EU law but rather must comply with its conditions. There is nonetheless room to allow space for choices, and in football those are increasingly made in a spirit of cooperation between the EU, in particular the Commission, and UEFA.[156] The arrangement for cooperation between the Commission and UEFA which was concluded in 2014 is emblematic.[157] Governing bodies have become users of EU law, rather than wishing it to be kept at bay. FFP is especially notable for UEFA working closely with the Commission and apparently succeeding in inducing it to accept the most favourable legal interpretation of the arrangements, applying also the approving brand of Article 165.[158] One consequence of the trends noted in this chapter is that the network of governance in football has become less straightforwardly hierarchical than would be suggested by a pyramid. There is a complex network engaging a large number of what one may call stakeholders, and less top-down hierarchy.[159] But even if the shape of the governance pyramid has been adjusted, it is still governing bodies which stand at its apex. EU law places conditions on their autonomy or, otherwise put, it puts their practices to the test, especially where regulatory functions overlap with commercial motivations, but it does not oust them from their position of primary responsibility in the organization of sport.

---

[155] cf A Duval, 'La Lex Sportiva Face au Droit de l'Union Européenne: Guerre et Paix dans l'Espace Juridique Transnational' (DPhil thesis, EUI Florence 2015) especially Titre I, 'Les nouveaux modes de co-production', available via <http://cadmus.eui.eu/handle/1814/36997> accessed 29 November 2016.

[156] cf B García, 'UEFA and the European Union: From Confrontation to Co-operation' (2007) 3 JCER 202; A Geeraert and E Drieskens, 'The EU Controls FIFA and UEFA: A Principal–Agent Perspective' (2015) 22 JEPP 1448.

[157] C (2014) 7378, 14 October 2014. See Ch 6.12.   [158] Barnier (n 121).

[159] A Geeraert, J Scheerder, and H Bruyninckx, 'The Governance Network of European Football: Introducing New Governance Approaches to Steer Football at the EU Level' (2013) 5 International Journal of Sport Policy and Politics 113.

11

Broadcasting

11.1 Introduction

The three landmark decisions of the Court of Justice in the development of EU sports law are *Walrave and Koch*,[1] the Court's first venture into the field which established its refusal to grant sport absolute autonomy from the application of EU law; *Bosman*,[2] the decision which vividly demonstrated the practical vitality of EU law as a means to challenge long-established features of sporting governance; and *Meca-Medina and Majcen v Commission*,[3] in which the Court spelled out the need for a careful case-by-case assessment of the compatibility of sporting practices with EU law which is infused by respect for, but not complete surrender to, the claim that sport is 'special'. None of these cases concerns broadcasting. But it is in the field of broadcasting—in which the landscape has altered radically over the last thirty years—that the collision between EU law and claims to sporting autonomy has been unusually vivid and certainly at its most commercially significant.

Four themes serve to illuminate the radical patterns according to which the broadcasting market affecting sport has been reshaped in recent times. These are deregulation, technological advance, commodification, and juridification. Deregulation of the broadcasting market has proceeded apace since the 1980s. It has led to a significant increase in the number of competing suppliers: the marketplace is very different, and immensely more varied, than it was thirty years ago when there were only a small number of television channels. This transformation has also been driven by technological advance, the second of the four animating themes in this narrative. It is no longer just terrestrial television that provides the means to supply viewers with access to sports events. Satellite and cable broadcasting are now common and the advent of the internet dramatically increased methods of broadcasting sport. The market has grown and for major events such as the football World Cup and the Olympics it is global. Commodification of the market for rights to broadcast sports events is the consequence of the explosion

---

[1] Case 36/74 *Walrave and Koch v Union Cycliste Internationale* [1974] ECR 1405.
[2] Case C-415/93 *Union royale belge des sociétés de football association ASBL v Jean-Marc Bosman* [1995] ECR I-4921.
[3] Case C-519/04P *Meca-Medina and Majcen v Commission* [2006] ECR I-6991.

in the number of methods by which to reach viewers. It is well understood that securing rights to broadcast the most popular events in sport is a centrally important method for establishing and maintaining a foothold in broadcasting markets more generally, especially if those rights can be acquired and sold on an exclusive basis where a premium price can be extracted from eager viewers with no other option. Commodification points to the rise of carefully nurtured brands, such as, to draw on football as the most vivid example, the Union of European Football Associations (UEFA) Champions League and the English Football Association Premier League (FAPL). The fourth theme is juridification, which means in short that legal questions and the threat of litigation have become more prominent. In some senses this is no more than a simple consequence of commodification. The financial stakes in sport are higher today than in the past and this breeds a greater readiness to go to law to defend or to advance commercial opportunities. There is, however, more to it: in particular, sport has long enjoyed a high level of autonomy from legal supervision and the rise of juridification in sport challenges that autonomy. It is fully in line with the thematic story told in this book that some aspects of the claim to autonomy are no more than cunning camouflage for a desire to maximize commercial advantage by sheltering from normal expectations of legal control, but some aspects of the claim to autonomy do hold water. Sport is sometimes special. The really interesting twists arise where legal assumptions clash with commercially significant custom and preference within sport. This is when the claim to autonomy receives its most rigorous scrutiny.

As far as EU law in particular is concerned, the many changes that sports broadcasting has undergone in recent years have not only been shaped by the prevailing legal environment but also in a more active sense they have demanded a legal response and, in particular, a response that is adequately sensitive to the peculiarities of the sector while at the same time protective of the assumptions of the EU's internal market. How far does (and should) the special character of sport dictate context-sensitive application of orthodox legal rules? That is precisely the overall thematic tension that animates this book. The tensions generated by deregulation, technological advance, commodification, and juridification are especially vivid in football, the commercially and culturally dominant sport in Europe and in most of the world. In this chapter it is the friction between, on the one hand, the law of the internal market, most of all competition law, and, on the other, the protection of property rights as an expression of commercial value-creation and of sporting autonomy which underpins the discussion. A degree of intricately detailed analysis is unavoidable, but the purpose of this chapter is not to supply a practical guide to drafting contracts to sell rights to broadcast sporting events, although that market forms most of the background to the discussion. The purpose of this chapter is to traverse the interconnected themes of deregulation, technological advance, commodification, and juridification in order to understand what the story of EU law's engagement with broadcasting reveals about the plausibility and scope of the claim that 'sport is special'.

11.2 The Law, Economics, and Technology
of the Broadcasting Sector

In early 2015 reports of the sale of the rights to broadcast matches in the English Premier League were accompanied by shock and awe. The rights for the period 2016–19 had been sold for a total of just over £5 billion. This amounted to roughly £10 million for each match to be shown live over the three seasons covered by the deal. This was literally front page news.[4]

The sum seemed huge. It was widely reported to be in excess of the seller's expectations. And it was a price that was a great deal larger than the Premier League had been able to command in previous rights sales. £3 billion was the price charged for 2013–16, amounting to roughly £6.6 million per game; £1.8 billion for 2010–13; £1.7 billion for 2007–10.[5] The English Premier League was created in 1992 and its first television deal, covering five seasons up to 1997, involved receipt of what now appears to be a relatively meagre £191 million. The price of televised football, especially televised *live* football, paid by broadcasters, most prominently today SKY Sports and BT Sport, and therefore by their consumers has increased by a rate that far outstrips the general rate of inflation, to the enormous glee of those who provide the product—most of all, football clubs and their players. Richard Scudamore, Chief Executive of the English Premier League, was reported as ruling out the possibility that higher prices for consumers would be the result of the spectacular deal struck early in 2015, relying on the intensity of competition in the market as a restraint on broadcasters' freedom of action.[6] This was either complacent or disingenuous. The very next month SKY, which had acquired the lion's share of the broadcasting rights on offer by paying over £4 billion, announced a price rise in its package that includes live Premier League matches which, moreover, was effective in April instead of September, the month it which had previously made its normal annual adjustment to subscription prices.[7] The demand for top-level sport is both strong and durable. As a headline that was better informed or at least more honest than Mr Scudamore captured it, 'As Long As Viewers are Sofa-bound and Spending, the Broadcasters will Shell Out'.[8]

And this glittering cascade of income spills over beyond domestic sales alone. In 2014–15 the English Premier League earned more than twice as much as any other football League in the world as a result of its deal with SKY and BT to show matches in the United Kingdom, but it was able to add £1.1 billion per season to its overall

---

[4] eg 'Premier League's £5.1bn TV Bonanza' *The Times* (London, 11 February 2015) 1; 'They Think It's Over £5bn ... It Is Now' *The Independent* (London, 11 February 2015) 1.

[5] 'TV Football Breaks the £3bn Barrier' *The Guardian* (London, 14 June 2012) 1; 'Sky Retains Premiership Title after £1.7bn TV Rights Auction' *The Independent* (London, 6 May 2006) 1.

[6] *The Times* (n 4).

[7] 'Sky Raises Prices after Premier League Auction: Pay-TV Channel Paid £300 Million More Than Expected for Rights' *Financial Times* (London, 18 March 2015) <https://www.ft.com/content/54473a9c-cda2-11e4-8760-00144feab7de> accessed 29 November 2016.

[8] *The Independent* (London, 11 February 2015) 4.

revenues thanks to sales to the rest of the world for the three-year period beginning in 2016, a figure which far exceeds the international sales of any sports league—not simply any *football* League—in the world.[9] In late 2016 it was announced that a new deal had been struck between the Premier League and a Chinese broadcaster worth £190 million a year—eleven times greater than the existing deal.[10] The English Premier League is hugely popular all over the world and rights to broadcast matches are priced accordingly. It is only twenty years since it was breathlessly reported that rights to show live games outside the United Kingdom 'earns the Premier League around £8 million a year' but that insiders predict a new deal 'will be worth close to £25 million'.[11] This now seems a quaint and distant world. The Premier League's income from the sale of broadcasting rights places it at the top of football's global League table. This is of course only part of the fast-developing story: most of the leading clubs in English football are now owned by interests from outside the United Kingdom.

The English Premier League is an extraordinarily successful export business.

The English football clubs that are known today across the world began to emerge in the second half of the nineteenth century as sport began to become the subject of centralized organization and rule-making. Notts County, formed in 1862, is the world's oldest football club currently playing at a professional level. The twelve clubs that participated in the first ever officially organized English football league season in 1888–89 were all based in the Midlands or the North of the country. Some, such as Aston Villa and the champions in that first season Preston North End, were adding football in the winter to existing commitments to the game of cricket in the summer. However, several of the great football clubs of England that dominated the early years of the competition grew out of the heat and grime of the Industrial Revolution. Manchester United first drew breath in 1902 as the successor to Newton Heath, formed in 1878 by workers on the Lancashire and Yorkshire Railway. The early years of Stoke City, one of the twelve founding clubs, were also shaped by railway apprentices. Manchester City joined the league in 1892 as Ardwick before adopting their current name two years later, and they grew out of the dark industrial heartland of Gorton in East Manchester. City moved across the city to Moss Side in 1923 where they stayed, playing at Maine Road, until 2003, but when they took occupation of their current home, then known as the Commonwealth Stadium and now as the Etihad, they were returning to their roots in East Manchester. Manchester City was formed to allow workers in the area to enjoy recreation and in part also to improve their health. And they, together with other clubs born in the later nineteenth century, grew alongside industries that sent goods, services, and know-how round the world, the driving force of the industrialization of the planet at the height of the British Empire.

---

[9] See Deloitte's Annual Review of Football Finance <https://www2.deloitte.com/uk/en/pages/sports-business-group/articles/annual-review-of-football-finance.html> accessed 29 November 2016.
[10] 'New Chinese TV Deal Worth £190m a Year' *The Times* (London, 18 November 2016) 65.
[11] 'Football's £20m TV Goal' *Independent on Sunday* (London, 9 February 1997) Business section, 1.

Most of the leading English football clubs are still located today more or less exactly where they began their life in distant Victorian times. But the heavy industry from which they drew their energy and their workers is largely vanished. England is no longer home to the factories that manufactured goods that were sold throughout the world. But it is the football clubs themselves that have taken over exactly that role. Football, not turbines or steel or huge ocean-going ships, is now in demand. What was working-class relief from hard manual labour has itself become a hugely successful export product.[12]

The broadcasting sector is central to this evolution. Whereas goods were once shipped across vast distances to eager export markets, today services flash from one side of the world to another in an instant. Football is prominent: the jewels include not only the English Premier League, but also the Champions League, and, once every four years, the World Cup. Formula 1 motor racing is highly prized, so too the Olympic Games. Vastly increased sums of money now flow into sport, and there is a higher quantity and quality of televised sport. It was announced that in 2014 the England and Wales Cricket Board had seen an increase in its annual revenues of 42 per cent (to £174.7 million), this was 'largely the result of selling the broadcast rights for England's test matches against India to ESPNStar for about $100m'.[13] American football commands the highest prices of all for a domestic market, but it is less international in its appeal. Broadcasters compete to buy rights to show these spectacular events in the certain knowledge that they acquire a means to secure large numbers of paying viewers and consequently lucrative opportunities to attract sponsors and advertisers. Sport is a 'battering ram':[14] acquiring rights to show popular sports events is a quick and dramatic way for a new supplier to establish a presence in a market. Equally for incumbents, buying prized sports rights is an effective way to consolidate existing advantage and exclude fresh competition. Media companies may go so far as to invest in clubs in order to strengthen their position in the market.[15] Most of all, broadcasters want to acquire *exclusive* rights to broadcast the most popular events to viewers: this is what attracts the keen fan.

The market is savagely competitive and wildly volatile. The four themes that animate the narrative provided in this chapter—deregulation, technological advance, commodification, and juridification—operate in concert. Thirty years ago there was little competition or choice in broadcasting markets. There were only a small number of television channels. All were terrestrial and free-to-air. The consumer of

---

[12] I borrow here from David Conn, *Richer than God: Manchester City, Modern Football and Growing Up* (Quercus 2012) 332.

[13] 'Cricket Runs into Form with Strong Revenues' *Financial Times* (London, 15 May 2015) 4.

[14] The phrase is conventionally associated with Rupert Murdoch: eg *The Independent* (London, 15 October 1996) <http://www.independent.co.uk/sport/sport-is-murdochs-battering-ram-for-pay-tv-1358686.html> accessed 29 November 2016. See P Smith, T Evens, and P Iosifidis, 'The Next Big Match: Convergence, Competition and Sports Media Rights' (2016) 31 European Journal of Communication 536.

[15] In 1999 BSkyB's purchase of Manchester United was blocked pursuant to UK Competition Law (Fair Trading Act 1973). See N Toms, 'Ownership and Control of Sports Clubs: The Manchester United Football Club "Buyout"' in S Greenfield and G Osborn (eds), *Law and Sport in Contemporary Society* (Frank Cass 2000) ch 9.

televised football in England could expect to watch only a small number of matches 'live' each season. Rights were sold to the BBC or ITV: they did not compete with each other. Presentation was grotesquely dull. Deregulation of the broadcasting sector allied to the astonishing technological changes that have transformed the range of methods to provide broadcasting services has led to an explosion in the number of companies on the demand-side of the market willing to buy rights from those who organize sporting events. In one of the first ever cases dealing with the intersection of EU law and the broadcasting sector, *Sacchi*, the Court rejected the submissions of the Italian and German governments that radio and television were organized as a form of public service and so should not be subjected to free movement law.[16] This had some analogies with the similarly fruitless attempts to deny the economic context of sport in *Walrave and Koch*, which was decided only a few months later.[17] But no one would even begin to make an argument of this type about the deregulated and ferociously competitive broadcasting market of today. Public broadcasters still exist: deregulation has ensured that they coexist with an array of private corporate broadcasters, all eager to buy rights to transmit sports events. This transformation has been accelerated by technological innovation. Satellite and cable broadcasting is now common, and the rise and mutation of the internet has changed the landscape still more dramatically. Transmission occurs through an increasing variety of media, and it is highly plausible that the pace of technological change will continue to throw up new forms of rapid mass communication, generating intensified fragmentation in the pattern of supply of audiovisual services.

Sellers—sports governing bodies, leagues, and clubs—have gone some way to meet the increased demand consequent on deregulation and technological change. This is commodification. Competitions such as the UEFA Champions League, which began life as the European Cup in 1956, and the English FAPL, the successor to the first ever league championship won in 1889, are today immensely popular and carefully managed brands which are of intense interest to broadcasters, but the supply of sporting events is not static. Demand generates supply: this explains the emergence of new tournaments such as the Confederations Cup, first staged by Fédération Internationale de Football Association (FIFA) in 1997, and FIFA's World Club Cup, which dates from 2000. It explains too the expansion in the size of existing tournaments, so that, for example, the World Cup, reserved to sixteen countries until 1978, now comprises thirty-two participant nations, and Gianni Infantino, who assumed the FIFA Presidency in early 2016, has proposed further expansion to forty or even forty-eight participants.[18] At club level, the Champions League is a vastly inflated project compared with its predecessor the European Cup, while Thursdays, long a football-free day, are now reserved for the Europa League. These represent attempts to increase supply in order to meet demand in order to extract further revenue. These expansionist trends underline the direct commercial

---

[16] Case 155/73 *Guiseppe Sacchi* [1974] ECR 409.
[17] *Walrave and Koch* (n 1). See Ch 4.2.
[18] eg <https://www.theguardian.com/football/2016/oct/03/world-cup-expand-48-teams-fifa-gianni-infantino-suggests> accessed 29 November 2016.

interest of governing bodies such as FIFA and UEFA in organizing the calendar, which was discussed in Chapter 10. The International Olympic Committee (IOC) is also involved in this sporting inflation. It is not sporting considerations alone that have led to football at the Olympic Games acquiring a higher profile in recent years, to the detriment of clubs. This was noted by Advocate General Cosmas in *Deliège v Ligue de Judo*:

… it is no coincidence that professional athletes [In particular in sports such as football and basketball] are now allowed to compete as a means of attracting public interest, nor that new sports with no connection with Olympic history are regularly being introduced for exactly the same reason.[19]

There could be no clearer demonstration of how economic incentives affect what might be thought to be purely sporting choices, confirming the conflict of interest to which sports governing bodies are prey. In similar vein, events are staged with scant regard for the welfare of athletes. The award of the 2022 World Cup to Qatar is the most egregious instance, but to expect the Olympic Marathon to be run in the summer heat of Athens (2004) and the smog of Beijing (2008) makes very clear that the principal priorities of the organizers are remote from concern for the well-being of the athletes. Even lesser events receive lavish coverage, as broadcasters aim to deepen the pool of events that appeal to paying viewers: even a sport as negligible as rugby league, popular only in Sydney and a few towns in Northern England, receives ample coverage. But despite all these attempts to increase the supply of events, it remains clear that a small pool of competitions retain a place at the pinnacle and it is events such as the World Cup and the Olympic Games which stand alone from the perspective of consumers and for which demand and consequently prices are at their highest. These are the events that broadcasters want to acquire most of all in order to distinguish themselves from their competitors, and they will pay accordingly.

This is a process of commodification. Sporting events are for sale. Sport at the elite level is awash with money in a way that would be beyond the comprehension of those who established the English football league in 1888 or the Olympic Games in 1896. The dynamic adaptation of the broadcasting sector, enhancing competition and choice, is centrally significant in provoking this avalanche of money. Sports and media feed off each other: they are tightly entwined in commercial motivation and success.[20]

This puts the ruling in *Bosman* into its proper context as an agent for change in sport in recent years.[21] Of course the judgment brought to an end intra-EU/EEA nationality discrimination in club football. This was examined in Chapter 8. By

---

[19] Cases C-51/96 and C-191/97 *Deliège v Ligue de Judo* [2000] ECR I-2549, para 55, Opinion of Cosmas AG.
[20] For a good overview, see K Lefever, *New Media and Sport: International Legal Aspects* (TMC Asser 2012) chs 2 and 6, describing a 'sports/media complex'.
[21] *Bosman* (n 2).

generating an adjustment of the scope of the transfer system, it altered the nature of the relationship between player and club. This was covered in Chapter 9. But the dominating issue in professional sport over the last two decades has been the transformation of the broadcasting sector and, in particular, the hunger to acquire the most lucrative rights. The alterations to the status of players wrought by *Bosman* are frankly a sideshow compared with this cascade of commercialization. The Nice Declaration on Sport of 2000 stated that 'The sale of television broadcasting rights is one of the greatest sources of income today for certain sports',[22] but even this has now been overtaken. As the Commission's 2007 White Paper put it: 'sport media rights are a decisive source of content for many media operators'; and 'Sport has been a driving force behind the emergence of new media and interactive television services'.[23] It further declares: 'Issues concerning the relationship between the sport sector and sport media (television in particular) have become crucial as television rights are the primary source of income for professional sport in Europe.'[24] This is a commercial pre-eminence to which Advocate General Jääskinen drew explicit attention, using almost the same language in his Opinion in *UEFA and FIFA v Commission*.[25] The applicants in the case had challenged restrictions on their commercial plans as violations of their right to property. Their claim was unsuccessful, as will be explained in section 11.9, but the fact that they had incentives to pursue it before the courts highlights the commercial significance of broadcasting deals.

This also draws attention to the fourth theme that animates this chapter: juridification. Law is far more significant in sport today than it was before the broadcasting revolution that has broken in recent years. In part this is simply the result of commodification. Litigation chases the money. UEFA and FIFA probably did not expect to win the case just mentioned, and elaborated more fully later in this chapter, but the sums of money at stake made it worth their while at least making the attempt. But there is a more intellectual seam to the pattern of juridification in markets for the sale of rights to broadcast sports events. Contracting to sell rights to broadcast sporting events is a simple matter of adding value. Sporting events are organized by governing bodies, and sale of rights to broadcast them, combined with associated commercial strategies including sponsorship and brand association as well as sale of tickets to watch the event 'live', offers choice to paying consumers. This is, in short, how markets work and why they are normally a good thing. It is the juice of competition that lubricates the process and which ensures that the interests and preferences of the ultimate consumer drive the process, not the desire of suppliers to maximize profit.

---

[22] Nice Declaration on Sport, para 15. See Ch 6.3: the full text is at <http://eur-lex.europa.eu/legal-content/EN/TXT/?uri=URISERV:l35007> accessed 29 November 2016.

[23] White Paper on Sport, COM (2007) 391, 11 July 2007, 17, available via <http://ec.europa.eu/sport/index_en.htm> accessed 29 November 2016. See Ch 6.5.

[24] ibid.

[25] Case C-201/11P *UEFA v Commission*, Case C-204/11P *FIFA v Commission*, and Case C-205/11P *FIFA v Commission*, judgments of 18 July 2013, para 33, Opinion of Jääskinen AG, 12 December 2012.

Buyers of rights to broadcast events have an interest in acquiring those rights exclusively: they are then able to market those rights to consumers on the basis that they alone are able to satisfy viewer demand. Exclusivity of this type is common in sports broadcasting. Sellers of rights have an interest in joining together: if the rights to broadcast all matches played in a particular League are sold centrally, instead of by individual participating clubs, then a buyer cannot play clubs off against each other. Collective selling of this type is orthodox in sports leagues. The buyer can take or leave the single collectively sold package. There are winners here, but there are potential losers too. This is where competition law looms. In fact, much of the material traversed in this chapter is applied competition law. The acquisition of exclusive rights makes perfect sense from the perspective of the successful buyer, who gains a valuable resource, and the seller too doubtless commands a premium price in agreeing the contract, but the consequence is that no other broadcaster has access to the rights. That is the whole point of exclusivity. This may damage competition in the market, to the detriment of other actual and potential suppliers of services and may also harm the ultimate consumer, who has but one single—doubtless expensive—source of supply. There is not at all an *inevitable* problem here: this is the market in action, and it would subvert the foundations of our economy to intervene heedlessly simply because X has been able to buy something that Y has not. But the tighter the constraint on competition which flows from the exclusive deal, the more that one may legitimately fear that the exercise of contractual freedom has caused anti-competitive consequences. Whether this is in fact so will depend on matters such as the availability of alternatives to the service sold exclusively and on the length of the exclusive tie. The more populated and competitive the market, the less strong is the case for intervention and, conversely, the more concentrated the power of an individual supplier in a market, the greater the case for legal control to protect the competitive process and ultimately the consumer. In similar vein, collective selling makes obvious sense from the point of view of the seller, because it suppresses competition (between clubs) on the supply-side and therefore increases the price that can be charged for the bundle of rights. This harms those on the demand-side, both the parties which are able to buy the package (for whom the price will be higher than it would otherwise be) and the parties shut out from the deal who have no alternative sources of supply, and ultimately it affects the consumer/viewer. Again this is not to argue that collective selling always deserves condemnation, but rather that a sensitive appreciation is required in order to determine whether in the particular context its benefits exceed its costs.

Sport has long enjoyed a high level of autonomy from legal supervision and the rise of juridification in sport challenges that autonomy. In particular, what is the norm in sport may not fit with orthodox understandings of applicable legal rules. One must then determine whether sport is special enough to deserve appropriately modified treatment under the law. Might collective selling be tolerated if it raises extra revenue which can be shared with the 'grass roots'? This would be to argue that sport is special because of its structures of vertical solidarity. This is explored later, in section 11.7. Might exclusivity be prevented even where it plainly improves the quality and value of the product or service in order to maximize the access of the public wishing to view events? This would be to argue that sport is special because of its high profile and great popularity. This is explored in section 11.9.

Citation of concern to 'maximize access of the public' to sporting events is a reminder that it is not competition law alone that is potentially engaged by the sale of rights to broadcasting events. The previously mentioned report heralding the vastly increased revenues of the England and Wales Cricket Board added that 'the number of people playing cricket in the UK fell by 7 per cent' in 2014.[26] Test match cricket, the pinnacle of the sport, has not been available live on free-to-air television in the UK since 2005. Causal effect is not easy to prove, but it is plausible that the exclusive rights sold to BSkyB, a subscription-only service which became SKY in 2014, have generated short-term profit but long-term decline in the sport's visibility and appeal. Moreover, although fans paying at the gate used to be the most important source of revenue for clubs, their displacement as the primary revenue source in favour of broadcasters and ultimately consumers who do not leave their front room or the pub means that the interests of those who prefer to watch the game 'live' are routinely ignored, as kick-off times are altered, often at short notice, to suit television audiences. The business model of sport has changed: and therefore so has the character of sport itself.[27] Greg Dyke, Chairman of the English FA at the time, defended the FA Cup Final's switch from its traditional 3 o'clock start to a slot later in the afternoon as a consequence of the contract struck between the FA and the broadcasters, on the basis that viewing figures were higher for the later time, and, he asked, 'What are we here for? We're here for people to watch football'.[28] It was plainly not supporters attending the match with which he was concerned, and especially not those from Northern England unable to travel home after the match by public transport because of the late kick-off. More generally, like it or not and certainly not always with benevolent effects, major sporting events play a role of sorts in defining and promoting a sense of common identity: should they therefore be accessible to all citizens to watch for free? Here questions arise which transcend competition law. They include whether there are certain sporting events that are of such significance that rights of access by citizens should prevail over the commercial profit-maximizing preferences of rights owners. Property rights clash with rights to information.

---

[26] See n 13.
[27] See generally eg S Morrow, *The People's Game? Football, Finance and Society* (Macmillan 2003); S Szymanski, *Money and Football: A Soccernomics Guide* (Avalon 2015); D Conn, *The Beautiful Game? Searching for the Soul of Football* (Yellow Jersey Press 2005). The Deloitte Annual Review (n 9) provides plentiful detail: eg the 2016 Report's Foreword notes that as recently as 1991–92 matchday revenue was the largest income source for Premier League clubs, but this has long been surpassed by income from the sale of broadcasting rights.
[28] <http://www.telegraph.co.uk/sport/football/competitions/fa-cup/10187282/FA-Cup-back-on-BBC-but-final-will-controversially-remain-a-5.15pm-kick-off.html> accessed 29 November 2016.

11.3 Property Rights Associated with the Sale
of Rights to Broadcast Sports Events

The rights associated with the sale of broadcasting rights are property rights. They initially fall to be determined and defined under national law. Article 345 TFEU is explicit on this point: 'This Treaty shall in no way prejudice the rules in Member States governing the system of property ownership.' There is no centralized EU property law, and it is accordingly plain that the relevant rights will differ state by state within the EU. The home club would typically enjoy a right to exclude a broadcaster from its stadium where it is the owner of the ground. Whether it enjoys such a right as a tenant would depend on the terms of the contract with the owner. It may also have a right of sorts over the product, the match. But the away team, though holding no property right in respect of the stadium, would commonly also have some claim to property in the match itself. It is not only the participating clubs that are implicated. The organizer of the competition—the League, typically—might also have a stake. Rules and practice vary across the Member States of the EU.[29]

What, however, is clear is that Article 345 TFEU does not immunize rules governing property ownership from the application of EU law. Where their *exercise* cuts across the objectives of the EU, they are subject to review. Therefore Article 345 is a lot less valuable as a defence of sporting autonomy in the matter of the sale of broadcasting rights than it might first appear to be. The Court first made this clear in cases in which it was urged that Article 345's intent was that property rights could not be addressed pursuant to EU law even where they obstructed cross-border trade. For example, *Alfredo Albore* concerned the exemption of Italian nationals from the requirement to obtain an authorization to buy property in certain parts of the national territory.[30] Article 345 provides a reason not to object to the existence in principle of such a requirement, but it does not permit the evasion of EU law's fundamental resistance to discrimination against nationals of other Member States nor of its control of restrictions on capital movements between Member States. Article 345 protects the autonomy of the Member States to structure their own systems of property ownership, but the way in which those systems are operated is subject to review for compatibility with the basic expectations of EU internal market law.[31] Put another way, there is neither centralized nor comprehensive EU property law, but there is an emerging influence of EU law on national property law which is bringing into focus a distinctive soft species of EU property law.[32] This is

---

[29] See T Margoni, 'The Protection of Sports Events in the EU: Property, Intellectual Property, Unfair Competition and Special forms of Protection' (2016) 47 International Review of Intellectual Property and Competition Law 386.

[30] Case C-423/98 [2000] ECR I-5965.

[31] cf eg J Rutgers, 'The Rule of Reason and Private Law or the Limits to Harmonization' in A Schrauwen (ed), *Rule of Reason: Rethinking Another Classic of European Legal Doctrine* (Europa Law Publishing 2005) ch 9; U Drobnig, HJ Snijders, and E Zippro (eds), *Divergences of Property Law, an Obstacle to the Internal Market* (Sellier 2006).

[32] See E Ramaekers, *European Union Property Law: From Fragments to a System* (Intersentia 2013).

fully in line with the EU's characteristic claim to assert a broad functionally-based review of national law and practice pursuant to the Treaty provisions underpinning the internal market.[33]

In the case of practices pertaining to broadcasting rights, it is primarily the Treaty competition rules which are at stake. The twin pillars of EU competition law, explained in Chapter 3, are Article 101 TFEU, which exercises control over bilateral and multilateral practices that harm the internal market, and Article 102 TFEU, which is aimed at prohibiting the abuse of a dominant position within the internal market by a single powerful undertaking. Here too the same analytical pattern applies: Article 345 TFEU ensures that the definition and scope of such rights belongs at national level, but it does not shelter the way in which the rights are exercised from examination in the light of Articles 101 and 102.

The Commission's *Champions League* decision clearly demonstrates this pattern.[34] The legal analysis proceeds on the plainly correct basis that there is no common concept in the Member States attached to ownership of the property rights associated with staging football matches, nor is there any EU concept. The Commission saw no need to make a final ruling on exactly what type of property right is at stake, except only to exclude that UEFA was the sole owner of the property rights involved. Had it treated the matter as one where UEFA was simply selling its own property, then Article 101 TFEU would not have been relevant—though Article 102 TFEU might have been. Instead it decided to proceed on the basis that there is co-ownership between the football clubs and UEFA for the individual matches, and that there are multiple owners of the media rights to the UEFA Champions League.[35] So the collective selling arrangement fell to be scrutinized in the light of Article 101. Article 345 TFEU did not save it—though, as is explained later, in section 11.5, Article 101(3) did.

Article 102 TFEU may apply where a sports federation which enjoys monopoly power in making the rules that govern the sport makes decisions with direct commercial implications. This may apply in the case of the sale of broadcasting rights and is especially likely to arise where the governing body has a powerful central organizing role which goes beyond that held by UEFA in *Champions League*. In *FIA (Formula One)* part of the Commission's objections related to rules that provided a financial disincentive for contracted broadcasters to show motor sports events that competed with Formula 1.[36] The Commission was satisfied with a solution according to which the FIA curtailed its influence in order to permit broadcasters to make their own commercial choices about which events to show. The crucial legal point, however, was that even though the case concerned property rights, Article 345 TFEU guaranteed only that their *existence* shall remain intact: it did not protect their *exercise* from EU competition law. Article 102 TFEU subjects the practices of sports governing bodies that have an economic

---

[33] See S Weatherill, *The Internal Market as a Legal Concept* (OUP 2017).
[34] Dec 2003/778 *Champions League* [2003] OJ L291/25, para 122, considered more fully later.
[35] ibid paras 123, 124.   [36] COMP 35.163, Notice published at [2001] OJ C169/5.

impact to control, and they are likely to be treated as abusive where their restrictive effects go beyond what is necessary for the functioning of the sport. This is applicable to the use to which governing bodies put their broadcasting rights as to any other asset at their disposal.

The Commission's rising interest in sport in recent years is primarily motivated by its concern to oversee the development of the broadcasting market to which professional sport has become commercially so intimately linked. It is, in short, less exercised by potential anti-competitive activity in sport than it is by pernicious practices in the deregulated and technologically dynamic broadcasting sector. Most of the relevant activity has focused on control of the selling of rights pursuant to Article 101 TFEU. The straightforward sale of rights is a purely contractual matter and in a market characterized by several competing buyers and sellers there is unlikely to be any problem of a type that would generate interest under competition law. But whether there really are adequate competitive influences depends on the particular market in which rights are being traded. In particular exclusivity, territorial restrictions, and collective selling all raise awkward competition law questions. In part they are questions that invite the application of EU competition law to sport in an orthodox manner. But—in line with the theme pursued diligently throughout this book—there may also be issues regarding the extent to which sport is special and accordingly demands more sensitive treatment. The autonomy of sport under EU law is conditional, not absolute, and the regulation of the market for the sale of broadcasting rights offers another fascinating case study into how to determine the precise contours of those governing conditions.

11.4 The Sale of Exclusive Rights

It has already been explained that there is a clear commercial attraction to the acquisition of a product or service on an exclusive basis. The buyer becomes the sole source from which other parties in downstream markets can acquire the product or service, and can set prices accordingly. This is true in any market: the market for the sale of rights to broadcast sporting events is simply one in which the lure of exclusivity is especially glittering. The question, raised earlier, is whether the foreclosing effect on the market which results from exclusivity should attract concern from the perspective of competition law. The answer, explained at length in the following section, is in short, 'sometimes—but it depends on the state of the market'.

11.4.1 The scope of Article 101(1) TFEU

Article 101 TFEU prohibits agreements which have as their object or effect the prevention, restriction, or distortion of competition within the internal market, subject only to the possibility of exemption in accordance with the criteria set out in Article 101(3). The prohibition is given bite by Article 101(2) which directs that prohibited agreements shall be automatically void. This is plainly designed to curtail contractual autonomy where it violates the requirements of EU law. Where a seller agrees to supply a buyer with rights to broadcast sports events on an exclusive basis, other would-be competitors are excluded from access to the content. But this cannot of itself lead to the application of Article 101. After all, any contract that involves a promise to do or not to do something is capable of being understood as a restriction on the freedom of the party making the promise. It would stretch competition law in general and Article 101 in particular too far to apply it in such indiscriminate fashion. It is instead necessary to focus in a more economically informed manner on what should be the proper reach of Article 101.

The sale of rights counts as a vertical deal. Such deals generally have pro-competitive implications because they increase the supply of goods or services in the market. Exclusivity is commonly a necessary element in a successful vertical deal. The grant of exclusivity is what makes the purchase attractive to the buyer, who may thereby be induced to invest much more confidently in the quality of the product—which is in itself a clear benefit to the consumer. That means that where, without exclusivity, there will be no deal at all, then the exclusivity is in fact pro-competitive. It would be wrong to subject it to Article 101 TFEU.

There is nothing new about this, nor indeed is there anything sport-specific about it. As long ago as 1966 the Court ruled in *Société Technique Minière v Maschinenbau Ulm GmbH* that 'competition must be understood within the actual context in which it would occur in the absence of the agreement in dispute' and that 'it may be doubted whether there is an interference with competition if the said agreement seems really necessary for the penetration of a new area by an undertaking'.[37] This meant that in order to determine whether the prohibition contained in (what is today) Article 101(1) TFEU bites, the grant of an exclusive right needed to be accompanied by assessment of its context. There should be appreciation of matters including the nature and quantity of the products covered by the agreement, the position and importance of the buyer and the seller in the market for the products concerned, the question whether the disputed agreement stands alone or instead forms part of a series of agreements, and the severity of the clauses intended to protect the holder of exclusive rights.

The case concerned the sale of equipment used by public utilities by a German producer to a French user. It was not about sport or broadcasting. But it asserted that, in short, the structure of the particular market in which the grant of exclusive rights is made needs to be taken seriously in deciding whether there is a reason to review the arrangement pursuant to Article 101(1). This is enduringly true.

The most important document in practice today is the 2010 Commission *Guidelines on Vertical Restraints*.[38] This sets out in careful detail how to apply Article 101(1) TFEU. It makes clear that unduly tight or lengthy restrictions will not escape subjection to Article 101. Nor will EU law countenance an exclusive licence which suppresses parallel trade—that is, one which seeks to achieve absolute territorial

---

[37] Case 56/65 [1966] ECR 235.
[38] European Commission, *Guidelines on Vertical Restraints*, SEC (2010) 411 [2010] OJ C130/1.

protection within the wider EU internal market. Moreover, an agreement conferring exclusive rights should be assessed in the context of any 'network effects' that
are involved if that is relevant in the particular market—that means, an agreement's
impact on competition must not be assessed in isolation if the economic reality is
that the agreement is not an isolated transaction.

This model is readily applicable to the sale of sports rights, which is commonly
conducted according to the sale of exclusive rights on a territorial basis. Careful
consultation of the Guidelines may lead to the drafting of an agreement which
does not fall within the scope of Article 101(1) at all. However, the more power
in the market the agreement confers on the buyer, the more valuable the exclusive
right becomes: while the more power in the market the agreement confers, the
more likely it is that it will in consequence affect competition to a sufficient degree
to bring it within the scope of Article 101(1). This does not mean it is inevitably
unlawful. It means instead that it survives only if capable of exemption pursuant to
Article 101(3). This is now considered.

11.4.2 Exemption

If an agreement does not fall within Article 101(1) TFEU, it is immune from intervention based on EU competition law. If an agreement falls within Article 101(1),
its compatibility with EU law depends on its compliance with Article 101(3),
which gives scope for exemption. So a sale of rights to broadcast sports events on an
exclusive basis could conceivably fall within Article 101(1), yet secure an exemption
pursuant to Article 101(3).

Article 101(3) TFEU contains two positive and two negative criteria that must
be satisfied by an agreement in order to secure entitlement to exemption. The practice must 'contribute to improving the production or distribution of goods or to
promoting technical or economic progress, while allowing consumers a fair share
of the resulting benefit'; and it must not 'impose on the undertakings concerned
restrictions which are not indispensable to the attainment of these objectives', nor
'afford such undertakings the possibility of eliminating competition in respect of a
substantial part of the products in question'.

In the case of the sale of rights to broadcast sports events on an exclusive basis in
circumstances where the matter is found to fall within the scope of Article 101(1)
TFEU, one could readily imagine that the deal could be presented as a contribution
to improving the production or distribution of goods or to promoting technical
or economic progress because of the incentives created by the grant of exclusivity
to penetrate new markets and to improve the quality of the product in order to
increase market share—all of which is perfectly conceivably in the interest of consumers. The precise conditions of the deal would need to be scrutinized in order to
be satisfied that it is not marred by restrictions which are not indispensable to the
attainment of its objectives. It would also be necessary to ensure that the parties to
the deal are not afforded the possibility of eliminating competition in respect of a
substantial part of the products in question, which plainly requires careful examination of the structure of the particular market in question. The Commission's

Notice on market definition is helpful and influential on this point.[39] None of this is sports-specific. In all cases careful examination of the prevailing market structure is essential in determining the application of not only Article 101(1) but also Article 101(3).

In law the key text is the Block Exemption Regulation on Vertical Restraints. The currently applicable text is Commission Regulation 330/2010 of 20 April 2010 on the application of Article 101(3) of the Treaty on the Functioning of the European Union to categories of vertical agreements and concerted practices.[40] It entered into force at the beginning of June 2010 and will expire at the end of May 2022. And it is usefully supplemented by the 2010 *Guidelines on Vertical Restraints*, which were mentioned earlier.[41]

The Regulation is based on an assumption, amplified in its Preamble, that vertical agreements are apt to improve economic efficiency by facilitating better coordination between the participating undertakings. Article 1(1)(a) defines the 'vertical agreement' as an agreement or concerted practice entered into between two or more undertakings each of which operates, for the purposes of the agreement or the concerted practice, at a different level of the production or distribution chain, and relating to the conditions under which the parties may purchase, sell, or resell certain goods or services; and Article 1(1)(b) adds that 'vertical restraint' means a restriction of competition in a vertical agreement falling within the scope of Article 101(1) TFEU. The disposition to take a favourable view of vertical agreements is captured by Recital 6 of the Regulation, which declares that 'certain types of vertical agreements can improve economic efficiency within a chain of production or distribution by facilitating better coordination between the participating undertakings'; so too 'they can lead to a reduction in the transaction and distribution costs of the parties and to an optimisation of their sales and investment levels'.

The purpose here is not to provide a nuts-and-bolts inspection of the precise detail of the shape and size of the 'window' through which agreements may pass in order to secure exemption: reading Regulation 330/2010 itself is quite enough to meet that need, and it is important in practice. The most revealing aspect of the scheme is its limit: the circumstances in which exemption pursuant to the Regulation is *not* available reveal the underlying fears that the enhancement in patterns of supply created by the sale of rights on an exclusive basis may be outweighed in some circumstances by potentially serious anti-competitive consequences.

The calculation is heavily affected by the market power of the undertakings concerned: to what extent is their commercial freedom of action confined by competition from other suppliers? The Regulation therefore establishes a threshold based on market share. Its Article 3 directs that exemption is conditional on falling below

---

[39] [1997] OJ C372/5.
[40] Regulation (EU) 330/2010 of 20 April 2010 on the application of Article 101(3) of the Treaty on the Functioning of the European Union to categories of vertical agreements and concerted practices [2010] OJ L102/1 (Block Exemption Regulation). It replaced, but did not significantly alter, Regulation 2790/99 [1999] OJ L336/21.
[41] *Guidelines on Vertical Restraints* (n 38).

defined market share thresholds. The supplier's market share shall not exceed 30 per cent of the relevant market on which it sells the contract goods or services and the market share held by the buyer shall not exceed 30 per cent of the relevant market on which it purchases the contract goods or services. Calculation of the market share is the subject of careful elaboration in Article 7 of the Regulation. Article 8 does the same job in relation to turnover. So where the market share held by each of the undertakings party to the agreement on the relevant market does not exceed 30 per cent the assumption is that, in short, the vertical agreement leads to an improvement in production or distribution and allows consumers a fair share of the resulting benefits, and so deserves exemption—a green light. Above the 30 per cent market share threshold, there is no such assumption that (in short) the benefits exceed the costs. This does not mean the deal is forbidden. The point is only that it lies outwith the safe harbour created by Regulation 330/2010 and so it needs individual examination.

Articles 4 and 5 of the Regulation are crucial in negotiating the tension between preserving, on the one hand, contractual autonomy and, on the other, protecting the interest in a competitive market which is moreover an internal market. Article 4 lists restrictions that remove the benefit of the block exemption—so-called hardcore restrictions which are not to be tolerated irrespective of the undertakings' market share. The target is 'restrictions which are likely to restrict competition and harm consumers or which are not indispensable to the attainment of the efficiency-enhancing effects'.[42] Article 4 directs that exemption shall not apply to vertical agreements which, directly or indirectly, in isolation or in combination with other factors under the control of the parties, have as their object one or more of a list of five matters. Those matters focus on restrictions associated with the price of goods and services and certain types of territorial protection. So exemption is not on offer where a vertical agreement restricts the territory into which, or of the customers to whom, a buyer may sell goods or services, except where, of the highest significance, the restriction applies to active sales into the exclusive territory or to an exclusive customer group reserved to the supplier or allocated by the supplier to another buyer, where such a restriction does not limit sales by the customers of the buyer.[43] There is, then, a decisive break between restriction of active selling into an exclusive territory (which is not allowed) and restrictions of more passive behaviour (which may be exempted). This, which has a long pedigree in the Court's case law,[44] is the attempt to manage the tension between preserving the integrity of the EU's internal market and the virtuous effect of granting territorial exclusivity as an inducement to intensified commercial activity.

Article 5 of the Regulation then adds a set of 'Excluded restrictions', where exemption is not on offer. These cover any direct or indirect non-compete obligation, the

---

[42] Block Exemption Regulation (n 40) Recital 10.

[43] ibid Art 4(b)(i). There is also special provision in Art 4(b) for (in particular) restriction of sales in a selective distribution system.

[44] eg Case 258/78 *Nungesser v Commission* [1982] ECR 2015. For detailed exploration, see R Whish and D Bailey, *Competition Law* (8th edn, OUP 2015) ch 16.

duration of which is indefinite or exceeds five years; any direct or indirect obligation causing the buyer, after termination of the agreement, not to manufacture, purchase, sell, or resell goods or services; any direct or indirect obligation causing the members of a selective distribution system not to sell the brands of particular competing suppliers. The broad concern is to preclude the possibility that participating undertakings may eliminate competition in respect of a substantial part of the products in question, which is a concern written into Article 101(3) TFEU itself.

11.4.3 Application to sport: defining markets

Deals may be treated as compatible with EU law because they are not within Article 101(1) TFEU at all or because they are within Article 101(1) but nevertheless able to benefit from the exemption available under Article 101(3). There is some practical significance in deciding which is the appropriate route. The burden of proof is different: it rests on the party making the allegation to show that a matter falls foul of Article 101(1), whereas the parties seeking exemption must show that their arrangements satisfy Article 101(3).[45] The similarities are, however, greater than the differences. Whether an arrangement is placed outwith Article 101(1) or treated as exempted pursuant to Article 101(3) the outcome is the same—it is not precluded by EU competition law. It is, moreover, plain that issues relevant to the examination are to some extent common. The structure of the market, and in particular the amount of competition within it, is significant in deciding whether a grant of exclusive rights falls within Article 101 in the first place. Then, if it does, a contract for sale of rights to broadcast sports events on an exclusive basis may fit within Regulation 330/2010—but here too market share will matter and concrete figures are stipulated in the Regulation, as explained in subsection 11.4.2.

The application of Article 101 TFEU depends on the precise nature of the practices under examination and it depends on the particular market. Obviously the more narrowly the market is defined the higher the market share and the deeper the anxieties about the exclusionary effect of the grant of exclusivity on other operators, and so the more likely it is that there will be a negative outcome from the application of EU competition law. This then translates into detailed decision-making. Examination of markets for the sale of rights to broadcast sports events is no more than a particular application of the general principles of EU competition law.

There are, however, prominent and distinctive features of the market for the sale of rights to broadcast sporting events: it is, to adopt the analogy used tirelessly elsewhere in this book, in important respects different from selling cars or sausages or financial services. Most of all, rights to broadcast top-level sports events are unusually attractive. They are eagerly watched by consumers (as viewers) and so they have become immensely important to broadcasters and suppliers of services using new audiovisual media which wish to protect or establish a powerful position in

---

[45] Council Regulation (EC) 1/2003 of 16 December 2002 on the implementation of the rules on competition laid down in Articles 81 and 82 of the Treaty [2003] OJ L1/1, Art 2.

these fast-moving and lucrative markets. This leads typically to the assumption that holders of rights to broadcast top-level sport are in a position of economic strength because consumers (as viewers) want to watch that event and will not be satisfied with another less intense sporting event or another form of entertainment, such as a film. The right holder has a large market share. This in turn leads to attentive supervision of the potentially anti-competitive implications associated with the sale of such rights, in particular output restrictions and exclusive selling. Because high-profile live sport events are simply 'must have' for many consumers, it is, in short, more likely that arrangements to sell those rights on an exclusive basis will attract more concern where sport is involved than in most other markets. Most of all, in its decisions in this area the Commission has shown itself thematically anxious to sustain the potential for dynamic growth in the technologically agile and (compared to thirty years ago) lightly regulated broadcasting sector, which feeds so hungrily off sport.

The special, though not unique, sensitivities of inquiry into the sport sector emerge from the Commission's decisional practice. Identifying market share presupposes an accurate definition of the market in the first place. This conventionally requires determination of the relevant market within which sales occur: both the relevant product market and the relevant geographical market. The inquiry is into the willingness of buyers to substitute products or services for each other, and to find a geographical location in which the conditions of competition are sufficiently homogeneous and distinct from those of neighbouring geographical areas. The Commission's Notice on the Definition of the Relevant Market is most prominently concerned with Article 102 TFEU but on this point it is of service to Article 101 as well.[46] The assessment of substitutability requires case-by-case examination. Where the event for which exclusive rights are held is really 'must see', the point is that there is an absence of discipline by competition, and so a high level of market power. It will obviously exceed the 30 per cent market share which is the crucial threshold under Block Exemption Regulation 330/2010 and will more generally provoke anxiety about the anti-competitive effects of any sale on an exclusive basis.

A paper written in 1998, as the combined effects of deregulation, technological change, commodification, and juridification were emerging, by an official in the Competition Directorate-General, Anne-Marie Wachtmeister, neatly captures what is at stake.[47] She noted that: 'Exclusivity is an accepted commercial practice in the broadcasting sector.' It maximizes profitability for the buyer and is the key to building up a new audience. But, she added, 'duration, quantity and upstream and downstream market power need to be examined in order to assess whether the exclusivity seriously restricts competition'.

Champions League, a Commission decision of 2003, is primarily important for its exploration of the application of Article 101 TFEU to the collective selling of

---

[46] [1997] OJ C372/5.

[47] A-M Wachtmeister, 'Broadcasting of Sports Events and Competition Law', Competition Policy Newsletter (Brussels, European Commission, No 2 of 1998 (June)), available via <http://ec.europa.eu/comm/competition/speeches/index_1998.html> accessed 29 November 2016.

television rights.[48] Its importance to such horizontal arrangements—those struck between parties at the same level in the supply chain—is examined later: the arrangements in question granted UEFA the right to sell commercial rights to the Champions League on behalf of the participating football clubs, and so eliminated any possibility of competition among the clubs as sellers. But the inquiry is relevant to vertical restraints too. For obvious commercial reasons, the arrangements in question involved a grant of rights by UEFA on an *exclusive* basis. The value of these rights is immense. The competition today known as the Champions League began life as the European Cup in season 1955–56, and entry was confined to clubs that had won their national championship in the previous season. Real Madrid were the first winners: in fact they won for the first five years. Beginning in 1992–93 the competition was re-named the Champions League. Re-naming was in truth mis-naming: this was a grubby triumph of branding over substance because the principal change was to widen participation to allow entry not only to national champions but also to clubs that had not won the national title in the previous season. The aim of including non-champions in the so-called Champions League was to enhance the level of involvement of rich clubs from the major leagues, most of them from Spain, Germany, Italy, and England, the four dominant powers of European club football. The purity of the original European Cup format, whereby a club had to win its own national title before aspiring to become Europe's champion club, was sacrificed to achieve a far more vigorous commercial model. The competition is immensely popular. It comprises over 200 matches, but it is the later knockout rounds, taking place after Christmas, which are the focus and which culminate in a Final played at the very end of the season each year. The competition is eagerly watched and broadcasters are able to charge premiums of between 10 and 50 per cent for advertising spots during Champions League matches not only because of that core popularity but also because football is 'a tool to reach a hard-to-get-to audience'.[49]

The Commission had issued a statement of objections in 2001, in which it objected to UEFA's practice of selling rights on an exclusive basis in a single bundle to a single television broadcaster per territory for several years in a row. So the problem was not exclusivity *per se*: the problem was the size and shape of the exclusivity. Moreover, the problem was not the sport sector: the problem was the broadcasting sector. The Commission noted in its 2003 Decision that 'in most countries football is not only the driving force for the development of pay-TV services but is also an essential programme item for free-TV broadcasters' and so where 'one broadcaster holds all or most of the relevant football TV rights in a Member State, it is extremely difficult for competing broadcasters to establish themselves successfully in that market'.[50] The arrangements were modified as a result of the Commission's intervention. In particular, UEFA agreed to split up rights into several different rights packages that would be offered for sale in separate packages to different third parties. The final Decision refers to the splitting up

---

[48] *Champions League* (n 34).   [49] ibid para 75.   [50] ibid para 20.

of collectively sold media rights to the Champions League into several different rights packages, which are offered for sale in a competitive bidding procedure open to all interested media operators. So, it is noted, this 'allows several media operators to acquire media rights of the UEFA Champions League from UEFA'.[51] And some rights were made available on a non-exclusive basis. This satisfied the Commission of the thematically central point that buyers had several possible sources of supply. This 'unbundling' is explained at careful length in the Commission Decision. And UEFA proposed, as a general principle, that media rights contracts be concluded for a period not exceeding three UEFA Champions League seasons.[52] This was import-ant enough for the Commission ultimately to grant an exemption for a period of six years, basing this explicitly on the duration of two cycles of contract periods of three years.[53] The crucial point, then, was the concern of the Commission to ensure that the sale of rights did not adversely affect conditions of competition in broadcasting markets.

Grant of exclusive rights to show matches in the UEFA Champions League would generate no cause for concern if viewers were perfectly happy to watch something else instead of top-level club football. It was central to the Commission Decision that this was not so: it was the identification of a narrow market and consequently a dominant market share held by UEFA which led to alarm about the anti-competitive implications for the broadcasting industry of such aggressively enforced exclusivity. The market analysis in the Commission's Decision is there-fore fundamentally important to its conclusions. Having examined the attitude of viewers, it decided that a separate market existed for the acquisition of television broadcasting rights of football events that are played regularly throughout every year—that is, covering matches in national league and cup events as well as the UEFA Champions League and UEFA Cup. Football, unlike other sports, allows broadcasters to achieve high viewing figures on a regular, sustained, and continu-ous basis if they can get access to these rights.[54] It considered that 'The TV rights of football events create a particular brand image for a TV channel and allow the broadcaster to reach a particular audience at the retail level that cannot be reached by other programmes'.[55] Prices charged for advertising were an important factor in sustaining this conclusion. The key finding, then, was that television rights to other sports events or other types of programmes, such as feature films, do not put a competitive restraint on the holder of the television rights to football events being played regularly throughout the year. This relatively narrow market defin-ition meant that international club competitions are part of the same market as national club competitions, but the market is not much wider than that. And the Commission expressed a similar view about the structure of markets emerging as a result of the development of new media.

Consumers will not watch sporting events of lower prestige or films in sub-stitution for top-level football of this type, and so prices are unchecked by the

---

[51] ibid para 194.   [52] ibid para 25.   [53] ibid para 200.   [54] ibid para 68.
[55] ibid para 63.

availability of other such content and broadcasters wishing to gain ground in the market cannot rely on such content to compensate for failure to win access to top-level sport. This approach to defining markets for rights to broadcast sports events taken by the Commission in *Champions League* was important but it was not path-breaking. *Eurovision* concerned collective buying, rather than selling, of broadcasting rights.[56] It was decided three years before *Champions League*. Relying on the preferences of viewers, the Commission had rejected the view pressed on it by the European Broadcasting Union that the relevant market covered the acquisition of the television rights to important sporting events in all disciplines of sport, irrespective of the national or international character of the event. It preferred a narrow understanding: it noted that for at least some sporting events, such as the summer Olympics, the winter Olympics, the Wimbledon Finals, and the Football World Cup, the behaviour of viewers does not appear to be influenced by the coincidence of other major sporting events being broadcast simultaneously. These major events stand alone: the Commission found a strong likelihood that there are separate markets for the acquisition of some major sporting events, most of them international, though it did not need to reach a final conclusion in the matter for the purposes of the case.[57] So too in *Newscorp/Telepiù*, concerning a merger, the affected market was that for the acquisition of exclusive broadcasting rights for football events played every year where national teams participate (the national league, primarily first division and cups, the UEFA Champions League, and the UEFA Cup), because 'this type of football contents constitutes a stand-alone "driver" content for pay-TV operators'.[58] This was a decision adopted in April 2003, just a few months before *Champions League*,[59] and clearly in the same vein. At stake was the acquisition of 'premium' sports rights on an exclusive basis for the purposes of making a pay-TV venture sufficiently attractive to viewers as consumers, and the consequent effect on buyers unable to gain access to such content was at the heart of the Commission's concern about the effect of the proposed merger on the market. It allowed the deal to proceed but only on condition that undertakings were given which were designed to eliminate unacceptable anti-competitive aspects to the deal. These included restrictions on the length of the contracts granting exclusive rights to the new media group. This is a sports-specific concern in so far as the valuable prize of top-level sport is the reason why anti-competitive consequences may attach to a race for the prize where there is only one winner, but the real anxiety is with the effect on broadcasting markets, and this could conceivably arise where other premium content is at stake. So in *Bertelsmann/Kirch/Premiere* the Commission found that a proposed merger between powerful players in the media sector would harm effective competition and therefore blocked it, in accordance with the supervisory

---

[56] Comm Dec 2000/400 *Eurovision* [2000] OJ L151/18, paras 38–45.

[57] Dec 2000/400 was annulled, but not on the point of market definition, in Cases T-185/00 *M6 and others v Commission* [2002] ECR II-3805.

[58] COMP/M.2876 *Newscorp/Telepiù* Dec 2004/311 [2004] OJ L110/73, para 66.

[59] The proceedings that led to *Champions League* (n 34) are mentioned in the *Newscorp/Telepiù* decision (n 58) at para 56 fn 20.

powers granted by the EU's Merger Regulation.[60] The Commission noted en route to this conclusion that a sufficiently attractive 'pay-TV bouquet' must include a combination of premium rights for the first broadcasts of films produced at the major Hollywood studios which, it added, are resources 'in short supply, since, as a general rule, the broadcasting rights for premium content of this kind are given on the basis of longer-term exclusive contracts'.[61] But even here the weighty importance of sport could not be escaped: the decision was based also on the importance of 'popular sporting events' as resources in short supply.[62] The theme is clear: the higher the market power acquired, the happier the buyer, but the more perturbed the competition authorities. This is general competition law, and to this extent sport is not special. But sport is unusual in generating rather narrow markets (for rights to the very top events) which are consequently marked by a typically high level of market power enjoyed by the organizer of the event, commonly the governing body of the sport.[63]

In *Champions League* the geographical market was defined as national. The Commission relied on the pattern of distribution, which is national due to the existence of local regulatory regimes, language barriers, and cultural factors.[64] This reflected a long-standing understanding that licensing on a territorial basis is not inevitably treated as artificial market-partitioning in the EU, but rather may reflect the reality of divergent tastes, preferences, linguistic ability, and regulatory conditions.[65] So *Champions League* fits with pre-existing practice which finds that markets in the broadcasting sector tend to be enduringly national.[66] This too is likely to be volatile: the Eurosport channel and the rise of SKY show the possibility for a slow emergence of a European sports media. But even global events, such as the World Cup and the Olympic Games, tend to be shown on a national basis.

The practical question which emerges from this examination of the treatment of the sale of exclusive rights to broadcast major sporting events is just what is permitted under EU competition law. The commercial value of exclusivity, without which a seller would quite likely not be able to find a willing buyer or at least only a buyer at a much reduced price, means that it cannot in principle be the subject of routine prohibition, but equally the potential harm it causes to the competitive process in broadcasting markets means that it must be policed with care.

The solution to this conundrum lies in placing conditions on the grant of exclusivity. The Commission's practice reveals concern to ensure that there is an open and

---

[60] Case IV/M.993 *Bertelsmann/Kirch/Premiere* [1999] OJ L53/1. The current version of the Merger Regulation is Council Regulation (EC) 139/2004 of 20 January 2004 on the control of concentrations between undertakings [2004] OJ L24/1.

[61] *Bertelsmann/Kirch/Premiere* (n 60) paras 48–49.   [62] ibid.

[63] The narrowest market definition of all did not arise in the broadcasting sector: it is found in the Commission's Decision on the 1998 Football World Cup in which the market for match tickets for the tournament stood alone from the perspective of the consumer: Comm Dec 2000/12 1998 *Football World Cup* [2000] OJ L5/55. A fine was imposed for sales practices discriminatory on grounds of nationality in breach of TFEU, Art 102.

[64] *Champions League* (n 34) paras 88, 90.

[65] eg Case 262/81 *Coditel II* [1982] ECR I-3381.

[66] eg *Bertelsmann/Kirch/Premiere* (n 60) para 23; *Newscorp/Telepiù* (n 58) paras 67, 72–73.

transparent tendering process rinsed of any hint of discrimination based on nationality; commonly that there should be 'unbundling' of the package on offer to allow space for more than one buyer (which becomes ever easier as technology generates new forms of distribution); that the duration of exclusivity should be limited, and a duration of three years has become more or less standard; and the grant shall not be automatically renewed. The aim is to balance the need to address concerns about the open and competitive structure of the market against the autonomy of the commercial parties involved to create value.

In the wake of *Champions League* the Commission dealt with two further instances of collective selling of rights to broadcast high-level football matches, and it demonstrated how *Champions League* had set a pattern. The two Decisions concerned first the German Bundesliga and then the English Premier League, two of Europe's four strongest national football Leagues (along with Italy's Serie A and the Spanish Primera Liga).

The Bundesliga decision concerned the central marketing of media rights (television but also cable, satellite, and radio) to matches in the two top professional men's football leagues in Germany, Bundesliga and Bundesliga II.[67] The collective dimension to the sale restricted supply, and the Commission explicitly noted the commercial importance of being able to supply football content and therefore the potential harm in downstream markets caused by restriction of supply.[68] This is examined further later. The geographical market was defined by applicable national law, the language and cultural characteristics, and was confined to Germany and potentially also German-speaking areas.[69] The Commission decided a green light should be shone after receipt of commitments from the Bundesliga. These focused on the offer of nine distinct packages of rights on a transparent and non-discriminatory basis and on a duration that would not exceed three years. The aim was to increase competition in the market and the Commission was satisfied that the arrangements would 'contribute to innovation and dampen the concentration tendencies in the media markets'.[70] The Commission concluded that there were no longer grounds for action on its part—although it did not make explicit whether this was because the matter fell outside the scope of Article 101(1) TFEU or instead within the criteria of exemption set out in Article 101(3). Either way, exclusivity was permitted, but on terms that demonstrated a concern to keep broadcasting markets fluid.

The Commission's 2006 Decision on the collective selling of the media rights to the English FA Premier League was similarly predominantly concerned with horizontal aspects of selling, which are examined later, but as part of the inquiry, it was necessary to consider precisely what was being sold by the FAPL to downstream markets.[71] At the time the Commission first took an interest in the FAPL's practices, the package sold typically covered three years, and was split between

---

[67] COMP 37.214 Dec 2005/396 *Joint selling of the media rights to the German Bundesliga* [2005] OJ L134/46.
[68] ibid para 23.   [69] ibid para 19.   [70] ibid para 41.
[71] COMP 38.173 *Joint selling of the media rights to the FA Premier League*, 22 March 2006. Summary of Commission Decision at [2008] OJ C7/18.

exclusive packages of live rights to televise matches, live rights for radio broadcast, and rights for use on mobile phones. There were also rights to show matches on a deferred basis. The Commission had opened an investigation in 2001, due to a suspicion that the arrangements restricted competition within the meaning of (what is now) Article 101(1) TFEU and that they were not entitled to exemption pursuant to Article 101(3). An extended period of negotiation ensued and a number of commitments were made by the Premier League with a view to securing a green light, which was eventually forthcoming in 2006. The Commission aligned its analysis explicitly with its Decisions in *Champions League* and *Bundesliga*. The broadcasting rights to premium football events played regularly through the season constitutes a distinct relevant product market. The geographical market was the UK market alone: the Commission noted once again that markets for media rights are usually defined on the basis of national or linguistic criteria. The Commission decided that the tendency to sell large packages of rights on an exclusive basis creates damage in downstream markets by raising barriers to entry, especially if there is only a single buyer. It is clear that the underlying primary concern is not sport but broadcasting: the link is the huge value of sports rights to broadcasters seeking to establish their presence. The changes made under adapted commitments of the FAPL included increased output (the availability of an increased number of matches), the sale of six packages of rights that would not be purchasable by a single buyer (though buying five of six was possible), splitting the sale of UK and Irish rights, sale on a transparent and non-discriminatory tendering basis, and that the duration of agreements would not exceed three years. The thematic concern was clear—more and fairer competition. The Commission concluded that there were no longer grounds for action on its part—although, as in *Bundesliga*, it did not make explicit whether this was because the matter was now outside the scope of Article 101(1) or instead within the criteria of exemption set out in Article 101(3).

Football is the main game in town, but in 2001 the Commission addressed Formula 1.[72] Broadcasters had acquired exclusive rights for the contracted territory that were, in the Commission's estimation, too long and therefore anti-competitive within the meaning of Article 101 TFEU. The agreed solution was to cap the length of new free-to-air broadcasting contracts at three years, albeit with exceptional provision for five-year deals where a particular need to encourage investment is present. The three decisions on collective selling in football just examined follow this preference for three years of contractually agreed exclusive rights as the norm: enough to generate the benefits of value-creation associated with exclusive rights but not so long as to harm competition in broadcasting markets. This is not a cast iron rule: assessment must depend on the particular market.[73] Acquisition of exclusive rights to broadcast a popular football competition will be handled differently from acquisition of rights to broadcast a sport of interest only to a minority of viewers, such as weightlifting or bog-snorkelling. The markets are different: a long-term exclusive

---

[72] COMP 35.163, Notice published at [2001] OJ C169/5.
[73] See further Lefever (n 20) ch 9.

deal would be highly unlikely to escape the application of Article 101 in the former case but may plausibly do so in the latter. The fundamental issue is whether broadcasters can access other sources of material that will allow them to compete effectively. The less plausible this is, the more serious the foreclosure effect felt by both existing and potential competing broadcasters and the more harm is done to the competitive potential of the market.

11.5 Collective Selling of Rights to Broadcast Matches

Rights to broadcast sports events are commonly sold on a collective basis. So it is typical, though not at all inevitable, that a sports league will sell rights to broadcast matches en bloc (perhaps on an exclusive basis, perhaps not), rather than leaving individual clubs to sell rights to broadcast individual matches. This is collective selling. It plainly raises questions about the application of the Treaty competition rules. By preventing buyers from choosing between clubs and instead imposing only a single centralized point of sale, this appears to be a rather plain instance of the suppression of potential competition on the supply-side of the market for rights to broadcast events. The collective arrangements replace the market that would otherwise exist for the purchase of rights from the individual participants in the league, and, on an orthodox understanding, restriction of competition on the supply-side of the market must lead to the extraction of higher prices from buyers on the demand-side.

This seems straightforward, and in fact it is straightforward, yet a pause is appropriate. Sports governing bodies have periodically attempted to make the case that collective selling is not anti-competitive, but rather a necessary element in the organization of sporting competition. Their aim in advancing this argument is thematically familiar. It is to maximize their autonomy and, through that, their ability to extract maximum commercial value from their activities. As so often the Arnaut Report, met and criticized in Chapter 5.5, offers the most shameless example of this strategy:

> Both the Nice Declaration and the Terms of Reference for this Review explicitly recognise that collective selling [of television rights] and mutualisation of the resulting revenue is a fundamental aspect of sporting organisation and an essential component in the solidarity structure inherent to European sport … the concept of individual selling or individual ownership of television rights cannot be accepted from an intellectual point of view.[74]

The simplest rebuke to this claim is that (at least at the time of the publication of the Arnaut Report) in Spain and in some other countries too clubs do precisely what Arnaut alleges is intellectually unacceptable![75] One of the reasons why, until very recent statutory reforms, Real Madrid and Barcelona have outstripped other

---

[74] The Arnaut Report, paras 3.76, 3.77 <http://eose.org/wp-content/uploads/2014/03/independant_european_sports_review1.pdf> accessed 29 November 2016.
[75] As noted in *Champions League* (n 34) para 131, examined later.

clubs in Spain is precisely that clubs sell rights to televise League matches on an individual basis, with the result that the more popular clubs are able to command much higher fees from broadcasters.[76] So the claim made in the Arnaut Report is at best mischievous and at worst mendacious, but it is fully in line with its strategic concern to maximize sporting autonomy from the application of the law. It must be emphasized that the claim is nevertheless wholly without foundation. True, the phenomenon of 'interdependence' in sports leagues requires that *some* matters are agreed collectively between participants, often via the authority charged with over-all responsibility for running the competition, in order to create and administer the competition. Such rules escape the scope of EU law. Examples include fixing the numbers of players per team[77] and the scheduling of fixtures and the appointment of referees. A similar approach has been taken to rules forbidding multiple ownership of football clubs.[78] Such rules suppress the risk that the outcome may be thought to be fixed in advance. In a sports league the horizontal relationship prevailing between the clubs is not the same as that found in a normal market and the law must take account of that, or else risk mishandling the peculiar economic context in which the sports league operates. As a matter of legal classification the best way to understand this is provided by the Court's *Wouters* formula,[79] explained in Chapters 5 and 7: the overall context in which sports governance occurs, built around pursuit of a broad objective of fair and balanced competition, produces effects which though apparently restrictive of competition are nonetheless inherent in the pursuit of those objectives, and this is sustained by Article 165 TFEU's direction to take account of the specific nature of sport. But the logic of action taken collectively pursuant to this relationship of interdependence cannot explain away all restrictions on competition that participants might wish to agree among themselves. Sport is sometimes special, but not always. Some agreements would not reflect a need to coordinate to create a viable competition, but would rather amount to simple horizontal anti-competitive restraints. Clubs would certainly not escape Article 101 TFEU by recourse to the *Wouters* formula if they agreed the prices they would seek from sponsors or the cost of replica kits. The choice to pursue collective selling of broadcasting rights is of this type too. If rights are available only on a collective basis—so that a purchaser can buy only the output of the whole League—then a market for acquisition of rights belonging to individual clubs has been suppressed. Fixtures cannot be arranged unilaterally—this is the nature of sport—but once clubs agree to play against each other, the subsequent decision to sell rights to broadcast matches on a collective basis is restrictive of competition

---

[76] Statutory reform is achieved by Real Decreto-ley 5/2015 <http://boe.es/boe/dias/2015/05/01/pdfs/BOE-A-2015-4780.pdf> accessed 29 November 2016. In summary, P Callol, 'Spain: Legislation—Sports Broadcasting' [2015] ECLR N-128; on persisting legal disputes, see B Keane, 'The Application of EU Competition Law in the Sports and Entertainment Sectors 2014/2015' (2015) 6 Journal of European Comparative Law and Practice 735, 739.

[77] cf *Deliège* (n 19). See Ch 4.10.

[78] COMP 37.806 *ENIC/UEFA*, IP/02/942, 27 June 2002. See Ch 5.2.

[79] Case C-309/99 *JCJ Wouters, JW Savelbergh, Price Waterhouse Belastingadviseurs BV v Algemene Raad van de Nederlandse Orde van Advocaten* [2002] ECR I-1577.

within the meaning of Article 101(1), in so far as it has an effect on inter-state trade. Such arrangements need to find rescue, if at all, via the exemption foreseen by Article 101(3).

It took some time for the Commission to address this issue. But *Champions League* confirms both that collective selling of broadcasting rights falls within the scope of Article 101(1) TFEU as a restriction of competition and also that there is room to secure exemption of such arrangements pursuant to Article 101(3).[80]

In July 2001 the Commission sent a statement of objections to UEFA, European football's governing body, complaining that its arrangements for the sale of broadcasting rights to the 'Champions League', the principal European club football competition, infringed what was then Article 81 of the Treaty Establishing the European Community (EC), now Article 101 TFEU.[81] Questions of exclusivity— vertical restraints—were considered earlier; the concern here is collective selling— horizontal restraints between parties operating at the same level of the supply chain, which here refers to football clubs. UEFA sells rights to broadcast Champions League matches collectively on behalf of all participating clubs. It is a single package, which explains why there is a single brand identity: broadcasts are familiar to viewers all over Europe and beyond, because of the consistent use, irrespective of jurisdiction or venue, of the UEFA Champions League logo, anthem, and official sponsors and advertisers. The Commission was careful in its preliminary inquiry to observe that it did not object to collective selling of sports rights as such.[82] However, it stated that it considered that UEFA's scheme constituted a substantial restriction on competition, in part because of the foreclosure of the market to potential entrants into a sector capable of dynamic evolution.

UEFA duly responded by proposing an amended system involving, in short, an 'unbundling' of the package of rights available for purchase. More operators, including internet content providers as well as more traditional public and private broadcasters, would be able to acquire a degree of involvement in the coverage of the Champions League. This is an important point with obvious thematic connections to the general attitude of the Commission to the importance of ensuring that deals have the minimum effect of foreclosing the possibility of entry into developing markets. So much restriction is tolerated—only so much. The Commission expressed itself favourably disposed to this plan for competitive diversification which, it considered, would benefit football fans while also assisting the growth of new technology in the media sector.[83] This, it should be noted, did not set aside the core concept of collective selling—the adjustments related only to what was in fact being sold (collectively).

The Commission concluded its investigation by adopting a formal Decision in the *Champions League* case in July 2003.[84] The Decision explains in detail the structure of the arrangements for selling and provides close legal examination. It

---

[80] *Champions League* (n 34).   [81] IP/01/1043, 20 July 2001
[82] 'Background Note', Memo 01/271, 20 July 2001.
[83] IP/02/806, 3 June 2002 [2002] OJ C196/3.   [84] *Champions League* (n 34).

concludes that the collective selling arrangements restrict competition within the meaning of Article 101(1) TFEU, but it agrees that they fit the conditions for exemption which are set by Article 101(3). The high significance of this Decision, as a formal statement which has set the tone for subsequent deal-making in the field of sports broadcasting and its regulation in the light of competition law, justifies that close attention be paid to it.

UEFA had pressed on the Commission that the analysis should take account of the peculiar context of a sports league, wherein clubs are not truly independent competitors. The purpose was to persuade the Commission that the matter of collective selling is simply the way things are necessarily done in the particular context of a sports league and so not a restriction of competition at all within the meaning of Article 101(1) TFEU. Such an approach would, if accepted, preserve sporting autonomy and, in addition, enhance UEFA's commercial flexibility. It is the argument advanced by the Arnaut Report, as mentioned previously. But the argument failed to persuade, and, for the reasons provided earlier, deservedly so. The Commission devoted part of the Decision explicitly to rejecting this analysis, under the heading 'The Special Characteristics of Sport'.[85] The Commission agreed that 'some form of cooperation among the participants is necessary to organise a football league and that there is, in this context, certain interdependence among clubs'.[86] Moreover, the Decision 'fully endorses the specificity of sport, as expressed for example in the declaration of the European Council in Nice in December 2000'.[87] But that was where the acceptance of the special character of sport stopped. The Commission noted that interdependence between clubs did not preclude them competing in the areas of sponsorship, stadium advertising, and merchandising, as well as for players, and it held that it did not preclude the possibility of them competing in the market for selling rights to broadcast matches either. Such arrangements were not necessary to stage a football league: collective selling is not 'an indispensable prerequisite for the redistribution of revenue'.[88]

Accordingly the Commission did not at all deny that the relationship between clubs in a sports league is special, but it found it not special enough to warrant a finding that there was in the circumstances no restriction of competition of the type that falls within the Article 101(1) TFEU net. Rather, this was a commercial choice reached by UEFA and the clubs, with significant implications for the competitive process. The Commission did not refer to *Wouters*.[89] And this was several years before *Meca-Medina* had given the Court the chance to analyse more closely and definitively the proper model of application of EU competition law to sport.[90] But the Commission could have convincingly framed its examination with reference to *Wouters*. The overall context in which a sports league is organized may require a degree of collaboration between participants in agreeing rules, and such indispensable arrangements should not be treated as restrictions on competition within the meaning of Article 101(1). But this logic cannot be stretched to cover collective

---

[85] ibid paras 125–31.   [86] ibid para 129.   [87] ibid para 131.
[88] ibid para 131.   [89] *Wouters* (n 79).   [90] *Meca-Medina* (n 3). See Ch 5.

selling of rights to broadcast matches. So any potential benefits of the scheme, including those alleged to be specific to sport, such as the possible need to protect weaker clubs through a cross-subsidization of funds from the richer to the poorer clubs, could not defuse the application of Article 101(1) and were pushed instead to the stage of the analysis encompassed by exemption pursuant to Article 101(3).

At the stage of exemption UEFA was successful. The Commission agreed that collective selling, though a restriction within the meaning of Article 101(1) TFEU, could be exempted pursuant to Article 101(3), and that the deal under scrutiny was worthy of exemption.

The system created a single point of sale for defined 'packages' of matches, which the Commission considered generated efficiencies that were of a particularly significant magnitude as a result of the elimination of the need for broadcasters to deal with many different clubs subject to different ownership structures in different jurisdictions across Europe. Transaction costs were kept relatively low. In fact, the identification of advantages of this nature was a key factor in the Commission's earlier favourable treatment of Eurovision, which involved collective selling of rights.[91] Moreover, collective selling of the 'Champions League' permitted UEFA a tight grip on the pattern of the competition's organization and allowed the commercially advantageous 'branding' of the competition as an unfragmented single product. The Decision notes the 'dressing-up' of the stadium facilities, the recording of the match and the on-screen presentation, on-screen signage, and the music as common elements which increased the attraction of the Champions League brand.[92] So, in one of the many comments contained in the Decision which will chill the soul of the football traditionalist but which captures the commercial aims at stake, the Commission accepted that 'definitions of UEFA Champions League branded products will optimise the global interaction between UEFA Champions League branded and club branded Products'.[93] Media operators would share in the advantages. The efficiencies realized would permit them to invest more in improving the quality of production and transmission technologies.

There was, in short, a sufficient level of economic benefit created by the deal that it deserved a green light notwithstanding the restrictions on competition that had dragged it within the scope of Article 101 TFEU in the first place.

This, the Commission added, would be likely to lead to a more intensive and innovative exploitation of the rights to the benefit of the ultimate consumer, the viewer. It is noticeable that the emphasis on the gains made by providers, rather than consumers, is stronger. The treatment of the ultimate consumer is relatively brief, and makes the type of hasty assumptions about the inevitable transmissions of benefits to the consumer in consequence on an improved product that is admittedly typical of the Commission's decisional practice under Article 101(3) TFEU generally, but open to criticism for its complacency and infidelity to the textual

---

[91] See n 56. The CFI annulled the Commission's Decisions in *Eurovision* (Case T-185/00, see n 57), but it did not take issue with the identification of these economic benefits flowing from the arrangements.
[92] *Champions League* (n 34) paras 154–57.   [93] ibid para 163.

demands of Article 101(3).[94] In this particular case, however, the Commission's assumption of an adequate consumer benefit from collective selling of rights seems to be justified.

To complete the conclusion that the elements necessary for exemption pursuant to Article 101(3) TFEU were present, the Commission found that the restrictions on competition were indispensable to provide these economic gains and that, moreover, competition would not be eliminated in respect of a substantial part of the media rights in question.

Champions League serves as an illuminating case study into how the detailed application of Article 101 TFEU promotes the broader regulatory concerns of the Commission in its handling of the dynamically evolving broadcasting sector. Collective selling has clear economic advantages, but it has costs too, specifically in the elimination of competition on the supply-side. At stake is a balance. The length of the contract is carefully scrutinized: the shape of exclusive rights is carefully examined. The importance of keeping open opportunities for new players to enter the market to acquire rights forms part of the assessment, especially where, as in markets of this type, technological progress holds out the possibility of significant and rapid innovation that is capable of yielding benefits to the consumer.[95] This is not even fifteen years ago: but the impact of the third generation of mobile telephony was yet to take clear shape. In this sense, the combined effects of deregulation, technological innovation, and commodification need to be managed in order to ensure that their overall impact remains beneficial, and juridification, in particular through the scrupulous application of the EU's competition rules, is the essential supplementary theme that is designed to secure that enduringly felicitous outcome.

11.6 *Champions League*—Application to Collective Selling at National Level

It was mentioned earlier, in section 11.4, in connection with the analysis of exclusive selling, that the Commission followed up its decision in *Champions League* with investigation of the sale of rights to matches in the German Bundesliga and the English Premier League, to which it applied a similar approach to that adopted in *Champions League*. Collective selling of rights is the norm in both the Bundesliga and the FAPL, and on this point too *Champions League* paved the way for the Commission's treatment of the German and English practices.

---

[94] With particular reference to the audiovisual sector, see eg B Van Rompuy, *Economic Efficiency: The Sole Concern of Modern Antitrust Policy?* (Wolters Kluwer 2012) ch 6; and more generally E Buttigieg, *Competition Law: Safeguarding the Consumer Interest. A Comparative Analysis of US Antitrust Law and EC Competition Law* (Kluwer Law International 2009). See also R Parrish and S Miettinen, 'Sports Broadcasting and Community Law' in I Blackshaw, S Cornelius, and R Siekmann (eds), *TV Rights and Sport: Legal Aspects* (TMC Asser 2009).

[95] On this aspect of the impact of *Champions League* as seen at the time, see N Petit, 'The Commission's Contribution to the Emergence of 3G Mobile Communications: an Analysis of Some Decisions in the Field of Competition Law' [2004] ECLR 429, 436–37.

In fact, even in advance of the Commission's Decision in 2003 on UEFA's arrangements for collective selling of rights to broadcast the Champions League, there had been some inquiry into selling by national leagues pursuant to national competition laws. In Germany, collective selling in the Bundesliga was condemned by the competition authorities but subsequently granted statutory approval.[96] The matter was also examined at some length by the UK's Restrictive Practices Court in its 1999 ruling which found in favour of the legality of collective selling arrangements practised within the English (football) Premier League.[97] This, however, was decided under the antiquated and subsequently repealed Restrictive Trade Practices Act 1976, now replaced by the Competition Act 1998 which is closely aligned with the EU model. In the wake of *Champions League*, collective selling at national level came to be reconsidered in the light of EU law.

In the case of the German Bundesliga the Commission's inquiry resulted in commitments to loosen the prevailing form of collective selling. These were made legally binding in the form of a Commission decision.[98] The Commission took the same approach to the finding of a restriction on competition as it had in *Champions League*. The central marketing and sale of media rights to matches in the Bundesliga restricted competition in the sense that it meant that the clubs had surrendered their right to sell rights on an individual basis. In consequence an adverse effect was exerted on downstream markets in television and in new media and the Commission expressly noted the importance in this regard of supplying football content.[99] The geographical market was defined by applicable national law, the language and cultural characteristics, and was confined to Germany and potentially also German-speaking areas.[100]

The key commitments made by the Bundesliga which persuaded the Commission to show a green light focused on the offer of nine distinct packages of rights to be offered on a transparent and non-discriminatory basis and subject to a duration that would not exceed three years.[101] The aim was to sustain competition in the broadcasting market and the Commission was satisfied that the arrangements would 'contribute to innovation and dampen the concentration tendencies in the media markets'.[102] The animating policy concerns are vividly captured by Neelie Kroes, the Commissioner responsible at the time for Competition, who noted that:

This decision benefits both football fans and the game. Fans benefit from new products and greater choice. Leagues and clubs benefit from the increased coverage of their games. Readily available premium content such as top football boosts innovation and growth in the media

---

[96] Gesetz gegen Wettbewerbsbeschraenkungen, s 31 as amended with effect from 1 January 1999.

[97] *Re the supply of services facilitating the broadcasting on television of Premier League football matches* [1999] UKCLR 258.

[98] COMP/C.2/37.214, Dec 2005/396 *Joint selling of the media rights to the German Bundesliga* [2005] OJ L134/46.

[99] ibid para 23.   [100] ibid para 19.

[101] Subsequently the power of a single buyer to acquire all rights has been removed: <http://uk.reuters.com/article/uk-soccer-germany-broadcasting-idUKKCN0X80UJ> accessed 29 November 2016.

[102] *Bundesliga* (n 98) para 41.

and information technology sectors. Moreover, open markets and access to content are an essential safeguard against media concentration.[103]

The Commission did not make explicit whether it treated the matter as beyond the scope of Article 101(1) TFEU or instead within the criteria of exemption set out in Article 101(3), but in practice the Decision adds to the store of understanding of what is permitted in the process of selling rights in markets for sports broadcasting.

Collective selling of rights to broadcast matches in the English Premier League (FAPL) has similarly been handled in the light of *Champions League*. It was explained earlier that money has cascaded into English football as a result of its appeal to broadcasters and ultimately to viewers. The rights for the period 2016 to 2019 cost just over £5 billion; £3 billion was the price charged for 2013 to 2016; £1.8 billion for 2010 to 2013; £1.7 billion for 2007 to 2010; and so on. The attentive reader will now have grasped why the deals span a three-year period: it is the influence of EU competition law and, in particular, the anxiety to prevent undue foreclosure of access to premium content in broadcasting markets. Moreover, the identity of the buyers of rights is in part influenced by the requirement to navigate the channel set by EU competition law. The package sold by the FAPL embraces rights for live radio broadcast, rights for use on other audiovisual media, and rights to show matches on a deferred basis (this is the source of the BBC's long-standing Saturday evening programme *Match of the Day*) but the jewel in the crown is undoubtedly the right to televise matches live. Under the 2004–07 deal (and earlier ones) the purchasing broadcaster of rights to show live matches was BSkyB, a subscription-only channel which became SKY in 2014. Its determination to acquire exclusive rights to show live matches in the FAPL was readily explained by its need to secure content that would attract a large body of paying viewers. The Commission, anxious about the damaging effect on actual and potential competition in broadcasting markets, opened an investigation in 2001. An extended period of protracted and occasionally acrimonious negotiation[104] ensued and a number of commitments were made by the Premier League with a view to securing a green light, which was eventually forthcoming in 2006.[105] The Commission aligned its analysis explicitly with its Decisions in *Champions League* and *Bundesliga*. So it once again found that the rights to broadcasting premium football events played regularly through the season constitutes a distinct relevant product market. The geographical market was the UK market alone: the Commission noted once again that markets for media rights are usually defined on the basis of national or linguistic criteria. The Commission focused on the grant to the FAPL of sole and exclusive rights to sell as the main problem. This replaces a competitive market populated by many (twenty) suppliers with instead a single

---

[103] IP/05/62, 19 January 2005.

[104] eg 'Sky and Brussels At War over Premiership Rights' *The Observer* (London, 11 September 2005) Business section, 1.

[105] COMP 38.173 *Joint selling of the media rights to the FA Premier League*, 22 March 2006: summary of Commission Decision at [2008] OJ C7/18.

organization: 'markets that would be demand-led thus become supply-driven'.[106] The tendency to sell large packages of rights on an exclusive basis creates damage in downstream markets by raising barriers to entry, especially if there is only a single buyer. It is clear that once again the underlying primary concern is not sport but broadcasting: the link is the huge value of sports rights to broadcasters seeking to acquire a presence in such markets. The changes made according to the adapted commitments of the FAPL, explained previously, included increased output (the availability of an increased number of matches and the availability of a wider range of rights, including those pertaining not only to television but also to mobile phones and the internet), the sale of six packages of rights to show matches on live television that would not be purchasable by a single buyer (though buying five out of six was possible),[107] the splitting of the sale of UK and Irish rights, sale on a transparent and non-discriminatory tendering basis, and agreement that the duration of agreements would not exceed three years.

The anxiety to prevent a monopoly, albeit one limited in time, that will tend to make the market rigid is evident. In fact, BskyB, which became SKY in 2014, retained its grip on the lion's share of matches. In the first sale of rights following the Commission intervention it bought four of the six packages while two were acquired by an Irish-based broadcaster, Setanta. Setanta, however, appears to have over-estimated its ability to exploit the rights it had bought: in 2009 its British arm was placed into administration and it no longer exists. Today there are two principal broadcasters of live matches played in the FAPL, SKY and BT, and the number of matches shown live has also increased.[108] Under the three-year deal that commenced in 2016, live FAPL games are regularly shown on Friday evening, Saturday lunchtime, and Saturday early evening, at several points on a Sunday, including the prized 4 pm slot which SKY has retained throughout the process, and on Monday evening. It is only at 3 pm on a Saturday afternoon that live FAPL matches are not screened in the United Kingdom, as a result of the UEFA rule that a window may be kept in place where televised football is blocked in order to encourage fans to attend matches in person.[109] Obviously, however, the increase in output of matches to be shown live at other times, which has characterized each new three-year deal, has the consequence that only a minority of FAPL games kick off at 3 pm on a Saturday in any event. It is, moreover, not difficult for any fan to find a way to watch a match live on the internet or in a pub even at 3 pm on a Saturday, given the technological difficulties involved in blocking feeds of a live match shown on a channel under the FAPL's deal to sell rights to markets outside the United Kingdom.

---

[106] ibid para 25.   [107] cf n 101 on requiring more than one buyer of *Bundesliga* rights.

[108] This increase was one reason for OFCOM's decision pursuant to the UK's Competition Act 1998 not to proceed with a complaint by Virgin Media about output restrictions: CW/01138/09/14 *Virgin Media* <https://www.ofcom.org.uk/about-ofcom/latest/bulletins/competition-bulletins/all-closed-cases/cw_01138> accessed 29 November 2016.

[109] Comm Dec 2001/478 *UEFA's Broadcasting Regulations* [2001] OJ L171/12. See Ch 6.4.

How far, if at all, the system truly improves the consumer's lot has been questioned. The Commission's early interventions had minimal impact on SKY's dominance in pay-TV sports markets.[110] It has been argued that the Commission's practice makes little inquiry into how changes in the patterns of supply have in fact affected the viewer.[111] The committed sports fan now has to buy two subscription packages, from both SKY and BT, not just one. The sale of rights in 2015 suggests that the turgidly slow increase in actual or potential competition on the demand-side is driving up prices extracted by the seller of collective rights, able to exploit the supply-side market power granted by the restriction on competition that is the consequence of collective action. This immediately led to price increases for the ultimate consumer too.[112] Perhaps, then, the limited success in fostering competition in the broadcasting sector, combined with willingness to endorse collective selling, comes at the expense of the consumer of live televised football.

In summary, the collective selling of rights to broadcast sports events on terms that include conferral of exclusivity on the buyer is capable of being structured in a way that complies with the demands of EU competition law. The EU does not set rules on how rights shall be sold. Instead it simply determines whether arrangements crafted by governing bodies and broadcasters are compatible with EU law and prohibits those that are not. In practice, however, the developing practice of the Commission serves to channel the available options and, as has also been observed in relation to matters such as the transfer system (Chapter 9) and Financial Fair Play (Chapter 10.9), the Commission is an influential actor.[113] Deals in practice typically follow common patterns which are shaped by the Commission's view of what must accompany collective selling of exclusive rights in order to evade condemnation as anti-competitive. Exclusivity must be time-limited, with three years emerging as the industry standard provoked by the Commission; tendering processes must be open, transparent, and non-discriminatory; there must be multiple and divisible packages of rights, as a means to maximize the number of buyers able to enjoy the benefit of premium sports content across the enormous and (helpfully) increasing range of feasible media. This approach, pioneered in *Champions League*, has set the tone and the pattern of sale of broadcasting rights within the EU. Collective selling on this model is the norm, both by UEFA in selling rights to the Champions League and, with effect from 2014, in selling rights not only to the Finals but also the qualifying stages for its EURO competition for national

---

[110] For criticism of the Commission's assumptions, see D Harbord and S Szymanski, 'Football Trials' [2004] ECLR 117; D Geey and M James, 'The Premier League-European Commission Broadcasting Negotiations' (2006) 4 ESLJ, available via <http://www.entsportslawjournal.com/16/volume/4/issue/1/> accessed 29 November 2016.

[111] eg K Lefever and B Van Rompuy, 'Ensuring Access to Sports Content: 10 Years of EU Intervention. Time to Celebrate?' (2009) 2 Journal of Media Law 243, 255–59.

[112] See n 7.

[113] That the Commission works with governing bodies to become a 'co-producer' of norms is an important theme sustained in A Duval, 'La Lex Sportiva Face au Droit de l'Union Européenne: Guerre et Paix dans l'Espace Juridique Transnational' PhD thesis defended at the EUI Florence (September 2015), available via <http://cadmus.eui.eu/handle/1814/36997> accessed 29 November 2016.

representative teams, and for national Leagues. There is no attempt here to offer an exhaustive survey of practice.[114]

11.7 Collective Selling—an Unresolved Question about the Place of 'Solidarity'

Champions League provides an important but not exhaustive treatment of the legal issues at stake in the collective sale of rights to broadcast sports events. In fact the Commission was able to avoid the issue which would have shed most light on the extent to which collective selling of rights to broadcast sporting events might be different from collective selling more generally. This concerns the place of solidarity within the sport.

In pursuit of exemption, UEFA advanced an argument founded on solidarity.[115] It argued that even though the collective basis on which rights were sold restricted supply-side competition and thereby raised prices paid by buyers above the (aggregate) price that would have been paid for rights sold on an individual basis by clubs, this was justified because the revenue so raised could be used to share income in pursuit of goals of solidarity. There are two distinct forms of solidarity that could feasibly be engaged. 'Horizontal solidarity' would refer to redistribution of income, in order to promote a degree of competitive equality designed to promote the appeal of the contest. 'Vertical solidarity' would concern the transmission of funding from elite level sport to the 'grassroots', in order to promote the general good of the sport.

These are sports-specific concerns: sausage-makers, car-makers, and suppliers of financial services do not support each other financially, nor do they subsidize amateur sausage-makers, amateur car-makers, or amateur suppliers of financial services. The question is whether sport is special enough for the interest in solidarity to play a legitimate role in the interpretation and application of EU competition law.

In *Champions League* the Commission was able to dodge the question. In response to UEFA's reliance on its interest in promoting solidarity, the Commission accepted the desirability of promoting a balance between clubs playing in a League. It also accepted the value in encouraging the supply of young players. These objectives may be realized by cross-subsidy from rich clubs to poor. This, of course, loudly echoes and is in line with *Bosman*.[116] The Commission expressed itself in favour of the 'financial solidarity' principle, and referred to its endorsement in the Nice Declaration on Sport. The legal question, however, was whether the quest for

---

[114] The European Competition Law Review frequently carries short notes addressing national practice: eg 'Romania' [2015] ECLR N-69. So does the International Sports Law Journal, eg 'Netherlands' (2004) 4(1–2) Intl Sports LJ 63. See also Lefever (n 20) ch 9; Van Rompuy (n 94) chs 5 and 6, especially at 343–59; S Moya Izquierdo and M Troncoso Ferrer, 'Football Broadcasting Business in the EU: Towards Fairer Competition?' (2014) 5 Journal of European Competition Law and Practice 353. There are 29 country reports in I Blackshaw, S Cornelius, and R Siekmann (eds), *TV Rights and Sport: Legal Aspects* (TMC Asser 2009).

[115] *Champions League* (n 34) paras 164–67.   [116] *Bosman* (n 2). See ch 4.

improved solidarity in the sport could override the damage done to the market by the restrictions on supply-side competition which lie at the heart of a system of collective selling. In *Champions League* the Commission did not need to answer this question, because it had already decided that the anti-competitive implications of the arrangements that brought them within the scope of Article 101(1) TFEU were outweighed by the economic benefits of the deal, such as the single identifiable brand and the reduction in transaction costs consequent on the single source of sale, which justified exemption pursuant to Article 101(3). That meant the Commission was able to deal with the matter without looking beyond the orthodox scope of Article 101. It did not need to 'stretch' the analysis to consider also the impact on solidarity in the sport. And, not needing to do so, it did not do so, and it chose not to offer any view on the merits of UEFA's reliance on solidarity as a reason to exempt an anti-competitive deal. Nor was the matter treated any more fully in the German or English decisions.

The question would require an answer if a collective selling arrangement were devised which did not generate economic benefits of a type that justified exemption pursuant to Article 101(3) TFEU. If the interest in promoting solidarity were regarded as enough for such commercial practices to be given a green light, then this would amount to a striking recognition that sport is truly special.

This is intriguing. As long ago as the Helsinki Report on Sport, published in 1999,[117] the Commission, emphasizing a 'European Sports Model' characterized by the notion of solidarity (among other features), mentioned tentatively the worth of an inquiry into 'the extent to which a link can be established between the joint sale of rights and financial solidarity between professional and amateur sport, the objectives of the training of young sportsmen and women and those of promoting sporting activities among the population'. In 2001 Mr Monti, the Commissioner responsible for Competition, cautiously suggested that 'financial solidarity between clubs or between professional and amateur sport' could be a relevant factor in assessing whether to grant an exemption to collective selling.[118]

In the same vein, the Nice Declaration, to which the Commission made reference in *Champions League*, includes the following:

15. The sale of television broadcasting rights is one of the greatest sources of income today for certain sports. The European Council thinks that moves to encourage the mutualisation of part of the revenue from such sales, at the appropriate levels, are beneficial to the principle of solidarity between all levels and areas of sport.[119]

The Commission's 2007 White Paper maintained a tone of cautious receptivity to the virtue of solidarity as an organizational principle in sport allied to unwillingness

---

[117] COM (1999) 644 and 644/2. See Ch 6.4.

[118] Speech delivered in Brussels at a conference on 'Governance in Sport', 26 February 2001, available as Speech/01/84 via <http://europa.eu/rapid/press-release_SPEECH-01-84_en.htm> accessed 29 November 2016.

[119] See Ch 6.3: the full text of the Nice Declaration on Sport is at <http://eur-lex.europa.eu/legal-content/EN/TXT/?uri=URISERV:l35007> accessed 29 November 2016.

to be legally precise.[120] It noted that in sport 'media rights are sometimes sold collectively by a sport association on behalf of individual clubs (as opposed to clubs marketing the rights individually)', adding that although this raises competition concerns, 'the Commission has accepted it under certain conditions'. It then stated:

Collective selling can be important for the redistribution of income and can thus be a tool for achieving greater solidarity within sports. The Commission recognises the importance of an equitable redistribution of income between clubs, including the smallest ones, and between professional and amateur sport.[121]

In its 2011 Communication the Commission described the collective selling of media rights as 'a good example of financial solidarity and redistribution mechanisms within sports'. It recommended that sport associations 'establish mechanisms for the collective selling of media rights to ensure adequate redistribution of revenues' but added too that this shall be 'in full compliance with EU competition law'.[122]

But what exactly *is* required to achieve 'full compliance with EU competition law'?

One could imagine in law that, drawing (as is thematically usual) on the *Wouters* formula,[123] it would be argued by governing bodies that it is necessary to achieve the objectives of intensified solidarity in sport by creating a system of restricted competition that, given its true context, is not in fact within the scope of Article 101 TFEU at all. The window through which special sensitivity to sport enters the analysis might be dressed by assertion of the horizontal influence in competition law of Article 165 TFEU's direction that sport has a 'specific nature' that must be taken into account; and that Article 165(2) TFEU's direction that Union action shall aim at 'promoting fairness and openness in sporting competitions' should count in favour of treating redistributive arrangements put in place as a basis for finding in favour of the legality of restrictions on competition.

The argument is not without merit, and structurally it is in line with *Wouters*. It must be cautioned that any chance of success would be conditional on demonstration that solidarity is in fact the aim of the selling arrangements and that schemes are in place effectively to deliver it. That is, the claim would certainly fail if it were revealed that this was in truth simply a means to maximize income—and so it would certainly fail if advanced by a breakaway 'closed' League of the type considered in Chapter 10.11. But even assuming the vitality of arguments about solidarity, a major problem is that what this in fact entails is that third parties, broadcasters, shall be required to pay for sport's internal interest in promoting solidarity. The restriction on competition caused by the collective agreement between clubs causes a diminution in choice and an increase in price. The system may indeed allow

---

[120] White Paper on Sport, COM (2007) 391, 11 July 2007, available via <http://ec.europa.eu/sport/index_en.htm> accessed 29 November 2016. See Ch 6.5.

[121] White Paper on Sport (n 120) 17.

[122] Commission Communication, 'Developing the European Dimension in Sport' COM (2011) 12 (January 2011) 8 <http://ec.europa.eu/sport/news/doc/communication/communication_en.pdf> accessed 29 November 2016. See Ch 6.11.

[123] *Wouters* (n 79). See Ch 5.

clubs to raise more revenue than would otherwise be possible and to distribute that income horizontally, among competing clubs, and vertically, to the grass roots, but the fundamental question is just why sport should be permitted to improve its position at the expense of third parties, a category here covering both existing broadcasters and potential broadcasters kept out of the market by the restrictions imposed on supply and ultimately viewers required to pay more to watch matches. Solidarity could be promoted without collective selling: it would be permissible and, if solidarity is truly a sporting concern, rational for participant clubs to work together to distribute proceeds from individually sold matches in a manner which reflects the collective need to sustain healthy competition and to nurture the grass roots. True, the sums raised would not be so high as under a collective scheme, but the prices paid by broadcasters would be dictated by competition in the market that is not restricted on the supply-side. That would be to argue that the sports-specific anxiety to sustain solidarity would and should come into play only after third party broadcasters have enjoyed the right to participate in a 'normal' competitive market for the sale of rights. Sport should find other means to promote solidarity which do not impose costs on third party broadcasters and ultimately on consumers, such as internally arranged sharing of income. It would only be if it can be shown that this is simply not feasible—perhaps because a sufficient majority among clubs cannot be assembled under the league's constitution—that collective selling that lacks features necessary for Article 101(3) TFEU exemption could plausibly be treated as lawful under EU law. In conclusion, the point was left deliberately open in *Champions League* and it remains open today, but the prejudicial effect of such arrangements on third parties is probably enough to rule out even this window of opportunity to save collective selling that, unlike *Champions League*, cannot satisfy the criteria for exemption set out in Article 101(3) TFEU.

11.8 Territorial Exclusivity

It was explained in the previous section that broadcasting markets are typically defined as national in consequence of patterns of regulatory control, language, and culture. Selling patterns therefore commonly coincide with national frontiers. The Block Exemption Regulation on Vertical Restraints, Regulation 330/2010,[124] does not rule out sales into particular territories nor does it exclude action to protect the rights held for a particular territory from cross-border competition, but it excludes, as EU law generally excludes, an attempt to achieve absolute territorial protection. The thematic tension is between the promise of the EU's border-free internal market and the commercial value of treating markets as severable along national lines.

EU law's brutal intolerance of absolute territorial protection was confirmed in a sports-specific context in the case commonly known as *Karen Murphy*—though in full it is *Football Association Premier League Ltd, NetMed Hellas SA, Multichoice*

---

[124] Block Exemption Regulation (n 40).

Hellas SA v QC Leisure, David Richardson, AV Station plc, Malcolm Chamberlain, Michael Madden, SR Leisure Ltd, Philip George Charles Houghton, Derek Owen; and Karen Murphy v Media Protection Services Ltd.[125] This ruling counts as a vivid demonstration of the compelling combined power of sport, money, and television.

11.8.1 The dispute

The background was straightforward in its basic outline and driven by obvious commercial incentives. The cases arose as a result of disputes concerning the marketing and use in the United Kingdom of decoding devices which gave access to satellite broadcasting services provided elsewhere. Football was the trigger—specifically, the lure of watching live broadcasts of matches played in the Football Association Premier League Ltd (FAPL), more commonly known simply as English Premier League. The League granted contractual licences to broadcast and exploit its matches. This was typically organized on a territorial basis, tied to a particular country, and it was typically a grant of exclusive rights for that territory—so, one broadcaster per territory, which in practice follows the national pattern according to which most broadcasters operate. Moreover, sale is on an exclusive basis, because such a model, which confers on the buyer a powerful position to attract consumers in the contract territory, maximizes income. The grant was time-limited—for three years at the material time, in line with the practice explained earlier.

In order to protect this territorial exclusivity, all broadcasters agreed as part of the licensing deal concluded with the FAPL to prevent viewers from receiving broadcasts outside the designated area. This was achieved by secure encryption of broadcasts capable of being received outside that territory (most notably at the material time by satellite) combined with a commitment by broadcasters to ensure that no decoding device apt to break the encryption be supplied to permit anyone to view their transmissions from outside the territory concerned. So supply of the decoding devices necessary to watch the matches was limited to persons resident in the Member State of broadcast. Viewers were provided with a decoding device. Restrictions included in the contracts forbade the circulation of authorized decoder cards outside the territory of each licensee.

This model of territorial exclusivity created a market in circumvention. The cost of watching English games in a market in continental Europe was typically much lower in price than that charged in the United Kingdom. This follows, because although the English Premier League is a hugely attractive product, in Europe it is England which is home to the most eager viewers. Anyone able to acquire a decoding device in a territory where the prices are relatively low—lower than in the United Kingdom—is able to use it to watch matches in a territory where prices are relatively high—most pertinently in the United Kingdom itself. So enterprising individuals simply brought decoding devices from markets in continental Europe, where they had been bought lawfully, to the United Kingdom and enabled the

---

[125] Joined Cases C-403/08 and C-429/08 [2011] ECR I-9083 (Grand Chamber).

watching of matches at a much lower cost than if they had bought directly from the licensee for the United Kingdom. This is what the Premier League and its authorized broadcaster for the United Kingdom, at the time BSkyB, which became SKY in 2014, was trying to stop in the several disputes that provoked litigation and reached Luxembourg as preliminary references. The devices at stake in the litigation had been acquired lawfully in Greece, where NetMed Helas was the owner of licensed rights, and brought to and used in the United Kingdom in breach of the terms of supply between NetMed Hellas and consumers. Naturally the size of the market and the relative level of demand meant that the prices charged by the Premier League to broadcasters and hence by broadcasters to viewers were far higher in England than in Greece. Dealers responded to demand and supplied the decoders. The most eager acquirers were restaurants and bars. But the individual consumer could benefit from this market in decoders by sitting at home to watch matches too.

Cases of both a civil and criminal nature were brought before the English courts against suppliers of equipment and satellite decoder cards that enable the reception of broadcasts, and also against licensees or operators of public houses that had screened live Premier League matches by using a foreign decoding device. Karen Murphy, the manager of a streetcorner pub called the Red, White and Blue in Southsea, fifteen minutes' walk from Portsmouth FC's cramped but much loved Fratton Park home, who had relied on a foreign decoder to pay only about a tenth of what she would have been require to pay to BSkyB directly, was faced by a criminal prosecution. She quickly became the media darling of the process, though she was not the only party involved in the sequence of litigation.

The matter was pursued before the English courts and a preliminary reference was made by the High Court in two separate cases, in which importation from Greece was the principal background issue. The cases were duly joined. Did such action, taken in protection of the commercial model of territorial segregation within the EU, comply with EU law? There was a free movement dimension and a competition law dimension: a commercial dimension and a sport-specific dimension.

This, then, led to the Grand Chamber ruling in the case in October 2011.

11.8.2 Free movement law—a restriction on inter-state trade

The obstacle to free movement was obvious and unashamed. It was the core of the FAPL's commercial model. As the Court summed it up, the 'strategy is to bring the competition to viewers throughout the world while maximising the value of the rights to its members, the clubs'.[126] To this end the whole system was designed to keep national markets separate: the trade in decoding devices brought competition of exactly the type that undermined the FAPL's business model. Unchecked, it would eventually result in an inability to charge a price any higher than that capable

---

[126] *Karen Murphy* (n 125) para 32. The commercial model is summarized at paras 32–35 of the judgment.

of being absorbed by the cheapest market in the whole EU, with the result that the model would need to shift towards a model of territorial exclusivity—for the entire EU. To which the adherent of consumer choice and competition in the EU might respond—a very good thing too. To which a more sceptical observer might respond—if low-price markets are permitted to undermine the value of high-price markets then it is probable that the Premier League will simply withdraw from low-price markets (such as Greece), which will help neither market integration nor consumer choice. So a rather exciting choice about the best way to promote an internal market lurks beneath the surface of the dispute. The core legal question was whether any justification could be found for the attempt to suppress the cross-market in decoding devices.

The core of the legal case made by the Premier League was copyright infringement.[127] In particular, the relevant statutory provisions, sections of the UK Copyright, Designs and Patents Act 1988, allowed for criminal prosecutions in connection with the provision of broadcasting services in this manner in addition to civil claims. Here lies the interest as a matter of EU law. It was argued that EU free movement law defeated any attempt to suppress the practices of which the League complained. Specifically the High Court asked whether Articles 28 or 49 EC, which are now Articles 34 and 56 TFEU, preclude enforcement of a provision of national law which makes it unlawful to import or sell a satellite decoder card which has been issued by the provider of a satellite broadcasting service in another Member State on the condition that the satellite decoder card is only authorized for use in that other Member State. So this pitted free movement law against contractual autonomy and the business model of the Premier League and BSkyB. In similar vein and intent, the preliminary reference asked how to examine the network of exclusive licences involving territorial restriction in the light of Article 81(1) EC, now Article 101 TFEU. So both state measures and contractual networks struck by private parties fell under scrutiny. Moreover, wrapped up in the inquiry were questions about the extent to which relevant EU secondary legislation, the Conditional Access Directive 98/84 and, of most relevance, the Copyright Directive 2001/29,[128] governed action taken to suppress the use of a device in the manner that had occurred beyond the authorization of the service provider.

The Court's examination of the matters of secondary legislation, and in particular those concerning the protection of intellectual property, are intricate in their detail. However, the essence of the Court's initial finding was that the Conditional Access Directive was not relevant, for the matter of national legislation which prevents the use of foreign decoding devices escaped its material scope. This then brought the Court to consider the Treaty rules on free movement of goods and services, and it is this which provides the central part of the judgment.

---

[127] In detail, ibid paras 46ff.
[128] Directive 98/84/EC of 20 November 1998 on the legal protection of services based on, or consisting of, conditional access [1998] OJ L320/54; Directive 2001/29/EC of 22 May 2001 on the harmonisation of certain aspects of copyright and related rights in the information society [2001] OJ L167/10.

The Court first decided that the legislation fell to be examined in the light of Article 56 TFEU: it concerned at heart services (the broadcasts) rather than goods (the devices).[129] However, this is a point of legal detail with no wider implications of principle. In most, though not all, important respects the provisions on free movement are interpreted in a convergent manner—as they should be, unless strong arguments for their segmentation can be constructed, since all are based on the same idea of the internal market as a legal concept.[130] There was, the Court readily proceeded to find, a restriction on the freedom to provide services within the meaning of Article 56 TFEU. It was, in fact, a case of national legislation backing up territorial restrictions located in private contracts.[131] So the main issue was whether the legislation could be objectively justified.

11.8.3 Free movement—justifying the restrictions

Two main bases were advanced in order to justify the legislation: that there was justification provided by the public interest in the protection of intellectual property rights and that there was justification rooted in the objective of encouraging the public to attend football stadiums. Neither claim was fully successful, but neither was rejected out of hand. Sport is special but, in an echo of *Bosman*, it was not reckoned to be special enough to justify the challenged model.

The Court concluded that the prohibition on using foreign decoding devices is capable of being justified by the public interest in the protection of intellectual property rights.[132] But in the particular circumstances it was not justified. In this sense the ruling prioritized the interest in free movement and consumer choice in the internal market ahead of the interest of the right holder in maximizing income from sales within the internal market. But the Court's reasoning was nuanced and left space for some degree of protection—just not to the full extent attempted at the time of the dispute by the Premier League and BSkyB. And it did not at all neglect the character of sport, as promoted by Article 165 TFEU. The Court, helped by a thoughtful and lengthy Opinion provided by Advocate General Kokott, with which it mostly agreed, deserves credit for an assiduous attempt to do justice to the complexities of the matter under examination.

Sporting events cannot be regarded as intellectual creations: football matches are subject to rules of the game, leaving no room for creative freedom, and so such events cannot be protected under copyright.[133] However, the Court proceeded to find that 'sporting events, as such, have a unique and, to that extent, original character which can transform them into subject-matter that is worthy of protection'.[134] This is an observation that has something in common with the Court's supple readiness in *Bosman* and *Meca-Medina* to find something distinctive and special about

---

[129] ibid paras 77–84.   [130] Weatherill (n 33).
[131] *Karen Murphy* (n 125) paras 84–89.
[132] ibid para 94, citing Case 62/79 *Coditel and others* ('*Coditel I*') [1980] ECR 881; and Joined Cases 55/80 and 57/80 *Musik-Vertrieb membran and K-tel International* [1981] ECR 147.
[133] *Karen Murphy* (n 125) paras 98–99.   [134] ibid para 100.

sport even in the absence of any mention of sport in the Treaty; but here, given that the reforms of the Lisbon Treaty effective from 2009 had finally brought sport within the explicit terms of the Treaty, the Court was able to supplement such general observations with an explicit anchoring of the argument that 'sport is special' in the Treaty itself. So it immediately cited Article 165(1) TFEU's direction that the EU is to contribute to the promotion of European sporting issues, while taking account of the specific nature of sport, its structures based on voluntary activity, and its social and educational function.[135] This was only the second judgment in which the Court had cited Article 165: the first was *Bernard*.[136] Reliance on Article 165 as a basis for recognizing the legitimacy of national protection of sporting events is significant, though there is nothing new about the Court's basic structural approach, which is to take a creative and broad approach to the scope of justification under free movement law, nor indeed is the admission that sport is special new either. So, as in *Bernard*, Article 165 seems here to be treated as a packaging of existing assumptions that were developed in advance of the entry into force of the Lisbon Treaty in 2009, the moment from which Article 165 became part of EU law. The Court then noted too that Directive 97/36 already recognized events organized by an undertaking legally entitled to sell the rights pertaining to that event.[137] So the Court found that national legislation conferring protection on sporting events is capable of being treated as justified even where it acts as a restriction on the free movement of services.

But the Court immediately supplemented this by asserting that such a restriction must not go beyond what is necessary in order to attain the objective in view. This is orthodox: free movement law is built on an assumption, frequently visible in the Court's case law, that both the end in view and also the means used must be justified. So this allowed the Court to determine just how far EU law goes in leaving space to protect the commercial value of the intellectual property concerned.[138] The grant of the licence to broadcast is the obvious starting point in making money out of the sporting event. This may involve territorial exclusivity. But the Court drew a line. It would not accept arrangements that guaranteed absolute territorial exclusivity. This went beyond what a right holder could expect.

Admittedly, in *Coditel* the Court had, as long ago as 1980, found no breach of EU free movement law where an assignee of the performing right in a film relied on that right to exclude the film from being shown on cable television in Belgium, where it had been transmitted after being broadcast in another Member State, Germany, by a third party with the consent of the original right holder.[139] The key point about *Coditel* was that there were two distinct rights being exploited: allocation of television rights on a territorial basis was justified and so too was action taken to restrain cross-border retransmission which would damage the exploitation of

---

[135] ibid para 101.
[136] Case C-325/08 *Olympique Lyonnais v Olivier Bernard, Newcastle United* [2010] ECR I-2177. See Ch 7.2.
[137] *Karen Murphy* (n 125) para 103. On protected events, see sect 11.9.
[138] ibid paras 106ff.   [139] *Coditel I* (n 132).

the rights to show the films in the cinema. But the situation now before the Court was different because there was no question of an attempt to prevent broadcasting of matches in order to protect a different means to exploit the right to show the match. Instead what was occurring was the partitioning of the EU internal market on national lines in order to maximize income.[140] The Court refused to sanction the partitioning of national markets, which would lead to artificial price differences. This, it found, was 'irreconcilable with the fundamental aim of the Treaty, which is completion of the internal market'.[141] As Advocate General Kokott put it: 'This impairment of freedom to provide services is particularly intensive as the rights in question not only render the exercise of freedom to provide services more difficult, but also have the effect of partitioning the internal market into quite separate national markets'.[142]

The separate attempt to find justification in the objective of encouraging the public to attend football stadiums was rebuffed briskly and crisply.[143] The 'closed period' rule, encountered earlier, in section 11.6,[144] prohibits the broadcasting in the United Kingdom of football matches on Saturday afternoons. It aims to sustain a lively atmosphere inside grounds by encouraging spectators to attend matches 'live'. This practice, which impeded the commercial freedom of broadcasters to show matches during the 'blocked' period, had been the subject of inspection by the Commission some ten years earlier. The Commission concluded that the rules fell outwith the scope of application of Article 81 EC, now Article 101 TFEU. This was routine competition law analysis: the rules did not appreciably restrict competition.[145] It explicitly stated that it therefore did not need to assess the extent to which the televising of football exerts a negative impact on attendance at matches: it had, in short, no need to inquire into whether sport is special.[146] In 2006 the Commission Decision on the collective selling of the media rights to the FAPL dealt exclusively with the horizontal aspects of selling and did not address the blocking rules.[147] In *Karen Murphy* the matter was addressed from the perspective of free movement law, but the outcome was the same: the Court, like the Commission previously, did not exclude the possibility that sport may have particular concerns associated with the need to encourage 'live' attendance but it was able to resolve the dispute under a conventional legal approach which did not require it to address or assess the significance of this sport-specific concern. It was pressed on the Court that the objective of 'blocking' broadcasts on Saturday afternoons would

---

[140] *Karen Murphy* (n 125) paras 117–20 of the Court's ruling; more fully in Opinion of Kokott AG, paras 193–200.
[141] ibid para 115.   [142] ibid para 175, Opinion of Kokott AG.
[143] ibid paras 122–24.   [144] Comm Dec 2001/478 [2001] OJ L171/12.
[145] *UEFA's Broadcasting Regulations* (n 109) paras 49–61 of the Decision. The Commission stated that it will monitor change in market structure, particularly in the wake of the 'Internet revolution', ibid para 56.
[146] ibid para 59. Regrettably the Press Release concerning this matter (IP/01/583, 20 April 2001) claims that the decision 'reflects the Commission's respect of the specific characteristics of sport and of its cultural and social function'. As explained in Ch 6.4, this is a misleadingly inflated account. It would be accurate to say that the decision reflects the absence of a need to take account of such matters.
[147] See n 71.

be thwarted if television viewers in the United Kingdom were able freely to watch Premier League matches which broadcasters transmit in other Member States. The Court pointed out that the claimed objective could be achieved by placing a limitation in the licence agreements so that broadcasters would be required not to broadcast those Premier League matches during closed periods. This would doubtless reduce the value of the rights. But it was not open to the Premier League to seek to justify restrictions that were not necessary to achieve the end in view by relying on their commercial interest in doing so. The Court therefore did not rule against the possibility to justify 'blocking' periods in principle, but it did rule against this method of achieving it. This aligns with EU internal market law more generally. A Member State which has a choice between various measures to attain the same objective is required to choose that which least restricts free movement. Otherwise the choice is disproportionately restrictive.[148]

Advocate General Kokott's treatment of the matter was helpfully fuller than that of the Court, although she agreed with the Court that no special concession could be made in the circumstances. Given that she, unlike the Court, made explicit use of Article 165 TFEU in reaching this conclusion, a paragraph's brief attention is warranted. She noted that the existence of 'closed periods' restricts output and reduces income, and this she accepted as 'primarily a sporting interest which is in principle to be recognised in European Union law', citing the Lisbon Treaty's reference to the specific nature of sport and its structures based on voluntary activity.[149] She conceded a broad margin of discretion to football authorities in fixing closed periods. But she then switched tone: since she could not rule out that the closed period was 'also based at least in part on safeguarding the economic interest of the most important members of the association in partitioning the internal market for live football transmissions' she insisted on the application of a 'particularly strict test' in appraising the need for closed periods.[150] And she expressed doubt as to whether closed periods are even capable of encouraging attendance at matches and participation in matches, and added that the majority of football associations impose no closed period.[151] So, in summary, she was not minded to interpret the Lisbon Treaty as granting a wider zone of autonomy to sport than previous practice had permitted. In this sense the Opinion has close associations with cases such as *MOTOE*,[152] in which claims that 'sport is special' in truth mask commercially motivated attempts to evade the normal assumptions of EU law, as well as less egregious instances of over-ambitious appeals to protect sporting autonomy such as *Bosman*.[153] The Court was less strident than its Advocate General, for it confined its rejection of the case for enforcing closed

---

[148] eg Case 261/81 *Walter Rau* [1982] ECR 3961; Case C-189/95 *Harry Franzén* [1997] ECR I-2471; Case C-170/04 *Klas Rosengren* [2007] ECR I-4071; Case C-333/14 *Scotch Whisky Association*, judgment of 23 December 2015.

[149] *Karen Murphy* (n 125) para 207, Opinion of Kokott AG.

[150] ibid para 208, Opinion of Kokott AG.   [151] ibid para 209, Opinion of Kokott AG.

[152] Case C-49/07 *Motosykletistiki Omospondia Ellados NPID (MOTOE) v Elliniko Dimosio* [2008] ECR I-4863. See Ch 10.

[153] *Bosman* (n 2).

periods through restrictions on cross-border trade in decoders to the observation that this could be achieved simply by doing so via the terms of the original licensing—by refusing to sell rights to broadcast matches played during the 'closed period' in any jurisdiction.

11.8.4 Competition law

The Court's treatment of competition law in *Karen Murphy* was relatively brief.[154] Competition law stands with free movement law as a pillar of the EU's internal market, but, not least since its principal preoccupation is private practices not measures of public authorities, its detail is not exactly the same.[155] The ruling accordingly deals with the detailed ingredients of Article 101 TFEU which are distinct from those associated with Article 56 TFEU, such as, most importantly, the need to find that the arrangements had as their object or effect the prevention, restriction, or distortion of competition. The Court explained that a right holder may in principle grant to a sole licensee the exclusive right to broadcast protected subject matter by satellite and may include territorial restrictions. However, in the light of the Treaty objective of establishing an internal market, agreements which are aimed at partitioning national markets according to national borders or which make the interpenetration of national markets more difficult must be regarded as restrictive of competition within the meaning of Article 101(1).[156] So the problem resided in the additional obligations, beyond exclusivity, designed to ensure compliance with the territorial limitations in the contract: the obligation not to supply decoding devices for use outside the territory covered by the licence agreement. In short, the problem was *absolute territorial exclusivity*. And the Court, cross-referring to the substantive examination carried out in relation to free movement of services, found in predominantly the same vein that the agreements could not be tolerated under EU law. Here the Court's treatment was in tune with the general evolution of EU competition law explained previously: the grant of exclusive rights on a territorial basis is not necessarily incompatible with EU law even though it may appear to cause a fragmentation along national lines. But there are limits to this willingness to leave space for the expression of contractual autonomy and a limit is fatally crossed where parties seek to achieve absolute territorial protection.

11.8.5 Copyright law: public houses and private consumers

The Court's ruling makes an important distinction between the private consumer and the proprietors of the restaurants and public houses in question in the litigation. It is a distinction which flows from the Copyright Directive and the Related

[154] *Karen Murphy* (n 125) paras 134–46.   [155] See Ch 7.3.

[156] *Karen Murphy* (n 125) para 139, the Court comments 'see, by analogy, in the field of medicinal products, Joined Cases C-468/06 to C-478/06 Sot. Lélos kai Sia and Others [2008] ECR I-7139, paragraph 65, and GlaxoSmithKline Services and Others v Commission and Others, paragraphs 59 and 61'. So this is not a sport-specific examination.

Rights Directive.[157] It was identified by the Court after an intricate analysis of the relevant provisions.[158] It found that the Copyright Directive:

… must be interpreted as meaning that the reproduction right extends to transient fragments of the works within the memory of a satellite decoder and on a television screen, provided that those fragments contain elements which are the expression of the authors' own intellectual creation, and the unit composed of the fragments reproduced simultaneously must be examined in order to determine whether it contains such elements.[159]

Only the technologically savvy will grasp what this means. In fact, it refers to the decoration of a television broadcast with matters such as the opening video sequence, the Premier League anthem, pre-recorded films showing highlights of recent Premier League matches, or various graphics which are protectable under copyright.[160] The point, then, is that, as the Court had already found, sporting events cannot be protected under copyright but they may carry an original character which can transform them into subject matter that is worthy of protection should national law so choose, but associated features of the broadcast may be covered by copyright, as foreseen by the Copyright Directive. The ruling therefore induces broadcasters to lard their transmissions with further protectable adornments, such as logos. Then, the Court found that the Copyright Directive allows a right holder to receive reward, inter alia, on the occasion of 'communication to the public'. The Court chose to interpret this broadly.[161] It concluded that it covered transmission of the broadcast works, via a television screen and speakers, to the customers present in a public house which was, as the Court chose to note, pursued with profit-making in view.[162] This may be restrained as an infringement of copyright in the absence of authorization and, crucially, payment. But this clearly does not cover the private consumer in his or her own home, who may watch matches with the imported decoding device without any fear of being held to account for breach of copyright. EU law protects him or her, although this does not preclude actions on the contracts for breach elsewhere in the chain of supply.

11.8.6 Reacting to the judgment in *Karen Murphy*

To sum up, the use of legislation to enforce the prohibition on using foreign decoding devices shaped by the contracts in place could not be justified in the light of the objective of protecting intellectual property rights or by the objective of encouraging the public to attend football stadiums. It went too far. The same conclusion was reached in connection with the application of competition law to the

---

[157] Directive 2001/29/EC (n 128); Directive 2006/115/EC of 12 December 2006 on rental right and lending right and on certain rights related to copyright in the field of intellectual property [2006] OJ L376/28.
[158] *Karen Murphy* (n 125) para 147ff.   [159] ibid para 159.
[160] ibid paras 149, 152.   [161] ibid para 186.
[162] This is one of the few points on which the Court departed from AG Kokott, who did not find the matter to constitute a communication to the public within the meaning of the Directive 2001/29/EC on copyright.

contracts. Objectives permissible in principle were pursued by means that were unduly restrictive—a common theme in EU internal market law. The judgment stands for a strong protection of the internal market's long-standing mistrust of absolute territorial protection.[163]

The ruling in *Karen Murphy* left open what—albeit certainly reduced—level of protection could be maintained.[164] In line with the pattern seen thematically throughout this book, the intervention of EU law directed what may *not* be done. It is left to the private parties involved—rights holders and purchasing broadcasters—to decide what shall be done. But clearly the effect of EU law is to channel the available options. The Premier League's autonomy is conditional on compliance with EU law.

The ruling avoids any empirical inquiry into the likely consequences of loosening the FAPL's relatively secure grip on the cross-border trade in decoders.[165] The obvious fear is that the Premier League might simply respond by refusing to supply Greek and other low-price markets at all, which would do little for either market integration or consumer choice. Absolute territorial protection is anathema to EU law: intolerance to it places an outer limit on the autonomy of the seller of rights and the commercial reward available under licensing backed up by intellectual property. Whether that implacable distrust of absolute territorial protection is a coherent and consistently expressed thematic norm in EU law or an expression of militant refusal to permit commercial reality to disturb the fetish for market-making whatever the practical consequences—or both—is a tension that permeates all of EU internal market law, and has long done so.[166] *Karen Murphy* is a clear example of the orthodoxy that internal market law is not applied with detailed concern for empirical inquiry.

11.8.7 Concluding comments

Poor Karen Murphy had more in common with Jean-Marc Bosman than she might have wished. Her victory was hollow. She was able to defeat the criminal conviction

---

[163] See eg E Szyszczak, 'Karen Murphy: Decoding Licences and Territorial Exclusivity' (2012) 3 Journal of European Competition Law and Practice 169; S De Vries, 'Sport, TV and IP rights: Premier League and Karen Murphy' (2013) 50 CML Rev 591; K Pijetlovic and K Nyman-Metcalf, 'Liberalising the Service Market for Satellite Transmission' (2013) 13 Intl Sports LJ 82.

[164] On the options, see D Doukas, 'The Sky Is Not the (Only) Limit—Sports Broadcasting without Frontiers and the Court of Justice: Comment on *Murphy*' (2012) 37 EL Rev 605, especially 621–25; A Kaburakis, J Lindholm, and R Rodenberg, 'British Pubs, Decoder Cards, and the Future of Intellectual Property Licensing after *Murphy*' (2011–12) 18 Col J Eur L 307, especially 319–22. See also T Margoni, 'The Protection of Sports Events in the EU: Property, Intellectual Property, Unfair Competition and Special Forms of Protection' (2016) 47 International Review of Intellectual Property and Competition Law 386.

[165] Kokott AG does not ignore this, but has little to say: see *Karen Murphy* (n 125) paras 201–202, Opinion of Kokott AG.

[166] eg a critical account of the story of Johnny Walker Whisky (*Distillers Co Ltd* [1978] OJ L50/16) is a staple of successive editions of V Korah, *An Introductory Guide to EC Competition Law and Practice* (9th edn, Hart 2007) ch 8.6.1.

because she had paid for her decoder card (albeit it was sourced in Greece) and she had not acted dishonestly.[167] She celebrated 'with a bottle of Sambuca'.[168] But she could no longer show matches for free.[169] Following the ruling, the Premier League has continued to pursue pubs that show matches without authorization, and therefore without having paid a fee, and it has periodically secured the award of several thousands of pounds as compensation for copyright infringement.[170] The match itself is beyond the scope of copyright, but the League has adjusted its production values to maximize the amount of content that is covered in law by copyright.[171] Territorial separation, and differential pricing, can no longer be protected as aggressively as in the past, but restrictions caused by the language used for commentary go some way to preserving the pre-existing patterns.[172] The ruling did not address the licensing of rights to watch matches online, and this is doubtless the next frontier in charting the tension between the desire to maximize revenues from the sale of rights, on the one hand, and sustaining the principle of the internal market, on the other. The intolerance of absolute territorial protection, where exclusive territorial licences are tipped over the edge by supplementary restrictions that go too far, doubtless remains the watermark for future investigation and planning.

However, the incentives for pubs to continue to attract customers by showing matches illicitly remains strong, and it is the direct result of the discrepancy between the rights charged to commercial premises in the UK by SKY and the price of a purely domestic subscription in a low-price territory. One does not have to be too skilful or alert to find a pub in which to watch a Premier League match live on a Saturday afternoon in the towns and cities of England. And it takes a special kind of incompetent not to be able to find a site with links to watch any Premier League game anywhere in the world on the internet for free,[173] even if sometimes accompanied by a commentary in a language that is harder to decipher than some of the refereeing decisions in favour of the bigger clubs. Borderless technology rather than EU law is the main threat to the prevailing sports broadcasting business models.

---

[167] *Karen Murphy v Media Protection Services Ltd* [2012] EWHC 466 (Admin). For a further restraint, limiting the intervention of trading standards authorities funded by the FAPL against traders in decoders, *Helidon Vuciterni, ALSAT UK* [2012] EWCA 2140 (Admin).

[168] <http://www.bbc.co.uk/news/business-17150054> accessed 29 November 2016.

[169] In the English courts, see eg *FAPL v QC Leisure* [2012] EWHC 108 (Ch).

[170] eg 'Pub [New Inn, Stratton] fined £7,000 over TV football' *Swindon Advertiser* (Swindon, 22 November 2014) <http://www.swindonadvertiser.co.uk/news/11619530.Pub_fined___7_000_over_TV_football/?ref=mr> accessed 29 November 2016.

[171] R Boyle, 'Battle for Control? Copyright, Football and European Media Rights' (2015) 37 Media, Culture and Society 359. See also A Andreangeli, 'Weathering the Murphy Storm: Domestic IP Litigation and Industrial Consolidation as Pragmatic Responses to the Court of Justice's Decision?' (2016) 8 Journal of Media Law 173.

[172] Boyle (n 171).

[173] Exactly such possibilities, albeit in connection with hockey, provoked Case C-279/13 *C More Entertainment AB v Sandberg*, judgment of 26 March 2015 (Directive 2001/29/EC on copyright (n 128)).

11.9 Sporting Jewels: 'Protected' or 'Listed' Events

Legislation governing 'protected' or 'listed' events counts as one of the most misunderstood of all the EU's interventions into sport. It is, moreover, a misunderstanding that is in part a direct result of the obscurity of the rules, judged on both their detail and their purpose. This is another example of how concern for the operation of the broadcasting sector has incidental effects for the autonomy of sport, but in this instance it is striking how sport finds that its commercial ambitions are constrained under a rather obscurely defined notion of rights of public access to the jewels of the sporting calendar.

11.9.1 The legislative framework

The relevant rules are contained in the codified version of the Audiovisual Media Services Directive, Directive 2010/13.[174] This is the significantly amended successor to the original EU regime covering the sector, introduced in 1989 by the so-called 'Television without Frontiers' Directive,[175] and the subsequent re-naming of the measure as the Audiovisual Media Services Directive reflects both the widening of its scope beyond television broadcasting and more generally it provides a good example of the law panting in pursuit of fast-developing technology.[176]

The provisions of most direct significance to sport appear as Articles 14 and 15 in Chapter V of Directive 2010/13, entitled 'Provisions concerning exclusive rights' and 'short news reports in television broadcasting'. Their broad purpose is to place two distinct types of limitation on the autonomy of a holder of exclusive broadcasting rights and, in particular, to soften that exclusivity in favour of granting wider access. It is, however, important to appreciate just how and why the EU claims authority to address such matters. Articles 14 and 15 are simply part of the wider sweep of harmonized rules governing the integration and regulation of broadcasting markets across the EU. The driving concern of the EU's legislative *acquis* in this area is the establishment of the internal market. Directive 2010/13 is based on Articles 53(1) and 62 TFEU, the Treaty provisions governing the coordination of laws in the establishment and services sectors: its predecessors too have been

---

[174] Directive 2010/13/EU of 10 March 2010 on the coordination of certain provisions laid down by law, regulation or administrative action in Member States concerning the provision of audiovisual media services [2010] OJ L95/1 (Audiovisual Media Services Directive).
[175] Directive 89/552/EEC of 3 October 1989 on the coordination of certain provisions laid down by law, regulation or administrative action in Member States concerning the pursuit of television broadcasting activities [1989] OJ L298/23, amended by Directive 97/36/EC of 30 June 1997 amending Directive 89/552 on the coordination of certain provisions laid down by law, regulation or administrative action in Member States concerning the pursuit of television broadcasting activities [1997] OJ L202/60 and Directive 2007/65/EC of 11 December 2007 amending Directive 89/552 on the coordination of certain provisions laid down by law, regulation or administrative action in Member States concerning the pursuit of television broadcasting activities [2007] OJ L332/27.
[176] For a summary of the pattern of revision, see P Valcke and K Lefever, *Media Law in the EU* (Wouters 2012) 48–50.

of precisely this type. They are accordingly measures of market integration. The rationale for EU intervention holds that the national regulation of broadcasting markets took a variety of forms and shapes, with the result that the construction of a common commercial strategy apt to realize the benefits of the EU's internal market was hampered. Therefore the EU should intervene to replace that regulatory diversity with its own common rules.[177] This foundation of regulatory homogeneity permits the pursuit of an integrated trading strategy across the whole territory of the EU, while also locating at EU level, in replacement for national level, the responsibility to select the style and type of regulation appropriate (in common) for the sector in question. So, in short, the EU's constitutional basis for asserting authority over the autonomy of the holder of exclusive rights to broadcast sporting events is rooted in the fact that, in the past, national rules in this vein were different in scope and nature, to the detriment of the EU's internal market. Articles 14 and 15 of Directive 2010/13 are just part of a much broader framework aimed at achieving an integrated market for broadcasting in the EU, based on defined allocation of responsibilities between states from which signals are sent and those where they are received, and including detailed rules on matters such as the quality and quantity of advertising, product placement, the promotion of European works, and the protection of minors.[178] The EU does not regulate the content and method of supply of broadcasting services in general or the exercise of exclusive rights in particular for their own sake, but rather as part of its mission to achieve a market without internal frontiers in the EU for (inter alia) broadcasting, but that quest leads it unavoidably to become a site where sensitive regulatory choices about the sector come to be taken.

This is the logic behind EU legislative harmonization generally. The adoption of common rules serves the internal market while also meeting the regulatory expectations previously pursued (in different ways) at national level and mandated at EU level by horizontal Treaty provisions such as Article 12 on consumer protection and Article 167(4) on cultural diversity and the functionally parallel commitments found in Articles 38 and 22 of the Charter of Fundamental Rights of the European Union, respectively. This is how pursuit of trade integration spills over into other sectors. Because states have taken a stance on patterns of intervention designed to limit market freedoms, the EU, devising a regulatory framework for a broader European market, must respond by making its own choices about the content of the regime that shall be adopted at European level.[179] In Directive 2010/13 this phenomenon is seen in the context of sport and culture, in respect of which the EU lacks any general legislative competence, but which it affects as a result of the

---

[177] This theme is readily visible in the Recitals to Directive 2010/13 (n 174), eg 11, 24, and 50, though it is even more explicit in the original Directive 89/552 (n 175): 'Whereas the laws, regulations and administrative measures in Member States concerning the pursuit of activities as television broadcasters and cable operators contain disparities, some of which may impede the free movement of broadcasts within the Community and may distort competition within the common market'.

[178] In detail, Valcke and Lefever (n 176) ch 3, section 1.

[179] See Weatherill (n 33) ch 13.

wide-ranging functional impact of the programme of harmonization and coordination of laws in the service of building an internal market.

11.9.2 The rules: defining the listed or the protected event

Articles 14 and 15 of Directive 2010/13 are a rather unusual example of the EU's
programme of legislative harmonization. They did not exist in the original 1989
Directive, but rather they were added on amendment in 1997.[180] Given the sensitivity of the issues at stake, there is no question of intrusion into exclusive broadcasting rights and sporting autonomy being dealt with exhaustively at EU level.
In fact, the EU rules are alarmingly opaque. Article 14 on 'protected events' is
the more complicated and it is examined first; Article 15 on short news reports is
addressed later, in subsection 11.9.5.

Article 14 of Directive 2010/13 concerns protected events. These are explained
in Article 14(1) as events which are regarded by a Member State as being 'of major
importance for society'. It is open to each Member State to take measures in accordance with Union law to ensure that broadcasters under its jurisdiction do not
broadcast on an exclusive basis such events 'in such a way as to deprive a substantial
proportion of the public in that Member State of the possibility of following such
events by live coverage or deferred coverage on free television'.[181]

The central concept of an event of 'major importance for society' is not the subject of definition in the Directive. Recital 52 amplifies it:

Events of major importance for society should, for the purposes of this Directive, meet certain criteria, that is to say be outstanding events which are of interest to the general public
in the Union or in a given Member State or in an important component part of a given
Member State and are organised in advance by an event organiser who is legally entitled to
sell the rights pertaining to those events.

Recital 49 refers—purely by way of illustration and non-exhaustively—to events
'such as the Olympic Games, the Football World Cup and the European football
championship'.

The Member State which chooses to take advantage of this regime is required to
draw up a list of events which it chooses to designate as being of major importance
for society, and it is required to do so in a clear and transparent manner in due
time.[182] It is provided by Article 14(2) that Member States shall notify measures
taken to the Commission. The Commission is required to verify that the measures
are compatible with Union law and to communicate them to the other Member

---

[180] Directive 97/36/EC (n 175). See R Craufurd Smith and B Boettcher, 'Football and Fundamental
Rights: Regulating Access to Major Sporting Events on Television' (2002) 8 European Public Law 107.
[181] Audiovisual Media Services Directive (n 174) Art 14(1). According to ibid Recital 53 'free television' means broadcasting on a channel, either public or commercial, of programmes which are
accessible to the public without payment in addition to the modes of funding of broadcasting that
are widely prevailing in each Member State (such as licence fee and/or the basic tier subscription fee
to a cable network).
[182] ibid Art 14(1).

States. Measures taken are duly published in the Official Journal. The list reveals that most Member States do *not* feel the need to designate events as major for these purposes: only nine of the twenty-eight Member States have notified lists to the Commission.[183] Those Member States that do choose to intervene take varying approaches. This is in part because of local preference for idiosyncratic sports that are of interest only in some parts of the EU. So cricket is listed only by the United Kingdom, rugby only by the United Kingdom, Ireland, and France. But there is variation too even with regard to the same event which is of general interest. So, for example, the football World Cup Finals are listed in their entirety by Belgium and the United Kingdom, whereas Austria, France, Germany, and Ireland list only the opening match, the semi-Finals and Finals, and (should the team qualify) matches involving the national team of that state. Moreover, the lists are periodically changed. Denmark, for example, notified the Commission of its list in 1999 but withdrew this with effect from the beginning of 2002 and it now operates no list of the type recognized by Directive 2010/13.[184] The United Kingdom used to require that home Test matches be broadcast live on free-to-air television, but from 2006 it has required only that secondary coverage (ie highlights) be available free-to-air. So after the tumultuous 2005 Ashes series in which England beat Australia for the first time since 1987, live coverage migrated from its long-standing home on the BBC to SKY's subscription sports channel, where many more hours were devoted to the sport but the viewing audience was significantly smaller. In the short term, a great deal more money was earned by cricket: in the long-term, fans of the sport fear that a great deal of affection for it and even awareness of it, especially among younger people, will be lost. It is clear that choosing which events to 'list' is highly sensitive.[185]

An unsafe product in one Member State is in principle an unsafe product in every other Member State.[186] An unfair commercial practice in one Member State is in principle an unfair commercial practice in every other Member State.[187] But an event of major sporting interest in one Member State is not necessarily an event of major sporting interest in every other Member State. Rights to broadcast certain events are not to be sold exclusively to providers that are not free-to-air, but this is in essence a coordinating regime, not one that sets a common and comprehensive set of mandatory rules at EU level. The regime applies only if a state chooses to opt in to it, by designating certain events to be of major importance for society. This is perfectly clear from both the wording and intent of Article 14, which indeed begins

---

[183] The list is at <http://ec.europa.eu/digital-agenda/avmsd-list-major-events> accessed 29 November 2016. A consolidated list was published at [2008] OJ C17/7, but it is now out of date, as the website makes clear. On practice and definition, see Lefever (n 20) 229–35, 259–62, 265–68.

[184] The list was an 'utter failure', L Halgreen, *European Sports Law* (Forlaget Thomson 2004) 131.

[185] eg 'Governing Bodies Line Up to Criticise TV "Crown Jewels" Review' *The Guardian* (London, 14 November 2009) Sports section, 9; 'Cricketers Fear Ashes TV Rights Googly' *Financial Times* (London, 12 November 2009) 5.

[186] Directive 2001/95/EC of 3 December 2001 on general product safety [2002] OJ L11/4.

[187] Directive 2005/29/EC of 11 May 2005 concerning unfair business-to-consumer commercial practices in the internal market [2005] OJ L149/22.

with the formula: 'Each Member State *may* take measures …' (emphasis added). The Commission too has long properly emphasized that this is a 'voluntary provision'.[188] The EU's legislative system facilitates the preservation of those national choices within the context of the wider internal market.

11.9.3 What is the obligation imposed on the listing state?

The underlying anxiety is plainly that broadcasters to whom a fee must be paid by viewers to secure access to transmissions will acquire exclusive rights to major events with the consequence that the general population will be deprived of the opportunity to view such events for free. As explained, such events are certainly of great interest to the commercial model of providers of pay-per-view services, but they are of interest to citizens more broadly too. The EU regime requires that, if a Member State has chosen to list an event, the free broadcaster gets its chance. As a Commission website chattily has it: 'A Football World Cup final or the Olympic Games only on pay-TV, these are the scenarios which the EU wanted to prevent from happening'.[189] The commodification of sports events shall have limits.[190]

But what exactly does Article 14 entail? Once a state draws up the list of events that it perceives as being of 'major importance for society', if it chooses to do so, it is entitled to take measures to ensure that broadcasters do not broadcast those events on an exclusive basis 'in such a way as to deprive a substantial proportion of the public in that Member State of the possibility of following such events via live coverage or deferred coverage on free television'. It is, however, far from clear just what is envisaged. At one extreme on the spectrum of interpretation the buyer of exclusive rights must make the event available for free, either on its own channel or by permitting a free-to-air channel free access to the rights. This will rob it of subscribers willing to pay, for there will be no need to pay. This will plainly dramatically reduce the price that the broadcaster is willing to pay to the owner of the rights, typically the sport's governing body: the commercial glitter of exclusivity as a means to attract a portfolio of subscribers and interested advertisers is lost. At the other extreme the regime might be thought to mean merely that a free-to-air broadcaster is guaranteed access only to the bidding process on a non-discriminatory and transparent basis, so that there is a 'possibility' for the general population to have the opportunity of viewing the event free-to-air, but that it has no legal basis for complaint if exclusive rights are ultimately awarded to a pay-per-view broadcaster which bids more for the rights. Occasionally a free-to-air broadcaster may be able to promise a larger audience which may be more attractive to a sporting body aiming

---

[188] Third Report on the application of Directive 89/552, COM (2001) 9, p 8.

[189] <http://ec.europa.eu/archives/information_society/avpolicy/reg/tvwf/events/index_en.htm> accessed 29 November 2016.

[190] There are instances elsewhere in the world, see eg action pursuant to The Broadcasting Services Act 1992 in Australia (regulation is known as 'anti-siphoning') <https://www.communications.gov.au/policy/policy-listing/anti-siphoning> accessed 29 November 2016.

to enhance its long-term popularity and to satisfy its sponsors than the short-term profit represented by a higher fee paid by a broadcaster whose services are not available free of charge to the viewer, but normally the higher bidder will win, and this interpretation might seem to defeat the point of Article 14. A more moderate interpretation would hold that the free-to-air broadcaster is entitled to show the event but that it must pay a price to the rights holder (the organizer or another broadcaster who has bought them). The Directive, however, is silent on how any such price falls to be calculated or what happens in the event of a dispute. There is no ruling of the Court of Justice on how to choose between these competing interpretations of the legal obligation placed on the listing state.

It is clear that both the possibility of intrusion into the autonomy of the rights holder and the uncertainty about the depth of intrusion will lower the price tag for 'listed' major events. The more moderate interpretation, in between the two extremes, is certainly the most plausible attempt to balance the underlying tensions caused by, on the one hand, the value that a grant of exclusivity adds to the right to broadcast a sports event and, on the other, accessibility of that event to the wider population. It is, moreover, the interpretation that seems in practice to be guiding the operation of the EU regime in the minority of Member States that choose to 'list' events.[191] In the United Kingdom, the process is managed by OFCOM according to a Code of Practice published pursuant to the Broadcasting Act 1996.[192] This makes explicit that the scheme 'is concerned with providing an opportunity for live coverage to be made available', but that it 'does not require or guarantee live coverage of listed events'.[193] The Code sets out the circumstances in which OFCOM will permit a listed event to be shown exclusively live on a subscription channel: there must have been an opportunity, not taken, for a free-to-air broadcaster to acquire the rights on fair and reasonable terms.

It is a condemnation of the EU's regime that its precise legal shape is open to doubt. This is largely the consequence of a lack of clear articulation of the underlying policy pursued by the Directive, which deserves to be addressed later, after further legal obscurities are exposed.

11.9.4 What is the obligation imposed on states other than the listing state?

It is plain that it is not possible for a Member State acting unilaterally to achieve the objectives foreseen by the Directive. Its aspirations to secure its citizens' access to major events would be thwarted if rights were purchased on an exclusive basis by a broadcaster based in another Member State. Cooperation across borders is

---

[191] Lefever (n 20) 243–45.
[192] OFCOM, Code of Practice <https://www.ofcom.org.uk/tv-radio-and-on-demand/broadcast-codes/code-sports-events> accessed 29 November 2016. See M Milne, *The Transformation of Television Sport: New Methods, New Rules* (Palgrave Macmillan 2016) ch 5.
[193] OFCOM, Code of Practice (n 192) para 1.10.

required. So Article 14(3) of Directive 2010/13 provides that Member States shall take steps to ensure that broadcasters under their jurisdiction do not exercise exclusive rights which they have purchased in such a way that a substantial proportion of the public in *another* Member State is deprived of the possibility of following events designated by that other Member State in accordance with Article 14.

This is necessarily a mandatory rather than a voluntary provision as far as Member State authorities are concerned; were it otherwise, one state's choices would be readily undermined by another's lack of concern in so far as broadcasters established in the latter state have acquired rights 'listed' by the former state.

But here too the question arises of what this entails. What level of intrusion into the autonomy of the right holder is envisaged in order to secure the position of a substantial proportion of the viewing public in another Member State? Here too neither the Directive nor the Court of Justice offer anything usefully more detailed.

The decision of the UK House of Lords in *R v Independent Television Commission, ex parte TV Danmark 1 Ltd* is not authoritative as a matter of EU law, but offers insight into the interpretative choices at stake.[194] TV Danmark, a satellite television company established in England but targeting the Danish market, had acquired exclusive rights to broadcast World Cup football matches of the Danish national team, which were events that Denmark had chosen to 'list' under the Directive. TV Danmark had bought these rights on an exclusive basis after a bidding process in which they had, as part of a (commercially familiar) strategy to secure a presence in the market, offered a higher price than Danish public broadcasters, who would have been able to broadcast the games to at least 90 per cent of the Danish population, the threshold laid down under Danish law and which TV Danmark, with a relatively small pool of subscribers, would not be able to cross. This was, then, exactly the situation envisaged by what is now Article 14 of Directive 2010/13, although the dispute in fact had the earlier, though materially identical, legislative regime as its background.[195]

Under the UK rules in force, which implemented the predecessor to what is today Directive 2010/13, TV Danmark could show the matches only after securing the prior consent of the Independent Television Commission (ITC).[196] So the question in law was how, as a matter of EU law, the ITC should deal with the matter. The House of Lords took the view that the Directive's instruction to prevent the exercise by broadcasters of exclusive rights in such a way that a substantial proportion of the population in another Member State would be deprived of the possibility of watching a listed event on television meant that it was not mandatory for the ITC to grant its consent to a broadcaster in TV Danmark's position. This, in short, lends a higher priority to the Danish choice about the importance of access to viewing the matches and correspondingly less to the vigour of market forces and the interests of an undertaking that had won the rights in question. Lord

---

[194] [2001] 1 WLR 1604.   [195] Audiovisual Media Services Directive (n 174).
[196] The ITC's responsibilities in the field are today exercised by OFCOM (n 192).

Hoffman, who gave the main speech in the House of Lords, regarded the Directive as having carved out a defined circumstance in which competition in the market and unhampered enjoyment of purchased contractual rights would be restrained. Lord Hoffman assumed that the point of the regime is that an exclusive right holder must in such circumstances always make an offer of a share in the rights to a free-to-air broadcaster—though plainly this will greatly affect the price which a channel in TV Danmark's position would be prepared to bid for the rights in the first place.

The Court of Justice was not permitted the opportunity to explore this intriguing terrain. The House of Lords made no preliminary reference to Luxembourg. For its part the Commission did no more than briefly mention the case in its fourth report on the application of Directive 89/552 in the context of a broad comment that application of its Article 3a in the period under review had been 'satisfactory',[197] a bland approval repeated in the Discussion Paper released in April 2003 as part of the Commission's consultation exercise on the reform of the Directive.[198] At that point the trail goes cold. The true legal intent behind Article 14 of Directive 2010/13 is left unaddressed in the Commission's subsequently produced abundant documentation on the regime, including in the most recent and strikingly anodyne Commission report on the operation of the regime, published in 2012.[199] But one can understand reluctance to get involved in such obscure material. It is the Directive itself, not the Commission, that is the problem.

11.9.5 Short news reports

Article 15 of Directive 2010/13 concerns short news reports. It is stipulated that Member States shall ensure that for the purpose of short news reports any broadcaster established in the Union has access 'on a fair, reasonable and non-discriminatory basis to events of high interest to the public which are transmitted on an exclusive basis by a broadcaster under their jurisdiction'. Simply put, the purchased exclusivity is forcibly broken under the framework of management designed to ensure access which is foreseen by Article 15. This is not limited to sport, but sport is clearly one area in which relevant demand will arise. These short extracts shall be used solely for general news programmes and may be used in on-demand audiovisual media services only if the same programme is offered on a deferred basis by the same media service provider.[200] Article 15, unlike Article 14, expressly mentions compensation: this is a matter to be determined by Member States, but where compensation is provided for, it shall not exceed the additional costs incurred in providing access.[201]

---

[197] COM (2002) 778, p 10.

[198] Available via <http://ec.europa.eu/archives/information_society/avpolicy/reg/history/consult/consultation_2003/index_en.htm> accessed 29 November 2016.

[199] COM (2012) 203.

[200] Audiovisual Media Services Directive (n 174) Art 15(5). The rules do *not* cover radio broadcasts; cf E001313/12 (written question) [2013] OJ C96E/160.

[201] Audiovisual Media Services Directive (n 174) Art 15(6).

11.9.6 The nature and purpose of the regime

The point of both Articles 14 and 15 of Directive 2010/13, in short, is to leave space in the internal market framework governing an integrated broadcasting market for intervention to ensure that certain events are not to be sold exclusively to providers that are not free-to-air. It was the rise of 'pay-TV' that was the main anxiety, though technological advance has widened the relevant types of content provider. What is loosely at stake here is the perception that the commercial virtues of exclusivity as a means to maximize the attraction of and consequently the revenue raised from the sale of rights requires the possibility of modification where the value of dissemination of information carries particular weight. This is, however, to presuppose some form of balancing between interests that compete: mandatory loosening of exclusivity reduces the value of rights and so shifts resources away from rights holders to citizens generally. This is the tension at the heart of the regime.[202] It entails that commodification of sports events is limited. The subjection of private rights to action taken in the public interest is a perfectly familiar feature of modern democracies, but the calculation of why this should be done should be laid bare.

The lack of *legal* precision has been exposed. The reason for this ambiguity is largely the accompanying lack of *policy* precision.

A 1996 Resolution of the European Parliament declared 'it essential for all spectators to have a right of access to major sports events, just as they have a right to information'.[203] But what of the costs that right holders incur as a result of the legal designation of such a 'right', which presumably in turn reduces the funding available to improve the quality of the product? This unbalanced attitude seems to have carried influence in the negotiation that led to the creation of the protected events procedure when the original 1989 Directive was revised. So in this vein Recital 18 to Directive 97/36 refers to a 'right to information' and to ensuring 'wide access by the public to television coverage' of events of major importance to society. This is now taken over and absorbed in the Recitals to the currently applicable measure, Directive 2010/13. They assert the cultural worth of audiovisual media services alongside their economic role.[204] They assert too the importance of freedom of information, diversity of opinion, and media pluralism, including recognition of the role in this vein of Article 11 of the EU Charter of Fundamental Rights.[205] Article 11 directs (inter alia) that 'Everyone has the right to ... receive and impart information and ideas without interference by public authority and regardless of frontiers', which mirrors Article 10 of the European Convention for the Protection of Human Rights and Fundamental Freedoms (ECHR). The Court too has been content to adopt this reasoning to reject a challenge to the Directive's validity on the basis that the legislature had validly concluded that obstacles were justified by

---

[202] cf R Parrish, 'Access to Major Events on Television under European Law' (2008) 31 Journal of Consumer Policy 79.
[203] Resolution on the broadcasting of sports events [1996] OJ C166/109.
[204] Audiovisual Media Services Directive (n 174) Recitals 5, 6, and 7.
[205] ibid Recitals 5, 16, 48, 49, and 55.

the objective of protecting the right to information and ensuring wide public access to television coverage of the events in question.[206] This litigation is considered further later.

Information is power and the discourse of fundamental rights is deservedly prominent in analysis of law and policy in the broadcasting sector.[207] The promotion of pluralism in media markets has an intimate connection with sustaining the vibrancy of our democracies. And there is no constitutional objection to the 'decisive factor' in an EU measure of legislative harmonization being formed by a regulatory concern recognized by the Treaty such as the promotion of culture, provided only that the measure also serves to promote the functioning of the internal market, here in the broadcasting sector.[208]

The commercial impact of this regime is very real. Central to the narrative of this chapter is that growth on the demand-side of the market for the rights to show major sporting events, supply of which is limited, has led to dramatic price increases in recent years. This is deregulation combined with technological advance, which breeds commodification. Free-to-air broadcasters may be priced out of the market by eager subscription-based suppliers. So, for perfectly obvious reasons of self-interest, in the consultation process on reform of the regime conducted by the Commission in 2003, the BBC stressed the 'crucial' importance of access to events of major importance and pressed that the scheme 'should be maintained and, possibly, strengthened';[209] and the subsequently produced Commission Communication entitled 'The Future of European Regulatory Audiovisual Policy' noted a clear division between private broadcasters, critical of the regime, and more eagerly positive public service broadcasters.[210] The designation of a sporting event by a national government as 'listed' helps the free-to-air broadcaster and its viewers, but it means that because the right holder is prevented from selling untouchably exclusive rights, the value to the subscription-based broadcaster is decreased and so the price that the sale will command will typically fall. It is certainly not inevitable that the right holder will be prejudiced by these rules on 'protected events'—a sports body might on occasion be pleased to find that free television is required to show an event because this maximizes the audience for its sport and through such added exposure

---

[206] Case C-201/11P *UEFA v Commission*, paras 102–104, Case C-204/11P *FIFA v Commission*, paras 110–12, and Case C-205/11P *FIFA v Commission*, paras 126–27, judgments of 18 July 2013.

[207] See generally R Craufurd Smith, *Broadcasting Law and Fundamental Rights* (Clarendon Press 1997); J Oster, *Media Freedom as a Fundamental Right* (CUP 2015); see also R Parrish and S Miettinen, 'Sports Broadcasting and Community Law' in I Blackshaw, S Cornelius, and R Siekmann (eds), *TV Rights and Sport: Legal Aspects* (TMC Asser 2009).

[208] eg Case C-380/03 *Germany v Parliament and Council* [2006] ECR I-11573; Case C-210/03 *Swedish Match* [2004] ECR I-11893; Joined Cases C-154/04 and C-155/04 *Alliance for Natural Health* [2005] ECR I-6451; Case C-58/08 *Vodafone, O2 et al v Secretary of State* [2010] ECR I-4999; Weatherill (n 33) ch 13. I Katsirea, 'Why the European Broadcasting Quota should be Abolished' (2003) 28 EL Rev 190 adopts a contrary view, but now seems to have been overtaken by the Court's accumulated case law.

[209] <http://ec.europa.eu/archives/information_society/avpolicy/docs/reg/modernisation/2003_review/contributions/wc_bbc.pdf> accessed 29 November 2016.

[210] COM (2003) 784, para 3.3.

attracts more sponsors and, in the longer term, more public affection for the event in particular and the sport in general. A suggested example is the Epsom Derby.[211] However, although the regime does not prevent the sale of rights to a pay-per-view broadcaster, it does entail that a grant of exclusivity is conditional on the—as explained, ambiguous—impact of national choices recognized by the Directive, and so a common complaint is that the value of the rights is tarnished. Cricket's governing body successfully resisted suggestions that live Test Match coverage, sold on an exclusive basis to SKY from 2006, should be mandatorily restored to free-to-air access for games against Australia by claiming that the value of the rights would have been diminished by £137 million.[212] Inhibited exploitation of an extraordinarily lucrative market is likely to diminish the level of investment in the quality of the product, which is likely to be to the detriment of consumers.[213]

But the rules improve citizen access to major events. The right of the public to receive information lies comfortably within the scope of Article 10 ECHR and Article 11 of the Charter. There is scope to interpret this right as capable of application to freedom of information in connection with sporting events: big sporting events are popular and may even count as an element in fostering a shared sense of experience and community, tending towards national pride and identity. On the other hand, to garland such events with the status of a facility to which the public is entitled to access would feel exaggerated even were the EU regime on protected events carefully tailored to such aims, but given its voluntary and fragmented nature it is a stretch too far to seek to justify it in the language of fundamental rights.[214] Even more critically, one may go so far as to condemn such an approach to the glorious triviality of sport as apt to demean the quality and dignity of discourse about fundamental rights.

So the EU's regime asserts a peculiarly shaped intrusion into the commodification of sport and, moreover, it disturbs affected broadcasters' own claims to freedom of expression. It is frankly troubling that this occurs in the absence of any clearly articulated policy, which explains just why this reduction in commercial and sporting autonomy is thought appropriate. The regime represents a brittle compromise between the virtues of open markets and of public interest regulation. The language of fundamental rights seems to fit the Article 15 regime on short news reports a great deal more readily than it fits Article 16 on listed events of major importance. It is hard to believe that Article 14 of Directive 2010/13 and the state choices it seeks to protect deserves elevation to a status whereby the state is treated

---

[211] G Wood, 'Downgrading the Derby could be Long-Term Turn-Off' *The Guardian* (London, 17 November 2009) Sports section, 9.

[212] 'Ashes on Free TV "Will Cost ECB £137m"' *The Independent* (London, 20 March 2010) 21. It is noted that 'ECB officials resent cricket being handed back to it [the BBC] on a golden platter'; '... the return of Test cricket to terrestrial television ... would be a disaster!', Chairman's Report, Annual Report and Statement of Accounts for the year ended 30 September 2009 of Gloucestershire County Cricket Club, 2.

[213] eg K Lefever and B Van Rompuy, 'Ensuring Access to Sports Content: 10 Years of EU Intervention. Time to Celebrate?' (2009) 2 Journal of Media Law 243, 264–66.

[214] By contrast see Lefever (n 20) who *would* make the stretch, especially at 71, 98–99, 239–40, 314.

as fulfilling a positive obligation to ensure its citizens have access to the World Cup and the Olympic Games on free-to-air television. Much of EU sports law involves a sceptical assessment of inflated claims to autonomy made by governing bodies: in this instance the scepticism is deservedly aimed at the basis for interfering with that autonomy.

11.9.7 Litigating the legislative regime: listed or protected events

It is no surprise that juridification follows in the wake of the combined effects on the broadcasting market of deregulation, technological change, and commodification. An appetite for litigation is the inevitable outcome of this legislatively mis-shapen and commercially sensitive set of rules. But so far the litigation has not disturbed the validity of the regime. The structure of the regime, based on discretionary choices at national level combined with its (admittedly poorly articulated) claim to pursue a balance of rights has so far shielded it from any judicial interference.

In *Infront WM AG v Commission* the applicant (formerly the Kirch Media Group) objected to the United Kingdom's list, which affected rights which it owned and which consequently affected its commercial position.[215] However, the decision of the Court of First Instance (today the General Court) casts no light on the regime generally. Infront challenged the letter sent by the Commission to the British authorities advising them that it had no objections to the notified measures. The Court concluded that this letter was susceptible to judicial review because, by triggering the mechanism of mutual recognition foreseen by the Directive, it was endowed with binding legal effect and it also found the applicant to possess the necessary standing for the purposes of Article 230(4) EC (today Article 263(4) TFEU). The Court then annulled the decision for procedural reasons. Before the Court of Justice the Commission failed to dislodge the Court of First Instance's reasoning and the appeal was dismissed.[216] The Commission repaired the identified procedural errors by simply re-making all its relevant Decisions.[217]

The ruling in *Infront* demonstrates that access to the courts for disgruntled rights holders is possible and it led to procedural renovation, but the decision reveals nothing about more profound questions concerning the willingness of the Union's judicature to inquire into the Commission's role under the Directive and/or the choices made by Member States. A much more thorough workout was pursued in three cases with closely similar subject matter which were decided on the same day in July 2013.

The Third Chamber of the Court resisted attempts by UEFA and FIFA to subvert the system.[218] Provided that these rulings set a consistent tone for the future,

---

[215] Case T-33/01 *Infront WM AG v Commission* [2005] ECR II-5897.

[216] Case C-125/06P *Commission v Infront WM* [2008] ECR I-1451.

[217] This is why the list at [2008] OJ C17/7 (n 183) contains references to action taken in 2007. See Commission's Sixth Report on the application of Directive 89/552, COM (2007) 452, para 2.2.

[218] Case C-201/11P *UEFA v Commission*, Case C-204/11P *FIFA v Commission*, and Case C-205/11P *FIFA v Commission*, judgments of 18 July 2013.

they do much to insulate the regime from effective legal supervision. The Court's review is light: the rulings assume a generous grant of discretionary decision-making power to the Commission and the 'listing' Member States.

The cases were appeals from rulings of the General Court[219] in which, in each instance, the General Court had dismissed an application for partial annulment of two Commission Decisions. The first and third cases, brought by UEFA and FIFA respectively, were directed against Decision 2007/730, which expressed the Commission's view that measures taken by the United Kingdom to 'list' the Finals of the European Football Championships (EURO) and the World Cup in their entirety were compatible with EU law;[220] the second, brought by FIFA, was directed against Decision 2007/479, which expressed the same view in respect of measures taken by Belgium to 'list' the Finals of the World Cup in their entirety. The Decisions had their basis in common: the measures had been taken pursuant to Directive 89/552, the predecessor of the procedure currently set out in Article 14 of Directive 2010/13, and they had been duly communicated to the Commission, as foreseen by the Directive.

UEFA and FIFA had a powerful financial interest in the matter, and this is illuminatingly recorded in the Decisions. Of the revenue generated by the sale of the commercial rights relating to the final stage of the EURO, 64 per cent comes from the sale of television broadcasting rights for the matches,[221] while FIFA's primary source of income is the sale of television broadcasting rights to the Finals of the World Cup, which it organizes.[222]

The Decisions, quoted in the judgments, noted that the Commission was satisfied that the events listed met at least two of the four criteria considered to be reliable indicators of the importance of events for society: (a) a special general resonance within the Member State, and not simply a significance to those who ordinarily follow the sport or activity concerned; (b) a generally recognized, distinct cultural importance for the population in the Member State, in particular as a catalyst of cultural identity; (c) involvement of the national team in the event concerned in the context of a competition or tournament of international importance; and (d) the fact that the event has traditionally been broadcast on free television and has commanded large television audiences.

The applicants pieced together a long list of grounds on which to base the appeal. Most ran in common across the three cases. But none was successful. They failed to persuade the Court that the requirements of clarity and transparency were violated by the United Kingdom or by Belgium. The more substantive allegation that the Commission could not conclude that the United Kingdom had validly considered the entire final stage of the EURO to be an event of major importance, and that in UEFA's view, the United Kingdom could designate as events of major importance

---

[219] Case T-55/08 *UEFA v Commission* [2011] ECR II-271, Case T-385/07 *FIFA v Commission* [2011] ECR II-205, Case T-68/08 *FIFA v Commission* [2011] ECR II-349, respectively.
[220] In fact the Decision was adopted to fill the gap left by the measure annulled in Case T-33/01 *Infront WM v Commission* (n 215).
[221] Case C-201/11P (n 218) para 5.   [222] Case C-204/11P (n 218) para 5.

only so-called 'gala' matches, namely the final and semi-finals, and the matches involving the national teams of that Member State, also failed. FIFA made the same unsuccessful complaint about the United Kingdom and Belgian listing of the World Cup Finals in their entirety. It was plainly true that the United Kingdom and Belgium were more avaricious listers than most Member States, but the Court found that the competition may reasonably be regarded as a single event as a whole rather than as a series of individual events divided up into 'gala' and 'non-gala' matches—even if the preferred designation may differ from one Member State to another. Moreover Belgium and the United Kingdom's relatively wide-ranging choice, which would plainly bring some games within the bundle that were less popular than others, was based on all the games having special general resonance at national level and also carrying specific interest for those who do not generally follow football. Note was taken that the tournament as a whole, and so including 'non-gala matches', had traditionally been broadcast on free television channels and had commanded large television audiences.[223]

The Court's approach upholds the flexibility on which the Directive itself is based. The Court's Preliminary Observations in the rulings emphasize the Member States' 'broad discretion' in choosing what, if anything, to place on their list, against an assumption that the EU has opted not to harmonize practice but instead to respect the considerable social and cultural differences which exist within the EU in gauging the importance of intervening to make such events available for free. In exactly this vein of allowing room for local particularity, the Court relies on the deliberate absence in the Directive of 'detailed criteria' governing the exercise of the discretion.[224] It is an approach which, a few months later, the EFTA Court adopted in rejecting a challenge by FIFA to approval by the ESA (the EFTA Surveillance Authority which here performs a function analogous to the Commission within the EU) of Norway's listing of all matches in the World Cup Finals. The EFTA Court, moving down the track already set by the three Court of Justice rulings of 2013, emphasized the scope for local choices determined by social and cultural particularities and it found the measure lawful.[225]

It is crucial that the Commission does not exercise its own power of decision when notified of lists by Member States. Rather it exercises only a power of review.[226] And that power of review is limited. Intransparent or wholly irrational choices by a Member State may be invalid. But assuming procedural scrupulousness, the Commission's power of review must be limited to determining whether the Member States have committed any manifest errors of assessment in designating events of major importance.[227] This is a test inspired by the general approach to

---

[223] The Court found the General Court had mishandled this examination by failing to demand sufficient reasoning by the Commission, but this did not affect the final result for there were adequate grounds elsewhere in the judgment.

[224] Case C-201/11P (n 218) paras 10–21, Case C-204/11P (n 218) paras 11–22, C-205/11P (n 218) paras 12–23.

[225] Case E-21/13 *FIFA v EFTA Surveillance Authority*, judgment of 3 October 2014.

[226] Case C-201/11P (n 218) para 109; also Case E-21/13 (n 225) para 61.

[227] Case C-201/11P (n 218) paras 10–21, Case C-204/11P (n 218) paras 11–22, Case C-205/11P (n 218) paras 12–23.

review of EU legislative measures according to which a broad discretion is permitted in an area which entails political, economic, and social choices, and complex assessments.[228] It is a test that is, and it is intended to be, deferential to the autonomy of the decision-maker. It was argued in Chapter 7.4 that a test of this type, which recognizes a sporting margin of appreciation, is a good way to understand the conditional autonomy granted to sports governing bodies in the application of EU internal market law: here it is used to shelter the Commission from challenge by those very sports governing bodies.

Claims based on the right to property, and specifically on Article 17(1) of the Charter of Fundamental Rights, failed in the same way in all three decisions of the Court. The use of property may be regulated by law in so far as this is necessary for the general interest. Here the Court drew on its own preliminary observations in the ruling.[229] There it had found that the designation envisaged by the Directive had 'unavoidable consequences' for the freedom to provide services, the freedom of establishment, the freedom of competition, and the right to property, but that— relying on Recital 18 in the Preamble to Directive 97/36 (which is now Recital 49 of Directive 2010/13)—it is essential that Member States should be able to take measures to protect the right to information and to ensure wide access by the public to television coverage of national or non-national events of major importance for society. The Court drew too on a recital that placed this motivation also in the context of the public interest in cultural diversity and media pluralism. And it then applied this reasoning to reject this ground of challenge.[230]

This is certainly important. There was an admitted interference with property rights. The EU rules reduced FIFA and UEFA's earning power by taking away the possibility to sell rights on an exclusive basis to a broadcaster whose services are not provided free to viewers. But the right to property, though long recognized and protected by EU law, has never been treated as an absolute right. Instead, as the Court has put it, it 'must be viewed in relation to its social function' and the Court has no objection to legislative restriction on its exercise 'provided that those restrictions in fact correspond to objectives of general interest ... and do not constitute a disproportionate and intolerable interference, impairing the very substance of the rights guaranteed'.[231] A margin is allowed to the EU legislature in deciding to intervene in property rights. The Court attributes no absolute status to property rights or to the freedom to conduct a business, but rather accepts that in principle their exercise may be limited by market regulation in the general interest.

---

[228] eg Case C-491/01 *Ex parte British American Tobacco (Investments) and Imperial Tobacco* [2002] ECR I-11453, para 123; Case C-547/14 *Philip Morris Brands*, judgment of 4 May 2016, para 166.
[229] Case C-201/11P (n 218) paras 10–21, Case C-204/11P (n 218) paras 11–22, Case C-205/11P (n 218) paras 12–23.
[230] Case C-201/11P (n 218) paras 102–104, Case C-204/11P (n 218) paras 110–12, of Case C-205/11P (n 218) paras 126–27. See also Case E-21/13 (n 225).
[231] eg Case C-491/01 *R v Secretary of State, ex p BAT and Imperial Tobacco* [2002] ECR I-11543, para 149; Case C-280/93 *Germany v Council* [1994] ECR I-4973, para 78; Cases C-184/02 and C-223/02 *Spain and Finland v Parliament and Council* [2004] ECR I-7789, para 52.

This is not a sports-specific concern. Nor is it the exclusive preserve of the Charter of Fundamental Rights—in fact the Court's case law long pre-dates the Charter's acquisition of binding effect in 2009 and the Charter is in effect simply a confirmation of the Court's basis for review of EU measures that regulate the exercise of property rights. The overall theme is clear. It holds that the Court will not lightly set aside legislative reconciliation of competing interests. It requires that the legislative process shall strike 'a fair balance between them', but rarely does it find that this test has not been met.[232] The three cases brought without success by FIFA and UEFA fully conform to this trend.

So too does another case that arose in connection with Directive 2010/13. This is *Sky Österreich GmbH*, which deals with Article 15 of the Directive on short news reports.[233] Directive 2010/13's bite into the contractual freedom of the exclusive holder of broadcasting rights was held valid because of the public interest in permitting other broadcasters the right to use short extracts from events of high interest to the public in their own coverage. As is the norm in such cases, the freedom to conduct a business recognized by Article 16 of the Charter was not treated as absolute, but instead fell to be assessed in the light of its social function. The Court asserted that 'the freedom to conduct a business is not absolute, but must be viewed in relation to its social function'; and added that 'the freedom to conduct a business may be subject to a broad range of interventions on the part of public authorities which may limit the exercise of economic activity in the public interest'.[234] It then found that what was at stake was a 'balance' between, on the one hand, the importance of safeguarding the fundamental freedom to receive information and the freedom and pluralism of the media guaranteed by Article 11 of the Charter and, on the other, the protection of the freedom to conduct a business guaranteed by Article 16 of the Charter. The limitations on SKY's freedom to conduct a business were not disproportionate and so they were lawful. The Directive properly pursued 'the necessary balancing of the rights and interests at issue'.[235] This was so even though, as the Court carefully noted, the Directive meant that SKY, as the holder of exclusive broadcasting rights, could not demand remuneration greater than the additional costs directly incurred in providing access to the satellite signal, which were non-existent in this case.

The ruling in *Sky* is cited in the trio of cases involving UEFA and FIFA in support of the proposition that the marketing on an exclusive basis of events of high interest to the public is liable to restrict considerably the access of the general public

---

[232] eg dismissing challenges to the validity of EU acts, Case C-544/10 *Deutsches Weintor eG v Land Rheinland-Pfalz*, judgment of 6 September 2012, para 47, citing Case C-275/06 *Promusicae* [2008] ECR I-271 which was decided before the grant of binding force to the Charter; Case C-12/11 *Denise McDonough v Ryanair Ltd*, judgment of 31 January 2013; Case C-101/12 *Herbert Schaible*, judgment of 17 October 2013; Case C-157/14 *Neptune Distribution*, judgment of 17 December 2015; Case C-547/14 *Philip Morris* (n 228).
[233] Case C-283/11 *Sky Österreich GmbH*, judgment of 22 January 2013. See W Hins, 'Annotation' (2014) 51 CML Rev 665.
[234] *Sky Österreich GmbH* (n 233) paras 45, 46.   [235] ibid para 67.

to information relating to those events, and that, in a democratic and pluralistic society, the right to receive information is of particular importance.[236]

Ultimately the trio of judgments of July 2013, almost identical triplets, strongly uphold the Commission's management of the political choices made by the EU in the Directive and by the Member States pursuant to the Directive. *Sky* underlines in similar vein the Court's reluctance to protect commercial autonomy from regulatory intervention, provided there is no manifest error in the legislative act. This legislative regime is in its detail poorly shaped and its policy aims poorly articulated. But the Court will not find legal reasons to disturb it. The message of the rulings is that disgruntled right holders need to operate within the national political process to lobby to have their event removed from the list of protected events.

11.10 Conclusion

The narrative provided in this chapter is built on an assessment of the combined influence of deregulation, technological innovation, and commodification in the market for the sale of rights to broadcast sporting events. Juridification, in particular through the application of the EU's competition rules, is the necessary supplementary theme which asserts a concern to manage the process of change in a way that takes account of all affected interests.

Some of this is not sports-specific. The emphasis on market definition and market power which lies at the heart of orthodox approaches under EU competition law is perfectly appropriate in its deployment in the case of the sale of rights to broadcast sports events. Exclusivity and collective selling are common in markets for sports rights, but far from unknown elsewhere. There are no decided issues which are *unique* to sport, though it is certainly true that the Commission's sensitivity to the acquisition of exclusive rights to 'premium' events for an extended period reflects the profound concern about the damage to market flexibility which may be inflicted in such circumstances on the technologically and commercially volatile broadcasting sector. It is at least possible that one *undecided* issue—the issue left untouched in *Champions League* concerning the potential for pursuit of solidarity in sport to justify an agreement to sell rights on a collective basis falling within Article 101(1) TFEU but inapt for exemption pursuant to Article 101(3)—will reveal a sports-specific feature of the regulation of broadcasting markets, but it has been argued that this is a stretch too far.[237] By contrast, the restrictions on the sale of 'protected' or 'listed' events are sports-specific. They reveal an incursion into sporting autonomy which is generally regarded as unwelcome by governing bodies. This is to some extent an inversion of most of the material traversed in this book. I have frequently suggested that sporting bodies tend to dress up commercially

---

[236] See Case C-201/11P (n 218) para 11, Case C-204/11P (n 218) para 12, and Case C-205/11P (n 218) para 13.
[237] See sect 11.7.

motivated rules with the camouflage of tradition and sporting need: EU internal market law sometimes, but not always, demands change. In the case of the protected events legislation it is the EU and the public authorities in (some of) the Member States which claim to be acting on behalf of a perceived need to treat sport as a public good, and it is the commercial position of sporting bodies which suffers.

The combination of national and EU legislation governing 'protected events' diminishes the commercial value of the rights to broadcast such events by interfering in the ability of the holder of the rights to extract the highest price the market would yield. There is a loose similarity between the use of Article 101 TFEU to ensure that buyers of rights do not lock out actual or potential competition in the market and the use of the listing regime to open up particular events to the party that is not necessarily the one with the deepest pockets, but whereas the former is aimed at ensuring an adequate level of market access without dictating who shall win the competition, the latter entail public authorities making choices about who shall win, and not on the basis of price. This is a vivid proof of the notion that although broadcasting markets have become increasingly deregulated in recent years, thereby exchanging sector-specific regulation for more general application of 'normal' competition law, there remain some very idiosyncratic vestiges of assumptions that broadcasting, like sport, is special, but to a controversial and not always well-defined degree. Sporting bodies, commonly eager to make the case that their activities are 'special' as a means to maximize autonomy, are bitten by their own lofty rhetoric. If the integrative and social virtues of professional sport are advanced to secure favourable treatment under free movement and competition law, here those virtues are deployed to take away the opportunity to take maximum commercial advantage of those very activities.

12

The Principles of EU Sports Law

The core concern of this book is to explore the extent to which sport deserves autonomy from legal supervision, in particular in the context of EU law. Sport is special, but how special? And how should the perception that sport is—to some contested extent—special affect the application of legal rules? This inquiry forms the intellectual heart of sports law and the need to pursue it is the reason why sports law deserves to be treated as a distinct discipline, and not simply as an instance of the application to sport of an accumulation of existing and diverse legal rules.

Three interconnected themes animate the narrative. First, sport enjoys a conditional autonomy from EU law; second, in shaping the terms of this conditional autonomy sporting bodies and the institutions of the EU, most of all the Commission, have been incrementally induced into a relationship of cooperation rather than one based on top-down command and control; and third, EU law secures its legitimacy in application to sport by adding value to the patterns according to which it is organized. These three themes combine to show the way in which the frictions caused by collision between the concern for cross-border competition in a market cleansed of nationality discrimination under EU law and the claims to autonomy made in the name of the *lex sportiva* have been mediated.

The first theme, that of conditional autonomy, is based on willing recognition that sport possesses features that distance it from ordinary economic activity. Chapter 1 of this book demonstrates proper acceptance that sport is special in important respects. Participants in sport operate under conditions of mutual interdependence: a single supplier in most markets enjoys the bounties of economically dominant power, a single club in a sports league produces only the sound of one hand clapping. Moreover, governing bodies in sport legitimately appeal to their aspiration to preside over a truly global pattern of rule-making and rule enforcement within which sporting expertise informs the operation of the system. Sport, they argue with some justice, should not be fragmented along national lines as a consequence of the intrusion of local jurisdiction-specific peculiarities which, moreover, may not be attuned to the particular features of sport.

Motivated by these anxieties, sporting bodies have devised important strategies to achieve an insulation of sporting autonomy from the law of states or of the EU. This is the subject matter of Chapter 2. The system over which the Court of Arbitration for Sport (the CAS) presides represents an increasingly dense and sophisticated terrain on which is developed the *lex sportiva*. It is a contractually based separation of a system that is sensitive to sport's special character—and which claims uniform global application—from supervision by 'normal' law. It goes so far as to challenge what we mean by 'law', in the sense that it provokes reflection on the quality of norms that have come to exert powerful influence on the organization of sport without being subject to the type of democratic legitimation that is conventionally found at state level. Moreover, sport has an economic and political power that on occasion secures it a shield from the normal expectations of the legal order of states within which it operates. This ability to extract legislative concessions to the claim to sporting autonomy is peculiarly successful where the prize of hosting the top level of international sport, the Olympic Games and the World Cup, is at stake. However, neither the contractual nor the legislative route to securing sporting autonomy is watertight. The EU routinely displaces the claim of the CAS that its rulings should be treated as final both by equipping the Commission to investigate matters that offend against EU internal market law even if they have been the subject of a final CAS ruling and by requiring the national courts of EU Member States to apply EU internal market law as rules of public policy to supervise matters decided through the arbitral process. And since the EU has neither a sports team of its own nor an interest in bidding to host a major event in its own right it is immune to the blandishment of governing bodies seeking commercially attractive concessions from legal norms.

As is shown in the conclusion to Chapter 2, it is sometimes the case that sporting bodies must instead resort to the third of the three available strategies in order to protect the *lex sportiva* from legal supervision from 'outside' the world of sport. This is the interpretative or adjudicative solution, which involves claims before ordinary courts that sport is special enough to deserve a degree of tolerant and context-sensitive treatment in the application of legal rules to sporting activities. There is a contested zone within which it is necessary to determine whether practices pursued in sport which are not found in other sectors of economic activity are truly a reflection of the special character of sport or in truth simply anachronisms or, worse, commercially motivated arrangements dressed up as sporting specificity. In practical terms this route has long been regarded with scepticism or even downright hostility by sporting bodies, for it requires them to engage with and persuade institutions that are no part of the *lex sportiva*—normally judges but also sometimes administrative bodies, such as, in the EU, the Commission—that sport deserves a degree of insulation from orthodox legal rules. However, intellectually this is the very heart of sports law, for challenges of this type require a decision on how far sport is special, and what this should entail for the interpretation and application of legal rules. Moreover, in the EU practice has moved on, since Article 165 of the Treaty on the Functioning of the European Union (TFEU) represents a culmination of the process whereby sports governing bodies were made to realize that securing a constitutional exclusion from EU law was unavailable, and that instead they must accept inclusion but on terms that they could seek to mould in favour of a practical concordance between the assumptions of EU law and those of the *lex sportiva*. This is the second theme mentioned earlier which animates this book: the emergence of a relationship of cooperation (of sorts) between regulator and regulated. What really matters is the shaping of the conditions attached to sporting autonomy under

EU law, and to an extent this is developing as a joint enterprise engaging governing bodies in sport and the European Commission, albeit ultimately the authoritative voice is that of the Court of Justice.

So the principal strategy that must be pursued by sporting bodies intent on a mediation between their practices—the *lex sportiva*—and EU law is the adjudicative or interpretative route.

Chapter 3 shows how sport is in principle treated as subject to EU law wherever its organizing structures and practices fall within its scope, which is commonly and readily found to be the case given the sweeping application of EU law to economic activity exerting effects on the territory of the twenty-eight Member States. This draws in the law of the internal market—free movement, competition, and non-discrimination on the basis of nationality—and, since 2009, it engages too the carefully constrained legislative competence found in Article 165 TFEU, which asserts the EU's mandate to respect the specific nature of sport. So the assertion of constitutional principle that the EU operates within the limits set by its Treaties under Article 5 of the Treaty on European Union (TEU)—the so-called 'principle of conferral'—is revealed in practice to entail a generous grant of competence to review practices with economic effects even in sectors where the EU is provided with no explicit competence by its Treaties (which was true of sport until 2009) or where that competence is of only limited scope (which is true of sport today). This is why sporting ambition to achieve *absolute* autonomy from the application of EU law is so commonly thwarted. Chapter 3 sets out the basic framework of EU law and the detail is elaborated in the chapters that follow.

This is the material on which to rely in order to make good the case that EU law secures its legitimacy in application to sport by adding value to the patterns according to which it is organized. This is the third of this book's three themes mapped earlier. The argument throughout this book is that in the application of free movement and competition law, the EU only rarely displaces the choices made by sporting bodies. There is no absolute autonomy granted to sport, so sporting practices are routinely put to the test, but the conditional autonomy that is granted by EU law is openly sensitive to sport's claimed special character, and sport's preferences usually survive the test. For the long period prior to 2009, before the arrival in the Treaty of Article 165's commitment to the specific character of sport, the Court and the Commission were vigorously determined to make sure that EU law did not treat sport as an economic activity like any other. The landmarks in the case law examined in this book all reveal receptivity to the argument that 'sport is special', even if the argument is not always made good in the particular circumstances that have generated litigation. Since 2009 the application of EU law explicitly entails taking into account the specific nature of sport recognized by Article 165 TFEU. This provides no general exception, but rather serves only to repackage the pre-existing orientation of the Court and Commission. Sport enjoys a 'conditional autonomy' under EU law: it enjoys an autonomy from the orthodox demands of non-discrimination, free movement, and competition law *on condition that* it is shown that its practices, which would otherwise offend against such EU values, are necessary for the pursuit of the relevant sporting activity. The model of 'conditional autonomy' first emerged in admittedly but necessarily ad hoc fashion as the Court grappled with the intersection of EU internal market law, first free movement and later competition, and sporting practices. From *Walrave and Koch* through *Bosman* to *Meca-Medina and Majcen* it found ways to articulate the notion that sport cannot in principle be immunized from the application of the rules of EU law but that its special features shall form part of the interpretation and application of those rules, even if the precise jurisprudential character of that concession was elusive. This was the subject matter of Chapter 4 in the context of free movement and Chapter 5 in application to competition law. Ultimately, in *Meca-Medina and Majcen* the Court settled on the necessity for a case-by-case analysis in order to determine whether sporting practices passed the test—that is, whether the conditions for autonomy were met. And in doing so it drew on the wider pattern of EU internal market law: it is not that sport *alone* is special, but rather that the assessment of restrictive effects must also be made in context, with assessment included of the objectives pursued to check whether they are legitimate and of the methods used to ensure they do not violate the demands imposed by the proportionality principle. The Commission too followed in this vein, first in its decision-making practice in the field of EU competition law (Chapter 5) and then more generally in the elaboration of policy orientation, most conspicuously in the highly successful and influential 2007 White Paper, examined in Chapter 6 and notable for the Commission's sophisticated and thoughtful depiction of the specificity of sport.

Chapter 6 also explains the road to Article 165 TFEU and, the second theme mentioned earlier, coexistence between affected parties and an end to terse rejection by sporting bodies of the EU's pretensions. Article 165 creates an EU legislative competence in matters of sport for the first time—albeit, as detailed in Chapter 6, a slender one. It puts an end to the protest advanced with wearying frequency in the past by sporting bodies that EU law in general and the EU's institutions in particular have no business addressing sport. At the same time, as Chapter 6 shows, there is no hint (so far) that the EU aspires to assume a powerful role in directing sports policy. Article 165 (so far) is used to frame the EU's contribution to the shape of sport alongside, not above, that of other relevant private and public, national and international, actors. The Commission's attempts to promote, but not impose, improved patterns of governance in sport, examined in Chapter 10.12, provide a good example, even if they are considerably less high-profile than the raids on FIFA headquarters conducted in 2015 by officials of the US Department of Justice (Chapter 2.3.4). EU sports law and policy is now built constitutionally on Article 165 TFEU and the direction therein that the EU 'shall contribute to the promotion of European sporting issues, while taking account of the specific nature of sport, its structures based on voluntary activity and its social and educational function' and that EU action shall be aimed at 'developing the European dimension in sport, by promoting fairness and openness in sporting competitions and cooperation between bodies responsible for sports, and by protecting the physical and moral integrity of sportsmen and sportswomen, especially the youngest sportsmen and sportswomen'.

'Fairness' and 'openness' both have some potential to carry interpretative force as principles of EU sports law. Fairness might be invoked by sports bodies to argue that practices which restrain competition should nonetheless be treated as compatible with the Treaty in so far as they achieve a better balanced distribution of wealth within a sport. Chapter 11.7 explores this in connection with the promotion of solidarity through collective selling of broadcasting rights. Fairness may also be invoked in support of UEFA's arrangements for Financial Fair Play, examined in Chapter 10.9. 'Openness' has similar interpretative potential. Chapter 8.12 considers whether EU law, interpreted in the light of Article 165(2) TFEU, tolerates rules that exclude non-nationals from competitions designed to crown a national champion. In Chapter 10.8 it was asked whether the organization of Leagues along national lines is compatible with 'openness' as enshrined in Article 165 in so far as it leads to the suppression of cross-border club mobility. The suggestion is that such an attack on sporting structures will fail but the point is that Article 165 offers a vocabulary apt to challenge the durability of sporting autonomy in the shadow of EU law.

However, the argument presented in this book is *not* that Article 165 TFEU possesses transformative force. The principal function of Article 165 is not to produce new solutions but rather to reinforce the pre-existing trajectory of EU law applied to sport. As Chapter 7 explains, the evolved pattern of internal market law is helpfully wrapped up in Article 165's embrace of 'the specific nature of sport'. It is not altered by it. Chapter 7's main message is to show a route to understanding Article 165 as a basis for an integrated EU sports law which claims legitimacy through its capacity to add value to the *lex sportiva*. The application of EU law is structured around a sporting margin of appreciation which serves to mediate the tension between the assumptions of EU law and those associated with the defence of sporting autonomy. This summary brings together: (a) the Court's famous paragraph 106 in *Bosman*, in which, as explained in Chapter 4.6, it acknowledged 'the considerable social importance of sporting activities and in particular football' and treated 'the aims of maintaining a balance between clubs by preserving a certain degree of equality and uncertainty as to results and of encouraging the recruitment and training of young players' as legitimate; (b) its identification in *Deliège v Ligue de Judo* of rules governing selection as 'inherent' in the organization of sport (Chapter 4.10); and (c) the contextually sensitive appreciation of sporting practices in the light of EU competition law pursued in *Meca-Medina*, where, as elucidated in Chapter 5.3.4, the Court, addressing a sanction imposed for violation of anti-doping rules, assessed effects restrictive of competition in the light of the objectives to maintain a clean sport pursued by the governing body. It is this package of judicial practice, supplemented by the Commission's 2007 White Paper, which interrogates the 'specificity' of sport (Chapter 6.5), and endorsed by Article 165's depiction of 'the specific nature of sport' (Chapters 3.5, 6.9), which leads to the argument presented in Chapter 7.3 for a convergent understanding of EU law applied to sport and to the presentation in Chapter 7.4 of a sporting margin of appreciation in the application of EU law to sport. This is the conditional autonomy granted to sport by EU law.

It is compelling that the more slender the EU's legislative competence, so the more lenient should be the review practised in the name of EU internal market law. The relatively rare occasions on which sporting practices have been condemned as violations of EU law are readily understood as corrections of choices that reflect severe imbalances in power and indefensibly anachronistic choices. This is visible in Chapter 8, concerning nationality rules in club football, Chapter 9 in relation to a transfer system that trapped even out-of-contract players, and in Chapter 10 where governance arrangements that allow sports bodies to leverage their regulatory power to achieve commercial advantage—the 'conflict of interest'—are exposed as peculiarly vulnerable to attack driven by EU law in a number of different areas of rule-making and organizational practice in sport. In these areas, reform provoked by EU law has typically still permitted retention of a system that is reflective of sporting specificity—discrimination on the basis of nationality in international football, a sustained though narrowed transfer system, the prohibition of owner-ship of more than one football club, monopoly power for the governing body as regulator—only requiring that it be adjusted to take full account of the interests of all affected parties, including professional athletes. It is argued in Chapters 8, 9, and 10, in particular, that EU law contains an inexplicit but identifiable scepticism about the permissibility of restraints imposed in the labour market in circumstances where the objective in view may be secured through arrangements which burden only clubs. The net result is that employees in sport are not treated identically to those in 'normal' occupations—there is, for example, still a transfer system, albeit reduced in scope, and there are still restrictions on switching between international representative teams. However, their status has become a good deal less atypical as a result of the modification of the *lex sportiva* which has followed its interaction with the requirements of EU law. Not only players but also clubs have been able to rely on the leverage provided by EU law to induce change in patterns of governance: the system applicable to the release of players for international representative football examined in Chapter 10.7 provides a good example of this dynamic process, which involves both legal and extra-legal pressures and incentives.

The aggrieved squawking of governing bodies deserves to be treated as exaggeration. EU law puts sporting practices to the test when they collide with the demands of the internal market, but that test is flexible and context-specific and it is applied with a margin of appreciation. EU law takes the rough edges off sporting practices and it induces better governance, but it does not demand a retreat to the banality of sausage-making or the provision of financial services. Sport remains—to an extent—special. Moreover, recent developments, above all the embrace of inclusion rather than exclusion which lies at the heart of Article 165 TFEU, demonstrate that a more stable and cooperative relationship between all bodies with interests in sport is emerging in Europe.

It is increasingly apparent that sporting bodies and the institutions of the EU, most of all the Commission, are engaged in a joint enterprise in fleshing out the multiple interactions between EU law and the *lex sportiva*. Chapter 9's treatment of the renovation of the transfer system is a clear example of this trend towards institutional cooperation; it is visible too in the development of UEFA's Financial

Fair Play scheme, addressed in Chapter 10.9; and Chapter 11 provides another case study in its discussion of the relatively permissive attitude taken by the Commission to the collective selling of rights to broadcast sporting events, commonly on an exclusive basis.

EU law secures its legitimacy in application to sport by adding value to the patterns according to which sport is organized. Over forty years since *Walrave and Koch* and over twenty years since *Bosman*, EU sports law deserves to be treated as an intellectually distinct discipline. Its foundational concern is to interrogate the strength of the claim that sport deserves autonomy from legal supervision in consequence of its economic and cultural peculiarities—that in a sports league there is inter-dependence among participants that is absent from most markets and that sport is typically governed by global rule-making bodies which claim expertise in their field. EU law is sensitive to these claims that sport should be treated in its true context. Sport has, in the language of Article 165 TFEU, a specific nature. But the autonomy which EU law grants is conditional, not absolute. Sport enjoys a conditional autonomy from EU law, and the most intriguing issues in EU sports law concern the elucidation of those conditions. Their shape gives content to the specific nature of sport asserted by Article 165 TFEU. This is the heart of EU sports law, and exploration and critical evaluation of the conditions which EU law places on the autonomy of those engaged in sport-related activity provides most of the content of this book.

Index